HISTORIC
DOCUMENTS
OF
1991

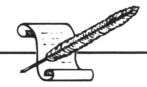

HISTORIC
DOCUMENTS
OF
1991

Cumulative Index, 1987-1991
Congressional Quarterly Inc.

Printed in the United States of America

Congressional Quarterly Inc.
1414 22nd St. N.W., Washington, D.C. 20037

The Library of Congress cataloged the first issue of this title as follows:

Historic documents.   1972—
    Washington. Congressional Quarterly Inc.

    1. United States — Politics and government — 1945— — Yearbooks. 2. World politics — 1945— —Yearbooks. I. Congressional Quarterly Inc.

E839.5H57   917.3'03'9205   72-97888

ISBN 0-87187-665-5

ISSN 0892-080X

Historic Documents of 1991

Editor: Hoyt Gimlin
Assistant Editor: Jamie R. Holland
Contributors: Carolyn Goldinger, James R. Ingram, Jenny K. Philipson,
   Richard C. Schroeder, D. Park Teter, Margaret C. Thompson
Indexer: Rhonda Holland

Congressional Quarterly Inc.

Andrew Barnes   *Chairman*
Andrew P. Corty   *Vice Chairman*
Neil Skene   *Editor and Publisher*
Robert W. Merry   *Executive Editor*
John J. Coyle   *Associate Publisher*
Michael L. Koempel   *Director of Information Services*
Robert E. Cuthriell   *Director of Development*

Book Division

Patrick Bernuth   *General Manager*

Book Editorial

David R. Tarr   *Director, Book Department*
Nancy A. Lammers   *Assistant Director*
Brenda W. Carter   *Acquisitions Editor*
Jeanne Ferris   *Acquisitions Editor*
Shana Wagger   *Developmental Editor*
Carolyn Goldinger   *Senior Editor*
Ann Davies   *Project Editor*
Colleen McGuiness   *Project Editor*
Jamie R. Holland   *Production Editor*
Ann F. O'Malley   *Production Editor*
Jerry A. Orvedahl   *Production Editor*
Jenny K. Philipson   *Production Editor*
Laura Carter   *Editorial Assistant*
Christopher M. Karlsten   *Editorial Assistant*
Linda White   *Administrative Assistant*

Book Marketing

Kathryn C. Suárez   *Director, Book Marketing*
Jacqueline A. Davey   *Manager, Library and Professional Marketing*
Kate Quinlin   *College Marketing Manager*
Kimberly B. Hatton   *Marketing Coordinator*
Kim Murt   *Marketing Administrator*
Dianne Clack   *Administrative Assistant*

Production

I. D. Fuller   *Production Manager*
Michael Emanuel   *Assistant Production Manager*
Jhonnie G. Bailey   *Assistant to the Production Manager*

PREFACE

Historic Documents of 1991 marks the twentieth year of a Congressional Quarterly project that began with *Historic Documents of 1972*. The purpose of this continuing series is to give students, librarians, journalists, scholars, and others convenient access to important documents in a range of world issues.

Each document is preceded by an introduction that provides background information and, when relevant, an account of continuing developments during the year. We believe that these introductions will become increasingly useful as memories of current times fade.

The year 1991 was punctuated with momentous events. It began with the onset of the Persian Gulf War and ended with the slow collapse of the Soviet Union. The year was only eight days old when Congress, for the first time since World War II, directly confronted the question of sending large numbers of American troops into combat. Once the U.S.-led allied forces were committed to battle against Iraq, victory came swiftly. By February 27 President George Bush could declare, "Kuwait is liberated," and on March 6, "The war is over." Victory, however, was incomplete. Though humiliated and politically weakened, Saddam Hussein continued to rule most of his devastated country.

In the first flush of triumph, the president spoke of a "new world order" in which peace would be ensured by cooperative nations—much the same as in the effort he had organized against Hussein. As if fulfilling that ideal, the parties to a sixteen-year-old Angolan civil war signed a peace agreement soon afterward. But peace remained elusive in much of the world. In Yugoslavia old hatreds between Serbs and Croats turned into civil war, splintering the country's fragile unity.

The Soviet Union's breakup, though relatively bloodless, unfolded from August to December. It began with President Mikhail Gorbachev's kidnapping in a coup attempt by old guard Communists. The coup failed but harmed Gorbachev politically; he no longer could keep the restive Soviet republics from asserting their independence and forming the new Commonwealth of Independent States. On Christmas Day he resigned as

---

How to Use This Book

The documents are arranged in chronological order. If you know the approximate date of the report, speech, statement, court decision, or other document you are looking for, glance through the titles for that month in the table of contents.

If the table of contents does not lead you directly to the document you want, turn to the index at the end of the book. There you may find references not only to the particular document you seek but also to other entries on the same or a related subject. The index in this volume is a five-year cumulative index of *Historic Documents* covering the years 1987-1991.

The introduction to each document is printed in italic type. The document itself, printed in roman type, follows the spelling, capitalization, and punctuation of the original or official copy. Where the full text is not given, omissions of material are indicated by the customary ellipsis points.

---

president of a Communist empire that, after sixty-nine years, had ceased to exist. Its long, agonizing death was aptly characterized by President Bush as "one of the greatest dramas of the 20th century."

America's euphoria over the Persian Gulf military victory faded as the nation's economy faltered. In January the president spoke optimistically of the country quickly overcoming a "temporary interruption" in its economic growth. But unemployment continued to rise while business statistics worsened. City and state governments, hurt by falling tax revenues, made deep budget cuts to make ends meet. Bridgeport, Connecticut, filed for bankruptcy—claiming to be the first major U.S. municipality to do so. On technical grounds, the city was refused the court's protection from debtors.

Americans were diverted from the economy, and almost everything else, by nationally televised Senate hearings into sexual harassment allegations against Bush's Supreme Court nominee Clarence Thomas. He went on to win—narrowly—Senate confirmation for the seat vacated by Justice Thurgood Marshall, the Court's first black member. Thomas was also black but, unlike Marshall, added his voice to the Court's conservative majority.

Basketball superstar Earvin "Magic" Johnson startled his legions of fans by disclosing that he had tested positive for HIV (human immunodeficiency virus), which can lead to AIDS (acquired immune deficiency syndrome), a fatal disease that often is transmitted sexually. By identifying himself as an HIV carrier, Johnson was praised for helping to raise the public's awareness of the disease and its rapid spread in recent years.

By year's end Bush gave in, conceding that the country was indeed suffering from a recession. At that time, on the eve of a presidential election year, his high public approval rating of 89 percent, as recorded on a Gallup Poll at the war's end, had dropped below 50 percent.

Terry Anderson, the last American hostage to be held by Arab radicals in Lebanon, was released December 4. His captivity lasted 2,454 days. When all the Americans were freed, several who had returned earlier felt free to give a full account of the often-brutal treatment their captors had inflicted.

Those were but some of this volume's topics of national and international interest presented in texts of official statements, news conferences, speeches, special studies, and court decisions. In our judgment, the documents chosen for this volume will be of lasting interest. Where space limitations prevent reproduction of a full text, excerpts provide essential details.

Hoyt Gimlin, Editor
Washington, D.C., February 1992

CONTENTS

January

February

March

June

July

August

September

October

November

CONTENTS

December

HISTORIC DOCUMENTS OF 1991

January

CONGRESS ON WAR WITH IRAQ
January 8, 10, and 12, 1991

A sharply divided Congress voted January 12 to authorize President George Bush to begin a war against Iraq if Iraq failed to withdraw from Kuwait by January 15, as ordered by the United Nations. The historic vote marked the first time since America's entry into World War II that Congress had directly confronted the question of sending large numbers of American troops into combat.

For months after Iraq's invasion of Kuwait August 2, 1990, Bush refused to acknowledge that Congress had a formal role in deciding whether to use force against Iraq. But as the deadline drew near and the Senate opened debate on his Persian Gulf policy, Bush sent identical letters to key congressional leaders urging that Congress formally endorse a UN Security Council resolution of the previous November 29. That resolution authorized "all means necessary" to remove Iraq's military forces from Kuwait if the Iraqis did not remove themselves by January 15. In previous months the Security Council had imposed an economic boycott and other punitive measures on Iraq, but the November 29 action marked the first time since the outset of the Korean War in 1950 that the UN had authorized force against a member country. (Deadline Pressure on Saddam Hussein, Historic Documents of 1990, p. 767)

Bush told Congress to send Iraqi president Saddam Hussein "the clearest possible message" of America's resolve in the crisis by passing a war resolution such as he requested. In so doing, Bush prepared the nation for battle, while momentarily quieting a longstanding constitutional argument over the president's power in foreign affairs. (War Powers Debate, Historic Documents of 1990, p. 663)

Deep Division on Sanctions vs. Combat

After months of indecision and conflict with the president over its appropriate role in deciding how to confront Saddam Hussein, Congress's divided vote revealed doubts as to the wisdom of going to war. The Senate voted 54-40 for the "Authorization of Military Force Against Iraq Resolution." Only minutes after the senators cast their votes, House members approved an identical resolution by a majority of 250-183. An unusual combination of Republicans, Northeastern liberals, and conservative Democrats overcame the opposition of the Democratic leadership in both houses to approve the measure.

Underscoring much of the debate was a sense that the legislative branch had acted too late to have any real choice except to back Bush in his showdown with the Iraqi leader. Sen. Charles S. Robb, D-Va., who supported Bush, said it would be a "fundamental mistake to give even the appearance of withdrawing our trust and support."

Those opposing the resolution, including Sen. Sam Nunn, D-Ga., chairman of the Senate Armed Services Committee, explained that they backed the goal of forcing an Iraqi withdrawal, but argued that if economic sanctions were given more time, military force might not be necessary. In opening the Senate debate, Majority Leader George Mitchell, D-Maine, also made a strong plea for economic sanctions. However, Senate Minority Leader Bob Dole, R-Kan., argued that the time required for sanctions to take effect "gives Saddam Hussein a holiday from the threat that we might use force."

Similarly, in the House, Speaker Thomas S. Foley, D-Wash., backed sanctions over force, while the chairman of the House Armed Services Committee, Rep. Les Aspin, D-Wis., concluded that, in the circumstances, war was "a reasonable option" and therefore supported the president. Rep. Dante B. Fascell, D-Fla., chairman of the House Foreign Affairs Committee, also took this view. Before Bush's resolution came to a vote, the House voted down (183-250) a nonbinding resolution that favored sanctions, and the Senate rejected (46-53) a resolution that gave Congress sole power to declare war and allowed economic sanctions against Iraq to continue.

During the three days of debate, a nationwide television audience watched as, for the first time in memory, Congress debated openly and extensively over whether the president should be allowed to take the country, unprovoked by a direct attack, into war.

Memories of Vietnam War

Congress's last formal declaration of war followed Japan's attack on Pearl Harbor in 1941. The United States went to war in Korea under the UN flag and without any special authorization by Congress. In 1964 Congress passed the so-called Gulf of Tonkin resolution, which President Lyndon B. Johnson considered equivalent to a declaration of war against North Vietnam. In response to a purported North Vietnamese attack on

U.S. warships in the gulf, Congress declared its support of "the determination of the President . . . to take all necessary measures to repel any armed attack against the forces of the United States." Florida Democratic representatives Charles E. Bennett and Sam M. Gibbons, both World War II veterans, spoke of the deep burden they felt for having voted for the Gulf of Tonkin resolution. They urged colleagues not to repeat the mistake. But Minority Leader Robert H. Michel, R-Ill., another veteran of World War II, made an emotional plea to members not to forget a different lesson from the past. "Those of our generation know from bloody experience," he said, alluding to the appeasement of Hitler before World War II, "that unchecked aggression against a small nation is a prelude to international disaster."

Sen. Daniel K. Inouye, D-Hawaii, who lost his right arm in World War II combat, cautioned against hasty military action. He was followed in Senate debate by Minority Leader Bob Dole, R-Kan., who lost the use of his right hand in the same war but asked his fellow lawmakers not to give Saddam Hussein a "holiday" by refusing to authorize force. But two other Republican senators, Charles E. Grassley of Iowa and John C. Danforth of Missouri, spoke of agonizing personal struggles to make their decisions, which ultimately opposed their party's president.

Some members of Congress offered prayers for the country, the president, and the U.S. armed forces in the Persian Gulf region. "In twenty-six years in the House of Representatives," said Foley, "I have never seen this House more serious nor more determined to speak its heart and mind on a question than they are at this time on this day."

Losers Vow to Support War Effort

Throughout the debate, the galleries in both houses were packed with onlookers who sat in silence and watched intently. But on January 11 this pensive mood was shattered in the Senate when about a dozen antiwar protesters began to shout, "No war for Bush!" and "No blood for oil!" Although brief, the outburst appeared to unsettle the senators. Some of them had questioned earlier whether the nation would again be torn apart as it had been by the Vietnam War.

Senator Nunn, whose speech was interrupted by the protests, resumed with words intended for Saddam Hussein. "We may disagree in this chamber," he said, "but when the vote is over . . . we are going to stand united." Once the voting was over, many who opposed the war resolution insisted that they would support the nation's war effort. Even the winners seemed subdued. "Normally, after a bipartisan victory, for me there's jubilation," said Michel. "This time it's different."

> *Following are President George Bush's letter of January 8 requesting Congress's formal support of the UN resolution to use force against Iraq; excerpts from speeches in the Senate debate by Sens. Sam Nunn, George J. Mitchell, and Bob Dole, and the resolution passed by Congress on January 12:*

5

BUSH REQUESTS CONGRESSIONAL RESOLUTION

The current situation in the Persian Gulf, brought about by Iraq's unprovoked invasion and subsequent brutal occupation of Kuwait, threatens vital U.S. interests. The situation also threatens the peace. It would, however, greatly enhance the chances for peace if Congress were now to go on record supporting the position adopted by the UN Security Council on twelve separate occasions. Such an action would underline that the United States stands with the international community and on the side of law and decency; it would also help dispel any belief that may exist in the minds of Iraq's leaders that the United States lacks the necessary unity to act decisively in response to Iraq's continued aggression against Kuwait.

Secretary of State Baker is meeting with Iraq's Foreign Minister on January 9. It would have been most constructive if he could have presented the Iraqi government a Resolution passed by both houses of Congress supporting the UN position and in particular Security Council Resolution 678. As you know, I have frequently stated my desire for such a Resolution. Nevertheless, there is still opportunity for Congress to act to strengthen the prospects for peace and safeguard this country's vital interests.

I therefore request that the House of Representatives and the Senate adopt a Resolution stating that Congress supports the use of all necessary means to implement UN Security Council Resolution 678. Such action would send the clearest possible message to Saddam Hussein that he must withdraw without condition or delay from Kuwait. Anything less would only encourage Iraqi intransigence; anything else would risk detracting from the international coalition arrayed against Iraq's aggression.

Mr. Speaker, I am determined to do whatever is necessary to protect America's security. I ask Congress to join with me in this task. I can think of no better way than for Congress to express its support for the President at this critical time. This truly is the last best chance for peace.

Sincerely,

George Bush

SPEECH BY SENATOR NUNN

... Mr. President, I still believe there is room for some hope that diplomacy can succeed in avoiding war. But as January 15th approaches, as so many of my colleagues have already observed, the Congress must act. Article 1, section 8 of the Constitution provides that the Congress clearly has the authority and the duty to decide whether the Nation should go to war. In many past instances it is true that military actions have occurred without congressional authorization. Pursuant to the authority assumed by the President in his constitutional capacity as Commander-in-Chief in today's fast-moving, interconnected world with instant communications, a world plagued with nuclear weapons and international terrorism, there are certainly instances when United States military force must be used without congressional authorization.

There are many gray areas where the Congress, by necessity, has permitted and even encouraged and supported military action by the Commander-in-Chief without specific authorization and without a declaration of war. I do not deem every military action taken as war. I think there is always room for debate on definitions. But a war against Iraq to liberate Kuwait initiated by the United States and involving over 400,000 American forces is not a gray area.

In this case, I believe the Constitution of the United States is absolutely clear. It is essential, to comply with the Constitution and to commit the Nation, that Congress give its consent before the President initiates a large-scale military offensive against Iraq. I think the founding Fathers had a great deal of wisdom when they put this provision in the Constitution. One of the main reasons, of course, was to prevent one person from being King. They did not want that. But I also believe that there was another purpose, and that is to make sure that when this Nation goes to war and asks its young men and, increasingly, young women also to put their lives on the line, the Nation must commit itself before we ask them to lay down their lives.

The President's January 8th request that Congress approve the use of military force presents Congress with an issue, simply stated, but profound in its consequences; not simply short term but also long term. Many of us strongly believe a war to liberate Kuwait should be the last resort and that sanctions and diplomacy combined with a threat—a continuing threat of force—should be given more time. Should we give the President—after all of these debates when the die is cast—should we give him blanket authority to go to war against Iraq to liberate Kuwait? This is the question we face. There are numerous questions that will have to be answered in the minds of each of us before casting our vote.

... We all agree with the goal of restoring Kuwaiti sovereignty; no doubt about that. But have we concluded here that the liberation of Kuwait in the next few weeks is so *vital* to our Nation's security that we must take military action *now* instead of waiting a few months—waiting a period of time to allow the economic embargo and blockage to take its toll?

Back in August and September when the embargo was successfully— and I'd say very skillfully brought about by President Bush, through what I think was his superb leadership—no one thought or predicted the embargo was going to be over by January. No one predicted we were going to be able to bring about the termination of the Iraqi presence in Kuwait by January. None of the intelligence experts or other experts who testified felt the embargo was really going to have much effect before April or May of 1991 and almost all of them said it would take at least a year. There was no surprise about that. I'm absolutely amazed when people say well, we've waited four months and five months and the embargo is not working. They must not have been there at the beginning or they must not have talked to anybody at the beginning about how long it was going to take. It's very puzzling to me how someone could give up on the embargo after five months when nobody that I know of predicted that it was going to last less than nine months to a year, and most people said a year to eighteen months from the time of inception, which was August of last year.

When we talk about the question of vital—a lot of times we in Washington throw that word around as if it's just another word. Sometimes we use so many words in the course of debate that we don't think carefully about what we mean. I recall very clearly President Reagan's 1982 declaration that Lebanon was vital to the *security* of the United States. Shortly thereafter, following the tragic death of more than 200 Marines, we pulled out of Lebanon, we pulled out of a country that only a few weeks before had been declared vital. Today, as we debate this, eight years later, while pursuing our newly proclaimed vital interest in Kuwait. It was not vital before August 2nd. Nobody had said it was vital then. There was no treaty. In fact, when we were protecting Kuwaiti vessels coming out of the Gulf for several years during the Iran/Iraq war, the Kuwaitis didn't even let us refuel, as I recall....

All of a sudden it's vital—vital....

In more recent history, we defined Panama and Nicaragua as vital, and we used force in the case of Panama directly. In the case of Nicaragua, we supported force. I supported both of those decisions. But after achieving our short-term goals in both these countries ... we seem to have forgotten their on-going economic and political agony.... Both the Bush Administration and the Congress have unfulfilled responsibilities regarding those two countries.

My point is, Mr. President, we throw around the word "vital" very carelessly.... We have an obligation as leaders to distinguish between important interests which are worthy of economic, political, and diplomatic efforts and interests that are vital, that are worth the calling by the leaders of this Nation on our young men and women in uniform to sacrifice, if necessary, their lives....

Are there reasonable alternatives to war? What is the likelihood that sanctions will work? In testimony before the Congress, and in public and private statements as recently as January 3, the Bush Administration stopped short of saying that sanctions cannot get Iraq out of Kuwait. The Administration acknowledges the significant economic impact sanctions have had on Iraq but now says there is "no guarantee" whether or not they will bring about an Iraqi decision to withdraw from Kuwait. Last August, President Bush asserted himself, saying, quoting him "Economic sanctions, in this instance, if fully enforced, can be very, very effective ... and nobody can stand up forever to total economic deprivation." That is from President Bush.

The international sanctions are, indeed, having a devastating effect on Iraq's economy, for two basic reasons. The Iraqi economy is based on oil, which accounts for about 50 percent of the country's GNP and almost 100 percent of the country's hard currency earnings....

The net result to date is that the international sanctions have cut off more than 90 percent of Iraq's imports, almost 100 percent of Iraq's exports, including virtually all of Iraqi oil exports. Iraqi industrial and military plants are receiving from abroad virtually no raw materials, no spare parts, no new equipment, no munitions, no lubricants. . . .

The question is: can anyone guarantee that Iraq will abandon Kuwait when their GNP goes down 70 percent? Can anybody guarantee that? The answer is no. We can't guarantee that. But the other options we have also must be held to the same standard. A sanctions policy is not perfect. There are no guarantees here. But it has to be weighed against the alternatives. . . . What guarantees do we have that the war will be brief and that American casualties will be light? No one can say whether a war will last five days, five weeks, or five months. We know we can win, and we will win. There is no doubt about that. There is no doubt about who wins this war. Our policy and our military planning, however, cannot be based on an expectation that the war will be concluded quickly and easily. . . .

Mr. President, in weighing the costs of the military option, one must also consider our long-term interests in the region. Has there been any in-depth analysis in the Administration about what happens in the Middle East after we win? And we will win. The President's declared goals include establishing stability in the Persian Gulf and protecting U.S. citizens abroad. Considering the wave of Islamic reaction, anti-Americanism and terrorism that is likely to be unleashed by a highly destructive war with many Arab casualties, it is difficult to conceive of the Middle East as a more stable region where Americans will be safe. . . .

In summary, Mr. President, I believe that on balance there is a reasonable expectation that continued economic sanctions, backed up by the threat of military force and international isolation, can bring about Iraqi withdrawal from Kuwait. I believe that the risks associated with continued emphasis on sanctions are *considerably less* than the very real risks associated with war and, most importantly, the aftermath of war in a very volatile region of the world. . . .

. . . [I]n conclusion, a message to Saddam Hussein: You are hearing an impassioned debate emanating from the U.S. Capitol, both the House and the Senate. These are the voices of Democracy. Don't misread the debate. If war occurs, the Constitutional and policy debates will be suspended and Congress will provide the American troops in the field whatever they need to prevail. There will be no cutoff of funds for our troops while they engage Iraq in battle. President Bush, the Congress, and the American people are united that you must leave Kuwait. We differ on whether these goals can best be accomplished by administering pain slowly with an economic blockade or by dishing it out in large doses with military power. Either way, Saddam Hussein, you lose.

SPEECH BY SENATOR MITCHELL

. . . In its simplest form, the question is whether Congress will give the President an unlimited blank check to initiate war against Iraq, at some unspecified time in the future, under circumstances which are not now known and cannot be foreseen. or whether, while not ruling out the use of force if all other means fail, we will now urge continuation of the policy of concerted international economic and diplomatic pressure.

This is not a debate about whether force should ever be used. No one proposes to rule out the use of force. We cannot and should not rule it out. The question is should war be truly a last resort when all other means fail? Or should we start with war, before other means have been fully and fairly exhausted?

This is not a debate about American objectives in the current crisis.

There is broad agreement in the Senate that Iraq must, fully and unconditionally, withdraw its forces from Kuwait.

The issue is how best to achieve that goal.

Most Americans and most Members of Congress, myself included, supported the President's initial decision to deploy American forces to Saudi Arabia to deter further Iraqi aggression.

We supported the President's effort in marshalling international diplomatic pressure and the most comprehensive economic embargo in history against Iraq.

I support that policy. I believe it remains the correct policy, even though the President abandoned his own policy before it had time to work.

The change began on November 8, when President Bush announced that he was doubling the number of American troops in the Persian Gulf to 430,000 in order to attain a "credible offensive option."

The President did not consult with Congress about that decision. He did not try to build support for it among the American people. He just did it.

In so doing, President Bush transformed the United States' role and its risk in the Persian Gulf crisis.

In effect, the President—overnight, with no consultation and no public debate—changed American policy from being part of a collective effort to enforce economic and diplomatic sanctions into a predominantly American effort relying upon the use of American military force....

Certainly the United States has a high responsibility to lead the international community in opposing aggression.

But this should not require the U.S. to assume a greater burden and a greater responsibility than other nations with an equal or even greater stake in the resolution of the crisis. That's what's happening. And it's wrong....

The arguments for and against sanctions have been made in detail.

I simply restate my firm conviction that the best course now for the President and the nation is to "stay the course," to continue the policy the President himself so clearly established at the outset of this crisis....

Let no one be under any illusions about the differences between these two resolutions. They are fundamentally different.

One authorizes immediate war. The other does not....

I urge my colleagues to vote for the first resolution, the Nunn Resolution, to vote for continuing economic sanctions and diplomatic pressure. I urge my colleagues to vote against the second resolution, to vote against an authorization for immediate war.

SPEECH BY SENATOR DOLE

... I guess when you ask the question how can you look someone in the eye or the parents and say, "This is worth it," I guess that has always been a question in any war.

To some of us, we see it differently. Sanctions, without a credible military threat, in my view, are not going to work for a long time. But it also seems to some of us that the best way to have peace is for Saddam Hussein to clearly understand the consequences.

Someone sent me a note yesterday saying that they had it on very credible authority that Saddam Hussein was waiting for the Senate vote. He still had some hope that he would prevail, not that anybody wants him to prevail, but that the outcome would mean to him he was going to have a little holiday. Nobody knows how long the holiday would be because there is not any deadline in the Nunn holiday resolution. It is not 1 day, 3 days, 3 months, 3 years.

I think everyone would agree that sanctions without a credible military threat would never have any severe impact on Iraq or Saddam Hussein.

I have said to the President of the United States in a meeting with Republicans and Democrats that we need to pursue every avenue for peaceful solution.

I have said to the President of the United States, when I look into the eyes of a young man in the desert in Saudi Arabia I see his parents, maybe his children, his spouse, and if we talk about burden sharing as we have in the dollar terms, when do we start counting the deaths; how many Egyptians? How many Americans? How many Saudis? How many British? This is the real burden sharing.

I have implored the President, who also has been there in World War II, that what we are attempting to do in the Congress of the United States is to strengthen his hand for peace, not to give him a license to see how fast we can become engaged in armed conflict. As far as this Senator knows, there is nothing in the U.N. resolution that says on January 15 you have to do something. But I think on January 15 Saddam Hussein will understand that if he wants peace, he can have it.

Mr. President, I know that everyone in this Chamber wants Saddam Hussein to get out of Kuwait, and some have additional demands they would make on Saddam Hussein.

I happen to believe that the resolution we are about to vote on does exactly the wrong thing. As I have indicated, it actually gives Saddam Hussein a holiday from the threat that we might use force, if I tell you, well, on January 15 we are going to let sanctions work some interminable length of time—not 6 months.

WAR RESOLUTION

Whereas the Government of Iraq without provocation invaded and occupied the territory of Kuwait on August 2, 1990; and

Whereas both the House of Representatives (in H.J. Res. 658 of the 101st Congress) and the Senate (in S. Con. Res. 147 of the 101st Congress) have condemned Iraq's invasion of Kuwait and declared their support for international action to reverse Iraq's aggression; and

Whereas Iraq's conventional, chemical, biological, and nuclear weapons and ballistic missile programs and its demonstrated willingness to use weapons of mass destruction pose a grave threat to world peace; and

Whereas the international community has demanded that Iraq withdraw unconditionally and immediately from Kuwait and that Kuwait's independence and legitimate government be restored; and

Whereas the U.N. Security Council repeatedly affirmed the inherent right of individual or collective self-defense in response to the armed attack by Iraq against Kuwait in accordance with Article 51 of the U.N. Charter; and

Whereas, in the absence of full compliance by Iraq with its resolutions, the U.N. Security Council in Resolution 678 has authorized member states of the United Nations to use all necessary means, after January 15, 1991, to uphold and implement all relevant Security Council resolutions and to restore international peace and security in the area: and

Whereas Iraq has persisted in its illegal occupation of, and brutal aggression against Kuwait: Now, therefore, be it

Resolved by the Senate and House of Representatives of the United States of America in Congress assembled,

SECTION 1. SHORT TITLE.

This joint resolution may be cited as the "Authorization for Use of Military Force Against Iraq Resolution".

SEC. 2. AUTHORIZATION FOR USE OF UNITED STATES ARMED FORCES.

(a) AUTHORIZATION.

—The President is authorized, subject to subsection (b), to use United States Armed Forces pursuant to United Nations Security Council Resolution 678 (1990) in order to achieve implementation of Security Council Resolutions 660, 661, 662, 664, 665, 666, 667, 669, 670, 674, and 677.

(b) REQUIREMENT FOR DETERMINATION THAT USE OF MILITARY FORCE IS NECESSARY.

—Before exercising the authority granted in subsection (a), the President shall make available to the Speaker of the House of Representatives and the President pro tempore of the Senate his determination that—

(1) the United States had used all appropriate diplomatic and other peaceful means to obtain compliance by Iraq with the United Nations Security Council resolutions cited in subsection (a); and

(2) those efforts have not been and would not be successful in obtaining such compliance.

(c) War Powers Resolution Requirements.—

(1) Specific Statutory Authorization.

—Consistent with section 8(a)(1) of the War Powers Resolution, the Congress declares that this section is intended to constitute specific statutory authorization within the meaning of section 5(b) of the War Powers Resolution.

(2) Applicability of Other Requirements.

—Nothing in this resolution supersedes any requirement of the War Powers Resolution.

SEC. 3. REPORTS TO CONGRESS.

At least once every 60 days, the President shall submit to the Congress a summary on the status of efforts to obtain compliance by Iraq with the resolutions adopted by the United Nations Security Council in response to Iraq's aggression.

PRELUDE AND ONSET
OF WAR WITH IRAQ
January 9, 12, 15, and 16

The United States went to war with Iraq on January 16, engaging American forces in their biggest conflict since the Vietnam War. That evening President George Bush told an expectant nation and world that all peace efforts had failed and combat had begun. As he spoke military targets in Iraq were under attack from U.S. and allied aircraft. The preceding week had been marked by a final but futile round of diplomacy aimed at resolving the crisis that had begun the previous August 2 with Iraq's seizure of Kuwait. To the end, Iraqi president Saddam Hussein remained defiant in the face of pleas from fellow Arab leaders and demands from the United Nations that he withdraw his army from Kuwait.

Since August the UN Security Council had passed a dozen resolutions condemning the invasion and occupation of Kuwait and imposing various trade sanctions on Iraq. The last of the twelve, No. 678, approved November 29, set a January 15 deadline for Iraq to comply or face attack by a U.S.-led multinational military force. Twenty-eight nations provided warplanes, troops, ships, or other support services to this military operation, which bore the code name Operation Desert Storm. But the American deployment was by far the greatest. It comprised more than half a million troops, an armada of warships, and ample air power to dominate the skies of Iraq. Hussein appeared unimpressed by the buildup, boasting on one occasion that if American troops attacked they would "swim in their own blood."

Any lingering hope for a peaceful solution virtually disappeared on January 9 when Secretary of State James P. Baker III reported at the conclusion of a meeting in Geneva with Foreign Minister Tariq Aziz of

Iraq that the two sides remained sharply at odds. Their long-awaited talk was the first and last between high officials of the two countries during the entire crisis. Bush said he had sent Baker to Geneva "not to negotiate but to communicate ... just how determined we are that the Iraqi forces leave Kuwait without condition or further delay." The tenor of the meeting was characterized by Aziz's refusal to deliver to Hussein a letter of warning from Bush.

After the Geneva failure, UN Secretary General Javier Perez de Cuellar undertook a peace mission to Baghdad—his second since August—but returned to New York empty-handed. He then publicly issued a final, unanswered appeal to Iraq January 15, only hours before the Security Council deadline expired. That occurred at the stroke of midnight on the U.S. East Coast—mid-morning in the Persian Gulf region. After that it was just a matter of waiting for the war to start.

"The liberation of Kuwait has begun," President George Bush announced in a brief statement read to White House reporters January 16 at 7:08 p.m. EST. He went on television at 9:01 p.m., speaking from his Oval Office of the failure of "all reasonable efforts" to resolve the crisis peacefully. "Now the 28 countries with forces in the Gulf area ... have no choice but to drive Saddam from Kuwait by force," Bush said. "We will not fail."

"I have instructed our military commanders to take every necessary step to prevail as quickly as possible ... this will not be another Vietnam," the president added. Unlike Vietnam, the war in the Persian Gulf was to end in military victory—more swiftly and with far fewer allied casualties than anticipated. It would greatly boost American morale, the president's popularity, and the U.S. position in world councils. But it appeared to bring neither peace nor political stability to the Middle East. (Victory in the Gulf, p. 97)

> *Following are President George Bush's announcement at a White House news conference, January 9, 1991, of the failure of that day's Geneva talks; Bush's undelivered letter to Iraqi president Saddam Hussein, dated January 5 and publicly released January 12; an appeal to Iraq on behalf of the United Nations from Secretary General Javier Perez de Cuellar in New York on January 15; and Bush's television address January 16 stating that military attacks on Iraq had begun:*

BUSH ON GENEVA TALKS

... I have spoken with Secretary of State Jim Baker, who reported to me on his nearly 7 hours of conversation with Iraqi Foreign Minister Tariq Aziz. Secretary Baker made it clear that he discerned no evidence whatsoever that Iraq was willing to comply with the international community's demand to withdraw from Kuwait and comply with the United Nations resolutions.

Secretary Baker also reported to me that the Iraqi Foreign Minister rejected my letter to Saddam Hussein—refused to carry this letter and give it to the President of Iraq. The Iraqi Ambassador here in Washington did the same thing. This is but one more example that the Iraqi Government is not interested in direct communications designed to settle the Persian Gulf situation.

The record shows that whether the diplomacy is initiated by the United States, the United Nations, the Arab League, or the European Community, the results are the same, unfortunately. The conclusion is clear: Saddam Hussein continues to reject a diplomatic solution.

I sent Secretary Jim Baker to Geneva not to negotiate but to communicate. And I wanted Iraqi leaders to know just how determined we are that the Iraqi forces leave Kuwait without condition or further delay. Secretary Baker made clear that by its full compliance with the 12 relevant United Nations Security Council resolutions, Iraq would gain the opportunity to rejoin the international community. And he also made clear how much Iraq stands to lose if it does not comply.

Let me emphasize that I have not given up on a peaceful outcome—it's not too late. I've just been on the phone, subsequent to the Baker press conference, with King Fahd [of Saudi Arabia], with President [François] Mitterrand [of France]—to whom I've talked twice today—Prime Minister [Brian] Mulroney [of Canada]. And others are contacting other coalition partners to keep the matter under lively discussion. It isn't too late. But now, as it's been before, the choice of peace or war is really Saddam Hussein's to make....

BUSH'S LETTER TO SADDAM HUSSEIN

We do not believe it is appropriate as a general matter to release diplomatic correspondence. However, the President's letter to Saddam Hussein has now appeared in the news media. Stories containing large segments of the letter have appeared on major wire services. This published letter is not, however, the final letter as presented to Foreign Minister [Tariq] Aziz. Therefore, we are today releasing the President's actual letter to Saddam Hussein.

Mr. President:

We stand today at the brink of war between Iraq and the world. This is a war that began with your invasion of Kuwait; this is a war that can be ended only by Iraq's full and unconditional compliance with UN Security Council Resolution 678.

I am writing you now, directly, because what is at stake demands that no opportunity be lost to avoid what would be a certain calamity for the people of Iraq. I am writing, as well, because it is said by some that you do not understand just how isolated Iraq is and what Iraq faces as a result. I am not in a position to judge whether this impression is correct; what I can do, though, is try in this letter to reinforce what Secretary of State Baker told your Foreign Minister and eliminate any uncertainty or ambiguity that might exist in your mind about where we stand and what we are prepared to do.

The international community is united in its call for Iraq to leave all of Kuwait without condition and without further delay. This is not simply the policy of the United States; it is the position of the world community as expressed in no less than twelve Security Council resolutions.

We prefer a peaceful outcome. However, anything less than full compliance with UN Security Council Resolution 678 and its predecessors is unacceptable. There can be no reward for aggression. Nor will there be any negotiation. Principle cannot be compromised. However, by its full compliance, Iraq will gain the opportunity to rejoin the international community. More immediately, the Iraqi military establishment will escape destruction. But unless you withdraw from Kuwait completely and without condition, you will lose more than Kuwait. What is at issue here is not the future of Kuwait—it will be free, its government will be restored—but rather the future of Iraq. This choice is yours to make.

The United States will not be separated from its coalition partners. Twelve Security Council resolutions, 28 countries providing military units to enforce them, more than one hundred governments complying with sanctions—all highlight the fact that it is not Iraq against the United States, but Iraq against the world. That most Arab and Muslim countries are arrayed against you as well should reinforce what I am saying. Iraq cannot and will not be able to hold on to Kuwait or exact a price for leaving.

You may be tempted to find solace in the diversity of opinion that is American democracy. You should resist any such temptation. Diversity ought not to be confused with division. Nor should you underestimate, as others have before you, America's will.

Iraq is already feeling the effects of the sanctions mandated by the United Nations. Should war come, it will be a far greater tragedy for you and your country. Let me state, too, that the United States will not tolerate the use of chemical or biological weapons or the destruction of Kuwait's oil fields and installations. Further, you will be held directly responsible for terrorist actions against any member of the coalition. The American people would demand the strongest possible response. You and your country will pay a terrible price if you order unconscionable acts of this sort.

I write this letter not to threaten, but to inform. I do so with no sense of satisfaction, for the people of the United States have no quarrel with the people of Iraq. Mr. President, UN Security Council Resolution 678 establishes the period before January 15 of this year as a "pause of good will" so that this crisis may end without further violence. Whether this pause is used as intended, or merely becomes a prelude to further violence, is in your hands, and yours alone. I hope you weigh your choice carefully and choose wisely, for much will depend upon it.

SECRETARY GENERAL'S APPEAL TO IRAQ

As 15 January advances, and the world stands poised between peace and war, I most sincerely appeal to President Saddam Hussein to turn the course of events away from catastrophe and towards a new era of justice and harmony based on the principles of the United Nations Charter.

All our efforts in this direction will fail unless Iraq can signify its readiness to comply with the relevant resolutions of the Security Council, beginning with Resolution 660.

If this commitment is made, and clear and substantial steps taken to implement these resolutions, a just peace, with all its benefits, will follow. I therefore urge President Saddam Hussein to commence, without delay, the total withdrawal of Iraqi forces from Kuwait.

Once this process is well under way, I wish to assure him, on the basis of the understandings I have received from governments at the highest level, that neither Iraq nor its forces will be attacked by those arrayed in the international coalition against his country.

Further, with the commencement of withdrawal, as Secretary General of the United Nations, I would, with the consent of the parties concerned, and the agreement of the Security Council, be prepared immediately to deploy United Nations observers and, if necessary, United Nations forces to certify the withdrawal and to insure that hostilities do not erupt on the ground.

In addition, with compliance of the resolutions, I would urge the Security Council to review its decisions imposing sanctions against Iraq.

I would also encourage a process whereby foreign forces deployed in the area would be phased out.

Peace in the region requires that all of its problems be resolved justly and equitably, in accordance with the principles of the Charter of the United Nations.

I have every assurance, once again from the highest levels of government, that with the resolution of the present crisis, every effort will be made to address, in a comprehensive manner, the Arab-Israeli conflict, including the Palestinian question. I pledge my every effort to this end.

As I stated to the council last night, all of us are aware of the extreme gravity of the decisions to be made in the period ahead. No one and no nation can—except with a heavy heart—resort to the other "necessary means" implied by Resolution 678, knowing in advance that tragic and unpredictable consequences can follow.

I trust, in the circumstances, that wisdom and statesmanship will prevail in all quarters in order to move decisively away from conflict. In appealing to President Saddam Hussein today, I wish him to know that I will readily devote my every capacity to working with him, and with all others concerned, to this end.

In the 10th and final year of my tenure as Secretary General of the United Nations, no cause would give me greater satisfaction than to set the Middle East as a whole on the road to a just and lasting peace. And no disappointment would be greater and more tragic than to find the nations of the world engaging in a conflict that none of their peoples want.

BUSH'S WAR ADDRESS

Just 2 hours ago, allied air forces began an attack on military targets in Iraq and Kuwait. These attacks continue as I speak. Ground forces are not engaged.

This conflict started August 2d when the dictator of Iraq invaded a small and helpless neighbor. Kuwait—a member of the Arab League and a member of the United Nations—was crushed; its people, brutalized. Five months ago, Saddam Hussein started this cruel war against Kuwait. Tonight, the battle has been joined.

This military action, taken in accord with United Nations resolutions and with the consent of the United States Congress, follows months of constant and virtually endless diplomatic activity on the part of the United Nations, the United States, and many, many other countries. Arab leaders sought what became known as an Arab solution, only to conclude that Saddam Hussein was unwilling to leave Kuwait. Others traveled to Baghdad in a variety of efforts to restore peace and justice. Our Secretary of State, James Baker, held an historic meeting in Geneva, only to be totally rebuffed. This past weekend, in a last-ditch effort, the Secretary-General of the United Nations went to the Middle East with peace in his heart—his second such mission. And he came back from Baghdad with no progress at all in getting Saddam Hussein to withdraw from Kuwait.

Now the 28 countries with forces in the Gulf area have exhausted all reasonable efforts to reach a peaceful resolution—have no choice but to drive Saddam from Kuwait by force. We will not fail.

As I report to you, air attacks are underway against military targets in Iraq. We are determined to knock out Saddam Hussein's nuclear bomb potential. We will also destroy his chemical weapons facilities. Much of Saddam's artillery and tanks will be destroyed. Our operations are designed to best protect the lives of all the coalition forces by targeting Saddam's vast military arsenal. Initial reports from General [Norman] Schwarzkopf are that our operations are proceeding according to plan.

Our objectives are clear: Saddam Hussein's forces will leave Kuwait. The legitimate government of Kuwait will be restored to its rightful place, and Kuwait will once again be free. Iraq will eventually comply with all relevant United Nations resolutions, and then, when peace is restored, it is our hope that Iraq will live as a peaceful and cooperative member of the family of nations, thus enhancing the security and stability of the Gulf.

Some may ask: Why act now? Why not wait? The answer is clear: The world could wait no longer. Sanctions, though having some effect, showed no signs of accomplishing their objective. Sanctions were tried for well over 5 months, and we and our allies concluded that sanctions alone would not force Saddam from Kuwait.

While the world waited, Saddam Hussein systematically raped, pillaged, and plundered a tiny nation, no threat to his own. He subjected the people of Kuwait to unspeakable atrocities—and among those maimed and murdered, innocent children.

While the world waited, Saddam sought to add to the chemical weapons arsenal he now possesses, an infinitely more dangerous weapon of mass destruction—a nuclear weapon. And while the world waited, while the world talked peace and withdrawal, Saddam Hussein dug in and moved massive forces into Kuwait.

While the world waited, while Saddam stalled, more damage was being done to the fragile economies of the Third World, emerging democracies of Eastern Europe, to the entire world, including to our own economy.

The United States, together with the United Nations, exhausted every means at our disposal to bring this crisis to a peaceful end. However, Saddam clearly felt that by stalling and threatening and defying the United Nations, he could weaken the forces arrayed against him.

While the world waited, Saddam Hussein met every overture of peace with open contempt. While the world prayed for peace, Saddam prepared for war.

I had hoped that when the United States Congress, in historic debate, took its resolute action, Saddam would realize he could not prevail and would move out of Kuwait in accord with the United Nation[s] resolutions. He did not do that. Instead, he remained intransigent, certain that time was on his side.

Saddam was warned over and over again to comply with the will of the United Nations: Leave Kuwait, or be driven out. Saddam has arrogantly rejected all warnings. Instead, he tried to make this a dispute between Iraq and the United States of America.

Well, he failed. Tonight, 28 nations—countries from 5 continents, Europe and Asia, Africa, and the Arab League—have forces in the Gulf area standing shoulder to shoulder against Saddam Hussein. These countries had hoped the use of force could be avoided. Regrettably, we now believe that only force will make him leave.

Prior to ordering our forces into battle, I instructed our military commanders to take every necessary step to prevail as quickly as possible, and with the greatest degree of protection possible for American and allied servicemen and women. I've told the American people before that this will not be another Vietnam, and I repeat this here tonight. Our troops will have the best possible support in the entire world, and they will not be asked to fight with one hand tied behind their back. I'm hopeful that this fighting will not go on for long and that casualties will be held to an absolute minimum.

This is an historic moment. We have in this past year made great progress in ending the long era of conflict and cold war. We have before us the opportunity to forge for ourselves and for future generations a new world order—a world where the rule of law, not the law of the jungle, governs the conduct of nations. When we are successful—and we will be—

we have a real chance at this new world order, an order in which a credible United Nations can use its peacekeeping role to fulfill the promise and vision of the U.N.'s founders.

We have no argument with the people of Iraq. Indeed, for the innocents caught in this conflict, I pray for their safety. Our goal is not the conquest of Iraq. It is the liberation of Kuwait. It is my hope that somehow the Iraqi people can, even now, convince their dictator that he must lay down his arms, leave Kuwait and let Iraq itself rejoin the family of peace-loving nations.

Thomas Paine wrote many years ago: "These are the times that try men's souls." Those well-known words are so very true today. But even as planes of the multinational forces attack Iraq, I prefer to think of peace, not war. I am convinced not only that we will prevail but that out of the horror of combat will come the recognition that no nation can stand against a world united. No nation will be permitted to brutally assault its neighbor.

No president can easily commit our sons and daughters to war. They are the Nation's finest. Ours is an all-volunteer force, magnificently trained, highly motivated. The troops know why they're there. And listen to what they say, for they've said it better than any President or Prime Minister ever could.

Listen to Hollywood Huddleston, Marine lance corporal. He says, "Let's free these people, so we can go home and be free again." And he's right. The terrible crimes and tortures committed by Saddam's henchmen against the innocent people of Kuwait are an affront to mankind and a challenge to the freedom of all.

Listen to one of our great officers out there, Marine Lieutenant General Walter Boomer. He said: "There are things worth fighting for. A world in which brutality and lawlessness are allowed to go unchecked isn't the kind of world we're going to want to live in."

Listen to Master Sergeant J. P. Kendall of the 82d Airborne: "We're here for more than just the price of a gallon of gas. What we're doing is going to chart the future of the world for the next 100 years. It's better to deal with this guy now than 5 years from now."

And finally, we should all sit up and listen to Jackie Jones, an Army lieutenant, when she says, "If we let him get away with this, who knows what's going to be next?"

I have called upon Hollywood and Walter and J. P. and Jackie and all their courageous comrades-in-arms to do what must be done. Tonight, America and the world are deeply grateful to them and to their families. And let me say to everyone listening or watching tonight: When the troops we've sent in finish their work, I am determined to bring them home as soon as possible.

Tonight, as our forces fight, they and their families are in our prayers. May God bless each and every one of them, and the coalition forces at our side in the Gulf, and may He continue to bless our nation, the United States of America.

SUPREME COURT ON
SCHOOL DESEGREGATION
January 15, 1991

The Supreme Court for the first time January 15 sought to determine the point at which lower federal courts could release local school boards from court-ordered desegregation plans. The plans invariably involved mandatory busing (transporting children from one-race neighborhoods to sometimes distant schools) to achieve a racial mixture in the community's classrooms.

A majority of five justices held that the courts should end their supervision if school boards complied "in good faith" and eliminated "vestiges of past discrimination . . . to the extent practicable." If those conditions were met, the reappearance of one-race schools as a result of housing patterns or private choice should not keep a judge from lifting a desegregation order, said Chief Justice William H. Rehnquist.

Without saying how to define "vestiges" or "extent practicable," the Court sent the case involving Oklahoma City public schools back to the local federal district court to determine if the school board had met the new criteria. The decision, in Board of Education v. Dowell, *reversed a 1989 ruling by a federal appeals court in Denver. Rehnquist said that the appellate court, in refusing to remove all judiciary control over the schools, had applied too strict a standard.*

The Dowell *decision was not viewed as an outright retreat from the principle that school districts must eliminate the effects of segregation policies, which the Court set forth in the 1954 landmark case of* Brown v. Board of Education. *However, some legal analysts viewed it as an indication that the era of court-imposed and -supervised school desegregation plans might be coming to an end.*

Nationwide Problem

The Justice Department was at the time involved in about 500 school desegregation cases nationally, and four of them had reached the Supreme Court. In addition to the Oklahoma City case, the Court had been asked to review similar cases arising from Atlanta, Denver, and Topeka, Kansas, site of the original Brown case. The Court deferred action on all three until it decided the Oklahoma City case, which it had previously agreed to review.

It was expected that once the Oklahoma City case was decided, the other three cases would be sent back to lower federal courts with instructions to apply the new standard. However, on February 19 the Supreme Court, without explanation, announced that it would also hear the Atlanta (DeKalb County School District) case, Freeman v. Pitts, but not the Denver case, School Board No. 1 v. Keys. The Topeka case was not mentioned, raising the prospect that its outcome would be determined by the Atlanta decision, which would probably be issued in the Court's 1991-1992 term.

The justices' acceptance of the Atlanta case so soon after issuing the Dowell decision indicated that the lower courts needed more guidance than it had set forth. Chief Justice Rehnquist was joined in that decision by Justices Byron R. White, Sandra Day O'Connor, Antonin Scalia, and Anthony M. Kennedy. Justice Thurgood Marshall wrote a dissenting opinion, in which Justices Harry A. Blackmun and John Paul Stevens concurred. Justice David H. Souter, who joined the Court after the case was argued, did not vote.

Case's Litigation Since 1961

Marshall, who as a civil rights lawyer had argued the Brown case before the Supreme Court, contended that the re-emergence of some predominantly black and predominantly white schools in Oklahoma City was a relevant vestige of de jure, or officially imposed, segregation. Litigation in the case had begun nearly thirty years earlier. In 1961, seven years after the Brown decision struck down the "separate but equal" doctrine of school segregation, a group of black students and their parents sued the Oklahoma City school board, charging it with unlawfully operating a segregated school system.

Two years later a federal district court agreed, saying that the city had intentionally created both segregated housing and schools. Determining in 1965 and again in 1972 that the school board's efforts had not brought about integration, the district court ordered the board to achieve it through busing. In 1977 the district court agreed that the board had acted in "substantial compliance" with the order and lifted it.

Then in 1984 the school board adopted a student reassignment plan that retained busing only for the older children. The next year a group of plaintiffs, seeking to reopen the case, told the district court that the city's schools were becoming more segregated. They lost in that court but won *in 1986 and again in 1989 on appeal to the U.S. Circuit Court of Appeals, in Denver. At issue before the Supreme Court was the appellate court's reasoning in its 1989 ruling that reinstated judicial jurisdiction over the school board.*

> *Following are excerpts from the Supreme Court's majority and dissenting opinions in* Board of Education v. Dowell, *issued January 15, 1991, returning an Oklahoma City school desegregation case to federal district court with a new standard for determining such cases:*

<u>No. 89-1080</u>

Board of Education of Oklahoma City Public Schools, Independent School District No. 89, Oklahoma County, Oklahoma, Petitioner
v.
Robert L. Dowell et al.

On writ of certiorari to the United States Court of Appeals for the Tenth Circuit

[January 15, 1991]

CHIEF JUSTICE REHNQUIST delivered the opinion of the Court.

Petitioner Board of Education of Oklahoma City sought dissolution of a decree entered by the District Court imposing a school desegregation plan. The District Court granted relief over the objection of respondents Robert L. Dowell, et al., black students and their parents. The Court of Appeals for the Tenth Circuit reversed, holding that the Board would be entitled to such relief only upon " '[n]othing less than a clear showing of grievous wrong evoked by new and unforeseen conditions. . . .' " We hold that the Court of Appeals' test is more stringent than is required either by our cases dealing with injunctions or by the Equal Protection Clause of the Fourteenth Amendment.

I

This school desegregation litigation began almost 30 years ago. In 1961, respondents, black students and their parents, sued petitioners, the Board of Education of Oklahoma City (Board), to end *de jure* [officially sanctioned] segregation in the public schools. In 1963, the District Court found that Oklahoma City had intentionally segregated both schools and housing in the past, and that Oklahoma City was operating a "dual" school system—one that was intentionally segregated by race. *Dowell* v. *School Board of Oklahoma City Public Schools* (WD Okla.). In 1965, the District Court found that the School Board's attempt to desegregate by using neighborhood zoning failed to remedy past segregation because residential segregation resulted in one-race schools. Residential segregation had once been state imposed, and it lingered due to discrimination by some realtors and financial institutions. The District Court found that school segregation had caused some housing segregation. In 1972, finding that previous efforts had not been successful at eliminating state imposed segregation, the District Court ordered the Board to adopt the "Finger Plan," under which kindergarteners would be assigned to neighborhood schools unless their parents opted otherwise; children in grades 1-4 would attend formerly all white schools, and thus black children would be bused to those schools; children in grade five would attend formerly all black schools, and thus white children would be bused to those schools; students in the upper grades would be bused to various areas in order to maintain integrated schools; and in integrated neighborhoods there would be stand-alone schools for all grades.

In 1977, after complying with the desegregation decree for five years, the Board made a "Motion to Close Case." The District Court held in its "Order Terminating Case":

> "The Court has concluded that [the Finger Plan] worked and that substantial compliance with the constitutional requirements has been achieved....
> Jurisdiction in this case is terminated ... subject only to final disposition of any case now pending on appeal."

This unpublished order was not appealed.

In 1984, the School Board faced demographic changes that led to greater burdens on young black children. As more and more neighborhoods became integrated, more stand-alone schools were established, and young black students had to be bused farther from their inner-city homes to outlying white areas. In an effort to alleviate this burden and to increase parental involvement, the Board adopted the Student Reassignment Plan (SRP), which relied on neighborhood assignments for students in grades K-4 beginning in the 1985-1986 school year. Busing continued for students in grades 5-12. Any student could transfer from a school where he or she was in the majority to a school where he or she would be in the minority. Faculty and staff integration was retained, and an "equity officer" was appointed.

In 1985, respondents filed a "Motion to Reopen the Case," contending that the School District had not achieved "unitary" status and that the SRP was a return to segregation. Under the SRP, 11 of 64 elementary schools would be greater than 90% black, 22 would be greater than 90% white plus other minorities, and 31 would be racially mixed. The District Court refused to reopen the case.... The District Court found that the School Board, administration, faculty, support staff, and student body were integrated, and transportation, extracurricular activities and facilities within the district were equal and nondiscriminatory. Because unitariness had been achieved, the District Court concluded that court-ordered desegregation must end.

The Court of Appeals for the Tenth Circuit [in 1986] . . . reasoned that the finding that the system was unitary merely ended the District Court's active supervision of the case, and because the school district was still subject to the desegregation decree, respondents could challenge the SRP. The case was remanded to determine whether the decree should be lifted or modified.

On remand, the District Court found that demographic changes made the Finger Plan unworkable, that the Board had done nothing for 25 years to promote residential segregation, and that the school district had bused students for more than a decade in good-faith compliance with the court's orders. The District Court found that present residential segregation was the result of private decisionmaking and economics, and that it was too attenuated to be a vestige of former school segregation. . . .

The Court of Appeals again reversed [in 1989], holding that " 'an injunction takes on a life of its own and becomes an edict quite independent of the law it is meant to effectuate.' " That court approached the case "not so much as one dealing with desegregation, but as one dealing with the proper application of the federal law on injunctive remedies." Relying on *United States* v. *Swift & Co.* (1932), it held that a desegregation decree remains in effect until a school district can show "grievous wrong evoked by new and unforeseen conditions." . . .

We granted the Board's petition for certiorari to resolve a conflict between the standard laid down by the Court of Appeals in this case and that laid down in *Spangler* v. *Pasadena City Board of Education* (CA9 1979), and *Riddick* v. *School Bd. of City of Norfolk* (CA4 1986). We now reverse the Court of Appeals.

II

We must first consider whether respondents may contest the District Court's 1987 order dissolving the injunction which had imposed the desegregation decree. Respondents did not appeal from the District Court's 1977 order finding that the school system had achieved unitary status, and petitioners contend that the 1977 order bars respondents from contesting the 1987 order. We disagree, for the 1977 order did not dissolve the desegregation decree and the District Court's unitariness finding was too ambiguous to bar respondents from challenging later action by the Board.

The lower courts have been inconsistent in their use of the term "unitary." Some have used it to identify a school district that has completely remedied all vestiges of past discrimination. Under that interpretation of the word, a unitary school district is one that has met the mandate of *Brown* v. *Board of Education* (1955), and *Green* v. *New Kent County School Board* (1968). Other courts, however, have used "unitary" to describe any school district that has currently desegregated student assignments, whether or not that status is solely the result of a court-imposed desegregation plan. In other words, such a school district could be called unitary and nevertheless still contain vestiges of past discrimination. . . .

We think it is a mistake to treat words such as "dual" and "unitary" as if they were actually found in the Constitution. The constitutional command of the Fourteenth Amendment is that "[n]o State shall ... deny to any person ... the equal protection of the laws." Courts have used the terms "dual" to denote a school system which has engaged in intentional segregation of students by race, and "unitary" to describe a school system which has been brought into compliance with the command of the Constitution. We are not sure how useful it is to define these terms more precisely, or to create subclasses within them. But there is no doubt that the differences in usage described above do exist.

III

The Court of Appeals relied upon language from this Court's decision in *United States* v. *Swift and Co., supra,* for the proposition that a desegregation decree could not be lifted or modified absent a showing of "grievous wrong evoked by new and unforeseen conditions." ...

In *Swift,* several large meat-packing companies entered into a consent decree whereby they agreed to refrain forever from entering into the grocery business. The decree was by its terms effective in perpetuity. The defendant meat-packers and their allies had over a period of a decade attempted, often with success in lower courts, to frustrate operation of the decree. It was in this context that the language relied upon by the Court of Appeals in this case was used.

United States v. *United Shoe Machinery Corp.* (1968), explained that the language used in *Swift* must be read in the context of the continuing danger of unlawful restraints on trade which the Court had found still existed. ... In the present case, a finding by the District Court that the Oklahoma City School District was being operated in compliance with the commands of the Equal Protection Clause of the Fourteenth Amendment, and that it was unlikely that the school board would return to its former ways, would be a finding that the purposes of the desegregation litigation had been fully achieved. No additional showing of "grievous wrong evoked by new and unforeseen conditions" is required of the school board. ...

Petitioners urge that we reinstate the decision of the District Court terminating the injunction, but we think that the preferable course is to remand the case to that court so that it may decide, in accordance with this opinion, whether the Board made a sufficient showing of constitutional compliance as of 1985, when the SRP was adopted, to allow the injunction to be dissolved. The District Court should address itself to whether the Board had complied in good faith with the desegregation decree since it was entered, and whether the vestiges of past discrimination had been eliminated to the extent practicable. ...

After the District Court decides whether the Board was entitled to have the decree terminated, it should proceed to decide respondent's challenge to the SRP. A school district which has been released from an injunction imposing a desegregation plan no longer requires court authorization for the promulgation of policies and rules regulating matters such as assignment of students and the like, but it of course remains subject to the mandate of the Equal Protection Clause of the Fourteenth Amendment. . . .

The judgment of the Court of Appeals is reversed, and the case is remanded to the District Court for further proceedings consistent with this opinion.

It is so ordered.

JUSTICE MARSHALL, with whom JUSTICE BLACKMUN and JUSTICE STEVENS join, dissenting.

Oklahoma gained statehood in 1907. For the next 65 years, the Oklahoma City School Board maintained segregated schools—initially relying on laws requiring dual school systems; thereafter, by exploiting residential segregation that had been created by legally enforced restrictive covenants. In 1972—18 years after this Court first found segregated schools unconstitutional—a federal court finally interrupted this cycle, enjoining the Oklahoma City School Board to implement a specific plan for achieving actual desegregation of its schools.

The practical question now before us is whether, 13 years after that injunction was imposed, the same School Board should have been allowed to return many of its elementary schools to their former one-race status. The majority today suggests that 13 years of desegregation was enough. The Court remands the case for further evaluation of whether the purposes of the injunctive decree were achieved sufficient to justify the decree's dissolution. However, the inquiry it commends to the District Court fails to recognize explicitly the threatened reemergence of one-race schools as a relevant "vestige" of *de jure* segregation.

In my view, the standard for dissolution of a school desegregation decree must reflect the central aim of our school desegregation precedents. In *Brown* v. *Board of Education* (1954) *(Brown I)*, a unanimous Court declared that racially "[s]eparate educational facilities are inherently unequal." . . . Remedying this evil and preventing its recurrence were the motivations animating our requirement that formerly *de jure* segregated school districts take all feasible steps to *eliminate* racially identifiable schools. See *Green* v. *New Kent County School Bd.* (1968); *Swann* v. *Charlotte-Mecklenburg Bd. of Education* (1971).

I believe a desegregation decree cannot be lifted so long as conditions likely to inflict the stigmatic injury condemned in *Brown I* persist and there remain feasible methods of eliminating such conditions. Because the record here shows, and the Court of Appeals found, that feasible steps could be taken to avoid one-race schools, it is clear that the purposes of the decree have not yet been achieved and the Court of Appeals' reinstatement of the decree should be affirmed. I therefore dissent.

I

In order to assess the full consequence of lifting the decree at issue in this case, it is necessary to explore more fully than does the majority the history of racial segregation in the Oklahoma City schools. This history reveals nearly unflagging resistance by the Board to judicial efforts to dismantle the City's dual education system.... In addition to laws enforcing segregation in the schools, racially restrictive covenants, supported by state and local law, established a segregated residential pattern in Oklahoma City. Petitioner Board of Education of Oklahoma City (Board) exploited this residential segregation to enforce school segregation, locating "all-Negro" schools in the heart of the City's northeast quadrant, in which the majority of the City's Afro-American citizens resided....

Parents of Afro-American children relegated to schools in the northeast quadrant filed suit against the Board in 1961. Finding that the Board's special transfer policy was "designed to perpetuate and encourage segregation," the District Court struck down the policy as a violation of the Equal Protection Clause. Undeterred, the Board proceeded to adopt another special transfer policy which, as the District Court found in 1965, had virtually the same effect as the prior policy.... Rather than promote integration through new school locations, the District Court found that the Board destroyed some integrated neighborhoods and schools by adopting inflexible neighborhood school attendance zones that encouraged whites to migrate to all-white areas....

Thus, by 1972, 11 years after the plaintiffs had filed suit ... the School Board continued to resist integration and in some respects the Board had worsened the situation.... The District Court concluded: "This litigation has been frustratingly interminable ... because of the unpardonable recalcitrance of the ... Board." Consequently, the District Court ordered the Board to implement the only available plan that exhibited the promise of achieving actual desegregation—the "Finger Plan" offered by the plaintiffs.

In 1975, after a mere three years of operating under the Finger Plan, the Board filed a "Motion to Close Case," arguing that it had " 'eliminated all vestiges of state imposed racial discrimination in its school system.' " In 1977, the District Court granted the Board's motion and ... concluded that the Board had "operated the [Finger] Plan properly" and stated that it did not "foresee that the termination of ... jurisdiction will result in the dismantlement of the [Finger] Plan or any affirmative action by the defendant to undermine the unitary system." The order ended the District Court's active supervision of the school district but did not dissolve the injunctive decree. The plaintiffs did not appeal this order.

The Board continued to operate under the Finger Plan until 1985, when it implemented the Student Reassignment Plan (SRP). The SRP superimposed attendance zones over some residentially segregated areas. As a result, considerable racial imbalance reemerged in 33 of 64 elementary schools in the Oklahoma City system with student bodies either greater than 90% Afro-American or greater than 90% non-Afro-American....

In response to the SRP, the plaintiffs moved to reopen the case. Ultimately, the District Court dissolved the desegregation decree, finding that the school district had been "unitary" since 1977 and that the racial imbalances under the SRP were the consequence of residential segregation arising from "personal preferences." The Court of Appeals reversed, finding that the Board had not met its burden to establish that "the condition the [decree] sought to alleviate, a constitutional violation, has been eradicated."

II

I agree with the majority that the proper standard for determining whether a school desegregation decree should be dissolved is whether the purposes of the desegregation litigation, as incorporated in the decree, have been fully achieved.... I strongly disagree with the majority, however, on what must be shown to demonstrate that a decree's purposes have been fully realized. In my view, a standard for dissolution of a desegregation decree must take into account the unique harm associated with a system of racially identifiable schools and must expressly demand the elimination of such schools.

A

Our pointed focus in *Brown I* upon the stigmatic injury caused by segregated schools explains our unflagging insistence that formerly *de jure* segregated school districts extinguish all vestiges of school segregation. The concept of stigma also gives us guidance as to what conditions must be eliminated before a decree can be deemed to have served its purpose.

In the decisions leading up to *Brown I*, the Court had attempted to curtail the ugly legacy of *Plessy* v. *Ferguson* (1896), by insisting on a searching inquiry into whether "separate" Afro-American schools were genuinely "equal" to white schools in terms of physical facilities, curricula, quality of the faculty and certain "intangible" considerations. In *Brown I*, the Court finally liberated the Equal Protection Clause from the doctrinal tethers of *Plessy*, declaring that "in the field of public education the doctrine of 'separate but equal' has no place. Separate educational facilities are inherently unequal."

The Court based this conclusion on its recognition of the particular social harm that racially segregated schools inflict on Afro-American children.... Remedying and avoiding the recurrence of this stigmatizing injury have been the guiding objectives of this Court's desegregation jurisprudence ever since. These concerns inform the standard by which the Court determines the effectiveness of a proposed desegregation remedy....

Similarly, avoiding reemergence of the harm condemned in *Brown I* accounts for the Court's insistence on remedies that ensure lasting integration of formerly segregated systems. Such school districts are required to "make every effort to achieve the *greatest possible degree of actual desegregation* and [to] be concerned with the elimination of one-race schools." ... This focus on "achieving and *preserving* an integrated school system," stems from the recognition that the reemergence of racial separation in such schools may revive the message of racial inferiority implicit in the former policy of state-enforced segregation.

Just as it is central to the standard for evaluating the formation of a desegregation decree, so should the stigmatic injury associated with segregated schools be central to the standard for dissolving a decree. The Court has indicated that "the ultimate end to be brought about" by a desegregation remedy is "a unitary, nonracial system of public education." We have suggested that this aim is realized once school officials have "eliminate[d] from the public schools *all* vestiges of state-imposed segregation"... Although the Court has never explicitly defined what constitutes a "vestige" of state-enforced segregation, the function that this concept has performed in our jurisprudence suggests that it extends to any condition that is likely to convey the message of inferiority implicit in a policy of segregation. So long as such conditions persist, the purposes of the decree cannot be deemed to have been achieved.

B

The majority suggests a more vague and, I fear, milder standard. Ignoring the harm identified in *Brown I*, the majority asserts that the District Court should find that the purposes of the decree have been achieved so long as "the Oklahoma City School District [is now] being operated in compliance with the commands of the Equal Protection Clause" and "it [is] unlikely that the school board would return to its former ways." Insofar as the majority instructs the District Court, on remand, to "conside[r] whether the vestiges of *de jure* segregation ha[ve] been eliminated as far as practicable," the majority presumably views elimination of vestiges as part of "operat[ing] in compliance with the commands of the Equal Protection Clause." But as to the scope or meaning of "vestiges," the majority says very little.

By focusing heavily on present and future compliance with the Equal Protection Clause, the majority's standard ignores how the stigmatic harm identified in *Brown I* can persist even after the State ceases actively to enforce segregation.... In sum, our school-desegregation jurisprudence establishes that the *effects* of past discrimination remain chargeable to the school district regardless of its lack of continued enforcement of segregation, and the remedial decree is required until those effects have been finally eliminated....

[III omitted]

IV

Consistent with the mandate of *Brown I*, our cases have imposed on school districts an unconditional duty to eliminate *any* condition that perpetuates the message of racial inferiority inherent in the policy of state-sponsored segregation. The racial identifiability of a district's schools is such a condition. Whether this "vestige" of state-sponsored segregation will persist cannot simply be ignored at the point where a district court is contemplating the dissolution of a desegregation decree. In a district with a history of state-sponsored school segregation, racial separation, in my view, *remains* inherently unequal.

I dissent.

STATE OF THE UNION ADDRESS
AND DEMOCRATIC RESPONSE
January 29, 1991

President George Bush used his second annual State of the Union address January 29 to rally the nation behind his Persian Gulf policy, on which his political future seemed destined to stand or fall. Only thirteen days earlier he had committed the United States to war with Iraq, and there was yet no certainty that it would end in a swift victory with few American casualties. (Prelude and Onset of War with Iraq, p. 15)

The president sketched out his rationale for American military action in the Middle East and his vision of a "new world order" to follow. His nationally televised speech before a joint session of Congress evoked rhetoric from other wars. With a phrase echoing Winston Churchill's "our finest hour," Bush spoke of standing with his countrymen at a "defining hour." He said Americans have a "unique responsibility to do the hard work of freedom."

"What is at stake is more than one small country," Bush said. "It is a big idea: a new world order, where diverse nations are drawn together in common cause to achieve the universal aspirations of mankind: peace and security, freedom and the rule of law." He suggested that the end of the Cold War with the Soviet Union and its involvement in the U.S.-led effort of the United Nations to "repel [Iraq's] lawless aggression" foretold a new spirit of cooperation in world affairs. In attempting to articulate America's war aims, the president tried to counter criticism that, despite broad public support for the war and his wartime leadership, he had not made clear why the United States was engaged in combat in the Middle East.

Bush's popularity had surged since the late summer when he assumed the leadership in lining up international support to force Iraq to withdraw from Kuwait, which it invaded August 2. A Washington Post/ABC News *poll released January 27 showed that 79 percent of the people surveyed approved his handling of his job. It was his highest rating since he had assumed the presidency two years earlier.*

Significantly, however, on his handling of the economy, Bush received an approval rating of only 45 percent. The president said little about what sacrifices might be demanded if the Middle East fighting turned into a protracted land war, or about the economic recession that had beset the country since the previous summer.

State of the Economy

In the Democrats' response, which immediately followed Bush's speech on national television, Senate majority leader George J. Mitchell of Maine said: "The president says he seeks a new world order. We ask him to join us in putting our own house in order." But Democrats, like Bush, were hemmed in by the constraints of war, recession, and record budget deficits in trying to fashion a domestic agenda.

Bush acknowledged that the country was in an economic recession, but vowed, "We will get this recession behind us and return to growth soon." He characterized the recession as a "temporary interruption" in a long period of national prosperity.

To stimulate economic growth, Bush called for tax breaks for family savings accounts and first-time home buyers, and a reduction in the tax rate on capital gains. The inclusion of capital gains was cheered by conservative Republicans as a triumph over party pragmatists who wanted to avoid refighting the issue. In 1990 the president's futile insistence on capital gains tax cuts stalled budget negotiations between Congress and the White House. (Bush on Taxes, Historic Documents of 1990, p. 409)

The president brought up capital gains with a new twist, which some interpreted as an effort to shelve the issue. He proposed having Federal Reserve Board chairman Alan Greenspan conduct a study to resolve what Bush called "technical differences"—disputes over whether the ultimate effect would be to increase or decrease revenues.

Domestic Agenda

The speech included several other references to the ideas of a group of young Republican conservatives who had been pushing domestic initiatives under the concept of "empowerment" of individuals through government policies. Bush mentioned parental choice in education and other ideas espoused by these conservatives, who included House minority whip Newt Gingrich, of Georgia. But his address lacked the partisan edge they had advocated for drawing clear lines between Republican and Democratic solutions to social ills.

One of the few proposals that was new to Bush's agenda was to eliminate about $15 billion in federal social programs and give the money *to the states in a single grant. However, the idea was reminiscent of President Ronald Reagan's "new federalism" and drew heavy criticism in Congress and from some governors, who argued that the funds were not sufficient for the projects they would encompass.*

Elaborate Security Precautions

Because of concern regarding war-related terrorism, unusually elaborate security precautions were in effect the evening of the address. Despite some suggestions that the speech be postponed or cancelled, Bush insisted it would be delivered as scheduled. "I am not going to be held a captive in the White House by Saddam Hussein of Iraq," he said January 25 at a news conference.

Additional Capitol police officers, with bomb-sniffing dogs, patrolled the Capitol and manned numerous checkpoints in and around the building. For two hours before the speech began, at 9:00 p.m. EST, traffic was banned on streets for several blocks around the Capitol. As is customary at every State of the Union address, one cabinet member did not attend; in the event of a catastrophe at the Capitol, someone in the line of presidential succession would survive. The designated cabinet member in 1991 was Secretary of the Interior Manuel Lujan, Jr.

Following is the 1991 State of the Union address delivered by President George Bush to a joint session of Congress and the nation on January 29, and the response by Majority Leader George J. Mitchell on behalf of congressional Democrats. (The bracketed headings have been added by Congressional Quarterly to highlight the organization of the text.):

STATE OF THE UNION ADDRESS

Mr. President, Mr. Speaker, members of the United States Congress. I come to this House of the people, to speak to you and all Americans, certain that we stand at a defining hour. Halfway around the world, we are engaged in a great struggle in the skies and on the seas and sands. We know why we're there. We are Americans: part of something larger than ourselves.

For two centuries, we've done the hard work of freedom. And tonight we lead the world in facing down a threat to decency and humanity. What is at stake is more than one small country; it is a big idea: a new world order, where diverse nations are drawn together in common cause to achieve the universal aspirations of mankind: peace and security, freedom and the rule of law. Such is a world worthy of our struggle and worthy of our children's future.

The community of nations has resolutely gathered to condemn and repel lawless aggression. [Iraqi President] Saddam Hussein's unprovoked invasion, his ruthless, systematic rape of a peaceful neighbor, violated everything the community of nations holds dear. The world has said this aggression would not stand—and it will not stand.

Together, we have resisted the trap of appeasement, cynicism and isolation that gives temptation to tyrants. The world has answered Saddam's invasion with 12 United Nations resolutions, starting with a demand for Iraq's immediate and unconditional withdrawal—and backed up by forces from 28 countries of six continents. With few exceptions, the world now stands as one.

The end of the Cold War has been a victory for all humanity. A year and a half ago, in Germany, I said that our goal was a Europe whole and free. Tonight, Germany is united. Europe has become whole and free—and America's leadership was instrumental in making it possible.

Our relationship with the Soviet Union is important, not only to us but to the world. That relationship has helped to shape these and other historic changes. But like many other nations, we have been deeply concerned by the violence in the Baltics, and we have communicated that concern to the Soviet leadership.

The principle that has guided us is simple: Our objective is to help the Baltic peoples achieve their aspirations, not to punish the Soviet Union.

In our recent discussions with the Soviet leadership, we have been given representations, which, if fulfilled, would result in the withdrawal of some Soviet forces, a reopening of dialogue with the republics and a move away from violence. We will watch carefully as the situation develops. And we will maintain our contact with the Soviet leadership to encourage continued commitment to democratization and reform.

[Victory Over Tyranny]

If it is possible, I want to continue to build a lasting basis for U.S.-Soviet cooperation, for a more peaceful future for all mankind. The triumph of democratic ideas in Eastern Europe and Latin America—and the continuing struggle for freedom elsewhere all around the world—all confirm the wisdom of our nation's founders. Tonight, we work to achieve another victory, a victory over tyranny and savage aggression.

We in this union enter the last decade of the 20th century thankful for our blessings, steadfast in our purpose, aware of our difficulties and responsive to our duties at home and around the world.

For two centuries, America has served the world as an inspiring example of freedom and democracy. For generations, America has led the struggle to preserve and extend the blessings of liberty. And today, in a rapidly changing world, American leadership is indispensable. Americans know that leadership brings burdens and sacrifices.

But we also [know] why the hopes of humanity turn to us.

We are Americans: We have a unique responsibility to do the hard work of freedom. And when we do—freedom works.

The conviction and courage we see in the Persian Gulf today is simply the American character in action. The indomitable spirit that is contributing to this victory for world peace and justice is the same spirit that gives us the power and the potential to meet our toughest challenges at home.

We are resolute and resourceful. If we can selflessly confront the evil for the sake of good in a land so far away, then surely we can make this land all that it should be.

If anyone tells you that America's best days are behind her, they're looking the wrong way.

[An Appeal for Renewal]

Tonight, I come before this House and the American people with an appeal for renewal. This is not merely a call for new government initiatives, it is a call for new initiative in government, in our communities and from every American to prepare for the next American century.

America has always led by example. So who among us will set the example? Which of our citizens will lead us in this American century? Everyone who steps forward today to get one addict off drugs, to convince one troubled teenager not to give up on life, to comfort one AIDS patient, to help one hungry child.

We have within our reach the promise of a renewed America. We can find meaning and reward by serving some higher purpose than ourselves—a shining purpose, the illumination of a thousand points of light. And it is expressed by all who know the irresistible force of a child's hand, of a friend who stands by you and stays there, a volunteer's generous gesture, an idea that is simply right.

The problems before us may be different, but the key to solving them remains the same: It is the individual—the individual—who steps forward. And the state of our union is the union of each of us, one to the other; the sum of our friendships, marriages, families and communities.

We all have something to give. So if you know how to read, find someone who can't. If you've got a hammer, find a nail. If you're not hungry, not lonely, not in trouble—seek out someone who is.

Join the community of conscience. Do the hard work of freedom. And that will define the state of our union.

Since the birth of our nation, "We, the people" has been the source of our strength. What government can do alone is limited, but the potential of the American people knows no limits.

We are a nation of rock-solid realism and clear-eyed idealism. We are Americans: We are the nation that believes in the future; we are the nation that can shape the future.

And we've begun to do just that—by strengthening the power and choice of individuals and families.

Together, these last two years, we've put dollars for child care directly in the hands of parents, instead of bureaucracies. Unshackled the potential of Americans with disabilities. Applied the creativity of the marketplace in the service of the environment, for clean air. And made home ownership possible for more Americans.

The strength of a democracy is not in bureaucracy, it is in the people and their communities. In everything we do, let us unleash the potential of our most precious resource—our citizens, our citizens themselves. We must return to families, communities, counties, cities, states and institutions of every kind the power to chart their own destiny, and the freedom and opportunity provided by strong economic growth. And that's what America is all about.

I know, tonight, in some regions of our country, people are in genuine economic distress. And I hear them.

['My Heart Is Aching']

Earlier this month, Kathy Blackwell of Massachusetts wrote me about what can happen when the economy slows down, saying, "My heart is aching, and I think that you should know: Your people out here are hurting badly."

I understand. And I'm not unrealistic about the future. But there are reasons to be optimistic about our economy.

First, we don't have to fight double-digit inflation. Second, most industries won't have to make big cuts in production, because they don't have big inventories piled up. And, third, our exports are running solid and strong. In fact, American businesses are exporting at a record rate.

So let's put these times in perspective. Together, since 1981, we've created almost 20 million jobs, cut inflation in half and cut interest rates in half.

And, yes, the largest peacetime economic expansion in history has been temporarily interrupted. But our economy is still over twice as large as our closest competitor.

We will get this recession behind us and return to growth soon.

We will get on our way to a new record of expansion and achieve the competitive strength that will carry us into the next American century.

We should focus our efforts today on encouraging economic growth, investing in the future, and giving power and opportunity to the individual.

We must begin with control of federal spending.

And that's why I'm submitting a budget that holds the growth in spending to less than the rate of inflation. And that's why, amid all the sound and fury of last year's budget debate, we put into law new enforceable spending caps so that future spending debates will mean a battle of ideas, not a bidding war.

Though controversial, the budget agreement finally put the government on a pay-as-you-go plan — and cut the growth of debt by nearly $500 billion. And that frees funds for saving and job-creating investment.

Now, let's do more. My budget again includes tax-free family savings accounts; penalty-free withdrawals from IRA's for first-time home buyers; and, to increase jobs and growth, a reduced tax for long-term capital gains.

I know there are differences among us about the impact and the effects of a capital gains incentive. So tonight I am asking the congressional leaders and the Federal Reserve to cooperate with us in a study, led by Chairman Alan Greenspan, to sort out our technical differences so that we can avoid a return to unproductive partisan bickering.

But just as our efforts will bring economic growth now and in the future, they must also be matched by long-term investments for the next American century.

[Investment in the Future]

And that requires a forward-looking plan of action—and that's exactly what we will be sending to the Congress. We have prepared a detailed series of proposals that include:

A budget that promotes investment in America's future —in children, education, infrastructure, space and high technology.

Legislation to achieve excellence in education—building on the partnership forged with the 50 governors at the Education Summit, enabling parents to choose their children's schools and helping to make America No. 1 in math and science.

A blueprint for a new national highway system, a critical investment in our transportation infrastructure.

A research and development agenda that includes record levels of federal investment and a permanent tax credit to strengthen private R&D and to create jobs.

A comprehensive national energy strategy that calls for energy conservation and efficiency, increased development and greater use of alternative fuels.

A banking reform plan to bring America's financial system into the 21st century so that our banks remain safe and secure and can continue to make job-creating loans for our factories, businesses and home buyers. You know, I do think there has been too much pessimism. Sound banks should be making sound loans, now—and interest rates should be lower, now.

In addition to these proposals, we must recognize that our economic strength depends upon being competitive in world markets. We must continue to expand American exports. A successful Uruguay Round of world trade negotiations will create more real jobs and more real growth— for all nations. You and I know that if the playing field is level, America's workers and farmers can outwork and outproduce anyone, any time, anywhere.

And with a Mexican free trade agreement and our Enterprise for the Americas Initiative, we can help our partners strengthen their economies and move toward a free trade zone throughout this entire hemisphere.

The budget also includes a plan of action right here at home to put more power and opportunity in the hands of the individual. And that means new incentives to create jobs in our inner cities by encouraging investment through enterprise zones. It also means tenant control and ownership of public housing. Freedom and the power to choose should not be the privilege of wealth. They are the birthright of every American.

Civil rights are also crucial to protecting equal opportunity.

Every one of us has a responsibility to speak out against racism, bigotry and hate.

We will continue our vigorous enforcement of existing statutes, and I will once again press the Congress to strengthen the laws against employment discrimination without resorting to the use of unfair preferences.

We're determined to protect another fundamental civil right—freedom from crime and the fear that stalks our cities. The attorney general will soon convene a crime summit of our nation's law enforcement officials. And to help us support them, we need tough crime-control legislation, and we need it now.

And as we fight crime, we will fully implement our national strategy for combating drug abuse. Recent data show we are making progress, but much remains to be done. We will not rest until the day of the dealer is over forever.

Good health care is every American's right and every American's responsibility. And so we are proposing an aggressive program of new prevention initiatives—for infants, for children, for adults and for the elderly—to promote a healthier America and to help keep costs from spiraling.

[Eliminating PACs]

It's time to give people more choice in government by reviving the ideal of the citizen politician who comes not to stay but to serve. And one of the reasons there is so much support for term limitations is that the American people are increasingly concerned about big-money influence in politics. So we must look beyond the next election to the next generation. And the time has come to put the national interest above the special interest and totally eliminate political action committees [PACs].

And that would truly put more competition in elections and more power in the hands of individuals. And where power cannot be put directly in the hands of the individual, it should be moved closer to the people—away from Washington. The federal government too often treats government programs as if they are of Washington, by Washington and for Washington. Once established, federal programs seem to become immortal. It's time for a more dynamic program life cycle: Some programs should increase, some should decrease, some should be terminated, and some should be consolidated and turned over to the states.

My budget includes a list of programs for potential turnover totaling more than $20 billion. Working with Congress and the governors, I propose we select at least $15 billion in such programs and turn them over to the states in a single consolidated grant, fully funded, for flexible management by the states.

The value of this turnover approach is straightforward. It allows the federal government to reduce overhead. It allows states to manage more flexibly and more efficiently. It moves power and decision-making closer to the people. And it reinforces a theme of this administration: appreciation and encouragement of the innovative power of "states as laboratories."

This nation was founded by leaders who understood that power belongs in the hands of people. And they planned for the future. And so must we, here and all around the world. As Americans, we know there are times when we must step forward and accept our responsibility to lead the world away from the dark chaos of dictators toward the brighter promise of a better day. Almost 50 years ago we began a long struggle against aggressive totalitarianism. Now we face another defining hour for America and the world.

There is no one more devoted, more committed to the hard work of freedom, than every soldier and sailor, every Marine, airman, and Coast Guardsman, every man and woman now serving in the Persian Gulf.

[Bush interrupted by extended applause.]

What a wonderful fitting tribute to them. Each of them has volunteered, volunteered to provide for this nation's defense—and now they bravely struggle, to earn for America, for the world, and for future generations a just and lasting peace.

Our commitment to them must be the equal of their commitment to their country. They are truly America's finest.

[War in the Gulf]

The war in the gulf is not a war we wanted. We worked hard to avoid war. For more than five months we, along with the Arab League, the European Community, and the United Nations, tried every diplomatic avenue. U.N. Secretary General Perez de Cuellar; Presidents [Mikhail S.] Gorbachev [of the Soviet Union], [François] Mitterrand [of France], [Turgut] Ozal [of Turkey], [Hosni] Mubarak [of Egypt], and [Chadli] Benjedid [of Algeria]; Kings Fahd [of Saudi Arabia] and Hassan [of Morocco]; Prime Ministers [John] Major [of Britain] and [Giulio] Andreotti [of Italy]—just to name a few—all worked for a solution. But time and again, Saddam Hussein flatly rejected the path of diplomacy and peace. The world well knows how this conflict began and when: It began on Aug. 2nd, when Saddam invaded and sacked a small, defenseless neighbor. And I am certain of how it will end. So that peace can prevail, we will prevail.

Tonight, I am pleased to report that we are on course. Iraq's capacity to sustain war is being destroyed. Our investment, our training, our planning—all are paying off. Time will not be Saddam's salvation. Our purpose in the Persian Gulf remains constant: to drive Iraq out of Kuwait, to restore Kuwait's legitimate government and to ensure the stability and security of this critical region. Let me make clear what I mean by the region's stability and security. We do not seek the destruction of Iraq, its culture or its people. Rather, we seek an Iraq that uses its great resources not to destroy, not to serve the ambitions of a tyrant, but to build a better life for itself and its neighbors. We seek a Persian Gulf where conflict is no longer the rule, where the strong are neither tempted nor able to intimidate the weak.

Most Americans know instinctively why we are in the gulf. They know we had to stop Saddam now, not later. They know that this brutal dictator will do anything, will use any weapon, will commit any outrage, no matter how many innocents must suffer. They know we must make sure that control of the world's oil resources does not fall into his hands, only to finance further aggression. They know that we need to build a new, enduring peace—based not on arms races and confrontation, but on shared principles and the rule of law. And we all realize that our responsibility to be the catalyst for peace in the region does not end with the successful conclusion of this war.

Democracy brings the undeniable value of thoughtful dissent—and we have heard some dissenting voices here at home—some, a handful, reckless; most responsible. But the fact that all voices have the right to speak out is one of the reasons we've been united in purpose and principle for 200 years.

[A Strong Defense]

Our progress in this great struggle is the result of years of vigilance and a steadfast commitment to a strong defense. Now, with remarkable technological advances like the Patriot missile, we can defend against ballistic missile attacks aimed at innocent civilians.

Looking forward, I have directed that the SDI [strategic defense initiative] program be refocused on providing protection from limited ballistic missile strikes—whatever their source.

Let us pursue an SDI program that can deal with any future threat to the United States, to our forces overseas, and to our friends and allies. The quality of American technology, thanks to the American worker, has enabled us to successfully deal with difficult military conditions and help minimize precious loss of life. We have given our men and women the very best. And they deserve it.

We all have a special place in our hearts for the families of our men and women serving in the gulf. They are represented here tonight by Mrs. Norman Schwarzkopf.

We are all very grateful to Gen. [H. Norman] Schwarzkopf [commander of U.S. troops in the Persian Gulf] and to all those serving with him. And I might also recognize one who came with Mrs. Schwarzkopf, Alma Powell, wife of the distinguished chairman of the Joint Chiefs.

And to the families, let me say our forces in the gulf will not stay there one day longer than is necessary to complete their mission.

The courage and success of the R.A.F. [Royal Air Force] pilots—of the Kuwaiti, Saudi, French, the Canadians, the Italians, the pilots of Qatar and Bahrain—all are proof that for the first time since World War II, the international community is united. The leadership of the United Nations, once only a hoped-for ideal, is now confirming its founders' vision.

And I am heartened that we are not being asked to bear alone the financial burden of this struggle. Last year, our friends and allies provided the bulk of the economic costs of Desert Shield, and now, having received commitments of over $40 billion for the first three months of 1991, I am confident they will do no less as we move through Desert Storm.

[The Dictator of Iraq]

But the world has to wonder what the dictator of Iraq is thinking. If he thinks that by targeting innocent civilians in Israel and Saudi Arabia, that he will gain advantage, he is dead wrong.

And if he thinks that he will advance his cause through tragic and despicable environmental terrorism—he is dead wrong.

And if he thinks that by abusing the coalition prisoners of war, he will benefit—he is dead wrong.

We will succeed in the gulf. And when we do, the world community will have sent an enduring warning to any dictator or despot, present or future, who contemplates outlaw aggression. The world can therefore seize this opportunity to fulfill the long-held promise of a new world order—where brutality will go unrewarded and aggression will meet collective resistance.

Yes, the United States bears a major share of leadership in this effort. Among the nations of the world, only the United States of America has had both the moral standing and the means to back it up. We are the only nation on this Earth that could assemble the forces of peace. This is the burden of leadership—and the strength that has made America the beacon of freedom in a searching world. This nation has never found glory in war. Our people have never wanted to abandon the blessings of home and work for distant lands and deadly conflict. If we fight in anger, it is only because we have to fight at all. And all of us yearn for a world where we will never have to fight again.

Each of us will measure, within ourselves, the value of this great struggle. Any cost in lives, any cost, is beyond our power to measure. But the cost of closing our eyes to aggression is beyond mankind's power to imagine. This we do know: Our cause is just, our cause is moral, our cause is right.

Let future generations understand the burden and the blessings of freedom. Let them say, we stood where duty required us to stand. Let them know that together, we affirmed America and the world as a community of conscience.

The winds of change are with us now. The forces of freedom are together and united. And we move toward the next century more confident than ever that we have the will at home and abroad to do what must be done—the hard work of freedom.

May God bless the United States of America. Thank you very, very much.

MITCHELL'S DEMOCRATIC RESPONSE

Across the Persian Gulf, dawn is now breaking. For Americans there, another night of danger is passing. Another day of combat begins.

In the skies over Iraq, aboard the ships in the gulf, on the sands of Arabia, they're Americans—not Republicans or Democrats—but Americans who've answered their country's call.

Before the war began, we debated openly, as democracy demands. We agreed that Iraq's aggression was brutal and illegal and that Iraq must leave Kuwait, by force if necessary.

The difference was not in the goals but in the means: whether force should be used immediately or only as a last resort if other means failed. No one will ever know if that other course would have worked. Now that war has begun, we'll work to see that it's swift and decisive, with the least possible loss of life.

Our hearts go out to the prisoners of war who've endured brutality and exploitation. We honor their bravery. We care for their families. We warn their captors that they'll pay a heavy price for mistreating our men.

[Supporting the Troops]

There's nothing a democratic society can do that's more difficult than to ask a few to risk everything in behalf of the many who risk nothing. We've done that. Our troops deserve our full support. They have mine and that of the Congress.

Our support will not end when the fighting ends.

Those who risk their lives in our behalf, and their families, must know that a grateful nation cares about them, not just during but also after the war.

And then, when the war's over, there's one lesson we must never forget: The dictator we help today may turn his weapons on us tomorrow. For 10 years, U.S. policy favored Iraq. We can't repeat that kind of mistake.

Out of the tragedy of war, we seek a world where the force of law is more powerful than the force of arms.

We seek a world where justice and human rights are respected everywhere. Students massacred in China, priests murdered in Central America, demonstrators gunned down in Lithuania — these acts of violence are as wrong as Iraqi soldiers killing civilians. We cannot oppose repression in one place and overlook it in another.

We seek a world where the burdens of freedom are shared by all who enjoy its benefits.

For half a century, from the Berlin airlift to the Persian Gulf, America has done its part. Those allies who've prospered behind the shield of a common defense must contribute their fair share. They're not doing it yet. It's time they did.

One nation, Israel, has done much by its brave refusal to be provoked. This crisis has given us powerful new proof of the importance of Israel's friendship.

[Crisis at Home]

But as critical as the gulf conflict is, the other business of the nation won't wait. The president says he seeks a new world order. We ask him to join us in putting our own house in order. We have a crisis abroad. But we also have a crisis here at home.

We're in a recession. More than a million Americans who had jobs last year are out of work today. Bankruptcies are rising. The banking system is in trouble. People are worried about their economic future.

We can meet this crisis by providing for the well-being of the American family. That's our strength. Working families, the men and women who toil in industry, tend our farms, work our computers and run our small businesses, the children and students who are the future—they're the true measure of our national vitality.

In just two weeks, this war has shown us the enormous potential of our people and of our technology.

We've combined superior equipment with concentrated training, high skill with great courage, to do the work of war. Now we should apply our talent and technology to the work of peace.

If we can make the best smart bomb, can't we make the best VCR? If we can build a high-speed Patriot missile, can't we build a high-speed train? I believe we can.

Our first priority must be economic growth.

A skilled and dedicated work force, modern equipment and innovation are essential to a rising standard of living. And economic growth solves many problems. The old saying is true: The best social program is a good job.

[Sensible Energy Policy]

The first step to growth is a sensible energy policy.

We should have learned the lessons of the two oil price shocks of the 70's. But we didn't.

For 10 years, we've had no energy policy. We've just relied on imported oil. We must change that. We need a new energy program which encourages conservation, promotes the use of alternative fuels and reduces our dependence on imported oil.

We're outraged by the environmental disaster in the Persian Gulf. But there's a broader threat: to the global environment. We must combat pollution before it makes much of the Earth unfit for life.

We must strengthen the banking system now, before it's a full national crisis, not after.

Last year the Senate passed a good bill to limit spending in political campaigns and to eliminate political action committees.

We're going to pass it again this year and push until it becomes law.

We want a better society, not just for our returning servicemen and women but for their children and all children.

We owe them not just a safer world but safer streets at home. So we'll put the emphasis and the resources where they belong—at the state and local level. That's the front line of the war on drugs and crime.

We'll provide care, food and early education for the millions of children who don't get them.

We spend more on health care than any other country. We get the best of care—but only for those who can afford it. That leaves out a lot of Americans.

Thirty-seven million don't have any health insurance.

And we don't have any policy on what will be the crisis of this decade: long-term care for the elderly.

We can provide better health care at less cost. We all have to do more with less.

Your families have to. Government must do the same, to be more careful with your tax dollars.

For 10 years, we've had record budget deficits and record trade deficits. We've lost a lot of American jobs.

[Lowering the Deficit]

We've got to bring the deficits down and the jobs home.

The president's way to do that is to give huge tax cuts to those with incomes over $200,000 a year.

We disagree.

It's working men and women, the middle class, whose taxes should be cut. They're already bearing most of the tax burden.

They're also bearing the burden of war.

Not many kids whose families earn more than $200,000 a year volunteer to join the Army. It's mostly the children of working people, the middle class and the poor who'll do the fighting and dying. Their families shouldn't have to bear all the burdens.

What they need, what all Americans need most of all is opportunity— the chance to succeed through hard work.

Before I entered the Senate, I served as a federal judge. It's a position of great power.

But what I enjoyed most was presiding at citizenship ceremonies. People who'd come from all over the world gathered before me in a federal courtroom.

There, in the final act, I administered to them the oath of allegiance to the United States, and they became Americans.

After every ceremony, I spoke personally with each new American. I asked them how and why they came. Through their answers ran a common theme, best expressed by a young man who said, in halting English, "I came because here in America everyone has a chance."

He summed up America in a sentence: Here everyone has a chance.

I know that's true. I know that in America you can go as high and as far as your talent and willingness to work will take you.

[Quality Education]

That means there must be a quality education for every American child. There must be jobs, fairness in the workplace, with no discrimination, with equal rights and economic independence for women. No guarantees for anyone but an equal chance to succeed for everyone.

So tonight, as we take stock of our country, we acknowledge our good fortune to be Americans, citizens of the most free, the most open, the most just society in human history, even as we recognize that there remain wrongs to be righted.

But most of all, we think of our grave responsibility:

To half a million of our fellow citizens who bear the burden of battle. To support them now and to respect them when they return.

I think tonight about a young airman from Winslow, Maine. I met him in December in Saudi Arabia. He has four children, including 1-year-old twins. He hadn't seen them for months and didn't know when he would. But he didn't complain. He was quiet, but it was the quiet strength of someone committed to his country and his duty.

Our duty now is to support the men and women serving in the Persian Gulf, to work and pray for their swift and safe return home and to build an America worthy of them and their children.

May God bless and watch over each of them.

Thank you and good night.

February

DE KLERK ON RACIAL LAWS; BUSH ON ECONOMIC SANCTIONS
February 1 and July 10, 1991

President F. W. de Klerk urged South Africa's Parliament February 1 to discard race separation laws, calling them "the cornerstones of apartheid." He set in motion a chain of events that led to decisions by the twelve-nation European Community and the United States to lift economic sanctions against South Africa.

President George Bush announced his decision on July 10, after the International Olympic Committee had voted July 9 to let South African athletes again participate in Olympic events. They had been barred for twenty-one years because of the country's refusal to field racially integrated teams.

Those actions signaled South Africa's return to the good graces of the international community, bolstering the country's economic outlook as well as de Klerk's political position at home. The removal of sanctions would reopen markets for South African exports and promote investments from abroad. But Bush's decision drew strong objections from many black leaders in South Africa and the United States. They contended that sanctions should be continued until a power-sharing arrangement was worked out with South Africa's black majority.

De Klerk's Anti-Apartheid Measures

De Klerk used his presidential election victory in September 1989 to promise "a totally changed South Africa ... free of domination or oppression," but he insisted that formal power sharing must await the outcome of negotiations between the South African government and the country's black leaders over the nation's future political structure. Such negotiations began in 1990 but repeatedly broke down, only to resume and again falter in 1991. (South African President's Inaugural Address, Historic Documents of 1989, p. 545)

In his opening-day address to Parliament, de Klerk outlined a number of steps for bringing about "a peaceful transition to a new society." Some reforms, he said, could not be started until a constitution was written and put into effect. However, he said that repealing the remaining basic apartheid laws need not await that development. De Klerk asked the lawmakers to discard laws that reserved four-fifths of the nation's land for its white minority and classified all citizens into one of four racial categories: black, white, mixed, or Asian.

De Klerk's unexpected call for repeal of the race classification law, formally called the Population Registration Act of 1950, evoked jeers and an angry walkout by members of the minority Conservative party. At the other end of the political spectrum, Nelson Mandela, leader of the African National Congress (ANC), seemed surprised but expressed cautious approval. It was the second straight year in which de Klerk had handed new parliamentary sessions anti-apartheid agendas whose boldness was even greater than his own Nationalist party expected. From the same podium a year earlier, the president had announced he would release Mandela and several other political prisoners, and negotiate with them for a new constitutional order. (De Klerk and Mandela on South African Changes, Historic Documents of 1990, p. 65)

Factional Strife Among Blacks

Mandela and de Klerk's dealings were troubled by factional and often fatal strife within South Africa's black townships. Mandela accused the government of connivance in that turmoil. De Klerk, in turn, accused the ANC of seeking to exploit the violence for its own political ends. Many of the deaths in 1990 and 1991 had occurred in fighting between supporters of the ANC and followers of Inkatha, a political movement of Zulu origin. Desmond M. Tutu, the black Anglican archbishop and Nobel laureate, in a widely publicized sermon in April 1991 blamed much of the violence on political rivalries.

Violence reached into Mandela's own household. His wife, Winnie, was tried and found guilty of kidnapping in connection with her bodyguards' removal of four black youths from a church home in December 1988. She was accused in court of trying to coerce the youths to say they had been sexually mistreated by a white Methodist minister. They were severely beaten, and one was later found murdered. Mrs. Mandela's chief bodyguard, Jerry Richardson, was found guilty of the killing and sentenced to death before she went on trial. On May 14 she drew a six-year prison sentence, which was promptly appealed.

Mandela assured South Africans that he would not let his wife's trial interfere with negotiations he was conducting with de Klerk. On May 18, however, he broke off the talks, citing the government's refusal to stop the violence in black townships. In a public relations sense, the walkout appeared to benefit the government as it continued to strike down racial barriers. By the time Parliament adjourned in mid-June, the legislators had repealed the apartheid laws as de Klerk had requested, leaving South Africa without a legal underpinning for race separation for the first time since the Nationalist party came to power in 1948.

There followed in July the first plenary meeting of the African National Congress ever held on South African soil. In previous years the ANC was forced to meet abroad. As the meeting ended July 7 at Durban, many observers concluded that Mandela and other moderate leaders had won the upper hand over more militant rivals and appeared intent on transforming the organization into a genuine political party.

Bush Lifts Economic Sanctions

On July 10 Bush announced he would lift U.S. economic sanctions. The State Department, he said, assured him that South Africa had met all the conditions Congress had imposed in 1986 when it passed the Comprehensive Apartheid Act. That law permitted the president, subject to a congressional veto within thirty days, to lift the sanctions when the following conditions had been met: all political prisoners released, the state of emergency ended, apartheid laws repealed, the legality of banned political parties restored, and "good faith negotiations with truly representative members of the black majority without preconditions" begun. Other sanctions imposed by separate U.S. legislation remained in effect.

In September, the two rival black groups signed an agreement to work together politically and try to end the factional violence. The accord led to the opening of negotiations on December 20 between de Klerk's government and black political parties to form an interim government that included black members. The interim government would function until a new constitution could be drafted for a permanent sharing of authority between South Africa's black majority and white minority. De Klerk promised that a referendum on proposals for an interim government would be open to voters of all races. Further talks were scheduled in 1992.

Following are excerpts from the speech of President F. W. de Klerk of South Africa to Parliament on February 1 asking for the repeal of remaining basic race separation laws, and from President George Bush's news conference July 10, at which he announced he was removing U.S. economic sanctions against South Africa:

DE KLERK ADDRESS

From this Chamber a year ago tomorrow South Africa was placed finally on a new course. Events succeeded one another in rapid succession and I have no doubt that our country is irrevocably on the road to a new dispensation. The goal with the removal of discrimination is to give all South Africans full rights in every sphere of life. . . .

The initiatives of the past year have prepared the way for a new South Africa. Our task this year will be to give greater content to our vision of what the new South Africa should be like. . . .

In South Africa the task of nation-building is formidable because of the diversity of our population. We lack the natural cohesion of a single culture and language that frequently forms the cornerstone of nationhood. Consequently we shall have to rely heavily on the other cornerstone—of common values and ideals.

I have taken the liberty on the basis of an analysis of the views of a wide spectrum of leaders of formulating a set of these common values and ideals. Without laying claim to it being complete or the last word on the subject, I believe that it may serve as a point of departure in the search for a national consensus.

The full text will be released today under the title "Manifesto for the new South Africa."

I believe that these values and ideals could provide the cohesiveness of a new South African nation, of a nation that will include all peace-loving South Africans on a equal footing. Furthermore a Manifesto such as this will be able to be associated with a Bill of Human Rights to which the Government is already committed. It should also give direction to the constitutional negotiations that lie ahead.

In a nutshell the basic values and ideals as formulated in the Manifesto and as they have crystallised out of the national debate could be summarised thus:

The basis of the new South Africa should be justice. The great majority of South Africans desire a just state which will guarantee basic liberties, rule out arbitrary actions and domination and which will require and assure responsible citizenship. Everyone desires a just dispensation in which fairness will be the point of departure.

On this basis South Africans ask that the new South Africa should epitomise the following objectives:

- They want peace. They wish to be assured that they and their families and their property will be safe.
- They want prosperity. They wish to share in a sound and growing economy that will make employment opportunities and better living conditions possible for everybody and allow everybody to reap the fruits of their labours.
- They want progress. They wish to have effective educational, health and welfare services as well as adequate housing and recreational facilities.
- They want participation in democratic institutions. They wish to feel that they are part of government on every level, that they are not dominated and that they may be proud together of our country, South Africa. . . .

If we build the new South African nation on the foundation of these values and ideals, a good future awaits us and our children. . . .

To this I commit myself. And I ask every leader to support me in this. If South Africans make the essence of a Manifesto such as this their own, then the foundations of our new nation will have been firmly laid. . . .

Naturally, the adoption of these values is merely a first step. Giving them constitutional content will require long and thorough negotiation. And before that can happen, agreement will have to be reached on the nature of the negotiations, procedures and structures.

Multi-Party Conference

. . . [M]ost of the major political groupings are now ready to attend multi-party exploratory talks. I trust that these talks will begin soon.

I am also convinced that this approach is the best way to ensure that the process, as well as the outcome, will be legitimate, durable and acceptable to the majority of South Africans.

In this connection, the Government declares its opposition to the idea of an elected constituent assembly. It is of the opinion that the negotiation of a new constitution should be the responsibility of the representatives of all political parties which enjoy proven support and are committed to a peaceful and negotiated solution.

In respect of constitutional development I wish, further, to state the Government's point of view clearly on an interim government. The idea that the present, legally-constituted Government should relinquish its powers and simply hand over its responsibilities to some or other temporary regime, cannot be considered in a sovereign, independent state. Effective government and administration in terms of existing constitutional legislation has to continue until a new constitution has been negotiated and been implemented after the acquisition of a mandate.

However, consideration may be given to certain transitional arrangements on the various legislative and executive levels to give the leaders of the negotiating parties a voice in the formulation of important policy decisions.

Local Government

Other interim measures may be considered as well. Local Government is an example.

The Government has been giving attention to reform at the local authority level for quite some time. The options concerning possible models, as contained in the report of the Co-ordinating Council for Local Government Affairs, have stimulated debate at the local level.

In many cases, discussions opened doors to co-operation which could not be implemented because of legal impediments. This leads to frustration which has a negative influence on the process of reform.

The Government does not wish to anticipate the national process of negotiation in any way. Therefore, without wishing to establish a final structure at the local level, the decision has been taken to initiate interim steps to accommodate the dynamics of co-operation which have developed in many communities in respect of co-operation, and to give legal sanction to agreed joint actions and joint structures. . . .

Removal of Statutory Discrimination

The elimination of racial discrimination goes hand in hand with the constitutional process. The Government has expressed its intention repeatedly to remove discriminatory laws and practices. Many of them have been abolished already. Those remaining could not be repealed out of hand, because their complex nature required in-depth investigation.

These investigations have now been completed to the extent that I am able to make certain announcements today.

Legislation is to be tabled [presented] shortly for the repeal of the Land Acts of 1913 and 1936, the Group Areas Act of 1966 and the Development of Black Communities Act of 1984, as well as all other stipulations that determine rights concerning land according to membership of population groups.

The Government will also table a White Paper in which it will fully state its approach to the future treatment of land and land questions. Both the White Paper and the relevant legislation will be at the disposal of members shortly.

No-one dare under-estimate the emotions and even the conflict potential relating to land rights. . . . On the one hand, there is a need for the protection of private property rights and security of title and tenure with due consideration for common and indigenous law. On the other, land ownership and financing for it have to be accessible to all in a non-discriminatory manner. . . .

The Population Registration Act of 1950 has been subjected to scrutiny as well.

On the part of the Government, the view was held that the Population Registration Act would have to be repealed eventually, but that this could not be done immediately because the Act was technically necessary for the maintenance of the present constitutional dispensation. Therefore, it would be possible to repeal the Act only once a new constitution had been implemented.

Following investigation, it would, in fact, appear possible to repeal this Act, provided that this is accompanied by the adoption of temporary transitional measures towards the acceptance of a new constitution. Consequently, I announce that legislation to this effect will be tabled during this session of Parliament.

Should Parliament adopt the Government's proposals, the South African statute book will be devoid, within months, of the remnants of racially discriminatory legislation which have become known as the cornerstones of apartheid.

Own Community Life

The ending of apartheid and the repeal of these last remaining discriminatory laws will bring us to the end of an era—an era in which it was sought to deal with the reality of a diversity of peoples and communities within the same national boundaries by means of discriminatory coercion.

However, the removal of discrimination and coercion, which is now being completed, does not alter the reality of the existence of a variety of peoples and communities. . . .

This is not unique to South Africa either.

Throughout the world, there are certain communities within countries and states that have maintained a specific identity.

Individuals, who feel attracted to certain communities and feel happy and secure in them, are also allowed to do so.

In South Africa, too, a deeply-rooted desire exists among some communities for a system in which certain human needs may continue to be met in a community context—without coercion, without discrimination and without apartheid.

The Government is convinced that recognition has to be given to this reality in any new dispensation. Therefore, it remains committed to ensuring community rights for those who desire them and believes that they will have to be accommodated in the new South Africa.

The Government's points of departure in this respect are that: people cannot be coerced into communities; the authorities may not discriminate against certain communities in favour of others; a community life of one's own has to be sustained by one's own inherent will and abilities and not by statutory coercion; community recognition has to be based on freedom of association, as it is recognised constitutionally and otherwise by various countries in the world. . . .

Legal Reform

The concept of an own community life may be associated logically and meaningfully with the concept of a bill of human rights. As is already known the Government favours such a bill of rights and is currently awaiting the final report of the South African Law Commission.

In the widest context, the Government wishes to bring the aims it has concerning community life, into line with the concept of a just state in which the rule of law prevails, a state which does not seek to prescribe communities or community life, nor force them upon anybody, but which maintains the legal principles, measures and courts that will make it possible for people to feel secure in the communities of their choosing.

Our legal system has to be subjected to continuous scrutiny to ensure that it meets the needs of the ever-changing demands of our society. In this regard the recognition of indigenous law, alongside common law, remains important.

The maintenance of the independence of our courts is indispensable to a stable and secure future. . . .

Against the background of the world-wide trend towards simplifying legal procedures, making the legal process more accessible and involving the community with it to a great extent, several further initiatives are now indicated. . . .

Education

... It is well-known that the Government is fully aware of, and deeply concerned about, serious problems in education.

Problems such as inadequate vocational emphasis in our school syllabuses, fragmented state administration, equal financial treatment for all pupils, finding alternative sources of finance for education, the adequate provision of facilities, liaison between formal education and the informal sector, and distance education as an alternative mode of providing education, receive continuous and urgent attention. To equip the individual better for his task, renewal in the education dispensation is essential to make it more career-oriented and more closely-related to the economy.

Therefore, the Government announced an investigation into a comprehensive educational renewal strategy last year already. The results are expected soon. Thereafter, the matter will be taken further seriously....

We are determined that our ultimate system of education shall enjoy the acceptance and support of the majority of our population. It will have to be an educational system that will be affordable and in which appropriate education is offered. In addition, it will have to keep abreast of changing needs and trends in our society.

The Economy

One other great imperative facing us in this closing decade of the twentieth century is economic reconstruction. It is the only way through which we will be able to return to a high growth path and meet the reasonable aspirations of all our people. No economy, least of all that of a developing society, can do this overnight; but we can and must promote the creation of employment opportunities and the generation of incomes to meet the basic needs of our rapidly growing population in the shortest possible space of time.

Economic growth and constitutional reform have to be mutually reinforcing. Unless the pressing problems of poverty and unemployment are alleviated, constitutional models will be of little avail to us....

Of special importance has been our new access, in Eastern Europe and elsewhere, to markets long closed to our exports, as well as our readmission to capital markets in Western Europe. These and other opportunities resulting from positive international reaction to the Government's initiatives, have to be grasped firmly and decisively....

All concerned South Africans working for a peaceful transition to a new society wish to see the reduction and ultimate elimination of the disparities that still exist. Restructuring the economy and allocating resources to specific needs are essential to this end. Equally important, however, are the channels for deploying the resources, the involvement of the peoples concerned, and their acceptance of mutual responsibility....

To achieve even the goal of parity in social expenditure will require hard work and stern discipline over the next decade and beyond. Attempts to shorten this inevitably incremental process by militant action in the labour or other fields, will merely serve to lengthen it. . . .

The Government places a high premium on job and income-creating growth. In broad terms, this requires:

> Firstly, that maximum private sector development be encouraged.
>
> Secondly, that the State's economic involvement be reduced in consequence to a minimum, with its residual activities based increasingly on business principles.
>
> Thirdly, that Government policy and actions be geared to the fullest utilization of national resources. This includes a shift from import replacement and strategic self-sufficiency to an export-oriented strategy, involving limited protection of domestic industry, and aimed at maximum productivity and cost-effectiveness. . . .

Given the expected slowdown in the world economy, quite apart from the Gulf crisis, the economic outlook for South Africa in 1991 is one of consolidation of the gains already made, and a continuation of the restructuring process. . . .

Foreign Affairs

. . . It is remarkable how the convergence of South African and international events has brought about greater harmony between us and the rest of the world.

The fundamental change of course we embarked upon a year ago, was motivated primarily by our national interests. Yet, the progress we have made since then has created an entirely new situation for South Africa internationally. I am happy to be able to say that we have succeeded in breaking out of the dead end of isolation.

The exploitation of regional conflict in our part of the world to further ideology and power has come to an end. Political opportunism, diplomatic blackmail and playing off the two major powers against one another for the achievement of questionable political objectives cannot be used effectively against us any longer. Revolution is no longer a marketable product in the world today. The resources of the destabilisation and propaganda campaigns against South Africa are drying up. The anti-South African industry is facing insolvency. Sanctions are withering away. . . .

Regional development is of decisive importance to Southern Africa. The eleven states of Southern Africa have a combined population of more than 100 million. The region is endowed with valuable natural resources and has the potential to become one of the most prosperous regions in the world. However, the nations comprising the region, divided for so long by colonialism, wars, conflicts and racial strife, will have to join forces, work together and plan together.

If we succeed in this, our region should be able to realise the common aim of a better future. If we work together, we will succeed in obtaining active involvement by Europe, the US and other developed countries in the developing economies of Southern Africa.

Security

This positive picture, which I was able to sketch over a wide area is contrasted by the high level of political and criminal lawlessness in the country. It is worrying and unacceptable. It has the potential to abet serious delays and even undermine the progress already made. Therefore, everything is being done to create a more conducive climate....

Mass action has to take place peacefully, responsibly and within the law. Should the current trend towards the abuse of this method continue in any way, the Government will be obliged to apply stronger measures to prevent abuse.

Of course it is not the task of the Government alone to act in this respect. The pressure and demands exerted on our security forces—on the Police Force as well as the Defence Force—are already enormous. Political and community leaders have to accept co-responsibility for settling disputes, controlling supporters and creating a climate for negotiation.

By and large our security forces are doing an excellent job and do not deserve the vilification to which they are subjected from many quarters. I wish to urge all the inhabitants of South Africa to give their full support to the security forces. If the authority and integrity of our police are undermined, all of us will have to pay a heavy price.

On the part of the Government, everything possible will be done as a matter of high priority to make our police force more effective and efficient....

BUSH'S NEWS CONFERENCE

President Bush: Let me begin with a statement, then I will take a few questions.

First, let me state that apartheid must be eliminated, and we've worked with the nations of the world to bring an end to this system of racial prejudice by every means possible. Political and economic pressure had been brought against the government of South Africa by the United States and by other nations for the last several years. And progress has been slow and often painful. But progress has definitely been made.

And during the last two years, we've seen a profound transformation in the situation in South Africa. Since coming to office in 1989 President [F. W.] de Klerk has repealed the legislative pillars of apartheid and opened up the political arena to prepare the way for constitutional negotiations, and as I've said on several occasions, I really firmly believe that this progress is irreversible.

Much remains to be done, let's be very clear on that point, but I've been impressed with the commitment by President de Klerk, by Nelson Mandela [president of the African National Congress], by [Zulu leader] Chief [Mangosuthu G.] Buthelezi, and many others, to continue to build a constitutional democracy in South Africa, and we will use all available means to encourage this process through to its successful conclusion.

The Congress anticipated this situation in what is known as the Comprehensive Anti-Apartheid Act of 1986, which placed economic sanctions against South Africa. That law anticipated the benefit of lifting these sanctions as a means of encouraging the government of South Africa and the people of South Africa to continue the progress that has been made in eliminating apartheid, and I have today just signed and issued an executive order terminating the sanctions against South Africa.

And in doing so, based on [a] recommendation from Secretary [of State] [James A.] Baker [III], I have determined that the South African government has met all five of the conditions for these sanctions to end, as set forth very clearly in the act, and other measures, sanctions, including the arms embargo and restrictions on our ability to support South Africa at the IMF [International Monetary Fund] are unaffected.

These other sanctions remain in effect. This morning I talked just now to Nelson Mandela, a fairly long talk with him to tell him personally of the commitment by the people of the United States to support equality in South Africa.

And I told him of my personal belief that lifting the sanctions at this time is the right thing to do in order to encourage continued change in his country, to help provide a more stable and dynamic economy in which the blacks of South Africa can participate.

And tomorrow I intend to call President de Klerk to indicate to him that we expect the progress that he has made so far to continue. And incidentally on the Mandela call, we've been in reasonably frequent touch, and I told him that certainly that consultation will certainly continue. And he seemed to be understanding and pleased about that.

The peaceful transition to the new South Africa will not occur in a vacuum. South Africa must achieve full economic health through a strong rate of growth if it is to meet the expectations of all South Africans for a better life.

The end of sanctions on trade and investment will encourage this process. And we hope that state and local governments and private institutions in the United States will take note of our action and act accordingly to help build a new South Africa, to help build employment opportunity in South Africa.

And so my appeal here and my appeal at this G-7 meeting [of the leaders of the seven leading industrialized nations] that I'm fixing to go to will be that we all must help now. And I'm therefore directing that our assistance to black South Africans be doubled from its present level of $40 million, and these funds will be used to expand our efforts, to prepare black South Africans to participate fully in the revitalization of their economy and to help meet the most pressing needs of blacks in the areas of housing and education.

This is a moment in history which many believed would never be attained. But we've done so through the efforts of many people in South Africa and around the world. And in that sense, this is a time for reflection.

And it's also [a] time when all who care about the future of South Africa, as I do, should rededicate themselves to stay the course in the interest of peace and democracy.

There has been dramatic change. The law says when the five conditions are met the sanctions will come off signed that day. But all is not totally well there, and we will continue to be actively involved—as actively involved as we can be.

So that is my statement, and now I'll refer to Tom Rolf for the first question.

Q: Mr. President, do you have any concerns or reservations on moving now to remove the sanctions? You might actually have the effect of undermining some of the progress that has been made rather than—

P: Well, I think—I had no flexibility in considering that. But my view is we will not be undermining the progress. Sometimes one wants to recognize the changes, the very constructive changes, that have taken place, and then see what the next best—next step is.

And in my view, the mandate by Congress is a proper one, and I think now that our role should be encouraging consultation between the parties, all of them, Buthelezi, Mandela, de Klerk, to see that progress made can be built on.

So I don't have any thoughts like that at all.

Q: Can I follow up, sir?

P: Yes.

Q: What do you say to groups like the NAACP and Amnesty International and even House Speaker Tom Foley [D-Wash.] that all of the five conditions have not been met, and there are in fact still political prisoners in South Africa?

P: I say to him—well, as a matter of fact, under our definition, there are not. Mr. Mandela pointed out to me that under different definitions of the law of the prisoner—what can constitute a prisoner, there may be people who are prisoners.

Under the way the Congress defined prisoner—and I'm going to refer these technical questions to Secretary Cohen [Assistant Secretary of State for African Affairs Herman J.] who has done a fantastic job on all of this— we are complying fully.

But in terms of how I respond to critics on this, I say, look, one, we're complying with the law you people wrote; and secondly, I happen to think it's the right thing to do.

I believe that this will result in more progress toward racial equity instead of less, and certainly, in more economic opportunity rather than less. So the time has come to do it.

Q: Mr. President, are you willing now to acknowledge that you were wrong on the question of sanctions—

P: No.

Q: —that you opposed? And you seem to think that they're pretty good for Iran and Iraq?

P: The answer is no.

Q: You think that none of this progress came as a result of our tightening the screws?

P: Well, I can't say that, no, in fairness, I can't say that none came as a result of that. But I think what really turned the difference was when South Africa came in with a new regime and they decided to move forward.

But I don't think it was strictly because they wanted to get rid of two sanctions while others remain.

Q: Well, it wasn't the question of (inaudible) mammoth change in the whole society.

P: No question. No question about it. But you're saying, do I credit sanctions totally? And the answer is no.

Q: I didn't say totally.

P: Well, I did. . . .

BUSH'S BUDGET MESSAGE
February 4, 1991

President George Bush sent his budget requests to Congress February 4, asking for $1.4 trillion in expenditures for fiscal year 1992 starting October 1, 1991. The budget anticipated a deficit for the year of $280.9 billion, the highest ever, eclipsing the record $268.7 billion deficit in fiscal 1991. A stubborn recession pushed later estimates for the 1992 budget well beyond $300 billion.

The farthest-reaching plans presented in the fiscal 1992 budget were for a comprehensive restructuring of America's military forces. Drawn up before the war in the Persian Gulf, the six-year spending plan reflected political changes in Eastern Europe and the Soviet Union that effectively ended the Cold War. In 1992 the budget called for the first outright reduction in defense spending in twenty years—spending of some $290.8 billion, down from about $300 billion in 1991.

New Budget Rules

In his message to Congress accompanying the budget, Bush said the figures were "consistent with the 5-year deficit reduction law enacted last fall." That landmark law was passed by Congress October 27, 1990, at the end of long and bruising negotiations between congressional leaders and White House officials.

Under terms of that agreement, Congress was left with little room for budgetary maneuvering. A prohibition against moving funds from one major budget category—defense, international, or domestic—to another category blocked the traditional transfers of money by Congress. The budget agreement also penalized discretionary spending above specific limits.

But the agreement left loopholes for excess spending deemed not the "fault" of Congress—for example, the Persian Gulf war. Still, over the five-year life of the 1990 budget agreement, the plan was expected by many economists to lower the annual deficits substantially.

A Leaner Military

The broad Department of Defense plan proposed in the president's budget was designed to reduce the U.S. armed forces by one-quarter of their current strength by 1995. Offered by Secretary of Defense Dick Cheney, the program also represented the strategic views of Gen. Colin L. Powell, Jr., chairman of the Joint Chiefs of Staff, and Paul Wolfowitz, undersecretary of defense for policy. As proposed, the number of active Army divisions would be reduced to twelve (from eighteen) and the number of Navy ships to 451 (from 545) by the end of 1995. But only one of thirteen naval aircraft carriers would be retired.

For decades, U.S. military policy had been shaped by a perceived need to block a sudden Soviet thrust into Western Europe. Under the new administration plan, the U.S. military potential would be reoriented toward the rapid deployment of forces to distant trouble spots. A number of defense requests pointed to that goal. For instance, about $2 billion would be used over the next six years to improve the long-range movement of men and materiel.

Other Proposals

The 1992 budget recommended increased spending for 250 domestic programs, decreased spending for 109, and the elimination of 238. It also recommended significant increases in spending on science, space programs, and highways. In his message, Bush said he wanted to "reduce governmental subsidies for those who are not in need." With that as a goal, he urged a tripling of monthly Medicare premiums paid by elderly persons with incomes above $125,000 a year. And he proposed to end crop subsidies to farmers with nonfarm income of more than $125,000 a year.

As in previous years, Bush asked for a reduction in the capital gains tax, arguing that it would encourage long-term investments. Because he had called for a study of the issue in 1990, many observers believed the administration would not press as hard for the tax cut in 1991 as it had before.

Economic Outlook

Democratic critics of the budget, led by Sen. Jim Sasser, D-Tenn., and Rep. Leon E. Panetta, D-Calif., chairmen of the Senate and House Budget Committees, pointed to the omission of any measures to counter a recession that began in July 1990. Richard G. Darman, director of the Office of Management and Budget (OMB), told the two committees February 6 that forecasts indicated that any antirecessionary legislation Congress might pass would take effect only after a recovery was under way. Such an outcome, he said, would add to inflationary pressures.

Short-term economic forecasts by OMB were similar to those of private economists. The agency predicted that growth in real gross national product from the fourth quarter of 1990 to the fourth quarter of 1991 would be 0.9 percent and that inflation over the year would average 4.3 percent. But OMB's longer-range forecasts, through 1996, were rosier than those of many economists elsewhere.

Block Grants

In a move that quickly drew resistance in Congress and in many of the nation's statehouses, Bush recommended that Congress turn over to the states about $15 billion a year in a single block grant and give them responsibility for a variety of federal programs. He said such action would move "power and decision-making closer to the people."

Anticipating objections, the president promised that programs relegated to the states would be "fully funded." Many of the programs enacted in past years specified narrowly how funds were to be spent. Congress traditionally opposes block grants that transfer control to the statehouses. Many mayors, preferring to deal directly with Washington rather than with the state capitals, also oppose block grants.

Following is President George Bush's message to Congress, February 4, 1991, accompanying his proposed federal budget for fiscal year 1992:

To the Congress of the United States:

I am pleased to present the *Budget of the United States Government for Fiscal Year 1992.*

The budget is consistent with the 5-year deficit reduction law enacted last fall. It recommends discretionary spending levels that fall within the statutory caps for defense, international, and domestic discretionary programs. It implements the entitlement savings and reforms enacted in the Budget Agreement. It conforms to the new pay-as-you-go-requirements.

By holding the overall rate of growth of Federal Government spending to approximately 2.6 percent—below the inflation rate—the budget puts into effect the concept of a "flexible freeze," which is an essential means of bringing the budget into long-term balance.

The longest period of peacetime economic expansion in history has been temporarily interrupted. We can, however, return to growth soon—and proceed on the path to a new era of expansion. With that goal in mind, the budget places special priority on policies that will enhance America's potential for long-term economic growth, and that will give individuals the power to take advantage of the opportunity America uniquely offers.

To this end, I am again proposing tax incentives to increase savings and long-term investment.

On the spending side of the budget, the existence of a cap on domestic discretionary outlays rightly creates a competition for resources. Priorities must be set. This budget proposes that domestic investment be increased in the following key areas:

Education and Human Capital. The budget proposes investments to prepare children better for school, to promote choice and excellence in our educational system, to improve math and science education, and to increase the access of low-income Americans to higher education.

Prevention and the Next Generation. The budget includes proposals to help reduce illness and death from preventable diseases, and to reverse the long-term trend of underinvestment in children.

Research and Development and the Human Frontier. The budget recommends an increase of $8.4 billion in the Federal investment in research and development, with special emphasis on basic research, high performance computing, and energy research and development. It proposes to extend permanently the tax credit for research and experimentation to encourage private sector R&D investment. In addition, the budget reflects the Administration's continued commitment to expanding human frontiers in space and biotechnology.

Transportation Infrastructure. The budget supports an expansion of the Federal Government's investment in highways and bridges to over $20 billion within 5 years, and proposes substantial increases to improve the condition of the Nation's airports, to modernize the air traffic control system, and to continue to develop the transportation infrastructure for exploration and use of space.

America's Heritage and Environmental Protection. The budget includes increased funds for the expansion and improvement of America's treasury of parks, forests, wildlife refuges, and other public lands; for the implementation of the Clean Air Act and other key environmental statutes; for the cleanup of pollution at various Federal facilities and at Superfund sites; and for protection and enhancement of coastal areas and wetlands.

Choice and Opportunity. The budget provides: funds to help give parents greater choice in child care, health care, education, and housing; the resources to allow *all* Americans, especially those with low incomes, to seize the opportunities that such choice provides; and a proposal to establish Enterprise Zones to bring hope to our inner cities and distressed rural areas.

Drugs and Crime. The budget further increases the Administration's investment in drug prevention, treatment, and law enforcement. And the budget substantially increases the resources available to help the Federal Bureau of Investigation fight crime, the Federal prosecutors prosecute criminals, and the Federal prison system accommodate those convicted of crimes.

To make such investments possible, the budget includes recommendations to terminate or reduce Federal investment in certain low-return programs, and proposes reforms to slow the continuing growth of mandatory entitlement programs and to increase fairness in the distribution of the benefits these programs provide.

In addition, the budget contains a new proposal to fund various programs now carried out by the States through a comprehensive block grant. The States are continuing to develop new and innovative ways to deliver services more effectively. The budget not only highlights several of these innovations; it proposes to reinforce and build upon them.

The budget contains several proposals that reflect my commitment to managing government better. These include measures to improve accountability, to reduce waste, to reform regulation, to employ risk management budgeting in addressing threats to health and safety, and to set clear objectives and measure performance in meeting them.

Finally, consistent with the statutory caps enacted last year, the budget provides the resources necessary to maintain national security, and to better advance American interests abroad. As the budget goes to press, the timing of the resolution of the multinational coalition's efforts to reverse the aggression in the Persian Gulf is uncertain. For this reason, the budget reflects only a placeholder for Operation Desert Shield. A supplemental request for the incremental costs of Desert Shield, which includes Desert Storm, will be forwarded to the Congress in the coming weeks.

The priority investments embodied in this budget will help America prepare for the requirements and opportunities presented by a rapidly changing world. I look forward to working with the Congress in developing a budget that lays the groundwork for a brighter future, protects our national interests, and helps create the conditions for long-term economic growth and prosperity.

PRESIDENT'S ECONOMIC REPORT, ECONOMIC ADVISERS' REPORT

February 12, 1991

Striking a markedly optimistic tone, President George Bush and his Council of Economic Advisers (CEA) presented their annual economic reports to Congress February 12. The reports reached policymakers and the public at a time when the country's economy was in its first recession since 1982.

In his report, Bush said, "This temporary interruption to America's economic growth does not signal a decline in the basic long-term vitality of the U.S. economy." A year earlier in his first economic report, Bush hailed "the longest peacetime expansion on record." But the expansion turned to recession during the summer of 1990. (President's Economic Report, Economic Advisers' Report, Historic Documents of 1990, p. 81)

The economic advisers were equally upbeat in their assessment of the country's economic prospects. They wrote that there was "no fundamental obstacle" to an economic expansion in the 1990s "at least as long and strong as the expansion" of the 1980s. However, unemployment figures for March showed that 2 million Americans had lost their jobs since the previous summer. In that time, indexes of consumer confidence also dropped sharply. In April, the National Bureau of Economic Research dated the beginning of the recession as July 1990.

The president's economists attributed the downturn to three factors, apparently all beyond the control of the Bush administration. First, they said, was a sudden rise in oil prices after Iraq's invasion of Kuwait (UN Action Against Iraq, Historic Documents of 1990, p. 533); the second was a steep drop in consumer confidence. The third factor was a pervasive "credit crunch" as bank lending tightened under new federal regulations in an effort to stem a growing number of bankruptcies among savings institutions. (Bank Failures' Toll on Deposit Insurance Funds, Historic Documents of 1990, p. 815)

Economic Recovery

Bush predicted that the recession would be "mild and brief by historical standards." The economists thought the recovery would begin in the summer of 1991. Their report also predicted that the economy would grow by 0.9 percent in 1991 and by 3.6 percent in 1992. A more somber assessment of the economy came from Alan Greenspan, chairman of the Federal Reserve Board, in testimony before the Senate Banking Committee February 2. He said that of all the uncertainties in the economy at that time the most serious was the continuing reluctance of banks to lend money. Vigorous moves by the Federal Reserve Board to stimulate bank lending had not worked, Greenspan said.

The reports of the president and his economic advisers hewed closely to views traditionally identified with the Republican party. For example, Bush said that the "simple secret of America's economic success" in the 1980s had been "a government policy that allowed the private sector to serve as the engine of economic growth."

Report Recommendations

To improve the nation's hard-pressed banking system, the report recommended that commercial firms be allowed to affiliate with banks in some circumstances. Commercial firms, the economists' report said, "offer a potentially large source of new capital and innovative ideas" for the financial services industry. Also among new recommendations was a proposal for far-reaching changes in the public education system. The CEA report said the system should be restructured in such a way that schools would compete for students.

Bush and his economists again urged enactment of a lower capital gains tax. To encourage private savings, the reports for the second year recommended Family Savings Accounts. Withdrawals from Family Savings Accounts, after seven years, would not be taxed. Bush said his administration would continue to press for the establishment of "enterprise zones" in distressed areas. The zones would be designed to encourage entrepreneurship, investment, and job creation.

Both the president and his advisers emphasized the importance the administration attached to legislation for establishing a United States-Mexico free trade zone. The economists said that a free trade agreement would "boost the international competitiveness of both U.S. and Mexican firms." A free trade pact with Canada was adopted in 1988.

> *Following is the text of the Economic Report of the President and excerpts from the Annual Report of the Council of Economic Advisers, both issued February 12, 1991, by the White House:*

ECONOMIC REPORT OF THE PRESIDENT

To the Speaker of the House of Representatives and the President of the Senate:

Just over 8 years ago the longest peacetime economic expansion in U.S. history began. By the start of the 1990s the unemployment rate had fallen to levels not seen since the early 1970s, and inflation remained relatively low and remarkably stable when compared with the 1970s. More than 20 million new jobs were created by our dynamic and diverse market economy—the largest and the most productive in the world. Reflecting both the evolving needs and wants of the American people and the rapid advance of technology, some industries and regions experienced much more robust job growth than others. And, as is normal during economic expansions, the rate of growth of the Nation's output varied from year to year.

The events of 1990 were a reminder that even a healthy economy can suffer shocks and short-term setbacks. In early August, Iraq invaded and occupied its small, defenseless neighbor Kuwait and threatened Saudi Arabia. Oil prices rose substantially on the world market, and business and consumer confidence plummeted. These shocks hit an economy that was already growing slowly for several reasons, including worldwide increases in interest rates, tightened credit conditions, and the lingering effects of a successful attempt begun in 1988 by the Federal Reserve to prevent an acceleration of inflation. U.S. output turned down in the fourth quarter of 1990, and it became clear that the economy had entered a recession. I know that in some regions of our country, people are in genuine economic distress.

This temporary interruption in America's economic growth does not signal a decline in the basic long-term vitality of the U.S. economy. Indeed, there were important economic achievements in 1990. Even though many analysts had earlier forecast increased inflation, the underlying rate of inflation was contained and showed clear signs of declining by the end of the year. Low inflation is essential to lower interest rates and strong economic growth. The U.S. trade deficit declined for the third year in a row, and U.S. firms remained competitive in world markets. Exports of American products reached an all-time high in 1990 and exceeded those of any other nation. Productivity in U.S. manufacturing continued to grow impressively. Some regions and industries experienced relatively strong job growth.

My Administration's economic policies are designed both to mitigate the current downturn and to provide for a solid recovery and the highest possible rate of sustainable economic growth. Because these policies are credible and systematic, they reduce uncertainty and pave the way to higher growth with sustained job-creating expansions. With these policies in place, the current recession is expected to be mild and brief by historical standards.

Economic growth is projected to recover by the middle of this year.

Inflation and interest rates are expected to decline. With the adoption of my pro-growth initiatives, the recovery and ensuing expansion are projected to be strong and sustained, and to be accompanied by continued progress toward lower inflation.

As the Nation proceeds into the 1990s, it is important to remember the simple secret of America's economic success in the 1980s: a government policy that allowed the private sector to serve as the engine of economic growth. We must also remember that economic growth is the fundamental determinant of the long-run success of any nation, the basic source of rising living standards, and the key to meeting the needs and desires of the American people.

The process of growth necessarily involves change. Advances in technology, shifts in world market conditions, and changes in tastes and demographics have created major new industries and dramatically altered the fortunes of existing industries. The lesson of history is clear. Attempts to protect special interests by blocking the economy's natural, market-driven evolution—through regulation, subsidy, or protection from competition—reduce the economy's flexibility and impair its ability to grow and to create jobs. Growth and prosperity are enhanced by strengthening and extending the scope of market forces, not by substituting government dictates for the free choices of workers, consumers, and businesses.

Toward Renewed Growth

The budget law enacted last fall gives fiscal policy a strong and credible medium-term framework. It increases the ability of the fiscal system to dampen the impact of the current recession, while providing for strong controls to reduce Federal spending as a percentage of our gross national product. A major reason that the budget deficit is expected to increase this year—before declining steadily thereafter—is the increase in payments to those adversely affected by the current downturn and the reduction in tax receipts as incomes grow more slowly. These automatic responses to the recession will help cushion its effects.

I am committed to maintaining a tax system that will sustain strong economic growth. My proposal to reduce the tax rate of capital gains would give a needed boost to the economy and set it on a strong course of economic growth and job creation for years to come. A lower capital gains tax rate would encourage entrepreneurial activity, which plays a critical role in creating new jobs, new products, and new methods of production. It would reduce the bias in favor of debt financing and thereby decrease the financial risks borne by U.S. corporations and their workers and shareholders.

The Federal Reserve's control of inflation throughout the recent long expansion has given it the credibility necessary to mitigate the current downturn significantly without triggering an increase in inflationary expectations. Federal Reserve action in recent months will also help to alleviate tight credit market conditions that have hampered the economy. It is important that the Federal Reserve sustain money and credit growth necessary for the maintenance of sustained economic growth, especially during an economic downturn. And, while unwarranted risks should be avoided, I believe that sound banks should be making more sound loans.

Comprehensive banking reform will help to alleviate tight credit conditions by reducing unnecessary restrictions on the banking sector. Healthier depository institutions are essential for a sound financial system. Lifting restrictions on interstate banking activities and on the ability of banks to combine with commercial and other financial firms will increase banks' competitiveness. These changes will enhance banks' ability to attract capital and reduce the risk of a contraction in lending.

Some have argued that the government should react to the recent oil price shock by reregulating energy markets. They would do well to remember the lessons of the 1970s, when regulation worsened the impacts of two oil shocks and forced Americans to waste many hours in long and unnecessary lines at gas stations. Long-term uncertainties about energy prices make it vital that U.S. energy policy be based, in both the short run and the long run, on the flexibility and efficiency that only well-functioning markets can provide.

My Administration's National Energy Strategy calls for removing unnecessary barriers to market forces so that ample supplies of reasonably priced energy can continue to foster economic growth. The Strategy also outlines initiatives to enhance the energy security of the United States and its friends and allies, to encourage cost-effective conservation and efficiency measures, to increase the use of alternative fuels, and to continue to mitigate the environmental consequences of energy use.

Supporting Long-Run Growth

The Federal Government cannot mandate or effectively direct economic growth, but it can and should create conditions that encourage market-driven growth. That requires reducing barriers to saving, investing, working, and innovating. Encouraging growth also requires sustaining and expanding the role of market forces and, thereby, enhancing the economy's flexibility. Attempts to second-guess the market and to direct government support to particular firms, industries, or technologies in the name of promoting growth are inevitably counterproductive.

The multiyear Federal deficit reduction package adopted last year, the largest and most comprehensive such package in U.S. history, will reduce the Federal budget deficit by nearly a half-trillion dollars over the next 5 years relative to baseline projections. This substantial reduction in government borrowing will raise the national saving rate and increase the pool of funds available to finance job-creating private investment in new productive capacity and new technology.

My Administration remains firmly committed to taking additional steps to lower the cost of capital and to encourage entrepreneurship, saving, investment, and innovation. I have again asked the Congress to reduce the tax rate on long-term capital gains and to make the research and experimentation tax credit permanent. To encourage private saving, my budget again includes Family Savings Accounts and penalty-free withdrawals from Individual Retirement Accounts for first-time homebuyers. My Administration will seek increased Federal support for research that has broad national benefits, and we will make the results of government-supported research more accessible to the private sector so that they can be brought more quickly to market.

Strong economic growth will continue to require a sound national transportation infrastructure. My Administration's proposals for restructuring highway programs, centered around a new National Highway System program, would make a substantial contribution to meeting those demands.

Economic growth requires skilled and adaptable workers as well as modern capital and new technology. Excellence in education is the key to increasing the quality of the U.S. labor force. My Administration is strongly committed to making the U.S. educational system second to none, so that U.S. workers can continue to compete effectively with their peers in other nations. To meet this goal, the performance of U.S. elementary and secondary education must be dramatically improved. More money will not ensure excellence; America is already a world leader in spending on education. Fundamental reform is necessary.

Government policies should be designed to put power in the hands of individuals and families—to give them the tools and incentives to improve their own lives. Thus students and their families must be given greater freedom to choose among competing schools, and talented and skilled individuals must be freed from unnecessary obstacles to entering the teaching profession. My Administration will seek enactment of a new Educational Excellence Act that would support choice in education, alternative certification for teachers and principals, rewards for outstanding teachers and for schools that improve their students' achievements, and innovative approaches to mathematics and science education.

The Immigration Act of 1990, the first major reform of legal immigration in a quarter-century, will substantially increase the overall level of immigration, particularly of skilled workers. These new workers will contribute to U.S. economic growth, as well as to the Nation's social and cultural vitality.

The Americans with Disabilities Act is the most significant extension of civil rights legislation in two decades. It will enable more of our citizens with disabilities to enter the economic mainstream and thus to better their own lives while contributing to the Nation's economic strength.

Last year important legislation passed that will give power and opportunity to individuals. The expansion of the Earned Income Tax Credit, the new health insurance credit, and the other child care provisions in the 1990s budget legislation will put dollars for child care directly in the hands of parents, instead of bureaucracies. The Homeownership and Opportunity for People Everywhere (HOPE) initiative in the National Affordable Housing Act will expand homeownership and give more families a stake in their communities. My Administration strongly supported the expansion of Medicaid to provide health insurance to more pregnant women and children in low-income families.

But there is more to be done. My Administration will continue to press for the establishment of enterprise zones to encourage entrepreneurship, investment, and job creation in distressed communities. We will propose initiatives focused on infant mortality, preventive measures, and nutrition to improve the health of those least able to provide for their own needs.

Flexibility and Regulation

The remarkable flexibility of the U.S. economy, which stems from its reliance on free markets, is a major national asset. Flexibility enables the economy to cushion the effects of adverse developments, such as oil price shocks, and to take full advantage of innovations and other new opportunities. Indeed, the responsiveness of the economy to new opportunities is an important spur to innovation and a source of economic dynamism.

Government regulation generally serves to reduce economic flexibility and thus should have a very limited role. Where regulation is necessary, regulatory programs should pass strict cost-benefit tests and should seek to harness the power of market forces to serve the public interest, not to distort or diminish those forces.

The lesson of the savings and loan crisis, to which my Administration responded swiftly, is not that competition and innovation are incompatible with safety and soundness in the financial sector. Rather, this experience shows that poorly designed regulation, inadequate supervision, and limits on risk-reducing diversification can combine to produce behavior that undermines creditors' confidence and imposes unnecessary burdens on taxpayers.

We can and must ensure the safety and soundness of our banking system and continue to provide full protection for insured deposits while allowing competition to improve efficiency and encourage innovation. My Administration's proposals for comprehensive reform of the regulatory system governing banks will achieve these goals. In addition, these reforms will enhance the ability of U.S. banks to compete in the global markets for financial services.

Last year's farm legislation embodied important steps toward a market-oriented agricultural policy and away from government domination of this vital and progressive sector. Farmers have been given additional flexibility in planting decisions, in a way that will both sustain farmers' incomes and save taxpayers' money.

Market-based initiatives can and should play a key role in environmental policy as well. In 1989 my Administration proposed comprehensive legislation to combat air pollution. This proposal broke a logjam that had blocked congressional action for more than a decade, and a landmark clean air bill was enacted last year—the most significant air pollution legislation in the Nation's history. The centerpiece of this bill is an innovative, market-based program for controlling—at the least possible cost to the economy—the emissions that produce acid rain. All provisions of this legislation will be implemented so as to minimize unnecessary burdens on American workers and firms.

Economic growth and environmental protection are compatible, but only if environmental goals reflect careful cost-benefit analysis and if environmental regulation provides maximum flexibility to meet those goals at least cost. My Administration will continue to be guided by the responsibilities of global stewardship; we will seek both to protect the environment and to maintain economic growth to give all the world's children the chance to lead better lives than their parents.

Leadership in the Global Economy

Throughout the postwar period, the United States has led the world toward a system of free trade and open markets. The benefits of global economic integration and expanded international trade have been enormous, at home and abroad. U.S. firms gain from access to global markets; U.S. workers benefit from foreign investment in America; and U.S. consumers can buy goods and services from around the world. Competition and innovation have been stimulated, and businesses have increased their efficiency by locating operations around the globe. The phenomenal prosperity and vitality of market-oriented economies—and the bankruptcy of the socialist model—point the way to future progress and growth.

My Administration will continue to push aggressively for open markets in all nations, including our own, and will continue to oppose protectionism. Protectionist trade barriers impose burdens on the many to serve the interests of the few and can only reduce the Nation's competitiveness. Government attempts to overrule the decisions of the international marketplace and to manage trade or investment flows inevitably reduce economic flexibility and lower living standards.

My Administration's top trade policy priority continues to be the successful completion of the Uruguay Round negotiations of the General Agreement on Tariffs and Trade (GATT). Success in the Uruguay Round would open agricultural markets, lower or eliminate tariffs on many products, strengthen the GATT system, and extend it to cover important new areas—such as services, investment, and intellectual property— critical to U.S. economic vitality. These improvements would significantly increase the ability of the global economy to raise living standards in the United States and around the world. Failure, on the other hand, would increase trade frictions and could lead to a destructive new round of protectionism.

In addition, my Administration has moved to pave the way toward a hemispheric zone of free trade. We have announced our intention to begin negotiations on a free-trade agreement with Mexico. My Enterprise for the Americas Initiative promises to fuel growth and prosperity throughout this hemisphere by removing barriers to trade and investment. This initiative also aims to provide official debt reduction to countries engaged in significant economic reforms and thereby to build on my Administration's ongoing support for commercial debt reduction.

America remains a beacon of hope to peoples around the world. Our Nation continues to demonstrate by shining example that political democracy and free markets reinforce each other and together lead to liberty and prosperity. Nations in this hemisphere and the emerging democracies of Eastern Europe are eagerly moving to follow America's example. The challenges these nations face as they fundamentally restructure their economies are enormous. My Administration will continue its strong support and assistance for their vital and historic efforts.

In my *Economic Report* last year I stated that I looked forward to the 1990s with hope and optimism. Despite the economic events of 1990, we have reason for both hope and optimism in full measure as the Nation approaches the next American century.

Following sound economic policy principles, my Administration seeks to achieve the maximum possible rate of sustainable economic growth. We must continue to adhere to those principles if we are to soften the impacts of the current recession and to strengthen the foundation for strong growth in the years to come. Economic growth remains the key to raising living standards for all Americans, to expanding job opportunities, and to maintaining America's global economic leadership.

THE ANNUAL REPORT OF THE COUNCIL OF ECONOMIC ADVISERS

Recent Developments and Prospects

The downturn in the U.S. economy in the latter part of 1990 does not signal any decline in its long-run underlying health or basic vitality. As stated in last year's *Report,* economic expansions end because of external shocks, imbalances in demand, or policy mistakes. The oil price shock of 1990 makes clear that the economy is episodically buffeted by external shocks. If sound fiscal, monetary, regulatory, and trade policies are maintained, however, such shocks will have smaller effects on the economy, downturns will be shallower and shorter, and expansions will be longer. In fact, with such policies now in place, the current downturn is expected to be shorter and milder than the average post-World War II recession.

Developments in 1990

The oil price shock, the sudden drop in consumer and business confidence, and the uncertainty about when the Persian Gulf crisis would end were undoubtedly the key factors in the downturn in late 1990. Oil prices more than doubled between July and October, before declining toward the end of the year and again in early 1991 after the outbreak of hostilities in the Gulf. Consumer and business confidence may have been reduced by the superficial similarity of this oil price shock to those of the 1970s, when unemployment and inflation soared.

The oil price shock hit an economy that was already growing slowly. A worldwide rise in long-term interest rates early in the year—partly due to anticipated increases in the demand for capital in Eastern Europe and to concerns about accelerating inflation—put upward pressure on borrowing rates in the United States and slowed the growth of consumer and business spending. This rise occurred when long-term interest rates were already high, in part because of large Federal budget deficits and the prospect that they might continue indefinitely.

The Federal Reserve had initiated a more restrictive monetary policy in the spring of 1988 to ward off an increase in the underlying inflation rate. The lagged effects of this policy also slowed the economy in 1989 and 1990, as higher interest rates discouraged spending. This tightening successfully contained inflationary pressures, and left monetary policy with much more latitude—compared with the inflationary policies of the 1970s—to ameliorate the adverse effects of the oil price shock.

Tighter credit markets reduced the availability of loans to some creditworthy borrowers, and this also contributed to the slowdown. Banks and other financial institutions tightened lending standards for a number of reasons: A slowing economy increased the risks of lending to businesses. The value of collateral on residential and commercial real estate loans fell with declining real estate values. Overly zealous bank examiners discouraged some banks from making new loans. And the need to increase the ratio of capital to loan assets to meet minimum capital requirements forced some banks to curtail loan growth. Stricter lending standards for commercial and residential loans slowed business investment and housing construction. . . .

The Outlook

The Administration projects that real economic growth will be 0.9 percent over the four quarters of 1991, with the downturn continuing through the first quarter and a recovery beginning near the middle of the year. Inflation is expected to remain under control, declining substantially from the temporarily high levels reached as a result of the oil price shock. Continued progress in gradually lowering the underlying rate of inflation is also expected. Interest rates are projected to be lower on average in 1991 than in 1990, reflecting slower growth in credit demand during the downtown, as well as lower inflation rates.

The current downturn is expected to be short and shallow for several reasons. Most firms have kept inventories low relative to sales, reducing the need for a sharp cut in production to work off excess inventories. Such inventory corrections accounted for much of the decline in output in earlier postwar recessions. Moreover, net exports are projected to improve, both because the Nation's major trading partners are expected on average to experience stronger growth than the United States, and because the decline in the value of the dollar since 1989 has lowered the price of U.S. exports on world markets. Oil prices remain a source of uncertainty in the outlook, but they have declined substantially since their peak in October, particularly since the start of Operation Desert Storm. Finally, both fiscal and monetary policies are well positioned to mitigate the downturn. There is a downside risk that the tightness in credit markets evident in 1990 will continue into 1991, a consideration that poses special challenges for monetary policy.

Assuming adoption of the Administration's growth initiatives—including a lower tax rate on long-term capital gains, tax incentives to reduce barriers to household saving, reforms to strengthen the financial sector, and increased investment in children, education, infrastructure, space, and high technology, all within the context of lower structural budget deficits—the long-term outlook is excellent. Growth is expected to strengthen in 1992, with the economy in a relatively high-growth recovery through 1993 before returning to a solid, sustainable expansion. With sound economic policies in place, there is no fundamental obstacle to an expansion in the 1990s at least as long and strong as the record expansion of the 1980s. . . .

Encouraging Investment and Improving Education

Continued growth in productivity and living standards requires investment in new buildings and equipment, advances in technology, and improvements in the skills of U.S. workers. All these must be encouraged if America is to leave its children a legacy of global economic leadership.

Investment in plant, equipment, and commercial technologies is the task of the private sector. Because market forces guide investment funds to their most productive uses, the government can generally only slow economic growth by second-guessing private investment decisions. Government's primary task is to create conditions under which high levels of productive investment, guided by market forces, can fuel rapid growth. The multiyear deficit reduction program enacted in 1990 is an important step in this direction. Reducing the tax rate on long-term capital gains and enacting the Administration's proposals to increase private saving would also significantly reduce barriers to robust long-term economic growth.

In addition, of course, governments at all levels must recognize their shared responsibility to provide an efficient U.S. transportation infrastructure, which is necessary for sustained economic growth. Legislation passed in 1990 will make it easier for airports to finance needed capacity expansions. The Administration will seek both increases in Federal funding for highways and a restructuring of highway programs that will give the States greater flexibility, while ensuring that the 150,000 miles of roads in the National Highway System will be maintained, rehabilitated, and expanded.

The Federal Government has an important role to play in the process of technological change. Some research projects offer the potential of large benefits to the economy as a whole but do not offer much prospect of profit to any private firm that might undertake them. The knowledge generated by these projects would be valuable, but no firm could prevent others from capturing most of that value. Such "spillovers" are important in the case of basic research, the results of which cannot generally be directly incorporated into a marketable product or process. The Administration has proposed substantial increases in Federal support for basic research, and the President has announced his intention to double the budget of the National Science Foundation.

Some areas of applied research promise advances in generic, precompetitive technologies that would also have large spillovers. The Administration will seek increased support for such research and will make the results of government-supported research more readily available to the private sector for speedier commercialization. Adoption of the Administration's proposed reform of the antitrust law governing joint ventures would increase the ability of the private sector to take advantage of research opportunities with industry-specific benefits. Finally, the Administration will again seek to make the research and experimentation tax credit permanent to enhance incentives for private-sector investment in new technology.

Education is the key to increasing the skills of the U.S. labor force. If America's children continue to learn less in school than their counterparts abroad, America's workers will not long continue to earn more. The United States already spends more per pupil in elementary and secondary education than all its major competitors, but it does not receive an adequate educational return on this investment.

The Administration will continue its strong support of the fundamental reform necessary to achieve excellence in U.S. elementary and secondary education. The key to successful reform is to harness the power of market forces: Schools should be able to compete for students. Parents and students must be afforded more choice among schools, and unnecessary barriers to entry into the teaching profession must be swept away.

The Administration will introduce a new Educational Excellence Act, which will stimulate fundamental reform and restructure the Nation's education system by promoting educational choice and alternative certification for teachers and principals. And, to help ensure that all students enter school ready to learn, the Administration has significantly expanded the Head Start program. The President will continue his close work with the Nation's Governors to advance the vital cause of educational excellence. . . .

U.S. Leadership in the Global Economy

The principle that market forces, not government planners, are the best source of lasting prosperity is as valid in global markets as it is within individual economies. The Administration accordingly remains strongly committed to removing barriers to trade and investment in all nations, to opposing pressures for protectionism and government management of trade, to supporting market-oriented reform around the world, and to pursuing macroeconomic policies conducive to strong noninflationary growth in the United States and the world economy. . . .

Sustained strong worldwide growth in the 1990s will depend on continued progress toward a free and open multilateral trading regime. Completing the Uruguay Round of multilateral trade negotiations, under the auspices of the General Agreement on Tariffs and Trade (GATT), remains the top trade priority of the Administration. In the Uruguay Round the United States has sought a significant agreement that reduces or eliminates tariffs in all nations in several broad sectors of manufacturing and that phases out other barriers to trade in textiles and agriculture. A key aim of the negotiations is to strengthen and modernize GATT rules and to extend them to new areas such as services, investment, and intellectual property.

In 1990 the Administration undertook several other market-opening initiatives that will both spur growth in this hemisphere and support the wave of market-oriented reform sweeping Latin America. A U.S.-Mexico free-trade agreement was endorsed by the Presidents of both countries. The Enterprise for the Americas Initiative aims to expand trade through free-trade agreements, to encourage liberalization of investment regimes in order to increase capital formation in the region, and to reduce official debt of countries pursuing strong economic reform programs. Additional measures to reduce trade barriers were also undertaken to help support cooperation on anti-narcotics efforts with Andean countries. As the benefits of these programs to the United States and its trading partners in the hemisphere become apparent, a clear signal of the gains from freer trade and sound economic policies will be sent around the world....

The U.S. Economy in 1990

Real GNP grew only 0.3 percent during 1990, well below the very strong 4¼-percent annual rate during 1987-88. Growth in the first part of 1990 was an extension of the modest growth in 1989, when real GNP grew 1.8 percent. But in the last part of 1990 the economy turned down. The unemployment rate rose 0.8 percentage point during the last 6 months of 1990. Despite the increase, the unemployment rate was low compared with the average over the previous 15 years. Consumer price increases excluding food and energy—a measure of core, or underlying, inflation—accelerated in the first quarter but were slowing at the end of the year. These developments in 1990 were influenced by, and in turn, affected monetary policy, fiscal policy, and conditions in credit markets.

Monetary Policy and Credit Markets

Monetary policy and credit market developments in 1990 were influenced by policy actions and developments that occurred in previous years. For example, the rapid economic growth in 1987 and 1988 pushed capacity utilization to high levels and reduced unemployment rates to the lowest levels since the early 1970s, but it also spurred serious concern about the possibility of rising inflation. In the spring of 1988, the Federal Reserve began to reduce the flow of money and credit gradually and to increase interest rates. The Federal Reserve's goal was to reduce inflationary pressures by engineering a "soft landing"; that is, by reducing overall demand slowly enough to avoid causing a recession. Since then, the difficulties inherent in distinguishing more permanent threats of rising inflation from temporary but sharp price-level changes, coupled with the long and variable lags through which monetary policy affects economic activity, have complicated the task of predicting the economic consequences of any given level of monetary restraint....

Long-Term Interest Rates

While short-term interest rates were relatively stable in the first half of the year, long-term interest rates were more volatile. After declining somewhat in the second half of 1989, long-term rates rose sharply in the first few months of 1990. The yield on 10-year Treasury bonds increased 75 basis points between December 1989 and March 1990.

Concern about a possible increase in the underlying inflation rate caused by the temporary jump in inflation in the first quarter may have contributed to the rise in long-term rates. A more important factor, however, was the anticipated increase in the demand for capital associated with developments in Eastern Europe and the unification of Germany....

Credit Market Developments

By midyear, surveys indicated that bank lending standards had tightened and that credit was becoming more difficult to obtain. As the year progressed, the effects of the tightening began to appear in aggregate bank lending figures. From August through October commercial and industrial loans at commercial banks fell at an annual rate of 3.3 percent. In addition, a Federal Reserve survey of senior bank lending officers in October reported that nearly two-thirds of respondents had tightened their lending standards for construction and land development loans in the previous 3 months, and almost half had tightened their standards on commercial and industrial loans. Overall, bank credit increased about 5.1 percent during 1990, compared to a 6.9-percent rise during 1989.

Tightened lending standards and slower growth in bank lending were partly the result of a sluggish economy. Demand for credit usually falls as the overall economy weakens. Moreover, as the economy slows, the probability of bankruptcy increases. To compensate for the increased risk of lending, lending standards may have become stricter. Concerns about overzealous bank examiners may have discouraged some banks from making loans, and declining real estate values reduced the value of collateral on residential and commercial real estate loans....

Federal Budget Developments

Federal spending, tax, and borrowing activities have an important influence over economic activity. The slowdown in the economy and the large financial transactions associated with the resolution of the savings and loan (S&L) crisis require that particular care be taken in describing budgetary and deficit changes for 1990 and beyond.. . .

The Federal Deficit

From 1979 to 1983 the consolidated Federal budget deficit as a percentage of GNP increased steadily to 6.3 percent, its highest level since World War II. (The difference between Federal outlays and receipts is the deficit.) The deficit-to-GNP ratio was around 5.2 percent between 1984 and 1986, and then fell to its recent low of 3 percent in 1989, primarily as a consequence of reductions in Federal spending. Since 1980 the ratio of tax receipts to GNP has been 19 percent, while the ratio of outlays to GNP has been 23.1 percent.

The ratio of the deficit to GNP rose in 1990, mostly due to spending increases. The ratio was expected to remain high, which led to concerns that interest rates would also remain high, harming prospects for long-run growth. *These concerns led to enactment of the Omnibus Budget Reconciliation Act, signed in November 1990. The budget law is expected to reduce future deficits substantially from what they would have been in the absence of the act.* Nevertheless, by all conventional measures the current deficit is large and will remain large during the next few years.

Federal budget accounting distinguishes between *on-budget* and *off-budget* outlays and receipts. The more comprehensive *consolidated budget* combines both on-budget and off-budget accounts. Some items are classified as off-budget based on economic reasons; others, for legislative or government accounting reasons. Currently, outlays and receipts of the Social Security trust funds are off-budget, yet changes in these trust funds affect total government saving and thereby the net borrowing requirements of the Federal Government. In fiscal 1990 Social Security receipts exceeded outlays, which was the main factor leading to an off-budget surplus of $57 billion. As a result, the fiscal 1990 on-budget deficit of $277 billion substantially exceeded the $220 billion *consolidated budget* deficit.

The financial transactions of the Resolution Trust Corporation (RTC) and other deposit insurance programs have made the interpretation of the effect of the budget on the economy more complex. The RTC reimburses federally insured depositors in failed savings and loan institutions. The funds required to pay the full value of these deposits are large, and the problems created by the incentives associated with deposit insurance have had negative effects on the economy. . . .

Industrial Production and Capacity Utilization

Sluggish consumer spending on goods, falling residential construction, and slowing export growth caused manufacturing output to fall during 1990 after slowing substantially in 1989. Sharp declines in the fourth quarter led to a 1.4-percent fall in overall industrial production during 1990, as production of motor vehicles fell more than 20 percent. Excluding motor vehicles and parts, industrial production fell 0.5 percent during 1990, compared with a 1.8-percent rise during 1989.

Slowing production in the first half and falling production in the second half pushed down capacity utilization in the industrial sector 3.3 percentage points during 1990. In December capacity utilization in manufacturing fell to 79.3 percent, well below the 85-percent rate in April 1989, its recent peak. Utilization rates generally declined across all industries. Utilization in motor vehicle manufacturing fell to 57 percent.

Employment

The civilian unemployment rate rose in the second half of 1990, after remaining around a 15-year low for most of 1989 and the first half of 1990. By December the unemployment rate had risen to 6.1 percent, about where it had been in mid-1987. From June to December the jobless rate for men rose 0.9 percentage point, while the rate for women rose 0.7 percentage point. In the second half of the year, the unemployment rate rose 1.5 percentage points for blacks and 1.9 percentage points for teenagers. For the entire year the civilian unemployment rate averaged 5.5 percent. . . .

Productivity

Growth in labor productivity in the nonfarm business sector fell 0.8 percent in 1990. Low or negative labor productivity growth is typical in an economic slowdown, as firms tend to keep workers even when demand slows in order to avoid costly search and training when demand increases again.

Manufacturing productivity continued its recent trend of relatively strong growth compared with other sectors. Manufacturing productivity grew 3 percent in 1990, compared with 3.3 percent in 1989. Rising labor productivity in manufacturing helped to hold the growth of unit labor costs to 0.3 percent, after a 0.6-percent rise in 1989. Very slow growth of unit labor costs in manufacturing is one indicator that underlying inflationary pressures did not rise in 1990. . . .

Broad-based measures of inflation indicated that inflation was contained in 1990. The GNP fixed-weighted price index, a measure that includes prices of all goods and services in the economy rather than just consumer goods and services, was up 4.5 percent in 1990, the same as in 1989. After rising substantially in the first quarter of 1990, inflation measured by this index was below the 1989 average in each of the last three quarters of the year. . . .

The Iraqi invasion of Kuwait in early August and its impact on oil prices dominated price-level movements in the second half of 1990. Crude oil prices jumped from $22 a barrel on August 1, the day before the invasion, to their 1990 peak of $40 a barrel in the middle of October. Prices retreated below $26 a barrel before ending the year at around $28 a barrel. Oil prices fell rapidly to around $20 a barrel in early 1991, following the beginning of Operation Desert Storm. . . .

The Economic Outlook

The Administration projects that the downturn in the economy is likely to continue into the early part of 1991 and that recovery is likely to begin by the middle of the year. After the recovery, the economy is then expected to return to a strong growth path of around 3 percent through the mid-1990s. In the long run, projected reductions in labor force growth may lead to lower real GNP growth, unless they are offset by increased immigration or greater labor force participation.

The Outlook for the Short Term

Reductions in real consumer income during the last two quarters of 1990, low levels of consumer and business confidence, and continued tight credit conditions all point to a further decline in real activity in the first quarter of this year.

There have been eight other recessions since World War II. The average recession lasted 11 months, two lasted 16 months, and one was only 6 months. The typical recession has been associated with a 2.6-percent decline in real GNP from peak to trough, although declines have been as high as 4.3 percent and as low as 1 percent.

Compared with the average of these previous recessions, the current downturn is likely to be shallow and relatively short, and the prospects for a recovery of economic growth by mid-1991 are good. The economy continues to have low inventories relative to sales, indicating that a prolonged period of inventory liquidation is not likely in the short term. More importantly, in the early stages of previous downturns both inflation and interest rates were either high or rising. In 1982, for example, the Federal Reserve had to follow a stringent monetary policy to reduce entrenched inflation expectations. In the current situation, the core inflation rate is moderating and is far lower than in the 1974-75 and 1981-82 recessions, partly because the Federal Reserve has followed a credible, systematic policy in recent years. Moderating inflation, coupled with Federal Reserve credibility in fighting inflation, leaves room for the Federal Reserve's policy to soften the downturn without raising expectations of higher inflation.

Additional developments in 1990 point to growth recovering in the second half of 1991. Lower long-term interest rates will begin to have positive effects on investment spending. The loosening of monetary policy that occurred in the fourth quarter of 1990 and early 1991 will also begin to affect consumer and business spending in the middle of 1991. . . .

Inflation in 1991 should be lower than in 1990, barring a resurgence of oil price rises or other price shocks. The economic slowdown in 1990 created excess capacity in many industries and eased tightness in labor markets, which will contribute to downward pressure on underlying inflation during the year.

In 1992, growth is expected to be robust as the economy continues to rebound from its sluggish growth in 1989-90 and the downturn that began in late 1990. Business investment and construction activity are expected to be especially strong. The unemployment rate is projected to decline. . . .

Education Reform for an Adaptable Work Force

A key determinant of the flexibility of the economy is the quality of its work force. Education raises skill levels that increase job performance and productivity. Well-educated workers have the basic skills necessary to adapt to the changing demands of a dynamic economy and are able to complete with their peers in other nations.

Unfortunately, primary and secondary education in this country does an inadequate job of producing such workers. Parental involvement and student dedication—especially to homework—is essential to the success of any school system. But greater parental and student effort alone cannot ensure success. Comprehensive reform of American elementary and secondary education is necessary....

The Current State of Education

Evidence of the inadequacy of education in the United States can be found in the workplace and in the schools themselves.

Evidence from the Workplace

Today's high school graduate is often ill-prepared for the world of work. The 1990 National Assessment of Educational Progress, which reported the results of a nationwide test of students conducted between 1986 and 1988, found that only 6 percent of 17-year old students demonstrate the capacity to solve multistep problems and use basic algebra; only 8 percent have the ability to draw conclusions and infer relationships using scientific knowledge; and only 5 percent can synthesize and learn from specialized reading materials.

Firms are finding it increasingly necessary to develop remedial training programs in reading and mathematical skills; they spend an estimated $20 billion annually on such programs. Even institutions of higher learning are adapting their course offerings to reflect the poor preparation of many freshmen; the fraction of colleges offering remedial instruction has increased from 79 percent to more than 90 percent since 1980....

Programs of Choice

The U.S. public educational system must be opened to the invigorating and challenging forces of market competition by enabling teachers, parents, and students to choose their schools. Over time, the schools that survive will be the most innovative and effective institutions, those capable of responding to the changing educational needs of society.

Schools that must compete for students will work harder to deliver quality education. A school choice program can become the catalyst for greater diversity and help eliminate mediocrity in the educational system. An important step in this direction is the magnet school concept in which schools specialize in particular subject areas or interests—such as science, mathematics, or the performing arts—and students and their parents choose which school to attend....

Health Care: Dynamic Technology and Changing Demographics

Health care has been one of the fastest growing and most innovative sectors of the U.S. economy during the last three decades. Although many factors have contributed to the rapid pace of change, the fundamental driving forces have been technological advances and shifts in the demographic makeup of the population. These forces, along with the lack of market incentives for cost-conscious behavior, have resulted in escalating costs and much concern about lack of access to health care for many Americans—particularly the 33 million people who lack health insurance coverage. While government programs finance care for many of the poor and elderly, increasing government involvement in the health care financing system has aggravated the problems of cost and access. . . .

Perceived Problems of the Existing System

Despite the beneficial effects of much spending on health care, there is a general perception that the U.S. health care system should perform better than it does. Costs are seen to be out of control, and millions of households do not have health insurance and are perceived to have inadequate access to care.

Rising Government Health Care Costs

Health care costs paid by Federal, State, and local governments have exploded. The combined total spent by all levels of government on health care rose from $28.1 billion in 1960 (in 1989 dollars) to $253.3 billion in 1989 and is expected to continue to rise. These escalating costs place great stress on the ability of governments to fund current and future liabilities in health care.

Medicare, the principal program for providing medical care to the elderly and disabled, illustrates the changes in government spending on health. Medicare expenditures were $17.6 billion (in 1989 dollars) in 1967, the first full year of the program, and 19.5 million people were enrolled. By 1989 the Federal Government was spending $100 billion on Medicare, and 33.6 million elderly and disabled Americans were enrolled. *The enormous increase in outlays for Medicare can be traced to the increase in the number of people covered by the program, general increases in medical care expenses, and the increased share of program costs borne by the Federal Government. . . .*

Medicaid, the program that funds health care for some of the poor, illustrates the effect of changing demographics on both the type of care received and increasing government costs. Started in 1965, Medicaid was initially designed as a joint Federal/State program to provide health care for women and children receiving welfare payments and the disabled. Medicaid eligibility has expanded in recent years, but even today it is not designed to provide medical care for all poor Americans. Total Medicaid expenditures in 1967 were only $7.6 billion (in 1989 dollars). In 1989, the

Federal Government financed 57 percent of a total Medicaid bill of $59.3 billion. . . .

Health Care Price Inflation

Rapid increases in the real price of health care have contributed to the overall rise in health care spending. From 1980 to 1989 the price index for medical care rose by 99 percent, twice as fast as the average for all goods and services, though difficulties in measuring the inflation rate in technologically dynamic sectors suggest that the real difference in inflation rates was probably somewhat less. Those rapid price increases, combined with growth in the volume of services demanded, raised total health care expenses.

The health care sector has responded to cost escalation in several innovative ways. One of the most significant changes is the growth in health maintenance organizations (HMOs) and preferred provider organizations (PPOs). HMOs charge a fixed annual fee for medical services, rather than a separate fee for each service provided. In a PPO, a group of providers negotiates prices and patient volume with a large health care purchaser, such as an insurance company or employer. Through their greater potential for supplying cost-effective care, HMOs and PPOs provide competitive alternatives to traditional fee-for-service insurance policies. The rapid growth of HMOs and PPOs illustrates both the important role of competition and the ability of the health care sector to respond innovatively to the challenge of cost escalation.

The Medically Uninsured

One of the most critical deficiencies of the U.S. health care delivery system is the large number of people who lack health insurance. Although estimates vary, *recent calculations place the number of uninsured Americans at around 33 million.* Because the very poor are usually covered by government programs such as Medicaid, many of the uninsured are employed workers or children and spouses of workers. They may lack insurance coverage because their employers cannot afford to offer it, they cannot afford to purchase it on their own, and they do not qualify for government-subsidized programs. . . .

Why Health Care Markets Perform Poorly

Why is the health care sector able to perform so well in meeting certain demands yet unable to control costs or provide adequate services to all who need them? The institutional structure of the U.S. health care delivery system and the poor incentives for cost control it provides are at least partially to blame.

Health Insurance and "Third-Party Payments"

The most important institutional feature of the existing system is the prevalence of Federal or private insurance policies. People purchase insurance because they want to be protected from the costs of accidents, fire, or, in the case of health insurance, disease and sickness. But one consequence of insurance coverage is that those who are protected from harm by an insurance policy have less reason to take actions to reduce the probability that any harm will occur. . . .

Employer-Based Insurance and Tax-Free Health Benefits

One fundamental characteristic of the U.S. private health insurance system is that it is predominantly employer-based; that is, most Americans with health insurance obtain it through their employer. Providing insurance through employment is a natural mechanism for achieving the risk-sharing benefits of insurance. Economies in administrative, sales, and purchase costs also enhance the desirability of employer-based group insurance.

By covering everyone in a large group, insurers avoid the problem of "adverse selection," which occurs because those most likely to need expensive care, such as the chronically ill, are also the most likely to seek insurance. However, these advantages pertain primarily to large employers. Small firms are less likely to offer insurance if they have employees particularly likely to need care, and the economies in administrative expenses are much reduced for small groups. Firms with fewer than 50 workers incur administrative costs of about 25 to 40 percent of total claims, versus only 5.5 percent for firms with 10,000 or more employees. . . .

Reform in the Financial Sector

The financial sector provides services that are essential for economic growth, and thus it is important for this sector to operate effectively. Reform required to ensure that the financial system functions smoothly and efficiently is well under way. The Financial Institutions Reform, Recovery, and Enforcement Act of 1989 was only the first step in this program. The Federal Credit Reform Act of 1990, enacted as part of the Omnibus Budget Reconciliation Act of 1990, will help the government make better use of the resources it puts into its Federal credit programs, while comprehensive reforms recently proposed by the Administration, if enacted, will substantially alter the role the Federal Government plays as regulator of depository institutions and insurer of their deposits.

Context for Depository Institution Reform

Since the insurance program and many of the rules regulating banks and thrifts were drawn up during the Great Depression, dramatic developments have changed the financial sector. Many of the conditions that created the problems of the 1930s no longer exist today. More efficient means of addressing those that still remain may now be available. Moreover, any regulatory reform should allow the market to play its role in efficiently allocating resources.

The goal of reforming banks and thrifts should be to ensure that the financial system is efficient, competitive, and free from the danger of disruptive panics. The reforms of the 1930s succeeded in eliminating panics, but the constraints those reforms created and under which banks and thrifts still operate hinder their efficiency and competitiveness in today's environment. . . .

Issues in Deposit Insurance Reform

President Franklin Roosevelt was one of many who initially opposed the creation of a Federal deposit insurance system for fear that it would encourage excessively risky bank operations. "The minute the Government starts to do that the Government runs into a probable loss . . . ," Roosevelt said. "We do not wish to make the United States Government liable for the mistakes and errors of individual banks, and put a premium on unsound banking in the future."

Roosevelt's fears were unfounded in the years following enactment of the insurance program. With only limited competition, banks and thrifts had little reason to pursue excessively risky strategies. Limited competition increased profitability and the value of holding a bank or thrift charter. Excessively risky strategies put this value at risk and, therefore, were not generally pursued.

As competition increased, however, profit opportunities for banks and thrifts eroded and the value of their charters decreased, causing a gradual decline of the economic capital in depository institutions. High interest rates accelerated the decline of economic capital among S&Ls. For banks, the erosion of economic capital has been more gradual and less severe. In fact, most banks have substantial tangible capital and remain well-capitalized. Nonetheless, losses in economic capital, due to the deterioration of charter value, combined with deposit insurance premiums that are insensitive to risk-taking, have given weak banks increased incentives to take undue risks. With less to lose, they are willing to take greater risks.

In most industries, incentives to take excessive risks are kept in check by the market. The cost of capital for firms pursuing risky strategies increases. The mechanism operates weakly in banking since banks are largely financed through insured deposits. The government guarantee virtually eliminates any concern insured depositors might have about the actual operations of a bank or thrift. Thus, these investors in a bank or thrift offer no discipline to the managers. This lack of market discipline not only makes it easier for poorly managed institutions to operate, it also makes business difficult for prudent managers who compete with poorly managed institutions for both loans and deposits.

Pros and Cons of a Federal Role in Deposit Insurance

Deposit insurance is generally recognized as having been quite successful in eliminating banking panics and the credit contractions and recessions associated with such panics. However, some have argued that the current problems in the banking and thrift industries reflect a fundamental danger in having the Federal Government extend a broad blanket of protection over deposits—a danger that can only be eliminated by curtailing the government's role.

These observers contend that well-organized political pressures to forbear in closing insolvent institutions, to extend the insurance guarantee to uninsured depositors, and to underprice coverage all undermine regulatory supervision. In the long run, they argue, the nature of our political process and its incentives for government policymakers are inconsistent with a sound insurance operation. In this view, the recently exposed flaws in Federal deposit insurance policies are no accident. They reflect a basic bias in the political process.

Another argument made against Federal deposit insurance is that government regulation and supervision are inherently less effective than market forces in balancing risk with depositor protection. Although regulators may be competent, dedicated, and well-intentioned, their incentives to monitor banking institutions carefully are unlikely to match the incentives for monitoring that the private sector is able to generate. Moreover, private market participants are unlikely to be subject to political pressure that may result in costly delays or inaction.

Supporters of continued Federal involvement in deposit insurance argue that because the potential liabilities are so large, only Federal insurance is credible. Depositors, they say, simply will not be so certain that the private market will be able to guarantee their deposits, and that uncertainty can lead to the kind of bank panics that the Federal deposit insurance system has so successfully eliminated. It is also argued that a private deposit insurance system would not appropriately assess the risks to check clearing and interbank fund transfer systems and to the overall economy that might be associated with the forced closure of very large institutions. . . .

The too-big-to-fail dilemma comes down to a conflict between principle and practicality. If the cost of bailing out an insolvent institution is clearly exceeded by the likely costs to the overall economy of allowing it to fail, then even if one agrees in principle that no institution should be considered too big to fail, it would be impractical to allow the failure. The key to resolving this conflict is to minimize the costs of such failures. Potential costs associated with systemic risks to the payments system have been greatly reduced by recent improvements in the public and private payment systems. Contagious uninsured depositor runs are less likely if uninsured depositors have confidence in other large banks. Banking reform that provides for the accurate measurement of capital and prompt corrective action before institutions are on the brink of failure should significantly reduce the possibility that the public would lose confidence in several large institutions at the same time.

Deposit Insurance Reform: Inducing Market-Based Incentives

Under the current system of deposit insurance, incentives on the part of poorly capitalized banks and thrifts to take undue risks must be constrained by regulation. In essence, examiners must question the decisions made by management. *Prudent management from the bank or thrift owners' perspective differs from prudent management from the regulators' perspective.* Regulators want to hold down costs to the insurance fund by minimizing the likelihood that the institution will fail. Institution owners want to maximize the value of their wealth.

For weak institutions, particularly those on the verge of failure, these divergent goals lead to clear conflict between regulators and management and require the imposition of tight and detailed regulatory constraints. The managers are trying to get funds out of the institutions and to the owners, while regulators want to keep funds in the institution to reduce the cost of failure to the insurance fund. Managers inevitably have superior information, and regulators thus face a task that is both difficult and critical.

The level of regulation and pressure on regulators might be reduced if the incentives of owners and the deposit insurer were more closely aligned. Before considering possible means to this end, it is important to emphasize that *a reduction in the regulation of depository institutions does not imply a reduction in their supervision.* The distinction needs to be clear. Regulations specify what types of activities institutions can and cannot engage in. Supervision entails observing what an institution does, but intervening only when the actions taken expose the institution to undue risks that could threaten the solvency of the institution. Thus, a healthy, well-capitalized institution might be allowed great flexibility but would still be carefully supervised. In fact, reduced regulation might on balance entail more, not less, supervision. . . .

VICTORY IN THE GULF
February 22, 23, 26, and 27

"Kuwait is liberated," President George Bush told the nation February 27. "Iraq's army is defeated," he said. "Our military objectives are met." He made the announcement in a brief televised address from the White House shortly after 9 p.m. EST. At midnight, the president said, a cease-fire would take effect, bringing the six-week-old war to an end, just 100 hours after the ground phase of the fighting commenced.

The relative ease with which the United States and its coalition allies had smashed Saddam Hussein's army and lifted Iraq's occupation of Kuwait stunned military analysts and elated the American people. The huge numbers of casualties that many feared from a ground war against Iraq never materialized. America suffered only 148 combat deaths—less than the toll sometimes incurred in a single week of fighting in Vietnam, where 47,000 Americans died in action.

"It's a proud day for America and, by God, we've kicked the Vietnam syndrome once and for all," Bush emphatically told a gathering of state legislators in Washington on March 1. On numerous occasions, the president had spoken out against a "Vietnam mentality" and vowed he would provide his commanders in the Persian Gulf with adequate military strength to achieve victory. More than half a million servicemen and women were sent to the region, after Iraq seized Kuwait on August 2, 1990. This constituted the biggest buildup of U.S. forces abroad since the Vietnam War. The American forces formed the largest national contingent among the twenty-eight countries comprising the UN-sponsored and U.S.-led coalition.

In a dozen resolutions, the UN Security Council condemned the seizure and set forth measures for the international community to undertake against Iraq. These included a trade boycott and other economic sanctions. The last of the twelve resolutions, approved November 29, called for the use of "all means necessary" to expel Iraq from Kuwait. (Deadline Pressure on Saddam Hussein, Historic Documents of 1990, p. 767) Bush additionally received explicit congressional authority on January 12 to commit U.S. troops to combat. (Congress on War With Iraq, p. 3)

Ground War

Iraq's army was the fourth largest in the world, widely assumed to be well equipped and battle-hardened after eight years of war with Iran from 1980 to 1988. (Iran-Iraq Truce, Historic Documents of 1988, p. 529) But once the allied land campaign began on February 24, Iraq's supposedly formidable border defenses were easily breached, and the Iraqis never used their huge stockpile of chemical weapons. Many of the defenders surrendered on the first contact with allied troops.

The land warfare followed thirty-eight days of incessant bombings, which had ravaged Iraq's military infrastructure and eviscerated its navy and air force. Some of Iraq's best warplanes were shot down or destroyed on the ground in the opening days of the air war; others were flown to safety in Iran and subsequently impounded by the Iranians. Iraqi ground units were left starved for supplies, badly damaged, and virtually blind to allied movements.

Allied military planners were able to deploy large forces without enemy detection for surprise attacks on February 24. While shipboard Marine combat forces feinted an attack on the Kuwaiti coast, pinning down 125,000 Iraqi defenders along the beaches, three columns pushed northward toward Kuwait City, the capital. One was composed of two Marine divisions and an Army tank brigade; the second of Saudi and Kuwaiti troops; and the third of two Egyptian divisions, a Syrian division, and units from Kuwait and Bahrain, as well as the United Arab Emirates.

Farther west, along the Saudi-Iraqi border, a flanking operation was taking place. American armored, infantry, and helicopter-borne assault divisions—aided by British and French armored units—moved northeastward in a great arc into southern Iraq, reaching the Euphrates River and cutting off escape routes for retreating Iraqi forces. The retreat from Kuwait became a rout, leaving the roads cluttered with men and vehicles, subject to devastating allied air attacks.

Iraq's Heavy Losses

Gen. H. Norman Schwarzkopf, the allied field commander, said in the final phase of the ground war that allied forces had put twenty-nine Iraqi divisions out of action and captured or destroyed most of the army's tanks. The surviving Iraqi forces north of the Euphrates—including some elite Republican Guard units never committed to battle—would still constitute the largest army in the region but would have relatively few tanks—"unless someone chooses to arm it in the future," the general said. "Barring that," he added, "there's not enough left of it . . . to be a regional threat."

Allied commanders refused to provide numbers of Iraqi battlefield casualties, but estimates from other sources ran as high as 50,000. The number of civilian casualties from allied bombings was not known at the war's end. A UN team visited Iraq in March and reported that the bombing had relegated the country "to a preindustrial age." Although the allied policy was to attack only industrial targets, the survey reported that 9,000 Iraqi homes had been destroyed or damaged beyond repair, casting 72,000 people homeless.

In Kuwait, Iraqi occupiers looted homes and national treasures and brutalized the civilian population. In an apparent attempt to foul Saudi Arabian water distillation plants along the Persian Gulf, the Iraqis created one of the world's largest oil spills by releasing oil from a Kuwaiti loading port and offshore tankers. Finally, in retreat, Iraqis set fire to about 650 Kuwaiti oil wells, enveloping much of the small country in acrid smoke. The last fire was extinguished November 6.

Soviet-Sponsored Peace Initiative

In the two weeks preceding Bush's victory declaration, Iraq had sought either directly or through the Soviet Union to stop the fighting, but on terms unacceptable to Washington. The Iraqi Revolutionary Command Council issued a vague statement February 15 suggesting that it might be willing to abide by Security Council Resolution No. 660 of August 8, which demanded that Iraq "withdraw immediately" from Kuwait. But the statement premised such action on a long list of demands, including Israel's withdrawal from the West Bank, Gaza Strip, and Golan Heights, which it had occupied since the 1967 Arab-Israeli war.

On February 18 Iraqi foreign minister Tariq Aziz met in Moscow with Soviet president Mikhail S. Gorbachev and out of that meeting came another peace proposal. Although the specifics of the plan were not made public, it was widely reported to have called for Iraq's withdrawal in return for Soviet assurances that Iraqi president Saddam Hussein would be protected from harm and that other Middle East issues—including the future of Palestinians in Israeli-occupied territories—would be dealt with.

Defusing the Palestine Issue

From the beginning of the crisis, Iraqi president Saddam Hussein had championed the Palestinians in his effort to win the support of fellow Arab leaders and divide the United Nations coalition that opposed him. Bush, in contrast, worked as vigorously to keep the Kuwait and Palestine issues separate. To avoid giving offense to Saudi Arabia and Egypt, the key Arab members of the UN coalition of forces, the United States worked diligently to avoid the involvement of Israeli military power against Iraq, its foremost enemy.

Keeping Israel on the sidelines became doubly difficult early in the war when Iraq began to fire Soviet-built Scud missiles at Israeli population centers, principally Tel Aviv, causing some civilian deaths and inflicting damage to several residential areas. The United States rushed to Israel's defense by providing several batteries of Patriot missiles, which were proving to have an exceptional ability to intercept the incoming Scud warheads before they reached their targets. Israel's uncharacteristic restraint in the face of attack brought words of praise from Washington officials and set the stage in Congress for added foreign-aid funding for Israel.

Bush's Ultimatum to Hussein

Bush brushed aside the Moscow peace initiative and another one that came three days later. By now, administration officials were fearful that Iraq's ambiguous statements about its willingness to withdraw could create pressure in allied capitals in Europe to undertake extensive negotiations that might undermine the U.S. military advantage. After Moscow's second offer, and a speech by Hussein portraying himself as peace-minded, Bush acted.

On the morning of February 22, he made a brief televised address, saying, "I have decided that the time has come to make public with specificity just exactly what is required of Iraq if a ground war is to be avoided." He said Hussein had until noon the next day to "begin his immediate and unconditional withdrawal from Kuwait." Soon afterward the White House issued a more detailed statement, but Hussein met none of the conditions it listed, and the ground war began.

> *Following are the texts of President George Bush's ultimatum to Iraq, February 22, 1991; his address the next day saying he had directed the ground war to begin; excerpts from the February 26 broadcast of Iraqi president Saddam Hussein declaring that "the mother of battles has succeeded" in producing a victory; and the text of Bush's announcement February 27 that "Kuwait is liberated":*

BUSH'S ULTIMATUM

Good morning.

The United States and its coalition allies are committed to enforcing the United Nations resolutions that call for Saddam Hussein to immediately and unconditionally leave Kuwait. In view of the Soviet initiative—which, very frankly, we appreciate—we want to set forth this morning the specific criteria that will ensure Saddam Hussein complies with the United Nations mandate.

Within the last 24 hours alone we have heard a defiant, uncompromising address by Saddam Hussein, followed less than 10 hours later by a statement in Moscow that, on the face of it, appears more reasonable. I say "on the face of it" because the statement promised unconditional Iraqi withdrawal from Kuwait, only to set forth a number of conditions. And needless to say, any conditions would be unacceptable to the international coalition and would not be in compliance with the United Nations Security Council Resolution 660's demand for immediate and unconditional withdrawal.

More importantly and more urgently, we learned this morning that Saddam has now launched a scorched-earth policy against Kuwait, anticipating perhaps that he will now be forced to leave. He is wantonly setting fires to and destroying the oil wells, the oil tanks, the export terminals, and other installations of that small country. Indeed, they're destroying the entire oil production system of Kuwait. At the same time that that Moscow press conference was going on and Iraq's Foreign Minister was talking peace, Saddam Hussein was launching Scud missiles.

After examining the Moscow statement and discussing it with my senior advisers here late last evening and this morning, and after extensive consultation with our coalition partners, I have decided that the time has come to make public with specificity just exactly what is required of Iraq if a ground war is to be avoided.

Most important, the coalition will give Saddam Hussein until noon Saturday to do what he must do—begin his immediate and unconditional withdrawal from Kuwait. We must hear publicly and authoritatively his acceptance of these terms. The statement to be released, as you will see, does just this and informs Saddam Hussein that he risks subjecting the Iraqi people to further hardship unless the Iraqi Government complies fully with the terms of the statement.

We will put that statement out soon. It will be in considerable detail. And that's all I'll have to say about it right now.

Thank you very much.

BEGINNING OF GROUND WAR

Good evening. Yesterday, after conferring with my senior national security advisers, and following extensive consultations with our coalition partners, Saddam Hussein was given one last chance—set forth in very explicit terms—to do what he should have done more than 6 months ago: withdraw from Kuwait without condition or further delay, and comply fully with the resolutions passed by the United Nations Security Council.

Regrettably, the noon deadline passed without the agreement of the Government of Iraq to meet demands of United Nations Security Council Resolution 660, as set forth in the specific terms spelled out by the coalition to withdraw unconditionally from Kuwait. To the contrary, what we have seen is a redoubling of Saddam Hussein's efforts to destroy completely Kuwait and its people.

I have, therefore, directed General Norman Schwarzkopf, in conjunction with coalition forces, to use all forces available, including ground forces, to eject the Iraqi army from Kuwait. Once again, this was a decision made only after extensive consultations within our coalition partnership.

The liberation of Kuwait has now entered a final phase. I have complete confidence in the ability of the coalition forces swiftly and decisively to accomplish their mission.

Tonight, as this coalition of countries seeks to do that which is right and just, I ask only that all of you stop what you are doing and say a prayer for all the coalition forces, and especially for our men and women in uniform who this very moment are risking their lives for their country and for all of us.

May God bless and protect each and every one of them. And may God bless the United States of America. Thank you very much.

HUSSEIN'S 'WITHDRAWAL' SPEECH

In the name of God, the merciful, the compassionate. O great people; O stalwart men in the forces of holy war and faith, glorious men of the mother of battles; O zealous, faithful and sincere people in our glorious nations, and among all Muslims and all virtuous people in the world; O glorious Iraqi women:

... We start by saying that on this day, our valiant armed forces will complete their withdrawal from Kuwait.... It was an epic duel which lasted for two months, which came to clearly confirm a lesson that God has wanted as a prelude of faith, impregnability and capability for the faithful, and a prelude of an [abyss], weakness and humiliation which God Almighty has wanted for the infidels, the criminals, the traitors, the corrupt and the deviators.

To be added to this time is the time of the military and nonmilitary duel, including the military and the economic blockade, which was imposed on Iraq and which lasted throughout 1990 until today, and until the time God Almighty wishes it to last.

Before that, the duel lasted, in other forms, for years before this period of time. It was an epic struggle between right and wrong; we have talked about this in detail on previous occasions.

It gave depth to the age of the showdown for the year 1990, and the already elapsed part of the year 1991.

Hence, we do not forget, because we will not forget this great struggling spirit, by which men of great faith stormed the fortifications and the weapons of deception and the Croesus [Kuwaiti rulers] treachery on the honorable day of the call. They did what they did within the context of legitimate deterrence and great principled action.

All that we have gone through or decided within its circumstances, obeying God's will and choosing a position of faith and chivalry, is a record of honor, the significance of which will not be missed by the people and nation and the values of Islam and humanity.

Their days will continue to be glorious and their past and future will continue to relate the story of a faithful, jealous and patient people, who believed in the will of God and in the values and stands accepted by the Almighty for the Arab nation in its leading role and for the Islamic nation in the essentials of its true faith and how they should be.

These values—which had their effect in all those situations, offered the sacrifices they had offered in the struggle, and symbolized the depth of the faithful character in Iraq—will continue to leave their effects on the souls. . . .

The harvest in the mother of battles has succeeded. After we have harvested what we have harvested, the greater harvest and its yield will be in the time to come, and it will be much greater than what we have at present, in spite of what we have at present in terms of the victory, dignity and glory that was based on the sacrifices of a deep faith which is generous without any hesitation or fear.

It is by virtue of this faith that God has bestowed dignity upon the Iraqi mujahedeen, and upon all the depth of this course of holy war at the level of the Arab homeland and at the level of all those men whom God has chosen to be given the honor of allegiance, guidance and honorable position, until He declares that the conflict has stopped, or amends its directions and course and the positions in a manner which would please the faithful and increase their dignity.

O valiant Iraqi men, O glorious Iraqi women. Kuwait is part of your country and was carved from it in the past.

Circumstances today have willed that it remain in the state in which it will remain after the withdrawal of our struggling forces from it. It hurts you that this should happen.

We rejoiced on the day of the call when it was decided that Kuwait should be one of the main gates for deterring the plot and for defending all Iraq from the plotters. We say that we will remember Kuwait on the great day of the call, on the days that followed it, and in documents and events, some of which date back 70 years.

The Iraqis will remember and will not forget that on 8 August, 1990, Kuwait became part of Iraq legally, constitutionally and actually. They remember and will not forget that it remained throughout this period from 8 August 1990 and until last night, when withdrawal began, and today we will complete withdrawal of our forces, God willing.

Today certain circumstances made the Iraqi Army withdraw as a result of the ramifications which we mentioned, including the combined aggression by 30 countries. Their repugnant siege has been led in evil and aggression by the machine and the criminal entity of America and its major allies.

. . . Everyone will remember that the gates of Constantinople were not opened before the Muslims in the first struggling attempt. . . . The confidence of the nationalists and the faithful mujahedeen and the Muslims has grown bigger than before, and great hope more and more.

Slogans have come out of their stores to strongly occupy the facades of the pan-Arab and human holy war and struggle. Therefore, victory is [great] now and in the future, God willing. . . .

O you valiant men; you have fought the armies of 30 states and the capabilities of an even greater number of states which supplied them with the means of aggression and support. Faith, belief, hope and determination continue to fill your chests, souls and hearts.

They have even become deeper, stronger, brighter and more deeply rooted. God is great; God is great; may the lowly be defeated.

Victory is sweet with the help of God.

KUWAIT LIBERATION

Kuwait is liberated. Iraq's army is defeated. Our military objectives are met. Kuwait is once more in the hands of Kuwaitis, in control of their own destiny. We share in their joy, a joy tempered only by our compassion for their ordeal.

Tonight the Kuwaiti flag once again flies above the capital of a free and sovereign nation. And the American flag flies above our Embassy.

Seven months ago, America and the world drew a line in the sand. We declared that the aggression against Kuwait would not stand. And tonight, America and the world have kept their word.

This is not a time of euphoria, certainly not a time to gloat. But it is a time of pride: pride in our troops; pride in the friends who stood with us in the crisis; pride in our nation and the people whose strength and resolve made victory quick, decisive, and just. And soon we will open wide our arms to welcome back home to America our magnificent fighting forces.

No one country can claim this victory as its own. It was not only a victory for Kuwait but a victory for all the coalition partners. This is a victory for the United Nations, for all mankind, for the rule of law, and for what is right.

After consulting with Secretary of Defense [Dick] Cheney, the Chairman of the Joint Chiefs of Staff, General [Colin] Powell, and our coalition partners, I am pleased to announce that at midnight tonight eastern standard time, exactly 100 hours since ground operations commenced and 6 weeks since the start of Desert Storm, all United States and coalition forces will suspend offensive combat operations. It is up to Iraq whether this suspension on the part of the coalition becomes a permanent cease-fire.

Coalition political and military terms for a formal cease-fire include the following requirements:

Iraq must release immediately all coalition prisoners of war, third country nationals, and the remains of all who have fallen. Iraq must release all Kuwaiti detainees. Iraq also must inform Kuwaiti authorities of the location and nature of all land and sea mines. Iraq must comply fully with all relevant United Nations Security Council resolutions. This includes a rescinding of Iraq's August decision to annex Kuwait, and acceptance in principle of Iraq's responsibility to pay compensation for the loss, damage, and injury its aggression has caused.

The coalition calls upon the Iraqi Government to designate military commanders to meet within 48 hours with their coalition counterparts at a place in the theater of operations to be specified, to arrange for military aspects of the cease-fire. Further, I have asked Secretary of State Baker to request that the United Nations Security Council meet to formulate the necessary arrangements for this war to be ended.

This suspension of offensive combat operations is contingent upon Iraq's not firing upon any coalition forces and not launching Scud missiles against any other country. If Iraq violates these terms, coalition forces will be free to resume military operations.

At every opportunity, I have said to the people of Iraq that our quarrel was not with them but instead with their leadership and, above all, with Saddam Hussein. This remains the case. You, the people of Iraq, are not our enemy. We do not seek your destruction. We have treated your POW's with kindness. Coalition forces fought this war only as a last resort and look forward to the day when Iraq is led by people prepared to live in peace with their neighbors.

We must now begin to look beyond victory and war. We must meet the challenge of securing the peace. In the future, as before, we will consult with our coalition partners. We've already done a good deal of thinking and planning for the postwar period, and Secretary [of State James P.] Baker has already begun to consult with our coalition partners on the region's challenges. There can be, and will be, no solely American answer to all these challenges. But we can assist and support the countries of the region and be a catalyst for peace. In this spirit, Secretary Baker will go to the region next week to begin a new round of consultations.

This war is now behind us. Ahead of us is the difficult task of securing a potentially historic peace. Tonight though, let us be proud of what we have accomplished. Let us give thanks to those who risked their lives. Let us never forget those who gave their lives. May God bless our valiant military forces and their families, and let us all remember them in our prayers.

Good night, and may God bless the United States of America.

SENATE ETHICS COMMITTEE ON THE "KEATING FIVE"

February 27, 1991

The Senate Ethics Committee rebuked five senators February 27 after a long inquiry into whether they improperly intervened with federal regulators to help political fundraiser Charles H. Keating, Jr., with his troubled savings and loan empire. The committee announced that all five "exercised poor judgment." But against only one of them, Sen. Alan Cranston, D-Calif., did the panel find "substantial creditable evidence" of misconduct. It concluded that Cranston engaged in "an impermissible pattern of conduct in which fundraising and official activities were substantially linked." The five senators, the so-called Keating Five, together accepted about $1.5 million in campaign contributions from Keating.

Among the other four (Sens. Dennis DeConcini, D-Ariz., Donald W. Riegle, D-Mich., John Glenn, D-Ohio, and John McCain, R-Ariz.), the ethics committee determined that DeConcini and Riegle gave "an appearance" of improper conduct. But like Glenn and McCain, they were admonished only for using poor judgment. All four declared themselves cleared of any wrongdoing.

Cranston portrayed himself as a scapegoat and contested the findings, delaying the committee's final report until November 20. In a compromise between Republican members who demanded formal censure and Democrats who opposed, the committee reprimanded him for "improper and repugnant" conduct. Chairman Howell Heflin, D-Ala., read to the Senate the committee resolution based on a 126-page submission of finding for the record. In a separate statement, Sen. Warren B. Rudman, the vice-chairman, gave a more detailed account of Cranston's conduct. Cranston expressed regret that some people thought he acted improperly,

*but he said he had not. "My behavior did not violate established norms,"
he told his colleagues. "Here, but for the grace of God, stand you."*

*Members looking for retribution were left unsatisfied because the
Ethics Committee had entered into an unprecedented plea bargain with
the ailing seventy-seven-year-old liberal stalwart. He had been undergoing treatment for prostate cancer. Senators were required to watch
Cranston be reprimanded as they sat silently at their desks on the floor,
but they were not to judge his behavior by voting, leaving his defiant
retort unchallenged by the full Senate.*

*Rudman grew visibly angry. When Cranston was done, he said in rage:
"After accepting this committee's recommendation, what I have heard in
a statement I can only describe as arrogant, unrepentant and a smear on
this insitiution. Everybody does not do it."*

*It was previously announced that Heflin would leave the committee
when the Cranston case was decided and be replaced by Sen. Richard D.
Bryan, D-Nev. Sen. Terry Sanford, D-N.C., was named the new chairman. Sen. Jesse Helms, R-N.C., would be replaced by Sen. Gordon Slade,
R-Wash.*

Keating's Role in S&L Scandal

*The Keating Five senators had been under the glare of publicity since
October 1989, when Common Cause, the public interest group, asked the
Justice Department and the Senate Ethics Committee to investigate
Keating's contributions of some $1 million to Cranston and a total of
nearly $500,000 to the other four senators between 1982 and 1987. During
that time Keating's financial affairs had come under the scrutiny of the
Securities and Exchange Commission and the Federal Home Loan Bank.*

*The government in April 1989 seized his Lincoln Savings and Loan
Association in California, and five months later it sued him and his
associates, charging fraud, racketeering, breach of fiduciary duties, and
other acts leading to losses of $1.1 billion. Later estimates ran to $2
billion. Lincoln's demise became symbolic of S&L bankruptcies and
scandals occurring across the nation. Those failures required massive
bailouts by the government to pay off federally insured depositors.*
(President Bush's Remarks on Signing S&L Bailout Bill, Historic Documents of 1989, p. 463)

*The Senate Ethics Committee in November 1989 hired a special
counsel, Robert S. Bennett, to investigate, and the next month it opened
a formal inquiry. His investigative report was followed by twenty-six days
of televised hearings and more than thirty-three hours of closed deliberations by the committee.*

Findings of Ethics Committee

*The committee concluded that the five senators had nothing to do with
Lincoln's collapse, and that each had ample information to justify
contacting regulators about the fairness of the treatment Keating was
receiving.*

The contributions the senators received from Keating were not inherently improper, the committee ruled. But because of the size and frequency of those to Cranston, and the proximity of the contributions to actions he took on Keating's behalf, the committee found "substantial evidence that . . . Sen. Cranston may have engaged in improper conduct which may reflect upon the Senate."

As for DeConcini and Riegle, the panel found an appearance of improper conduct but chose not to recommend further action against them because the Senate rules on such appearances of impropriety were unclear. With Glenn and McCain, even an appearance of impropriety was lacking, it said.

Reaction to the Rulings

The committee's findings were called a "sophisticated whitewash" by Fred Wertheimer, president of Common Cause. The New York Times *declared in a March 2 editorial, "This may satisfy the Senate. But the public, already angry at the costly excesses of politically powerful financiers, has been had. . . . The Keating Five is now the Keating Eleven: five senators who got caught and six committee members who let most of them go."*

From the outset of the inquiry, hope was expressed in Congress and the press that it would bring some definition—or at least some guidance—to an institution whose members seemed uncertain as to the bounds of propriety in serving their constituents and contributors. But the committee was hampered by fuzzy rules that its decision was expected to clarify. Instead, the committee recommended that the Senate create two bipartisan committees—one to set guidelines for determining how far senators can go in helping constituents, and the other to recommend campaign finance reforms.

Publicity from the case appeared to increase a sense of uneasiness that had been felt among members of Congress since the resignation of House Speaker Jim Wright in 1989 over a question of ethics. (Ethics Committee Reports, Wright's Resignation Speech, Historic Documents of 1989, p. 239) "There will be some chilling effect on constituent service, and that's not all bad," said Sen. William S. Cohen, R-Maine. Sen. Phil Gramm, R-Texas, said the case had "induced every member of Congress to go back and look at how they operate their offices."

> *Following is the text of the Senate Ethics Committee's conclusions, released February 27, 1991, after its investigation of whether five senators who had received campaign funds from entrepreneur Charles H. Keating, Jr., improperly tried to intervene with federal regulators on his behalf:*

Introduction

The United States Senate Select Committee on Ethics initiated Preliminary Inquiries into allegations of misconduct by Senator Alan Cranston

[D-Calif.], Senator Dennis DeConcini [D-Ariz.], Senator John Glenn [D-Ohio], Senator John McCain [R-Ariz.], and Senator Donald [W.] Riegle [Jr., D-Mich.], in connection with their actions on behalf of Charles H. Keating, Jr. and Lincoln Savings and Loan Association. In the course of its Preliminary Inquiries, the Committee held hearings over a two month period which began November 15, 1990. These hearings were conducted for the purpose of determining whether there is sufficient credible evidence of possible violations by any of the five Senators involved in the Preliminary Inquiries. Because this process was investigatory in nature, a wide net was cast and evidence was admitted with few limitations.

The Committee has met on more than a dozen occasions to consider the evidence produced at the hearings and the written arguments of Special Counsel and counsel for each of the Respondent Senators. The task of the Committee has been to sort through this exhaustive record to ascertain the relevant facts, and to identify any evidence of wrongdoing and any exculpatory evidence.

Findings and Recommendations

Having deliberated at length upon the issues presented, the Committee has weighed the relevant evidence and makes the following findings and recommendations:

Administrative Process

It is a necessary function of a Senator's office to intervene with officials of the executive branch and independent regulatory agencies on behalf of individuals when the facts warrant, and it is a Senator's duty to make decisions on whether to intervene without regard to whether they have contributed to the Senator's campaigns or causes. Ample evidence was received during the hearings showing that Senators should and do provide essential constituent services. In this case, each of the Senators under inquiry had information that reasonably caused concern about the fairness of the Federal Home Loan Bank's examination of Lincoln Savings and Loan Association (Lincoln), and which was sufficient to justify the Senator's contacting Bank Board personnel.

The degree of intervention with the regulators varied as to each Senator. The evidence clearly shows that their contacts with federal regulators regarding Lincoln did not cause the eventual failure of Lincoln or the thrift industry in general.

Prior to April 1987, four of the Senators (Cranston, DeConcini, Glenn, and McCain) had officially expressed opposition to or raised questions about the adoption of a "Direct Investment Rule," promulgated by the Federal Home Loan Bank Board (FHLBB). This Rule was opposed by many Members of Congress and a large number of thrift organizations. The Committee has concluded that, when considered without regard to any contribution or other benefit, the opposition expressed or the questions raised about the Direct Investment Rule did not violate any law or Senate rule.

There were two meetings between Federal Home Loan Bank personnel and groups of Senators. The first, on April 2, 1987, between Federal Home Loan Bank Board Chairman Edwin [J.] Gray and four Senators (Cranston, DeConcini, Glenn, and McCain), ended when Chairman Gray advised the Senators that he had no knowledge about the Lincoln examination being conducted by the San Francisco Federal Home Loan Bank (FHLB), and indicated that he would arrange a meeting with, and suggested that they could obtain the information they sought from, the San Francisco FHLB personnel. When considered without regard to any contribution or other benefit, no Senator violated any law or Senate rule by merely attending the meeting.

One week later, on April 9, 1987, there was a second meeting in Washington between four representatives of the San Francisco Federal Home Loan Bank and five Senators (DeConcini, Glenn, McCain, Riegle; and Cranston making a one-minute appearance). One of the FHLB personnel wrote an account of the meeting in reasonable detail, which was amplified by testimony. The Committee finds that, when considered without regard to any contributions or other benefit, no Senator, merely by virtue of his attendance at this meeting, violated any law or Senate rule. At this second meeting, the FHLB representatives advised the Senators that a "criminal referral" was going to be filed relative to the conduct of certain unnamed officials of Lincoln.

Following the two meetings, neither Senator McCain nor Senator Riegle took any action on behalf of Lincoln.

Ten months after the April meetings, Senator Glenn was host at a luncheon meeting he arranged for Mr. Charles Keating to meet House Speaker Jim Wright. There is disputed evidence as to whether Lincoln's problems with the FHLBB were discussed at this meeting. The weight of the evidence indicates that Senator Glenn's participation did not go beyond serving as host, and there is no evidence that Senator Glenn was asked to or did take any action on behalf of Lincoln.

Between February and mid-April 1989, Senator DeConcini made several telephone calls to FHLBB members and other regulatory officials urging prompt consideration of applications for the sale of Lincoln.

In 1987 following the April meetings, and in 1988, Senator Cranston set up a meting between FHLBB Chairman M. Danny Wall and Mr. Keating, and made several telephone inquiries to Chairman Wall on behalf of Lincoln. Additionally, in 1989, Senator Cranston made calls to FHLB Board members and other regulatory officials urging consideration of applications for the sale of Lincoln.

The Committee finds that, when considered without regard to any contribution or other benefit, none of the activities of Senator Cranston, Senator DeConcini, or Senator Glenn concerning Mr. Keating or Lincoln, following the April 1987 meetings, violated any law or Senate rule.

Official Actions and Campaign Contributions

While the Committee has concluded that none of the Senators' actions described above, when considered without regard to any contribution or other benefit, violated any law or Senate rule, each act must also be examined against more general ethical standards to determine if there was any impropriety because of any relation between those actions and campaign contributions or other benefits provided by Mr. Keating and his associates.

It is a fact of life that candidates for the Senate must solicit and receive assistance in their campaigns, including the raising of campaign funds. Such fundraising is authorized and regulated by law, and contributions and expenditures under the Federal Election Campaign Act are required to be publicly disclosed. Additionally, contributions under the Federal Election Campaign Act are not personal gifts to candidates.

Mr. Keating, his associates and his friends contributed $49,000 for Senator Cranston's 1984 Presidential Campaign and his 1986 Senatorial Campaign. Mr. Keating also gave corporate funds at the behest of Senator Cranston: $85,000 to the California Democratic Party 1986 get-out-the-vote campaign; $850,000 in 1987 and 1988 to several voter registration organizations with which Senator Cranston was affiliated; and $10,000 to a PAC [political action committee] affiliated with Senator Cranston in January 1989. Mr. Keating's Lincoln Savings and Loan also made a $300,000 line of credit available to Senator Cranston's campaign in the fall of 1986 on an expedited basis, although the loan was not used.

Mr. Keating, his associates and his friends contributed $31,000 to Senator DeConcini's 1982 Senatorial Campaign and $54,000 to his 1988 Senatorial Campaign.

Mr. Keating contributed a total of $200,000 in corporate funds to the non-federal account of Senator Glenn's multi-candidate PAC in 1985 and 1986. Mr. Keating, his associates, and his friends contributed $24,000 for Senator Glenn's Senatorial Campaign, and $18,200 for his Presidential Campaign. Senator Glenn received no contribution from or through Mr. Keating after February 1986.

Mr. Keating, his associates, and his friends contributed $56,000 for Senator McCain's two House races in 1982 and 1984, and $54,000 for his 1986 Senate race. Mr. Keating also provided his corporate plan and/or arranged for payment for the use of commercial or private aircraft on several occasions for travel by Senator McCain and his family, for which Senator McCain ultimately provided reimbursement when called upon to do so. Mr. Keating also extended personal hospitality to Senator McCain for vacations at a location in the Bahamas in each of the calendar years 1983 through 1986.

Mr. Keating organized and hosted a Riegle re-election campaign fundraising event in March 1987 in Detroit at his company's Pontchartrain Hotel. As a result of Mr. Keating's efforts, approximately $78,250 was raised from Keating associates and friends for Senator Riegle's 1988 campaign.

Based on all the available evidence, the Committee has concluded that in the case of each of the five Senators, all campaign contributions from

Mr. Keating and his associates under the Federal Election Campaign Act were within the established legal limits, and were properly reported. Similarly, from the available evidence the Committee concludes that the Senators' solicitation or acceptance of all contributions made in these cases to state party organizations, political action committees, and voter registration organizations were, standing alone, not illegal or improper; nor did any such contribution constitute a personal gift to any Senator.

With respect to each Senator, there remains the question of whether any actions taken by the Senator, standing alone or in combination with contributions or other benefits, constitutes improper conduct or an appearance of impropriety. The Committee has examined the specific conduct of each Senator and has determined that under the totality of the circumstances: The conduct of each of the five Senators reflected poor judgment; the conduct of some of the Senators constituted at least an appearance of improper conduct; and the conduct of one Senator may have been improper.

The Committee believes that every Senator must always endeavor to avoid the appearance that he, the Senate, or the governmental process may be influenced by campaign contributions or other benefits provided by those with significant legislative or governmental interests. Nonetheless, if an individual or organization which contributed to a Senator's campaigns or causes has a case which the Senator reasonably believes he is obliged to press because it is in the public interest or the cause of justice or equity to do so, then the Senator's obligation is to pursue that case. In such instances, the Senator must be mindful of the appearance that may be created and take special care to try to prevent harm to the public's trust in him and the Senate.

The Committee believes that appearances of impropriety are particularly likely to arise where a Senator takes action on behalf of a contributor. Such appearances are even more difficult to avoid when large sums are being raised from individuals or corporations for unregulated "soft money" accounts and for independent expenditures by third parties. Over 80 percent of the funds raised by Mr. Keating for or on behalf of the five Senators was "soft money."

A full report respecting the Committee's decisions will be issued at the earliest possible date. The Final Report will also contain at least two recommendations (summarized below) for further Senate action.

Specific Findings

The Committee finds that there is substantial credible evidence that provides substantial cause for the Committee to conclude that Senator Cranston may have engaged in improper conduct reflecting upon the Senate and, therefore, has voted to proceed to an Investigation (see attached). The Investigation will proceed as expeditiously as possible.

The Committee's conclusions in the cases concerning the other four Senators are also set forth in attachments.

Recommendations to the Senate

Section 2(a)(3) of Senate Resolution 338 (88th Congress) places a duty upon the Committee to recommend additional rules or regulations to the Senate, where the Committee has determined that such rules or regulations are necessary or desirable to ensure proper standards of conduct by Members, officers, and employees in the performance of their official duties.

In fulfilling its duty under this section, the Committee will make the following recommendations to the Senate in its Final Report on the Preliminary Inquiries.

Recommendation for a Bipartisan Task Force on Constituent Service

As noted in the course of the Committee's hearings, the Senate has no specific written standards embodied in the Senate rules respecting contact or intervention with federal executive or independent regulatory agency officials. While unknown to many Senators, there are general guidelines. These are best expressed in House Advisory Opinion No. 1 and the writings of Senator Paul Douglas.

The Committee believes that the Senate should adopt written standards in this area. A specific proposal should be developed either by the Senate Rules Committee or by a bipartisan Senate Task Force created for this purpose. The Rules Committee or Task Force will, of course, need to address the special ethical problems which may arise when such contact or intervention is sought by individuals who have contributed to the Senator's campaigns or causes.

Such standards could be similar to House Advisory Opinion No. 1 or could be more specific. Until such time as such Committee or Task Force has finished its work and the Senate has adopted specific standards respecting contact or intervention with executive or independent regulatory agencies, all Senators are encouraged to use House Advisory Opinion No. 1 as a source of guidance for their actions.

The Committee hopes that the adoption of specific standards governing contact or intervention by Senators with executive or independent regulatory agencies will minimize the potential for appearances of impropriety. Members of the Committee are especially mindful that the success of any democratic government, designed to execute the will of a free people, is ultimately dependent on the public's confidence in the integrity of the governmental process and those who govern.

Recommendation for Bipartisan Campaign Reform

The inquiries in these five cases have shown the obvious ethical dilemmas inherent in the current system by which political activities are financed. The Committee notes that over 80 percent of the funds at issue were not disclosed funds raised by candidates for Senate or House campaigns under the Federal Election Campaign Act. Rather, such funds were undisclosed, unregulated funds raised for independent expenditures, political party "soft money," and a non-federal political action committee. Any campaign finance reform measure will have to address these mechanisms for political activities, as well as campaign fund raising and expenditures directly by candidates, in order to deal meaningfully and effectively with the issues presented in these cases.

The Committee urges the leadership and Members of both the Senate and the House to work together in a bipartisan manner to address the urgent need for comprehensive campaign finance reform. The reputation and honor of our institutions demand it.

Resolution for Investigation

Whereas, the Select Committee on Ethics on December 21, 1989, initiated a Preliminary Inquiry into allegations of misconduct by Senator Alan Cranston, and notified Senator Cranston of such action; and

Whereas, the Committee retained Special Counsel Robert S. Bennett to assist the Committee in conducting the Preliminary Inquiry into the allegations, and received and considered a report related thereto; and

Whereas, in the course of its Preliminary Inquiry the Committee held hearings from November 15, 1990, through January 16, 1991, and heard evidence relating to the allegations; and

Whereas, the Committee received and considered post-hearing memoranda from Special Counsel and counsel for Respondent Senators;

It is therefore RESOLVED:

(a) That the Committee finds that there is substantial credible evidence that provides substantial cause for the Committee to conclude that, in connection with his conduct relating to Charles H. Keating, Jr. and Lincoln Savings and Loan Association, Senator Cranston may have engaged in improper conduct that may reflect upon the Senate, as contemplated in Section 2(a)(1) of S. Res. 338, 88th Congress, as amended. To wit, there is substantial credible evidence that provides substantial cause for the Committee to conclude, based upon the totality of the circumstances, including but not limited to the following conduct or activities, that Senator Cranston engaged in an impermissible pattern of conduct in which fundraising and official activities were substantially linked:

(1) From April 1987 through April 1989, Senator Cranston personally, or through Senate staff, contacted the Federal Home Loan Bank Board on behalf of Lincoln, during a period when Senator Cranston was soliciting and accepting substantial contributions from Mr. Keating. On at least four occasions, these contacts were made in close connection with the solicitation or receipt of contributions. These four occasions are as follows:

(i) As a result of a solicitation from Senator Cranston in early 1987, Mr. Keating, on March 3, 1987, contributed $100,000 to America Votes, a voter registration organization. This contribution was made during the period leading to Senator Cranston's participation in the April 2 and April 9 meetings with Federal Home Loan Bank Board Chairman Edwin J. Gray and the San Francisco regulators.

(ii) In the fall of 1987, Senator Cranston solicited from Mr. Keating a $250,000 contribution, which was delivered to the Senator personally by Mr. Keating's employee James J. Grogan on November 6, 1987. When the contribution was delivered, Mr. Grogan and Senator Cranston called Mr. Keating, who asked if the Senator would contact new Federal Home Loan Bank Board Chairman M. Danny Wall about Lincoln. Senator Cranston agreed to do so, and made the call six days later.

(iii) In January 1988, Mr. Keating offered to make an additional contribution and also asked Senator Cranston to set up a meeting for him with Chairman Wall. Senator Cranston did so on January 20, 1988, and Chairman Wall and Mr. Keating met eight days later. On February 10, 1988, Senator Cranston personally collected checks totaling $500,000 for voter registration groups.

(iv) In early 1989, at the time that Senator Cranston was contacting Bank Board officials about the sale of Lincoln, he personally or through Joy Jacobson, his chief fundraiser, solicited another contribution. (This contribution was never made. American Continental Corporation declared bankruptcy on April 13, 1989.)

(2) Senator Cranston's Senate office practices further evidenced an impermissible pattern of conduct in which fundraising and official activities were substantially linked. For example, Joy Jacobson (who was not a member of his Senate staff and who had no official Senate duties or substantive expertise) engaged in the following activities with Senator Cranston's knowledge, permission, at his direction, or under his supervision:

(i) Senator Cranston's fundraiser repeatedly scheduled and attended meetings between Senator Cranston and contributors in which legislative or regulatory issues were discussed.

(ii) Senator Cranston's fundraiser often served as the intermediary for Mr. Keating or Mr. Grogan when they could not reach the Senator or Carolyn Jordan, the Senator's banking aide.

(iii) Senator Cranston received several memoranda from Ms. Jacobson which evidenced her understanding that contributors were entitled to special attention and special access to official services. Senator Cranston never told her that her understanding was incorrect, nor did he inform her that such a connection between contributions and official actions was improper.

(b) That the Committee, pursuant to Committee Supplementary Procedural Rules 3(d)(5) and 4(f)(4), shall proceed to an Investigation under Committee Supplementary Procedural Rule 5; and

(c) That Senator Cranston shall be given timely written notice of this resolution and the evidence supporting it, and informed of a respondent's rights pursuant to the Rules of the Committee.

Decision of the Committee Concerning Senator McCain

Based on the evidence available to it, the Committee has given consideration to Senator McCain's actions on behalf of Lincoln Savings & Loan

Association. The Committee concludes that Senator McCain exercised poor judgment in intervening with the regulators. The Committee concludes that Senator McCain's actions were not improper nor attended with gross negligence and did not reach the level of requiring institutional action against him. The Committee finds that Senator McCain took no further action after the April 9, 1987, meeting when he learned of the criminal referral.

The Committee reaffirms its prior decision that it does not have jurisdiction to determine the issues of disclosure or reimbursement pertaining to flights provided by American Continental Corporation while Senator McCain was a Member of the House of Representatives. The Committee did consider the effect of such on his state of mind and judgment in taking steps to assist Lincoln Savings & Loan Association.

Senator McCain has violated no law of the United States or specific Rule of the United States Senate; therefore, the Committee concludes that no further action is warranted with respect to Senator McCain on the matters investigated during the preliminary inquiry.

Decision of the Committee Concerning Senator Glenn

Based on the evidence to it, the Committee has given consideration to Senator Glenn's actions on behalf of Lincoln Savings & Loan Association. The Committee concludes that Senator Glenn, although believing that the Lincoln matter was in the process of resolution, exercised poor judgment in arranging a luncheon meeting between Mr. Keating and Speaker Wright in January, 1988, some eight months after Senator Glenn learned of the criminal referral. There is disputed evidence as to whether Lincoln's problems with the Federal Home Loan Bank Board (FHLBB) were discussed at that meeting. The evidence indicates that Senator Glenn's participation did not go beyond serving as host. The Committee further concludes that Senator Glenn's actions were not improper or attended with gross negligence and did not reach the level requiring institutional action against him.

Senator Glenn has violated no law of the United States or specific Rule of the United States Senate; therefore, the Committee concludes that no further action is warranted with respect to Senator Glenn on the matters investigated during the preliminary inquiry.

Decision of the Committee Concerning Senator Riegle

Based on evidence available to it, the Committee has given consideration to Senator Riegle's actions on behalf of Lincoln Savings & Loan Association. The Committee finds that Senator Riegle took steps to assist Lincoln Savings & Loan Association with its regulatory problems at a time that Charles Keating was raising substantial campaign funds for Senator Riegle. During the course of the hearings, possible conflicts arose concerning actions on the part of Senator Riegle that caused the Committee concern, but the Committee finds that the evidence indicates no deliberate intent to deceive. The evidence shows that Senator Riegle took no further action after the April 9, 1987, meeting where he learned of the criminal referral.

While the Committee concludes that Senator Riegle has violated no law of the United States or specific Rule of the United States Senate, it emphasizes that it does not condone his conduct. The Committee has concluded that the totality of the evidence shows that Senator Riegle's conduct gave the appearance of being improper and was certainly attended with insensitivity and poor judgment. However, the Committee finds that his conduct did not reach a level requiring institutional action.

The Committee concludes that no further action is warranted with respect to Senator Riegle on the matters investigated during the preliminary inquiry.

Decision of the Committee Concerning Senator DeConcini

Based on the evidence available to it, the Committee has given consideration to Senator DeConcini's actions on behalf of Lincoln Savings & Loan Association. While aggressive conduct by Senators in dealing with regulatory agencies is sometimes appropriate and necessary, the Committee concludes that Senator DeConcini's aggressive conduct with the regulators was inappropriate. The Committee further concludes that the actions of Senator DeConcini after the April 9, 1987, meeting where he learned of the criminal referral, were not improper in and of themselves.

While the Committee concludes that Senator DeConcini has violated no law of the United States or specific Rule of the United States Senate, it emphasizes that it does not condone his conduct. The Committee has concluded that the totality of the evidence shows that Senator DeConcini's conduct gave the appearance of being improper and was certainly attended with insensitivity and poor judgment. However, the Committee finds that his conduct did not reach a level requiring institutional action.

The Committee therefore concludes that no further action is warranted with respect to Senator DeConcini on the matters investigated during the preliminary inquiry.

March

BUSH ON WAR VICTORY AND
MIDEAST PEACE PLANS
March 6, 1991

"As President, I can report to the nation: Aggression is defeated. The war is over." Those words of President George Bush, delivered to a special joint session of Congress and a national broadcast audience March 6, set off fervent cheering among the assembled, flag-waving lawmakers. They seemed to care little that Iraq's defeat and Kuwait's liberation was not news. America was still savoring the swift victory by U.S.-led allied forces in the Persian Gulf War. (Victory in the Gulf, p. 97)

As the architect of that victory, Bush was invited to the Capitol to receive the plaudits of Congress. The legislators had consented to American combat in the Persian Gulf after an agonizing debate in which a majority of Democrats and a few Republicans in each house urged delaying military action in favor of trying to strangle Iraq with an existing United Nations economic boycott. (Congress on War with Iraq, p. 3)

Some Republicans, attempting to portray the war as a Republican triumph, were now asking, "Who won Iraq?" The question carried echoes from the 1950s when their party's attempt to blame Democrats for the communist takeover in China was summed up in the question "Who lost China?" With Republicans threatening to make an issue of the war vote in the 1992 elections, Democrats in Congress had recently been at pains to explain to their colleagues and constituents that they, too, fully supported the president in the war once the debate was concluded.

Bush's speaking invitation was issued by the Democratic leadership of the House and Senate. Democrats appeared to cheer his speech as heartily as Republicans. House Speaker Thomas S. Foley, D-Wash., for instance, *noted that it was customary to introduce Bush to Congress "directly and without further comment." But, he added, "I wish to depart from tradition tonight and express to you on behalf of the Congress and the country, and through you to members of our Armed Forces, our warmest congratulations on the brilliant victory of the Desert Storm Operation."*

The president, buoyed by a historically high public approval rating of 89 percent (as measured by the Gallup Poll), left the partisan attacks to others and focused on trying to translate his popularity into congressional support for a domestic and foreign affairs agenda.

Middle East Peace Plan

Beyond affirming victory, the president acknowledged that the Middle East would be his primary area of interest. He placed a large portion of his political capital on the line in search of a resolution to the region's oldest dispute, the Arab-Israeli conflict. He essentially reasserted what Secretary of State James A. Baker III had called the "pillars of peace" in two days of congressional testimony in February. This "framework," in Bush's words, rested on meeting four "challenges." They were, in addition to achieving an Arab-Israeli settlement, creating new security arrangements to assure stability in the region, stopping the spread of weapons of mass destruction in the Middle East, and promoting economic growth there.

"By now, it should be plain to all parties that peacemaking in the Middle East requires compromise," Bush said, echoing sentiments expressed by former president Jimmy Carter in 1978. That year Carter persuaded Egypt and Israel to sign the Camp David accords, enabling them to settle outstanding grievances and establish diplomatic relations. But no other diplomatic breakthroughs between Israel and Arab states followed in the intervening thirteen years. (Camp David Accords, Historic Documents of 1978, p. 605)

Bush said a "comprehensive peace" must be grounded in the "principle of territory for peace"—permitting Palestinians in Israeli-occupied territories some measure of self-rule in return for Arab guarantees of Israel's sovereignty. Baker, beginning the first of several successive peace missions to the Middle East during the year, made his first visit to Israel on March 11 and briefed officials there of what he called "new thinking" from Arab nations on peace with Israel.

The previous day, foreign ministers of Egypt, Syria, Saudi Arabia, and the Persian Gulf states of Kuwait, Qatar, Oman, Bahrain, and the United Arab Emirates met in Riyadh, the Saudi capital, and generally endorsed the concept of an international peace conference on the Middle East under United Nations auspices. But the agreement masked wide differences among Arab states, and Israel appeared very reluctant to enter any negotiations that might result in international pressure to give up territories it had occupied since the 1967 Arab-Israeli War. But a Middle East peace conference was convened in Madrid on October 30, leading to direct negotiations between Israel and its Arab neighbors. (Madrid Conference on Mideast Peace, p. 719)

War's Aftermath

Other events in the Middle East seemed to mock the celebrations of a military victory. For weeks after the war's end, violence continued in Iraq and Kuwait. Liberated Kuwaitis retaliated against many foreigners whom they suspected of collaborating with Iraq during its occupation of their country. In Iraq, Saddam Hussein's surviving troops bloodily ended a Kurdish rebellion in the north and a Shiite Moslem rebellion in the south after the fighting stopped between allied and Iraqi forces. (UN Peace Terms; Iraq's Acceptance, p. 191)

Despite defeat and humiliation, Hussein remained in control of the Iraqi government and what was left of his army, provoking questions as to whether Bush should have agreed to a cease-fire before his foe was removed from power. Bush expressed condolences for all of the "victims of war," including the Iraqi people who, he said, "have never been our enemy." He expressed hope that "one day we will once again welcome them as friends into the community of nations."

Following is President George Bush's address to a joint session of Congress, March 6, 1991, declaring victory in the Persian Gulf and outlining his goal for a postwar political settlement in the Middle East:

... Members of Congress, 5 short weeks ago I came to this House to speak to you about the state of the Union. We met then in time of war. Tonight, we meet in a world blessed by the promise of peace.

From the moment Operation Desert Storm commenced on January 16th until the time the guns fell silent at midnight 1 week ago, this nation has watched its sons and daughters with pride—watched over them with prayer. As Commander in Chief, I can report to you our armed forces fought with honor and valor. And as President, I can report to the Nation aggression is defeated. The war is over.

This is a victory for every country in the coalition, for the United Nations. A victory for unprecedented international cooperation and diplomacy, so well led by our Secretary of State, James Baker. It is a victory for the rule of law and for what is right.

Desert Storm's success belongs to the team that so ably leads our Armed Forces: our Secretary of Defense and our Chairman of the Joint Chiefs, Dick Cheney and Colin Powell. And while you're standing—[*laughter*]— this military victory also belongs to the one the British call the "Man of the Match"—the tower of calm at the eye of Desert Storm—General Norman Schwarzkopf.

And recognizing this was a coalition effort, let us not forget Saudi General Khalid, Britain's General de la Billiere, or General Roquejoffre of France—and all the others whose leadership played such a vital role. And most importantly, most importantly of all, all those who served in the field.

I thank the Members of this Congress—support here for our troops in battle was overwhelming. And above all, I thank those whose unfailing love and support sustained our courageous men and women—I thank the American people.

Tonight, I come to this House to speak about the world—the world after war. The recent challenge could not have been clearer. Saddam Hussein was the villain; Kuwait, the victim. To the aid of this small country came nations from North America and Europe, from Asia and South America, from Africa and the Arab world—all united against aggression. Our uncommon coalition must now work in common purpose: to forge a future that should never again be held hostage to the darker side of human nature.

Tonight in Iraq, Saddam walks amidst ruin. His war machine is crushed. His ability to threaten mass destruction is itself destroyed. His people have been lied to—denied the truth. And when his defeated legions come home, all Iraqis will see and feel the havoc he has wrought. And this I promise you: For all that Saddam has done to his own people, to the Kuwaitis, and to the entire world, Saddam and those around him are accountable.

All of us grieve for the victims of war, for the people of Kuwait and the suffering that scars the soul of that proud nation. We grieve for all our fallen soldiers and their families, for all the innocents caught up in this conflict. And, yes, we grieve for the people of Iraq—a people who have never been our enemy. My hope is that one day we will once again welcome them as friends into the community of nations. Our commitment to peace in the Middle East does not end with the liberation of Kuwait. So tonight, let me outline four key challenges to be met.

First, we must work together to create shared security arrangements in the region. Our friends and allies in the Middle East recognize that they will bear the bulk of the responsibility for regional security. But we want them to know that just as we stood with them to repel aggression, so now America stands ready to work with them to secure the peace. This does not mean stationing U.S. ground forces in the Arabian Peninsula, but it does mean American participation in joint exercises involving both air and ground forces. It means maintaining a capable U.S. naval presence in the region—just as we have for over 40 years. Let it be clear: Our vital national interests depend on a stable and secure Gulf.

Second, we must act to control the proliferation of weapons of mass destruction and the missiles used to deliver them. It would be tragic if the nations of the Middle East and Persian Gulf were now, in the wake of war, to embark on a new arms race. Iraq requires special vigilance. Until Iraq convinces the world of its peaceful intentions—that its leaders will not use new revenues to rearm and rebuild its menacing war machine—Iraq must not have access to the instruments of war.

And third, we must work to create new opportunities for peace and stability in the Middle East. On the night I announced Operation Desert Storm, I expressed my hope that out of the horrors of war might come new momentum for peace. We've learned in the modern age geography cannot guarantee security and security does not come from military power alone.

All of us know the depth of bitterness that has made the dispute between Israel and its neighbors so painful and intractable. Yet, in the conflict just concluded, Israel and many of the Arab States have for the first time found themselves confronting the same aggressor. By now, it should be plain to all parties that peacemaking in the Middle East requires compromise. At the same time, peace brings real benefits to everyone. We must do all that we can to close the gap between Israel and the Arab states—and between Israelis and Palestinians. The tactics of terror lead absolutely nowhere. There can be no substitute for diplomacy.

A comprehensive peace must be grounded in United Nations Security Council Resolutions 242 and 338 and the principle of territory for peace. This principle must be elaborated to provide for Israel's security and recognition and at the same time for legitimate Palestinian political rights. Anything else would fail the twin test of fairness and security. The time has come to put an end to Arab-Israeli conflict.

The war with Iraq is over. The quest for solutions to the problems in Lebanon, in the Arab-Israeli dispute, and in the Gulf must go forward with new vigor and determination. And I guarantee you: No one will work harder for a stable peace in the region than we will.

Fourth, we must foster economic development for the sake of peace and progress. The Persian Gulf and Middle East form a region rich in natural resources—with a wealth of untapped human potential. Resources once squandered on military might must be redirected to more peaceful ends. We are already addressing the immediate economic consequences of Iraq's aggression. Now, the challenge is to reach higher—to foster economic freedom and prosperity for all the people of the region.

By meeting these four challenges we can build a framework for peace. I've asked Secretary of State Baker to go to the Middle East to begin the process. He will go to listen, to probe, to offer suggestions—to advance the search for peace and stability. I've also asked him to raise the plight of the hostages held in Lebanon. We have not forgotten them, and we will not forget them.

To all the challenges that confront this region of the world there is no single solution—no solely American answer. But we can make a difference. America will work tirelessly as a catalyst for positive change.

But we cannot lead a new world abroad if, at home, it's politics as usual on American defense and diplomacy. It's time to turn away from the temptation to protect unneeded weapons systems and obsolete bases. It's time to put an end to micromanagement of foreign and security assistance programs—micromanagement that humiliates our friends and allies and hamstrings our diplomacy. It's time to rise above the parochial and the pork barrel, to do what is necessary, what's right, and what will enable this nation to play the leadership role required of us.

The consequences of the conflict in the Gulf reach far beyond the confines of the Middle East. Twice before in this century, an entire world was convulsed by war. Twice this century, out of the horrors of war hope emerged for enduring peace. Twice before, those hopes proved to be a distant dream, beyond the grasp of man. Until now, the world we've known has been a world divided—a world of barbed wire and concrete block, conflict, and cold war.

Now, we can see a new world coming into view. A world in which there is the very real prospect of a new world order. In the words of Winston Churchill, a world order in which "the principles of justice and fair play protect the weak against the strong...." A world where the United Nations—freed from cold war stalemate—is poised to fulfill the historic vision of its founders. A world in which freedom and respect for human rights find a home among all nations. The Gulf war put this new world to its first test. And my fellow Americans, we passed that test.

For the sake of our principles—for the sake of the Kuwaiti people—we stood our ground. Because the world would not look the other way, Ambassador al-Sabah, tonight, Kuwait is free. And we're very happy about that.

Tonight, as our troops begin to come home, let us recognize that the hard work of freedom still calls us forward. We've learned the hard lessons of history. The victory over Iraq was not waged as "a war to end all wars." Even the new world order cannot guarantee an era of perpetual peace. But enduring peace must be our mission. Our success in the Gulf will shape not only the world order we seek, but our mission here at home.

In the war just ended, there were clear-cut objectives—timetables—and, above all, an overriding imperative to achieve results. We must bring that same sense of self-discipline, that same sense of urgency, to the way we meet challenges here at home. In my State of the Union Address and in my budget, I defined a comprehensive agenda to prepare for the next American century.

Our first priority is to get this economy rolling again. The fear and uncertainty caused by the Gulf crisis were understandable. But now that the war is over, oil prices are down, interest rates are down, and confidence is rightly coming back. Americans can move forward to lend, spend, and invest in this, the strongest economy on Earth.

We must also enact the legislation that is key to building a better America. For example, in 1990, we enacted an historic Clean Air Act. And now we've proposed a national energy strategy. We passed a child care bill that put power in the hands of parents. And today, we're ready to do the same thing with our schools and expand choice in education. We passed a crime bill that made a useful start in fighting crime and drugs. This year, we're sending to Congress our comprehensive crime package to finish the job. We passed the landmark Americans with Disabilities Act. And now we've sent forward our civil rights bill. We also passed the aviation bill. This year, we've sent up our new highway bill. And these are just a few of our pending proposals for reform and renewal.

So, tonight I call on Congress to move forward aggressively on our domestic front. Let's begin with two initiatives we should be able to agree on quickly—transportation and crime. And then, let's build on success with those and enact the rest of our agenda. If our forces could win the ground war in 100 hours, then surely the Congress can pass this legislation in 100 days. Let that be a promise we make tonight to the American people.

When I spoke in this House about the state of our Union, I asked all of you: If we can selflessly confront evil for the sake of good in a land so far away, then surely we can make this land all that it should be. In the time since then, the brave men and women of Desert Storm accomplished more than even they may realize. They set out to confront an enemy abroad, and in the process, they transformed a nation at home. Think of the way they went about their mission—with confidence and quiet pride. Think about their sense of duty, about all they taught us about our values, about ourselves.

We hear so often about our young people in turmoil—how our children fall short, how our schools fail us, how American products and American workers are second-class. Well, don't you believe it. The America we saw in Desert Storm was first-class talent. And they did it using America's state-of-the-art technology. We saw the excellence embodied in the Patriot missile and the patriots who made it work. And we saw soldiers who know about honor and bravery and duty and country and the world-shaking power of these simple words. There is something noble and majestic about the pride, about the patriotism that we feel tonight.

So, to everyone here—and everyone watching at home—think about the men and women of Desert Storm. Let us honor them with our gratitude. Let us comfort the families of the fallen and remember each precious life lost.

Let us learn from them as well. Let us honor those who have served us by serving others. Let us honor them as individuals—men and women of every race, all creeds and colors—by setting the face of this nation against discrimination, bigotry, and hate. Eliminate them.

I'm sure that many of you saw on the television the unforgettable scene of four terrified Iraqi soldiers surrendering. They emerged from their bunkers—broken, tears streaming from their eyes, fearing the worst. And then there was an American soldier. Remember what he said? He said: "It's okay. You're all right now. You're all right now." That scene says a lot about America, a lot about who we are. Americans are a caring people. We are a good people, a generous people. Let us always be caring and good and generous in all we do.

Soon, very soon, our troops will begin the march we've all been waiting for—their march home. And I have directed Secretary Cheney to begin the immediate return of American combat units from the Gulf. Less than 2 hours from now, the first planeload of American soldiers will lift off from Saudi Arabia, headed for the U.S.A. It will carry men and women of the 24th Mechanized Infantry Division bound for Fort Stewart, Georgia. This is just the beginning of a steady flow of American troops coming home. Let their return remind us that all those who have gone before are linked with us in the long line of freedom's march.

Americans have always tried to serve, to sacrifice nobly for what we believe to be right. Tonight, I ask every community in this country to make this coming Fourth of July a day of special celebration for our returning troops. They may have missed Thanksgiving and Christmas, but I can tell you this: For them and for their families, we can make this a holiday they'll never forget.

In a very real sense, this victory belongs to them—to the privates and the pilots, to the sergeants and the supply officers, to the men and women in the machines, and the men and women who made them work. It belongs to the regulars, to the reserves, to the National Guard. This victory belongs to the finest fighting force this nation has ever known in its history.

We went halfway around the world to do what is moral and just and right. We fought hard and, with others, we won the war. We lifted the yoke of aggression and tyranny from a small country that many Americans had never even heard of, and we shall ask nothing in return.

We're coming home now—proud, confident, heads high. There is much that we must do, at home and abroad. And we will do it. We are Americans.

May God bless this great nation, the United States of America. Thank you all very, very much.

KNIGHT REPORT ON REFORMING COLLEGE ATHLETICS

March 19, 1991

The Knight Foundation Commission on Intercollegiate Athletics issued a report March 19 calling on university presidents to take charge of varsity sports programs and cleanse them of pervasive abuses. If they do not act, the report warned, Congress will likely do so. The report cited a poll conducted by Louis Harris Associates in February that showed that 70 percent of the college trustees who were questioned, and three-fourths of the people generally, said they thought college athletics were out of control.

"We sense that public concern about abuse is growing," said the commission's cochairmen, former presidents Theodore M. Hesburgh of Notre Dame University and William C. Friday of the North Carolina university system, in a letter accompanying the report. "The public appears ready to believe that many institutions achieve their athletic goals not through honest effort but through equivocation, not by hard work and sacrifice but by hook or crook."

Their letter was to Lee Hills, board vice chairman of the Knight Foundation, which commissioned the report in October 1989. The foundation's president was Creed C. Black, publisher of the Lexington, Kentucky, Herald Leader, *a newspaper that had recently won a Pulitzer Prize for disclosing violations in athletic recruiting by the University of Kentucky.*

Several of twenty-two commission members had prominent backgrounds in education, sports, business, and politics. They included Lamar Alexander, president of the University of Tennessee and former governor of the state, who subsequently became President George Bush's secretary of education. Another member was Rep. Tom McMillen, D-Md., who had been a basketball star at the University of Maryland and played in the National Basketball Association.

Extent of the Study

The commission conducted what some commentators called the most extensive look at intercollegiate athletics since 1929. That year, as the Knight report states, the Carnegie Fund for the Advancement of Teaching "identified many of the difficulties still with us today," including the commercialization and professionalization of supposedly amateur sports, the recruitment of academically deficient athletes, and the separation of athletic budgets from other university finances. As cited in the report, big-time athletic programs were more beholden to booster clubs and outside financial interests, especially television networks, than to the students. Revenue-producing sports, especially football and basketball, were emphasized at the expense of "minor" and women's sports.

The report said: "The problems described to the commission—in more than a year of meetings and discussions with athletic directors, faculty representatives, coaches, athletes, [athletic] conference leaders, television officials and accrediting associations—are widespread.... [T]hey are most apparent within major athletic programs and are concentrated most strongly in those sports for which collegiate participation serves the talented few as an apprenticeship for professional careers."

In quest of academic and financial integrity, the commission said its "bedrock conviction is that university presidents are the key to successful reform. They must be in charge—and be understood to be in charge—on campuses, in conferences and in the decision-making councils of the NCAA [National Collegiate Athletic Association]." The association is the supervisory body for twenty-one varsity sports in which men and women compete at 828 colleges and universities.

The commission recommended that every NCAA institution undergo independent audits to verify that athletic departments follow institutional goals, that fiscal controls are sound, and that "athletes in each sport resemble the rest of the student body in admissions, academic progress and graduation rates."

Reaction to the Report

McMillen expressed doubt that college sports can be reformed "internally" because "there's so much money now." His comments came at a news conference in Washington at which the report was released. Asked if he was suggesting federal involvement, he recalled that President Theodore Roosevelt's threat of action against college football caused it to write new, safer rules and to create the NCAA as a policing agent.

Murray Sperber, author of the book College Sports, Inc., *said the commission offered mere "symbolic reform." He contended that "the system isn't working" and "needs radical reform." In contrast, a number of sports writers on metropolitan daily newspapers praised the report.*

Thomas Boswell of the Washington Post *called it "a grouchy, high-toned blue-ribbon jeremiad, tending toward the utopian. But it also has excellent practical suggestions, strewn in among the fine type, that might make for hard times for the bad guys."*

Following are excerpts from the Report of the Knight Foundation's Commission on Intercollegiate Athletics, "Keeping Faith with the Student-Athlete: A New Model for Intercollegiate Athletics," released March 19, 1991:

... The value and successes of college sport should not be overlooked. They are the foundation of our optimism for the future. At the 828 colleges and universities which comprise the National Collegiate Athletic Association (NCAA), over 254,000 young men and women participate in 21 different sports each year in about one quarter of a million contests. At the huge majority of these institutions, virtually all of these young athletes participate in these contests without any evidence of scandal or academic abuse. This record is one in which student-athletes and university administrators can take pride and from which the Knight Foundation Commission takes heart.

All of the positive contributions that sports make to higher education, however, are threatened by disturbing patterns of abuse, particularly in some big-time programs. These patterns are grounded in institutional indifference, presidential neglect, and the growing commercialization of sport combined with the urge to win at all costs. The sad truth is that on too many campuses big-time revenue sports are out of control.

The assumption of office by a new executive director of the NCAA coincides with renewed vigor for major reform on the part of athletics administrators and university presidents. Reform efforts are well underway. One conference has voted to bar from athletics participation all students who do not meet NCAA freshman-eligibility standards. One state has decided to require all students in publicly supported institutions to maintain a "C" average in order to participate in extracurricular activities, including intercollegiate sports. Judging by the tone of recent NCAA conventions, concern for the university's good name and the welfare of the student-athlete—irrespective of gender, race or sport—will be the centerpiece of athletics administration as we approach a new century. We do not want to interfere with that agenda. We hope to advance it.

The Problem

The problems described to the Commission—in more than a year of meetings and discussions with athletics directors, faculty representatives, coaches, athletes, conference leaders, television officials and accrediting associations—are widespread. They are not entirely confined to big schools ... or to football or basketball ... or to men's sports. But they are most apparent within major athletics programs and are concentrated most strongly in those sports for which collegiate participation serves the talented few as an apprenticeship for professional careers.

Recruiting, the bane of the college coach's life, is one area particularly susceptible to abuse. While most institutions and coaches recruit ethically and within the rules, some clearly do not. Recruiting abuses are the most frequent cause of punitive action by the NCAA. Even the most scrupulous coaching staffs are trapped on a recruiting treadmill, running through an interminable sequence of letters, telephone calls and visits. The cost of recruiting a handful of basketball players each year exceeds, on some campuses, the cost of recruiting the rest of the freshman class.

Athletics programs are given special, often unique, status within the university; the best coaches receive an income many times that of most full professors; some coaches succumb to the pressure to win with recruiting violations and even the abuse of players; boosters respond to athletic performance with gifts and under-the-table payments; faculty members, presidents and other administrators, unable to control the enterprise, stand by as it undermines the institution's goals in the name of values alien to the best the university represents.

These programs appear to promise a quick route to revenue, recognition and renown for the university. But along that road, big-time athletics programs often take on a life of their own. Their intrinsic educational value, easily lost in their use to promote extra-institutional goals, becomes engulfed by the revenue stream they generate and overwhelmed by the accompanying publicity. Now, instead of the institution alone having a stake in a given team or sport, the circle of involvement includes the television networks and local stations that sell advertising time, the corporations and local businesses buying the time, the boosters living vicariously through the team's success, the local economies critically dependent on the big game, and the burgeoning population of fans who live and die with the team's fortunes.

In this crucible, the program shifts from providing an exciting avenue of expression and enjoyment for the athletes and their fans to maximizing the revenue and institutional prestige that can be generated by a handful of highly-visible teams. The athletics director can become the CEO [chief executive officer] of a fair-sized corporation with a significant impact on the local economy. The "power coach," often enjoying greater recognition throughout the state than most elected officials, becomes chief operating officer of a multi-million dollar business.

Within the last decade, big-time athletics programs have taken on all of the trappings of a major entertainment enterprise. In the search for television revenues, traditional rivalries have been tossed aside in conference realignments, games have been rescheduled to satisfy broadcast preferences, the number of games has multiplied, student-athletes have been put on the field at all hours of the day and night, and university administrators have fallen to quarrelling among themselves over the division of revenues from national broadcasting contracts.

But the promise of easy access to renown and revenue often represents fool's gold. Recognition on the athletic field counts for little in the academic community. Expenses are driven by the search for revenues and the revenue stream is consumed, at most institutions, in building up the program to maintain the revenue. Renown for athletic exploits can be a two-edged sword if the university is forced to endure the public humiliation of sanctions brought on by rules violations. Above all, the fragile institution of the university often finds itself unable to stand up against the commitment, the energy and the passion underlying modern intercollegiate athletics.

In the circumstances we have described, it is small wonder that three out of four Americans believe that television dollars, not administrators, control college sports. But the underlying problems existed long before the advent of television. A 1929 report from the Carnegie Fund for the Advancement of Teaching identified many of the difficulties still with us today. In college athletics, it said, recruiting had become corrupt, professionals had replaced amateurs, education was being neglected, and commercialism reigned. That document still rings true today, reminding us that it is an oversimplification to blame today's problems on television alone. Even so, the lure of television dollars has unquestionably added a new dimension to the problems and must be addressed.

At the root of the problem is a great reversal of ends and means. Increasingly, the team, the game, the season and "the program"—all intended as expressions of the university's larger purposes—gain ascendancy over the ends that created and nurtured them. Non-revenue sports receive little attention and women's programs take a back seat. As the educational context for collegiate athletics competition is pushed aside, what remains is, too often, a self-justifying enterprise whose connection with learning is tainted by commercialism and incipient cynicism.

In the short term, the human price for this lack of direction is exacted from the athletes whose talents give meaning to the system. But the ultimate cost is paid by the university and by society itself. If the university is not itself a model of ethical behavior, why should we expect such behavior from students or from the larger society?

Pervasive though these problems are, they are not universal. This is true even if the universe is restricted to the roughly 300 institutions playing football or basketball at the highest levels. But they are sufficiently common that it is no longer possible to conclude they represent the workings of a handful of misguided individuals or a few "rotten apples." One recent analysis indicates that fully one-half of all Division I-A institutions (the 106 colleges and universities with the most competitive and expensive football programs) were the object of sanctions of varying severity from the NCAA during the 1980s. Other institutions, unsanctioned, graduate very few student-athletes in revenue-producing sports.

The problems are so deep-rooted and long-standing that they must be understood to be systemic. They can no longer be swept under the rug or kept under control by tinkering around the edges. Because these problems are so widespread, nothing short of a new structure holds much promise for restoring intercollegiate athletics to their proper place in the university.

This report of the Knight Foundation Commission is designed to suggest such a structure.

We are at a critical juncture with respect to the intercollegiate athletics system. We believe college sports face three possible futures:

- higher education will put its athletics house in order from within;
- athletics order will be imposed from without and college sports will be regulated by government; or
- abuse—unchecked—will spread, destroying not only the intrinsic value of intercollegiate athletics but higher education's claim to the high moral ground it should occupy.

Concern for the health of both intercollegiate athletics and American higher education makes the choice clear.

Focus on Students

Even clearer, in the Commission's view, is the need to start with the student-athlete. The reforms we deem essential start with respect for the dignity of the young men and women who compete and the conviction that they occupy a legitimate place as students on our campuses. If we can get that right, everything else will fall into place. If we cannot, the rest of it will be all wrong.

Regulations governing the recruitment of student-athletes—including letters-of-intent, and how and under what conditions coaches may contact athletes—take up 30 pages of the *NCAA Manual*. But there is no requirement that the prospective student-athlete be found academically admissible before accepting a paid campus visit. A prospective player can very easily agree to attend an institution even though the admissions office does not know of the student's existence. Similarly, student-athletes deemed eligible in the fall can compete throughout the year, generally regardless of their academic performance in the first term.

It is hard to avoid the conclusion that there are few academic constraints on the student-athlete. Non-academic prohibitions, on the other hand, are remarkable. Athletics personnel are not permitted to offer rides to student-athletes. University officials are not permitted to invite a student-athlete home for dinner on the spur of the moment. Alumni are not allowed to encourage an athlete to attend their alma mater....

...Some rules have been developed to manage potential abuse in particular sports, at particular schools, or in response to the particular circumstances of individual athletes. Whatever the origin of these regulations, the administration of intercollegiate athletics is now so overburdened with legalism and detail that the *NCAA Manual* more nearly resembles the IRS Code than it does a guide to action....

A New Model: "One-Plus-Three"

Individual institutions and the NCAA have consistently dealt with problems in athletics by defining most issues as immediate ones: curbing particular abuses, developing nationally uniform standards, or creating a "level playing field" overseen by athletics administrators.

But the real problem is not one of curbing particular abuses. It is a more central need to have academic administrators define the terms under which athletics will be conducted in the university's name. The basic concern is not nationally uniform standards. It is a more fundamental issue of grounding the regulatory process in the primacy of academic values. The root difficulty is not creating a "level playing field." It is insuring that those on the field are students as well as athletes.

We reject the argument that the only realistic solution to the problem is to drop the student-athlete concept, put athletes on the payroll, and reduce or even eliminate their responsibilities as students.

Such a scheme has nothing to do with education, the purpose for which colleges and universities exist. Scholarship athletes are already paid in the most meaningful way possible: with a free education. The idea of intercollegiate athletics is that the teams represent their institutions as true members of the student body, not as hired hands. Surely American higher education has the ability to devise a better solution to the problems of intercollegiate athletics than making professionals out of the players, which is no solution at all but rather an unacceptable surrender to despair.

It is clear to the Commission that a realistic solution will not be found without a serious and persistent commitment to a fundamental concept: intercollegiate athletics must reflect the values of the university. Where the realities of intercollegiate competition challenge those values, the university must prevail.

The reform we seek takes shape around what the Commission calls the "one-plus-three" model. It consists of the "one"—presidential control—directed toward the "three"—academic integrity, financial integrity and accountability through certification. . . .

The "One"—Presidential Control

. . . The following recommendations are designed to advance presidential control:

1. **Trustees should explicitly endorse and reaffirm presidential authority in all matters of athletics governance.** The basis of presidential authority on campus is the governing board. If presidential action is to be effective, it must have the backing of the board of trustees. We recommend that governing boards:

   - Delegate to the president administrative authority over financial matters in the athletics program.
   - Work with the president to develop common principles for hiring, evaluating and terminating all athletics administrators, and affirm the president's role and ultimate authority in this central aspect of university administration.
   - Advise each new president of its expectations about athletics administration and annually review the athletics program.

- Work with the president to define the faculty's role, which should be focused on academic issues in athletics.

2. **Presidents should act on their obligation to control conferences.** We believe that presidents of institutions affiliated with athletics conferences should exercise effective voting control of these organizations. Even if day-to-day representation at conference proceedings is delegated to other institutional representatives, presidents should formally retain the authority to define agendas, offer motions, cast votes or provide voting instructions, and review and, if necessary, reshape conference decisions.

3. **Presidents should control the NCAA.** The Knight Commission believes hands-on presidential involvement in NCAA decision-making is imperative. As demonstrated by the overwhelming approval of their reform legislation at the 1991 NCAA convention, presidents have the power to set the course of the NCAA—if they will use it. The Commission recommends that:

   - Presidents make informed use of the ultimate NCAA authority— their votes on the NCAA convention floor. They should either attend and vote personally, or familiarize themselves with the issues and give their representatives specific voting instructions. Recent procedural changes requiring that pending legislation be published for review several months before formal consideration simplify this task enormously.
   - The Presidents Commission follow up its recent success with additional reform measures, beginning with the legislation on academic requirements it proposes to sponsor in 1992. The Commission can and should consolidate its leadership role by energetic use of its authority to draft legislation, to determine whether balloting will be by roll call or paddle, and to order the convention agenda.
   - Presidents stay the course. Opponents of progress have vowed they will be back to reverse recent reform legislation. Presidents must challenge these defenders of the status quo. They cannot win the battle for reform if they fight in fits and starts—their commitment to restoring perspective to intercollegiate athletics must be complete and continuing.

4. **Presidents should commit their institutions to equity in all aspects of intercollegiate athletics.** The Commission emphasizes that continued inattention to the requirements of Title IX (mandating equitable treatment of women in educational programs) represents a major stain on institutional integrity. It is essential that presidents take the lead in this area. We recommend that presidents:

   - Annually review participation opportunities in intercollegiate programs by gender.

- Develop procedures to insure more opportunities for women's participation and promote equity for women's teams in terms of schedules, facilities, travel arrangements and coaching.

5. Presidents should control their institution's involvement with commercial television. The lure of television dollars has clearly exacerbated the problems of intercollegiate athletics. Just as surely, institutions have not found the will or the inclination to define the terms of their involvement with the entertainment industry. Clearly, something must be done to mitigate the growing public perception that the quest for television dollars is turning college sports into an entertainment enterprise. In the Commission's view it is crucial that presidents, working through appropriate conference and NCAA channels, immediately and critically review contractual relationships with networks. It is time that institutions clearly prescribe the policies, terms and conditions of the televising of intercollegiate athletics events. Greater care must be given to the needs and obligations of the student-athlete and the primacy of the academic calendar over the scheduling requirements of the networks.

The "Three": Academic Integrity

The first consideration on a university campus must be academic integrity. The fundamental premise must be that athletes are students as well. They should not be considered for enrollment at a college or university unless they give reasonable promise of being successful at that institution in a course of study leading to an academic degree. Student-athletes should undertake the same courses of study offered to other students and graduate in the same proportion as those who spend comparable time as full-time students. Their academic performance should be measured by the same criteria applied to other students.

Admissions. At some Division I institutions, according to NCAA data, every football and basketball player admitted in the 1988-89 academic year met the university's regular admissions policy. At others, according to the same data, not a single football or basketball player met the regular requirements. At half of all Division I-A institutions, about 20 percent or more of football and basketball players are "special admits," i.e. admitted with special consideration. That rate is about 10 times as high as the rate for the total student body.

The Commission believes that the freshman eligibility rule known as Proposition 48 has improved the academic preparation of student-athletes. Proposition 48 has also had some unanticipated consequences. Virtually unnoticed in the public discussion about Proposition 48 is the requirement that the high school grade point average be computed for only 11 units of academic work. Out of 106 Division I-A institutions, 97 of them (91 percent) require or recommend more than 11 high school academic units for the typical high school applicant. In fact, 73 Division I-A institutions, according to their published admissions criteria, require or recommend 15 or more academic high school units from all other applicants.

Academic Progress. The most recent NCAA data indicate that in one-half of all Division I institutions about 90 percent of all football and basketball players are meeting "satisfactory" progress requirements and are, therefore, eligible for intercollegiate competition. Under current regulations, however, it is possible for a student-athlete to remain eligible each year but still be far from a degree after five years as a full-time student. The 1991 NCAA convention began to address this issue in enacting provisions requiring that at the end of the third year of enrollment, student-athletes should have completed 50 percent of their degree requirements.

The 1991 convention also made significant headway in reducing the excessive time demands athletic participation places on student-athletes. Throughout the 1980s, according to recent NCAA research, football and basketball players at Division I-A institutions spent approximately 30 hours a week on their sports in season, more time than they spent attending or preparing for class. Football and basketball are far from the only sinners. Baseball, golf and tennis players report the most time spent on sports. Many other sports for both men and women, including swimming and gymnastics, demand year-round conditioning if athletes are to compete successfully. . . .

Graduation Rates. At some Division I institutions, 100 percent of the basketball players or the football players graduate within five years of enrolling. At others, none of the basketball or football players graduate within five years. In the typical Division I college or university, only 33 percent of basketball players and 37.5 percent of football players graduate within five years. Overall graduation rates for all student-athletes (men and women) in Division I approach graduation rates for all students in Division I according to the NCAA—47 percent of all student-athletes in Division I graduate in five years.

Dreadful anecdotal evidence about academic progress and graduation rates is readily available. But the anecdotes merely illustrate what the NCAA data confirm: About two-thirds of the student-athletes in big-time, revenue-producing sports have not received a college degree within five years of enrolling at their institution.

The Commission's recommendations on academic integrity can be encapsulated in a very simple concept—"No Pass, No Play." That concept, first developed for high school athletics eligibility in Texas, is even more apt for institutions of higher education. It applies to admissions, to academic progress and to graduation rates.

The following recommendations are designed to advance academic integrity:

1. **The NCAA should strengthen initial eligibility requirements.** Proposition 48 has served intercollegiate athletics well. It has helped insure that more student-athletes are prepared for the rigors of undergraduate study. It is time to build on and extend its success. We recommend that:

   - By 1995 prospective student-athletes should present 15 units of high school academic work in order to be eligible to play in their first year.
   - A high school student-athlete should be *ineligible* for reimbursed campus visits or for signing a letter of intent until the admissions office indicates he or she shows reasonable promise of being able to meet the requirements for a degree.
   - Student-athletes transferring from junior colleges should meet the admissions requirements applied to other junior college students. Moreover, junior college transfers who did not meet NCAA Proposition 48 requirements when they graduated from high school should be required to sit out a year of competition after transfer.
   - Finally, we propose an NCAA study of the conditions under which colleges and universities admit athletes. This study should be designed to see if it is feasible to put in place admissions requirements to insure that the range of academic ability for incoming athletes, by sport, would approximate the range of abilities for the institution's freshman class.

2. **The letter of intent should serve the student as well as the athletics department.** Incoming freshmen who have signed a letter of intent to attend a particular institution should be released from that obligation if the head coach who recruited them leaves the institution, or if the institution is put on probation by the NCAA, before they enroll. Such incoming student-athletes should be automatically eligible to apply to any other college or university, except the head or assistant coach's new home, and to participate in intercollegiate athletics. Currently, student-athletes are locked into the institution no matter how its athletics program changes—a restriction that applies to no other student.

3. **Athletics scholarships should be offered for a five-year period.** In light of the time demands of athletics competition, we believe that eligibility should continue to be limited to a period of four years, but athletics scholarship assistance routinely should cover the time required to complete a degree, up to a maximum of five years. . . .

4. **Athletics eligibility should depend on progress toward a degree.** In order to retain eligibility, enrolled athletes should be able to graduate within five years and to demonstrate progress toward that goal each semester. At any time during the student-athlete's

undergraduate years, the university should be able to demonstrate that the athlete can meet this test without unreasonable course loads. Further, eligibility for participation should be restricted to students who meet the institution's published academic requirements, including a minimum grade point average when applicable.

5. **Graduation rates of athletes should be a criterion for NCAA certification.** The Commission believes that no university should countenance lower graduation rates for its student-athletes, in any sport, than it is willing to accept in the full-time student body at large. Fundamental to the restoration of public trust is our belief that graduation rates in revenue-producing sports should be a major criterion on which NCAA certification depends.

The "Three": Financial Integrity

An institution of higher education has an abiding obligation to be a responsible steward of all the resources that support its activities—whether in the form of taxpayers' dollars, the hard-earned payments of students and their parents, the contributions of alumni, or the revenue stream generated by athletics programs. In this respect, the responsibility of presidents and trustees is singular.

Costs. A 1990 College Football Association study indicated that in the prior four years, the cost of operating an athletics department increased 35 percent while revenues increased only 21 percent. For the first time in its surveys, said the CFA, average expenses exceeded average income. Overall, 39 of 53 institutions responding—including some of the largest and presumably the most successful sports programs—are either operating deficits or would be without institutional or state support. More comprehensive data from the NCAA confirm that, on average, the athletics programs of Division I-A institutions barely break even. When athletics expenses are subtracted from revenues, the average Division I-A institution is left with $39,000.

The Larger Economic Environment. Big-time sports programs are economic magnets. They attract entertainment and business interests of a wide variety. They support entire industries dedicated to their needs and contests. But while college sports provide a demonstrably effective and attractive public showcase for the university, potential pitfalls abound because of the money involved....

The Commission recommends that:

1. **Athletics costs must be reduced.** The Commission applauds the cost control measures—including reductions in coaching staff sizes, recruiting activities and the number of athletics scholarships—approved at the 1991 NCAA convention. It is essential that presidents monitor these measures to insure that, in the name of "fine tuning," these provisions are not watered down before they become

fully effective in 1994. . . .

2. **Athletics grants-in-aid should cover the full cost of attendance for the very needy.** Despite the Commission's commitment to cost reduction, we believe existing grants-in-aid (tuition, fees, books, and room and board) fail to adequately address the needs of some student-athletes. Assuming the ten percent reduction in scholarship numbers approved at the 1991 NCAA convention is put in place, we recommend that grants-in-aid for low-income athletes be expanded to the "full cost of attendance," including personal and miscellaneous expenses, as determined by federal guidelines.

3. **The independence of athletics foundations and booster clubs must be curbed.** Some booster clubs have contributed generously to overall athletics revenues. But too many of these organizations seem to have been created either in response to state laws prohibiting the expenditure of public funds on athletics or to avoid institutional oversight of athletics expenditures. Such autonomous authority can severely compromise the university. . . . All funds raised for athletics should be channeled into the university's financial system and subjected to the same budgeting procedures applied to similarly structured departments and programs.

4. **The NCAA formula for sharing television revenue from the national basketball championship must be reviewed by university presidents.** The new revenue-sharing plan for distributing television and championship dollars has many promising features—funds for academic counseling, catastrophic injury insurance for all athletes in all divisions, a fund for needy student-athletes, and financial support for teams in all divisions, including increased transportation and per diem expenses. Nonetheless, the testimony before this Commission made it clear that a perception persists that the plan still places too high a financial premium on winning and that the rich will continue to get richer. The Commission recommends that the plan be reviewed annually by the Presidents Commission during the seven-year life of the current television contract and adjusted as warranted by experience.

5. **All athletics-related coaches' income should be reviewed and approved by the university.** The Commission believes that in considering non-coaching income for its coaches, universities should follow a well-established practice with all faculty members: If the outside income involves the university's functions, facilities or name, contracts for particular services should be negotiated with the university. As part of the effort to bring athletics-related income into the university, we recommended that the NCAA ban shoe and equipment contracts with individual coaches. If a company is eager to have an institution's athletes using its product, it should approach the institution not the coach.

6. **Coaches should be offered long-term contracts.** Academic tenure is not appropriate for most coaches, unless they are *bona fide*

members of the faculty. But greater security in an insecure field is clearly reasonable. The Commission suggests that within the first five years of contractual employment, head and assistant coaches who meet the university's expectations, including its academic expectations, should be offered renewable, long-term contracts. . . .

7. **Institutional support should be available for intercollegiate athletics.** The Commission starts from the premise that properly administered intercollegiate athletics programs have legitimate standing in the university community. In that light, general funds can appropriately be used when needed to reduce the pressure on revenue sports to support the entire athletics program. There is an inherent contradiction in insisting on the one hand that athletics are an important part of the university while arguing, on the other, that spending institutional funds for them is somehow improper.

The "Three": Certification

. . . The academic and financial integrity of college athletics is in such low repute that authentication by an outside agency is essential. . . . [T]he commission therefore recommends:

1. **The NCAA should extend the certification process to all institutions granting athletics aid.** The NCAA is now in the midst of a pilot effort to develop a certification program which will, when in place, certify the integrity of athletics programs. We recommend that this pilot certification process be extended on a mandatory basis to all institutions granting athletics aid. . . .

2. **Universities should undertake comprehensive, annual policy audits of their athletics program.** We urge extending the annual financial audit now required by the NCAA to incorporate academic issues and athletics governance. The new annual review should examine student-athletes' admissions records, academic progress and graduation rates, as well as the athletics department's management and budget. . . .

SUPREME COURT ON FETAL PROTECTION
March 20, 1991

The Supreme Court ruled March 20 that an employer cannot exclude women from jobs that might harm an unborn child. The Court said the woman who holds or seeks such a job—not the employer—must decide whether to accept the health risk.

At issue was the "fetal protection" job policy of Johnson Controls, a Milwaukee-based maker of batteries. Since 1982 the company permitted women to hold jobs that exposed them to lead, a battery ingredient, only if they could prove they were infertile. Medical studies had shown that lead in the bloodstream of pregnant women caused birth defects.

The decision in Automobile Workers v. Johnson Controls *was a victory for a coalition of women's and labor organizations. They contended that fetal protection policies in industry were often used as an excuse to deny women good jobs or to infringe on their right to privacy. A congressional staff study conducted in 1990 estimated that as many as 20 million jobs in the United States exposed workers to reproductive or fetal health hazards.*

Although industry officials tended to view the figure as a gross overestimation, the Court's ruling would nevertheless require changes in the work rules of many companies, including several of the nation's biggest. Among them, according to the American Civil Liberties Union's Women's Rights Project, were American Cyanamid, Olin, General Motors, Gulf Oil, B. F. Goodrich, Dow Chemical, DuPont, Union Carbide, and Monsanto.

More than that, in the view of the victors in the case, Automobile Workers v. Johnson Controls *was one of the most important sex discrimi-*

nation cases to be decided by the Supreme Court in years. In its first examination of fetal protection policies, the Court in effect told American employers that they could almost never cite gender as a reason from keeping a woman from holding a specific job.

All nine justices agreed that the policy at Johnson Controls violated the Pregnancy Discrimination Act of 1978, an amendment to the 1964 Civil Rights Act, in which Congress prohibited discrimination in the workplace on the basis of pregnancy or potential pregnancy. But the Court was divided over whether such policies could ever be justified under the law. Four justices suggested the possibility in other situations. Their thoughts were expressed in two separate opinions—one written by Justice Byron R. White, in which Justice Anthony M. Kennedy and Chief Justice William H. Rehnquist joined, and the other by Justice Antonin Scalia. Both opinions, while setting out divergent views, technically concurred with the majority opinion written by Justice Harry A. Blackmun, and which Justices Thurgood Marshall, John Paul Stevens, Sandra Day O'Connor, and David H. Souter joined.

The majority held, without reservation, that federal law did not permit an employer to take fetal welfare into account in awarding a job or promotion. "Congress has left this choice to the woman as hers to make," Blackmun wrote. He said that Congress had set a high level of job protection for women that could not be overridden by either health concerns for the fetus or the possibility of future lawsuits against the employer for injury to a fetus. While saying that more than forty states recognize an individual's right to sue for prenatal injury based on negligence, Blackmun discounted the likelihood of a rash of lawsuits.

Concern Over Employer's Liability

"Such speculation will be small comfort to employers," White retorted in his separate opinion. He said "it is far from clear" that federal law will preempt state laws on the matter of prenatal injuries, "and the Court offers no support for that proposition." White further said that although health warnings issued by employers "may preclude claims by injured employees, [his emphasis], they will not preclude claims by injured children because the general rule is that parents cannot waive causes of action on behalf of their children, and the parents' negligence will not be imputed to the children."

Business groups had argued that the decision increased the liability of employers for workers whose babies are born with birth defects. Johnson Controls said it imposed its job-restriction policy after the lead content in the blood of eight pregnant female workers was detected at a level considered critical by the federal Occupational Health and Safety Administration.

Several workers at Johnson Controls, including a fifty-year-old divorcee and a woman who had been sterilized to avoid losing her job, filed a class-action suit in federal district court in Milwaukee charging that the company's policy violated federal law. The court certified as class-action plantiffs members of United Auto Workers bargaining units at nine Johnson Controls plants who had been affected by the policy. However, the court dismissed the case. The dismissal was upheld by a 7-4 majority on the U.S. Federal Court of Appeals for the Seventh Circuit, in Chicago.

Question of Correct Defense Test

The Supreme Court said the appellate court erred in upholding the dismissal and sent the case back to the federal district court for reconsideration. From the beginning the case provoked the question of what legal defense Johnson Controls could use. The appellate court said the company's policy was justified on either of two legal principles and permitted it to use a "business necessity" defense that generally favors the employer in rebutting statistical evidence that a policy, perhaps unintentionally, has a discriminatory effect.

The other defense, a "bona fide occupational qualification" (BFOQ) test, is usually more difficult for an employer to meet. All nine justices agreed that Johnson Controls had to meet the BFOQ test. Blackmun defined the test as permitting an employer to set "job-related skills and aptitudes" for the employment, and nothing more. White interpreted it more broadly, to take into account not only the employee's ability but possibility of injury to "third parties," including fetuses. Scalia argued that the majority erred in saying that costs alone cannot support a BFOQ defense. "I think, for example," Scalia wrote, "that a shipping company may refuse to hire pregnant women as crew members on long voyages because the on-board facilities for foreseeable emergencies . . . would be inordinately expensive." But he noted that Johnson Controls did not assert a cost defense.

Following are excerpts from the Supreme Court's majority and concurring opinions in International Union, United Automobile, Aerospace & Agricultural Implement Workers of America, et al., v. Johnson Controls Inc., *March 20, 1991, declaring that a company cannot bar a female worker from a job because of the potential harm to her unborn child:*

<u>No. 89-1215</u>

International Union, United Automobile, Aerospace and Agricultural Implement Workers of America, UAW, et al., Petitioners *v.* Johnson Controls, Inc.	On writ of certiorari to the United States Court of Appeals for the Seventh Circuit

[March 20, 1991]

JUSTICE BLACKMUN delivered the opinion of the Court.

In this case we are concerned with an employer's gender-based fetal-protection policy. May an employer exclude a fertile female employee from certain jobs because of its concern for the health of the fetus the woman might conceive?

I

Respondent Johnson Controls, Inc., manufactures batteries. In the manufacturing process, the element lead is a primary ingredient. Occupational exposure to lead entails health risks, including the risk of harm to any fetus carried by a female employee.

Before the Civil Rights Act of 1964 became law, Johnson Controls did not employ any woman in a battery-manufacturing job. In June 1977, however, it announced its first official policy concerning its employment of women in lead-exposure work:

> "[P]rotection of the health of the unborn child is the immediate and direct responsibility of the prospective parents. While the medical profession and the company can support them in the exercise of this responsibility, it cannot assume it for them without simultaneously infringing their rights as persons.

> ". . . . Since not all women who can become mothers wish to become mothers (or will become mothers), it would appear to be illegal discrimination to treat all who are capable of pregnancy as though they will become pregnant."

Consistent with that view, Johnson Controls "stopped short of excluding women capable of bearing children from lead exposure" but emphasized that a woman who expected to have a child should not choose a job in which she would have such exposure. The company also required a woman who wished to be considered for employment to sign a statement that she had been advised of the risk of having a child while she was exposed to lead. The statement informed the woman that although there was evidence "that women exposed to lead have a higher rate of abortion," this evidence was "not as clear . . . as the relationship between cigarette smoking and cancer," but that it was, "medically speaking, just good sense not to run that risk if you want children and do not want to expose the unborn child to risk, however small. . . ."

Five years later, in 1982, Johnson Controls shifted from a policy of warning to a policy of exclusion. Between 1979 and 1983, eight employees became pregnant while maintaining blood lead levels in excess of 30 micrograms per deciliter. This appeared to be the critical level noted by the Occupational Health and Safety Administration (OSHA) for a worker who was planning to have a family. The company responded by announcing a broad exclusion of women from jobs that exposed them to lead:

> ". . . [I]t is [Johnson Controls'] policy that women who are pregnant or who are capable of bearing children will not be placed into jobs involving lead exposure or which could expose them to lead through the exercise of job bidding, bumping, transfer or promotion rights."

The policy defined "women ... capable of bearing children" as "[a]ll women except those who inability to bear children is medically documented." It further stated that an unacceptable work station was one where, "over the past year," an employee had recorded a blood lead level of more than 30 micrograms per deciliter or the work site had yielded an air sample containing a lead level in excess of 30 micrograms per cubic meter.

II

In April 1984, petitioners filed in the United States District Court for the Eastern District of Wisconsin a class action challenging Johnson Controls' fetal-protection policy as sex discrimination that violated Title VII of the Civil Rights Act of 1964, as amended. Among the individual plaintiffs were petitioners Mary Craig, who had chosen to be sterilized in order to avoid losing her job, Elsie Nason, a 50-year-old divorcee, who had suffered a loss in compensation when she was transferred out of a job where she was exposed to lead, and Donald Penney, who had been denied a request for a leave of absence for the purpose of lowering his lead level because he intended to become a father. Upon stipulation of the parties, the District Court certified a class consisting of "all past, present and future production and maintenance employees" in United Auto Workers bargaining units at nine of Johnson Controls' plants "who have been and continue to be affected by [the employer's] Fetal Protection Policy implemented in 1982."

The District Court granted summary judgment for defendant-respondent Johnson Controls. Applying a three-part business necessity defense derived from fetal-protection cases in the Courts of Appeals for the Fourth and Eleventh Circuits, the District Court concluded that while "there is a disagreement among the experts regarding the effect of lead on the fetus," the hazard to the fetus through exposure to lead was established by "a considerable body of opinion"; that although "[e]xpert opinion has been provided which holds that lead also affects the reproductive abilities of men and women ... [and] that these effects are as great as the effects of exposure of the fetus ... a great body of experts are of the opinion that the fetus is more vulnerable to levels of lead that would not affect adults"; and that petitioners had "failed to establish that there is an acceptable alternative policy which would protect the fetus." The court stated that, in view of this disposition of the business necessity defense, it did not "have to undertake a bona fide occupational qualification's (BFOQ) analysis."

The Court of Appeals for the Seventh Circuit, sitting en banc, affirmed the summary judgment by a 7-to-4 vote. The majority held that the proper standard for evaluating the fetal-protection policy was the defense of business necessity; that Johnson Controls was entitled to summary judgment under that defense; and that even if the proper standard was a BFOQ, Johnson Controls still was entitled to a summary judgment.

The Court of Appeals first reviewed fetal-protection opinions from the Eleventh and Fourth Circuits. Those opinions established the three-step business necessity inquiry: whether there is a substantial health risk to the fetus; whether transmission of the hazard to the fetus occurs only through women; and whether there is a less discriminatory alternative equally capable of preventing the health hazard to the fetus. . . .

Applying this business necessity defense, the Court of Appeals ruled that Johnson Controls should prevail. Specifically, the court concluded that there was no genuine issue of material fact about the substantial health-risk factor because the parties agreed that there was a substantial risk to a fetus from lead exposure. The Court of Appeals also concluded that, unlike the evidence of risk to the fetus from the mother's exposure, the evidence of risk from the father's exposure, which petitioners presented, "is, at best, speculative and unconvincing." Finally, the court found that petitioners had waived the issue of less discriminatory alternatives by not adequately presenting it. . . .

Having concluded that the business necessity defense was the appropriate framework and that Johnson Controls satisfied that standard, the court proceeded to discuss the BFOQ defense and concluded that Johnson Controls met that test, too. The en banc majority ruled that industrial safety is part of the essence of respondent's business, and that the fetal-protection policy is reasonably necessary to further that concern. . . .

With its ruling, the Seventh Circuit became the first Court of Appeals to hold that a fetal-protection policy directed exclusively at women could qualify as a BFOQ. We granted certiorari to resolve the obvious conflict between the Fourth, Seventh, and Eleventh Circuits on this issue, and to address the important and difficult question whether an employer, seeking to protect potential fetuses, may discriminate against women just because of their ability to become pregnant.

III

The bias in Johnson Controls' policy is obvious. Fertile men, but not fertile women, are given a choice as to whether they wish to risk their reproductive health for a particular job. Section 703(a) of the Civil Rights Act of 1964 prohibits sex-based classifications in terms and conditions of employment, in hiring and discharging decisions, and in other employment decisions that adversely affect an employee's status. Respondent's fetal-protection policy explicitly discriminates against women on the basis of their sex. The policy excludes women with childbearing capacity from lead-exposed jobs and so creates a facial classification based on gender. . . .

Nevertheless, the Court of Appeals assumed, as did the two appellate courts who already had confronted the issue, that sex-specific fetal-protection policies do not involve facial discrimination. These courts analyzed the policies as though they were facially neutral, and had only a discriminatory effect upon the employment opportunities of women. Consequently, the courts looked to see if each employer in question had established that its policy was justified as a business necessity. The business necessity standard is more lenient for the employer than the statutory BFOQ defense. The Court of Appeals here went one step further and invoked the burden-shifting framework set forth in *Wards Cove*

Packing Co. v. *Atonio* (1989), thus requiring petitioners to bear the burden of persuasion on all questions. The court assumed that because the asserted reason for the sex-based exclusion (protecting women's unconceived offspring) was ostensibly benign, the policy was not sex-based discrimination. That assumption, however, was incorrect.

First, Johnson Controls' policy classifies on the basis of gender and childbearing capacity, rather than fertility alone. Respondent does not seek to protect the unconceived children of all its employees. Despite evidence in the record about the debilitating effect of lead exposure on the male reproductive system, Johnson Controls is concerned only with the harms that may befall the unborn offspring of its female employees. . . . Johnson Controls' policy is facially discriminatory because it requires only a female employee to produce proof that she is not capable of reproducing.

Our conclusion is bolstered by the Pregnancy Discrimination Act of 1978 (PDA), in which Congress explicitly provided that, for purposes of Title VII, discrimination "on the basis of sex" includes discrimination "because of or on the basis of pregnancy, childbirth, or related medical conditions." "The Pregnancy Discrimination Act has now made clear that, for all Title VII purposes, discrimination based on a woman's pregnancy is, on its face, discrimination because of her sex." *Newport News Shipbuilding & Dry Dock Co.* v. *EEOC* (1983). . . .

. . . [T]he absence of a malevolent motive does not convert a facially discriminatory policy into a neutral policy with a discriminatory effect. Whether an employment practice involves disparate treatment through explicit facial discrimination does not depend on why the employer discriminates but rather on the explicit terms of the discrimination. . . .

IV

Under § 703(e)(1) of Title VII, an employer may discriminate on the basis of "religion, sex, or national origin in those certain instances where religion, sex, or national origin is a bona fide occupational qualification reasonably necessary to the normal operation of that particular business or enterprise." We therefore turn to the question whether Johnson Controls' fetal-protection policy is one of those "certain instances" that come within the BFOQ exception.

The BFOQ defense is written narrowly, and this Court has read it narrowly. . . .

In *Dothard* v. *Rawlinson* [1977], this Court indicated that danger to a woman herself does not justify discrimination. We there allowed the employer to hire only male guards in contact areas of maximum-security male penitentiaries only because . . . the employment of a female guard would create real risks of safety to others if violence broke out because the guard was a woman. Sex discrimination was tolerated because sex was related to the guard's ability to do the job—maintaining prison security. . . .

Similarly, some courts have approved airlines' layoffs of pregnant flight attendants at different points during the first five months of pregnancy on the ground that the employer's policy was necessary to ensure the safety of passengers.... We stressed that in order to qualify as a BFOQ, a job qualification must relate to the "essence," or to the "central mission of the employer's business." ...

Our case law, therefore, makes clear that the safety exception is limited to instances in which sex or pregnancy actually interferes with the employee's ability to perform the job.... Johnson Controls suggests, however, that we expand the exception to allow fetal-protection policies that mandate particular standards for pregnant or fertile women. We decline to do so....

[V Omitted]

VI

A word about tort liability and the increased cost of fertile women in the workplace is perhaps necessary. One of the dissenting judges in this case expressed concern about an employer's tort liability and concluded that liability for a potential injury to a fetus is a social cost that Title VII does not require a company to ignore. It is correct to say that Title VII does not prevent the employer from having a conscience. The statute, however, does prevent sex-specific fetal-protection policies. These two aspects of Title VII do not conflict.

More than 40 States currently recognize a right to recover for a prenatal injury based either on negligence or on wrongful death. According to Johnson Controls, however, the company complies with the lead standard developed by OSHA and warns its female employees about the damaging effects of lead.... If, under general tort principles, Title VII bans sex-specific fetal-protection policies, the employer fully informs the woman of the risk, and the employer has not acted negligently, the basis for holding an employer liable seems remote at best....

VII

Our holding today that Title VII, as so amended, forbids sex-specific fetal-protection policies is neither remarkable nor unprecedented. Concern for a woman's existing or potential offspring historically has been the excuse for denying women equal employment opportunities. Congress in the PDA prohibited discrimination on the basis of a woman's ability to become pregnant. We do no more than hold that the Pregnancy Discrimination Act means what it says.

It is no more appropriate for the courts than it is for individual employers to decide whether a woman's reproductive role is more important to herself and her family than her economic role. Congress has left this choice to the woman as hers to make.

The judgment of the Court of Appeals is reversed and the case is remanded for further proceedings consistent with this opinion.

It is so ordered.

JUSTICE WHITE, with whom THE CHIEF JUSTICE and JUSTICE KENNEDY join, concurring in part and concurring in the judgment.

The Court properly holds that Johnson Controls' fetal protection policy overtly discriminates against women, and thus is prohibited by Title VII unless it falls within the bona fide occupational qualification (BFOQ) exception. . . . The Court erroneously holds, however, that the BFOQ defense is so narrow that it could never justify a sex-specific fetal protection policy. I nevertheless concur in the judgment of reversal because on the record before us summary judgment in favor of Johnson Controls was improperly entered by the District Court and affirmed by the Court of Appeals.

I

In evaluating the scope of the BFOQ defense, the proper starting point is the language of the statute. Title VII forbids discrimination on the basis of sex, except "in those certain instances where . . . sex . . . is a bona fide occupational qualification reasonably necessary to the normal operation of that particular business or enterprise." For the fetal protection policy involved in this case to be a BFOQ, therefore, the policy must be "reasonably necessary" to the "normal operation" of making batteries, which is Johnson Controls' "particular business." Although that is a difficult standard to satisfy, nothing in the statute's language indicates that it could *never* support a sex-specific fetal protection policy.

On the contrary, a fetal protection policy would be justified under the terms of the statute if, for example, an employer could show that exclusion of women from certain jobs was reasonably necessary to avoid substantial tort liability. Common sense tells us that it is part of the normal operation of business concerns to avoid causing injury to third parties, as well as to employees, if for no other reason than to avoid tort liability and its substantial costs. This possibility of tort liability is not hypothetical; every State currently allows children born alive to recover in tort for prenatal injuries caused by third parties, and an increasing number of courts have recognized a right to recover even for prenatal injuries caused by torts committed prior to conception.

The Court dismisses the possibility of tort liability by no more than speculating that if "Title VII bans sex-specific fetal-protection policies, the employer fully informs the woman of the risk, and the employer has not acted negligently, the basis for holding an employer liable seems remote at best." Such speculation will be small comfort to employers. First, it is far from clear that compliance with Title VII will pre-empt state tort liability, and the Court offers no support for that proposition. Second, although warnings may preclude claims by injured *employees,* they will not preclude claims by injured children because the general rule is that parents cannot waive causes of action on behalf of their children, and the parents' negligence will not be imputed to the children. . . . Compliance with OSHA standards, for example, has been held not to be a defense to state tort or criminal liability. Moreover, it is possible that employers will be held strictly liable, if, for example, their manufacturing process is considered "abnormally dangerous.". . .

Prior decisions construing the BFOQ defense confirm that the defense is broad enough to include considerations of cost and safety of the sort that could form the basis for an employer's adoption of a fetal protection policy. . . .

The Pregnancy Discrimination Act (PDA), contrary to the Court's assertion, did not restrict the scope of the BFOQ defense. The PDA was only an amendment to the "Definitions" section of Title VII, and did not purport to eliminate or alter the BFOQ defense. Rather, it merely clarified Title VII to make it clear that pregnancy and related conditions are included within Title VII's antidiscrimination provisions. As we have already recognized, "the purpose of the PDA was simply to make the treatment of pregnancy consistent with general Title VII principles." . . .

In enacting the BFOQ standard, "Congress did not ignore the public interest in safety." The court's narrow interpretation of the BFOQ defense in this case, however, means that an employer cannot exclude even *pregnant* women from an environment highly toxic to their fetuses. It is foolish to think that Congress intended such a result, and neither the language of the BFOQ exception nor our cases requires it.

II

Despite my disagreement with the Court concerning the scope of the BFOQ defense, I concur in reversing the Court of Appeals because that court erred in affirming the District Court's grant of summary judgment in favor of Johnson Controls. First, the Court of Appeals erred in failing to consider the level of risk-avoidance that was part of Johnson Controls' "normal operation." Although the court did conclude that there was a "substantial risk" to fetuses from lead exposure in fertile women, it merely meant that there was a high risk that *some* fetal injury would occur absent a fetal protection policy. That analysis, of course, fails to address the *extent* of fetal injury that is likely to occur. If the fetal protection policy insists on a risk-avoidance level substantially higher than other risk levels tolerated by Johnson Controls such as risks to employees and consumers, the policy should not constitute a BFOQ.

Second, even without more information about the normal level of risk at Johnson Controls, the fetal protection policy at issue here reaches too far. This is evident both in its presumption that, absent medical documentation to the contrary, all women are fertile regardless of their age, and in its exclusion of presumptively fertile women from positions that might result in a promotion to a position involving high lead exposure. There has been no showing that either of those aspects of the policy is reasonably necessary to ensure safe and efficient operation of Johnson Controls' battery-manufacturing business. Of course, these infirmities in the company's policy do not warrant invalidating the entire fetal protection program.

Third, it should be recalled that until 1982 Johnson Controls operated without an exclusionary policy, and it has not identified any grounds for believing that its current policy is reasonably necessary to its normal operations. Although it is now more aware of some of the dangers of lead exposure, it has not shown that the risks of fetal harm or the costs associated with it have substantially increased. . . .

Finally, the Court of Appeals failed to consider properly petitioners' evidence of harm to offspring caused by lead exposure in males. The court considered that evidence only in its discussion of the business necessity standard, in which it focused on whether *petitioners* had met their burden of proof. The burden of proving that a discriminatory qualification is a BFOQ, however, rests with the employer. . . .

JUSTICE SCALIA, concurring in the judgment.

I generally agree with the Court's analysis, but have some reservations, several of which bear mention.

First, I think it irrelevant that there was "evidence in the record about the debilitating effect of lead exposure on the male reproductive system." Even without such evidence, treating women differently "on the basis of pregnancy" constitutes discrimination "on the basis of sex," because Congress has unequivocally said so.

Second, the Court points out that "Johnson Controls has shown no factual basis for believing that all or substantially all women would be unable to perform safely . . . the duties of the job involved." In my view, this is . . . entirely irrelevant. By reason of the Pregnancy Discrimination Act, it would not matter if all pregnant women placed their children at risk in taking these jobs, just as it does not matter if no men do so. . . .

Last, the Court goes far afield, it seems to me, in suggesting that increased cost alone—short of "costs . . . so prohibitive as to threaten survival of the employer's business"—cannot support a BFOQ defense. I agree with JUSTICE WHITE's concurrence that nothing in our prior cases suggests this, and in my view it is wrong. I think, for example, that a shipping company may refuse to hire pregnant women as crew members on long voyages because the on-board facilities for foreseeable emergencies, though quite feasible, would be inordinately expensive. In the present case, however, Johnson has not asserted a cost-based BFOQ.

I concur in the judgment of the Court.

AMBASSADOR GLASPIE ON
PRE-WAR MEETING WITH HUSSEIN
March 20, 1991

April C. Glaspie, the U.S. ambassador to Iraq, made long-awaited appearances before the Senate Foreign Relations Committee and the next day before the House Foreign Affairs' Subcommittee on Europe and the Middle East March 20 and 21 to give her version of a meeting she had with Iraqi president Saddam Hussein July 25, 1990—only eight days before Iraq invaded Kuwait. She accused Hussein of doctoring the record of that meeting in Baghdad to make it appear that she was trying to appease him—and thus had misled him about Washington's position on Iraq's quarrel with Kuwait. After the United States condemned the invasion and began organizing an international force to repel it, Iraq on September 11 released its account of the meeting, which, until Glaspie testified March 20, had gone publicly and officially unchallenged.

Secretary of State James A. Baker III had appeared to distance himself from the ambassador, and the State Department repeatedly rebuffed attempts by congressional committees to get Glaspie to testify. She had been widely depicted as a scapegoat of the Bush administration for a "soft" pre-invasion policy toward Iraq.

Glaspie Says "Stupid" Hussein Lied

Glaspie attributed the long silence to the administration's greater concern with conducting a war than with "retrospectives." The ambassador answered most questions with a forcefulness and confidence that belied the image of the obsequious diplomat pictured in the Iraqi transcript. If there was any error in America's dealings with Hussein, she said, it was a failure "to realize that he was stupid—that he did not believe our clear and repeated warnings that we would support our vital interests."

As for the Iraqi account of the July 25 meeting, Glaspie told the Foreign Relations Committee: "This is fabrication. This is disinformation. This is not a transcript." For instance, the document quoted her as saying that the United States had "no opinion on the Arab-Arab conflicts, like your border disagreement with Kuwait," but Glaspie testified that her remark was in response to hints by Saddam that the U.S. should side with him in the border dispute. She said she made clear to him that "it was emphatically our business that they [Iraq and Kuwait] make the settlement in a nonviolent way."

Glaspie's explanations of what occurred in the private meeting with the reclusive Iraqi leader—the first he had granted since she reported to Baghdad in 1988—seemed to satisfy members of both panels. But Rep. Lee H. Hamilton, D-Ind., chairman of the House subcommittee, questioned her contention that U.S. policy had been made clear. Sen. Claiborne Pell, D-R.I., the Foreign Relations chairman, said he did not fault Glaspie for carrying out her instructions, but, rather, "I question the instructions." He recalled that the administration opposed repeated attempts in Congress to impose some sanctions against Iraq well before it went to war in Kuwait.

Senators Doubt Ambassador's Explanations

Whatever points Glaspie scored with questioning senators at the March 20 hearing were dissipated after the Foreign Relations Committee requested and obtained several secret cables from the State Department, including the ambassador's own account of her meeting with Hussein. On July 11, Pell wrote Baker, saying that Glaspie's March 20 testimony was inconsistent with her classified report to the department about the meeting. The next day Sen. Alan Cranston, D-Calif., a member of the committee, accused her of deliberately misleading Congress.

Deputy Secretary of State Lawrence S. Eagleburger requested that he and Glaspie be allowed to appear together before the committee to set the record straight, although the department had not decided whether to declassify the cables and make them public. Some information attributed to the cables had been reported in the press. Whatever the outcome of the Glaspie matter, investigation into U.S. pre-war policy in the Persian Gulf region was likely to be pursued further in Congress.

Following are excerpts from the testimony of Ambassador April C. Glaspie before the Senate Foreign Relations Committee, March 20, 1991, as transcribed by Reuters Information Services:

Ambassador Glaspie: I'm sure that you will all remember that the first part of the year, 1990, in the Middle East, was dominated by Saddam Hussein's threats against Israel. We were pleased to have some senators visit us during that period, and they helped greatly in conveying to Saddam Hussein that the administration and the Congress were at one in their view that it was he that was responsible for heightened tensions in the area.

But suddenly, on July 17th, Saddam Hussein made a state of the union message—that's what he called it, in which he completely switched his focus from Israel and the threat that he declared he perceived from Israel, to Kuwait. And he announced in that speech, in the crudest and most unmistakable way, that if Kuwait and the United Arab Emirates did not revise their oil policy and produce according to their OPEC quotas, Iraq would take upon itself effective measures to make sure that they did. This was a naked threat, and it was made on Iraqi television, on the evening of the 17th of July.

Just hours later, we responded. We responded publicly and we responded privately. To the best of my knowledge, we were the only government ever to respond publicly on behalf of Kuwait. Publicly, you recall, Margaret Tutwiler, on behalf of the United States government said that we would certainly, under any circumstances, we would defend our vital interests. She said we were strongly committed to the individual and collective self-defense of our friends in the gulf. That's a pretty clear statement, I think.

The senior Iraqi diplomat in the United States, who was, of course, the ambassador, was summoned to the State Department. He was given the same words. Additionally, and I want to read this, gentlemen, to you—he was told that we would continue to defend our vital interests in the gulf, and we would continue to support the sovereignty and integrity of the gulf states. He was reminded that while we would not take positions on the equities of bilateral Iraqi-Kuwaiti disputes, we would insist—I repeat insist—that disputes be settled peacefully and not by threat or intimidation.

Those points were cabled to American embassies in the area. All ambassadors were instructed to act upon them immediately. In the case of my colleagues, they were, of course, asked to consult with host governments to point out what we had said, what we were urging, and to ask them to undertake vigorous diplomacy as well.

You recall that the Arab states took the position that this was an Arab matter and we should stay out of it. In my case, I was instructed to find the highest available Iraqi official and impress upon him that we insisted that all disputes with Kuwait or with any, if fact, of Iraq's neighbors, be settled peacefully. I found the deputy foreign minister, who many of you may know, Nasir Hamdoun. I made those points to him. I also asked vigorously for clarification as to the reason for this statement. I got no clarification.

I went back the next day. I went back seven straight days. On the 20th of July, we picked up in Baghdad the first indication of military deployments to the south. This was the response to our request to the Iraqis for moderation—a deployment to the south.

We went back again to the Iraqis. We went back the next and the next day. They continued to deploy. Against the advice of our Arab friends, we decided that we must do more. Our Arab friends counseled publicly, in fact, as well as privately, that even a show of force would provoke the Arabs—would provoke the Iraqi government, and would be counter productive. It would likely lead to an Iraqi military move.

We did not take that advice, and neither did one of Iraq's neighbors— the United Arab Emirates agreed with us. Together, we announced a joint military exercise on July the 24th. We announced that in the afternoon of July 24th. This at last focused the mind of the Iraqi government. I was summoned at midnight in Baghdad, as was the UAE ambassador. I, of course, repeated our announcement and explained that we were a super-power and we intended to act like one. We had vital interests, and we would protect them, and that was that.

When dawn came, I had received Margaret Tutwiler's statement in writing. I took it down to the foreign ministry and delivered it. I came back to my office. Half an hour or so later, I was asked to go back to the foreign ministry, and I was ushered into one of the offices used by Saddam Hussein in the presidency.

It was clear that our show of force had caught his attention. It was also clear that the United Arab Emirates, very bravely, had no intention of backing down. It was clear to me that Saddam Hussein was enraged that we had taken this step. He I think felt stymied. In any case—and we can go back to the meeting, I just wanted to sketch out these two weeks—he surrendered; he spoke on the telephone to President Mubarak for some time, came back, told me that he had told President Mubarak and he wanted me to inform President Bush that he would not solve his problems with Kuwait by violence, period. He would not do it. He would take advantage of the Arab diplomatic framework which President Mubarak and King Fahd had set up. That's what he would do.

The next day every word about Kuwait, hostility towards Kuwait— anything about Kuwait at all—dropped from the Baghdad press. There are four main morning newspapers in Baghdad. Every day for the past 10 days the front pages had been crowded with insults toward Kuwait and its rulers. Every word of that was dropped, and, I might add, the Arab ambassadors, many of them dropped by and congratulated us on our tactics. They believed that he meant what he said.

On the 28th of July I received the same assurances, reiterated by the foreign minister. On the 29th of July they were reiterated to me by the minister of military industrialization, who was President Saddam's son in law, a very powerful minister. On the 1st of August, while the Kuwaiti-Iraqi conversations were going on in Jidda, the Iraqi delegation announced that the negotiations would resume in a very few days in Baghdad. I think it was four hours later Iraq invaded Kuwait.

That is what happened....

Senator Alan Cranston (D-Ca.): You didn't describe your session with Saddam Hussein in any detail, or touch upon it in that statement. Could you describe what happened there, the atmosphere, what you sensed about the situation from that session? Do you think anything that you could have said would have had any impact on his decision to proceed militarily?

Ambassador Glaspie: The main factor, I think, was that the Iraqis for some months, since February of the year, had been quite convinced that the United States, far from appeasing Iraq, as I have read sometimes in the press, was targeting Iraq. The Iraqis were very, very concerned about that; they complained about it all the time; they made formal representations to other members of the Arab League and two European states, asking them to come to us and we should get off the Iraqi back. Now, of course, you remember what it was that we were doing: we were arresting Iraqi spies and we were catching people who were illegally smuggling capacitors out of the country. But day after day the Iraqi media for all those months since February, literally every day, was full of these accusations.

And I think it was genuinely believed by Saddam Hussein—it certainly came through in that meeting. He reminded me of the previous Irangate business, which of course from the Iraqi point of view was a disaster; they believe that we gave their order of battle to the Iranians. He recalled previous years in which the Iraqis believed that with the shah we were actively supporting Kurdish rebels who were trying to overthrow the central government.

So this paranoia about the United States came through, and the other major factor that I sensed was that he was flummoxed, Senator. It had just occurred to him I think that we really might fight. I think he overcame that idea; I think it was just a passing fancy. The point is he thought that he had to take Kuwait. And there was also just a suspicion, I think, in his conversation with me of why. And one of the reasons why, of course, is he was broke. I remember he made a speech in February saying that he was overspending, but it didn't matter because oil prices were going up. The price of oil was $20; by July it was $14.

So overall I would say that, after I had repeated several times—and I might say, he had our written note to him in front of him when I came in. After I repeated several times that we would not countenance violence or in fact threat or intimidation, then it was clear that he was going to tell me that Iraq accepted that. It was a strange atmosphere, because he was conciliatory, and he normally is not. . . .

Senator Kassebaum: I would like to ask, because it has been something that's been commented on many times one way or another, and we have here the transcript that was handed out by the Iraqi embassy regarding your conversation with President Saddam Hussein.

I would like to hear your comment and explanation of the conversation on page 7, and what the context of that was, when you were quoted in this as saying, "We understand that and our opinion is that you should have the opportunity to rebuild your country, but we have no opinion on the Arab-Arab conflicts, like your border disagreement with Kuwait."

Ambassador Glaspie: That is, of course, one of the many inaccuracies in the so-called transcript. One way to edit maliciously is to cut off the second half of the sentence. The focus of my remarks and of course the focus of my instructions, as I read them to the committee, and certainly the focus of seven exhausting days of American diplomacy here and in Baghdad, was the other end of the sentence, if fact, the beginning of the sentence, which was that we would insist, we would insist on settlements being made in a nonviolent manner, not by threats, not by intimidation, and certainly not by aggression.

The issue of border disputes in the Middle East is a very broad one, as I'm sure you know, Senator. Unlike the Africans, the Middle Easterners did not decide after World War II to let the colonial borders stand. As you know, the Organization of African Unity takes that position. They don't normally question those borders in Africa. In the Middle East, it's not the case.

I can't think of an Arab country—I may be wrong, but at the moment, I can't think of an Arab country that does not have some border claim. And of course, the famous ones are Iraq-Iran. But there are many, many more, including between gulf states. We take no position on any of those disputes.

The context of that particular remark was really quite simple. Saddam Hussein was hinting that we should bully the Kuwaitis into paying up, that this would be an appropriate thing for the United States to do, that we should take the Iraqi position on their border dispute. My point was that it was not our business. It was Kuwait and Iraq's business to decide whether a border post should go one meter to the left or one meter to the right. And that of course is what the dispute was about.

But it was emphatically our business that they make the settlement in a nonviolent way....

Senator Pell: Could you then submit for the record the report you made of your conversation with Saddam Hussein?

Ambassador Glaspie: That, of course, is not my decision, Senator. I'd be glad to pass on your request.

Senator Pell: We would so request of the State Department.

Ambassador Glaspie: Could I just make a comment on that, as a professional Foreign Service officer? In my 25 years, I do not recall any government, other than Saddam Hussein, issuing a transcript of a confidential diplomatic exchange. There may well have been, but I have never heard of that, and I think the reason is very clear. If we're going to maintain confidence in our own confidentiality, no matter how great the temptation to expose the lies of the other side, I personally think it is wise not to begin issuing transcripts. But of course I will be glad to convey your request....

Senator Cranston: ... I'd like to ask you just two questions. One relates to the Diane Sawyer program and your comments to Saddam Hussein, according to the transcript about that. Is that an accurate transcript of your remarks in that respect?

Ambassador Glaspie: I have not met Ms. Sawyer, unfortunately. I admired her work. The video that I was talking about was in fact hers. We watched on Baghdad Television a video of her interview with Saddam Hussein. The Iraqis had cut out everything which involved her asking a hard question and Saddam Hussein unable to give a good answer. This is typical of the kinds of transcripts, whether they're video or audio or written, that he presents. . . .

Senator Cranston: Did you allude in any way at that time to the atrocities committed on the Kurds?

Ambassador Glaspie: Not in that context, but I can assure you, Senator, that I alluded to them constantly, and I hope that you have a chance to read our human rights report. The material in there was collected by my embassy at some risk to themselves, I might add, Senator.

So human rights, I would say, was perhaps the most constant subject of dialogue that I had with the Iraqi government in my two years there. . . .

Senator Cranston: Did you say "We have no opinion on the Arab-Arab conflicts, like your border disagreement with Kuwait"?

Ambassador Glaspie: Yes. That was one part of my sentence. The other part of my sentence was "but we insist that you settle your disputes with Kuwait nonviolently." And he told me he would do so. . . .

Senator Biden: . . . Does your cable back to Washington reflect what you just said? Does it say in your cable, without telling us the entirety of the cable, does it reflect what you just said, which is that we insist that you settle your disputes with Kuwait peacefully?

Ambassador Glaspie: Yes.

Senator Biden: It does reflect that?

Ambassador Glaspie: Yes, it does, sir.

Senator Biden: And did you indicate that we viewed Kuwait as in our vital interest? Was there any discussion about how important we thought Kuwait was?

Ambassador Glaspie: Yes. Before you came in, Senator, I read my instructions, which you will be pleased to know, were exactly the same as our public position. There's no secret diplomacy involved here. Our private and public positions were exactly the same. Saddam Hussein had before him in writing and I told him orally that we would defend our vital interests, we would support the right of self-defense of our friends in the gulf, we would support their sovereignty and integrity.

Senator Biden: Did we wait too long to change our position on Saddam Hussein, from thinking we could deal with him to concluding we couldn't?

Ambassador Glaspie: Well, we certainly, like every other government in the world, made a serious mistake about him, but I think the mistake is the one that Senator Kassebaum suggested. We did not understand—we, the whole world, and especially his neighbors who presumably know him better than we do—that he would be impervious to logic and diplomacy. . . .

Senator Lugar: . . . I am curious why was this meeting with Saddam Hussein the very first one that you had had?

Did he simply refuse to see you for months, or years of your tenure there?

Ambassador Glaspie: The last ambassador he received was in November 1984; he had seen no other ambassador since; he was totally isolated and extremely ignorant, and of course this was one of the problems. I mean anybody who would seriously parade American prisoners of war on television in the thought that this would weaken our resolve is obviously somebody who understands nothing about us. . . .

Senator John Kerry (D-Mass.): I'm a little bit, I guess, confused about one aspect of things. You cited Saddam Hussein's stupidity, you've talked about how he understood nothing about America, was ignorant of our way of operating so to speak, and of our standards, values, political system, et cetera.

Yet we were operating under National Security Directive Number 26 which basically espoused a policy of moderation, assuming that he was going to understand that and react to it.

Isn't there a contradiction there? I mean how could you expect some sort of normal reaction from a man who is and has proven himself to be all that you say?

Ambassador Glaspie: Sir, when the gulf war with Iran ended in August '88 we were looking at a very powerful and very ambitious president of Iraq. There were only two obvious ways to move forward; we would try to isolate him, and as I've tried to suggest in a different context, I don't think we could have succeeded. Or we could try to show him, demonstrate to him that a beginning of international political activity which was constructive, which we had never had from him before, would bring—to use the rawest word—rewards.

So we started very, very cautiously; we were trying to educate him; we weren't assuming that he was educated; quite the opposition; we were trying—what we told him in effect was that we would way down the road be willing to consider a correct or even some kind of normal relationship with Iraq when certain conditions were met. . . . So that was our effort, Senator, I think it was a reasonable one. . . .

The Iraqis have believed for years, as I mentioned early on, that we were trying to overthrow the Iraqi government. They believe they have historic reason for that. They go back to the days of the shah and their belief that we were working with the shah and with the Kurds against the central government of Iraq. And it's the same government as we have today.

They cite Irangate, a period when they believe that we provided their war secrets to the Iranians.

Whether we find it paranoid or not, and I do find it paranoid, they believe that we are trying to overthrow the government. Now my instructions, as surely every ambassador's, but certainly my instructions were to keep the lines of communication open, to try to clear up misunderstandings wherever possible. And it was not true that we were trying to overthrow the Iraqi government.

Senator Kerry: . . . The question I'm really asking is, whether or not, in Saddam Hussein's view, to have protested in the way that he did, and to be able to elicit a response from us that was, in effect, conciliatory and kind of keeping the lines open and sort of evidencing that we're really not willing to take a risk and break those communications or send a serious message, couldn't that contribute in a way to his sense of paper tiger, that we're the country that can't lose 10,000 people in one battle, the message he delivered to you later on?

Ambassador Glaspie: No, sir, I don't believe that. I really don't. I think it would be wrong not to correct the record on an issue as very basic as that one. I certainly never persuaded the Iraqi government that we were not trying to overthrow the government, but in order to try to influence the Iraqi government, which is what I was there for, I had to keep the lines of communication open, and I had to keep trying to persuade them that we weren't trying to get rid of them. . . .

UN REPORT ON
POSTWAR IRAQ
March 20, 1991

Allied bombings of Iraq during the Persian Gulf War "wrought near-apocalyptic results upon the economic infrastructure," relegating the country to a "pre-industrial age," a United Nations team reported after surveying civilian damage in Iraq. "[N]othing that we had seen or read had quite prepared us for the particular form of devastation which has now befallen the country," said the team director, Under Secretary General Martti Ahtisaari, in his report.

The report, submitted to Secretary General Javier Perez de Cuellar March 20 and publicly released the next day in New York, warned that "epidemic and famine" were likely to arise unless Iraqis promptly received large amounts of outside assistance. Ahtisaari, a Finn, headed a team of officials from several UN agencies and offices, including the World Health Organization and the Food and Agricultural Organization.

Health threats and food needs were emphasized, although the report covered a wide range of problems that the Iraqi people faced in the aftermath of war. A food importer even before the war, Iraq was more dependent than ever on food imports to stave off malnutrition and hunger but less able to provide them. At the same time, the report continued, many basic medical supplies were depleted.

Above all else, effective bombings of Iraq's electric power facilities had created dire conditions. Iraqi rivers are heavily polluted by raw sewage, and water levels are unusually low. "All sewage treatment and [water] pumping plants have been brought to a virtual standstill by the lack of power supply and the lack of spare parts," the report said. "Pools of sewage lie in the streets and villages. Health hazards will build in the weeks to come." It added that Baghdad's water supply was reduced to about 10 percent of the capital's prewar usage.

Pressure to Lift Sanctions

On March 22 the United Nations Security Council, in apparent reaction to the report, lifted its embargo on food shipments to Iraq and eased restrictions on items such as electrical generators, water purification facilities, and truck fuels. The Security Council had imposed the international embargo on trade with Iraq after it invaded Kuwait, August 2, 1990, triggering the Persian Gulf War. (UN Action Against Iraq, Historic Documents of 1990, p. 545)

The embargo remained in effect after the fighting ceased February 28, 1991. Under the peace terms Iraq was forced to accept; the embargo and other economic sanctions would not be removed until the Baghdad government fully revealed and relinquished its capacity to conduct nuclear, chemical, and biological warfare. Through the spring and summer, Iraqi leader Saddam Hussein was repeatedly accused of trying to hide the extent of Iraq's research and development of such weaponry. (UN Peace Terms; Iraq's Acceptance, p. 191)

Other accounts of dire conditions in Iraq continued to command attention through the following months. One came from a team of physicians, lawyers, and public health specialists from Harvard University who assessed the health situation in Iraq during a nine-day visit to hospitals in that country. Upon their return in mid-May, the members spoke of cholera and typhoid outbreaks. They said Iraqi hospitals often lacked bandages, antibiotics, infant formula, and other supplies. Their focus was especially on children, who were said to be dying of malnutrition in large numbers. They estimated that the death rate for children under five was two to three times higher than before the war. Dr. Aldo Benini, a Swiss representative of the International Red Cross, was quoted in the New York Times *on June 1 as saying that among children living in typical mud-and-reed homes in the poor fringes around Baghdad, 11 percent were suffering from malnutrition.*

Stories of civilian hardship in Iraq appeared often in American newspapers and magazines, but several dispatches from Iraq suggested the UN team's "near apocalyptic" description of Iraq's economy might have been exaggerated. The American media nevertheless sketched a picture of human need—often human misery—especially among the poor. For example, the July 15 Wall Street Journal *said, "Most Iraqis are spending almost all their income on food." The Baghdad correspondent, Tony Horwitz, explained that while sanctions permitted food imports, "Iraq can't export oil or get at its foreign assets to pay for adequate supplies. With the size of state rations diminishing, most families find that their monthly allotment lasts a week. So they must buy the rest on the open market, where prices are spiraling so fast that many merchants have stopped marking their goods."*

Keeping the Oil Export Ban

Pleading with the Security Council to remove economic sanctions, the Iraqi government reported that market surveys in July showed that the prices of many basic foods had risen 2,000 to 3,000 percent since the sanctions were imposed less than a year earlier.

Iraq resumed oil production in April but on a relatively small scale; many of its refineries and pipelines had been destroyed. According to press reports, the Central Intelligence Agency estimated that by the end of summer Iraq could be exporting about 1 million barrels a day—about one-third the prewar level—if it were permitted to do so. The Security Council decided August 7 to permit Iran to sell up to $1.6 billion worth of petroleum to buy food and medical supplies but otherwise continued the sanctions.

Following are excerpts from a United Nations report on humanitarian needs in Iraq, submitted to Secretary General Javier Perez de Cuellar, March 20, 1991, by an assistant, Martti Ahtisaari, who headed an on-the-scene survey:

General Remarks

I and the members of my mission were fully conversant with media reports regarding the situation in Iraq and, of course, with the recent WHO/UNICEF [World Health Organization/United Nations] report on water, sanitary and health conditions in the Greater Baghdad area. It should, however, be said at once that nothing that we had seen or read had quite prepared us for the particular form of devastation which has now befallen the country. The recent conflict has wrought near-apocalyptic results upon the economic infrastructure of what had been, until January 1991, a rather highly urbanized and mechanized society. Now, most means of modern life support have been destroyed or rendered tenuous. Iraq has, for some time to come, been relegated to a pre-industrial age, but with all the disabilities of post-industrial dependency on an intensive use of energy and technology.

My mandate was limited to assessing the need for urgent humanitarian assistance. It did not extend to the huge task of assessing the requirements for reconstructing Iraq's destroyed infrastructure, much less, to developmental matters. Accordingly, my report to you, in its several technical sections, seeks with as much exactitude as possible to convey the extent of needs in the primary areas of humanitarian concern: for safe water and sanitation, basic health and medical support; for food; for shelter; and for the logistical means to make such support actually available. Underlying each analysis is the inexorable reality that, as a result of war, virtually all previously viable sources of fuel and power (apart from a limited number of mobile generators) and modern means of communication are now, essentially, defunct. The far-reaching implications of this energy and communications' vacuum as regards urgent humanitarian support are of crucial significance for the nature and effectiveness of the international response.

These conditions, together with recent civil unrest in some parts of the country, mean that the authorities are as yet scarcely able even to measure the dimensions of the calamity, much less respond to its consequences, because they cannot obtain full and accurate data. Additionally, there is much less than the minimum fuel required to provide the energy needed for movement or transportation, irrigation or generators for power to pump water and sewage. For instance, emergency medical supplies can be moved to health centres only with extreme difficulty and, usually, major delay. Information regarding local needs is slow and sparse. Most employees are simply unable to come to work. Both the authorities and the trade unions estimate that approximately 90 per cent of industrial workers have been reduced to inactivity and will be deprived of income as of the end of March. Government departments have at present only marginal attendance. Prior to recent events, Iraq was importing about 70 per cent of its food needs. Now, owing to the fuel shortage, the inability to import and the virtual breakdown of the distribution system, the flow of food through the private sector has been reduced to a trickle, with costs accelerating upwards. Many food prices are already beyond the purchasing reach of most Iraqi families. Agricultural production is highly mechanized, and much land depends on pumped-water irrigation. Should the main harvest in June 1991 be seriously affected by a lack of energy to drive machines and pump water, then an already grave situation will be further aggravated. As shown below, prospects for the 1992 harvest could, for combined reasons, be in at least as much jeopardy. Having regard to the nature of Iraq's society and economy, the energy vacuum is an omnipresent obstacle to the success of even a short-term, massive effort to maintain life-sustaining conditions in each area of humanitarian need.

Food and Agriculture

Mission members held working sessions with counterparts from the relevant ministries, visited social centres where various vulnerable groups are cared for, agricultural production areas, a seed production centre, a veterinary health centre and a dairy production unit. The mission noted that Iraq has been heavily dependent on food imports which have amounted to at least 70 per cent of consumption needs. Seed was also imported. Sanctions decided upon by the Security Council had already adversely affected the country's ability to feed its people. New measures relating to rationing and enhanced production were introduced in September 1990. These were, however, in turn, negatively affected by the hostilities which impacted upon most areas of agricultural production and distribution.

Food is currently made available to the population both through government allocation and rations, and through the market. The Ministry of Trade's monthly allocation to the population of staple food items fell from 343,000 tons in September 1990 to 182,000 tons, when rationing was introduced, and was further reduced to 135,000 tons in January 1991 (39 per cent of the pre-sanctions level). While the mission was unable to gauge the precise quantities still held in government warehouses, all evidence indicates that flour is now at a critically low level, and that supplies of sugar, rice, tea, vegetable oil, powdered milk and pulses are currently at critically low levels or have been exhausted. Distribution of powdered milk, for instance, is now reserved exclusively for sick children on medical prescription.

Livestock farming has been seriously affected by sanctions because many feed products were imported. The sole laboratory producing veterinary vaccines was destroyed during the conflict, as inspected by the mission. The authorities are no longer able to support livestock farmers in the combat of disease, as all stocks of vaccine were stated to have been destroyed in the same sequence of bombardments on this centre, which was an FAO [Food and Agriculture Organization] regional project.

The country has had a particular dependence upon foreign vegetable seeds, and the mission was able to inspect destroyed seed warehouses. The relevant agricultural authorities informed the mission that all stocks of potatoes and vegetable seeds have been exhausted. Next season's planting will be jeopardized if seeds are not provided before October 1991.

This year's grain harvest in June is seriously compromised for a number of reasons, including failure of irrigation/drainage (no power for pumps, lack of spare parts); lack of pesticides and fertilizers (previously imported); and lack of fuel and spare parts for the highly-mechanized and fuel-dependent harvesting machines. Should this harvest fail, or be far below average, as is very likely barring a rapid change in the situation, wide-spread starvation conditions become a real possibility.

The official programme for the support of socially dependent groups of the population (the elderly, disabled, mothers and children, hospital patients, orphans, refugees, etc.) is affected by the overall grave deficiencies in the food situation.

The mission had the opportunity to conduct independent research relating to household costs and living standards in Baghdad. Such standards have declined rapidly in the last months, while food and fuel prices have climbed dramatically. Price increases in the August to January period reflected shortages of supply, but since January there has been a further acceleration of price increases reflecting both supply shortages and the breakdown of the transport system. Interviews with private wholesale food distributors revealed that their stocks are near depletion and they no longer have an organized private transport capacity, owing to fuel shortages. The government-initiated rationing system was designed to provide families with a fraction of their basic necessities at prices comparable to those prevailing before August. The system allows families either 5 kilograms per person, per month, of flour or 3 loaves of baked bread; 10 kilograms per family, per month, of liquid cooking gas; 1 bar of soap per person, per month, etc. However, independent surveys conducted by the mission in several diverse areas of Baghdad showed that many families cannot draw their full rations, since the distribution centres are often depleted and they have great difficulty in travelling to other centres. The quality of food distribution has itself deteriorated to the point of causing health problems. Most families also reported that they could not meet their needs through the private markets. Despite official price controls, the independent market surveys conducted by the mission showed hyperinflation since August. ... In contrast to this hyperinflation, many incomes have collapsed. Many employees cannot draw salaries, the banking system has in large measure closed down. ... In short, most families lack access to adequate rations or the purchasing power to meet normal minimal standards.

The mission recommends that, in these circumstances of present severe hardship and in view of the bleak prognosis, sanctions in respect of food supplies should be immediately removed, as should those relating to the import of agricultural equipment and supplies. The urgent supply of basic commodities to safeguard vulnerable groups is strongly recommended, and the provision of major quantities of the following staples for the general population: milk, wheat flour, rice, sugar, vegetable oil and tea. These are required to meet minimum general requirements until the next harvest. Safeguarding the harvest means the urgent importation of fertilizers, pesticides, spare parts, veterinary drugs, agricultural machinery and equipment, etc. The mission was able to quantify many of these needs. The disappearance of vegetables from the country's markets also appears likely by the summer, and seed importation is crucial.

The mission observes that, without a restoration of energy supplies to the agricultural production and distribution sectors, implementation of many of the above recommendations would be to little effect. Drastic international measures across the whole agricultural spectrum are most urgent.

Water, Sanitation and Health

As regards water, prior to the crisis Baghdad received about 450 litres per person supplied by seven treatment stations purifying water from the Tigris river. The rest of the country had about 200-250 litres per person per day, purified and supplied by 238 central water-treatment stations and 1,134 smaller water projects. All stations operated on electric power; about 75 per cent had standby diesel-powered generators. Sewage was treated to an acceptable standard before being returned to the rivers.

With the destruction of power plants, oil refineries, main oil storage facilities and water-related chemical plants, all electrically operated installations have ceased to function. Diesel-operated generators were reduced to operating on a limited basis, their functioning affected by lack of fuel, lack of maintenance, lack of spare parts and non-attendance of workers. The supply of water in Baghdad dropped to less than 10 litres per day but has now recovered to approximately 30-40 litres in about 70 per cent of the area (less than 10 per cent of the overall previous use). Standby generating capacity is out of order in several pumping stations and cessation of supplies will therefore ensue if current machinery goes out of order for any reason (spare parts are not available owing to sanctions). As regards the quality of water in Baghdad, untreated sewage has now to be dumped directly into the river—which is the source of the water supply—and all drinking-water plants there and throughout the rest of the country are using river water with high sewage contamination. Recently, the water authority has begun to be able to improve the quality of drinking water by adding more of the remaining stock of alum and chlorine. ... Chemical tests are now being conducted at the stations but no bacteriological testing and control is possible because of the lack of electricity necessary for the functioning of laboratories, the shortage of necessary chemicals and reagents and the lack of fuel for the collection of samples. No chlorine tests are being conducted because of the lack of fuel for sampling. While the water authority has warned that water must be boiled, there is little fuel to do this, and what exists is diminishing. Cool winter conditions have prevailed until recently.

Only limited information is available to authorities regarding the situation in the remainder of the country because all modern communications systems have been destroyed and information is now transmitted and received (in this sector as in all others) by person-to-person contact. In those areas where there are no generators, or generators have broken down, or the fuel supply is exhausted, the population draws its water directly from polluted rivers and trenches. This is widely apparent in rural areas, where women and children can be seen washing and filling water receptacles. The quantity and quality of water produced by treatment centres is very variable and in many locations there are no chemicals available for purification. No quality control—chlorine testing, chemical testing or bacteriological testing—is being conducted.

... A further major problem, now imminent, is the climate. Iraq has long and extremely hot summers, the temperature often reaching 50 degrees Celsius. This has two main implications: (a) the quantity of water must be increased, and a minimum target of 50 litres per person per day has to be attained (this entails a gross output of 65 litres per person at the source); and (b) the heat will accelerate the incubation of bacteria, and thus the health risks ascribable to the water quality (already at an unacceptable level) will be further exacerbated—especially viewed in the overall sanitary circumstances which have already led to a fourfold increase in diarrheal disease incidence among children under five years of age, and the impact of this on their precarious nutritional status.

As regards sanitation, the two main concerns relate to garbage disposal and sewage treatment. In both cases, rapidly rising temperatures will soon accentuate an existing crisis. Heaps of garbage are spread in the urban areas and collection is poor to non-existent. The work of collection vehicles is hampered by lack of fuel, lack of maintenance and spare parts and lack of labour, because workers are unable to come to work. Incinerators are in general not working, for these same reasons, and for lack of electric power. Insecticides, much needed as the weather becomes more torrid, are virtually out of stock because of sanctions and a lack of chemical supplies. ... Pools of sewage lie in the streets and villages. Health hazards will build in the weeks to come. ...

Refugees and Other Vulnerable Groups

Conditions described above affect the whole population of Iraq and, most especially, low-income groups. The mission paid particular attention to the plight of especially vulnerable groups, whether Iraqi or non-Iraqi. Thus, it found that care for orphans, the elderly and the handicapped had been in many instances disrupted, with residents of institutions having had to be moved and regrouped at various locations. It recommends the urgent implementation of a humanitarian programme aimed at enabling some 25 orphanages and 71 other social welfare centres to resume their normal activities and at providing their beneficiaries with essential relief supplies, and specifies essential inputs for this purpose.

As regards the displaced and the homeless, the authorities themselves have not yet been able fully to assess the impact of the recent hostilities. They have, however, calculated that approximately 9,000 homes were destroyed or damaged beyond repair during the hostilities, of which 2,500 were in Baghdad and 1,900 were in Basrah. This has created a new homeless potential total of 72,000 persons. Official help is now hampered by the conditions described throughout this report and, especially, a virtual halt in the production of local building materials and the impossibility to import. The input of essential materials should be permitted.

The mission was unable, in the time available and having regard to the incomplete data in the hands of the authorities, to ascertain the number of foreign workers of Arab and other nationalities still resident in Iraq. It has been estimated that approximately 750,000 were still present in January 1991. It can at this stage be no more than a matter of surmise whether a number of those remaining may be in need of support to return to their countries of origin.

Some 64,000 Iranian nationals, protected under either the Fourth Geneva Convention relative to the Protection of Civilian Persons in Time of War of 14 August 1949, or the 1951 Convention relating to the Status of Refugees, had previously resided in three camps in Iraq. There has been substantial dislocation of some of these persons. Others have indicated their desire for repatriation. Limited relief assistance is urgently needed for some of those who have been obliged to leave one of the camps. Additionally, some 80,000 Palestinians are resident in Iraq, including a group of 35,000 considered as refugees benefiting from the protection of the Iraqi Government. It has been reported that several hundred Palestinians have recently come to Baghdad from Kuwait and are now in need of emergency assistance. Certain measures have been developed to provide urgent assistance to those most in need.

Logistics: Transportation, Communications and Energy

... As regards transportation, the fact that the country has been on a war footing almost continuously since 1980 has undermined its capacity. At present, Iraq's sole available surface transport link with the outside world is via Amman to Aqaba [Jordan]. ... Internal transportation by road is now severely affected by a lack of spare parts and tires and, above all, by a lack of fuel. Some internal railway capability still exists on the Baghdad-Mosul line. The mission was informed that a total of 83 road bridges had been destroyed and a number were inspected.

As regards communications, the mission was informed that all internal and external telephone systems had been destroyed, with the exception of a limited local exchange in one town. It had the opportunity to inspect a number of war-damaged or destroyed facilities and experienced for itself the situation in the Greater Baghdad and other urban areas. Communication in Iraq is now on a person-to-person basis, as mail services have also disintegrated.

The role of energy in Iraq is especially important because of the level of its urbanization (approximately 72 per cent of the population lives in towns), its industrialization, and its prolonged, very hot, summers. ... Bombardment has paralyzed oil and electricity [power-generating] sectors almost entirely. Power output and refineries' production is negligible. ... The limited and sporadic power supply in some residential areas and for health facilities is provided by mobile generators. There have, officially, been virtually no sales of gasoline to private users since February. The mission was told that the only petrol, oil and lubricants (POL) products now available are heating oil (rationed to 60 litres per month, per family) and liquefied petroleum gas (LPG), which is rationed to one cylinder per month, per family. The authorities stated that stocks of these two products are close to exhaustion and that their distribution is expected to cease within the next 2-4 weeks. While work is under way to clear sites and assess damages, lack of communications and transport is retarding this activity. Initial inspections are said to show that necessary repairs to begin power generation and oil refining at minimal levels may take anywhere from 4 to 13 months. Minimal survival level to undertake humanitarian activities would require approximately 25 per cent of pre-war civilian domestic fuel consumption. ...

Observations

... I, together with all my colleagues, am convinced that there needs to be a major mobilization and movement of resources to deal with aspects of this deep crisis in the fields of agriculture and food, water, sanitation and health. Yet the situation raises, in acute form, other questions. For it will be difficult, if not impossible, to remedy these immediate humanitarian needs without dealing with the underlying need for energy, on an equally urgent basis. The need for energy means, initially, emergency oil imports and the rapid patching up of a limited refining and electricity production capacity, with essential supplies from other countries. Otherwise, food that is imported cannot be preserved and distributed; water cannot be purified; sewage cannot be pumped away and cleansed; crops cannot be irrigated; medicaments cannot be conveyed where they are required; needs cannot even be effectively assessed. It is unmistakable that the Iraqi people may soon face a further imminent catastrophe, which could include epidemic and famine, if massive life-supporting needs are not rapidly met. . . .

SUPREME COURT ON
COERCED CONFESSIONS
March 26, 1991

A divided Supreme Court declared March 26 that an outright ban on the use of coerced confessions in criminal trials no longer applied in all cases. In 1967 the Supreme Court, led by Chief Justice Earl Warren, imposed the ban in Chapman v. California. *The present chief justice, William H. Rehnquist, mustered a five-member majority to overturn the earlier ruling.*

David H. Souter, the Court's newest justice, cast the deciding vote for the chief justice's position that a coerced confession could be considered a harmless error and admitted as evidence in a criminal trial if it could be shown that other evidence was adequate to obtain a guilty verdict. Justices Sandra Day O'Connor, Antonin Scalia, and Anthony M. Kennedy also endorsed Rehnquist's view.

The case, Arizona v. Fulminante, *was argued October 10, 1990, just a day after Souter joined the Court. Souter replaced William J. Brennan, Jr., who, until his retirement the previous summer, had led the Court's liberal minority. (Judge Souter's Testimony to Senate Judiciary Committee, Historic Documents of 1990, p. 615) Court observers believe that Brennan's departure enabled the chief justice to prevail on this issue. The remaining members of the Court's liberal wing—Justices Thurgood Marshall, Harry A. Blackmun, and John Paul Stevens—opposed the ruling.*

White's Dissent

But it was Justice Byron R. White, usually identified with the Court's conservative majority, who wrote the opinion in which Marshall, Blackmun, and Stevens joined. White emphasized his disapproval by taking the unusual step of reading his dissent from the bench. "Permitting a coerced confession to be part of the evidence on which a jury is free to base its verdict of guilty is inconsistent with the thesis that ours is not an inquisitorial system of criminal justice," he said.

White defended the Court's precedent, set forth in Chapman v. California. *It identified three errors in a criminal trial that were too serious to be categorized as harmless: using a tainted confession against the defendant, depriving the defendant of counsel, and trying the defendant before a biased judge.*

Case's Realignment of Justices

Once the Rehnquist majority decided that the harmless-error test could be applied to coerced confessions, Scalia joined White, Marshall, Blackmun, and Stevens in declaring that the confession in the Fulminante *case had been coerced. Then, in still another lineup of justices, Kennedy joined White, Marshall, Blackmun, and Stevens in determining the ultimate disposition of the case. They held that this confession did not meet the harmless test. White wrote: "Absent the confessions, it is unlikely that Fulminante would have been prosecuted at all."*

The Court thus upheld an order by the Arizona Supreme Court for a retrial of Oreste C. Fulminante, who had been convicted and sentenced to death by a state trial court for the murder of his eleven-year-old stepdaughter, Jeneane Michelle Hunt, in 1982. He was a suspect in the slaying but was not charged with the crime until 1984.

Confession to FBI Informant

In the meantime, Fulminante had moved to New Jersey, where he was convicted on a firearms-possession charge and sent to Ray Brook Federal Correctional Institution in New York. There he was befriended by Anthony Sarivola, a paid FBI informant posing as an organized crime figure. Sarivola told Fulminante that he knew he was getting "some rough treatment" from other inmates and offered to protect him. Sarivola stated that at his urging Fulminante confided that he had killed Jeneane, and upon release from prison made a similar confession to Sarivola's fiancée. Prior to trial, Fulminante attempted unsuccessfully to suppress both statements, asserting that they had been coerced.

On Fulminante's appeal of his murder conviction, the state's high court initially ruled that his confession to the crime was admissible but on reconsideration held that it had been obtained through coercion and used against him in violation of his constitutional right to due process. Because of different views in the state and federal courts over the application of harmless-error analyses, the U.S. Supreme Court agreed to review the case before Fulminante was retried.

> *Following are excerpts from the Supreme Court's majority opinion in* Arizona v. Fulminante, *with separate opinions partly in concurrence and partly in dissent, issued March 26, 1991:*

No. 89-839

| Arizona, Petitioner
v.
Oreste C. Fulminante | On writ of certiorari to the
Supreme Court of Arizona |

[March 26, 1991]

JUSTICE WHITE delivered the opinion of the Court.

The Arizona Supreme Court ruled in this case that respondent Oreste Fulminante's confession, received in evidence at his trial for murder, had been coerced and that its use against him was barred by the Fifth and Fourteenth Amendments to the United States Constitution. The court also held that the harmless-error rule could not be used to save the conviction. We affirm the judgment of the Arizona court, although for different reasons than those upon which that court relied.

I

Early in the morning of September 14, 1982, Fulminante called the Mesa, Arizona, Police Department to report that his 11-year-old step-daughter, Jeneane Michelle Hunt, was missing. He had been caring for Jeneane while his wife, Jeneane's mother, was in the hospital. Two days later, Jeneane's body was found in the desert east of Mesa. She had been shot twice in the head at close range with a large caliber weapon, and a ligature was around her neck. Because of the decomposed condition of the body, it was impossible to tell whether she had been sexually assaulted.

Fulminante's statements to police concerning Jeneane's disappearance and his relationship with her contained a number of inconsistencies, and he became a suspect in her killing. When no charges were filed against him, Fulminante left Arizona for New Jersey. Fulminante was later convicted in New Jersey on federal charges of possession of a firearm by a felon.

Fulminante was incarcerated in the Ray Brook Federal Correctional Institution in New York. There he became friends with another inmate, Anthony Sarivola, then serving a 60-day sentence for extortion. The two men came to spend several hours a day together. Sarivola, a former police officer, had been involved in loansharking for organized crime but then became a paid informant for the Federal Bureau of Investigation. While at Ray Brook, he masqueraded as an organized crime figure. After becoming friends with Fulminante, Sarivola heard a rumor that Fulminante was suspected of killing a child in Arizona. Sarivola then raised the subject with Fulminante in several conversations, but Fulminante repeatedly denied any involvement in Jeneane's death. During one conversation, he told Sarivola that Jeneane had been killed by bikers looking for drugs; on another occasion, he said he did not know what had happened. Sarivola passed this information on to an agent of the Federal Bureau of Investigation, who instructed Sarivola to find out more.

Sarivola learned more one evening in October 1983, as he and

Fulminante walked together around the prison track. Sarivola said that he knew Fulminante was "starting to get some tough treatment and whatnot" from other inmates because of the rumor. Sarivola offered to protect Fulminante from his fellow inmates, but told him, " 'You have to tell me about it,' you know. I mean, in other words, 'For me to give you any help.' " Fulminante then admitted to Sarivola that he had driven Jeneane to the desert on his motorcycle, where he choked her, sexually assaulted her, and made her beg for her life, before shooting her twice in the head.

Sarivola was released from prison in November 1983. Fulminante was released the following May, only to be arrested the next month for another weapons violation. On September 4, 1984, Fulminante was indicted in Arizona for the first-degree murder of Jeneane.

Prior to trial, Fulminante moved to suppress the statement he had given Sarivola in prison, as well as a second confession he had given to Donna Sarivola, then Anthony Sarivola's fiancee and later his wife, following his May 1984 release from prison. He asserted that the confession to Sarivola was coerced, and that the second confession was the "fruit" of the first. Following the hearing, the trial court denied the motion to suppress, specifically finding that, based on the stipulated facts, the confessions were voluntary. The State introduced both confessions as evidence at trial, and on December 19, 1985, Fulminante was convicted of Jeneane's murder. He was subsequently sentenced to death.

Fulminante appealed. . . . After considering the evidence at trial as well as the stipulated facts before the trial court on the motion to suppress, the Arizona Supreme Court held that the confession was coerced, but initially determined that the admission of the confession at trial was harmless error, because of the overwhelming nature of the evidence against Fulminante. Upon Fulminante's motion for reconsideration, however, the court ruled that this Court's precedent precluded the use of the harmless-error analysis in the case of a coerced confession. The Court therefore reversed the conviction and ordered that Fulminante be retried without the use of the confession to Sarivola. Because of differing views in the state and federal courts over whether the admission at trial of a coerced confession is subject to a harmless-error analysis, we granted the State's petition for certiorari [to call up the case for review]. Although a majority of this Court finds that such a confession is subject to a harmless-error analysis, for the reasons set forth below, we affirm the judgment of the Arizona court.

II

We deal first with the State's contention that the court below [Arizona Supreme Court] erred in holding Fulminante's confession to have been coerced. The State argues that it is the totality of the circumstances that determines whether Fulminante's confession was coerced, but contends that rather than apply this standard, the Arizona court applied a "but for" test, under which the court found that but for the promise given by Sarivola, Fulminante would not have confessed. In support of this argument, the State points to the Arizona court's reference to *Bram* v. *United States* (1897).... [I]t is clear this passage from *Bram,* which under current precedent does not state the standard for determining the voluntariness of a confession, was not relied on by the Arizona court in reaching its conclusion. Rather, the court cited this language as part of a longer quotation from an Arizona case which accurately described the State's burden of proof for establishing voluntariness. Indeed, the Arizona Supreme Court stated that a "determination regarding the voluntariness of a confession ... must be viewed in a totality of the circumstances," and under that standard plainly found that Fulminante's statement to Sarivola had been coerced....

Although the question is a close one, we agree with the Arizona Supreme Court's conclusion that Fulminante's confession was coerced. The Arizona Supreme Court found a credible threat of physical violence unless Fulminante confessed. Our cases have made clear that a finding of coercion need not depend upon actual violence by a government agent; a credible threat is sufficient. As we have said, "coercion can be mental as well as physical, and ... the blood of the accused is not the only hallmark of an unconstitutional inquisition." *Blackburn* v. *Alabama* (1960)....

III

Four of us, JUSTICES MARSHALL, BLACKMUN, STEVENS, and myself, would affirm the judgment of the Arizona Supreme Court on the ground that the harmless-error rule is inapplicable to erroneously admitted coerced confessions. We thus disagree with the Justices who have a contrary view.

The majority today abandons what until now the Court has regarded as the "axiomatic [proposition] that a defendant in a criminal case is deprived of due process of law if his conviction is founded, in whole or in part, upon an involuntary confession, without regard for the truth or falsity of the confession.... The Court has repeatedly stressed that the view that the admission of a coerced confession can be harmless error because of the other evidence to support the verdict is "an impermissible doctrine.".... Today, a majority of the Court, without any justification overrules this vast body of precedent without a word and in so doing dislodges one of the fundamental tenets of our criminal justice system.

In extending to coerced confessions the harmless error rule of *Chapman* v. *California* (1967), the majority declares that because the Court has applied that analysis to numerous other "trial errors," there is no reason that it should not apply to an error of this nature as well. The four of us remain convinced, however, that we should abide by our cases that have refused to apply the harmless error rule to coerced confessions, for a coerced confession is fundamentally different from other types of erroneously admitted evidence to which the rule has been applied....

Chapman specifically noted three constitutional errors that could not be categorized as harmless error: using a coerced confession against a defendant in a criminal trial, depriving a defendant of counsel, and trying a defendant before a biased judge. The majority attempts to distinguish the use of a coerced confession from the other two errors listed in *Chapman* by drawing a meaningless dichotomy between "trial errors" and "structural defects" in the trial process. . . .

This effort fails, for our jurisprudence on harmless error has not classified so neatly the errors at issue. . . .

. . . [P]ermitting a coerced confession to be part of the evidence on which a jury is free to base its verdict of guilty is inconsistent with the thesis that ours is not an inquisitorial system of criminal justice. . . .

The search for truth is indeed central to our system of justice, but "certain constitutional rights are not, and should not be, subject to harmless-error analysis because those rights protect important values that are unrelated to the truth-seeking function of the trial." *Rose* v. *Clark*. The right of a defendant not to have his coerced confession used against him is among those rights. . . .

IV

Since five Justices have determined that harmless error analysis applies to coerced confessions, it becomes necessary to evaluate under that ruling the admissibility of Fulminante's confession to Sarivola. *Chapman* . . . made clear that "before a federal constitutional error can be held harmless, the court must be able to declare a belief that it was harmless beyond a reasonable doubt.". . . In so doing, it must be determined whether the State has met its burden of demonstrating that the admission of the confession to Sarivola did not contribute to Fulminante's conviction. Five of us are of the view that the State has not carried its burden and accordingly affirm the judgment of the court below reversing petitioner's conviction. . . .

First, the transcript discloses that both the trial court and the State recognized that a successful prosecution depended on the jury believing the two confessions. Absent the confessions, it is unlikely that Fulminante would have been prosecuted at all, because the physical evidence from the scene and other circumstantial evidence would have been insufficient to convict. Indeed, no indictment was filed until nearly two years after the murder. Although the police had suspected Fulminante from the beginning, as the prosecutor acknowledged in his opening statement to the jury: "[W]hat brings us to Court, what makes this case fileable, and prosecutable and triable is that later, Mr. Fulminante confesses this crime to Anthony Sarivola and later, to Donna Sarivola, his wife.". . .

Second, the jury's assessment of the confession to Donna Sarivola could easily have depended in large part on the presence of the confession to Anthony Sarivola. Absent the admission at trial of the first confession, the jurors might have found Donna Sarivola's story unbelievable. Fulminante's confession to Donna Sarivola allegedly occurred in May 1984, on the day he was released from Ray Brook, as she and Anthony Sarivola drove Fulminante from New York to Pennsylvania. Donna Sarivola testified that Fulminante, whom she had never before met, confessed in detail about

Jeneane's brutal murder in response to her casual question concerning why he was going to visit friends in Pennsylvania instead of returning to his family in Arizona. Although she testified that she was "disgusted" by Fulminante's disclosures, she stated that she took no steps to notify authorities of what she had learned. In fact, she claimed that she barely discussed the matter with Anthony Sarivola, who was in the car and overheard Fulminante's entire conversation with Donna. Despite her disgust for Fulminante, Donna Sarivola later went on a second trip with him. Although Sarivola informed authorities that he had driven Fulminante to Pennsylvania, he did not mention Donna's presence in the car or her conversation with Fulminante. Only when questioned by authorities in June 1985 did Anthony Sarivola belatedly recall the confession to Donna more than a year before, and only then did he ask if she would be willing to discuss the matter with authorities.

Although some of the details in the confession to Donna Sarivola were corroborated by circumstantial evidence, many, including details that Jeneane was choked and sexually assaulted, were not. . . .

Third, the admission of the first confession led to the admission of other evidence prejudicial to Fulminante. For example, the State introduced evidence that Fulminante knew of Sarivola's connections with organized crime in an attempt to explain why Fulminante would have been motivated to confess to Sarivola in seeking protection. Absent the confession, this evidence would have had no relevance and would have been inadmissible at trial. The Arizona Supreme Court found that the evidence of Sarivola's connections with organized crime reflected on Sarivola's character, not Fulminante's, and noted that the evidence could have been used to impeach Sarivola. This analysis overlooks the fact that had the confession not been admitted, there would have been no reason for Sarivola to testify and thus no need to impeach his testimony. Moreover, we cannot agree that the evidence did not reflect on Fulminante's character as well, for it depicted him as someone who willingly sought out the company of criminals. It is quite possible that this evidence led the jury to view Fulminante as capable of murder.

Finally, although our concern here is with the effect of the erroneous admission of the confession on Fulminante's conviction, it is clear that the presence of the confession also influenced the sentencing phase of the trial. Under Arizona law, the trial judge is the sentencer. At the sentencing hearing, the admissibility of information regarding aggravating circumstances is governed by the rules of evidence applicable to criminal trials. § 13-703(C). In this case, "based upon admissible evidence produced at the trial," the judge found that only one aggravating circumstance existed beyond a reasonable doubt, *i.e.*, that the murder was committed in "an *especially* heinous, cruel, and depraved manner." In reaching this conclusion, the judge relied heavily on evidence concerning the manner of the killing and Fulminante's motives and state of mind which could only be found in the two confessions. . . .

Because a majority of the Court has determined that Fulminante's confession to Anthony Sarivola was coerced and because a majority has determined that admitting this confession was not harmless beyond a reasonable doubt, we agree with the Arizona Supreme Court's conclusion that Fulminante is entitled to a new trial at which the confession is not admitted. Accordingly the judgment of the Arizona Supreme Court is

Affirmed.

Chief Justice REHNQUIST, with whom Justice O'CONNOR joins, Justice KENNEDY and Justice SOUTER join as to Parts I and II, and Justice SCALIA joins as to Parts II and III, delivering the opinion of the Court as to Part II, and dissenting as to Parts I and III.

The Court today properly concludes that the admission of an "involuntary" confession at trial is subject to harmless error analysis. Nonetheless, the independent review of the record which we are required to make shows that respondent Fulminante's confession was not in fact involuntary. And even if the confession were deemed to be involuntary, the evidence offered at trial, including a second, untainted confession by Fulminante, supports the conclusion that any error here was certainly harmless.

I

... The admissibility of a confession such as that made by respondent Fulminante depends upon whether it was voluntarily made. ...

The Supreme Court of Arizona stated that the trial court committed no error in finding the confession voluntary based on the record before it. But it overturned the trial court's finding of voluntariness based on the more comprehensive trial record before it, which included, in addition to the facts stipulated at the suppression hearing, a statement made by Sarivola at the trial that "the defendant had been receiving 'rough treatment from the guys, and if the defendant would tell the truth, he could be protected.' " ...

... I am at a loss to see how the Supreme Court of Arizona reached the conclusion that it did. Fulminante offered no evidence that he believed that his life was in danger or that he in fact confessed to Sarivola in order to obtain the proffered protection. Indeed, he had stipulated that "[a]t no time did the defendant indicate he was in fear of other inmates nor did he ever seek Mr. Sarivola's 'protection.' " Sarivola's testimony that he told Fulminante that "if [he] would tell the truth, he could be protected," adds little if anything to the substance of the parties' stipulation. ... The fact that Sarivola was a government informant does not by itself render Fulminante's confession involuntary, since we have consistently accepted the use of informants in the discovery of evidence of a crime as a legitimate investigatory procedure consistent with the Constitution. The conversations between Sarivola and Fulminante were not lengthy, and the defendant was free at all times to leave Sarivola's company. Sarivola at no time threatened him or demanded that he confess; he simply requested that he speak the truth about the matter. Fulminante was an experienced habitue of prisons, and presumably able to fend for himself. In concluding on these facts that Fulminante's confession was involuntary, the Court today embraces a more expansive definition of that term than is warranted by any of our decided cases.

II

Since this Court's landmark decision in *Chapman* ... in which we adopted the general rule that a constitutional error does not automatically require reversal of a conviction, the Court has applied harmless error analysis to a wide range of errors and has recognized that most constitutional errors can be harmless....

The common thread connecting these cases is that each involved "trial error"—error which occurred during the presentation of the case to the jury, and which may therefore be quantitatively assessed in the context of other evidence presented in order to determine whether its admission was harmless beyond a reasonable doubt. In applying harmless-error analysis to these many different constitutional violations, the Court has been faithful to the belief that the harmless-error doctrine is essential to preserve the "principle that the central purpose of a criminal trial is to decide the factual question of the defendant's guilt or innocence, and promotes public respect for the criminal process by focusing on the underlying fairness of the trial rather than on the virtually inevitable presence of immaterial error." ...

It is evident from a comparison of the constitutional violations which we have held subject to harmless error, and those which we have held not, that involuntary statements or confessions belong in the former category. The admission of an involuntary confession is a "trial error," similar in both degree and kind to the erroneous admission of other types of evidence. The evidentiary impact of an involuntary confession, and its effect upon the composition of the record, is indistinguishable from that of a confession obtained in violation of the Sixth Amendment ... or of a prosecutor's improper comment on a defendant's silence at trial.... When reviewing the erroneous admission of an involuntary confession, the appellate court, as it does with the admission of other forms of improperly admitted evidence, simply reviews the remainder of the evidence against the defendant to determine whether the admission of the confession was harmless beyond a reasonable doubt.

Nor can it be said that the admission of an involuntary confession is the type of error which "transcends the criminal process." This Court has applied harmless-error analysis to the violation of other constitutional rights similar in magnitude and importance and involving the same level of police misconduct. For instance, we have previously held that the admission of a defendant's statements obtained in violation of the Sixth Amendment is subject to harmless-error analysis....

Of course an involuntary confession may have a more dramatic effect on the course of a trial than do other trial errors—in particular cases it may be devastating to a defendant—but this simply means that a reviewing court will conclude in such a case that its admission was not harmless error; it is not a reason for eschewing the harmless error test entirely....

III

I would agree with the finding of the Supreme Court of Arizona in its initial opinion—in which it believed harmless-error analysis was applicable to the admission of involuntary confessions—that the admission of Fulminante's confession was harmless. Indeed, this seems to me to be a classic case of harmless error: a second confession giving more details of the crime than the first was admitted in evidence and found to be free of any constitutional objection. Accordingly, I would affirm the holding of the Supreme Court of Arizona in its initial opinion, and reverse the judgment which it ultimately rendered in this case.

Justice KENNEDY, concurring in the judgment.

For the reasons stated by The Chief Justice, I agree that Fulminante's confession to Anthony Sarivola was not coerced. In my view, the trial court did not err in admitting this testimony. A majority of the Court, however, finds the confession coerced and proceeds to consider whether harmless-error analysis may be used when a coerced confession has been admitted at trial.... For the reasons given by Justice WHITE in Part IV of his opinion, I cannot with confidence find admission of Fulminante's confession to Anthony Sarivola to be harmless error....

In the interests of providing a clear mandate to the Arizona Supreme Court in this capital case, I deem it proper to accept in the case now before us the holding of five Justices that the confession was coerced and inadmissible. I agree with a majority of the Court that admission of the confession could not be harmless error when viewed in light of all the other evidence; and so I concur in the judgment to affirm the ruling of the Arizona Supreme Court.

REAGAN ON GUN CONTROL
March 28, 1991

Ronald Reagan, a foe of federal gun control proposals during his presidency, declared his support for legislation before Congress to require a seven-day waiting period for the purchase of a handgun so that a background check of the buyer could be administered. Reagan's turn-about in favor of a gun control measure was voiced March 28 at a George Washington University convocation marking the tenth anniversary of an attempt on Reagan's life and his recovery at the university's hospital.

Outside the Washington Hilton Hotel on March 30, 1981, John W. Hinckley, Jr., wounded Reagan, White House press secretary James Brady, Secret Service agent Timothy J. McCarthy, and D.C. policeman Thomas Delahanty. Hinckley had a history of mental illness but easily bought his gun in Texas after giving false information on a gun-registration form. In 1991 all fifty states and the District of Columbia had some restrictions on public access to certain firearms. Seventeen states required a waiting period for obtaining handguns. But gun control advocates argued that many of those laws were weak; and even stringent laws could be circumvented if the purchaser went to a neighboring state with few or no restrictions.

Backers of federal legislation insisted that, if applied effectively nationwide, the waiting period would reduce firearm violence. By preliminary calculations, 23,220 murders were committed in America during 1990, breaking the previous record of 20,040 in 1980. Most of these homicides were committed with firearms, principally handguns. In many big cities, 1990 was merely the latest in a series of record-breaking years for firearms violence.

Reagan's Change of Heart

After the assassination attempt, Reagan continued to say that he viewed gun control laws as unenforceable. The emphasis on crime control should be elsewhere, he insisted. Before leaving office in January 1989 Reagan did endorse the idea of waiting periods for gun purchases but he thought the states should decide, not the federal government.

Addressing the convocation, at which Reagan and his wife Nancy were awarded honorary degrees, he readily acknowledged his membership in the National Rifle Association (NRA), a powerful foe of gun control. "My position on the right to bear arms is well known," the former president told his audience of physicians, hospital staff members, and others. But he added that "with the right to bear arms comes a great responsibility to use caution and common sense on handgun purchases."

Reagan urged Congress "without further delay" to pass the waiting-period legislation, known informally as the Brady bill. Brady has been left permanently disabled by his wounds. He and his wife, Sarah, became crusaders for Gun Control Inc., the nation's biggest and best-known lobbying organization of its kind.

Role in Brady Bill Passage

In 1988 a similar bill on which the Reagan White House took no position was rejected by the House of Representatives. And in 1990 another Brady bill was sidetracked before it reached the House floor for a vote. The outcome was different in 1991. On May 8, by a 239-186 vote, the House passed a package of anti-crime measures that included provisions for a seven-day waiting period for the purchase of a handgun.

As required by the House bill, handgun dealers would have to send police a sworn statement from a buyer saying that he or she was not a felon, drug addict, or mentally ill. The police could then check the buyer's background and determine if the purchase was legal. However, the police were not required to make the checks. At present, purchasers already had to swear to such statements, but they remained with the dealer. Although the lack of a mandatory police check in the Brady bill was a compromise to obtain enough votes for passage, its supporters called it a modest step toward keeping handguns from dangerous criminals.

Gun control activists said that Reagan's endorsement had helped them persuade some wavering House members to support the bill. There was also press speculation that Reagan's new position enabled President George Bush, also an NRA member, to relax his opposition to the measure. Immediately after Reagan spoke, he called on his successor at the White House. The next day Bush let it be known that he might be willing to sign the Brady bill if Congress accepted anti-crime proposals the administration wanted. These included invoking the death penalty for a number of crimes to which it did not then apply, and limiting the court appeals that could be filed by inmates awaiting execution. Those *provisions were included in the House-passed legislation.*

The size of the House vote, 239-186, encouraged the Senate to pass a similar measure June 28, 67-32. The Senate bill decreed a five-day waiting period during the next two and a half years and after that an instantaneous check. Differences in the two bills required a conference committee from the two chambers to come up with a compromise both could accept. That action was expected sometime after Congress returned from its August recess.

Following are excerpts from remarks by former president Ronald Reagan at a George Washington University convocation March 28, 1991:

I am deeply humbled and honored to be recognized by the George Washington University in this way. After all the time I spent with G.W. doctors, it seems fitting that I've now become one! And I am so flattered that you would name the Institute of Emergency Medicine for me. This is one of our country's true treasures and I know from personal experience how important it is, not only because of the events of 10 years ago. . . .

This University is part of history, many of your faculty and students have been key players in this town for decades. Our Administration borrowed heavily from your talented family and I will always be grateful for that. All of you should be proud of the contribution G.W. is making to America.

I want you to know how much it means to me that you would honor Nancy, too. There are no words to describe what she means to me and it makes me so proud to know that there will be a plaque in the emergency room to pay tribute to her and to help others who find themselves as she did that day 10 years ago.

For me it was easy—I just got on the gurney and let the wonderfully talented and dedicated people at the George Washington University Hospital do what they do best. But for Nancy, it was the greatest challenge of her life. To get the word that there had been a shooting, to have been told that I was OK, to rush to the hospital and then be told that not only was I not OK, but that my life was in great danger; then the waiting and worrying and yes, the praying—I can't even begin to imagine what it must have been like for her. But she held up. She was there at my side every moment—a source, as your plaque so eloquently states, of great comfort and strength. I couldn't have made it without her, and so I thank you from the bottom of my heart for recognizing her in this way.

It's hard to believe that a decade has passed since our lives came together in a way none of us could have ever imagined. You have all been told what happened on March 30, 1981. A seemingly routine public appearance came perilously close to being a very dark chapter in history.

But the people at the George Washington Hospital would have none of that. With no warning or time to get ready, they got the call—the one they had practiced for and thought about, but probably never expected would ever come—and made history. With speed, precision and unmatched skill, they did what they do best. I do not think it is an exaggeration to say that the Good Lord was looking out for Jim Brady, Tim McCarthy and me when he delivered us to the doors of G.W. Hospital. We were healed here and allowed to carry on. For that, we will always be grateful. And speaking of Jim Brady, I want to tell all of you here today something I'm not sure you know. You do know that I'm a member of the N.R.A. [National Rifle Association] and my position on the right to bear arms is well known. But I want you to know something else, and I am going to say it in clear, unmistakable language: I support the Brady Bill and I urge the Congress to enact it without further delay. With the right to bear arms comes a great responsibility to use caution and common sense on handgun purchases. And it's just plain common sense that there be a waiting period to allow local law enforcement officials to conduct background checks on those who wish to buy a handgun. The Brady Bill is good legislation and I hope my colleagues at the other end of Pennsylvania Avenue will do what's right for the people and that means enacting this Bill.

And I couldn't mention this Bill without adding a special word about its most dedicated supporter, Sarah Brady. Nancy [Reagan] and I have the greatest respect and affection for Sarah, who is not only an effective and articulate advocate, but an inspiring woman who we are honored to call our friend. . . .

My young friends, savor these moments. Keep the memories close to your heart. Cherish your family and friends. As I learned 10 years ago, we never really know what the future will bring. . . .

April

UN PEACE TERMS;
IRAQ'S ACCEPTANCE
April 3 and 6, 1991

The United Nations Security Council on April 3 dictated stringent peace terms to Iraq, which it grudgingly accepted three days later. Iraq's acceptance activated a "permanent" cease-fire and formally ended the Persian Gulf War. A temporary cease-fire, in effect since February 28, had silenced the desert battlefields in southern Iraq, where much of Saddam Hussein's army lay in ruins. A multinational military force, operating under UN auspices and U.S. leadership, had swiftly driven his army out of Kuwait, ending an occupation that began with Iraq's seizure of that small, oil-rich kingdom August 2, 1990. (Victory in the Gulf, p. 97)

However, internal hostilities continued in Iraq for weeks after the war had ended. Surviving units of the Iraqi army fought and suppressed rebellious Shiite Moslems in the south and minority Kurds in the north. Thousands of Kurds and Shiites died in the fighting. By the end of March massive numbers of Kurdish refugees—possibly as many as 2 million—were fleeing into Turkey and Iran, where they were confined to makeshift border camps on cold, barren mountainsides. Hunger was prevalent and disease took a heavy toll.

The Kurdish plight drew world attention and, by April 16, compelled President George Bush to overcome his earlier refusal to intervene in their behalf. But this time military intervention was for humanitarian purposes. Helicopters brought in food, clothing, and other necessities; international medical teams flew in to treat the ill, and soldiers rigged up sanitary facilities and communications networks.

Gradually the refugees were persuaded to go, under allied military escort, to "safe zones" that the UN declared in northern Iraq over objections from Baghdad. By June 1 all the border camps were closed and a specially formed UN security police force was beginning to supplant the approximately 20,000 soldiers from the United States and eight allied nations protecting the Kurds.

Key Peace Terms

The Kurdish and Shiite uprisings were not addressed in the peace terms, as set forth in Resolution 687, approved by the Security Council on April 3. However, they did require the creation of a zone nine miles wide along the Iraq-Kuwait border that would be monitored by a UN observer force. In all, the 4,000-word document, the longest ever drawn by the Security Council, laid out a lengthy list of conditions for Iraq to meet.

Among the key terms, Iraq was required to pay billions of dollars in compensation for damages caused by its invasion of Kuwait; accept borders with Kuwait that it renounced before the invasion; destroy and pledge not to reacquire ballistics missiles, nuclear materials, and chemical and biological weapons, and give up terrorist activities.

As those obligations were met in accordance with a Security Council timetable, that body would gradually lift the trade embargo and other economic sanctions it had imposed in August and September 1990. (UN Action Against Iraq, Historic Documents of 1990, p. 545) *Iraq's once-booming oil exports, the country's chief source of foreign earnings, had virtually disappeared. So had most of its imports, including many foods and everyday items, causing severe shortages.* (UN Report on Postwar Iraq, p. 165)

Iraq's Hidden Weapons

Iraqi Foreign Minister Ahmed Hussein, in an official response to the UN demands, wrote Secretary General Javier Perez de Cuellar that his country "has no choice but to accept this resolution." He called the peace terms "unjust" and "vengeful" and accused the Security Council of being an American "puppet."

The level of discourse did not improve in the following months. On May 17 Iraq agreed to let an international commission inspect its military and scientific installations. But inspectors were denied entry to several facilities, and on June 28 Bush accused Hussein of violating the cease-fire by trying to hide the full extent of Iraq's advanced weapons development. He hinted that the allies might bomb sites that the Iraqis refused to open.

Rolf Ekeus, head of a special UN commission in charge of the inspections, said July 3 that his inspectors had found four times more chemical weapons than Iran admitted having. Five days later the Iraqi government, feeling international pressure and perhaps a threat of renewed bombing, submitted a list of nuclear sites and materials that it had not revealed earlier. It also admitted to running three secret programs to enrich uranium for the manufacture of nuclear bombs.

That information startled many Western specialists, who concluded that Iraq was further advanced than they realized in its efforts to build a nuclear bomb. In August it was disclosed that Iraqi officials had conceded to UN investigators that the country had conducted biological warfare research. Iraq had insisted in its April 6 response to the peace terms that it did not possess "any biological weapons or related items," and that biological research was for purely peaceful purposes.

Following are excerpts from Resolution 687, approved by the UN Security Council, April 3, 1991, setting forth peace terms for Iraq, and from the acceptance statement of Foreign Minister Ahmed Hussein on behalf of the Iraqi government, submitted to UN officials April 6, 1991:

RESOLUTION 687 (1991)

Adopted by the Security Council at its 2981st meeting, on 3 April 1991

The Security Council,

Recalling its resolutions 660 (1990) of 2 August 1990, 661 (1990) of 6 August 1990, 662 (1990) of 9 August 1990, 664 (1990) of 18 August 1990, 665 (1990) of 25 August 1990, 666 (1990) of 13 September 1990, 667 (1990) of 16 September 1990, 669 (1990) of 24 September 1990, 670 (1990) of 25 September 1990, 674 (1990) of 29 October 1990, 677 (1990) of 28 November 1990, 678 (1990) of 29 November 1990 and 686 (1991) of 2 March 1991. . . .

1. *Affirms* all thirteen resolutions noted above, except as expressly changed below to achieve the goals of this resolution, including a formal cease-fire;

A

2. *Demands* that Iraq and Kuwait respect the inviolability of the international boundary and the allocation of islands set out in the "Agreed Minutes Between the State of Kuwait and the Republic of Iraq Regarding the Restoration of Friendly Relations, Recognition and Related Matters", signed by them in the exercise of their sovereignty at Baghdad on 4 October 1963 and registered with the United Nations and published by the United Nations in document 7063, United Nations, *Treaty Series*, 1964;

3. *Calls upon* the Secretary-General to lend his assistance to make arrangements with Iraq and Kuwait to demarcate the boundary between Iraq and Kuwait. . . .

4. *Decides* to guarantee the inviolability of the above-mentioned international boundary and to take as appropriate all necessary measures to that end in accordance with the Charter of the United Nations;

B

5. *Requests* the Secretary-General, after consulting with Iraq and Kuwait, to submit within three days to the Security Council for its approval a

plan for the immediate deployment of a United Nations observer unit to monitor the Khor Abdullah and a demilitarized zone, which is hereby established, extending ten kilometres into Iraq and five kilometres into Kuwait from the boundary. . . .

6. *Notes* that as soon as the Secretary-General notifies the Security Council of the completion of the deployment of the United Nations observer unit, the conditions will be established for the Member States cooperating with Kuwait in accordance with resolution 678 (1990) to bring their military presence in Iraq to an end consistent with resolution 686 (1991);

C

7. *Invites* Iraq to reaffirm unconditionally its obligations under the Geneva Protocol for the Prohibition of the Use in War of Asphyxiating, Poisonous or Other Gases, and of Bacteriological Methods of Warfare, signed at Geneva on 17 June 1925, and to ratify the Convention on the Prohibition of the Development, Production and Stockpiling of Bacteriological (Biological) and Toxin Weapons and on Their Destruction, of 10 April 1972;

8. *Decides* that Iraq shall unconditionally accept the destruction, removal, or rendering harmless, under international supervision, of:

(a) All chemical and biological weapons and all stocks of agents and all related subsystems and components and all research, development, support and manufacturing facilities;

(b) All ballistic missiles with a range greater than 150 kilometres and related major parts, and repair and production facilities;

9. *Decides*, for the implementation of paragraph 8 above, the following:

(a) Iraq shall submit to the Secretary-General, within fifteen days of the adoption of the present resolution, a declaration of the locations, amounts and types of all items specified in paragraph 8 and agree to urgent, on-site inspection as specified below;

(b) The Secretary-General, in consultation with the appropriate Governments and, where appropriate, with the Director-General of the World Health Organization, within forty-five days of the passage of the present resolution, shall develop, and submit to the Council for approval, a plan calling for the completion of the following acts within forty-five days of such approval:

  (i) The forming of Special Commission, which shall carry out immediate on-site inspection of Iraq's biological, chemical and missile capabilities. . . .

  (ii) The yielding by Iraq of possession to the Special Commission for destruction, removal or rendering harmless . . . of all items specified under paragraph 8 (a) above . . . and the destruction by Iraq, under the supervision of the Special Commission, of all its missile capabilities, including launchers, as specified under paragraph 8

(b) above;

(iii) The provision by the Special Commission of the Assistance and cooperation to the Director-General of the International Atomic Energy Agency required in paragraphs 12 and 13 below;

10. *Decides* that Iraq shall unconditionally undertake not to use, develop, construct or acquire any of the items specified in paragraphs 8 and 9 above and requests the Secretary-General, in consultation with the Special Commission, to develop a plan for the future ongoing monitoring and verification of Iraq's compliance with this paragraph, to be submitted to the Security Council for approval within one hundred and twenty days of the passage of this resolution;

11. *Invites* Iraq to reaffirm unconditionally its obligations under the Treaty on the Non-Proliferation of Nuclear Weapons of 1 July 1968;

12. *Decides* that Iraq shall unconditionally agree not to acquire or develop nuclear weapons or nuclear-weapons-usable material or any subsystems or components or any research, development, support or manufacturing facilities related to the above; to submit to the Secretary-General and the Director-General of the International Atomic Energy Agency within fifteen days of the adoption of the present resolution a declaration of the locations, amounts, and types of all items specified above; to place all of its nuclear-weapons-usable materials under the exclusive control, for custody and removal, of the International Atomic Energy Agency, with the assistance and cooperation of the Special Commission as provided for in the plan of the Secretary-General discussed in paragraph 9 (b) above; to accept, in accordance with the arrangements provided for in paragraph 13 below, urgent on-site inspection and the destruction, removal or rendering harmless as appropriate of all items specified above; and to accept the plan discussed in paragraph 13 below for the future ongoing monitoring and verification of its compliance with these undertakings;

13. *Requests* the Director-General of the International Atomic Energy Agency ... to carry out immediate on-site inspection of Iraq's nuclear capabilities based on Iraq's declarations and the designation of any additional locations by the Special Commission; to develop a plan for submission to the Security Council within forty-five days calling for the destruction, removal, or rendering harmless as appropriate of all items listed in paragraph 12 above; to carry out the plan within forty-five days following approval by the Security Council; and to develop a plan ... for the future ongoing monitoring and verification of Iraq's compliance with paragraph 12 above ... to be submitted to the Security Council for approval within one hundred and twenty days of the passage of the present resolution;

14. *Takes note* that the actions to be taken by Iraq in paragraphs 8, 9, 10, 11, 12 and 13 of the present resolution represent steps towards the goal of establishing in the Middle East a zone free from weapons of mass destruction and all missiles for their delivery and the objective of a global ban on chemical weapons;

D

15. *Requests* the Secretary-General to report to the Security Council on the steps taken to facilitate the return of all Kuwaiti property seized by Iraq, including a list of any property that Kuwait claims has not been returned or which has not been returned intact;

E

16. *Reaffirms* that Iraq ... is liable under international law for any direct loss, damage, including environmental damage and the depletion of natural resources, or injury to foreign Governments, nationals and corporations, as a result of Iraq's unlawful invasion and occupation of Kuwait;

17. *Decides* that all Iraqi statements made since 2 August 1990 repudiating its foreign debt are null and void, and demands that Iraq adhere scrupulously to all of its obligations concerning servicing and repayment of its foreign debt;

18. *Decides also* to create a fund to pay compensation for claims that fall within paragraph 16 above and to establish a Commission that will administer the fund;

19. *Directs* the Secretary-General to develop and present to the Security Council for decision, no later than thirty days following the adoption of the present resolution, recommendations for the fund to meet the requirement for the payment of claims established in accordance with paragraph 18 above and for a programme to implement the decisions in paragraphs 16, 17 and 18 above, including: administration of the fund; mechanisms for determining the appropriate level of Iraq's contribution to the fund based on a percentage of the value of the exports of petroleum and petroleum products from Iraq not to exceed a figure to be suggested to the Council by the Secretary-General, taking into account the requirements of the people of Iraq, Iraq's payment capacity as assessed in conjunction with the international financial institutions taking into consideration external debt service, and the needs of the Iraqi economy; arrangements for ensuring that payments are made to the fund; the process by which funds will be allocated and claims paid; appropriate procedures for evaluating losses, listing claims and verifying their validity and resolving disputed claims. . . .

F

20. *Decides,* effective immediately, that the prohibitions against the sale or supply to Iraq of commodities or products, other than medicine and health supplies, and prohibitions against financial transactions related thereto contained in resolution 661 (1990) shall not apply to foodstuffs notified to the Security Council Committee established by resolution 661 (1990) concerning the situation between Iraq and Kuwait or, with the approval of that Committee, under the simplified and accelerated "no-objection" procedure, to materials and supplies for essential civilian needs as identified in the report of the Secretary-General dated 20 March 1991,

and in any further findings of humanitarian need by the Committee;

21. *Decides* that the Security Council shall review the provisions of paragraph 20 above every sixty days in the light of the policies and practices of the Government of Iraq, including the implementation of all relevant resolutions of the Security Council, for the purpose of determining whether to reduce or lift the prohibitions referred to therein;

22. *Decides* that upon the approval by the Security Council of the programme called for in paragraph 19 above and upon Council agreement that Iraq has completed all actions contemplated in paragraphs 8, 9, 10, 11, 12 and 13 above, the prohibitions against the import of commodities and products originating in Iraq and the prohibitions against financial transactions related thereto contained in resolution 661 (1990) shall have no further force or effect;

23. *Decides* that, pending action by the Security Council under paragraph 22 above, the Security Council Committee established by resolution 661 (1990) shall be empowered to approve, when required to assure adequate financial resources on the part of Iraq to carry out the activities under paragraph 20 above, exceptions to the prohibition against the import of commodities and products originating in Iraq;

24. *Decides* that, in accordance with resolution 661 (1990) and subsequent related resolutions and until a further decision is taken by the Security Council, all States shall continue to prevent the sale or supply, or the promotion or facilitation of such sale or supply, to Iraq by their nationals, or from their territories or using their flag vessels or aircraft, of:

(a) Arms and related *matériel* of all types, specifically including the sale or transfer through other means of all forms of conventional military equipment, including for paramilitary forces, and spare parts and components and their means of production, for such equipment;

(b) Items specified and defined in paragraphs 8 and 12 above not otherwise covered above;

(c) Technology under licensing or other transfer arrangements used in the production, utilization or stockpiling of items specified in subparagraphs (a) and (b) above;

(d) Personnel or materials for training or technical support services relating to the design, development, manufacture, use, maintenance or support of items specified in subparagraphs (a) and (b) above;

25. *Calls upon* all States and international organizations to act strictly in accordance with paragraph 24 above, notwithstanding the existence of any contracts, agreements, licenses or any other arrangements;

26. *Requests* the Secretary-General, in consultation with appropriate Governments, to develop within sixty days, for the approval of the Security Council, guidelines to facilitate full international implementation of paragraphs 24 and 25 above and paragraph 27 below, and to make them available to all States and to establish a procedure for updating these guidelines periodically;

27. *Calls upon* all States to maintain such national controls and procedures and to take such other actions consistent with the guidelines to

be established by the Security Council under paragraph 26 above as may be necessary to ensure compliance with the terms of paragraph 24 above, and calls upon international organizations to take all appropriate steps to assist in ensuring such full compliance;

28. *Agrees* to review its decisions in paragraphs 22, 23, 24 and 25 above, except for the items specified and defined in paragraphs 8 and 12 above, on a regular basis and in any case one hundred and twenty days following passage of the present resolution, taking into account Iraq's compliance with the resolution and general progress towards the control of armaments in the region;

29. *Decides* that all States, including Iraq, shall take the necessary measures to ensure that no claim shall lie at the instance of the Government of Iraq, or of any person or body in Iraq, or of any person claiming through or for the benefit of any such person or body, in connection with any contract or other transaction where its performance was affected by reason of the measures taken by the Security Council in resolution 661 (1990) and related resolutions;

G

30. *Decides* that, in furtherance of its commitment to facilitate the repatriation of all Kuwaiti and third country nationals, Iraq shall extend all necessary cooperation to the International Committee of the Red Cross, providing lists of such persons, facilitating the access of the International Committee of the Red Cross to all such persons wherever located or detained and facilitating the search by the International Committee of the Red Cross for those Kuwaiti and third country nationals still unaccounted for;

31. *Invites* the International Committee of the Red Cross to keep the Secretary-General apprised as appropriate of all activities undertaken in connection with facilitating the repatriation or return of all Kuwaiti and third country nationals or their remains present in Iraq on or after 2 August 1990;

H

32. *Requires* Iraq to inform the Security Council that it will not commit or support any act of international terrorism or allow any organization directed towards commission of such acts to operate within its territory and to condemn unequivocally and renounce all acts, methods and practices of terrorism;

I

33. *Declares* that, upon official notification by Iraq to the Secretary-General and to the Security Council of its acceptance of the provisions above, a formal cease-fire is effective between Iraq and Kuwait and the Member States cooperating with Kuwait in accordance with resolution 678 (1990);

34. *Decides* to remain seized of the matter and to take such further

steps as may be required for the implementation of the present resolution and to secure peace and security in the area.

IRAQ'S REPLY

I have the honour to inform you that the Iraqi Government has taken note of the text of Security Council resolution 687 (1991), the authors of which are the first to recognize that it is unprecedented in the annals of the Organization. . . .

I. While in its preamble the resolution reaffirms that Iraq is an independent sovereign State, the fact remains that a good number of its iniquitous provisions impair that sovereignty. In fact, the resolution constitutes an unprecedented assault on the sovereignty, and the rights that stem therefrom, embodied in the Charter and in international law and practice. For example, where the question of boundaries is concerned, the Security Council has determined in advance the boundary between Iraq and Kuwait. And yet it is well known . . . that in international relations boundary issues must be the subject of an agreement between States, since this is the only basis capable of guaranteeing the stability of frontiers.

Moreover, the resolution fails to take into account Iraq's view, which is well known to the Council, that the provisions relating to the boundary between Iraq and Kuwait . . . have not yet been subjected to the constitutional procedures required for ratification of . . . the legislative branch and the President of Iraq, thus leaving the question of the boundary pending and unresolved. . . . By acting in this strange manner, the Council itself has also violated one of the provisions of resolution 660, which served as the basis for its subsequent resolutions. In its paragraph 3, resolution 660 calls upon Iraq and Kuwait to resolve their differences through negotiation. . . . Where the question of the boundary is concerned, the Council resolution is an iniquitous resolution which constitutes a dangerous precedent, a first in the annals of the international Organization and as some impartial members of the Council indicated in their statements when the resolution was voted on—an assault on the sovereignty of States.

It is also to be noted that the United States of America—the author of the draft resolution on which resolution 687, which imposes a solution to the boundary-related and other differences between Iraq and Kuwait, was based, refuses to impose any solution whatsoever on its ally, Israel, in accordance with conventions, United Nations resolutions and international law.

Furthermore, the United States of America is preventing the Security Council from assuming the responsibilities incumbent upon it with respect to the Arab-Zionist conflict, the Israeli policy of annexation of the occupied Arab territories, the establishment of settlements, the displacement of populations and the disregard for the rights of the Palestinian people and the neighbouring Arab countries, by vetoing any draft resolution approved by the remaining members of the Council, for the simple reason that Israel does not want a resolution which favours a just settlement of the conflict.

II. Iraq's position with regard to the prohibition of chemical and bacteriological weapons is clear. It is indeed a party to the Protocol for the Prohibition of the Use in War of Asphyxiating, Poisonous or Other Gases, and of Bacteriological Methods of Warfare, signed at Geneva in 1925. In a statement issued in September 1988, Iraq reiterated its attachment and adherence to the provisions of that Protocol. It also participated in the Conference of States Parties to the 1925 Geneva Protocol and Other Interested States, held at Paris from 7 to 11 January 1989, and signed the Declaration issued by the participating States. On that occasion, Iraq took a position which was unanimously shared by all the Arab countries, namely that all weapons of mass destruction, including nuclear weapons, must be eliminated from the Middle East region.

Iraq is also a party to the Treaty on the Non-Proliferation of Nuclear Weapons, of 1 July 1968. As the many reports of the International Atomic Energy Agency confirm, it is applying all the provisions of the Treaty. The Security Council resolution obliges only Iraq, and it alone, to undertake the destruction of the non-conventional weapons left to it after the heavy destruction inflicted both on these weapons and on the related installations by the military operations launched against Iraq by the 30 countries of the coalition. It does not deprive the other countries of the region, particularly Israel, of the right to possess weapons of this type, including nuclear weapons. Moreover, the Council has ignored its resolution 487 (1981), which calls on Israel to place all its nuclear facilities under international safeguards, and has not sought to ensure the implementation of that resolution in the same way as it is now seeking to impose the position it has taken against Iraq. It is thus clear that a double standard is being applied with respect to the elimination of weapons of mass destruction in the region, and an attempt being made to disrupt the military balance there, and this is, all the more apparent in that Iraq has not had recourse to weapons of this type.

The application of this provision of the resolution cannot but seriously endanger the regional balance, as indeed was confirmed by certain impartial members of the Security Council in their statements when the resolution was voted upon. There can be no doubt that Israel, an expansionist aggressor country which is occupying the territory of neighbouring countries, usurping the right of the Palestinian Arab people against which it daily commits the most horrible atrocities, and refusing to comply with the resolutions of the Security Council, which it holds in contempt, as well as all the resolutions of the international Organization, will be the first to benefit from this imbalance.

Whereas the resolution emphasizes the importance of all States adhering to the Convention on the Prohibition of the Development, Production and Stockpiling of Bacteriological (Biological) and Toxin Weapons, of a Convention on the Universal Prohibition of Chemical Weapons being drafted and of universal adherence thereto, it makes no mention whatsoever of the importance of universal adherence to the convention banning nuclear weapons or of the drafting of a convention on the universal prohibition of such weapons in the region. . . .

Proof of the resolution's biased and iniquitous nature is afforded by the Council's use of what it terms unprovoked attacks using ballistic missiles as grounds for calling for the destruction of all ballistic missiles with a range greater than 150 kilometres and of all repair and production facilities. The term unprovoked attacks is used of attacks against Israel, a country which itself launched an unprovoked attack in 1981, destroying Iraqi nuclear installations which were used for peaceful purposes and were under international safeguards. . . .

III. Furthermore, Iraq's internal and external security has been and remains seriously threatened, in that continuing efforts are being made to interfere, by force of arms, in the country's internal affairs. Thus the measures taken by the Council against Iraq to deprive it of its lawful right to acquire weapons and military *matériel* for defence directly contribute to the intensification of these threats and to the destabilization of Iraq, thus endangering the country's internal and external security and hence peace, security and stability throughout the region.

IV. Whereas the Council resolution provides for mechanisms for obtaining redress from Iraq, it makes no reference to Iraq's rights to claim redress for the considerable losses it sustained and the massive destruction inflicted on civilian installations and infrastructures as a result of the abusive implementation of resolution 678 (1990). . . . The Council has not explained to world public opinion and the conscience of mankind what the relationship is between its resolution 678 and the deliberate destruction of Iraq's infrastructure—generating stations, water distribution networks, irrigation dams, civilian bridges, telephone exchanges, factories producing powdered milk for infants and medicines, shelters, mosques, churches, commercial centres, residential neighbourhoods, etc. . . .

Further evidence of the resolution's biased and iniquitous nature is that it holds Iraq liable for environmental damage and the depletion of natural resources, although this liability has not been established; on the other hand, it makes no mention of Iraq's own right to obtain compensation for the established facts of damage to its environment and depletion of its natural resources as a result of more than 88,000 tons of explosives, or for the destruction of water distribution networks, generating stations and the road network, which has spread disease and epidemics and caused serious harm to the environment.

These provisions partake of a desire to exact vengeance and cause harm, not to give effect to the relevant provisions of international law. The direct concrete consequences of their implementation will affect the potential and resources of millions of Iraqis, and deprive them of the right to live in dignity.

V. After imposing compulsory and universal sanctions against Iraq by adopting resolution 661 (1990) in consequence, according to it, of Iraq's refusal to comply with the provisions of resolution 660 (1990), the Council has maintained most of them in force despite Iraq's acceptance of all the Council's resolutions and the implementation of a good number of their provisions. . . .

VI. The Council does not deal clearly and directly with the question of withdrawal of the foreign forces occupying part of Iraqi territory, although the resolution declares a formal cease-fire.

The very conditions invoked in support of the declaration of a formal cease-fire also necessitate the withdrawal. The fact that the withdrawal is not explicitly mentioned is tantamount to authorizing the occupation of Iraqi territory for a period whose duration is at the discretion of the occupying countries, which make no secret of their intention to exploit the occupation for political purposes and to make use of it as a trump card in their hand. This position on the part of the Council constitutes a flagrant violation of Iraq's sovereignty, independence and territorial integrity. . . .

VII. Numerous mechanisms are envisaged which will necessitate consultation in the context of the implementation of the resolution's provisions, but the resolution is not at all clear about Iraq's participation in these consultations. . . .

The questions raised in the resolution and discussed in the foregoing preliminary comments constitute, in substance, an injustice, a severe assault on the Iraqi people's right to life and a flagrant denial of its inalienable rights to sovereignty and independence and its right to exercise its free choice. . . .

By adopting this unjust resolution and by this selective treatment of the Iraqi people, the Council has merely confirmed the fact that we have never ceased to emphasize, namely that the Council has become a puppet which the United States of America is manipulating in order to achieve its political designs in the region, the prime objective being to perpetuate Israel's policy of aggression and expansion, despite the empty words about peace and justice in the Middle East uttered by one or another of the Council members which voted for this resolution.

It could not be more clear to all men of honour and justice that these iniquitous and vengeful measures against Iraq are not a consequence of the events of 2 August 1990 and the subsequent period, for the essential motive underlying these measures stems from Iraq's rejection of the unjust situation imposed on the Arab nation and the countries of the region for decades, a situation which has enabled Israel, a belligerent Power heavily armed with the most modern and fearsome conventional weapons and with weapons of mass destruction, including nuclear weapons, to exercise hegemony in the region. This reality confirms what Iraq had stated before the events of 2 August 1990, namely that it was the target of a plot aimed at destroying the potential it had deployed with a view to arriving at a just balance in the region which would pave the way for the institution of justice and of a lasting peace.

It is unfortunate that States whose intention was not in any way to help the United States of America and Israel attain their objectives should involuntarily have contributed to their attainment by voting for this iniquitous resolution.

As Iraq makes its preliminary comments on the juridical and legal aspects of this resolution, so as to encourage men of conscience in the countries, members of the international community and world public opinion to make an effort to understand the truth as it is and the need to ensure the triumph of justice, it has no choice but to accept this resolution.

I should be grateful if you would have this letter circulated as a document of the Security Council.

(*Signed*) Ahmed HUSSEIN
Minister for Foreign Affairs
of Iraq

SUPREME COURT ON
APPEALS FROM PRISONERS
April 16, 1991

The Supreme Court adopted new rules April 16 restricting the ability of prison inmates to challenge their convictions in federal courts. In refusing to further consider a Georgia death penalty case, the Court said in its 6-3 decision that second or subsequent petitions of habeas corpus from a prisoner must be rejected except in unusual circumstances.

Previously a prisoner was allowed to file an unlimited number of petitions. However, the judicial doctrine of "abuse of the writ" provided federal courts a practical way of winnowing out petitions repeating previously rejected claims or making arguments that could have been advanced earlier.

Chief Justice William Rehnquist had long argued that too many repetitive or spurious claims were still being made, placing excessive demands on the judicial system. In 1990 he attempted to persuade Congress to tighten the habeas corpus law, but his efforts were thwarted by senior federal judges and Democratic lawmakers.

Justice Thurgood Marshall, in a vigorous dissent joined by Justices Harry A. Blackmun and John Paul Stevens, accused the Court's six-member majority of accomplishing in McCleskey v. Zant *what Congress had refused to do. Marshall charged that "the majority exercises legislative power not properly belonging to this Court."*

Justice Anthony M. Kennedy wrote that the decision redefined the "abuse of the writ" doctrine to strengthen the ability of state prosecutors to attack all habeas corpus petitions after the initial one. He said the new standard "should curtail the abusive petitions that in recent years have threatened to undermine the integrity of the habeas corpus process." His view was endorsed by Chief Justice Rehnquist and Justices Byron R. White, Sandra Day O'Connor, Antonin Scalia, and David H. Souter.

Effect on Death Row Inmates

The ruling was expected to reduce the time inmates spend on death row between sentencing and execution, which averaged more than eight years, according to federal prison statistics. Habeas corpus filings are not limited to convicts under sentence of death, but traditionally such inmates have been prolific petitioners.

The petitioner at issue, Warren McCleskey, was convicted at a jury trial in December 1978 of a robbery and murder earlier that year. Recounts of the subsequent developments in the case, including habeas corpus filings and other appeals, filled nearly eight printed pages in the Supreme Court's decision.

The first federal habeas corpus petition filed on behalf of McCleskey, a black man, challenged the Georgia death penalty as racially discriminatory. The Supreme Court ruled against him in the 1987 case of McCleskey v. Kemp, *holding that a disproportionate number of blacks receiving the state's death penalty was not inherently discriminatory.*

State Conceals Informer

In a second petition, McCleskey's lawyers contended that his Sixth Amendment right to counsel had been violated by placing a police informer in the Atlanta jail cell next to his. According to court records, McCleskey had confessed to investigators that he took part in the robbery, but he renounced the confession at his trial. The prosecutors then called Offie Evans, the occupant of an adjoining cell in the Atlanta jail, as a witness. He testified that McCleskey confided that he had done the shooting. But for nearly a decade the state had withheld information that it had planted Evans in the cell purposely to draw a confession out of McCleskey. That information was obtained by defense lawyers in a twenty-one-page document extracted from state files under terms of Georgia's freedom-of-information act; a month later they filed the second petition. The federal district court in Atlanta granted McCleskey's new petition, ruling that his previous lack of proof about Evans's role excused his failure to make the Sixth Amendment argument in the first petition.

The U.S. Court of Appeals for the Eleventh Circuit, in Atlanta, disagreed. It said McCleskey had made a similar Sixth Amendment argument in an earlier state court appeal; not using it again in the first federal petition amounted to "deliberate abandonment" of the issue, and thus he was disqualified from raising it later.

Court's Reasoning; Bitter Dissent

The Supreme Court upheld the appellate court's decision, but applied different reasoning. Kennedy said there was no need to show "deliberate abandonment"; it was enough to show that McCleskey "had at least

*constructive knowledge all along of the facts he now claims to have
learned only from the 21-page document" and lacked "sufficient cause"
for not having raised the argument earlier.*

*Marshall accused the majority of rewarding "state misconduct and
deceit." He argued that the ruling "encourages state officials to conceal
[his emphasis] evidence" that would likely result in a habeas corpus
claim. He contended that the Court had changed the habeas corpus rules
on the petitioner; having done so, he added, it should send the case back
to federal district court to be reconsidered under the new rules. Instead,
the Court's action appeared to block further legal recourse in federal
courts.*

*Following are excerpts from the Supreme Court's majority
and dissenting opinions in* McCleskey v. Zant, *issued April
16, 1991, in which the Court restrictively redefined the rules
governing the ability of prisoners to file successive habeas
corpus petitions challenging their convictions:*

No. 89-7024

Warren McCleskey, Petitioner
v.
Walter D. Zant, Superintendent,
Georgia Diagnostic &
Classification Center

On writ of Certiorari to the United
States Court of Appeals for the
Eleventh Circuit

[April 16, 1991]

JUSTICE KENNEDY delivered the opinion of the Court.

The doctrine of abuse of the writ defines the circumstances in which
federal courts decline to entertain a claim presented for the first time in a
second or subsequent petition for a writ of habeas corpus. Petitioner
Warren McCleskey in a second federal habeas petition presented a claim
under *Massiah* v. *United States* (1964), that he failed to include in his first
federal petition. The Court of Appeals for the Eleventh Circuit held that
assertion of the *Massiah* claim in this manner abused the writ. Though our
analysis differs from that of the Court of Appeals, we agree that the
petitioner here abused the writ, and we affirm the judgment.

I

McCleskey and three other men, all armed, robbed a Georgia furniture
store in 1978. One of the robbers shot and killed an off duty policeman who
entered the store in the midst of the crime. McCleskey confessed to the
police that he participated in the robbery. When on trial for both the
robbery and the murder, however, McCleskey renounced his confession
after taking the stand with an alibi denying all involvement. To rebut
McCleskey's testimony, the prosecution called Offie Evans, who had

occupied a jail cell next to McCleskey's. Evans testified that McCleskey admitted shooting the officer during the robbery and boasted that he would have shot his way out of the store even in the face of a dozen policemen.

Although no one witnessed the shooting, further direct and circumstantial evidence supported McCleskey's guilt of the murder. An eyewitness testified that someone ran from the store carrying a pearl-handled pistol soon after the robbery. Other witnesses testified that McCleskey earlier had stolen a pearl-handled pistol of the same caliber as the bullet that killed the officer. Ben Wright, one of McCleskey's accomplices, confirmed that during the crime McCleskey carried a white-handled handgun matching the caliber of the fatal bullet. Wright also testified that McCleskey admitted shooting the officer. Finally, the prosecutor introduced McCleskey's confession of participation in the robbery.

In December 1978, the jury convicted McCleskey of murder and sentenced him to death. Since his conviction, McCleskey has pursued direct and collateral remedies for more than a decade. We describe this procedural history in detail, both for a proper understanding of the case and as an illustration of the context in which allegations of abuse of the writ arise.

On direct appeal to the Supreme Court of Georgia, McCleskey raised six grounds of error. A summary of McCleskey's claims on direct appeal, as well as those he asserted in each of his four collateral proceedings, is set forth in the Appendix to this opinion. The portion of the appeal relevant for our purposes involves McCleskey's attack on Evans' rebuttal testimony. McCleskey contended that the trial court "erred in allowing evidence of [McCleskey's] oral statement admitting the murder made to [Evans] in the next cell, because the prosecutor had deliberately withheld such statement" in violation of *Brady* v. *Maryland*. A unanimous Georgia Supreme Court acknowledged that the prosecutor did not furnish Evans' statement to the defense, but ruled that because the undisclosed evidence was not exculpatory, McCleskey suffered no material prejudice and was not denied a fair trial under *Brady*. The court noted, moreover, that the evidence McCleskey wanted to inspect was "introduced to the jury in its entirety" through Evans' testimony, and that McCleskey's argument that "the evidence was needed in order to prepare a proper defense or impeach other witnesses ha[d] no merit because the evidence requested was statements made by [McCleskey] himself." The court rejected McCleskey's other contentions, and affirmed his conviction and sentence. We denied certiorari [for Supreme Court review].

McCleskey then initiated postconviction proceedings. In January 1981, he filed a petition for state habeas corpus relief. The amended petition raised 23 challenges to his murder conviction and death sentence. Three of the claims concerned Evans' testimony. First, McCleskey contended that the State violated his due process rights under *Giglio* v. *United States* (1972), by its failure to disclose an agreement to drop pending escape charges against Evans in return for his cooperation and testimony. Second,

McCleskey reasserted his *Brady* claim that the State violated his due process rights by the deliberate withholding of the statement he made to Evans while in jail. Third, McCleskey alleged that admission of Evans' testimony violated the Sixth Amendment right to counsel as construed in *Massiah*.... On this theory, "[t]he introduction into evidence of [his] statements to [Evans], elicited in a situation created to include [McCleskey] to make incriminating statements without the assistance of counsel, violated [McCleskey's] right to counsel under the Sixth Amendment to the Constitution of the United States."

At the state habeas corpus hearing, Evans testified that one of the detectives investigating the murder agreed to speak a word on his behalf to the federal authorities about certain federal charges pending against him. The state habeas court ruled that the *ex parte* recommendation did not implicate *Giglio,* and it denied relief on all other claims. The Supreme Court of Georgia denied McCleskey's application for a certificate of probable cause, and we denied his second petition for a writ of certiorari.

In December 1981, McCleskey filed his first federal habeas corpus petition in the United States District Court for the Northern District of Georgia, asserting 18 grounds for relief. The petition failed to allege the *Massiah* claim, but it did reassert the *Giglio* and *Brady* claims. Following extensive hearings in August and October 1983, the District Court held that the detective's statement to Evans was a promise of favorable treatment, and that failure to disclose the promise violated *Giglio.* The District Court further held that Evans' trial testimony may have affected the jury's verdict on the charge of malice murder. On these premises it granted relief.

The Court of Appeals reversed the District Court's grant of the writ. The court held that the State had not made a promise to Evans of the kind contemplated by *Giglio,* and that in any event the *Giglio* error would be harmless. The court affirmed the District Court on all other grounds. We granted certiorari limited to the question whether Georgia's capital sentencing procedures were constitutional, and denied relief.

McCleskey continued his postconviction attacks by filing a second state habeas corpus action in 1987 which, as amended, contained five claims for relief. One of the claims again centered on Evans' testimony, alleging the State had an agreement with Evans that it had failed to disclose. The state trial court held a hearing and dismissed the petition. The Supreme Court of Georgia denied McCleskey's application for a certificate of probable cause.

In July 1987, McCleskey filed a second federal habeas action, the one we now review. In the District Court, McCleskey asserted seven claims, including a *Massiah* challenge to the introduction of Evans' testimony. McCleskey had presented a *Massiah* claim, it will be recalled, in his first state habeas action when he alleged that the conversation recounted by Evans at trial had been "elicited in a situation created to induce" him to make an incriminating statement without the assistance of counsel. The first federal petition did not present a *Massiah* claim. The proffered basis for the *Massiah* claim in the second federal petition was a 21-page signed statement that Evans made to the Atlanta Police Department on August 1, 1978, two weeks before the trial began. The department furnished the document to McCleskey one month before he filed his second federal petition.

The statement related pretrial jailhouse conversations that Evans had with McCleskey and that Evans overheard between McCleskey and Bernard Dupree. By the statement's own terms, McCleskey participated in all the reported jail-cell conversations. Consistent with Evans' testimony at trial, the statement reports McCleskey admitting and boasting about the murder. It also recounts that Evans posed as Ben Wright's uncle and told McCleskey he had talked with Wright about the robbery and the murder.

In his second federal habeas petition, McCleskey asserted that the statement proved Evans "was acting in direct concert with State officials" during the incriminating conversations with McCleskey, and that the authorities "deliberately elicited" inculpatory admissions in violation of McCleskey's Sixth Amendment right to counsel. Among other responses, the State of Georgia contended that McCleskey's presentation of a *Massiah* claim for the first time in the second federal petition was an abuse of the writ.

The District Court held extensive hearings in July and August 1987 focusing on the arrangement the jailers had made for Evans' cell assignment in 1978. Several witnesses denied that Evans had been placed next to McCleskey by design or instructed to overhear conversations or obtain statements from McCleskey. McCleskey's key witness was Ulysses Worthy, a jailer at the Fulton County Jail during the summer of 1978. McCleskey's lawyers contacted Worthy after a detective testified that the 1978 Evans statement was taken in Worthy's office. The District Court characterized Worthy's testimony as "often confused and self-contradictory." Worthy testified that someone at some time requested permission to move Evans near McCleskey's cell. He contradicted himself, however, concerning when, why, and by whom Evans was moved, and about whether he overheard investigators urging Evans to engage McCleskey in conversation.

On December 23, 1987, the District Court granted McCleskey relief based upon a violation of *Massiah*. The court stated that the Evans statement "contains strong indication of an *ab initio* [from the beginning] relationship between Evans and the authorities." In addition, the court credited Worthy's testimony suggesting that the police had used Evans to obtain incriminating information from McCleskey. Based on the Evans statement and portions of Worthy's testimony, the District Court found that the jail authorities had placed Evans in the cell adjoining McCleskey's "for the purpose of gathering incriminating information"; that "Evans was probably coached in how to approach McCleskey and given critical facts unknown to the general public"; that Evans talked with McCleskey and eavesdropped on McCleskey's conversations with others; and that Evans reported what he had heard to the authorities. These findings, in the District Court's view, established a *Massiah* violation.

In granting habeas relief, the District Court rejected the State's argument that McCleskey's assertion of the *Massiah* claim for the first time in the second federal petition constituted an abuse of the writ. The court ruled that McCleskey did not deliberately abandon the claim after raising it in his first state habeas petition. "This is not a case," the District Court reasoned, "where petitioner has reserved his proof or deliberately withheld his claim for a second petition." The District court also determined that when McCleskey filed his first federal petition, he did not know about either the 21-page Evans document or the identity of Worthy, and that the failure to discover the evidence for the first federal petition "was not due to [McCleskey's] inexcusable neglect."

The Eleventh Circuit reversed, holding that the District Court abused its discretion by failing to dismiss McCleskey's *Massiah* claim as an abuse of the writ. The Court of Appeals agreed with the District Court that the petitioner must "show that he did not deliberately abandon the claim and that his failure to raise it [in the first federal habeas proceeding] was not due to inexcusable neglect." Accepting the District Court's findings that at the first petition stage McCleskey knew neither the existence of the Evans statement nor the identity of Worthy, the court held that the District Court "misconstru[ed] the meaning of deliberate abandonment." Because McCleskey included a *Massiah* claim in his first state petition, dropped it in his first federal petition, and then reasserted it in his second federal petition, he "made a knowing choice not to pursue the claim after having raised it previously" that constituted a prima facie showing of "deliberate abandonment." The court further found the State's alleged concealment of the Evans statement irrelevant because it "was simply the catalyst that caused counsel to pursue the *Massiah* claim more vigorously" and did not itself "demonstrate the existence of a *Massiah* violation." The court concluded that McCleskey had presented no reason why counsel could not have discovered Worthy earlier. Finally, the court ruled that McCleskey's claim did not fall within the ends of justice exception to the abuse of the writ doctrine because any *Massiah* violation that may have been committed would have been harmless error.

McCleskey petitioned this Court for a writ of certiorari, alleging numerous errors in the Eleventh Circuit's abuse of the writ analysis. In our order granting the petition, we requested the parties to address the following additional question: "Must the State demonstrate that a claim was deliberately abandoned in an earlier petition for a writ of habeas corpus in order to establish that inclusion of that claim in a subsequent habeas petition constitutes abuse of the writ?"

II

The parties agree that the government has the burden of pleading abuse of the writ, and that once the government makes a proper submission, the petitioner must show that he has not abused the writ in seeking habeas relief. Much confusion exists though, on the standard for determining when a petitioner abuses the writ. Although the standard is central to the proper determination of many federal habeas corpus actions, we have had little occasion to define it. Indeed, there is truth to the observation that we have defined abuse of the writ in an oblique way, through dicta and denials of certiorari petitions or stay applications. . . . Today we give the subject our careful consideration. We begin by tracing the historical development of some of the substantive and procedural aspects of the writ, and then consider the standard for abuse that district courts should apply in actions seeking federal habeas corpus relief.

A

The Judiciary Act of 1789 empowered federal courts to issue writs of habeas corpus to prisoners "in custody, under or by colour of the authority of the United States." In the early decades of our new federal system, English common law defined the substantive scope of the writ. Federal prisoners could use the writ to challenge confinement imposed by a court that lacked jurisdiction, or detention by the executive without proper legal process.

. . . The major statutory expansion of the writ occurred in 1867, when Congress extended federal habeas corpus to prisoners held in state custody. For the most part, however, expansion of the writ has come through judicial decisionmaking. . . . [T]he Court began by interpreting the concept of jurisdictional defect with generosity to include sentences imposed without statutory authorization, and convictions obtained under an unconstitutional statute. Later, we allowed habeas relief for confinement under a state conviction obtained without adequate procedural protections for the defendant.

. . . With the exception of Fourth Amendment violations that a petitioner has been given a full and fair opportunity to litigate in state court, *Stone* v. *Powell* (1976), the writ today appears to extend to all dispositive constitutional claims presented in a proper procedural manner.

One procedural requisite is that a petition not lead to an abuse of the writ. . . .

[B omitted]

III

. . . [T]he doctrine of abuse of the writ refers to a complex and evolving body of equitable principles informed and controlled by historical usage, statutory developments, and judicial decisions. . . .

Although our decisions on the subject do not all admit of ready synthesis, one point emerges with clarity: Abuse of the writ is not confined to instances of deliberate abandonment. . . .

. . . Our recent decisions confirm that a petitioner can abuse the writ by raising a claim in a subsequent petition that he could have raised in his first, regardless of whether the failure to raise it earlier stemmed from a deliberate choice.

The inexcusable neglect standard demands more from a petitioner than the standard of deliberate abandonment. But we have not given the former term the content necessary to guide district courts in the ordered consideration of allegedly abusive habeas corpus petitions.... [A] review of our habeas corpus precedents leads us to decide that the same standard used to determine whether to excuse state procedural defaults should govern the determination of inexcusable neglect in the abuse of the writ context....

... If re-examination of a conviction in the first round of federal habeas stretches resources, examination of new claims raised in a second or subsequent petition spreads them thinner still. These later petitions deplete the resources needed for federal litigants in the first instance, including litigants commencing their first federal habeas action.... And if re-examination of convictions in the first round of habeas offends federalism and comity, the offense increases when a State must defend its conviction in a second or subsequent habeas proceeding on grounds not even raised in the first petition.

The federal writ of habeas corpus overrides all these considerations, essential as they are to the rule of law, when a petitioner raises a meritorious constitutional claim in a proper manner in a habeas petition. Our procedural default jurisprudence and abuse of the writ jurisprudence help define this dimension of procedural regularity. Both doctrines impose on petitioners a burden of reasonable compliance with procedures designed to discourage baseless claims and to keep the system open for valid ones; both recognize the law's interest in finality; and both invoke equitable principles to define the court's discretion to excuse pleading and procedural requirements for petitioners who could not comply with them in the exercise of reasonable care and diligence....

In procedural default cases, the cause standard requires the petitioner to show that "some objective factor external to the defense impeded counsel's efforts" to raise the claim in state court. Objective factors that constitute cause include " 'interference by officials' " that makes compliance with the state's procedural rule impracticable, and "a showing that the factual or legal basis for a claim was not reasonably available to counsel." In addition, constitutionally "ineffective assistance of counsel ... is cause." Attorney error short of ineffective assistance will not excuse a procedural default. Once the petitioner has established cause, he must show " 'actual prejudice' resulting from the errors of which he complains."

... When a prisoner files a second or subsequent application, the government bears the burden of pleading abuse of the writ. The government satisfies this burden if, with clarity and particularity, it notes petitioner's prior writ history, identifies the claims that appear for the first time, and alleges that petitioner has abused the writ. The burden to disprove abuse then becomes petitioner's. To excuse his failure to raise the claim earlier, he must show cause for failing to raise it and prejudice therefrom as those concepts have been defined in our procedural default decisions. . . . If petitioner cannot show cause, the failure to raise the claim in an earlier petition may nonetheless be excused if he or she can show that a fundamental miscarriage of justice would result from a failure to entertain the claim. . . .

The cause and prejudice standard should curtail the abusive petitions that in recent years have threatened to undermine the integrity of the habeas corpus process. . . .

We now apply these principles to the case before us.

IV

McCleskey based the *Massiah* claim in his second federal petition on the 21-page Evans document alone. Worthy's identity did not come to light until the hearing. The District Court found, based on the document's revelation of the tactics used by Evans in engaging McCleskey in conversation (such as his pretending to be Ben Wright's uncle and his claim that he was supposed to participate in the robbery), that the document established an *ab initio* relationship between Evans and the authorities. It relied on the finding and on Worthy's later testimony to conclude that the State committed a *Massiah* violation.

This ruling on the merits cannot come before us or any federal court if it is premised on a claim that constitutes an abuse of the writ. We must consider, therefore, the preliminary question whether McCleskey had cause for failing to raise the *Massiah* claim in his first federal petition. The District Court found that neither the 21-page document nor Worthy were known or discoverable before filing the first federal petition. Relying on these findings, McCleskey argues that his failure to raise the *Massiah* claim in the first petition should be excused. For reasons set forth below, we disagree.

That McCleskey did not possess or could not reasonably have obtained certain evidence fails to establish cause if other known or discoverable evidence could have supported the claim in any event. For cause to exist, the external impediment, whether it be government interference or the reasonable unavailability of the factual basis for the claim, must have prevented petitioner from raising the claim. Abuse of the writ doctrine examines *petitioner's* conduct: the question is whether petitioner possessed, or by reasonable means could have obtained, a sufficient basis to allege a claim in the first petition and pursue the matter through the habeas process. . . .

. . . It is essential at the outset to distinguish between two issues: (1) Whether petitioner knew about or could have discovered the 21-page document; and (2) whether he knew about or could have discovered the evidence the document recounted, namely the jail-cell conversations. The District Court's error lies in its conflation of the two inquiries, an error petitioner would have us perpetuate here.

The 21-page document unavailable to McCleskey at the time of the first petition does not establish that McCleskey had cause for failing to raise the *Massiah* claim at the outset. Based on testimony and questioning at trial, McCleskey knew that he had confessed the murder during jail-cell conversations with Evans, knew that Evans claimed to be a relative of Ben Wright during the conversations, and knew that Evans told the police about the conversations. Knowledge of these facts alone would put McCleskey on notice to pursue the *Massiah* claim in his first federal habeas petition as he had done in the first state habeas petition. . . .

By failing to raise the *Massiah* claim in 1981, McCleskey foreclosed the procedures best suited for disclosure of the facts needed for a reliable determination. . . .

As McCleskey lacks cause for failing to raise the *Massiah* claim in the first federal petition, we need not consider whether he would be prejudiced by his inability to raise the alleged *Massiah* violation at this late date.

We do address whether the Court should nonetheless exercise its equitable discretion to correct a miscarriage of justice. That narrow exception is of no avail to McCleskey. The *Massiah* violation, if it be one, resulted in the admission at trial of truthful inculpatory evidence which did not affect the reliability of the guilt determination. The very statement McCleskey now seeks to embrace confirms his guilt. . . .

The history of the proceedings in this case, and the burden upon the State in defending against allegations made for the first time in federal court some 9 years after the trial, reveal the necessity for the abuse of the writ doctrine. The cause and prejudice standard we adopt today leaves ample room for consideration of constitutional errors in a first federal habeas petition and in a later petition under appropriate circumstances. Petitioner has not satisfied this standard for excusing the omission of the *Massiah* claim from his first petition. The judgment of the Court of Appeals is

Affirmed.

JUSTICE MARSHALL, with whom JUSTICE BLACKMUN and JUSTICE STEVENS join, dissenting.

Today's decision departs drastically from the norms that inform the proper judicial function. Without even the most casual admission that it is discarding longstanding legal principles, the Court radically redefines the content of the "abuse of the writ" doctrine, substituting the strict-liability "cause and prejudice" standard of *Wainwright* v. *Sykes* for the good-faith "deliberate abandonment" standard of *Sanders* v. *United States* (1963). This doctrinal innovation, which repudiates a line of judicial decisions codified by Congress in the governing statute and procedural rules, was by no means foreseeable when the petitioner in this case filed his first federal habeas application. Indeed, the new rule announced and applied today was not even *requested* by respondent at any point in this litigation. Finally, rather than remand this case for reconsideration in light of its new standard, the majority performs an independent reconstruction of the record, disregarding the factual findings of the District Court and applying its new rule in a manner that encourages state officials to *conceal* evidence that would likely prompt a petitioner to raise a particular claim on habeas. Because I cannot acquiesce in this unjustifiable assault on the Great Writ, I dissent.

I

... The Court in *Sanders* distinguished successive petitions raising previously asserted grounds from those raising previously unasserted grounds. With regard to the former class of petitions, the Court explained, the district court may give "[c]ontrolling weight ... to [the] denial of a prior application" unless "the ends of justice would ... be served by reaching the merits of the subsequent application." With regard to the latter, however, the district court *must* reach the merits of the petition *unless* "there has been an abuse of the writ. In determining whether the omission of the claim from the previous petition constitutes an abuse of the writ, the judgment of the district court is to be guided chiefly by the " '[equitable] principle that a suitor's conduct in relation to the matter at hand may disentitle him to the relief he seeks.' "...

What emerges from *Sanders* and its predecessors is essentially a good-faith standard.... [S]o long as the petitioner's previous application was based on a good-faith assessment of the claims available to him, the denial of the application does not bar the petitioner from availing himself of "new or additional information" in support of a claim not previously raised.

"Cause and prejudice"—the standard currently applicable to procedural defaults in state proceedings—imposes a much stricter test. As this Court's precedents make clear, a petitioner has *cause* for failing effectively to present his federal claim in state proceedings only when "some objective factor external to the defense impeded counsel's efforts to comply with the State's procedural rule. ..." Under this test, the state of mind of counsel is largely irrelevant. Indeed, this Court has held that even counsel's *reasonable* perception that a particular claim is without factual or legal foundation does not excuse the failure to raise that claim in the absence of an objective, external impediment to counsel's efforts. In this sense, the cause component of the *Wainwright* v. *Sykes* test establishes a *strict-liability* standard.

Equally foreign to our abuse-of-the-writ jurisprudence is the requirement that a petitioner show "prejudice." Under *Sanders,* a petitioner who articulates a justifiable reason for failing to present a claim in a previous habeas application is not required in addition to demonstrate any particular degree of prejudice before the habeas court must consider his claim. If the petitioner demonstrates that his claim has merit, it is the State that must show that the resulting constitutional error was harmless beyond a reasonable doubt.

II

The real question posed by the majority's analysis is not *whether* the cause-and-prejudice test departs from the principles of *Sanders*—for it clearly does—but whether the majority has succeeded in *justifying* this departure as an exercise of this Court's common-lawmaking discretion. In my view, the majority does not come close to justifying its new standard.

A

Incorporation of the cause-and-prejudice test into the abuse-of-the-writ doctrine cannot be justified as an exercise of this Court's common-lawmaking discretion, because this Court has no discretion to exercise in this area. Congress has affirmatively ratified the *Sanders* good-faith standard in the governing statute and procedural rules, thereby insulating that standard from judicial repeal.

The abuse-of-writ doctrine is embodied in 28 U.S.C. § 2244(b) and in Habeas Corpus Rule 9(b)....

The majority concedes that § 2244(b) and Rule 9(b) codify *Sanders*, but concludes nonetheless that Congress did "not answer" all of the "questions" concerning the abuse-of-the-writ doctrine. The majority emphasizes that § 2244(b) refers to second or successive petitions from petitioners who have "deliberately withheld the newly asserted ground *or otherwise abused the writ*" without exhaustively cataloging the ways in which the writ may "otherwise" be "abused." From this "silenc[e]," the majority infers a congressional delegation of lawmaking power broad enough to encompass the engrafting of the cause-and-prejudice test onto the abuse-of-the-writ doctrine.

It is difficult to take this reasoning seriously.... Insofar as *Sanders* was primarily concerned with limiting dismissal of a second or subsequent petition to instances in which the petitioner had deliberately abandoned the new claim, the suggestion that Congress invested courts with the discretion to read this language out of the statute is completely irreconcilable with the proposition that § 2244(b) and Rule 9(b) codify *Sanders*....

The majority tacitly acknowledges this constraint on the Court's interpretive discretion by suggesting that "cause" is tantamount to "inexcusable neglect." This claim, too, is untenable. The majority exaggerates when it claims that the "inexcusable neglect" formulation—which this Court has never applied in an abuse-of-the-writ decision—functions as an independent standard for evaluating a petitioner's failure to raise a claim in a previous habeas application....

Confirmation that the majority today exercises legislative power not properly belonging to this Court is supplied by Congress' own recent consideration and rejection of an amendment to § 2244(b). It is axiomatic that this Court does not function as a backup legislature for the reconsideration of failed attempts to amend existing statutes. Yet that is exactly the effect of today's decision....

[B omitted]

III

The manner in which the majority applies its new rule is as objectionable as the manner in which the majority creates that rule. As even the majority acknowledges, the standard that it announces today is not the one employed by the Court of Appeals, which purported to rely on *Sanders*. Where, as here, application of a different standard from the one applied by the lower court requires an in-depth review of the record, the ordinary course is to remand so that the parties have a fair opportunity to address, and the lower court to consider, all of the relevant issues. . . .

The majority's analysis of this case is dangerous precisely because it treats as irrelevant the effect that the State's disinformation strategy had on counsel's assessment of pursing the reasonableness of the *Massiah* claim. For the majority, all that matters is that no external obstacle barred McCleskey from finding Worthy. But obviously, counsel's decision even to look for evidence in support of a particular claim has to be informed by what counsel reasonably perceives to be the prospect that the claim may have merit; in this case, by withholding the 21-page statement and by affirmatively misleading counsel as to the State's involvement with Evans, state officials created a climate in which McCleskey's first habeas counsel was perfectly justified in focusing his attentions elsewhere. The sum and substance of the majority's analysis is that McCleskey had no "cause" for failing to assert the *Massiah* claim because he did not try hard enough to pierce the State's veil of deception. Because the majority excludes from its conception of cause any recognition of how state officials can distort a petitioner's reasonable perception of whether pursuit of a particular claim is worthwhile, the majority's conception of "cause" creates an incentive for state officials to engage in this very type of misconduct. . . .

IV

Ironically, the majority seeks to defend its doctrinal innovation on the ground that it will promote respect for the "rule of law." Obviously, respect for the rule of law must start with those who are responsible for *pronouncing* the law. The majority's invocation of " 'the orderly adminis- tration of justice' " rings hollow when the majority itself tosses aside established precedents without explanation, disregards the will of Con- gress, fashions rules that defy the reasonable expectations of the persons who must conform their conduct to the law's dictates, and applies those rules in a way that rewards state misconduct and deceit. Whatever "abuse of the writ" today's decision is designed to avert pales in comparison with the majority's own abuse of the norms that inform the proper judicial function.

I dissent.

BUSH ON NATIONAL
EDUCATION STRATEGY
April 18, 1991

In a nationally televised address April 18, President George Bush unveiled an ambitious plan to revamp the nation's educational system. "For the sake of the future of our children, and of the Nation's, we must transform America's schools," he said. "The days of the status quo are over.... To those who want to see real improvement in American education, I say: 'There will be no renaissance without revolution.'"

The plan—called America 2000—focused on improving existing schools, creating "a new kind of school," fostering continuing education for adults, and challenging Americans to "cultivate communities where learning can happen." It was crafted largely by Education Secretary Lamar Alexander, who stood at Bush's side during the president's White House speech. Also present were business leaders, governors, members of Congress, and educators.

In March Alexander succeeded Lauro F. Cavazos, who had disappointed many educators by what they considered to be his lack of forceful leadership. Alexander, a former governor of Tennessee and president of the University of Tennessee, had served on the administration's Education Policy Advisory Committee. As the Republican governor, he had persuaded a Democratic-controlled legislature to increase the Tennessee sales tax to raise funds for school needs. In 1986, as chairman of the National Governors' Association (NGA), he directed a fifty-state education survey that, the president remarked, "put us on the path to the six national education goals that guide our efforts from now to the year 2000."

Plan Objectives

The new education plan mandated that standards be set in five "core" subjects—English, mathematics, science, history, and geography. The administration planned to ask governors to adopt a national test for fourth-, eighth-, and twelfth-graders. The test would be optional because of objections to federal oversight of curricula at the expense of the traditional local control. In addition, America 2000 called on the National Education Goals Panel, a group created by the administration and the NGA to set "new world standards" in the five core subjects and to oversee development of an "anchor test."

The plan would make it easier for parents to move their children to other schools. About $200 million in financial incentives would be given to states and local governments to develop school-choice policies. The federal government would not necessarily pay for students to go to private schools; it would only encourage local school districts to experiment with various choice options.

If Congress approved, schools could ignore federal rules governing their funding in order to cut through red tape and raise achievement levels. The federal government would award grants to schools that had made progress toward meeting the national goals—if Congress authorized the funds.

School districts would be urged to boost the pay of teachers who taught well, who taught core subjects, who taught in "dangerous" settings, or who were mentors for new teachers. The administration envisioned raising up to $200 million from the business community to finance the development of "non-traditional" schools. The president additionally asked Congress for $550 million to create 535 "New American Schools," one in each congressional district, by 1996.

To receive funds for a "New American School," a community would have to be designated an "AMERICA 2000 Community" by its governor. It would have to (1) adopt the education goals established by the Bush administration and the NGA in 1990, (2) draft a strategy to reach these goals, (3) develop a "report card" to assess progress, and (4) demonstrate readiness to support an experimental school. (Bush and Governors' Statements on Education Goals, Historic Documents of 1990, p. 153) *The adult-education part of the strategy would be administered primarily by the Department of Labor. It called on business and labor groups to establish job-related skill standards and proposed the creation of "skill centers" in communities and workplaces that would provide information to workers about skills needed for particular jobs and where to obtain training.*

Mixed Reaction to Plan

Many observers hailed the plan as a step by Bush toward fulfilling his 1988 campaign pledge to be "the education president." Governors and business executives generally supported the strategy. A group of business leaders, led by Paul H. O'Neill, chief executive officer of the Aluminum Company of America, pledged to establish a nonprofit organization called the "New American Schools Development Corporation."

Other observers were skeptical. "The glaring thing that's missing is the federal investment," said Edward R. Kealy, president of the Committee for Education Funding and director of federal programs for the National School Boards Association. "It didn't surprise us to find out we're dealing with some promises and rhetoric, but we don't see real muscle to flesh out a commitment to education." Kealy estimated that the federal government would have to double its spending on education—currently about $27 billion—to meet the new national goals. The administration estimated that AMERICA 2000 would cost the government far less, some $692 million. Bush insisted in his speech that "dollar bills don't educate students." He stated that per pupil costs had risen 33 percent—after inflation—since 1981 "and I don't think ... we've seen a 33 percent improvement in our schools' performance."

The disagreement over spending was dwarfed by controversy over Bush's revival of the "choice" proposal. Sen. Edward M. Kennedy, D-Mass., chairman of the Labor and Human Resources Committee, said the choice plan would reopen "the bitter and divisive policy and constitutional debates of the past about public aid to private schools."

Albert Shenker, president of the American Federation of Teachers, and Keith Geiger, president of the National Education Association, both criticized the concept of allowing education funds to "follow the child" to another school.

Critics of national testing argued that such a plan would lead to a national curriculum and harm minority students who performed disproportionately poorly on tests. Others (among them Kennedy) also pointed out that the program offered no new funding to strengthen early intervention programs such as Head Start for disadvantaged children.

Although congressional action would determine the fate of many parts of the plan, there was general agreement that its success would depend largely on acceptance by the states and localities. "These results are going to take a while," Alexander said after the president spoke. "It won't decide the result of the next presidential election. You won't see a transformation of education in the next two years."

Following is the text of President George Bush's televised address on a national education strategy, delivered from the White House, April 18, 1991:

Thank you all for joining us here in the White House today. Let me thank the Speaker for being with us, and the Majority Leader; other distinguished Members, committee heads and ranking members, and very important education committees here with us today. I want to salute the Governors, the educators, the business and the labor leaders, and especially want to single out the National Teachers of the Year. I believe we have 10 of the previous 11 Teachers of the Year with us here today, and that's most appropriate and most fitting.

But together, all of us, we will underscore the importance of a challenge destined to define the America that we'll know in the next century.

For those of you close to my age, the 21st century has always been a kind of shorthand for the distant future—the place we put our most far-off hopes and dreams. And today, that 21st century is racing towards us—and anyone who wonders what the century will look like can find the answer in America's classrooms.

Nothing better defines what we are and what we will become than the education of our children. To quote the landmark case *Brown* versus *Board of Education*, "It is doubtful that any child may reasonably be expected to succeed in life if he is denied the opportunity of an education."

Education has always meant opportunity. Today, education determines not just which students will succeed but also which nations will thrive in a world united in pursuit of freedom in enterprise. Think about the changes transforming our world: the collapse of communism and the cold war, the advent and acceleration of the Information Age. Down through history, we've defined resources as soil and stones, land and the riches buried beneath. No more. Our greatest national resource lies within ourselves— our intelligence, ingenuity—the capacity of the human mind.

Nations that nurture ideas will move forward in years to come. Nations that stick to stale old notions and ideologies will falter and fail. So I'm here today to say America will move forward. The time for all the reports and rankings, for all the studies and the surveys about what's wrong in our schools is past. If we want to keep America competitive in the coming century, we must stop convening panels to report on ourselves. We must stop convening panels that report the obvious. And we must accept responsibility for educating everyone among us, regardless of background or disability.

If we want America to remain a leader, a force for good in the world, we must lead the way in educational innovation. And if we want to combat crime and drug abuse, if we want to create hope and opportunity in the bleak corners of this country where there is now nothing but defeat and despair, we must dispel the darkness with the enlightenment that a sound and well-rounded education provides.

Think about every problem, every challenge we face. The solution to each starts with education. For the sake of the future of our children, and of the Nation's, we must transform America's schools. The days of the status quo are over.

Across this country, people have started to transform the American school. They know that the time for talk is over. Their slogan is: Don't dither, just do it. Let's push the reform effort forward. Use each experiment, each advance to build for the next American century—new schools for a new world.

As a first step in this strategy, we must challenge not only the methods and the means that we've used in the past but also the yardsticks that we've used to measure our progress. Let's stop trying to measure progress in terms of money spent. We spend 33 percent more per pupil in 1991 than we did in 1981—33 percent more in real, constant dollars—and I don't think there's a person anywhere who would say—anywhere in the country—who would say that we've seen a 33-percent improvement in our schools' performance.

Dollar bills don't educate students. Education depends on committed communities, determined to be places where learning will flourish; committed teachers, free from the noneducational burdens; committed parents, determined to support excellence; committed students, excited about school and learning. To those who want to see real improvement in American education, I say: There will be no renaissance without revolution.

We who would be revolutionaries must accept responsibilities for our schools. For too long, we've adopted a no-fault approach to education. Someone else is always to blame. And while we point fingers out there, trying to assign blame, the students suffer. There's no place for a no-fault attitude in our schools. It's time we held our schools—and ourselves—accountable for results.

Until now, we've treated education like a manufacturing process, assuming that if the gauges seemed right—if we had good pay scales, the right pupil-teacher ratios—good students would just pop out of our schools. It's time to turn things around—to focus on students, to set standards for our schools—and let teachers and principals figure out how best to meet them.

We've made a good beginning by setting the Nation's sights on six ambitious national education goals—and setting for our target the year 2000. Our goals have been forged in partnership with the Nation's Governors, several of whom are with us here today in the East Room. And those who have taken a leadership are well-known to everyone in this room. And for those who need a refresher course—there may be a quiz later on—let me list those goals right now.

By 2000, we've got to, first, ensure that every child starts school ready to learn; second one, raise the high school graduation rate to 90 percent; the third one, ensure that each American student leaving the 4th, 8th, and 12th grades can demonstrate competence in core subjects; four, make our students first in the world in math and science achievements; fifth, ensure that every American adult is literate and has the skills necessary to compete in a global economy and exercise the rights and responsibilities of citizenship; and sixth, liberate every American school from drugs and violence so that schools encourage learning.

Our strategy to meet these noble national goals is founded in common sense and common values. It's ambitious—and yet, with hard work, it's within our reach. And I can outline our strategy in one paragraph, and here it is: For today's students, we must make existing schools better and more accountable. For tomorrow's students, the next generation, we must create a new generation of American schools. For all of us, for the adults who think our school days are over, we've got to become a nation of students—recognize learning is a lifelong process. Finally, outside our schools we must cultivate communities where learning can happen. That's our strategy.

People who want Washington to solve our educational problems are missing the point. We can lend appropriate help through such programs as Head Start. But what happens here in Washington won't matter half as much as what happens in each school, each local community, and yes, in each home. Still, the Federal Government will serve as a catalyst for change in several important ways.

Working closely with the Governors, we will define new world-class standards for schools, teachers, and students in the five core subject: math and science, English, history and geography. We will develop voluntary—let me repeat it—we will develop voluntary national tests for 4th, 8th, and 12th graders in the five core subjects. These American Achievement Tests will tell parents and educators, politicians, and employers just how well our schools are doing. I'm determined to have the first of these tests for fourth graders in place by the time that school starts in September of 1993. And for high school seniors, let's add another incentive—a distinction sure to attract attention of colleges and companies in every community across the country—a Presidential Citation to students who excel on the 12th-grade test.

We can encourage educational excellence by encouraging parental choice. The concept of choice draws its fundamental strength from the principle at the very heart of the democratic idea. Every adult American has the right to vote, the right to decide where to work, where to live. It's time parents were free to choose the schools that their children attend. This approach will create the competitive climate that stimulates excellence in our private and parochial schools as well.

But the centerpiece of our national education strategy is not a program, it's not a test. It's a new challenge: To reinvent American education—to design new American schools for the year 2000 and beyond. The idea is simple but powerful: Put America's special genius for invention to work for America's schools. I will challenge communities to become what we will call America 2000 communities. Governors will honor communities with this designation if the communities embrace the national education goals, create local strategies for reaching these goals, devise report cards for measuring progress, and agree to encourage and support one of the new generation of America's schools.

We must also foster educational innovation. I'm delighted to announce today that America's business leaders, under the chairmanship of Paul O'Neill, will create the New American Schools Development Corporation—a private sector research and development fund of at least $150 million to generate innovation in education.

This fund offers an open-end challenge to the dreamers and the doers eager to reinvent, eager to reinvigorate our schools. With the results of this R&D in hand, I will urge Congress to provide $1 million in startup funds for each of the 535 New American Schools—at least one in every congressional district—and have them up and running by 1996.

The New American Schools must be more than rooms full of children seated at computers. If we mean to prepare our children for life, classrooms also must cultivate values and good character—give real meaning to right and wrong.

We ask only two things of these architects of our New American Schools: that their students meet the new national standards for the five core subjects, and that outside of the costs of the initial research and development, the schools operate on a budget comparable to conventional schools. The architects of the New American Schools should break the mold. Build for the next century. Reinvent—literally start from scratch and reinvent the American school. No question should be off limits, no answers automatically assumed. We're not after one single solution for every school. We're interested in finding every way to make schools better.

There's a special place in inventing the New American School for the corporate community, for business and labor. And I invite you to work with us not simply to transform our schools but to transform every American adult into a student.

Fortunately, we have a secret weapon in America's system of colleges and universities—the finest in the entire world. The corporate community can take the lead by creating a voluntary private system of world-class standards for the workplace. Employers should set up skill centers where workers can seek advice and learn new skills. But most importantly, every company and every labor union must bring the worker into the classroom and bring the classroom into the workplace.

We'll encourage every Federal agency to do the same. And to prove no one's ever too old to learn, Lamar, with his indefatigable determination and leadership, has convinced me to become a student again myself. Starting next week, I'll begin studying. And I want to know how to operate a computer. [Laughter] Very candidly—I don't expect this new tutorial to teach me how to set the clock on the VCR or anything complicated. [Laughter] But I want to be computer literate, and I'm not. There's a lot of kids, thank God, that are. And I want to learn, and I will.

The workplace isn't the only place we must improve opportunities for education. Across this nation, we must cultivate communities where children can learn—communities where the school is more than a refuge, more than a solitary island of calm amid chaos. Where the school is the living center of a community where people care—people care for each other and their futures—not just in the school but in the neighborhood, not just in the classroom but in the home.

Our challenge amounts to nothing less than a revolution in American education—a battle for our future. And now, I ask all Americans to be Points of Light in the crusade that counts the most: the crusade to prepare our children and ourselves for the exciting future that looms ahead.

What I've spoken about this afternoon are the broad strokes of this national education strategy: accountable schools for today, a new generation of schools for tomorrow, a nation of students committed to a lifetime of learning, and communities where all our children can learn.

There are four people here today who symbolize each element of this strategy and point the way forward for our reforms. Esteban Pagan—Steve—an award-winning eighth-grade student in science and history at East Harlem Tech, a choice school. Steve? right here, I think. Stand up, now.

Mike Hopkins, lead teacher in the Saturn School in St. Paul, Minnesota, where teachers have already helped reinvent the American school. Mike, where are you? Right here, sir. Thank you.

David Kelley, a high-tech troubleshooter at the Michelin Tire plant in Greenville, South Carolina. David has spent the equivalent of 1 full year of his 4 years at Michelin back at his college expanding his skills. David? There he is.

Finally, Michelle Moore, of Missouri, a single mother active in Missouri's Parents as Teachers program. She wants her year-old son, Alston, to arrive for his first day of school ready to learn. Michelle?

So, to sum it up, for these four people and for all the others like them, the revolution in American education has already begun. Now I ask all Americans to be Points of Light in the crusade that counts the most: the crusade to prepare our children and ourselves for the exciting future that looms ahead. At any moment in every mind, the miracle of learning beckons us all. Between now and the year 2000, there is not one moment or one miracle to waste.

Thank you all. Thank you for your interest, for your dedication. And may God bless the United States of America. Thank you very much.

May

PAPAL ENCYCLICAL
ON ECONOMIC QUESTIONS
May 1, 1991

Pope John Paul II issued an encyclical letter to the Catholic church May 1 addressing economic questions raised by the collapse of communism in Eastern Europe. His 25,000-word document, Centesimus Annus *(The Hundredth Year), commemorated the 100th anniversary of the encyclical* Rerum Novarum *(Of New Things) by Pope Leo XIII, which is widely credited with recasting the church's social teaching in terms of the industrial age. It departed in significant ways from an 1864 encyclical of Pope Pius IX (Syllabus of Errors) that condemned nineteenth-century modernism and liberalism.*

Rerum Novarum *recognized the Catholic worker movement and the existence of labor unions. But this position was balanced by an endorsement of private ownership. It denounced the evils of capitalism, but condemned socialism even more strongly. Similarly, in* Centesimus Annus, *John Paul seemed to seek a middle ground in his guidance for East European countries, including his native Poland, as they move from state-controlled economies toward free markets.*

"The free market is the most efficient instrument for utilizing resources and effectively responding to needs," the pontiff wrote. "But there are many human needs which find no place on the market," he added. He went on to say that "If by 'capitalism' is meant an economic system which recognizes the fundamental and positive role of business, the market, private property and the resulting responsibility for the means of production, as well as free human creativity in the economic sector, then the answer is certainly in the affirmative...." But if capitalism "is not circumscribed within a strong juridical framework

which places it at the service of human freedom ... then the reply is certainly negative."

The pope said alienation remained "a reality in Western societies," and warned against material abundance promoting a form of consumerism that becomes an end in itself. He said the excesses of capitalism threatened both the natural environment and the stability of family life.

John Paul went on to assert that the church had no economic model to present; rather it "offers her social teaching as an indispensable and ideal orientation, a teaching which ... recognizes the positive value of the market and of enterprise, but which at the same time points out that these need to be oriented toward a common good." This teaching, he added, "also recognizes the legitimacy of workers' efforts to obtain full respect for their dignity ... and [so participate] through the exercise of their intelligence and freedom."

Following are excerpts from the encyclical Centesimus Annus *(The Hundredth Year), issued by Pope John Paul II to the Catholic church, May 1, 1991, in English translation, as published by the U.S. Catholic Conference:*

[Introduction and Chapter I omitted]

Chapter II

Towards the "New Things" of Today

The commemoration of *Rerum Novarum* would be incomplete unless reference were also made to the situation of the world today. The document lends itself to such a reference, because the historical picture and the prognosis which it suggests have proved to be surprisingly accurate in the light of what has happened since then.

This is especially confirmed by the events which took place near the end of 1989 and at the beginning of 1990. These events, and the radical transformations which followed, can only be explained by the preceding situations which, to a certain extent, crystallized or institutionalized Leo XIII's predictions and the increasingly disturbing signs noted by his Successors. Pope Leo foresaw the negative consequences—political, social and economic—of the social order proposed by "socialism", which at that time was still only a social philosophy and not yet a fully structured movement. It may seem surprising that "socialism" appeared at the beginning of the Pope's critique of solutions to the "question of the working class" at a time when "socialism" was not yet in the form of a strong and powerful State, with all the resources which that implies, as was later to happen. However, he correctly judged the danger posed to the masses by the attractive presentation of this simple and radical solution to the "question of the working class" of the time—all the more so when one considers the terrible situation of injustice in which the working classes of the recently industrialized nations found themselves.

Two things must be emphasized here: first, the great clarity in perceiving, in all its harshness, the actual condition of the working class—men, women and children; secondly, equal clarity in recognizing the evil of a solution which, by appearing to reverse the positions of the poor and the rich, was in reality detrimental to the very people whom it was meant to help. The remedy would prove worse than the sickness. By defining the nature of the socialism of his day as the suppression of private property, Leo XIII arrived at the crux of the problem.

His words deserve to be re-read attentively: "To remedy these wrongs (the unjust distribution of wealth and the poverty of the workers), the Socialists encourage the poor man's envy of the rich and strive to do away with private property, contending that individual possessions should become the common property of all . . .; but their contentions are so clearly powerless to end the controversy that, were they carried into effect, the working man himself would be among the first to suffer. They are moreover emphatically unjust, for they would rob the lawful possessor, distort the functions of the State, and create utter confusion in the community. . . ."

. . . The Church is well aware that in the course of history conflicts of interest between different social groups inevitably arise, and that in the face of such conflicts Christians must often take a position, honestly and decisively. . . .

. . . [The papal encyclical] *Rerum Novarum* points the way to just reforms which can restore dignity to work as the free activity of man. These reforms imply that society and the State will both assume responsibility, especially for protecting the worker from the nightmare of unemployment. Historically, this has happened in two converging ways: either through economic policies aimed at ensuring balanced growth and full employment, or through unemployment insurance and re-training programmes capable of ensuring a smooth transfer of workers from crisis sectors to those in expansion. . . .

The Encyclical and the related social teaching of the Church had far-reaching influence in the years bridging the nineteenth and twentieth centuries. The influence is evident in the numerous reforms which were introduced in the areas of social security, pensions, health insurance and compensation in the case of accidents, within the framework of greater respect for the rights of workers.

These reforms were carried out in part by States, but in the struggle to achieve them *the role of the workers' movement* was an important one. This movement, which began as a response of moral conscience to unjust and harmful situations, conducted a widespread campaign for reform, far removed from vague ideology and closer to the daily needs of workers. . . .

Thus, as we look at the past, there is good reason to thank God that the great Encyclical was not without an echo in human hearts and indeed led to a generous response on the practical level. Still, we must acknowledge that its prophetic message was not fully accepted by people at the time. Precisely for this reason there ensued some very serious tragedies.

Reading the Encyclical within the context of Pope Leo's whole magisterium, we see how it points essentially to the socio-economic consequences of an error which has even greater implications. As has been mentioned, this error consists in an understanding of human freedom which detaches it from obedience to the truth, and consequently from the duty to respect the rights of others. The essence of freedom then becomes self-love carried to the point of contempt for God and neighbour, a self-love which leads to an unbridled affirmation of self-interest and which refuses to be limited by any demand of justice.

This very error had extreme consequences in the tragic series of wars which ravaged Europe and the world between 1914 and 1945. . . . Here we recall the Jewish people in particular, whose terrible fate has become a symbol of the aberration of which man is capable when he turns against God. . . .

While it is true that since 1945 weapons have been silent on the European continent, it must be remembered that true peace is never simply the result of military victory, but rather implies both the removal of the causes of war and genuine reconciliation between peoples. For many years there has been in Europe and the world a situation of non-war rather than genuine peace. Half of the continent fell under the domination of a Communist dictatorship, while the other half organized itself in defence against this threat. Many peoples lost the ability to control their own destiny and were enclosed within the suffocating boundaries of an empire in which efforts were made to destroy their historical memory and the centuries-old roots of their culture. As a result of this violent division of Europe, enormous masses of people were compelled to leave their homeland or were forcibly deported.

An insane arms race swallowed up the resources needed for the development of national economies and for assistance to the less developed nations. Scientific and technological progress, which should have contributed to man's well-being, was transformed into an instrument of war: science and technology were directed to the production of ever more efficient and destructive weapons. . . .

. . . [I]t should be remembered that after the Second World War, and in reaction to its horrors, there arose a more lively sense of human rights, which found recognition in a number of *International Documents* and, one might say, in the drawing up of a new "right of nations", to which the Holy See has constantly contributed. The focal point of this evolution has been the United Nations Organization. Not only has there been a development in awareness of the rights of individuals, but also in awareness of the rights of nations, as well as a clearer realization of the need to act in order to remedy the grave imbalances that exist between the various geographical areas of the world. In a certain sense, these imbalances have shifted the centre of the social question from the national to the international level.

While noting this process with satisfaction, nevertheless one cannot ignore that fact that the overall balance of the various policies of aid for development has not always been positive. The United Nations, moreover, has not yet succeeded in establishing, as alternatives to war, effective means for the resolution of international conflicts. This seems to be the most urgent problem which the international community has yet to resolve.

Chapter III

The Year 1989

It is on the basis of the world situation just described ... that the unexpected and promising significance of the events of recent years can be understood.... An important, even decisive, contribution was made by *the Church's commitment to defend and promote human rights.* In situations strongly influenced by ideology, in which polarization obscured the awareness of a human dignity common to all, the Church affirmed clearly and forcefully that every individual—whatever his or her personal convictions—bears the image of God and therefore deserves respect. Often, the vast majority of people identified themselves with this kind of affirmation, and this led to a search for forms of protest and for political solutions more respectful of the dignity of the person. ...

It cannot be forgotten that the fundamental crisis of systems claiming to express the rule and indeed the dictatorship of the working class began with the great upheavals which took place in Poland in the name of solidarity. It was the throngs of working people which foreswore the ideology which presumed to speak in their name. On the basis of a hard, lived experience of work and of oppression, it was they who recovered and, in a sense, rediscovered the content and principles of the Church's social doctrine. ...

The events of 1989 took place principally in the countries of Eastern and Central Europe. However, they have worldwide importance because they have positive and negative consequences which concern the whole human family. These consequences are not mechanistic or fatalistic in character, but rather are opportunities for human freedom to cooperate with the merciful plan of God who acts within history.

The first consequence was *an encounter* in some countries *between the Church and the workers' movement,* which came about as a result of an ethical and explicitly Christian reaction against a widespread situation of injustice. For about a century the workers' movement had fallen in part under the dominance of Marxism, in the conviction that the working class, in order to struggle effectively against oppression, had to appropriate its economic and materialistic theories.

In the crisis of Marxism, the natural dictates of the consciences of workers have re-emerged in a demand for justice and a recognition of the dignity of work, in conformity with the social doctrine of the Church. The worker movement is part of a more general movement among workers and other people of good will for the liberation of the human person and for the affirmation of human rights. It is a movement which today has spread to many countries, and which, far from opposing the Catholic Church, looks to her with interest.

The crisis of Marxism does not rid the world of the situations of injustice and oppression which Marxism itself exploited and on which it fed. To those who are searching today for a new and authentic theory and praxis of liberation, the Church offers not only her social doctrine and, in general, her teaching about the human person redeemed in Christ, but also her concrete commitment and material assistance in the struggle against marginalization and suffering. . . .

The fall of Marxism has naturally had a great impact on the division of the planet into worlds which are closed to one another and in jealous competition. It has further highlighted the reality of interdependence among peoples, as well as the fact that human work, by its nature, is meant to unite peoples, not divide them. Peace and prosperity, in fact, are goods which belong to the whole human race: it is not possible to enjoy them in a proper and lasting way if they are achieved and maintained at the cost of other peoples and nations, by violating their rights or excluding them from the sources of well-being.

In a sense, for some countries of Europe the real post-war period is just beginning. The radical re-ordering of economic systems, hitherto collectivized, entails problems and sacrifices comparable to those which the countries of Western Europe had to face in order to rebuild after the Second World War. It is right that in the present difficulties the formerly Communist countries should be aided by the united effort of other nations. Obviously they themselves must be the primary agents of their own development, but they must also be given a reasonable opportunity to accomplish this goal, something that cannot happen without the help of other countries. . . .

Assistance from other countries, especially the countries of Europe which were part of that history and which bear responsibility for it, represents a debt in justice. But it also corresponds to the interest and welfare of Europe as a whole, since Europe cannot live in peace if the various conflicts which have arisen as a result of the past are to become more acute because of a situation of economic disorder, spiritual dissatisfaction and desperation. . . .

Finally, development must not be understood solely in economic terms, but in a way that is fully human. It is not only a question of raising all peoples to the level currently enjoyed by the richest countries, but rather of building up a more decent life through united labour, of concretely enhancing every individual's dignity and creativity, as well as his capacity to respond to his personal vocation, and thus to God's call. The apex of development is the exercise of the right and duty to seek God, to know him and to live in accordance with that knowledge. In the totalitarian and authoritarian regimes, the principle that force dominates over reason was carried to the extreme. Man was compelled to submit to a conception of reality imposed on him by coercion, and not reached by virtue of his own reason and the exercise of his own freedom. . . .

Chapter IV

Private Property and the Universal Destination of Material Goods

In *Rerum Novarum*, Leo XIII strongly affirmed the natural character of the right to private property, using various arguments against the socialism of his time. This right, which is fundamental for the autonomy and development of the person, has always been defended by the Church up to our own day. At the same time, the Church teaches that the possession of material goods is not an absolute right, and that its limits are inscribed in its very nature as a human right.

While the Pope proclaimed the right to private ownership, he affirmed with equal clarity that the "use" of goods, while marked by freedom, is subordinated to their original common destination as created goods, as well as to the will of Jesus Christ as expressed in the Gospel. . . .

The Successors of Leo XIII have repeated this twofold affirmation: the necessity and therefore the legitimacy of private ownership, as well as the limits which are imposed on it. The Second Vatican Council likewise clearly restated the traditional doctrine in words which bear repeating: "In making use of the exterior things we lawfully possess, we ought to regard them not just as our own but also as common, in the sense that they can profit not only the owners but others too.". . . I have returned to this same doctrine, first in my address to the Third Conference of the Latin American Bishops at Puebla [Mexico, January 28, 1979], and later in the Encyclicals *Laborem Exercens* and *Sollicitudo Rei Socialis*. . . .

The original source of all that is good is the very act of God, who created both the earth and man, and who gave the earth to man so that he might have dominion over it by his work and enjoy its fruits (*Gen* 1:28). God gave the earth to the whole human race for the sustenance of all its members, without excluding or favouring anyone. This is *the foundation of the universal destination of the earth's goods*. The earth, by reason of its fruitfulness and its capacity to satisfy human needs, is God's first gift for the sustenance of human life. But the earth does not yield its fruits without a particular human response to God's gift, that is to say, without work. It is through work that man, using his intelligence and exercising his freedom, succeeds in dominating the earth and making it a fitting home. . . .

In history, these two factors—*work* and *the land*—are to be found at the beginning of every human society. However, they do not always stand in the same relationship to each other. At one time *the natural fruitfulness of the earth* appeared to be, and was in fact, the primary factor of wealth, while work was, as it were, the help and support for this fruitfulness. In our time, *the role of human work* is becoming increasingly important as the productive factor both of non-material and of material wealth. Moreover, it is becoming clearer how a person's work is naturally interrelated with the work of others. More than ever, work is *work with others* and *work for others:* it is a matter of doing something for someone else. . . .

In our time, in particular, there exists another form of ownership which is becoming no less important than land: *the possession of know-how, technology and skill.* The wealth of the industrialized nations is based much more on this kind of ownership than on natural resources. . . .

. . . Whereas at one time the decisive factor of production was *the land,* and later capital—understood as a total complex of the instruments of production—today the decisive factor is increasingly *man himself,* that is, his knowledge, especially his scientific knowledge, his capacity for interrelated and compact organization, as well as his ability to perceive the needs ' of others and to satisfy them.

However, the risks and problems connected with this kind of process should be pointed out. The fact is that many people, perhaps the majority today, do not have the means which would enable them to take their place in an effective and humanly dignified way within a productive system in which work is truly central. They have no possibility of acquiring the basic knowledge which would enable them to express their creativity and develop their potential. They have no way of entering the network of knowledge and intercommunication which would enable them to see their qualities appreciated and utilized. Thus, if not actually exploited, they are to a great extent marginalized; economic development takes place over their heads. . . . Allured by the dazzle of an opulence which is beyond their reach, and at the same time driven by necessity, these people crowd the cities of the Third World where they are often without cultural roots, and where they are exposed to situations of violent uncertainty, without the possibility of becoming integrated. Their dignity is not acknowledged in any real way, and sometimes there are even attempts to eliminate them from history through coercive forms of demographic control which are contrary to human dignity.

Many other people, while not completely marginalized, live in situations in which the struggle for a bare minimum is uppermost. These are situations in which the rules of the earliest period of capitalism still flourish in conditions of "ruthlessness" in no way inferior to the darkest moments of the first phase of industrialization. In other cases the land is still the central element in the economic process, but those who cultivate it are excluded from ownership and reduced to a state of quasi-servitude. In these cases, it is still possible today, as in the days of *Rerum Novarum,* to speak of inhuman exploitation. . . .

Unfortunately, the great majority of people in the Third World still live in such conditions. It would be a mistake, however, to understand this *"world"* in purely geographic terms. . . . [A]spects typical of the Third World also appear in developed countries, where the constant transformation of the methods of production and consumption devalues certain acquired skills and professional expertise, and thus requires a continual effort of re-training and updating. Those who fail to keep up with the times can easily be marginalized, as can the elderly, the young people who are incapable of finding their place in the life of society and, in general, those who are weakest or part of the so-called Fourth World. The situation of women too is far from easy in these conditions.

It would appear that, on the level of individual nations and of international relations, *the free market* is the most efficient instrument for utilizing resources and effectively responding to needs. But this is true only for those needs which are "solvent", insofar as they are endowed with purchasing power, and for those resources which are "marketable", insofar as they are capable of obtaining a satisfactory price. But there are many human needs which find no place on the market. It is a strict duty of justice and truth not to allow fundamental human needs to remain unsatisfied, and not to allow those burdened by such needs to perish. It is also necessary to help these needy people to acquire expertise, to enter the circle of exchange, and to develop their skills in order to make the best use of their capacities and resources. Even prior to the logic of a fair exchange of goods and the forms of justice appropriate to it, there exists *something which is due to man because he is man,* by reason of his lofty dignity. Inseparable from that required "something" is the possibility to survive and, at the same time, to make an active contribution to the common good of humanity.

In Third World contexts, certain objectives stated by *Rerum Novarum* remain valid, and, in some cases, still constitute a goal yet to be reached, if man's work and his very being are not to be reduced to the level of a mere commodity. These objectives include a sufficient wage for the support of the family, social insurance for old age and unemployment, and adequate protection for the conditions of employment.

Here we find a wide range of *opportunities for commitment and effort* in the name of justice on the part of trade unions and other workers' organizations. These defend workers' rights and protect their interests as persons, while fulfilling a vital cultural role, so as to enable workers to participate more fully and honourably in the life of their nation and to assist them along the path of development.

In this sense, it is right to speak of a struggle against an economic system, if the latter is understood as a method of upholding the absolute predominance of capital, the possession of the means of production and of the land, in contrast to the free and personal nature of human work. In the struggle against such a system, what is being proposed as an alternative is not the socialist system, which in fact turns out to be State capitalism, but rather *a society of free work, of enterprise and of participation.* Such a society is not directed against the market, but demands that the market be appropriately controlled by the forces of society and by the State, so as to guarantee that the basic needs of the whole of society are satisfied.

The Church acknowledges the legitimate *role of profit* as an indication that a business is functioning well. When a firm makes a profit, this means that productive factors have been properly employed and corresponding human needs have been duly satisfied. But profitability is not the only indicator of a firm's condition. It is possible for the financial accounts to be in order, and yet for the people—who make up the firm's most valuable asset—to be humiliated and their dignity offended. . . . We have seen that it is unacceptable to say that the defeat of so-called "Real Socialism" leaves capitalism as the only model of economic organization. . . .

In earlier stages of development, man always lived under the weight of necessity. His needs were few and were determined, to a degree, by the objective structures of his physical make-up. Economic activity was directed towards satisfying these needs. It is clear that today the problem is not only one of supplying people with a sufficient quantity of goods, but also of responding to a *demand for quality:* the quality of the goods to be produced and consumed, the quality of the services to be enjoyed, the quality of the environment and of life in general.

To call for an existence which is qualitatively more satisfying is of itself legitimate, but one cannot fail to draw attention to the new responsibilities and dangers connected with this phase of history. The manner in which new needs arise and are defined is always marked by a more or less appropriate concept of man and of his true good. A given culture reveals its overall understanding of life through the choices it makes in production and consumption. It is here that *the phenomenon of consumerism* arises. . . .

A striking example of artificial consumption contrary to the health and dignity of the human person, and certainly not easy to control, is the use of drugs. Widespread drug use is a sign of a serious malfunction in the social system; it also implies a materialistic and, in a certain sense, destructive "reading" of human needs. In this way the innovative capacity of a free economy is brought to a one-sided and inadequate conclusion. Drugs, as well as pornography and other forms of consumerism which exploit the frailty of the weak, tend to fill the resulting spiritual void.

It is not wrong to want to live better; what is wrong is a style of life which is presumed to be better when it is directed towards "having" rather than "being", and which wants to have more, not in order to be more but in order to spend life in enjoyment as an end in itself. It is therefore necessary to create life-styles in which the quest for truth, beauty, goodness and communion with others for the sake of common growth are the factors which determine consumer choices, savings and investments. . . .

. . . In his desire to have and to enjoy rather than to be and to grow, man consumes the resources of the earth and his own life in an excessive and disordered way. At the root of the senseless destruction of the natural environment lies an anthropological error, which unfortunately is widespread in our day. Man, who discovers his capacity to transform and in a certain sense create the world through his own work, forgets that this is always based on God's prior and original gift of the things that are. Man thinks that he can make arbitrary use of the earth, subjecting it without restraint to his will, as though it did not have its own requisites and a prior God-given purpose, which man can indeed develop but must not betray. Instead of carrying out his role as a cooperator with God in the work of creation, man sets himself up in place of God. . . .

The first and fundamental structure for "human ecology" is *the family,* in which man receives his first formative ideas about truth and goodness, and learns what it means to love and to be loved, and thus what it actually means to be a person. Here we mean the *family founded on marriage,* in which the mutual gift of self by husband and wife creates an environment in which children can be born and develop their potentialities, become aware of their dignity and prepare to face their unique and individual destiny. But it often happens that people are discouraged from creating the proper conditions for human reproduction and are led to consider themselves and their lives as a series of sensations to be experienced rather than as a work to be accomplished. The result is a lack of freedom, which causes a person to reject a commitment to enter into a stable relationship with another person and to bring children into the world, or which leads people to consider children as one of the many "things" which an individual can have or not have, according to taste, and which compete with other possibilities.

It is necessary to go back to seeing the family as the *sanctuary of life.* The family is indeed sacred: it is the place in which life—the gift of God— can be properly welcomed and protected against the many attacks to which it is exposed, and can develop in accordance with what constitutes authentic human growth. In the face of the so-called culture of death, the family is the heart of the culture of life.

Human ingenuity seems to be directed more towards limiting, suppressing or destroying the sources of life—including recourse to abortion, which unfortunately is so widespread in the world—than towards defending and opening up the possibilities of life. . . .

These criticisms are directed not so much against an economic system as against an ethical and cultural system. The economy in fact is only one aspect and one dimension of the whole of human activity. If economic life is absolutized, if the production and consumption of goods become the centre of social life and society's only value, not subject to any other value, the reason is to be found not so much in the economic system itself as in the fact that the entire socio-cultural system, by ignoring the ethical and religious dimension, has been weakened, and ends by limiting itself to the production of goods and services alone. . . .

[C]an it perhaps be said that, after the failure of Communism, capitalism is the victorious social system, and that capitalism should be the goal of the countries now making efforts to rebuild their economy and society? Is this the model which ought to be proposed to the countries of the Third World which are searching for the path to true economic and civil progress?

The answer is obviously complex. If by "capitalism" is meant an economic system which recognizes the fundamental and positive role of business, the market, private property and the resulting responsibility for the means of production, as well as free human creativity in the economic sector, then the answer is certainly in the affirmative, even though it would perhaps be more appropriate to speak of a "business economy", "market economy" or simply "free economy". But if by "capitalism" is meant a system in which freedom in the economic sector is not circumscribed within a strong juridical framework which places it at the service of human freedom in its totality, and which sees it as a particular aspect of that freedom, the core of which is ethical and religious, then the reply is certainly negative.

The Marxist solution has failed, but the realities of marginalization and exploitation remain in the world, especially the Third World, as does the reality of human alienation, especially in the more advanced countries. Against these phenomena the Church strongly raises her voice. Vast multitudes are still living in conditions of great material and moral poverty. The collapse of the Communist system in so many countries certainly removes an obstacle to facing these problems in an appropriate and realistic way, but it is not enough to bring about their solution. Indeed, there is a risk that a radical capitalistic ideology could spread which refuses even to consider these problems, in the *a priori* belief that any attempt to solve them is doomed to failure, and which blindly entrusts their solution to the free development of market forces.

The Church has no models to present; models that are real and truly effective can only arise within the framework of different historical situations, through the efforts of all those who responsibly confront concrete problems in all their social, economic, political and cultural aspects, as these interact with one another. For such a task the Church offers her social teaching as an *indispensable and ideal orientation,* a teaching which, as already mentioned, recognizes the positive value of the market and of enterprise, but which at the same time points out that these need to be oriented towards the common good. This teaching also recognizes the legitimacy of workers' efforts to obtain full respect for their dignity and to gain broader areas of participation in the life of industrial enterprises so that, while cooperating with others and under the direction of others, they can in a certain sense "work for themselves" through the exercise of their intelligence and freedom. ...

The obligation to earn one's bread by the sweat of one's brow also presumes the right to do so. A society in which this right is systematically denied, in which economic policies do not allow workers to reach satisfactory levels of employment, cannot be justified from an ethical point of view, nor can that society attain social peace. Just as the person fully realizes himself in the free gift of self, so too ownership morally justifies itself in the creation, at the proper time and in the proper way, of opportunities for work and human growth for all.

Chapter VI

Man is the Way of the Church

... Today, the Church's social doctrine focuses especially *on man* as he is involved in a complex network of relationships within modern societies. The human sciences and philosophy are helpful for interpreting *man's central place within society* and for enabling him to understand himself better as a "social being". However, man's true identity is only fully revealed to him through faith, and it is precisely from faith that the Church's social teaching begins. While drawing upon all the contributions made by the sciences and philosophy, her social teaching is aimed at helping man on the path of salvation.

The Encyclical *Rerum Novarum* can be read as a valid contribution to socio-economic analysis at the end of the nineteenth century, but its specific value derives from the fact that it is a document of the Magisterium and is fully a part of the Church's evangelizing mission, together with many other documents of this nature. Thus the Church's *social teaching* is itself a valid *instrument of evangelization*. As such, it proclaims God and his mystery of salvation in Christ to every human being, and for that very reason reveals man to himself. In this light, and only in this light, does it concern itself with everything else: the human rights of the individual, and in particular of the "working class", the family and education, the duties of the State, the ordering of national and international society, economic life, culture, war and peace, and respect for life from the moment of conception until death. . . .

SCHWARZKOPF'S HOMECOMING
ADDRESS TO CONGRESS
May 8, 1991

General H. Norman Schwarzkopf received a hero's welcome in a special appearance before the assembled members of Congress on May 8. They rose in applause as the blunt-spoken four-star general entered the House chamber, to a fanfare by the Army Band. At the rostrum, the commander of victorious allied forces in Operation Desert Storm thanked God, the president, Congress, the American people, and the troops for the willingness to "get the job done" and "kick the Iraqis out of Kuwait." Congress's enthusiastic reaction to the general reflected the nation's euphoria over the swift military victory which had been accomplished with far less American bloodshed than had been expected. (Victory in the Gulf, p. 97)

It "is a great day to be a soldier, and it is a great day to be an American," he said, giving special thanks to "our Commander in Chief for his wisdom and courage and the confidence he demonstrated in us by allowing us to fight this war in such a way that we were able to minimize our casualties—that is the right way to fight a war."

"We were black and white and yellow and brown and red and we noticed when our blood was shed in the desert it didn't separate by race but it flowed together, because that's what your military is," the general said. "We fought side by side with brothers and sisters at arms who were British and French and Saudi Arabian and Egyptian, Kuwaiti and members of many other Arab and Western nations...."

Schwarzkopf's address to Congress was but one of many honors he received after his return from the Persian Gulf on April 20. He led throng-filled victory parades down Broadway in New York City and Pennsylvania Avenue in Washington, D.C. In the nation's capital an accompanying display of military arms was the largest assembled in that city since Dwight D. Eisenhower led a parade down Pennsylvania Avenue at the end of World War II.

Britain's Queen Elizabeth II, on a visit to the United States, bestowed on Schwarzkopf an honorary knighthood. She expressed Britain's gratitude for his military leadership in the defeat of Iraq. Eisenhower was the only other American military commander to be so honored.

Schwarzkopf, commander in chief of the U.S. Central Command, had returned its headquarters back to Florida from temporary relocation in Saudi Arabia during the war. Before its outbreak in August 1990, the general was placed in charge of revising U.S. military contingency plans in the Middle East. Those plans were used in the deployment of more than half a million American and allied troops to that region to liberate Kuwait and protect Saudi Arabia.

Schwarzkopf, a 1956 graduate of West Point, was a decorated combat veteran of the Vietnam War who held a variety of command and staff assignments during his army career. Upon returning from the Middle East, he declined the offer to replace the retiring Gen. Carl E. Vuono as army chief of staff, opting instead to retire in June. This followed his signing of a contract with Bantam Books to write his autobiography, reportedly for a record $5 million. In the meantime, at least three biographies had been published, all complimentary.

He was not without detractors, however. Gregg Easterbrook, writing in the September 30 New Republic, *said Schwarzkopf's "reputation is based largely on showings at press appearances, though this has little to do with his performance as an officer." Easterbrook contended that the allied victory was achieved through an overwhelming superiority of arms.*

On one matter of considerable public speculation, Schwarzkopf said before and after his military retirement that he would not become a candidate for political office.

> *Following is Gen. H. Norman Schwarzkopf's address to Congress, May 8, 1991, as printed in the* Congressional Record:

Mr. Speaker, Members of Congress and distinguished guests, it is a great day to be a soldier, and it is a great day to be an American.

I want to thank you for the singular distinction of being allowed to speak to the special session of the Congress of the United States of America.

Indeed, I am awed and honored to be standing at the podium where so many notable men and women have stood before me. Unlike them, I do not stand here today for any great deed that I have done. Instead, I stand here because I was granted by our national leadership the great privilege of commanding the magnificent American service men and women who constituted the Armed Forces of Operation Desert Shield and Desert Storm.

Before I go further, I must, through their Representatives who are here today, tell each and every one of those extraordinary patriots that I have no idea of what the future holds in store for me, but I do know one thing, I will never, ever in my entire life receive a greater reward than the inspiration that I received every single day as I watched your dedicated performance, your dedicated sacrifice, your dedicated service to your country.

Since I was fortunate enough to command these great Americans and since you are the elected Representatives of the American people, I would presume today to speak for our service men and women, through you, to the people of our great Nation.

First of all, who were we? We were 541,000 soldiers, sailors, airmen, marines, and coastguardsmen. We were the thunder and lightning of Desert Storm. We were the U.S. military and we are damn proud of it. But we were more than that. We were all volunteers and we were regulars. We were Reservists and we were National Guardsmen, serving side-by-side as we have in every war, because that's what the U.S. military is. And we were men and women, each of us bearing our fair share of the load and none of us quitting because the conditions were too rough or the job was too tough, because that's what your military is. We were Protestants and Catholics and Jews and Moslems and Buddhists and many other religions fighting for a common and just cause, because that's what your military is. We were black and white and yellow and brown and red and we noticed when our blood was shed in the desert it didn't separate by race but it flowed together, because that's what your military is. We fought side by side with brothers and sisters at arms who were British and French and Saudi Arabian and Egyptian, Kuwaiti and members of many other Arab and Western nations; and we noticed the same thing when their blood was shed in the desert—it did not separate according to national origin. We left our homes and our families and traveled thousands of miles away and fought in places whose names we couldn't even pronounce simply because you asked us to and it therefore became our duty, because that's what your military does.

We now proudly join the ranks of those Americans who call themselves veterans. We are proud to share that title with those who went before us and we feel a particular pride in joining ranks with that special group who served their country in the mountains, and the jungles, and the deltas of Vietnam. We who were there and they served just as proudly as we served in the Middle East. And now that we have won a great victory, we dare to ask that, just as we were willing to sacrifice and fight to win the war, you be willing to sacrifice and search to win the peace.

We would like to offer our thanks. First, we would like to thank our God for the protection He gave us in the deserts of Kuwait and Iraq. Most of us came home safely. We ask Him to grant a special love to all of our fallen comrades who gave their lives for the cause of freedom and we ask that He embrace to His bosom not only the 147 of us who were killed in action but also the 188 of us who gave their lives both before the war during Desert

Shield and since the termination of Desert Storm. They, too, no less than our killed in action, died for the cause of freedom. We also ask that God grant special strength to our comrades who are still in hospitals with wounds and injuries they received during the war. By their example, we should all remember that the freedoms we enjoy in this great country of ours do not come without a price. They are paid for and protected by the lives, the limbs and the blood of American service men and women.

We would also like to thank our Commander in Chief for his wisdom and courage and the confidence he demonstrated in us by allowing us to fight this war in such a way that we were able to minimize our casualties—that is the right way to fight a war. We would like to thank the Congress and former administrations for giving us the finest tanks and aircraft and ships and military equipment in the whole world without question. Without question that is what gave us the confidence necessary to attack into the teeth of our enemy with the sure knowledge that we would prevail. And we would ask that in the years to come as we reduce the quantity of our Armed Forces that you never forget that it is the quality of our Armed Forces that wins wars. We want to say a special thanks to our comrades in uniform who stayed behind. You backed us up so we could carry the fight to the enemy. You maintained the peace so that we could win the war. We never could have done our job if you hadn't done yours. We also want to thank our families. It is you who endure the hardships and the separations simply because you choose to love a soldier, a sailor, an airman, a marine, or a coastguardsman. But it is your love that gave us strength in our darkest hours. You are truly the wind beneath our wings. Finally, and most importantly, to the great American people: The prophets of doom, the naysayers, the protesters, and the flag burners all said that you would never stick by us. But we knew better. We knew you would never let us down. By golly, you didn't. Since the first hour of Desert Shield until the last minute of Desert Storm, every day in every way all across America you shouted that you were with us. Millions of elementary school, high school and college students, millions and millions of families, untold numbers of civic organizations, veterans' organizations, countless offices, factories, companies and work places, millions of senior citizens and just plain Americans never let us forget that we were in your hearts and you were in our corner. Because of you when that terrible first day of the war came, we knew we would not fail, we knew we had the strength of the American people behind us and with that strength we were able to get the job done, kick the Iraqis out of Kuwait, and get back home. So, for every soldier, thank you America. For every sailor, thank you America. For every marine, thank you America. For every airman, thank you America. For every coastguardsman, thank you America. From all of us who proudly served in the Middle East in your Armed Forces, thank you to the great people of the United States of America.

QUEEN ELIZABETH II'S VISIT
TO THE UNITED STATES
May 16, 1991

Queen Elizabeth II became the first British monarch ever to address Congress when she spoke before a joint session May 16. She emphasized the ties of language, culture, and history that have bound Americans and Britons in common cause on twentieth-century battlefields, most recently in the Persian Gulf.

"Both our countries saw the invasion of Kuwait in just the same terms: an outrage to be reversed, both for the people of Kuwait and for the sake of the principle that naked aggression should not prevail," Queen Elizabeth said. "Our views were identical and so were our responses." She went on to "salute the outstanding leadership of your president, and the courage and prowess of the armed forces of the United States."

During their thirteen-day visit, the queen and her husband, Prince Philip, visited Maryland, Virginia, Florida, Texas, and Kentucky after an initial stay in Washington, D.C., where they were officially welcomed May 14 at a White House ceremony and state dinner. Following an exchange of greetings with President George Bush, televised from the White House Rose Garden, the sixty-five-year-old queen recalled that she first visited the United States "when Mr. Truman was president." That was in November 1951, three months before her coronation.

In her father's honor, Queen Elizabeth joined with President Bush in witnessing the planting of a tree on the White House lawn. It replaced a tree, badly damaged by a storm, that was planted on the occasion of her father's coronation in 1937.

At the White House dinner that evening, she said, "Now is the fourth time I have had the honor of proposing a toast to the President of the

United States in the very place my father once proposed a toast to President Roosevelt." Her father, King George VI, and her mother, Queen Elizabeth, visited the United States in 1939, shortly before the outbreak of World War II in Europe, a trip that was hailed as a public relations success.

Her last visit to Washington, she said to the dinner guests, was in 1976, when America was celebrating the bicentennial of its independence from British rule. There were no other allusions to the American Revolution in her public remarks, although her visit included a trip to George Washington's home at Mount Vernon.

Public Appearances

The royal couple, with the Bushes, attended an American League baseball game in Baltimore, where a stadium full of fans of royalty or baseball waved Union Jacks and joined in the pre-game singing of "God Save the Queen," which co-starred with the "Star-Spangled Banner." In their midst, a few protesters waved banners bearing demands that Britain get out of Northern Ireland. Some of the demonstrators identified themselves as Irish Americans working with Irish Northern Aid, or Noraid, an organization sometimes accused of smuggling weapons into Northern Ireland to arm the underground Irish Republican Army.

Rep. Joseph P. Kennedy II, D-Mass., and a few other lawmakers of Irish descent boycotted Queen Elizabeth's address to Congress in protest of what Kennedy described as "the British occupation in Northern Ireland." However, his uncle, Sen. Edward M. Kennedy, D-Mass., attended the queen's address and a luncheon that followed in her honor.

Rep. Gus Savage, D-Ill., and the Rev. Al Sharpton, a black activist from Brooklyn, urged black people to shun the queen's public appearances because of racial tensions in Britain and its recent decision to lift economic sanctions against South Africa. However, on a visit to Washington's inner city, the British monarch received a big hug from a black woman, an impulsive gesture of friendship that defied royal protocol.

Aside from the few protests, the queen was well received in all of her public appearances. In Congress, her brief speech was interrupted seven times by applause. The New York Times *observed that, as "arguably the most famous person in the world," she "created a fuss in Washington this week that no other national leader could match, not even Mikhail S. Gorbachev at the height of Gorbamania."*

Knighthood for Schwarzkopf

From Washington, the royal party flew to Florida, where the queen bestowed an honorary knighthood on Gen. H. Norman Schwarzkopf, who commanded the allied forces in the war against Iraq. He became the ninth American military commander since Gen. Dwight D. Eisenhower, the allied commander in World War II, to be knighted. Other Americans, including Ronald Reagan in 1989, had been similarly honored.

The royal party's journey continued to Texas, where a crowd of thousands welcomed the motorcade in Austin. From the state capitol steps, Elizabeth spoke briefly, acknowledging "the strength of Texas expertise" that "notably helped us find and use the oil fields in the North Sea." Then she drew wild cheers with the remark that "lesser mortals are pitied for their misfortune in not being born Texan."

The queen closed her American tour with a private visit to several horse farms in Kentucky.

Following is the address of Queen Elizabeth II of Britain to a special joint session of Congress, May 16, 1991, from the Congressional Record:

Mr. Speaker, Mr. President, distinguished Members of Congress, I know what a rare privilege it is to address a joint meeting of your two Houses. Thank you for inviting me.

The concept, so simply described by Abraham Lincoln as "government by the people, of the people, for the people," is fundamental to our two nations. Your Congress and our Parliament are the twin pillars of our civilisations and the chief among the many treasures that we have inherited from our predecessors.

We, like you, are staunch believers in the freedom of the individual and the rule of a fair and just law. These principles are shared with our European partners and with the wider Atlantic community. They are the bedrock of the Western World.

Some people believe that power grows from the barrel of a gun. So it can, but history shows that it never grows well nor for very long. Force, in the end, is sterile. We have gone a better way; our societies rest on mutual agreement, on contract and on consensus. A significant part of your social contract is written down in your Constitution. Ours rest on custom and will. The spirit behind both, however, is precisely the same. It is the spirit of democracy.

These ideals are clear enough, but they must never be taken for granted. They have to be protected and nurtured through every change and fluctuation. I want to take this opportunity to express the gratitude of the British people to the people of the United States of America for their steadfast loyalty to our common enterprise throughout this turbulent century. The future is, as ever, obscure. The only certainty is that it will present the world with new and daunting problems, but if we continue to stick to our fundamental ideals, I have every confidence that we can resolve them.

Recent events in the gulf have proved that it is possible to do just that. Both our countries saw the invasion of Kuwait in just the same terms; an outrage to be reversed, both for the people of Kuwait and for the sake of the principle that naked aggression should not prevail. Our views were identical and so were our responses. That response was not without risk, but we have both learned from history that we must not allow aggression to succeed.

I salute the outstanding leadership of your President, and the courage and prowess of the Armed Forces of the United States. I know that the servicemen and servicewomen of Britain, and of all the members of the coalition, were proud to act in a just cause alongside their American comrades.

Unfortunately, experience shows that great enterprises seldom end with a tidy and satisfactory flourish. Together, we are doing our best to reestablish peace and civil order in the region, and to help those members of ethnic and religious minorities who continue to suffer through no fault of their own. If we succeed, our military success will have achieved its true objective.

For all that uncertainty, it would be a mistake to make the picture look too gloomy. The swift and dramatic changes in Eastern Europe in the last decade have opened up great opportunities for the people of those countries. They are finding their own paths to freedom. But the paths would have been blocked if the Atlantic Alliance had not stood together— if your country and mine had not stood together. Let us never forget that lesson.

Britain is at the heart of a growing movement toward greater cohesion within Europe, and within the European Community in particular. This is going to mean radical economic, social, and political evolution. NATO, too, is adapting to the new realities in Eastern Europe and the Soviet Union, and to changing attitudes in the West. It is Britain's prime concern to ensure that the new Europe is open and liberal and that it works in growing harmony with the United States and the other members of the Atlantic community. All our history in this and earlier centuries underlines the basic point that the best progress is made when Europeans and Americans act in concert. We must not allow ourselves to be enticed into a form of continental insularity.

I believe this is particularly important now, at a time of major social, environmental, and economic changes in your continent, and in Asia and Africa. We must make sure that those changes do not become convulsions. For the primary interest of our societies is not domination but stability; stability so that ordinary men and women everywhere can get on with their lives in confidence.

Our two countries have a special advantage in seeking to guide the process of change because of the rich ethnic and cultural diversity of both our societies. Stability in our own countries depends on tolerance and understanding between different communities. Perhaps we can, together, build on our experience to spread the message we have learned at home to those regions where it has yet to be absorbed.

Whether we will be able to realise our hopes will depend on the maintenance of an acceptable degree of international order. In this we see the United Nations as the essential instrument in the promotion of peace and cooperation. We look to its Charter as the guardian of civilised conduct between nations.

In 1941 President Roosevelt spoke of "Freedom of speech and expression—everywhere in the world . . . freedom of every person to worship God in their own way—everywhere in the world . . . Freedom from want and . . . Freedom from fear." Just as our societies have prospered through their reliance on contract, not force, so too will the world be a better place for the spread of that mutual respect and good faith which are so fundamental to our way of life. Freedom under the rule of law is an international, as well as a national, concern.

That thought might be in the minds of those of you attending the 50th Anniversary Meeting for the British-American Parliamentary Group in July. Both our Houses are eager to greet you. They will, I know, tell you that our aim, as Britons and Europeans, is to celebrate and nurture our long-standing friendship with the people of the United States. We want to build on that foundation and to do better. And, if the going gets rough, I hope you can still agree with your poet Emerson, who wrote in 1847 "I feel, in regard to this aged England, with a kind of instinct, that she sees a little better on a cloudy day, and that, in storm of battle and calamity, she has a secret vigour and a pulse like a cannon." You will find us worthy partners, and we are proud to have you as our friends.

May God bless America.

WALESA'S APOLOGY IN ISRAEL FOR POLISH ANTISEMITISM

May 20, 1991

On the first visit of a Polish leader to Israel, President Lech Walesa apologized for Poland's role in the Holocaust and asked for reconciliation between Jews and Poles. In his impassioned address to the Israeli Knesset (parliament) May 20, Walesa recalled that Jews had lived in Poland for a thousand years and found it a haven. Before World War II Poland's 4 million Jews accounted for more than half of the world's Jewish population, but only a few thousand survived five and a half years of Nazi occupation. Many died in Polish-based concentration camps.

"We too, were victims of Nazism," Walesa said of his fellow Poles, but he acknowledged that "there were also malefactors among us" who aided in the killing of Jews. Such wrongs between nations could not be measured "by human reckoning," he said. "But here, in Israel, in the land of your birth and rebirth, I ask your forgiveness."

The Knesset audience included several Polish-born survivors of the Holocaust, including Prime Minister Yitzhak Shamir and his predecessor, Shimon Peres. In introducing Walesa, Shamir said he welcomed the prospect of "a new era in the relations of our two countries and our two peoples," and he praised the "new Poland" that Walesa had helped to create. (Speeches Marking Poland's New Era, Historic Documents of 1989, p. 523)

But the prime minister also said, "What happened on Polish soil for five and a half years will accompany the history of Poland and all of humanity until the end of time." Shamir, whose father was killed by a Pole, was once quoted as saying that "Poles suck [antisemitism] in their mother's milk."

*Walesa's presence in Israel drew mixed responses in the Israeli press.
The newspaper* Haaretz *accused the Polish leader of having used
antisemitism for political advancement but called him "one of today's
most outspoken opponents of antisemitism in Eastern Europe."*

*Before leaving for Israel, Walesa also apologized for his behavior
during his 1990 presidential election campaign. At that time he was
accused of exploiting antisemitic feelings by calling himself "100 percent
Polish."*

*As East European countries discarded Soviet controls in 1989 and
1990, many age-old ethnic hatreds were rekindled, including loud expressions of antisemitism. On December 19, 1990, the Catholic bishops of
Poland felt compelled to issue a statement expressing "sincere regret over
all cases of antisemitism which were committed on Polish soil" and
declaring antisemitism to be "against the spirit of the [Christian]
Gospel." The same statement also conceded that some Poles had aided in
the Nazi persecution of Jews in World War II.*

*Before leaving for a visit to the United States in September, Cardinal
Josef Glemp, the Roman Catholic primate of Poland, condemned
antisemitism as evil and issued an apology for saying in August 1989 that
Jewish demonstrators who scaled the walls of a convent at the site of the
wartime Auschwitz concentration camp had intended to harm the nuns.
The protesters objected to a Catholic religious edifice being placed where
thousands upon thousands of Jews had died.*

> *Following is an English translation of Polish president Lech
> Walesa's address to the Israeli Knesset in Jerusalem, May
> 20, 1991, asking for reconciliation between Poles and Jews
> and for forgiveness of Poland's role in the Nazi-era killing of
> Polish Jews:*

I wish to express my immense satisfaction at our meeting here today. It
has a singular meaning, just as the relationship uniting Poles and Jews is
singular. For a thousand years, the history has interwoven the fates of both
nations.

Jews from all over Europe had been coming to Poland, finding the
climate of tolerance and hospitality. They felt safe and could develop their
great culture. Outstanding Jewish intellectuals and religious leaders were
able to act and work. Poland was a common home for Poles and Jews.
There was a time when more than half of all Jews in the world lived in
Poland.

Before World War II, the diaspora in Poland was second in size in the
world. The second world war brought to the Jewish people the greatest
tragedy in their history. The Nazis prepared their total annihilation. The
invaders established ghettos and death camps in Auschwitz, Treblinka and
Sobibór.

We too, were victims of Nazism. Although for us, your younger brothers, the misery of that epoch was also difficult to bear and although we, too, were facing extermination, yet its horror was not as terrible, it was incomparable with shoach [the Holocaust]. We tried to help you according to our abilities. There were many Poles who were "righteous among nations," and these now have trees planted for them in the Avenue of the Righteous [in Jerusalem].

In the Talmud we read: "Whoever saves one human life, saves the whole world; whoever takes one human life, kills the whole world." There were also malefactors among us. I am a Christian, and so I cannot measure the wrongs between the two nations by human reckoning. But here, in Israel, in the land of your birth and rebirth, I ask your forgiveness.

The Uprising in Warsaw Ghetto, that bold outburst of people who understood that there are times when one has to die so that one's nation does not live on its knees, preceded Warsaw Uprising by almost a year. The cooperation between the Home Army and the Jewish Combat Organization is a tradition to which we often proudly refer. From you, our elder brethren, with whom we were not always successful in arranging our lives in the mother country, we can learn much about national solidarity, about building statehood and wielding the nation's spiritual resources.

Polish-Jewish relations were at their worst when foreign powers were ruling the country. In the postwar period, the same principle "divide and rule" was adopted by the communists. Deprived, as they were of state sovereignty, both our nations looked at, and perceived each other as if in a distorting mirror. How alike we are in our special mix of both good and bad features; in the tendency to give in to foreign influences, and in the quest for freedom; in contentiousness and the sense of solidarity; in generosity, and petty envy. How much aggressiveness is born out of these similarities.

Today, however, when Poland is rejoining the family of free nations into which, while herself not a sovereign state, she introduced Israel in 1948, let us open our minds to the past. As a representative of Poland which has regained her freedom and is regaining her independence, in the name of Polish honor, I ask you to view our common nature in fairness. We are now building a free and democratic Poland, shaping the state in which all citizens will feel at home and which will give equal rights and opportunities to all, irrespective of their origin and religion.

The independent Republic of Poland evokes the best Polish tradition. These are not just words. I have established The Council for Polish-Jewish Relations. Its task will be to give notice of anything that could hinder our cooperation. Long-term educational programs are being prepared. Young Poles will be able to acquire deeper knowledge of the common history of our nations. After an over 20 years long interval, our countries have resumed diplomatic relations. It is in getting to know each other that our future lies. So let us expand mutual contacts. Let young Poles and young Jews exchange visits. Let us promote our cultural, educational and economic cooperation.

I am greatly impressed by Israel's achievements. In the course of 40 years you have built a strong and democratic state. In spite of immense difficulties and impending dangers, your admirable experience will help us.

Poland is now living through a period of historic changes. We revert to such acknowledged and well-tested values as democracy, civil liberties, free market economy, and individual enterprise. Poland's foreign policy mirrors the profound political transformation and it helps to enhance respect for universal human values and for international law. The solidarity manifested by the allied countries during the war in the Persian Gulf has restored our faith in the validity of respecting the rules of international law. We in Poland watched with admiration the restraint and the sense of responsibility which marked Israel's behavior. Missiles were hitting your cities. But you refrained from military retaliation, thus helping to win the war, averting the danger of the conflict's expansion, and winning Israel international respect and admiration.

We support efforts to establish an equitable and permanent peace in the Middle East. We consider such a peaceful settlement feasible, provided it will ensure security and development to all countries of the region. We wish Israel such peace. We wish you success in building your country.

Dear Ladies and Gentlemen, I know what the state of Israel means to the Jewish people and to the Israelis. It is here that your great prophets had lived. It is here that God had entered into the Covenant with His chosen people. It is here that the ten commandments had been given. Then the Jewish state fell into ruins. Jerusalem was destroyed by the Romans. There began the Great Diaspora, but the Jewish people have survived even the worst. Thanks to your faith, you preserved your identity. You have returned to the land of your forefathers, which is an immense accomplishment of world-shaking proportions. It is a momentous day for me when, as President of the Republic of Poland I am addressing representatives of Israel.

May our present meeting help to erase all prejudices. May it become an impulse to intensify cooperation between Poland and Israel. May it foster brotherly relations between Poles and Jews in Poland, in Israel, and all over the world.

SUPREME COURT ON ABORTION ADVICE FROM FAMILY CLINICS

May 23, 1991

The Supreme Court, in a 5-4 decision May 23, upheld government regulations that prohibit employees from offering abortion advice at federally funded family-planning clinics. The ruling applied to 4,500 clinics serving about 4 million women each year.

Justice David H. Souter's vote for the regulations indicated that abortion foes might have attained enough support on the Court to reverse its 1973 Roe v. Wade *decision that made abortions legal. In 1989 the Court upheld a Missouri law that placed restrictions on abortions but stopped short of overturning* Roe. *Subsequently, Souter replaced Justice William J. Brennan, a supporter of abortion rights.* (Supreme Court on Abortion, Historic Documents of 1973, p. 101, and Supreme Court's Decision in Webster Abortion Case, Historic Documents of 1989, p. 365)

This case, Rust v. Sullivan, *was the first on an abortion-rights question in which Souter had participated since joining the Court in October 1990, an appointee of President George Bush. Souter's confirmation hearings and prior judicial record did not clearly reveal his position on abortion.*

The regulations the Court upheld forbid physicians and other employees at the clinics to discuss abortion services with the pregnant women they counsel. If a woman asks for abortion information, the regulations require that she be informed that the clinic "does not consider abortion an appropriate method of family planning." Those rules had been blocked by court challenges since they were issued by the Department of Health and Human Services (HHS) in 1988, the last year of the Reagan administration.

The case bore the names of plaintiff Irving Rust, medical director of the Hub, a South Bronx clinic run by Planned Parenthood of New York City, and defendant Louis W. Sullivan, who was HHS secretary when the case reached the Supreme Court. Another challenge to the regulations, filed by the city and state of New York, was consolidated with the Rust case. Both cases had been heard by the U.S. Court of Appeals for the Second Circuit, in New York, which upheld the regulations.

Two other federal appellate courts, for the First Circuit in Boston and the Tenth Circuit in Denver, held the regulations unconstitutional on challenges brought, respectively, by the state of Massachusetts and the Planned Parenthood Federation of America.

Interpreting the Language in Title X

The Supreme Court's ruling turned on what Congress meant in a twenty-one-word provision in Title X of the Public Health Service Act of 1970 which reads: "None of the funds appropriated under this subchapter shall be used in programs where abortion is a method of family planning." Until 1988 supervising HHS officials had interpreted the words as forbidding abortions but not abortion advice at federally funded clinics.

Rehnquist, writing for the Court, approvingly cited the 1984 case of Chevron v. Natural Resources Defense Council, in which the Court said that generally the judiciary should defer to the responsible agency's interpretation of an ambiguous law if the interpretation is "plausible"—even if the agency had reversed its previous interpretation.

He found the language about not using federal funds (to "promote abortion as a method of family planning") to be "ambiguous" but said that it "plainly allows" the agency's interpretation of it. The fact that HHS changed its reading of the law, from permitting to prohibiting abortion counseling, did not entitle the Court to second-guess the agency, Rehnquist wrote.

The chief justice dismissed arguments that the counseling restrictions violated the free speech rights of physicians and their patients, and interfered unduly with women's access to abortion. The government, he said, "is simply insisting that public funds be spent for the purpose for which they were authorized." Justices Byron R. White, Anthony M. Kennedy, Antonin Scalia, and Souter endorsed Rehnquist's view.

Blackmun's "Free Speech" Dissent

Justice Harry A. Blackmun disagreed strongly. "Until today," he wrote in the main dissenting opinion, "the Court never has upheld viewpoint-based suppression of speech simply because that suppression was a condition upon the acceptance of public funds." Blackmun— author of the 1973 Roe decision—said the regulations violated the free speech rights of clinic employees and amounted to "coercion" of indigent women to continue unwanted pregnancies by withholding abortion information from them. "For these women," he added, "the Government will have obliterated the freedom to choose as surely as *if it had banned abortions outright.''*

In a section of Blackmun's dissent joined by Justices Thurgood Marshall and Sandra Day O'Connor, he scoffed at the majority's "facile response" to arguments that the regulations violated First and Fifth Amendment rights. Regardless of whether the rules were authorized by law, he said, "it avoids reality to contend that they do not give rise to serious constitutional questions.''

Justice John Paul Stevens went farther in a separate dissent, saying that the rules went beyond what the law allowed. O'Connor, also writing separately, said that by declaring the regulations constitutional, the Court had ignored "our time-honored practice of not reaching constitutional questions unnecessarily." In this case, she wrote, "we need only tell the [HHS] Secretary that his regulations are not a reasonable interpretation of the statute.''

Reaction to Souter's Key Vote

Reaction to the decision was swift and predictable. "When David Souter showed his true colors today," said Judith Lichtman, director of the Women's Legal Defense Fund, "the majority of the Supreme Court put Roe versus Wade in immediate peril." In contrast, Wendy Stone, speaking for Americans United for Life, said it was "encouraging to have Justice Souter firmly on the record." The National Right to Life Committee issued a statement saying, "The Supreme Court has rejected the bizarre concept that the Constitution or medical ethics require that abortion be treated the same as contraception.''

Solicitor General Kenneth W. Starr, who argued on behalf of the government for upholding the regulations, said that the decision "reiterated the basic principle that when it is funding programs, the government is able ... to take sides ... to have viewpoints." Harvard Law School professor Kathleen Sullivan, one of the lawyers who challenged the regulations, retorted: "This says he who takes the king's shilling becomes the king's mouthpiece.''

Several family-planning groups across the nation said they would forgo federal funding rather than stop providing abortion counseling. Legislation was promptly introduced in Congress to change the wording of Title X to nullify the Court's ruling. Faye Wattleton, president of Planned Parenthood, spoke of organizing a lobbying campaign to assure enough votes to override a veto threat by President Bush.

> *Following are excerpts from the Supreme Court's majority and dissenting opinions in its* Rust v. Sullivan *decision, May 23, 1991, upholding government regulations that prohibit federally funded family-planning clinics from giving abortion advice to patients:*

Nos. 89-1391 and 89-1392

Irving Rust, etc., et al.,
Petitioners
v.
Louis W. Sullivan, Secretary of
Health and Human Services

New York, et al., Petitioners
v.
Louis W. Sullivan, Secretary of
Health and Human Services

On writs of certiorari to the
United States Court of Appeals
for the Second Circuit

[May 23, 1991]

CHIEF JUSTICE REHNQUIST delivered the opinion of the Court.

[I omitted]

II

We begin by pointing out the posture of the cases before us. Petitioners are challenging the *facial* validity of the regulations. Thus, we are concerned only with the question whether, on their face, the regulations are both authorized by the Act, and can be construed in such a manner that they can be applied to a set of individuals without infringing upon constitutionally protected rights. Petitioners face a heavy burden in seeking to have the regulations invalidated as facially unconstitutional. "A facial challenge to a legislative Act is, of course, the most difficult challenge to mount successfully, since the challenger must establish that no set of circumstances exists under which the Act would be valid. The fact that [the regulations] might operate unconstitutionally under some conceivable set of circumstances is insufficient to render [them] wholly invalid." *United States* v. *Salerno* (1987)....

A

We need not dwell on the plain language of the statute because we agree with every court to have addressed the issue that the language is ambiguous. The language of § 1008—that "[n]one of the funds appropriated under this subchapter shall be used in programs where abortion is a method of family planning"—does not speak directly to the issues of counseling, referral, advocacy, or program integrity....

The broad language of Title X plainly allows the Secretary's construction of the statute. By its own terms, § 1008 prohibits the use of Title X funds "in programs where abortion is a method of family planning." Title X does not define the term "method of family planning," nor does it enumerate what types of medical and counseling services are entitled to Title X funding. Based on the broad directives provided by Congress in Title X in general and § 1008 in particular, we are unable to say that the Secretary's construction of the prohibition in § 1008 to require a ban on counseling, referral, and advocacy within the Title X project, is impermissible. . . .

When we find, as we do here, that the legislative history is ambiguous and unenlightening on the matters with respect to which the regulations deal, we customarily defer to the expertise of the agency. Petitioners argue, however, that the regulations are entitled to little or no deference because they "reverse a longstanding agency policy that permitted nondirective counseling and referral for abortion," and thus represent a sharp break from the Secretary's prior construction of the statute. Petitioners argue that the agency's prior consistent interpretation of Section 1008 to permit nondirective counseling and to encourage coordination with local and state family planning services is entitled to substantial weight.

This Court has rejected the argument that an agency's interpretation "is not entitled to deference because it represents a sharp break with prior interpretations" of the statute in question. *Chevron* [1984]. In *Chevron*, we held that a revised interpretation deserves deference because "[a]n initial agency interpretation is not instantly carved in stone" and "the agency, to engage in informed rulemaking, must consider varying interpretations and the wisdom of its policy on a continuing basis.". . .

We find that the Secretary amply justified his change of interpretation with a "reasoned analysis." The Secretary explained that the regulations are a result of his determination, in the wake of the critical reports of the General Accounting Office (GAO) and the Office of the Inspector General (OIG), that prior policy failed to implement properly the statute and that it was necessary to provide "clear and operational guidance to grantees to preserve the distinction between Title X programs and abortion as a method of family planning." He also determined that the new regulations are more in keeping with the original intent of the statute, are justified by client experience under the prior policy, and are supported by a shift in attitude against the "elimination of unborn children by abortion." We believe that these justifications are sufficient to support the Secretary's revised approach. Having concluded that the plain language and legislative history are ambiguous as to Congress' intent in enacting Title X, we must defer to the Secretary's permissible construction of the statute.

B

We turn next to the "program integrity" requirements embodied at § 59.9 of the regulations, mandating separate facilities, personnel, and records. These requirements are not inconsistent with the plain language of Title X. Petitioners contend, however, that they are based on an impermissible construction of the statute because they frustrate the clearly expressed intent of Congress that Title X programs be an integral part of a broader, comprehensive, health-care system. They argue that this integration is impermissibly burdened because the efficient use of non-Title X funds by Title X grantees will be adversely affected by the regulations.

The Secretary defends the separation requirements of § 59.9 on the grounds that they are necessary to assure that Title X grantees apply federal funds only to federally authorized purposes and that grantees avoid creating the appearance that the government is supporting abortion-related activities. The program integrity regulations were promulgated in direct response to the observations in the GAO and OIG reports that "[b]ecause the distinction between the recipient's title X and other activities may not be easily recognized, the public can get the impression that Federal funds are being improperly used for abortion activities.". . .

III

Petitioners contend that the regulations violate the First Amendment . . . "free speech rights of private health care organizations that receive Title X funds, of their staff, and of their patients" by impermissibly imposing "viewpoint-discriminatory conditions on government subsidies" and thus penaliz[e] speech funded with non-Title X monies." Because "Title X continues to fund speech ancillary to pregnancy testing in a manner that is not evenhanded with respect to views and information about abortion, it invidiously discriminates on the basis of viewpoint." Relying on *Regan* v. *Taxation With Representation of Wash.,* [1983] and *Arkansas Writers Project, Inc.* v. *Ragland* (1987), petitioners also assert that while the Government may place certain conditions on the receipt of federal subsidies, it may not "discriminate invidiously in its subsidies in such a way as to 'ai[m] at the suppression of dangerous ideas.' "

There is no question but that the statutory prohibition contained in § 1008 is constitutional. In *Maher* v. *Roe* [1977] we upheld a state welfare regulation under which Medicaid recipients received payments for services related to childbirth, but not for nontherapeutic abortions. The Court rejected the claim that this unequal subsidization worked a violation of the Constitution. We held that the government may "make a value judgment favoring childbirth over abortion, and . . . implement that judgment by the allocation of public funds." Here the Government is exercising the authority it possesses under *Maher* and [*Harris* v.] *McRae* [1980] to subsidize family planning services which will lead to conception and child birth, and declining to "promote or encourage abortion." The Government can, without violating the Constitution, selectively fund a program to encourage certain activities it believes to be in the public interest, without at the same time funding an alternate program which seeks to deal with the problem in another way. . . .

. . . This is not a case of the Government "suppressing a dangerous idea," but of a prohibition on a project grantee or its employees from engaging in activities outside of its scope. . . . When Congress established a National Endowment for Democracy to encourage other countries to adopt democratic principles, it was not constitutionally required to fund a program to encourage competing lines of political philosophy such as Communism and Fascism. . . .

We believe that petitioners' reliance upon our decision in *Arkansas Writers Project, supra,* is misplaced. That case involved a state sales tax which discriminated between magazines on the basis of their content.

Relying on this fact, and on the fact that the tax "targets a small group within the press,". . . the Court held the tax invalid. But we have here not the case of a general law singling out a disfavored group on the basis of speech content, but a case of the Government refusing to fund activities, including speech, which are specifically excluded from the scope of the project funded.

Petitioners rely heavily on their claim that the regulations would not, in the circumstance of a medical emergency, permit a Title X project to refer a woman whose pregnancy places her life in imminent peril to a provider of abortions or abortion-related services. This case, of course, involves only a facial challenge to the regulations, and we do not have before us any application by the Secretary to a specific fact situation. On their face, we do not read the regulations to bar abortion referral or counseling in such circumstances. Abortion counseling as a "method of family planning" is prohibited, and it does not seem that a medically necessitated abortion in such circumstances would be the equivalent of its use as a "method of family planning." Neither § 1008 nor the specific restrictions of the regulations would apply. Moreover, the regulations themselves contemplate that a Title X project would be permitted to engage in otherwise prohibited abortion-related activity in such circumstances. Section 59.8(a)(2) provides a specific exemption for emergency care and requires Title X recipients "to refer the client immediately to an appropriate provider of emergency medical services." Section 59.5(b)(1) also requires Title X projects to provide "necessary referral to other medical facilities when medically indicated.". . .

Petitioners also contend that the restrictions on the subsidization of abortion-related speech contained in the regulations are impermissible because they condition the receipt of a benefit, in this case Title X funding, on the relinquishment of a constitutional right, the right to engage in abortion advocacy and counseling. Relying on *Perry* v. *Sindermann* (1972), and *FCC* v. *League of Women Voters of Cal.* (1984), petitioners argue that "even though the government may deny [a] . . . benefit for any number of reasons, there are some reasons upon which the government may not rely. It may not deny a benefit to a person on a basis that infringes his constitutionally protected interests—especially, his interest in freedom of speech."

Petitioners' reliance on these cases is unavailing, however, because here the government is not denying a benefit to anyone, but is instead simply insisting that public funds be spent for the purposes for which they were authorized. . . . The Title X *grantee* can continue to perform abortions, provide abortion-related services, and engage in abortion advocacy; it simply is required to conduct those activities through programs that are separate and independent from the project that receives Title X funds.

In contrast, our "unconstitutional conditions" cases involve situations in which the government has placed a condition on the *recipient* of the subsidy rather than on a particular program or service, thus effectively prohibiting the recipient from engaging in the protected conduct outside the scope of the federally funded program. In *FCC* v. *League of Women Voters of Cal.*, we invalidated a federal law providing that noncommercial television and radio stations that receive federal grants may not "engage in editorializing." Under that law, a recipient of federal funds was "barred absolutely from all editorializing" because it "is not able to segregate its activities according to the source of its funding" and thus "has no way of limiting the use of its federal funds to all noneditorializing activities." The effect of the law was that "a noncommercial educational station that receives only 1% of its overall income from [federal] grants is barred absolutely from all editorializing" and "barred from using even wholly private funds to finance its editorial activity." We expressly recognized, however, that were Congress to permit the recipient stations to "establish 'affiliate' organizations which could then use the station's facilities to editorialize with nonfederal funds, such a statutory mechanism would plainly be valid." Such a scheme would permit the station "to make known its views on matters of public importance through its nonfederally funded, editorializing affiliate without losing federal grants for its noneditorializing broadcast activities."

Similarly, in *Regan* we held that Congress could, in the exercise of its spending power, reasonably refuse to subsidize the lobbying activities of tax-exempt charitable organizations by prohibiting such organizations from using tax-deductible contributions to support their lobbying efforts. In so holding, we explained that such organizations remained free "to receive deductible contributions to support ... nonlobbying activit[ies].". . .

By requiring that the Title X grantee engage in abortion-related activity separately from activity receiving federal funding, Congress has, consistent with our teachings in *League of Women Voters* and *Regan*, not denied it the right to engage in abortion-related activities. Congress has merely refused to fund such activities out of the public fisc, and the Secretary has simply required a certain degree of separation from the Title X project in order to ensure the integrity of the federally funded program.

The same principles apply to petitioners' claim that the regulations abridge the free speech rights of the grantee's staff. Individuals who are voluntarily employed for a Title X project must perform their duties in accordance with the regulation's restrictions on abortion counseling and referral. The employees remain free, however, to pursue abortion-related activities when they are not acting under the auspices of the Title X project. The regulations, which govern solely the scope of the Title X project's activities, do not in any way restrict the activities of those persons acting as private individuals. The employees' freedom of expression is limited during the time that they actually work for the project; but this limitation is a consequence of their decision to accept employment in a project, the scope of which is permissibly restricted by the funding authority.

This is not to suggest that funding by the Government, even when coupled with the freedom of the fund recipients to speak outside the scope of the Government-funded project, is invariably sufficient to justify government control over the content of expression. For example, this Court has recognized that the existence of a Government "subsidy," in the form of Government-owned property, does not justify the restriction of speech in areas that have "been traditionally open to the public for expressive activity," *United States* v. *Kokinda* (1990).... Similarly, we have recognized that the university is a traditional sphere of free expression so fundamental to the functioning of our society that the Government's ability to control speech within that sphere by means of conditions attached to the expenditure of Government funds is restricted by the vagueness and overbreadth doctrines of the First Amendment, *Keyishian* v. *Board of Regents* (1967). It could be argued by analogy that traditional relationships such as that between doctor and patient should enjoy protection under the First Amendment from government regulation, even when subsidized by the Government. We need not resolve that question here, however, because the Title X program regulations do not significantly impinge upon the doctor-patient relationship. Nothing in them requires a doctor to represent as his own any opinion that he does not in fact hold. Nor is the doctor-patient relationship established by the Title X program sufficiently all-encompassing so as to justify an expectation on the part of the patient of comprehensive medical advice. The program does not provide postconception medical care, and therefore a doctor's silence with regard to abortion cannot reasonably be thought to mislead a client into thinking that the doctor does not consider abortion an appropriate option for her....

IV

We turn now to petitioners' argument that the regulations violate a woman's Fifth Amendment right to choose whether to terminate her pregnancy. We recently reaffirmed the long-recognized principle that " 'the Due Process Clauses generally confer no affirmative right to governmental aid, even where such aid may be necessary to secure life, liberty, or property interests of which the govenment itself may not deprive the individual.' " *Webster*, quoting *DeShaney* v. *Winnebago County Dept. of Social Services* (1989). The Government has no constitutional duty to subsidize an activity merely because the activity is constitutionally protected....

Petitioners also argue that by impermissibly infringing on the doctor/patient relationship and depriving a Title X client of information concerning abortion as a method of family planning, the regulations violate a woman's Fifth Amendment right to medical self-determination and to make informed medical decisions free of government-imposed harm. They argue that under our decisions in *Akron* v. *Akron Center for Reproductive Health, Inc.* (1983), and *Thornburg* v. *American College of Obstetricians and Gynecologists* (1986), the government cannot interfere with a woman's right to make an informed and voluntary choice by placing restrictions on the patient/doctor dialogue.

In *Akron*, we invalidated a city ordinance requiring *all* physicians to make specified statements to the patient prior to performing an abortion in order to ensure that the woman's consent was "truly informed." Similarly, in *Thornburg*, we struck down a state statute mandating that a list of agencies offering alternatives to abortion and a description of fetal development be provided to *every* woman considering terminating her pregnancy through an abortion.... [B]oth cases required *all* doctors within their respective jurisdictions to provide *all* pregnant patients contemplating an abortion a litany of information, regardless of whether the patient sought the information or whether the doctor thought the information necessary to the patient's decision. Under the Secretary's regulations, however, a doctor's ability to provide, and a woman's right to receive, information concerning abortion and abortion-related services outside the context of the Title X project remains unfettered. It would undoubtedly be easier for a woman seeking an abortion if she could receive information about abortion from a Title X project, but the Constitution does not require that the Government distort the scope of its mandated program in order to provide that information.

Petitioners contend ... that most Title X clients are effectively precluded by indigency and poverty from seeing a health care provider who will provide abortion-related services. But once again, even these Title X clients are in no worse position than if Congress had never enacted Title X....

The Secretary's regulations are a permissible construction of Title X and do not violate either the First or Fifth Amendments to the Constitution. Accordingly, the judgment of the Court of Appeals is

Affirmed.

JUSTICE BLACKMUN, with whom JUSTICE MARSHALL joins, with whom JUSTICE STEVENS joins as to Parts II and III, and with whom JUSTICE O'CONNOR joins as to Part I, dissenting.

Casting aside established principles of statutory construction and administrative jurisprudence, the majority in these cases today unnecessarily passes upon important questions of constitutional law. In so doing, the Court, for the first time, upholds viewpoint-based suppression of speech solely because it is imposed on those dependent upon the Government for economic support. Under essentially the same rationale, the majority upholds direct regulation of dialogue between a pregnant woman and her physician when that regulation has both the purpose and the effect of manipulating her decision as to the continuance of her pregnancy. I conclude that the Secretary's regulation of referral, advocacy, and counseling activities exceeds his statutory authority, and, also, that the Regulations violate the First and Fifth Amendments of our Constitution. Accordingly, I dissent and would reverse the divided-vote judgment of the Court of Appeals.

I

... Whether or not one believes that these Regulations are valid, it avoids reality to contend that they do not give rise to serious constitutional questions. . . . [T]he question squarely presented by the Regulations—the extent to which the Government may attach an otherwise unconstitutional condition to the receipt of a public benefit—implicates a troubled area of our jurisprudence in which a court ought not entangle itself unnecessarily. . . .

[T]he Regulations impose viewpoint-based restrictions upon protected speech and are aimed at a woman's decision whether to continue or terminate her pregnancy. In both respects, they implicate core constitutional values. This verity is evidenced by the fact that two of the three Courts of Appeals that have entertained challenges to the Regulations have invalidated them on constitutional grounds. See *Massachusetts* v. *Secretary of Health and Human Services* (CA1 1990); *Planned Parenthood Federation of America* v. *Sullivan* (CA10 1990). . . . That a bare majority of this Court today reaches a different result does not change the fact that the constitutional questions raised by the Regulations are both grave and doubtful.

Nor is this a case in which the statutory language itself requires us to address a constitutional question. Section 1008 of the Public Health Service Act, 84 Stat. 1508, 42 U.S.C. § 300a-6, provides simply: "None of the funds appropriated under this title shall be used in programs where abortion is a method of family planning." The majority concedes that this language "does not speak directly to the issues of counseling, referral, advocacy, or program integrity," and that "the legislative history is ambiguous" in this respect. . . . Indeed, it would appear that our duty to avoid passing unnecessarily upon important constitutional questions is strongest where, as here, the language of the statute is decidedly ambiguous. It is both logical and eminently prudent to assume that when Congress intends to press the limits of constitutionality in its enactments, it will express that intent in explicit and unambiguous terms. . . .

Because I conclude that a plainly constitutional construction of § 1008 "is not only 'fairly possible' but entirely reasonable," I would reverse the judgment of the Court of Appeals on this ground without deciding the constitutionality of the Secretary's Regulations.

II

A

. . . Until today, the Court never has upheld viewpoint-based suppression of speech simply because that suppression was a condition upon the acceptance of public funds. Whatever may be the Government's power to condition the receipt of its largess upon the relinquishment of constitutional rights, it surely does not extend to a condition that suppresses the recipient's cherished freedom of speech based solely upon the content or viewpoint of that speech. This rule is a sound one, for, as the Court often has noted: " 'A regulation of speech that is motivated by nothing more than a desire to curtail expression of a particular point of view on controversial issues of general interest is the purest example of a "law ... abridging the freedom of speech, or of the press." ' ". ...

It cannot seriously be disputed that the counseling and referral provisions at issue in the present cases constitute content-based regulation of speech. Title X grantees may provide counseling and referral regarding any of a wide range of family planning and other topics, save abortion. ...

The Regulations are also clearly viewpoint-based. While suppressing speech favorable to abortion with one hand, the Secretary compels anti-abortion speech with the other. For example, the Department of Health and Human Services' own description of the Regulations makes plain that "Title X projects are *required* to facilitate access to prenatal care and social services, including adoption services, that might be needed by the pregnant client to promote her well-being and that of her child, while making it abundantly clear that the project is not permitted to promote abortion by facilitating access to abortion through the referral process."

Moreover, the Regulations command that a project refer for prenatal care each woman diagnosed as pregnant, irrespective of the woman's expressed desire to continue or terminate her pregnancy. If a client asks directly about abortion, a Title X physician or counselor is required to say, in essence, that the project does not consider abortion to be an appropriate method of family planning. Both requirements are antithetical to the First Amendment.

The Regulations pertaining to "advocacy" are even more explicitly viewpoint-based. These provide: "A Title X project may not *encourage, promote or advocate* abortion as a method of family planning." They explain: "This requirement prohibits actions to *assist* women to obtain abortions or *increase* the availability or accessibility of abortion for family planning purposes." The Regulations do not, however, proscribe or even regulate anti-abortion advocacy. These are clearly restrictions aimed at the suppression of "dangerous ideas."

Remarkably, the majority concludes that "the Government has not discriminated on the basis of viewpoint; it has merely chosen to fund one activity to the exclusion of another." But the majority's claim that the Regulations merely limit a Title X project's speech to preventive or preconceptional services rings hollow in light of the broad range of non-preventive services that the Regulations authorize Title X projects to provide. By refusing to fund those family-planning projects that advocate abortion *because* they advocate abortion, the Government plainly has targeted a particular viewpoint. The majority's reliance on the fact that the Regulations pertain solely to funding decisions simply begs the question. Clearly, there are some bases upon which government may not rest its decision to fund or not to fund. For example, the Members of the majority surely would agree that government may not base its decision to support an activity upon considerations of race. As demonstrated above, our cases make clear that ideological viewpoint is a similarly repugnant ground upon which to base funding decisions.

The majority's reliance upon *Regan* in this connection is also misplaced.

That case stands for the proposition that government has no obligation to subsidize a private party's efforts to petition the legislature regarding its views. Thus, if the challenged Regulations were confined to non-ideological limitations upon the use of Title X funds for lobbying activities, there would exist no violation of the First Amendment. The advocacy Regulations at issue here, however, are not limited to lobbying but extend to all speech having the effect of encouraging, promoting, or advocating abortion as a method of family planning. Thus, in addition to their impermissible focus upon the viewpoint of regulated speech, the provisions intrude upon a wide range of communicative conduct, including the very words spoken to a woman by her physician. By manipulating the content of the doctor/patient dialogue, the Regulations upheld today force each of the petitioners "to be an instrument for fostering public adherence to an ideological point of view [he or she] finds unacceptable." This type of intrusive, ideologically based regulation of speech goes far beyond the narrow lobbying limitations approved in *Regan*, and cannot be justified simply because it is a condition upon the receipt of a governmental benefit.

B

The Court concludes that the challenged Regulations do not violate the First Amendment rights of Title X staff members because any limitation of the employees' freedom of expression is simply a consequence of their decision to accept employment at a federally funded project. But it has never been sufficient to justify an otherwise unconstitutional condition upon public employment that the employee may escape the condition by relinquishing his or her job....

The majority attempts to circumvent this principle by emphasizing that Title X physicians and counselors "remain free ... to pursue abortion-related activities when they are not acting under the auspices of the Title X project." "The regulations," the majority explains, "do not in any way restrict the activities of those persons acting as private individuals." Under the majority's reasoning, the First Amendment could be read to tolerate *any* governmental restriction upon an employee's speech so long as that restriction is limited to the funded workplace. This is a dangerous proposition, and one the Court has rightly rejected in the past....

In the cases at bar, the speaker's interest in the communication is both clear and vital. In addressing the family-planning needs of their clients, the physicians and counselors who staff Title X projects seek to provide them with the full range of information and options regarding their health and reproductive freedom. Indeed, the legitimate expectations of the patient and the ethical responsibilities of the medical profession demand no less. "The patient's right of self-decision can be effectively exercised only if the patient possesses enough information to enable an intelligent choice.... The physician has an ethical obligation to help the patient make choices from among the therapeutic alternatives consistent with good medical practice." Current Opinions, the Council on Ethical and Judicial Affairs of the American Medical Association pgh. 8.08 (1989)....

When a client becomes pregnant, the full range of therapeutic alternatives includes the abortion option, and Title X counselors' interest in providing this information is compelling.

The Government's articulated interest in distorting the doctor/patient dialogue—ensuring that federal funds are not spent for a purpose outside the scope of the program—falls far short of that necessary to justify the suppression of truthful information and professional medical opinion regarding constitutionally protected conduct. . . .

C

Finally, it is of no small significance that the speech the Secretary would suppress is truthful information regarding constitutionally protected conduct of vital importance to the listener. One can imagine no legitimate governmental interest that might be served by suppressing such information. Concededly, the abortion debate is among the most divisive and contentious issues that our Nation has faced in recent years. "But freedom to differ is not limited to things that do not matter much. That would be a mere shadow of freedom. The test of its substance is the right to differ as to things that touch the heart of the existing order." *West Virginia Board of Education* v. *Barnette* (1943).

III

By far the most disturbing aspect of today's ruling is the effect it will have on the Fifth Amendment rights of the women who, supposedly, are beneficiaries of Title X programs. . . .

Until today, the Court has allowed to stand only those restrictions upon reproductive freedom that, while limiting the availability of abortion, have left intact a woman's ability to decide without coercion whether she will continue her pregnancy to term. *Maher,* . . . *McRae,* and *Webster* [1989] are all to this effect. Today's decision abandons that principle, and with disastrous results.

Contrary to the majority's characterization, this is not a case in which individuals seek government aid in exercising their fundamental rights. The Fifth Amendment right asserted by petitioners is the right of a pregnant woman to be free from affirmative governmental *interference* in her decision. *Roe* v. *Wade* (1973), and its progeny are not so much about a medical procedure as they are about a woman's fundamental right to self-determination. Those cases serve to vindicate the idea that "liberty," if it means anything, must entail freedom from governmental domination in making the most intimate and personal of decisions. . . .

It is crystal-clear that the aim of the challenged provisions—an aim the majority cannot escape noticing—is not simply to ensure that federal funds are not used to perform abortions, but to "reduce the incidence of abortion." As recounted above, the Regulations require Title X physicians and counselors to provide information pertaining only to childbirth, to refer a pregnant woman for prenatal care irrespective of her medical situation, and, upon direct inquiry, to respond that abortion is not an "appropriate method" of family planning.

The undeniable message conveyed by this forced speech, and the one that the Title X client will draw from it, is that abortion nearly always is an improper medical option. Although her physician's words, in fact, are strictly controlled by the Government and wholly unrelated to her particular medical situation, the Title X client will reasonably construe them as professional advice to forgo her right to obtain an abortion. As would most rational patients, many of these women will follow that perceived advice and carry their pregnancy to term, despite their needs to the contrary and despite the safety of the abortion procedure for the vast majority of them. Others, delayed by the Regulations' mandatory prenatal referral, will be prevented from acquiring abortions during the period in which the process is medically sound and constitutionally protected.

In view of the inevitable effect of the Regulations, the majority's conclusion that "[t]he difficulty that a woman encounters when a Title X project does not provide abortion counseling or referral leaves her in no different position than she would have been if the government had not enacted Title X" is insensitive and contrary to common human experience. Both the purpose and result of the challenged Regulations is to deny women the ability voluntarily to decide their procreative destiny. For these women, the Government will have obliterated the freedom to choose as surely as if it had banned abortions outright. The denial of this freedom is not a consequence of poverty but of the Government's ill-intentioned distortion of information it has chosen to provide.

The substantial obstacles to bodily self-determination that the Regulations impose are doubly offensive because they are effected by manipulating the very words spoken by physicians and counselors to their patients. In our society, the doctor/patient dialogue embodies a unique relationship of trust. The specialized nature of medical science and the emotional distress often attendant to health-related decisions requires that patients place their complete confidence, and often their very lives, in the hands of medical professionals. One seeks a physician's aid not only for medication or diagnosis, but also for guidance, professional judgment, and vital emotional support. Accordingly, each of us attaches profound importance and authority to the words of advice spoken by the physician....

The manipulation of the doctor/patient dialogue achieved through the Secretary's Regulations is clearly an effort "to deter a woman from making a decision that, with her physician, is hers to make." As such, it violates the Fifth Amendment.

IV

In its haste further to restrict the right of every woman to control her reproductive freedom and bodily integrity, the majority disregards established principles of law and contorts this Court's decided cases to arrive at its preordained result. The majority professes to leave undisturbed the free speech protections upon which our society has come to rely, but one must wonder what force the First Amendment retains if it is read to countenance the deliberate manipulation by the Government of the dialogue between a woman and her physician. While technically leaving intact the fundamental right protected by *Roe* v. *Wade*, the Court, "through a relentlessly formalistic catechism," once again has rendered the right's substance nugatory. This is a course nearly as noxious as overruling *Roe* directly, for if a right is found to be unenforceable, even against flagrant attempts by government to circumvent it, then it ceases to be a right at all. This, I fear, may be the effect of today's decision.

JUSTICE STEVENS, dissenting.

In my opinion, the Court has not paid sufficient attention to the language of the controlling statute or to the consistent interpretation accorded the statute by the responsible cabinet officers during four different Presidencies and 18 years. . . .

The entirely new approach adopted by the Secretary in 1988 was not, in my view, authorized by the statute. The new regulations did not merely reflect a change in a policy determination that the Secretary had been authorized by Congress to make. Rather, they represented an assumption of policymaking responsibility that Congress had not delegated to the Secretary. . . .

Because I am convinced that the 1970 Act did not authorize the Secretary to censor the speech of grant recipients or their employees, I would hold the challenged regulations invalid and reverse the judgment of the Court of Appeals.

Even if I thought the statute were ambiguous, however, I would reach the same result for the reasons stated in JUSTICE O'CONNOR's dissenting opinion. As she also explains, if a majority of the Court had reached this result, it would be improper to comment on the constitutional issues that the parties have debated. . . .

JUSTICE O'CONNOR, disssenting.

"[W]here an otherwise acceptable construction of a statute would raise serious constitutional problems, the Court will construe the statute to avoid such problems unless such construction is plainly contrary to the intent of Congress." *Edward J. DeBartolo Corp.* v. *Florida Gulf Coast Building & Construction Trades Council* (1988). JUSTICE BLACKMUN has explained well why this long-standing canon of statutory construction applies in this case, and I join Part I of his dissent. Part II demonstrates why the challenged regulations, which constitute the Secretary's interpretation of § 1008 of the Public Health Service Act, 84 Stat. 1508, 42 U.S.C. § 300a-6, "raise serious constitutional problems": the regulations place content-based restrictions on the speech of Title X fund recipients, restrictions directed precisely at speech concerning one of "the most divisive and contentious issues that our Nation has faced in recent years."

One may well conclude, as JUSTICE BLACKMUN does in Part II, that the regulations are unconstitutional for this reason. I do not join Part II of the dissent, however, for the same reason that I do not join Part III, in which JUSTICE BLACKMUN concludes that the regulations are unconstitutional under the Fifth Amendment. The canon of construction that JUSTICE BLACKMUN correctly applies here is grounded in large part upon our time-honored practice of not reaching constitutional questions unnecessarily. . . .

This Court acts at the limits of its power when it invalidates a law on constitutional grounds. In recognition of our place in the constitutional scheme, we must act with "great gravity and delicacy" when telling a coordinate branch that its actions are absolutely prohibited absent constitutional amendment. In this case, we need only tell the Secretary that his regulations are not a reasonable interpretation of the statute; we need not tell Congress that it cannot pass such legislation. If we rule solely on statutory grounds, Congress retains the power to force the constitutional question by legislating more explicitly. It may instead choose to do nothing. That decision should be left to Congress; we should not tell Congress what it cannot do before it has chosen to do it. It is enough in this case to conclude that neither the language nor the history of § 1008 compels the Secretary's interpretation, and that the interpretation raises serious First Amendment concerns. On this basis alone, I would reverse the judgment of the Court of Appeals and invalidate the challenged regulations.

RULING ON PROTECTING
THE SPOTTED OWL
May 23, 1991

The northern spotted owl and the old-growth forests in which it lives won a courtroom victory May 23, adding another chapter to this environment-versus-jobs saga. The ruling by U.S. District Judge William L. Dwyer of Seattle suspended timber sales on 66,000 acres of the bird's habitat in the national forests of the Pacific Northwest. His intent was to protect this endangered species from the risk of extinction.

Dwyer sharply criticized "higher authorities in the executive branch" of government for "a deliberate and systematic refusal by the Forest Service and the FWS [Fish and Wildlife Service] to comply with the laws protecting wildlife." The Seattle Audubon Society had sued the Forest Service, challenging an administrative decision it made in 1988 to continue to sell old-growth timber to loggers in national forests despite its negative impact on the spotted owl. Shortly before that, another ruling in Seattle by federal judge Thomas Zilly forced the Fish and Wildlife Service to list the bird as endangered. It did so in June 1990, taking effect across the spotted owl's range in northern California, western Oregon, and Washington. Under the Endangered Species Act of 1973, any plant or animal designated as threatened must be protected from hunting, trading, or federal actions that could destroy its breeding and feeding grounds.

However, an interagency task force headed by Secretary of Agriculture Clayton Yeutter sought to exempt the Forest Service and the Bureau of Land Management from compliance with major environmental laws regulating logging on public lands, thereby nullifying the effect of the endangered-species listing. Moreover, the Fish and Wildlife Service balked at designating "critical habitat" areas, as required by law, until

Zilly ordered the agency to do so. In April 1991 it complied, designating 11.6 million acres.

The conflict reflected sharp differences over what should be done about forests in the huge federal domain. While environmentalists and many others wanted to protect the old forests of the Pacific Northwest, the timber industry objected bitterly, arguing that it would cost them jobs.

Timber cutting in the national forests of Washington and Oregon ranged from 4.4 billion to 5 billion board feet from 1985 through 1989, accounting for approximately one-third of the total taken in the two states over those years. In the June 25, 1990, issue of Time *magazine,* Ted Gup *wrote that "when scores of communities are imperiled, relief measures are necessary. In the case of the Northwest, the federal government should help retrain loggers and mill workers and provide towns with grants to spur economic diversification."*

But Judge Dwyer said job losses would continue "regardless of whether the spotted owl is protected." Losses had been heavy in the past decade, he said, due mainly to plant modernization, changes in demand for wood products, and "competition from elsewhere"—southeastern states in particular.

Both the Bush administration and Congress failed to resolve the dispute. Even the congressional delegations from the affected states were divided. However, the Dwyer ruling inspired several members of Congress to try again to devise legislation that would satisfy both environmentalists and timber-industry workers in the Pacific Northwest. The House Agriculture Subcommittee held a round of hearings in late May to ponder the matter once again.

An acceptable compromise did not appear easy. Lumber industry officials estimated that the Fish and Wildlife Service's "critical habitat" plan could cost more than 131,000 jobs directly or indirectly related to timber sales.

A group of logging and community groups filed suit in federal court August 30 challenging the plan. The plaintiffs said the Fish and Wildlife Service acted without regard for the economic consequences and without proper public participation.

Following are excerpts from a decision issued May 23, 1991, in U.S. District Court in Seattle by Judge William L. Dwyer, forbidding the sale of timber from national forest lands in the Pacific Northwest until the U.S. Forest Service revised plans to assure the survival of the spotted owl, an endangered species that inhabits those forests:

History of This Case and Recent Administrative Proceedings

The national forests are managed by the Forest Service under NEMA. Regulations promulgated under that statute provide that

[f]ish and wildlife shall be managed to maintain viable populations of existing native and desired non-native vertebrate species in the planning area.

A viable population is "one which has the estimated numbers and distribution of reproductive individuals to insure its continued existence is well distributed in the planning area." To insure viability, habitat must be provided to support at least a minimum number of reproductive individuals.

Since not every species can be monitored, "indicator species" are observed as signs of general wildlife viability. The northern spotted owl is an indicator species.

While having these conservation duties, the Forest Service is also charged with managing these lands to "provide for multiple use and sustained yield of goods and services from the National Forest System in a way that maximizes long term net public benefit in an environmentally sound manner."

In recent years logging and development have steadily reduced wildlife habitat in the Pacific Northwest. At the same time many local mills have experienced log shortages. The result is an intensified struggle over the future of the national forests.

In 1989 SAS [Seattle Audubon Society] and WCLA [Washington Contract Loggers Association] sued the Forest Service in this court, challenging the legality of an administrative decision adopting standards and guidelines for managing northern spotted owl habitat in the national forests. The administrative decision was set out in a Record of Decision ("ROD") issued on December 8, 1988. . . . For opposite reasons, the two sets of plaintiffs challenged the Forest Service's plan under NFMA [National Forest Management Act] and the National Environmental Policy Act ("NEPA"), and their implementing regulations.

The court consolidated the two cases. . . . On March 24, 1989, the court issued a temporary injunction deferring specified timber sales in Washington and Oregon for what then appeared to be a few weeks until the final hearing.

On May 11, 1989, the Forest Service moved for a stay of all proceedings pending completion of a conference process between itself and the [U.S.] Fish and Wildlife Service ("FWS"). In a separate case, Judge [Thomas] Zilly of this district had ruled that the FWS was acting arbitrarily and capriciously, and contrary to law, in failing to list the spotted owl as endangered or threatened under the Endangered Species Act ("ESA"). On April 25, 1989, having reconsidered in response to Judge Zilly's order, the FWS announced its intent to list the owl as "threatened" under the ESA. SAS and WCLA agreed that a stay of the present case was warranted so that the two agencies could consult. The Forest Service proposed a temporary ban on timber sales containing forty or more acres of spotted owl habitat. This was adopted by order of May 26, 1989.

The Forest Service said it would present within thirty days interim measures to protect spotted owl habitat during the FWS listing process. It did not do so. Instead it moved on August 24, 1989, for leave to go forward with eleven timber sales that had been deferred. At that point there was no spotted owl management plan in effect. The court on its own motion lifted the stay and ordered an expedited final hearing in these cases.

Congress in the meantime was debating legislation which would provide a short-term supply of national forest and Bureau of Land Management ("BLM") timber to mills in Washington and Oregon without having the usual type of agency action subject to judicial review. The final result was section 318 of the Department of the Interior and Related Agencies Appropriations Act for the Fiscal Year 1990.... The Congressional conference committee presented the bill as necessary "because of the failure of the ... Forest Service and the BLM [Bureau of Land Management] to take steps on their own to resolve these matters in a manner which could have prevented the current situation."

Section 318 included the following provisions, among others:

- It directed the Forest Service and the BLM to offer specified quantities of timber for sale in fiscal years 1989 and 1990. Subsection (a).
- It contained restrictions on the cutting of "ecologically significant old growth forest stands" except as necessary to meet the sales quota, barred logging in certain "spotted owl habitat areas," and adopted temporarily (with a few modifications) the standards and guidelines proposed in the Forest Service's December 1988 ROD. Subsections (b)(1), (2) and (3).
- It stated that Congress "determines and directs" that management of the forests for fiscal years 1989-90 according to its provisions "is adequate consideration for the purpose of meeting the statutory requirements that are the basis for [the present cases and a similar case pending in the District of Oregon]." Subsection (b)(6)(A).
- It directed the Forest Service to prepare a new spotted owl plan and have it in place by September 30, 1990....

On November 6, 1989, this court vacated the preliminary injunction because section 318 had become law as to 1989-90 timber sales. The court construed the statute as a temporary amendment of the environmental laws.... Over the next several months the parties proceeded under section 318. SAS brought a series of challenges to timber sales under the standards of the temporary statute. On May 11, 1990, this court entered an order on the first such challenge, enjoining [a] ... sale in the Umpqua National Forest.... Other challenges to 1990 timber sales followed.... The court enjoined three sales on the basis that the Forest Service had not complied with section 318; the agency withdrew two other sales after a motion for summary judgment was filed; and the court found for the Forest Service as to one sale. No party appealed from these rulings.

On September 18, 1990, the court of appeals [for the Ninth Circuit] issued an opinion, and on October 30 an amended opinion, finding the first sentence of section 318 (b)(6)(A) unconstitutional under the separation of powers doctrine.

The appeal to the Ninth Circuit concerned the part of section 318 in which Congress "determines and directs" that management of the forests in 1989-90 according to subsections (b)(3) and (b)(5) "is adequate consideration for the purpose of meeting the statutory requirements" underlying the cases in this district and in Oregon. The court of appeals ruled that this provision was not a temporary amendment of the environmental laws but rather an unconstitutional attempt to adjudicate rather than legislate. The requirements of section 318 were thus held to be in addition to, and not in lieu of, those of the general environmental statutes. The decision did not affect the other parts of section 318.

While the above-described events were taking place, federal administrative agencies took further action regarding the spotted owl. The Interagency Scientific Committee was established in 1989 by agreement of the Forest Service, the Bureau of Land Management of the Department of the Interior, the Fish and Wildlife Service, and the National Park Service. Its mission was "to develop a scientifically credible conservation strategy for the northern spotted owl in the United States."

In June 1990 the Fish and Wildlife Service, having completed its listing process, listed the owl as a threatened species under the Endangered Species Act.... The Forest Service did not comply by the deadline of September 30, 1990—or at all—with section 318's requirement that it adopt a revised plan to ensure the owl's viability.

On September 28, 1990, the Department of Agriculture gave notice that the Forest Service ... would manage timber sales in a manner "not inconsistent with" the ISC Report. This announcement was made without notice, hearing, environmental impact statement, or other rule-making procedures.

On December 18, 1990, this court enjoined the Forest Service from proceeding with twelve proposed fiscal year 1990 timber sales because the agency had failed to comply with NFMA by having any standards and guidelines for spotted owl viability in place. The order reaffirmed what the court of appeals had already held, i.e., that section 318 did not displace NFMA. Leave was granted to the Forest Service to pursue a newly-raised argument that its duty under NFMA to maintain the species ended when the listing under ESA occurred.

On February 26, 1991, Judge Zilly ruled ... that the FWS had again failed to comply with the law, stating:

> Upon the record presented, this Court finds the [Fish and Wildlife] Service has failed to discharge its obligations under the Endangered Species Act and its own administrative regulations. Specifically, the Service acting on behalf of the Secretary of the Interior, abused its discretion when it determined not to designate critical habitat concurrently with the listing of the northern spotted owl, or to explain any basis for concluding that the critical habitat was not determinable. These actions were arbitrary and capricious, and contrary to law.

The Forest Service's argument in this case that it was relieved of its NFMA duty to plan for the spotted owl's viability once the species was listed by the FWS as "threatened" was rejected in an order entered March 7, 1991. The court found not only that the argument was insupportable, but that "the Forest Service has understood at all times that its duties under NFMA and ESA are concurrent." Accordingly, summary judgment was granted determining that the Forest Service's proposal to log spotted owl habitat without complying with NFMA was unlawful.... WCLA was then allowed to intervene in the SAS action, and thus remains a party.

Amicus Curiae Brief of Siskiyou County

On May 16, 1991, a week after the evidentiary hearing ended, the board of Supervisors and Office of Education of Siskiyou County, California ("Siskiyou County"), sought leave to file a brief *amicus curiae* [friend of the court].... [T]he brief has been filed, and SAS has responded.

Siskiyou County's brief is untimely but has nevertheless been fully considered on the merits. It argues that SAS has no standing to seek relief relating to national forests in Northern California as distinguished from those in Washington and Oregon; and that, if SAS does have standing, any injunctive relief (even in the form proposed by the Forest Service) should exclude Northern California....

Nothing has been presented that would justify excluding the four Northern California forests, either on biological or economic grounds, from injunctive relief, regardless of whether SAS's or the Forest Service's proposed order is adopted.

Findings of Fact

... From the evidence admitted at the hearing the court makes and enters the following findings of fact:

A. Background Findings

1. The fate of the spotted owl has become a battleground largely because the species is a symbol of the remaining old growth forest....

2. An old growth forest consists not just of ancient standing trees, but of fallen trees, snags, massive decaying vegetation, and numerous resident plant and animal species, many of which live nowhere else.

3. A great conifer forest originally covered the western parts of Washington, Oregon, and Northern California, from the Cascade and Coast mountains to the sea. Perhaps ten percent of it remains. The spaces protected as parks or wilderness areas are not enough for the survival of the northern spotted owl.

4. The old growth forest sustains a biological community far richer than those of managed forests or tree farms....

5. The remaining old growth stands are valued also for their effects on climate, air, and migratory fish runs, and for their beauty....

6. Through most of the country's history there was little or no logging in the national forests. Intensive logging began with World War II and has accelerated.

7. NFMA was adopted in 1976, after three decades of heavy logging, in

the hope of serving both wilderness and industry values. Senator [Hubert H.] Humphrey of Minnesota, a sponsor of the act, stated:

> The days have ended when the forest may be viewed only as trees and trees viewed only as timber. The soil and the water, the grasses and the shrubs, the fish and the wildlife, and the beauty that is the forest must become integral parts of resource managers' thinking and actions.

8. Despite increasing concern over the environment, logging sales by the Forest Service have continued on a large scale. Timber harvests in the national forests in Washington and Oregon ranged from 4.448 billion to 5.082 billion board feet per year in 1985 through 1989, amounting to between 30% and 33% of the total harvested in those states in those years.

9. Some major firms in the Pacific Northwest have extensive private forests and need little or no wood from public sources. Many small mills and logging companies depend in whole or in part on federal timber.

10. Mill owners and loggers, and their employees, especially in small towns, have developed since World War II an expectation that federal timber will be available indefinitely, and a way of life that cannot be duplicated elsewhere.

11. The region's timber industry has been going through fundamental changes. The most important is modernization which increases productivity and reduces the demand for labor (i.e., the jobs available). There have also been recent changes in product demand, in competition from other parts of the country and the world. . . . The painful results for many workers, and their families and communities, will continue regardless of whether owl habitat in the national forests is protected.

B. Statutory Violations

12. The records . . . show a remarkable series of violations of the environmental laws. The Forest Service defended its December 1988 ROD persistently for nearly two years. Congress was persuaded in 1989 to adopt most of the ROD standards as a temporary measure in section 318. But in the fall of 1990 the Forest Service admitted that the ROD was inadequate after all—that it would fail to preserve the northern spotted owl. In seeking a stay of proceedings in this court in 1989 the Forest Service announced its intent to adopt temporary guidelines within thirty days. It did not do that within thirty days, or ever. When directed by Congress to have a revised ROD in place by September 30, 1990, the Forest Service did not even attempt to comply. The FWS, in the meantime, acted contrary to law in refusing to list the spotted owl as endangered or threatened. After it finally listed the species as "threatened" following Judge Zilly's order, the FWS again violated the ESA by failing to designate critical habitat as required. Another order had to be issued setting a deadline for the FWS to comply with the law.

13. The reasons for this pattern of behavior were made clear at the evidentiary hearing.

Dr. Eric Forsman, a research wildlife biologist with the Forest Service, testified, in regard to the 1988 ROD and other Forest Service plans for the spotted owl that preceded the ISC Report:

> Q. Were you satisfied at the time with the results of those previous works?
> A. No. On all of those plans, I had considerable reservations for a variety of reasons. But primarily because in every instance, there was a considerable—I would emphasize considerable—amount of political pressure to create a plan which was an absolute minimum. That is, which had a very low probability of success and which had a minimum impact on timber harvest.

George M. Leonard, associate chief of the Forest Service, testified that the agency experts began in early 1990 the work needed to have a revised plan in place by September 30 of that year, as Congress mandated in section 318. But the Secretaries of Agriculture and Interior decided to drop the effort. The public was not told of this decision to ignore what the law required. . . .

14. Had the Forest Service done what Congress directed it to do—adopt a lawful plan by last fall—this case would have ended some time ago.

15. More is involved here than a simple failure by an agency to comply with its governing statute. The most recent violation of NFMA exemplifies a deliberate and systematic refusal by the Forest Service and the FWS to comply with the laws protecting wildlife. This is not the doing of the scientists, foresters, rangers, and others at the working levels of these agencies. It reflects decisions made by higher authorities in the executive branch of government.

C. Time Needed for Forest Service to Comply With NFMA

16. The Forest Service seeks an allowance of fifteen more months, or until July 31, 1992, to prepare a new ROD and environmental impact statement. Another month would have to pass before the ROD could take effect. The agency thus proposes to accomplish by August 31, 1992, the step that Congress directed it to complete by September 30, 1990. . . .

17. Further delays of this magnitude are neither necessary nor tolerable.

18. In adopting section 318, which became law on October 23, 1989, Congress directed the Forest Service to have a revised spotted owl plan in effect eleven months later. In doing so Congress made clear that it expected full compliance. . . .

19. According to Mr. Leonard's testimony, the Forest Service began work in early 1990 to meet the congressional deadline. It had been directed in section 318 to consider the forthcoming ISC Report. The report came out in April. Work was then stopped by a decision made at the cabinet level.

20. The Forest Service now has advantages it lacked in early 1990. Much of the research and analysis has been done. . . .

21. With the knowledge at hand, there is no reason for the Forest Service to fail to develop quickly a plan to ensure the viability of the spotted owl in the national forests. . . . However . . . eleven months will be afforded. The time will run from April 1, 1991, when the court ordered the agency to proceed diligently in compliance with NFMA. A new ROD with

accompanying EIS (environmental impact statement] will thus be due on February 3, 1992, to take effect on March 5, 1992. The net result is that the agency has a seventeen-month extension to complete the job that Congress mandated be done by September 30, 1990.

D. Probability of Irreparable Harm

22. The northern spotted owl is now threatened with extinction ... *throughout* its range.

[Nos. 23-24 omitted]

25. The Forest Service estimates that an additional 66,000 acres of spotted owl habitat would be destroyed if logging went forward to the extent permitted by the ISC Report over the next sixteen months. That would be in addition to about 400,000 acres of habitat logged in the seven years since the agency began preparing these guidelines, all without having a lawful plan or EIS for the owl's management in place.

26. The ISC Report recommends standards and guidelines aimed at assuring the owl's long-term viability. The strategy contains seven major components: four categories of habitat conservation areas ("HCAs"), two different spacing requirements between HCAs, and the 50:11:40 rule. . . . [That rule requires that at least fifty percent of the forested landscape outside HCAs be maintained in stands of timber with an average diameter at breast height of eleven inches or greater, and at least 40% canopy closure.]

[Nos. 27-30 omitted]

31. The ISC Report has been described by experts on both sides as the first scientifically respectable proposal regarding spotted owl conservation to come out of the executive branch. However:

(a) To have a chance of success, the strategy would have to be adopted and followed by the agencies concerned. So far it has not been adopted by any agency. . . .

(b) The ISC proposal has not been put to the test of public comment and hearings.

(c) The ISC strategy may or may not prove to be adequate. While it is endorsed by well-qualified scientists, it is criticized by others, equally well-qualified, as over-optimistic and risky. . . .

(d) The ISC Report calls for diligent monitoring to sample the results once the program begins. . . . No monitoring scheme exists. . . .

32. To log tens of thousands of additional acres of spotted owl habitat before a plan is adopted would foreclose options that might later prove to have been necessary. . . .

33. Mr. Leonard of the Forest Service has testified that the agency will consider the alternative of preserving the remaining spotted owl habitat in the national forests. That alternative would be lost if extensive logging of habitat were to go forward now.

34. A review of proposed sales by the FWS would not be a substitute for compliance with NFMA. . . .

35. The logging of 66,000 acres of owl habitat, in the absence of a

conservation plan, would itself constitute a form of irreparable harm. Old growth forests are lost for generations. No amount of money can replace the environmental loss.

36. While the agency's proposal would involve logging an estimated one percent of the remaining habitat, the experts agree that cumulative loss of habitat is what has put the owl in danger of extinction. . . .

E. Economic and Social Consequences

37. The testimony on economic impact assumed a sixteen-month injunction. . . . The difference between protecting and not protecting habitat until the Forest Service develops its plan would thus be [the sale of] between 1.03 and 1.34 billion board feet [of lumber] during fiscal year 1991 and between 1.04 and 1.59 billion board feet during fiscal year 1992.

38. The injunction would not prohibit the logging of existing sales, but rather the sale of additional logging rights in owl habitat areas while the Forest Service was in the process of adopting a plan. Thus, timber sale reductions do not translate directly into harvest reductions.

39. The estimate used by all parties is that as of February 28, 1991, there were 4.778 billion board feet of uncut timber under contract in the "spotted owl" forests. . . .

40. Any after-effects of an injunction would be reduced by the fact that its period would be six months shorter than that requested by the agency and assumed by the economists who testified.

41. Additional timber supplies from private lands can reasonably be expected to enter the market if the price of timber stumpage increases, as it probably will do if Forest Service sales decline. In addition, some timber now exported will probably be diverted to the domestic market.

42. To the extent that Pacific Northwest mills have had supply shortages, the problem has been exacerbated by the export of raw logs. . . . The exported logs produce no mill jobs or added value in the United States. . . .

43. While some mills may experience log shortages during the period of an injunction, that would occur to some degree regardless of whether owl habitat is protected, and there is no way of assuring that the mills most in need of logs would get them if the Forest Service proposal were adopted. National forest timber sales must be awarded on competitive bids.

44. Over the past decade many timber jobs have been lost and mills closed in the Pacific Northwest. The main reasons have been modernization of physical plants, changes in product demand, and competition from elsewhere. . . .

45. Job losses in the wood products industry will continue regardless of whether the northern spotted owl is protected. A credible estimate is that over the next twenty years more than 30,000 jobs will be lost to worker-productivity increases alone.

46. A social cost is paid whenever an economic transformation of this nature takes place, all the more so when a largely rural industry loses sizeable numbers of jobs. Today, however, in contrast to earlier recession periods, states offer programs for dislocated workers that ease and

facilitate the necessary adjustments.

47. Counties in timber-dependent communities derive revenues from the harvest of national forest timber.... These public entities, however, do not expect to obtain revenues from sales made in violation of law.

48. The timber industry no longer drives the Pacific Northwest's economy. In Oregon, for example, the level of employment in lumber and wood products declined by seventeen percent between 1979 and 1989. In the same period, Oregon's total employment increased by twenty-three percent.

49. The wood products industry now employs about four percent of all workers in Western Oregon, two percent in Western Washington, and six percent in Northern California. Even if some jobs in wood products were affected by protecting owl habitat in the short term, any effect on the regional economy probably would be small.

50. The remaining wilderness contributes to the desirability of this region as a site for new industries and their employees....

The Public Interest and the Balance of Equities

The court must weigh and consider the public interest in deciding whether to issue an injunction in an environmental case. It must also consider the balance of equities among the parties.

The problem here has not been any shortcoming in the laws, but simply a refusal of administrative agencies to comply with them. This invokes a public interest of the highest order: the interest in having government officials act in accordance with law.... This is not the usual situation in which the court reviews an administrative decision and, in doing so, gives deference to agency expertise....

The loss of an additional 66,000 acres of spotted owl habitat, without a conservation plan being in place, and with no agency having committed itself to the ISC strategy, would constitute irreparable harm, and would risk pushing the species beyond a threshold from which it could not recover.

Any reduction in federal timber sales will have adverse effects on some timber industry firms and their employees, and a suspension of owl habitat sales in the national forests is no exception. But while the loss of old growth is permanent, the economic effects of an injunction are temporary and can be minimized in many ways.

To bypass the environmental laws, either briefly or permanently, would not fend off the changes transforming the timber industry. The argument that the mightiest economy on earth cannot afford to preserve old growth forests for a short time, while it reaches an overdue decision on how to manage them, is not convincing today. It would be even less so a year or a century from now.

For the reasons stated, the public interest and the balance of equities require the issuance of an injunction directing the Forest Service to comply with the requirements of NFMA by March 5, 1992, and preventing it from selling additional logging rights in spotted owl habitat until it complies with the law....

PEACE ACCORD IN ANGOLA
May 31, 1991

The government of Angola and that nation's largest rebel faction signed a peace agreement May 31, thereby ending a sixteen-year civil war and preparing the southern African country for free elections in 1992. A formal cease-fire then went into effect under supervision of a small United Nations' peacekeeping force, extending a truce the two sides had established several weeks earlier.

The signing ceremony took place in Lisbon, Portugal, where negotiations had been conducted for much of the past year. During that time Portugal served as a neutral third party in trying to mend the divisions that had beset Angola since it became independent of Portugal in 1975.

In hastily pulling out of Angola, Portugal left behind a transitional government composed of three disparate insurgent factions: the Marxist-dominated Movement for the Popular Liberation of Angola (MPLA); the National Union for the Total Independence of Angola, known as UNITA; and the National Liberation Front of Angola. Even before independence was formally proclaimed, that government collapsed, leaving the MPLA in control of the capital city of Luanda and large sections of the countryside. It proclaimed itself the People's Republic of Angola.

Combatants as Cold War Proxies

This set the stage for a proxy confrontation in Angola between the United States and the Soviet Union. The MPLA, armed by the Soviet Union and backed by Cuban troops, soon crushed the National Liberation Front. But UNITA, supported by South Africa and later the United States, continued to carry on a guerrilla warfare that was widespread at times. As the Cold War dissipated, Washington and Moscow looked for a way to end the conflict in Angola and a related one in neighboring Namibia.

A political settlement came first in Namibia. At American instigation, South Africa in 1988 withdrew its troops from Namibia, which it had long claimed as a colony in defiance of a United Nations decree. That December the parties to the Namibian dispute signed an agreement linking Namibian independence with the departure of Cuba's 50,000 troops from Angola by mid-1991. Namibia formally proclaimed its independence in March 1990. (Independence of Namibia, Historic Documents of 1990, p. 199)

Meanwhile, in June 1989, seven African presidents brought together Angolan president and MPLA leader José Eduardo dos Santos and UNITA leader Jonas Savimbi and hammered out a cease-fire agreement. It was soon violated, and some of the heaviest fighting of the long civil war occurred later that year in a Marxist offensive against UNITA. Savimbi then turned to Portugal for help in restoring the peace process.

U.S.-Soviet Leverage

Peace talks began in April 1990 but were bogged down until Washington and Moscow applied leverage to the separate sides in Angola. That December, Secretary of State James Baker III and Soviet Foreign Minister Eduard Shevardnadze met in Houston and agreed on joint proposals linking an immediate cease-fire to later elections. The plan was promptly presented to the two sides and Portugal at a follow-up meeting in New York. In April 1991 dos Santos announced that his government had accepted a refined version of the plan.

At the document signing in Lisbon, Portuguese prime minister Anibal Cavaco Silva said that this peace accord was "proof of an active cooperation and a meeting of interests between the United States and the Soviet Union." Baker praised Soviet cooperation in "resolving yet another issue that once deeply divided our countries...." The ceremony was also attended by Alexander Bessmertnykh, Shevardnadze's immediate successor, UN Secretary General Javier Perez de Cuellar, and Charles Crocker, a former U.S. assistant secretary of state who was the architect of the Namibian agreement.

The Task Ahead

Neither the words of praise from the attending dignitaries nor the peel of church bells throughout Lisbon that accompanied the signing could disguise the problems that lay ahead in Angola. The basic question was whether the Angolan people, and especially the two sets of enemies, could lay aside a generation of violence to work together. In the pact they agreed to build a unified armed force, strive for political pluralism, work toward free elections, and build a market economy. The ruling MPLA had retreated from its strident advocacy of Marxism as that ideology fell into disrepute in Eastern Europe and the Soviet Union.

The warring sides appeared to have come to the peace table out of wartime exhaustion and loss of outside sponsors rather than out of a desire for political harmony. By some estimates, more than 300,000 of Angola's 10 million people had died during the protracted strife. The civil war had impoverished the survivors in a country notably rich in natural resources, especially oil, nearly all of which is exported to the United States.

Following is a key document of the Angolan peace accords, "Fundamental Principles for the Establishment of Peace in Angola," signed in Lisbon, May 31, 1991, by president José Eduardo dos Santos of Angola and Angolan rebel leader Jonas Savimbi, as translated from Portuguese by the State Department:

Fundamental Principles for the Establishment of Peace in Angola

Point 1

Recognition by UNITA of the Angolan state, of President José Eduardo dos Santos, and of the Angolan government until the general elections are held.

Point 2

At the moment the cease-fire enters into force, UNITA will acquire the right to conduct and freely participate in political activities in accordance with the revised Constitution and the pertinent laws for the creation of a multi-party democracy.

Point 3

The Angolan government will hold discussions with all political forces in order to survey their opinions concerning the proposed changes in the Constitution. The Angolan government will then work with all the parties to draft the laws that will regulate the electoral process.

Point 4

Free and fair elections for a new government will take place following voter registration conducted under the supervision of international elections observers, who will remain in Angola until they certify that the elections were free and fair and that the results have been officially announced. At the time of the signature of the cease-fire, the parties will determine the period within which free and fair, elections must be held. The exact date of said elections will be established through consultation with all political forces in Angola.

Point 5

Respect for human rights and basic freedoms, including the right of free association.

Point 6

The process of creating the National Army will begin with the entry into force of the cease-fire and will be concluded on the date of the elections, under terms to be agreed on between the Government of the PRA and

UNITA. The neutrality of the National Army in the electoral process will be guaranteed by the Angolan parties, acting within the framework of the CCPM, with the support of the international monitoring group.

Point 7

Declaration and entry into force of the cease-fire throughout Angolan territory, in accordance with the agreement to be concluded on this subject between the Government of the PRA and UNITA.

Annex I.

1. The Government of the PRA and UNITA agree to the formation of a Joint Political-Military Commission (CCPM), to be established in Luanda at the time of the signature of the "Fundamental Principles for the Establishment of Peace in Angola."

2. The CCPM shall be composed of representatives of the Government of the PRA and of UNITA, as members, and by representatives of Portugal, the United States, and the Soviet Union, as observers. In addition, a representative of the United Nations may be invited to participate in the meetings of the CCPM.

3. It shall be the task of the CCPM to see that the peace accords are applied, thereby guaranteeing strict compliance with all political and military understandings, and to make the final decision on possible violations of those accords.

4. The CCPM shall have the authority necessary to approve all the rules relating to its functioning, particularly its own internal regulations. Its decisions will be made by consensus between the Government of the PRA and UNITA.

Concepts for Resolving the Issues Still Pending Between the Government of the People's Republic of Angola and UNITA

1. At the moment the cease-fire enters into force, UNITA will acquire the right to conduct and freely participate in political activities in accordance with the revised Constitution and the pertinent laws for the creation of a multi-party democracy. At the time of the signature of the cease-fire, the parties will determine the period within which they must hold free and fair elections. The exact date of said elections will be established through consultation with all political forces in Angola.

2. The Angolan government will hold discussions with all political forces in order to survey their opinions concerning proposed changes in the Constitution. The Angolan government will then work with all the parties to draft the laws that will regulate the electoral process.

3. The cease-fire agreement will oblige the parties to cease receiving lethal material. The United States, the USSR, and all other countries will support the implementation of the cease-fire and will refrain from furnishing lethal material to any of the Angolan parties.

4. Overall political supervision of the cease-fire process will be the responsibility of the Angolan parties, acting within the framework of the

CCPM. Verification of the cease-fire will be the responsibility of the international monitoring group. The United Nations will be invited to send monitors to support the Angolan parties, at the request of the Government of Angola. The governments that are to send monitors will be chosen by the Angolan parties, acting within the framework of the CCPM.

5. The process of creating the National Army will begin with the entry into force of the cease-fire and will be concluded on the date of the elections. The neutrality of the National Army in the electoral process will be guaranteed by the Angolan parties, acting within the framework of the CCPM, with the support of the international monitoring group. The Angolan parties reserve for later negotiations the discussions on the foreign assistance that may be necessary in order to form the National Army.

6. Free and fair elections for the new government will take place under the supervision of international elections observers, who will remain in Angola until they certify that the elections were free and fair and that the results have been officially announced.

The Protocol of Estoril

The Government of the People's Republic of Angola and UNITA, meeting in Estoril, Portugal, with the Portuguese government as mediator and in the presence of observers from the United States of America and the Union of Soviet Socialist Republics, have reached the following agreements and understandings regarding political and military matters:

   I. Elections
  II. The Joint Political-Military Commission (CCPM)
 III. Principles relating to the issue of internal security during the period between the entry into force of the cease-fire and the holding of elections
 IV. Political rights to be exercised by UNITA following the cease-fire
  V. Administrative Structures
 VI. Formation of the Angolan Armed Forces

I. Elections

1. Elections will take place in Angola to choose the President of the Republic and the National Assembly. The question of whether or not these elections will be held simultaneously will be decided through consultations among all Angolan political forces.

2. The President will be elected by direct and secret suffrage, through a majority system, with recourse to a second round, if necessary.

3. The National Assembly will be elected by direct and secret suffrage, through a system of proportional representation at the national level.

4. The elections will be preceded by an official election campaign period, the duration of which will be determined following a process of consultations involving all Angolan political forces. A technical opinion from a specialized international body such as the United Nations, for

example, will be obtained on the question of the desirable duration of the election campaign in Angola. That opinion, however, will not be considered binding by any of the parties.

5. All Angolan citizens of adult age may vote, participate in the election campaign, and stand for election without any discrimination or intimidation. The definition of what is to be understood as "adult age" will be dealt with in the election law, to be drafted following the cease-fire, after a process of consultations between the Government of the PRA and all Angolan political forces.

6. The voting will be secret, and special provisions will be made for those who cannot read or write. These provisions will be included in the election law, to be drafted following the cease-fire, after a process of consultations between the Government of the PRA and all Angolan political forces.

7. All political parties and interested persons will have the opportunity to organize and to participate in the elections process on an equal footing, regardless of their political positions.

8. Total freedom of expression, association, and access to the media will be guaranteed.

9. The parties have accepted the tripartite proposal by the delegations of Portugal in its capacity of mediator, and the United States, and the Soviet Union as observers, to the effect that September 1 through November 30, 1992, will be the period within which free and fair elections should be held in Angola, the cease-fire being signed in May 1991. The parties have reached an understanding that the following tripartite declaration is to be taken into consideration in the discussion of the precise date for the holding of elections:

"Taking into consideration the logistical difficulties in organizing the elections process, specifically the desirability that the elections be held during the dry season, and the need to reduce the high costs that the international community will have to bear in monitoring the cease-fire, the delegations of Portugal, the United States, and the Soviet Union heartily recommend that the elections be held during the first part of the suggested period, preferably between September 1 and October 1 of 1992."

II. Joint Political-Military Commission (CCPM)

1. According to the document entitled "Concepts for Resolving the Issues Still Pending Between the Government of the People's Republic of Angola and UNITA," and Annex I to the "Fundamental Principles for the Establishment of Peace in Angola," the Joint Political-Military Commission (CCPM) has as its mission the overall political supervision of the cease-fire process. It will have the duty to see that the Peace Accords are applied, thereby guaranteeing strict compliance with all political and military understandings, and to make the final decision on possible violations of those accords.

2. The CCPM will have the authority necessary to approve all rules relating to its own functioning, particularly its own internal regulations. Its

decisions will be made by consensus between the Government of the PRA and UNITA, after hearing the opinion of the Observers.

Sole Paragraph: The CCPM does not seek to replace the government of the PRA.

3. In light of the foregoing, the CCPM, with headquarters in Luanda, should structure itself so as to:

3.1 Guarantee the conditions of peace for the holding of free, fair, multi-party, and internationally verifiable elections;

3.2 Ensure the fulfillment of all the political understandings resulting from the Peace Accords relating to the electoral process;

3.3 Supervise the implementation of the Cease-Fire Agreement within the framework of the CMVF [Joint Verification and Monitoring Commission] and cooperate with the representatives of the United Nations;

3.4 Inform itself about possible threats to the territorial integrity of the country;

3.5 Discuss, within the sphere of its authority, questions relating to Angolan exiles.

4. The CCPM is to be constituted at the time of the signature of the Cease-Fire Agreement.

5. The CCPM shall be composed of representatives of the Government of the PRA and of UNITA, as members, and by representatives of Portugal, the United States, and the Soviet Union, as observers. The United Nations may be represented, in the capacity of invited guest.

5.1 Members and observers shall be supported by assistants and technical advisors for the areas assigned to them, namely:

(a) Joint Cease-Fire Verification and Monitoring Commission (CMVF);
(b) Joint Commission for the Formation of the Angolan Armed Forces (CCFA);
(c) The Political Commission.

Sole Paragraph: In the case of the members of the CCPM, the assistant and technical advisors will have to be Angolans.

6. The meetings of the CCPM shall be presided over, alternately in accordance with the principle of rotation, by the Government of the PRA and by UNITA, without prejudice to the principle of consensus in the decision-making process.

7. It shall be the responsibility of the CCPM to draft its internal regulations as well as to determine its budget.

8. The mandate of the CCPM ends on the date the elected government takes office.

III. Principles Relating to the Issue of Internal Security During the Period Between the Entry Into Force of the Cease-Fire and the Holding of Elections

1. All Angolans shall have the right to conduct and participate in political activities without intimidation, in accordance with the revised Constitution and pertinent laws for the creation of a multi-party democ-

racy, and the provisions of the Peace Accords.

2.1 The neutrality of the police, whose functions and activities are the responsibility of the Government of the PRA, shall be the object of verification and monitoring by teams of monitors composed of two members designated by the Government of the PRA, two members designated by UNITA, and one expert in police affairs to be designated by and subordinate to the United Nations Command structure.

2.2 Within the sphere of their authority, the monitoring teams shall have as their specific mandate the duty to visit police facilities, examine their activities, and investigate possible violations of political rights committed by the police. These teams may move freely throughout the entire territory of Angola.

2.3 The monitoring teams are subordinate to the CCPM, and must submit reports of their activities to that body.

2.4 In principle, there will be three monitoring teams for each Angolan province. The CCPM may modify the number of monitoring teams in accordance with the needs of each province.

3.1 Consonant with the invitation from the Government, UNITA will participate in the police force that is responsible for maintaining public order.

3.2 To that end, shortly after entry into force of the cease-fire, and as a means of strengthening trust between the parties, the availability of vacancies in the ranks of the police force to be filled by personnel designated by UNITA will be guaranteed, and those personnel will be given appropriate training.

4. UNITA will be responsible for the personal safety of its highest-ranking leaders. The Government of the PRA will grant police status to the member of UNITA in charge of guaranteeing that safety.

IV. Political Rights to Be Exercised by UNITA Following the Cease-Fire

1. According to the provisions contained in the document entitled "Concepts for Resolving the Issues Still Pending Between the Government of the People's Republic of Angola and UNITA," and in the document on "Fundamental Principles for the Establishment of Peace in Angola," at the time of entry into force of the cease-fire, UNITA will acquire the right to conduct and freely participate in political activities, according to the revised Constitution and the pertinent laws for the creation of a multi-party democracy, particularly including the following rights:

(a) Freedom of expression;
(b) The right to present, publish, and freely debate its political program;
(c) The right to recruit and enroll members;
(d) The right to hold meetings and demonstrations;
(e) The right of access to the government media;
(f) The right to free movement and personal safety of its members;

(g) The right to present candidates in the elections;

(h) The right to open headquarters and representative offices anywhere in Angola.

2. Without prejudice to the stipulations of the previous paragraph, which permit UNITA to exercise those rights immediately, UNITA must, after entry into force of the cease-fire, satisfy the formal requirements for its registration as a political party pursuant to the "Political Parties Law" of the People's Republic of Angola.

V. Administrative Structures

1. Both parties accept the principle of the extension of the Central Administration to those areas of Angola that are presently beyond the range of its authority.

2. Both parties recognize that such extension must not be made abruptly or endanger the free circulation of persons and goods, the activities of the political force, and the execution of the tasks related to the electoral process.

3. Both parties agree to leave for a later date the study of the actual implementation of such extension, which will be carried out within the framework of the CCPM by competent teams composed of representatives of the Government of the PRA and UNITA. Those teams may have recourse to international technical advisors.

VI. Formation of the Angolan Armed Forces

A. Identification and General Principles

Whereas the peace process between the Government of the PRA and UNITA presupposes the need to form an Armed Forces,

The Government of the PRA and UNITA agree to the following:

1. An Angolan Armed Forces [FAA] shall be formed.

2. The Angolan Armed Forces:

(a) Shall have as their overall mission the defense and safeguarding of independence and territorial integrity.

(b) May, in compliance with provisions of law, perform other missions of general interest that are the responsibility of the State, or collaborate in tasks related to satisfying the basic needs and improving the quality of life of the population, without prejudice to the aforesaid overall mission.

(c) Shall be composed exclusively of Angolan citizens; furthermore, its organizational structure is unitary for the entire territory.

(d) Shall have such composition, high command structure, troops, mechanisms, and equipment as determined in accordance with foreseeable external threats and the country's socio-economic conditions.

(e) Are nonpartisan and obey the competent organs of sovereignty, within the principle of subordination to political authority.

(f) Swear publicly to respect the Constitution and other laws of the Republic.

3. Members of the military on active duty shall enjoy active voting status, but may not use their duties or the structural units of the Angolan Armed Forces to interfere in any other partisan political or union activities.

4. The process of formation of the Armed Forces shall begin with the entry into force of the cease-fire and end on the date of the elections.

5. The process of formation of the Armed Forces shall evolve simultaneously with the assembly, disarmament, and integration into civilian life of the troops that are gradually being demobilized as a consequence of the cease-fire.

6. Recruitment into the Angolan Armed Forces during the period prior to the elections shall proceed in accordance with the principle of free will, drawing from the ranks of troops that are now part of the FAPLA and FALA.

7. It is mandatory that all military personnel incorporated into the Angolan Armed Forces prior to the date of the elections attend professional training courses with a view to achieving unification in terms of doctrine and procedure that is conducive to the development of an essential esprit de corps.

8. The neutrality of the Armed Forces during the period prior to the holding of the elections shall be guaranteed by the Angolan parties acting within the framework of the CCPM and the Joint Commission for the Formation of the Armed Forces (CCFA).

9. By the time the elections are held, only the Angolan Armed Forces shall exist; there may be no other troops whatsoever. All members of the present armed forces of each party who do not become members of the Angolan Armed Forces shall be demobilized prior to the holding of elections.

10. Both parties agree that individual rights acquired by military personnel of the Angolan Armed Forces during the period prior to the elections shall continue to be assured, and that the structural units created up to that point to consolidate those same Armed Force shall be safeguarded.

11. The units of the Angolan Armed Forces shall be formed beginning at the platoon level.

B. Troop Strength

1. The parties agree that the troop strength of the Angolan Armed Forces by the time of the elections shall be as follows:

Army 40,000
Air Force 6,000
Navy 4,000

2. Army personnel shall be distributed in accordance with the following plan:

- 15,000 operations soldiers, 7,200 of which shall belong to the Military Regions, 4,800 to the Army General Reserve, and 3,000 to the Special Forces.
- 15,000 soldiers for support services and administration
- 6,000 non-commissioned officers
- 4,000 officers

3. Each of the parties shall provide the Army with a total of 20,000 men, distributed as follows:

- 15,000 soldiers (of which 7,500 are to be operations personnel)
- 3,000 non-commissioned officers
- 2,000 officers

4. The first troops assigned to the Air Force and Navy shall be furnished from the respective branches of the FAPLA, inasmuch as the FALA does not have such units. As soon as the process of training the Angolan Armed Forces begins, UNITA will be able to participate in the Air Force and Navy under terms to be defined within the framework of the CCFA.

5. The Navy and the Air Force shall be subject to verification and monitoring, without prejudice to their being permitted to carry out controlled missions as a means of assuring their operationality and the defense of economic interests. As soon as the Navy and the Air Force units become part of the FAA, they shall be subordinate to the High Command of the FAA.

C. The Command Structures of the Angolan Armed Forces

1. General Principles

(a) A Joint Commission for the Formation of the Armed Forces (CCFA) shall exist, created specifically to direct the process of formation of the FAA and subordinate to the CCPM.

(b) The FAA Command Structure, including the High Command of the FAA and the commands of the three branches (Army, Air Force, and Navy) is shown on the diagram in Annex I.

(c) The entire command structure of the FAA, although derived during the period of its formation from the FAPLA and the FALA, is to become strictly non-partisan and will receive directives and orders from only the CCPM, the CCFA, and the FAA chain of command.

(d) Appointments to the FAA High Command and the commands of the three branches of the FAA are to be proposed by the CCFA and approved by the CCPM.

(e) The logistics of the FAA shall be joint, and a Logistical and Infrastructure Command, subordinate to the High Command of the FAA, shall be created for this purpose.

2. Joint Commission for the Formation of the Armed Forces

(a) The CCFA, which is directly subordinate to the CCPM, constitutes the transitional body, until the date of the elections, between the political-military echelon and the FAA echelon.

(b) The CCFA is to be composed of representatives of the FAPLA and the FALA as members, assisted by representatives of the country(ies) selected to advise them during the formation process of the FAA.

(c) The duties of the CCFA shall be as follows; however, other duties may be assigned to it by the CCPM:

- Propose to the CCPM the rules applicable to the FAA.
- Propose to the CCPM the budget to be allocated to the FAA [for the period] prior to the elections.
- Undertake strategic planning for the FAA [during the period] prior to the elections.
- Propose to the CCPM the criteria for selecting personnel from the FAPLA and FALA for purposes of forming the FAA.
- Propose to the CCPM the names of the principal commanding officers of the FAA, down to and including the brigade echelon.
- Draft directives concerning the phasing of the process of staffing the structural units of the FAA.

3. The FAA High Command

(a) The overall mission of the High Command of the FAA is to detail the generic directives received from the CCFA, with a view to staffing the structural units and supporting the forces.

(b) The High Command is composed [during the period] prior to the elections, of two general officers having equal rank, designated by each of the parties. Its decisions shall be valid only when signed by those two general officers.

(c) The High Command is assisted by EMGFAA [Angolan Armed Forces General Staff], which shall have at least the following staff units, headed by general officers or by field officers:

Office Staff
Planning and Organization Staff
Military Doctrine and Instruction Staff
Legislation Staff
Information Staff
Public Relations Staff
Justice and Discipline Staff
Operations Staff

4. The Army Command

(a) The Army Command shall be structured in due course by the High Command of the FAA, within the framework of the CCFA, and subject to approval by the CCPM.

(b) The structure of the Army Command shall accommodate the Military Regions and Military Zone(s) in a position directly subordinate to the General CEME [Army Chief of Staff], whose duties are yet to be defined, but which may include: organizing and preparing the forces, training, justice and discipline, and logistical support to the assigned forces.

(c) Each Military Region shall be commanded by a Commanding General, assisted by a Deputy General and by a Headquarters General. The Military Zones shall be commanded by general officers.

(d) The headquarters of the Military Regions and Zone(s) are as follows:

Northern Military Region, with headquarters in Uige
Central Military Region, in Huambo
Eastern Military Region, in Luene
Southern Military Region, in Lubango
The Cabinda Military Zone.

(e) The System of Forces shall be constituted on the basis of units at the brigade level and other forces that may be assigned to the Military Regions/Zone(s) or maintained in the Army Reserve or the FAA Reserve.

5. The Air Force

The Air Force shall be formed on the basis of the FAPLA Air Force, in accordance with the provision in section B, items 4 and 5 above. The details will be contained in directives issued by the CCFA.

6. The Navy

The Navy shall be formed on the basis of the FAPLA navy, in accordance with the provision in section B, items 4 and 5 above. The details will be contained in directives to be issued by the CCFA.

7. The Logistical and Infrastructure Command

(a) The Logistical and Infrastructure Command (CLI) is to be created, and is to be directly subordinate to the High Command of the FAA.

(b) The CLI shall have as its overall function to plan and propose administrative and logistical support for the FAA and guarantee that it is provided to the FAA via common services. In particular, it will be responsible for the logistics of production and procurement.

(c) The CLI is to be commanded by a General, assisted by a Second Commander (a general officer) and by a General Staff that, initially, will include the following:

- Infrastructure Staff
- Common Services Staff
- Re-equipment Staff
- Finance Staff

(d) The CLI has command over those support units that may be assigned to it.

8. Phasing and Establishing the Timetable for the Process

(a) The process of forming the Angolan Armed Forces shall proceed in phases, as follows:

- 1st phase: appointment of the CCFA—prior to the entry into force of the cease-fire.
- 2nd phase: appointment of the FAA High Command.
- 3rd phase: appointment of the commands of the sub-units.
- 4th phase: appointment of the commanders of the Military Regions and the brigade commanders.
- 5th phase: appointment of the commands of the three branches.

(b) Immediately following the appointment of each command, the respective General Staffs are to be organized.

(c) The administrative and logistical support system is organized within the principle of transformation, without loss or rupture of existing structures, in accordance with EMGFAA plans approved by the CCFA.

D. Technical Assistance from Foreign Countries

The parties will inform the Portuguese government, not later than the date of notification of their acceptance of the accords, as to which country or countries will be invited to render assistance in the FAA formation process.

E. Demobilization

The accommodation of the demobilized forces constitutes a national problem that must be studied jointly by the two parties and submitted to the CCPM for review and a decision. The same treatment should be given the problem of people who have been physically disabled by the war.

June

BRIDGEPORT'S MAYOR ON CITY'S BANKRUPTCY

June 6, 1991

Bridgeport, Connecticut, calling itself "the first major municipality in the United States" to file for bankruptcy, went to court June 6 asking for federal protection from accumulating debt and a state-ordered increase in the city's property taxes. Though refused, Bridgeport's request captured the attention of a recession-mired nation in which a multitude of local and state governments were operating under severe financial constraints. They were characterized, typically, by increasingly higher taxes and a steady reduction of public services.

A city of 141,000, Bridgeport had stopped cleaning its streets, eliminated its recreation programs, and halved its funding of libraries and services for the elderly. The city's finances had been under review by a state-created Financial Review Board since a previous budget crisis in 1988. To keep the city's $319 million budget in balance, the board had decreed an 18 percent increase in property taxes—the chief source of income for Bridgeport and most other municipalities—to take effect June 7.

In filing for bankruptcy, the city sidetracked the tax increase—at least temporarily. Mayor Mary C. Moran argued that, on the basis of per capita income, Bridgeport was the third-poorest city in the state but already had the highest taxation of real estate and personal property. "The City believes that its taxpayers cannot bear the burden of any further tax increase," she said in a statement to the City Council accompanying the bankruptcy filing. An increase, it continued, would depress property values, deter economic development, and consequently decrease rather than increase revenues, resulting in a demoralized citizenry and even-harsher cuts in services.

State Opposes Bankruptcy Petition

Connecticut challenged Bridgeport's right to defy the board, which had ordered the city not to file for bankruptcy. Judge Alan H. W. Shiff of the U.S. Bankruptcy Court in Bridgeport ruled that the board lacked authority to bar the city from doing so. But the judge agreed with the state that Bridgeport was not entirely insolvent and thus could not legally claim to be bankrupt. The judge appeared to leave the city the option of returning with a new bankruptcy petition when it did exhaust the last of its funds. The bankruptcy law pertaining to cities, known as Chapter 9, was enacted during the Depression for municipalities to use as a last resort.

The outcome left the tax increase in doubt. The state attorney general, Richard Blumenthal, said that he and William J. Cibes, the head of the review board, would study what might be done to help Bridgeport balance its budget without raising taxes. But the city could expect no help from the state. The state legislature and Gov. Lowell Weicker had been engaged since February in a test of wills over how to finance a state budget deficit estimated at $707 million. The governor thrice vetoed budget bills, causing most state government employees to be out of work and pay for nearly a week in July. Finally on August 22 the lawmakers passed a budget with the provision he wanted: it required Connecticut to impose an income tax.

In Maine and Pennsylvania many state employees were also idled by similar budget impasses that briefly stopped the flow of state funds. By one count, no fewer than twenty-eight states were struggling in mid-summer with ways to overcome budget deficits. Almost everywhere, state governments were trimming employment rolls, reducing services, or adding taxes.

For local officials, budget problems were often compounded by state policies. States facing deficits often cut aid to localities or passed on to them charges that the states once paid. In New York, for instance, Gov. Mario M. Cuomo lopped from the legislature's budget $145 million in unrestricted aid to local governments. Sylvan Leabman, a budget officer for Milwaukee County, calculated that state-mandated programs took 46 percent of the country's property tax fund, up from 32 percent in 1988.

The National League of Cities reported in July that every fourth city it had surveyed faced severe budget gaps. The National Association of Counties said that among the nation's 443 counties with populations above 100,000, some 40 percent were incurring deficits. About the same percentage had raised property taxes to the legal limit.

Following are excerpts from a statement by Mayor Mary C. Moran of Bridgeport, Connecticut, to the City Council on June 6, 1991, explaining the city's decision to file for bankruptcy to avert a tax increase and gain debt protection:

I come before you tonight with what is perhaps the most significant action in Bridgeport's history. Our fiscal crisis of many years had been addressed this evening in an unprecedented manner.

This action should assure long-term stability and fiscal restructuring that will afford much-needed tax relief and provide the services our residents deserve.

Accordingly, as the city's chief executive, I am providing notice of the fact that the City of Bridgeport has filed a Chapter 9 petition that will allow an adjustment of our debts through a plan of reorganization.

At this time I wish to inform all department heads, employees and citizens of the city that day-to-day operations will continue as usual, without disruption. Your jobs are secure and your co-operation is encouraged and invited.

This is not a time for sadness or uncertainty, but a time to all move forward together with renewed optimism to that prosperity that always eluded us.

For further clarification, I am submitting for the record a copy of the preamble submitted with our petition.

Statement of Purpose

The City of Bridgeport files the annexed Petition pursuant to Chapter 9 of the United States Bankruptcy Code with full recognition that it is the first major municipality in the United States to have made the difficult decision to solve its fiscal problems through the bankruptcy process as provided for under Federal Law. In order to clarify the intended effect of this filing, the City of Bridgeport submits this statement so that its citizens and those with whom it does business will have an accurate understanding of why this Petition is being filed, what the City of Bridgeport hopes to accomplish by this process, and what substantive areas of its fiscal obligations the City wishes to modify under its proposed Plan for the adjustment of the City's debts (referred to hereafter as the "Plan").

The City's Intentions

The City wishes to emphasize that the Plan which it shall submit to the court will, subject to the Court's approval, guarantee the full payment of its debts with municipal bond holders and trade creditors. During the pendency of the City's Petition, and until confirmation of its Plan, the City will pay all bond holders and trade creditors in a timely fashion. Bond holders are protected by tax revenues intercepted into a trust fund on a daily basis for making bond payments. The City does not anticipate any disruption of its daily operations during the Chapter 9 Proceedings.

The City, then, files for adjustment of its debts under the Court's protection in an effort to effectuate a broad restructuring plan to save Bridgeport from unbearable consequences. The City's primary purpose in filing the annexed Petition is to utilize the provisions of the Bankruptcy Code to adjust its debts, and specifically to modify certain onerous and economically burdensome contracts. Without such modifications, the City is unable to balance its fiscal year 1991-1992 and future budgets. The City is presently confronted with two alternatives to balance its budget: 1) drastic tax increases coupled with elimination of critical services, or 2) avail itself of the opportunity to adjust its debt through Chapter 9. The City believes that its taxpayers cannot bear the burden of any further tax increase. The Chapter 9 alternative is the only viable course at this point.

Increased Taxation

Taxation of real estate and personal property in the City of Bridgeport presently is the highest effective rate in the State of Connecticut. Coupled with the fact that Bridgeport is the third poorest city in the State, based upon median per capita income, and suffers major health and public safety problems (e.g., high infant mortality and extreme violent crime), any further increase in taxes would not only be counter-productive, but economically devastating to the City and its residents.

... To balance its budget for the fiscal year beginning July 1, 1991, the City would be required to impose an eighteen (18%) percent increase in taxes. Even if such an increase were to be instituted, the City would also be required to drastically cut necessary services to unacceptable and dangerous levels.

The effect of such a large increase in taxes will: (a) further diminish tax collection; (b) depress real estate and property values; and (c) deter economic development. In addition to such adverse effects, at a time when the City's Grand List is stagnant, its citizenry will become even more demoralized, especially in that there would of necessity be a reduction or elimination of essential services in the following areas: (a) law enforcement; (b) refuse collection; (c) parks and recreation; and (d) libraries.

The City believes that given the inability of its residents to pay the prospective large increase in taxes, which would be required to balance the fiscal year 1991-1992 budget, and the devastating effect which such a tax increase would have on the local economy, a tax increase of the required magnitude is completely impractical if not impossible.

Historical Perspective

The root causes for the City's present fiscal crisis are the result of a combination of factors, including:

- (a) inequitable State and Federal government tax structure, including, but not limited to, increasing payments in lieu of taxes (PILOT) to 100% reimbursement levels;
- (b) the binding arbitration statutes governing the settlement of municipal labor contract negotiations and other factors resulting in labor contracts that the City is unable to pay and which are much too costly vis-a-vis the prevailing standards for such contracts.
- (c) unfunded State mandates;
- (d) refusal of surrounding suburban areas to contribute to and share

the burden of social services presently provided by the City to persons from throughout the region, including:

health and welfare;
hospitals;
affordable housing;
education;
homeless shelters;
drug treatment and counseling.

- (e) unfair Minimum Expenditure Requirement ("MER") formula imposed upon the City.

Federal and State government presently mandates that local municipalities provide services without funding. At the same time, revenue sharing has been reduced, eliminated, or is otherwise nonexistent. Urban areas such as the City of Bridgeport cannot support themselves except to the extent they can rely upon the regressive system of real and personal property taxation which presently exists in this State. These problems have been exacerbated by the recent and present downturn in economic conditions throughout Connecticut and the Northeastern United States which have significantly increased the demand for services and entitlements, while decimating the City's tax base.

Alternatives Pursued by the City

Every effort has been made to pursue traditional alternatives to balance the present budget (i.e., reductions in force, spending controls, elimination of City services). The City has filed the ... Chapter 9 Petition only after first exploring all the alternatives available to it. ...

RULING TO UPHOLD ALL-MALE POLICY AT VMI

June 14, 1991

*A federal judge ruled June 14 that the policy of excluding female
students at Virginia Military Institute (VMI) promoted "diversity in
education" and did not violate federal antidiscrimination laws. The case
had been filed by the Justice Department on behalf of a young woman
who was disqualified from attending the state-supported college because
of her sex. In April Judge Jackson L. Kiser conducted a six-day trial in
Roanoke, Virginia, during which numerous expert witnesses testified for
and against single-sex education and on whether the presence of women
strengthened or weakened military-training programs.*

*Judge Kiser's ruling was based largely on a 1982 Supreme Court
decision,* Mississippi University for Women v. Hogan, *in which the Court
ruled that the university had violated antidiscrimination laws by refusing
to admit a male student to its nursing program for academic credit. In
that case the Court concluded that the college did not meet an "intermediate scrutiny" test requiring it to have "a legitimate and substantial
goal" for denying admission. The university had argued that the presence
of males would adversely affect teaching, student performance, and
educational goals. Judge Kiser concluded that VMI passed the* Hogan
*test and offered needed diversity in Virginia's system of higher educa-
tion. All other publicly funded colleges in the state were coeducational.*

*The judge further cited "exceedingly persuasive" evidence from nu-
merous experts that both men and women benefited from attending
single-sex colleges. Moreover, he said, the presence of women would
significantly alter VMI's unique "adversarial" model of rigorous educational and personal discipline. He cited testimony that cadets at VMI are*

subjected to far more stressful demands than those at the U.S. military, naval, and air force academies. "Even if the female could physically and psychologically undergo the rigors of the life of a male cadet, her introduction into the process would change it," Kiser wrote. "Thus, the very experience she sought would no longer be available."

Kiser repeatedly cited research by three prominent educators: Alexander W. Astin, director of the Higher Education Research Institute at the University of California at Los Angeles; Dr. Richard C. Richardson, Jr., professor of educational leadership and policy studies at Arizona State University; and Dr. David Reisman, professor emeritus of sociology at Harvard University, the author of several books on higher education.

Astin, who declined VMI's request to testify, had concluded in a 1977 study that some students benefited from single-sex education, but in an interview following the VMI ruling, said his research was outdated and called VMI an "anachronistic institution." Richardson, on the other hand, testified that it would be wrong to force VMI to admit women. Reisman, testifying from Boston via videotape, restated his longstanding support for single-sex institutions and expressed the opinion that the adversarial model of education was inappropriate for most women.

A fourth expert witness, Dr. Clifton Conrad, professor of higher education at the University of Wisconsin at Madison, testified on behalf of the Justice Department but stated that he was a "believer in single-sex education."

Reaction to the Ruling

The ruling was widely praised by VMI supporters and staff. It was "a victory for single-sex education, educational diversity, and common sense," said Robert H. Patterson, Jr., attorney for the school. Lt. Gen. Claudius E. Watts III, president of the Citadel—an all-male military institution in South Carolina—said, "A very dark cloud has been lifted from VMI and the Citadel."

Richard F. Rosser, president of the National Association of Independent Colleges and Universities, called the decision "a positive vote for diversity in higher education." He said a ruling against VMI might have produced challenges to private single-sex colleges.

A number of women's organizations and some politicians expressed strong objections to the ruling. It "missed the point altogether," said Marcia D. Greenberger, president of the National Women's Law Center. "[G]ender discrimination hurts both men and women, in that it pigeonholes them in artificial ways that don't reflect individual abilities," she said. Emilie F. Miller, the Virginia state senator who had introduced legislation to require VMI to become coeducational, said the ruling was "an outrage to the men and women in Virginia who believe in equality." In one of his last acts as attorney general, Dick Thornburgh issued a statement in August saying that the department intended to appeal the case.

Following are excerpts from the June 14, 1991, decision by Judge Jackson L. Kiser of the U.S. District Court for the Western District of Virginia in United States of America v. Commonwealth of Virginia, *ruling that the Virginia Military Institute did not violate antidiscrimination laws by refusing to admit women:*

No. 90-0126-R

United States of America, Plaintiff v. Commonwealth of Virginia, et al., Defendants	In the United States District Court for the Western District of Virginia

[June 14, 1991]

The Controversy

It was in May of 1864 that the United States and the Virginia Military Institute (VMI) first confronted each other. That was a life-and-death engagement that occurred on the battlefield at New Market, Virginia. The combatants have again confronted each other, but this time the venue is in this court. Nonetheless, VMI claims the struggle is nothing short of a life-and-death confrontation—albeit figurative.

The conflict between the parties arises out of the United States' challenge to VMI's all-male admissions policy. The United States asserts that as a state-supported college, VMI's refusal to admit females to the Institute, regardless of their qualifications, violates the Equal Protection Clause of the Fourteenth Amendment. VMI counters by saying that although it discriminates against women, the discrimination is not invidious but rather to promote a legitimate state interest—diversity in education. Thus, the issue to be resolved is whether VMI's practice of excluding women can pass muster under the equal protection clause, as glossed by the decisions of the Supreme Court. I find that it can, for the reasons that I hereafter state. . . .

Procedural Background

This case originated from a complaint filed by the United States Department of Justice on behalf of a female high school student who wanted to be considered for admission to VMI. . . .

A six-day trial was held beginning April 4, 1991. Nineteen witnesses testified, including four experts on education, one expert on college facilities, and one expert on human physiology. . . .

Standard of Review

The VMI Board of Visitors decides the admissions policy of VMI. The seventeen members of this Board are appointed by the Governor of Virginia, subject to approval by the General Assembly, including the State Adjutant General, who is a member *ex officio*. . . . Twelve of the members must be VMI alumni.

All parties recognize that this case concerns educational policy, and the proper standard of review should be derived from cases concerning higher education. The principle of academic freedom, an aspect of the freedom of association guaranteed by the First Amendment, has been recognized by the Supreme Court as a reason to defer to academic decisionmaking by a university. *Regents of the University of California v. Bakke* (1978). The essential freedoms of a university include the freedom to choose who may be admitted to study. . . . While *Bakke* involved diversity within a single graduate program, other courts have extended the rationale of that decision to include the freedom to create different missions at different state universities, in order to promote diverse educational opportunities within the state. . . .

However, deference to university decisions is not absolute. The Supreme Court ordered racial integration of graduate programs long before it ordered desegregation of lower public schools. . . . Courts have, in some cases, entered injunctions that have the effect of overruling discretionary educational decisions of individual colleges, where those decisions tend to perpetuate unconstitutional discrimination. In *Board of Visitors of the College of William & Mary v. Norris* (1971), a three-judge panel of the Fourth Circuit entered an injunction preventing Richard Bland College, a two-year branch of the College of William and Mary, from expanding into a four-year college, because that would have impeded desegregation of nearby Virginia State College.

Sex Discrimination

The first court challenge to sex segregation in Virginia higher education appeared in *Kirstein v. Rector and Visitors of the University of Virginia* (1970). In that case . . . the court encouraged a settlement that required the university to admit women. But the court refused to enter an order requiring Virginia to admit both sexes to all of its universities:

> We are urged to go further and to hold that Virginia may not operate any educational institution separated according to the sexes. We decline to do so. Obvious problems beyond our capacity to decide on this record readily occur. One of Virginia's educational institutions is military in character. Are women to be admitted on an equal basis, and, if so, are they to wear uniforms and be taught to bear arms?

Another early Fourth Circuit decision, affirmed by the Supreme Court, involved Winthrop College in Rock Hill, South Carolina. *Williams v. NcNair* [1970]. In that case, male students wanted to attend an all-female college. The Court noted that South Carolina had one public all-male college (The Citadel, which like VMI offers a military program), and several coeducational institutions. The court noted,

> It is conceded that recognized pedagogical opinion is divided on the wisdom of maintaining "single-sex" institutions of higher education but it is stipulated that there is a respectable body of educators who believe that "a single-sex institution can advance the quality and effectiveness of its instruction by concentrating upon areas of primary interest to only one sex."

Unlike *Kirstein,* there was no feature of Winthrop College other than its single-sex status that made it distinctive, and the plaintiffs' interest in attending college in the town where they lived was found to be less than compelling. The denial of admission to them was not an equal protection violation. [*Mississippi University for Women v. Hogan,* 458 U.S. 718 (1982)]

Hogan . . . guides my decision in this case. In *Hogan,* the Supreme Court conducted a factual inquiry into the justification for the policy of the Mississippi University for Women of allowing men to audit courses in the nursing program, but not granting them academic credit. It concluded that the policy denied equal protection to the plaintiff, who wished to earn credit for advanced nursing courses at the school.

The *Hogan* court applied the "intermediate scrutiny" test:

> [T]he party seeking to uphold a statute that classifies individuals on the basis of their gender must carry the burden of showing an exceedingly persuasive justification for the classification. The burden is met only by showing at least that the discrimination serves important governmental objectives and that the discriminatory means employed are substantially related to the achievement of those objectives.

Where a state offers an educational opportunity to only one gender,

> The issue is not whether the benefited class profits from the classification, but whether the State's decision to confer a benefit only upon one class by means of a discriminatory classification is substantially related to achieving a legitimate and substantial goal.

Finally,

> [a]lthough the test for determining the validity of a gender-based classification is straightforward, it must be applied free of fixed notions concerning the roles and abilities of males and females. Care must be taken in ascertaining whether the statutory objective itself reflects archaic and stereotypic notions. Thus, if the statutory objective is to exclude or "protect" members of one gender because they are presumed to suffer from an inherent handicap or to be innately inferior, the objective itself is illegitimate.

Hogan involved admission of a single student into the nursing school, and the Court did not purport to extend its ruling to cover other programs at the school. . . . These determinations require a fact-intensive examination of the practical considerations underlying the challenged policy.

Many of the facts underlying the Supreme Court's rejection of the justification proffered in *Hogan* are not present here. In *Hogan,* Justice O'Connor's majority opinion emphasized that the uncontroverted record reveals that admitting men to nursing classes does not affect teaching style, . . . that the presence of men in the classroom would not affect the performance of the female nursing students, . . . and that men in coeducational nursing schools do not dominate the classroom. . . . In sum, the record in this case is flatly inconsistent with the claim that excluding men from the School of Nursing is necessary to reach any of MUW's educational goals.

The record in this case is directly to the contrary. The record is replete with testimony that single gender education at the undergraduate level is beneficial to both males and females. Moreover, the evidence establishes that key elements of the adversative VMI educational system, with its focus on barracks life, would be fundamentally altered, and the distinctive ends of the system would be thwarted, if VMI were forced to admit females and to make changes necessary to accommodate their needs and interests.

One of the most striking differences in the two cases is the reasons proffered to justify the discrimination. In *Hogan,* Mississippi maintained that a female-only admission policy at MUW was affirmative action which was justified to compensate women for past discrimination whereas, here, Virginia urges that a male-only admission policy at VMI promotes diversity within its statewide system of higher education. The Court found that Mississippi's proffered explanation failed both prongs of the intermediate scrutiny test, i.e., that it was not an important governmental objective and that the means of advancing the objective were not substantially related to the achievement of that objective. In contrast, diversity in education has been recognized both judicially and by education experts as being a legitimate objective. The sole way to attain single-gender diversity is to maintain a policy of admitting only one gender to an institution. . . .

Single-sex Education is a Constitutionally Legitimate Form of Diversity

A substantial body of "exceedingly persuasive" evidence supports VMI's contention that some students, both male and female, benefit from attending a single-sex college. For those students, the opportunity to attend a single-sex college is a valuable one, likely to lead to better academic and professional achievement. . . . Most importantly, Dr. [Clifton] Conrad, the United States' expert witness on higher education, called himself a "believer in single-sex education." He believed that single-sex education should be provided only by the private sector, because he also believes that public institutions should be open to all citizens to the extent possible. He concedes that his public/private dichotomy is a personal, philosophical preference rather than one born of educational-benefit considerations. . . .

One empirical study in evidence, not questioned by any expert, demonstrates that single-sex colleges provide better educational experiences than coeducational institutions. Students of both sexes become more academically involved, interact with faculty frequently, show larger increases in intellectual self-esteem and are more satisfied with practically all aspects of college experience (the sole exception is social life) compared with their counterparts in coeducational institutions. Attendance at an all-male college substantially increases the likelihood that a student will carry out career plans in law, business and college teaching, and also has a substantial positive effect on starting salaries in business. Women's colleges increase the chances that those who attend will obtain positions of leadership, complete the baccalaureate degree, and aspire to higher degrees. [citing] Alexander Astin, *Four Critical Years* (1977). This research was cited favorably by Justice [Lewis] Powell in his dissenting opinion in *Hogan*. Viewed in the light of this very substantial authority favoring single-sex education, the VMI Board's decision to maintain an all-male institution is fully justified even without taking into consideration the other unique features of VMI's method of teaching and training.

Openness and equal treatment by public institutions is a valid legislative goal, but legislators or other decisionmakers may also take other goals into account, even when adopting a policy that discriminates on the basis of sex. The VMI Board has decided that providing a distinctive, single-sex educational opportunity is more important than providing an education equally available to all.

Effect of Coeducation at VMI

When one considers VMI's methods of education and the effect that admission of women into the institution will have, the Board's decision to remain an all-male institution is further reinforced. Expert testimony established that, even though some women are capable of all of the individual activities required of VMI cadets, a college where women are present would be significantly different from one where only men are present. . . . In addition to converting VMI from a single-gender institution to a coeducational institution, changes in methods of instruction and living conditions would occur.

As West Point's experience in converting to coeducation bears out, the presence of women would tend to distract male students from their studies. It would also increase pressures relating to dating, which would tend to impair the *esprit de corps* and the egalitarian atmosphere which are critical elements of the VMI experience.

Allowance for personal privacy would have to be made. Doors would have to be locked, and the windows on all of the doors would have to be covered. This would alter the adversative environment that VMI students must now endure.

Physical education requirements would have to be altered, at least for the women. . . . which would remove one important part of the VMI system of education. . . .

Dr. [David] Riesman testified that the adversative model of education is simply inappropriate for the vast majority of women. He felt that if VMI were to admit women, it would eventually find it necessary to drop the adversative system altogether, and adopt a system that provides more nurturing and support for the students. Evidence supports this theory, including the West Point experience.... The changes, which all parties agreed would occur, provide sufficient constitutional justification for continuing the single-sex policy....

I find that both VMI's single-sex status and its distinctive educational method represent legitimate contributions to diversity in the Virginia higher education system, and that excluding women is substantially related to this mission.... VMI has, therefore, met its burden under *Hogan* of showing a substantial relationship between the single-sex admission policy and achievement of the Commonwealth's objective of educational diversity....

Absence of Comparable Opportunity for Women

Ironically, although much of the testimony at trial concerned the ways that men and women are different, my ruling is based on a trait that men and women share: Both men and women can benefit from a single-sex education. Indeed, it appears that demand for single-sex education is greater among women, and that the beneficial effects of single-sex education are stronger among women than among men.

Gender discrimination, as a rule, works to the benefit of one group and to the detriment of another. But in a real sense of the word, that is not true in this case because, as the testimony of experts demonstrates, it would be impossible for a female to participate in the "VMI experience." Even if the female could physically and psychologically undergo the rigors of the life of a male cadet, her introduction into the process would change it. Thus, the very experience she sought would no longer be available. Consequently, it seems to me that the criticism which might be directed toward Virginia's higher educational policy is not that it maintains VMI as an all-male institution, but rather that it fails to maintain at least one all-female institution. But this issue is not before the Court. ...

Conclusion

... VMI is a different type of institution. It has set its eye on the goal of citizen-soldier and never veered from the path it has chosen to meet that goal. VMI truly marches to the beat of a different drummer, and I will permit it to continue to do so. ...

SUPREME COURT ON LIBEL FROM MISQUOTATION

June 20 and 24, 1991

In two important freedom-of-the-press rulings, the Supreme Court sought in the final week of its 1990-1991 term to define when a published misquotation is libelous and to determine if a newspaper can be punished for breaking a pledge of confidentiality to a news source. In the first case, Masson v. New Yorker Magazine, *the Court on June 20 reinstated a seven-year-old libel suit that had drawn wide attention in literary and journalistic circles.*

In the second case, Cohen v. Cowles Media Company, *the Court ruled June 24 that the Minnesota Supreme Court erred in dismissing a damage suit against the state's two biggest newspapers, the* Minneapolis Star Tribune *and the* St. Paul Pioneer Press Dispatch *for reneging on a promise not to identify a news source. That court had ruled that the papers' First Amendment right to publish news of public value overrode other legal considerations. In Washington, a five-member majority of justices held that "generally applicable" laws apply to the press even if they incidentally inhibit news gathering and reporting.*

Although the two cases were reinstated, putting the defendant publications at risk of financial losses, the rulings clearly could not be regarded as outright victories for the plaintiffs. Justice Byron R. White, writing for the majority in Cohen, *said that the Minnesota court might find the papers shielded by state law—even if not by the federal Constitution.*

In the Masson *ruling, lawyers for the magazine expressed relief that standard First Amendment protections for libel had been left intact. To win a libel suit, a public figure must prove that erroneous information about him harmed his reputation and was published with "actual malice," defined as deliberate or reckless falsity. Moreover, Justice Anthony M. Kennedy's opinion on behalf of the Court seemed sensitive to the difficulties a news interviewer might encounter in recording a subject's precise words in proper context.*

Libel Case Over Alleged Misquotations

Jeffrey M. Masson, a psychoanalyst-author, sued the New Yorker *and the Alfred A. Knopf book publishing company for $10 million, accusing writer Janet Malcolm of deliberately misquoting him in a long, unflattering two-part article that appeared in the magazine in December 1982 and later as a book. The book's title,* In the Freud Archives, *referred to a place near London where writings, letters, and the personal library of the psychiatrist Sigmund Freud are kept. Masson, who had been projects director at that repository, became disillusioned with Freudian theory and gained a measure of fame by writing a book denouncing it. He was dismissed from his job.*

For the article, Malcolm taperecorded about forty hours of conversations with Masson, in person and by telephone. She denied that any of the quotations she used were fabricated, although some were not on the recordings. She said the others were from scribbled notes, subsequently discarded after their contents were typewritten. After legal wrangling in federal district court in California, where the suit was filed, the number of challenged passages was winnowed to six.

"Intellectual Gigolo" Quotation

In one instance Masson was quoted as describing how Freud's daughter Anna and the archives director viewed him: "I was like an intellectual gigolo—you get your pleasure from him but you don't take him out in public." On tape, he had said: "They liked me when I was alone in their living room, and I could talk and chat and tell them the truth about things and they would tell me that I was, in a sense, much too junior within the hierarchy of analysis, for these important training analysts to be caught dead with me."

All nine justices agreed that a federal appellate court in San Francisco had erred in dismissing the case before it went to trial on grounds that even if the quotations were fabricated they would not be libelous because they represented a "rational interpretation" of what Masson said. Kennedy asserted that such a standard would "give journalists the freedom to place statements in their subjects' mouths without fear of liability" and "diminish to a great degree the trustworthiness of the printed word."

Violation of News Source's Confidentiality

The Cohen *case on violation of confidentiality arose during the 1982 Minnesota gubernatorial election campaign. Dan Cohen sued the two papers after they identified him as the person who tipped their reporters to information potentially damaging to his candidate's opponent. Fired* *from his job, he sued the papers for lost income and punitive damages. Charging breach of contract, Cohen was awarded $700,000 by a state court jury. An intermediate state court allowed only $200,000, and the Minnesota Supreme Court disallowed any compensation. It held that the newspapers' First Amendment rights to publish news of public value overrode other legal considerations.*

In Washington, a five-member Supreme Court majority interpreted the law differently. White said Minnesota law "simply requires those making promises to keep them" and saw no constitutional reason to keep it from applying to this case.

David H. Souter, participating in his first press-freedom case since joining the Court in October 1990, wrote a dissenting opinion saying that the state's interest in enforcing a promise was outweighed by the nature of the published information. "There can be no doubt that Cohen's identity expanded the universe of information relevant to the choice faced by Minnesota voters.... An election could turn on just such a factor; if it should, I am ready to assume that it would be to the greater public good, at least over the long run...."

Following are the Supreme Court's majority, concurring, and dissenting opinions in the cases of Masson v. New Yorker Magazine, *June 20, 1991, declaring that prevailing standards for determining libel applied to the misquotation of public figures, and of* Cohen v. Cowles Media Company, *June 24, 1991, ruling that "generally applicable" laws apply to the press even if they incidentally inhibit news gathering and reporting:*

No. 89-1799

Jeffrey M. Masson, Petitioner *v.* New Yorker Magazine, Inc., Alfred A. Knopf, Inc. and Janet Malcolm	On writ of certiorari to the United States Court of Appeals for the Ninth Circuit

[June 20, 1991]

JUSTICE KENNEDY delivered the opinion of the Court.

In this libel case, a public figure claims he was defamed by an author who, with full knowledge of the inaccuracy, used quotation marks to attribute to him comments he had not made. The First Amendment protects authors and journalists who write about public figures by requiring a plaintiff to prove that the defamatory statements were made with what we have called "actual malice," a term of art denoting deliberate or reckless falsification. We consider in this opinion whether the attributed quotations had the degree of falsity required to prove this state of mind, so that the public figure can defeat a motion for summary judgment and proceed to a trial on the merits of the defamation claim.

I

Petitioner Jeffrey Masson trained at Harvard University as a Sanskrit scholar, and in 1970 became a professor of Sanskrit & Indian Studies at the University of Toronto. He spent eight years in psychoanalytic training, and qualified as an analyst in 1978. Through his professional activities, he came to know Dr. Kurt Eissler, head of the Sigmund Freud Archives, and Dr. Anna Freud, daughter of Sigmund Freud and a major psychoanalyst in her own right. The Sigmund Freud Archives, located at Maresfield Gardens outside of London, serves as a repository for materials about Freud, including his own writings, letters, and personal library. The materials, and the right of access to them, are of immense value to those who study Freud, his theories, life and work.

In 1980, Eissler and Anna Freud hired petitioner as Projects Director of the Archives. After assuming his post, petitioner became disillusioned with Freudian psychology. In a 1981 lecture before the Western New England Psychoanalytical Society in New Haven, Connecticut, he advanced his theories of Freud. Soon after, the Board of the Archives terminated petitioner as Projects Director.

Respondent Janet Malcolm is an author and a contributor to respondent The New Yorker, a weekly magazine. She contacted petitioner in 1982 regarding the possibility of an article on his relationship with the Archives. He agreed, and the two met in person and spoke by telephone in a series of interviews. Based on the interviews and other sources, Malcolm wrote a lengthy article. One of Malcolm's narrative devices consists of enclosing lengthy passages in quotation marks, reporting statements of Masson, Eissler, and her other subjects. . . .

Petitioner brought an action for libel under California law in the United States District Court for the Northern District of California. During extensive discovery and repeated amendments to the complaint, petitioner concentrated on various passages alleged to be defamatory, dropping some and adding others. The tape recordings of the interviews demonstrated that petitioner had, in fact, made statements substantially identical to a number of the passages, and those passages are no longer in the case. We discuss only the passages relied on by petitioner in his briefs to this Court.

Each passage before us purports to quote a statement made by petitioner during the interviews. Yet in each instance no identical statement appears in the more than 40 hours of taped interviews. Petitioner complains that Malcolm fabricated all but one passage; with respect to that passage, he claims Malcolm omitted a crucial portion, rendering the remainder misleading. . . .

Malcolm submitted to the District Court that not all of her discussions with petitioner were recorded on tape, in particular conversations that occurred while the two of them walked together or traveled by car, while petitioner stayed at Malcolm's home in New York, or while her tape recorder was inoperable. She claimed to have taken notes of these unrecorded sessions, which she later typed, then discarding the handwritten originals. Petitioner denied that any discussion relating to the substance of the article occurred during his stay at Malcolm's home in New York, that Malcolm took notes during any of their conversations, or that Malcolm gave any indication that her tape recorder was broken.

Respondents moved for summary judgment. The parties agreed that petitioner was a public figure and so could escape summary judgment only if the evidence in the record would permit a reasonable finder of fact, by clear and convincing evidence, to conclude that respondents published a defamatory statement with actual malice as defined by our cases. The District Court analyzed each of the passages and held that the alleged inaccuracies did not raise a jury question. The court found that the allegedly fabricated quotations were either substantially true, or were " 'one of a number of possible rational interpretations' of a conversation or event that ' bristled with ambiguities,' " and thus were entitled to constitutional protection. The court also ruled that the " he had the wrong man" passage involved an exercise of editorial judgment upon which the courts could not intrude.

The Court of Appeals affirmed, with one judge dissenting. The court assumed for much of its opinion that Malcolm had deliberately altered each quotation not found on the tape recordings, but nevertheless held that petitioner failed to raise a jury question of actual malice, in large part for the reasons stated by the District Court....

II

A

Under California law, "[l]ibel is a false and unprivileged publication by writing ... which exposes any person to hatred, contempt, ridicule, or obloquy, or which causes him to be shunned or avoided, or which has a tendency to injure him in his occupation." False attribution of statements to a person may constitute libel, if the falsity exposes that person to an injury comprehended by the statute....

The First Amendment limits California's libel law in various respects. When, as here, the plaintiff is a public figure, he cannot recover unless he proves by clear and convincing evidence that the defendant published the defamatory statement with actual malice, i.e., with "knowledge that it was false or with reckless disregard of whether it was false or not." [quoting] New York Times Co. v. Sullivan (1964). Mere negligence does not suffice. Rather, the plaintiff must demonstrate that the author "in fact entertained serious doubts as to the truth of his publication," [quoting] St. Amant v. Thompson (1968), or acted with a "high degree of awareness of ... probable falsity," [quoting] Garrison v. Louisiana (1964)....

B

In general, quotation marks around a passage indicate to the reader that the passage reproduces the speaker's words verbatim. They inform the reader that he or she is reading the statement of the speaker, not a paraphrase or other indirect interpretation by an author. By providing this information, quotations add authority to the statement and credibility to the author's work. . . .

A fabricated quotation may injure reputation in at least two senses, either giving rise to a conceivable claim of defamation. First, the quotation might injure because it attributes an untrue factual assertion to the speaker. An example would be a fabricated quotation of a public official admitting he had been convicted of a serious crime when in fact he had not.

Second, regardless of the truth or falsity of the factual matters asserted within the quoted statement, the attribution may result in injury to reputation because the manner of expression or even the fact that the statement was made indicates a negative personal trait or an attitude the speaker does not hold. . . .

Of course, quotations do not always convey that the speaker actually said or wrote the quoted material. "Punctuation marks, like words, have many uses. Writers often use quotation marks, yet no reasonable reader would assume that such punctuation automatically implies the truth of the quoted material." In *Baker* [v. *Los Angeles Examiner*], a television reviewer printed a hypothetical conversation between a station vice president and writer/producer, and the court found that no reasonable reader would conclude the plaintiff in fact had made the statement attributed to him. . . . In other instances, an acknowledgement that the work is so-called docudrama or historical fiction, or that it recreates conversations from memory, not from recordings, might indicate that the quotations should not be interpreted as the actual statements of the speaker to whom they are attributed.

The work at issue here, however, as with much journalistic writing, provides the reader no clue that the quotations are being used as a rhetorical device or to paraphrase the speaker's actual statements. To the contrary, the work purports to be nonfiction, the result of numerous interviews. At least a trier of fact could so conclude. The work contains lengthy quotations attributed to petitioner, and neither Malcolm nor her publishers indicate to the reader that the quotations are anything but the reproduction of actual conversations. Further, the work was published in The New Yorker, a magazine which at the relevant time seemed to enjoy a reputation for scrupulous factual accuracy. These factors would, or at least could, lead a reader to take the quotations at face value. A defendant may be able to argue to the jury that quotations should be viewed by the reader as nonliteral or reconstructions, but we conclude that a trier of fact in this case could find that the reasonable reader would understand the quotations to be nearly verbatim reports of statements made by the subject.

C

The constitutional question we must consider here is whether, in the framework of a summary judgment motion, the evidence suffices to show that respondents acted with the requisite knowledge of falsity or reckless disregard as to truth or falsity. This inquiry in turn requires us to consider the concept of falsity; for we cannot discuss the standards for knowledge or reckless disregard without some understanding of the acts required for liability. We must consider whether the requisite falsity inheres in the attribution of words to the petitioner which he did not speak.

In some sense, any alteration of a verbatim quotation is false. But writers and reporters by necessity alter what people say, at the very least to eliminate grammatical and syntactical infelicities. If every alteration constituted the falsity required to prove actual malice, the practice of journalism, which the First Amendment standard is designed to protect, would require a radical change, one inconsistent with our precedents and First Amendment principles. Petitioner concedes this absolute definition of falsity in the quotation context is too stringent, and acknowledges that "minor changes to correct for grammar or syntax" do not amount to falsity for purposes of proving actual malice. We agree, and must determine what, in addition to this technical falsity, proves falsity for purposes of the actual malice inquiry.

Petitioner argues that, excepting correction of grammar or syntax, publication of a quotation with knowledge that it does not contain the words the public figure used demonstrates actual malice. The author will have published the quotation with knowledge of falsity, and no more need be shown. Petitioner suggests that by invoking more forgiving standards the Court of Appeals would permit and encourage the publication of falsehoods. . . .

We reject the idea that any alteration beyond correction of grammar or syntax by itself proves falsity in the sense relevant to determining actual malice under the First Amendment. An interviewer who writes from notes often will engage in the task of attempting a reconstruction of the speaker's statement. That author would, we may assume, act with knowledge that at times she has attributed to her subject words other than those actually used. Under petitioner's proposed standard, an author in this situation would lack First Amendment protection if she reported as quotations the substance of a subject's derogatory statements about himself.

Even if a journalist has tape recorded the spoken statement of a public figure, the full and exact statement will be reported in only rare circumstances. The existence of both a speaker and a reporter; the translation between two media, speech and the printed word; the addition of punctuation; and the practical necessity to edit and make intelligible a speaker's perhaps rambling comments, all make it misleading to suggest that a quotation will be reconstructed with complete accuracy. . . .

. . . If an author alters a speaker's words but effects no material change in meaning, including any meaning conveyed by the manner or fact of expression, the speaker suffers no injury to reputation that is compensable as a defamation....

... [W]e reject any special test of falsity for quotations, including one which would draw the line at correction of grammar or syntax. We conclude, rather, that the exceptions suggested by petitioner for grammatical or syntactical corrections serve to illuminate a broader principle.

The common law of libel takes but one approach to the question of falsity, regardless of the form of the communication. It overlooks minor inaccuracies and concentrates upon substantial truth. As in other jurisdictions, California law permits the defense of substantial truth, and would absolve a defendant even if she cannot "justify every word of the alleged defamatory matter; it is sufficient if the substance of the charge be proved true, irrespective of slight inaccuracy in the details." ... In this case, of course, the burden is upon petitioner to prove falsity....

We conclude that a deliberate alteration of the words uttered by a plaintiff does not equate with knowledge of falsity ... unless the alteration results in a material change in the meaning conveyed by the statement....

... In the case under consideration, readers of In the Freud Archives may have found Malcolm's portrait of petitioner especially damning because so much of it appeared to be a self-portrait, told by petitioner in his own words. And if the alterations of petitioner's words gave a different meaning to the statements, bearing upon their defamatory character, then the device of quotations might well be critical in finding the words actionable.

D

The Court of Appeals applied a test of substantial truth which, in exposition if not in application, comports with much of the above discussion. The Court of Appeals, however, went one step beyond protection of quotations that convey the meaning of a speaker's statement with substantial accuracy and concluded that an altered quotation is protected so long as it is a "rational interpretation" of an actual statement.... Application of our protection for rational interpretation in this context finds no support in general principles of defamation law or in our First Amendment jurisprudence ... because many of the quotations at issue might reasonably be construed to state or imply factual assertions that are both false and defamatory, we cannot accept the reasoning of the Court of Appeals on this point....

The protection for rational interpretation serves First Amendment principles by allowing an author the interpretive license that is necessary when relying upon ambiguous sources. Where, however, a writer uses a quotation, and where a reasonable reader would conclude that the quotation purports to be a verbatim repetition of a statement by the speaker, the quotation marks indicate that the author is not involved in an interpretation of the speaker's ambiguous statement, but attempting to convey what the speaker said. This orthodox use of a quotation is the quintessential "direct account of events that speak for themselves"....

... Were we to assess quotations under a rational interpretation standard, we would give journalists the freedom to place statements in their subjects' mouths without fear of liability. By eliminating any method of distinguishing between the statements of the subject and the interpretation of the author, we would diminish to a great degree the trustworthiness of the printed word, and eliminate the real meaning of quotations. Not only public figures but the press doubtless would suffer under such a rule....

III

A

We apply these principles to the case before us. On summary judgment, we must draw all justifiable inferences in favor of the nonmoving party, including questions of credibility and of the weight to be accorded particular evidence. So we must assume, except where otherwise evidenced by the transcripts of the tape recordings, that petitioner is correct in denying that he made the statements attributed to him by Malcolm, and that Malcolm reported with knowledge or reckless disregard of the differences between what petitioner said and what was quoted....

[A]t this stage, the evidence creates a jury question whether Malcolm published the statements with knowledge or reckless disregard of the alterations.

[B omitted]

C

Because of the Court of Appeals' disposition with respect to Malcolm, it did not have occasion to address petitioner's argument that the District Court erred in granting summary judgment to The New Yorker Magazine, Inc., and Alfred A. Knopf, Inc. on the basis of their respective relations with Malcolm or the lack of any independent actual malice. These questions are best addressed in the first instance on remand.

The judgment of the Court of Appeals is reversed, and the case is remanded for further proceedings consistent with this opinion.

It is so ordered.

JUSTICE WHITE, with whom JUSTICE SCALIA joins, concurring in part and dissenting in part.

[In] *New York Times Co.* v. *Sullivan* (1964), "malice" means deliberate falsehood or reckless disregard for whether the fact asserted is true or false. As the Court recognizes, the use of quotation marks in reporting what a person said asserts that the person spoke the words as quoted. As this case comes to us, it is to be judged on the basis that in the instances identified by the Court, the reporter, Malcolm, wrote that Masson said certain things that she knew Masson did not say. By any definition of the term, this was "knowing falsehood": Malcolm asserts that Masson said these very words, knowing that he did not. The issue, as the Court recognizes, is whether Masson spoke the words attributed to him, not whether the fact, if any, asserted by the attributed words is true or false. In my view, we need to go no further to conclude that the defendants in this case were not entitled to summary judgment on the issue of malice with respect to any of the six erroneous quotations. . . .

This seems to me to be the straightforward, traditional approach to deal with this case. Instead, the Court states that deliberate misquotation does not amount to *New York Times* malice [standard set in *New York Times* v. *Sullivan* (1964)] unless it results in a material change in the meaning conveyed by the statement. This ignores the fact that under *New York Times*, reporting a known falsehood—here the knowingly false attribution—is sufficient proof of malice. The falsehood, apparently, must be substantial; the reporter may lie a little, but not too much. . . .

No. 90-634

Dan Cohen, Petitioner *v.* Cowles Media Company, DBA Minneapolis Star and Tribune Company, et al.	On writ of certiorari to the Supreme Court of Minnesota

[June 24, 1991]

JUSTICE WHITE delivered the opinion of the Court.

The question before us is whether the First Amendment prohibits a plaintiff from recovering damages, under state promissory estoppel law, for a newspaper's breach of a promise of confidentiality given to the plaintiff in exchange for information. We hold that it does not.

During the closing days of the 1982 Minnesota gubernatorial race, Dan Cohen, an active Republican associated with Wheelock Whitney's Independent-Republican gubernatorial campaign, approached reporters from the St. Paul Pioneer Press Dispatch (Pioneer Press) and the Minneapolis Star and Tribune (Star Tribune) and offered to provide documents relating to a candidate in the upcoming election. Cohen made clear to the reporters that he would provide the information only if he was given a promise of confidentiality. Reporters from both papers promised to keep Cohen's identity anonymous and Cohen turned over copies of two public court records concerning Marlene Johnson, the Democratic-Farmer-Labor candidate for Lieutenant Governor. The first record indicted that Johnson had been charged in 1969 with three counts of unlawful assembly, and the second that she had been convicted in 1970 of petit theft. Both newspapers interviewed Johnson for her explanation and one reporter tracked down the person who had found the records for Cohen. As it turned out, the unlawful assembly charges arose out of Johnson's participation in a protest of an alleged failure to hire minority workers on municipal construction projects and the charges were eventually dismissed. The petit theft conviction was for leaving a store without paying for $6.00 worth of sewing materials. The incident apparently occurred at a time during which Johnson was emotionally distraught, and the conviction was later vacated.

After consultation and debate, the editorial staffs of the two newspapers independently decided to publish Cohen's name as part of their stories concerning Johnson. In their stories, both papers identified Cohen as the source of the court records, indicated his connection to the Whitney campaign, and included denials by Whitney campaign officials of any role in the matter. The same day the stories appeared, Cohen was fired by his employer.

Cohen sued respondents, the publishers of the Pioneer Press and Star Tribune, in Minnesota state court, alleging fraudulent misrepresentation and breach of contract. The trial court rejected respondents' argument that the First Amendment barred Cohen's lawsuit. A jury returned a verdict in Cohen's favor, awarding him $200,000 in compensatory damages and $500,000 in punitive damages. The Minnesota Court of Appeals, in a split decision, reversed the award of punitive damages after concluding that Cohen had failed to establish a fraud claim, the only claim which would support such an award. However, the court upheld the finding of liability for breach of contract and the $200,000 compensatory damage award.

A divided Minnesota Supreme Court reversed the compensatory damages award....

... [T]he court concluded that "in this case enforcement of the promise of confidentiality under a promissory estoppel theory would violate defendants' First Amendment rights." ...

Respondents initially contend that the Court should dismiss this case without reaching the merits because the promissory estoppel theory was not argued or presented in the courts below and because the Minnesota Supreme Court's decision rests entirely on the interpretation of state law. These contentions do not merit extended discussion. It is irrelevant to this Court's jurisdiction whether a party raised below and argued a federal-law issue that the state supreme court actually considered and decided....

The initial question we face is whether a private cause of action for promissory estoppel involves "state action" within the meaning of the Fourteenth Amendment such that the protections of the First Amendment are triggered. For if it does not, then the First Amendment has no bearing on this case. The rationale of our decision in *New York Times Co. v. Sullivan* (1964), and subsequent cases compels the conclusion that there is state action here. Our cases teach that the application of state rules of law in state courts in a manner alleged to restrict First Amendment freedoms constitutes "state action" under the Fourteenth Amendment. In this case, the Minnesota Supreme Court held that if Cohen could recover at all it would be on the theory of promissory estoppel, a state-law doctrine which, in the absence of a contract, creates obligations never explicitly assumed by the parties. These legal obligations would be enforced through the official power of the Minnesota courts. Under our cases, that is enough to constitute "state action" for purposes of the Fourteenth Amendment.

Respondents rely on the proposition that "if a newspaper lawfully obtains truthful information about a matter of public significance then state officials may not constitutionally punish publication of the information, absent a need to further a state interest of the highest order." [quoting] *Smith* v. *Daily Mail Publishing Co.* (1979)....

This case, however, is not controlled by this line of cases but rather by the equally well-established line of decisions holding that generally applicable laws do not offend the First Amendment simply because their enforcement against the press has incidental effects on its ability to gather and report the news. As the cases relied on by respondents recognize, the truthful information sought to be published must have been lawfully acquired.... It is therefore beyond dispute that "[t]he publisher of a newspaper has no special immunity from the application of general laws. He has no special privilege to invade the rights and liberties of others." [quoting] *Associated Press* v. *NLRB* (1937). Accordingly, enforcement of such general laws against the press is not subject to stricter scrutiny than would be applied to enforcement against other persons or organizations.

There can be little doubt that the Minnesota doctrine of promissory estoppel is a law of general applicability. It does not target or single out the press. Rather, in so far as we are advised, the doctrine is generally applicable to the daily transactions of all the citizens of Minnesota. The First Amendment does not forbid its application to the press....

... Moreover, JUSTICE BLACKMUN'S reliance on cases like *The Florida Star* and *Smith* v. *Daily Mail* is misplaced. In those cases, the State itself defined the content of publications that would trigger liability. Here, by contrast, Minnesota law simply requires those making promises to keep them. The parties themselves, as in this case, determine the scope of their legal obligations and any restrictions which may be placed on the publication of truthful information are self-imposed.

Also, it is not at all clear that Respondents obtained Cohen's name "lawfully" in this case, at least for purposes of publishing it. Unlike the situation in *The Florida Star*, where the rape victim's name was obtained through lawful access to a police report, respondents obtained Cohen's name only by making a promise which they did not honor. The dissenting opinions suggest that the press should not be subject to any law, including copyright law for example, which in any fashion or to any degree limits or restricts the press' right to report truthful information. The First Amendment does not grant the press such limitless protection.

Nor is Cohen attempting to use a promissory estoppel cause of action to avoid the strict requirements for establishing a libel or defamation claim. As the Minnesota Supreme Court observed here, "Cohen could not sue for defamation because the information disclosed [his name] was true." Cohen is not seeking damages for injury to his reputation or his state of mind. He sought damages in excess of $50,000 for a breach of a promise that caused him to lose his job and lowered his earning capacity....

Respondents and *amici* [supporting petitioners] argue that permitting

Cohen to maintain a cause of action for promissory estoppel will inhibit truthful reporting because news organizations will have legal incentives not to disclose a confidential source's identity even when that person's identity is itself newsworthy. JUSTICE SOUTER makes a similar argument. But if this is the case, it is no more than the incidental, and constitutionally insignificant, consequence of applying to the press a generally applicable law that requires those who make certain kinds of promises to keep them. ... Accordingly, the judgment of the Minnesota Supreme Court is reversed, and the case is remanded for further proceedings not inconsistent with this opinion.

So ordered.

JUSTICE BLACKMUN, with whom JUSTICE MARSHALL and JUSTICE SOUTER join, dissenting.

I agree with the Court that the decision of the Supreme Court of Minnesota rested on federal grounds and that the judicial enforcement of petitioner's promissory estoppel claim constitutes state action under the Fourteenth Amendment. I do not agree, however, that the use of that claim to penalize the reporting of truthful information regarding a political campaign does not violate the First Amendment. Accordingly, I dissent.

... In my view, the [Minnesota Supreme] Court's decision is premised, not on the identity of the speaker, but on the speech itself. Thus, the court found it to be of "critical significance," that "the promise of anonymity arises in the classic First Amendment context of the quintessential public debate in our democratic society, namely, a political source involved in a political campaign".... The majority's admonition that " '[t]he publisher of a newspaper has no special immunity from the application of general laws,' " and its reliance on the cases that support that principle, are therefore misplaced....

To the extent that truthful speech may ever be sanctioned consistent with the First Amendment, it must be in furtherance of a state interest "of the highest order." Because the Minnesota Supreme Court's opinion makes clear that the State's interest in enforcing its promissory estoppel doctrine in this case was far from compelling, I would affirm that court's decision.

I respectfully dissent.

JUSTICE SOUTER, with whom JUSTICE MARSHALL, JUSTICE BLACKMUN and JUSTICE O'CONNOR join, dissenting.

I agree with Justice Blackmun that this case does not fall within the line of authority holding the press to laws of general applicability where commercial activities and relationships, not the content of publication, are at issue....

... There can be no doubt that the fact of Cohen's identity expanded the universe of information relevant to the choice faced by Minnesota voters in that State's 1982 gubernatorial election, the publication of which was thus of the sort quintessentially subject to strict First Amendment protection.

The propriety of his leak to respondents could be taken to reflect on his character, which in turn could be taken to reflect on the character of the candidate who had retained him as an adviser. An election could turn on just such a factor; if it should, I am ready to assume that it would be to the greater public good, at least over the long run. . . .

Because I believe the State's interest in enforcing a newspaper's promise of confidentiality insufficient to outweigh the interest in unfettered publication of the information revealed in this case, I respectfully dissent.

NEW YORK REPORT ON
MULTICULTURAL TEXTBOOKS
June 20, 1991

A special committee for the New York commissioner of education issued a report June 20 recommending that the state's public schools revise their social science courses to identify the contributions of America's diverse racial and ethnic traditions to the nation's cultural heritage. The courses would de-emphasize an "Anglo-American" model of history and highlight instead a variety of interpretations.

The ninety-seven page report, titled "One Nation, Many Peoples: A Declaration of Cultural Independence" renewed a lively and often emotional national debate over "multicultural education," which promotes giving full recognition of the contributions of racial and ethnic groups to the nation's culture and economy. The report quickly drew detractors and defenders.

While generally acceptable as a concept, the report produced bitter academic infighting on many university campuses over conflicting views of history and how it should be taught. The traditional understanding of Europe as the fount of Western civilization was widely challenged—often by black students and their allies who would substitute an "Afrocentric" for a "Eurocentric" view.

In a book that gained wide attention during 1991, Illiberal Education, author Dinesh D'Souza argued that demands by minority scholars and their supporters for greater faculty representation and curriculum changes were squelching academic freedom on campus. Those who disagreed were said to be coerced into silence.

Still another quarrel arose during the year over questions of diversity and pluralism on campus. Secretary of Education Lamar Alexander accused the Middle States Association of Colleges and Schools, an accrediting agency, of unfairly demanding that colleges within its jurisdiction diversify the makeup of their student bodies and faculties as to race, sex, age, and ethnic backgrounds. Alexander said the diversity standard could undermine academic freedom and create race-based hiring quotas.

Fight Over Multicultural Education

Such was the climate of debate into which the report was issued. In New York, as elsewhere, few quarreled with the stated intent of the report, as expressed in its introduction. "If the United States is to continue to prosper in the 21st century," it said, "then all of its citizens, whatever their race or ethnicity, must believe that they and their ancestors have shared in the building of a country and have a stake in its success."

But there were fears that multicultural education might divide rather than unify American society—a possibility strongly expressed by two noted historians, Kenneth T. Jackson and Arthur Schlesinger, Jr. Both served the committee—Jackson as a member and Schlesinger as an observer—and appended dissenting statements to the report.

Jackson wrote that "within any single country, one culture must be accepted as the standard" if that nation "is to survive in peace." The English language and British political and legal traditions prevailed in the United States, he contended, and to argue over whether it should have been otherwise "is beside the point."

Schlesinger wrote that the ethnic interpretation of history "reverses the historic theory of America ... which has been the creation of a new culture and new national identity." While saying that he favored more inclusive interpretations of past and present, "I do not believe that we should magnify ethnic and racial themes at the expense of the unifying ideals that precariously hold our differentiated society together." Referring to the U.S. motto, "E pluribus unum" (out of many, one), he commented that the report "is saturated with pluribus and neglectful of unum."

Another committee member stating his concern was Harvard sociologist Nathan Glazer, coauthor of the influential book, Beyond the Melting Pot, *which argued that the traditional American goal of assimilating its immigrants remained incomplete. Glazer warned against considering specific ethnic groups as monolithic in outlook. He said that, like the nation as a whole, they were fragmented by class, intermarriage, and degree of assimilation. Ethnicity, he said, tended to be in a state of change and should not be regarded as "something that establishes itself as a distinct and permanent element in American society and polity."*

New York Follows California

The twenty-four member panel was under the cochairmanship of Drs. Edmund G. Gordon, a professor of African-American studies at Yale

University, and Francis Roberts, superintendent of public schools in Cold Spring, New York. They submitted the report to Education Commissioner Thomas Sobol, who asked and received permission on July 25 from the Board of Regents, the policy-making body for New York state's schools, to proceed with the curriculum revision.

In that regard, New York followed California and other states in revising its teaching of the social sciences. In 1987 the California Board of Education adopted a curriculum that stretched the study of American and world history to three years in the public schools and introduced social studies in the early grades. The board demanded that California schools "accurately portray the cultural and racial diversity of our society." Textbooks tailored to the California curriculum subsequently were adopted in Arkansas, Indiana, Oregon, and West Virginia.

Following are excerpts from a report by the New York State Social Studies and Review Committee, "One Nation, Many People: A Declaration of Cultural Independence," issued June 20, 1991:

Preamble

The United States is a microcosm of humanity today. No other country in the world is peopled by a greater variety of races, nationalities, and ethnic groups. But although the United States has been a great asylum for diverse peoples, it has not always been a great refuge for diverse cultures. The country has opened its doors to a multitude of nationalities, but often their cultures have not been encouraged to survive or, at best, have been kept marginal to the mainstream.

Since the 1960s, however, a profound reorientation of the self-image of Americans has been under way. Before this time the dominant model of the typical American had been conditioned primarily by the need to shape a unified nation out of a variety of contrasting and often conflicting European immigrant communities. But following the struggles for civil rights, the unprecedented increase in non-European immigration over the last two decades and the increasing recognition of our nation's indigenous heritage, there has been a fundamental change in the image of what a resident of the United States is.

With this change, which necessarily highlights the racial and ethnic pluralism of the nation, previous ideals of assimilation to an Anglo-American model have been put in question and are now slowly and sometimes painfully being set aside. Many people in the United States are no longer comfortable with the requirement, common in the past, that they shed their specific cultural differences in order to be considered American. Instead, while busily adapting to and shaping mainstream cultural ideals commonly identified as American, in recent decades many in the United States—from European and non-European backgrounds—have been encouraging a more tolerant, inclusive, and realistic vision of American identity than any that has existed in the past.

This identity, committed to the democratic principles of the nation and the nation-building in which all Americans are engaged, is progressively evolving from the past model toward a new model marked by respect for pluralism and awareness of the virtues of diversity. This situation is a current reality, and a multicultural education, anchored to the shared principles of a liberal democracy, is today less an educational innovation than a national priority.

It is fitting for New York State, host to the Statue of Liberty, to inaugurate a curriculum that reflects the rich cultural diversity of the nation. The beacon of hope welcomes not just the "wretched and poor" individuals of the world, but also the dynamic and rich cultures all people bring with them.

Two centuries after this country's founders issued a Declaration of Independence, focused on the political independence from which societies distant from the United States have continued to draw inspiration, the time has come to *recognize cultural interdependence*. We propose that the principle of respect for diverse cultures is critical to our nation, and we affirm that a right to cultural diversity exists. We believe that the schoolroom is one of the places where this cultural *interdependence* must be reflected.

It is in this spirit that we have crafted this report, "One Nation, Many Peoples." We see the social studies as the primary avenue through which the school addresses our cultural diversity and interdependence. But the study of cultural diversity and interdependence is only one goal. It is through such studies that we seek to strengthen our national commitment and world citizenship, with the development of intellectual competence in our students as the foundation. We see the social studies as directed at the development of intellectual competence in learners, with the capacity to view the world and understand it from multiple perspectives as one of the main components of such competence. Multicultural knowledge in this conception of the social studies becomes a vehicle and not a goal. Multicultural content and experience become instruments by which we enable students to develop their intelligence and to function as human and humane persons.

I. Introduction

Affirmation of Purpose

This Committee affirms that multicultural education should be a source of strength and pride. Multicultural education is often viewed as divisive and even as destructive of the values and beliefs which hold us together as Americans. Certainly, contemporary trends toward separation and dissolution in such disparate countries as the Soviet Union, South Africa, Canada, Yugoslavia, Spain, and the United Kingdom remind us that different ethnic and racial groups have often had extraordinary difficulty remaining together in nation-states. But national unity does not require that we eliminate the very diversity that is the source of our uniqueness and, indeed, of our adaptability and viability among the nations of the world. *If the United States is to continue to prosper in the 21st century, then all of its citizens, whatever their race or ethnicity, must believe that they and their ancestors have shared in the building of the country and have a stake in its success.* Thus, multicultural education, far from being a source of dissolution, is necessary for the cultural health, social stability, and economic future of New York State and the nation.

The Committee believes that to achieve these ends, the teaching of social studies should emphasize the following:

First, beginning in the earliest grades social studies should be taught from a global perspective. The earth is humankind's common home. Migration is our common history. The earth's peoples, cultures, and material resources are our common wealth. Both humankind's pain and humankind's triumphs must be shared globally. The uniqueness of humankind is our *many ways of being human,* our remarkable range of cultural and physical diversity within a common biological unity.

Second, the social studies will very likely continue to serve nation-building purposes, among others, even as we encourage global perspectives. With efforts to respect and honor the diverse and pluralistic elements in our nation, special attention will need to be given to those values, characteristics, and traditions which we share in common. Commitment to the presentation of multiple perspectives in the social studies curriculum encourages attention to the traditional and dominant elements in our society, even as we introduce and examine minority elements which have been neglected or those which are emerging as a result of new scholarship and newly recognized voices.

Third, the curriculum must strive to be informed by the most up-to-date scholarship. It must be open to all relevant input, to new knowledge, to fresh perspectives. Human history is to be seen as ongoing, often contradictory, and subject to reasonable differences based on contrasting perceptions and distinct viewpoints.

Fourth, students need to see themselves as active makers and changers of culture and society; they must be helped to develop the tools by which to judge, analyze, act, and evaluate.

Fifth, the program should be committed to the honoring and continuing examination of democratic values as an essential basis for social organization and nation-building. The application of democracy to social organization should be viewed as a continuing process which sometimes succeeds and sometimes fails, and thus requires constant effort.

Sixth, one of the central aims of the social studies is the development of the intellect; thus, the social studies should be taught not solely as information, but rather through the critical examination of ideas and events rooted in time and place and responding to social interests. The social studies should be seen not as some dreary schoolroom task of fact mastery to be tested and forgotten, but as one of the best curricular vehicles for telling the story of humanity in a way that motivates and inspires all of our children to continue the process of responsible nation-building in a world context. . . .

Background: The Social Studies and the Changing Society

Recent debate concerning change in New York State's social studies curriculum often implies that the curriculum stands as a fixed and unchanging prescription for the classroom, its stability protecting the inculcation of basic values from shifting political and economic winds. Closer examination, however, reveals that the curriculum has grown and been transformed over time in response to societal change, as a few examples will show. . . .

Unlike literature and languages, the social studies and their parent disciplines of history and geography were not a major part of the mainstream of the school curriculum until the present century. In 1899, a Committee of Seven of the American Historical Association (founded in 1884) made a recommendation which led to the study of European and American history and government in schools, including those of New York State. Other subject-matter organizations, as they were formed, also began to press for inclusion in the school curriculum (the American Political Science Association and the American Sociological Association, for example, founded respectively in 1903 and 1905).

In the second decade of this century, the need to accommodate the surge of immigration led to the view that the schools should help students develop the attitudes and skills necessary for good citizenship. In 1916 a Committee on the Social Studies of the American Historical Association declared this to be the goal of schooling, bringing the term "social studies" into formal use. In 1951, responding to the mood of national insecurity reflected in McCarthyism, New York State dropped the term "social studies" in favor of "citizenship education," and the amount of American history in the secondary curriculum was greatly increased ("social studies" re-emerged in 1960). Between 1965 and the late 1980s, as international communication and commerce increased, the curriculum was enlarged to include more global studies, such as year-long courses in Asian and African Studies (grade 9) and European Studies (grade 10). Since 1987, these in turn have been replaced by a two-year global studies sequence.

Indeed, the processes of contest, debate, and transformation are integral parts of the rich history of education in the United States. That history has reflected the society of which it is a part, and societal changes over the past 30 years have brought with them rising interest in the study of diverse cultures in the United States and the world. In the universities, scholarly attention has turned to previously neglected groups (those that have historically been minorities in the United States and women) and topics (social history, ethnic and cultural studies). Such scholarship has brought to light much that had been omitted from U.S. and world history, as traditionally studied.

In the 1970s and early 1980s, elementary and secondary schools, like colleges and universities, were faced with the recognition that much of the experience, cultural values, and collective pasts of their students was not identified or represented in the curriculum. Corresponding to what James A. Banks has termed the "demographic imperative" of increasing numbers of minority students enrolled in public schools, parents, students and communities served by the schools became more forceful in demanding that their children learn about their own pasts. There was a new recognition that the teaching of social studies as a single officially sanctioned story was inaccurate as to the facts of conflict in American history, and further, that it was limiting for white students and students of color alike.

Much of the heat of debate concerning the importance of valuing cultural difference in the schools arises from divergent opinions on whether preparing students to become members of U.S. society necessarily means assimilation. While the goal of assimilation has historically been relatively explicit in American schooling, in recent years many thoughtful writers and educators have argued against assimilation when interpreted as erasure of distinctive cultural identities. *Education must respond to the joint imperatives of educating toward citizenship in a common polity while respecting and taking account of continuing distinctiveness.* Even more, as we have argued, the perspectives of a number of major groups in American society must be recognized and incorporated. Nor is assimilation essential to educate citizens who value this country's ideals and participate in its polity and economy....

Over the past two decades, elementary, middle, and secondary schools and postsecondary institutions have seen efforts to restructure the curriculum in order to represent more adequately the diverse cultures of the student body and the world in which students must eventually function. Shifts in curriculum design in such states as California, Oregon, Iowa, Ohio and Florida reflect an increasing awareness that children and society are inadequately served when study is limited to the intellectual monuments of Western civilization. Comprehensive study of multiple cultures is increasingly recognized as having critical relevance for students who will face a national economy and political structures that grow more globally interdependent and increasingly diverse....

[II and III omitted]

IV. The State Syllabi

The Syllabi in Relation to the Other Components of a Program

The current New York State Social Studies syllabi include a series of twelve publications: one booklet each for kindergarten and grades 1, 2, 3, 4, 5, 6, and 11; one for grades 7-8; one for 9-10; one for the first half of grade 12, and another for the second half. The publications vary in length from 73 to 202 pages. They are reviewed and updated periodically by committees of teachers and professors under the guidance of the Bureau of Social Studies Education. All of the current publications carry dates of revision between 1987 and 1989.

Statewide syllabi are not found in most other states, but in New York, with its long history of attempting to direct education from the top down, State syllabi are regarded as very important policy documents. And because such a large and influential state does officially adopt these documents, they acquire much more importance and visibility than do the locally and regionally developed curriculum outlines and syllabi elsewhere. It is vital, therefore, that the syllabi be accurate and comprehensive, and that they reflect up-to-date scholarship. The present syllabi were drawn up with participation of content specialists and practitioners, and the Committee recognizes the effort that was made to be comprehensive and to include subject matter about all parts of the world, about women, and about groups that have been minorities in the U.S. population. . . .

Specific Findings and Illustrations with Regard to the Present New York State Syllabi and Social Studies Program

Number One:

Finding: Need for Multiple Perspectives. The Committee noted how frequently social studies slips into a "we-they" framework. All too often when communities are perceived as monolithic, it is common to teach from one perspective, usually that of the so-called dominant culture. For example, in the primary grades children examine neighborhoods and communities. Educators need to be aware that many of the typical features cited for study (such as banks, government buildings, department stores, and other major economic institutions) may not necessarily be present in inner-city or rural communities. Students need to be exposed to the strengths and potential of what does exist in their community, despite obstacles such as drugs and high visibility of crime. What does exist in the students' immediate real world should be used to help them become more aware of and sensitive to their civic responsibilities and possibilities in building their community. To take another instance, the story of the early colonization in the eastern U.S. has too often been told from the perspective of the colonists, not the Native Americans already settled on the land. Or the story of the western United States is told as one of westward expansion, assuming the perspective of the migrating Easterners and disregarding the native men and women already there or the long-established Hispanic influence and settlements in the West.

Related Finding: Unequal regard for the importance of national/ regional boundaries and distinctions. For example:

- In the syllabus for grades 9-10, all nations south of the United States are lumped together in the unit entitled "Latin America," tending to omit the information that a number of islands in the Caribbean and nations in Central and South America trace their traditions to non-Latin European nations, to Africa, India, and Indonesia, as well as to native roots. Attention is rarely paid to the complex and controversial relationship between Puerto Rico and the United States.
- The syllabus for grades 9/10 suggests: "Using pictures of Greek, Roman, and Oriental art and architecture, students could identify

similarities." Does the term "Oriental" refer to Asians? If so, which Asians? The reference should be to specific Asian people, corresponding with the Greeks and Romans.

- Northern Africa often is implicitly or explicitly incorporated in the "Middle East" in the teaching of social studies at grade 6.

Related Finding: A disregard for the understanding and study of indigenous social, political, economic, and technological structures, and the precolonial histories of indigenous peoples. For example, the treatment of the European colonization of Africa in the syllabi inadequately addresses the great loss of lives and the eradication of many varieties of traditional culture and knowledge. Similarly, the long and rich history of India before the British conquest is not properly treated. The K-6 syllabi, for example, focus on celebrations such as Thanksgiving and Columbus Day without examining other perspectives than those of Europeans, such as the perspectives of Native Americans.

Related Finding: Effects are often seen as unidirectional (with the European participants as the actors) rather than bi-directional. For example, the syllabus for grades 9/10 recommends that teachers explore the effects of European rule on Africa with their students, but the effects that contact with Africa had on Europe—or the dehumanizing effects on Europeans of their role as colonizers—are not mentioned. In the syllabus for grades 7/8, the connection between Toussaint L'Ouverture's defeat of Napoleon in Haiti and the Louisiana Purchase is not made. In the grade 9/10 syllabus, the influence of Islam upon the religious, cultural, economic and political systems of lands extending from Spain to Sumatra is highlighted, but not the impact upon Islam of the peoples of these lands.

Related Finding: Complex and large-scale issues are often simplified because they are seen from a single, implicit perspective. For example, superficial discussions of the origins and eventual abolition of slavery in the Americas frequently omit the economic basis for the persistence of slavery as an institution. The syllabi for grades 7/8 and 11 do not adequately address the incarceration of Japanese Americans; nor do they discuss the deportation from the U.S. of thousands of people of Mexican origin in the 1920s, regardless of citizenship.

Recommendation: Social Studies should be taught from multiple perspective, global in scope. Beyond the successes, the complexities and shortcomings of U.S. policy should be explored.

Number Two:

Finding: Language Sensitivity. Although specific terms fall into and out of currency and the language of the syllabi may not be deliberately or intentionally sexist, racist, or prejudicial from the point of view of diversity and inclusiveness, the language used is often dated, narrow, and in some cases insensitive. For example, the syllabi refer to "slaves" or "the everyday life of a slave," as if being a slave were one's role or status, similar to that of gardener, cook, or carpenter. To refer, rather, to "enslaved persons" would call forth the essential humanity of those enslaved, helping students to understand from the beginning the true meaning of slavery (in contrast to the sentimental pictures of contented slaves, still found in some texts).

Many geographical terms are Western-derived, sometimes almost unconsciously. Terms like "the Far East" should be replaced by ones like "East Asia." Ideally, even the term "Middle East" should become "Southwest Asia and North Africa." To Native Americans, the Western Hemisphere is not "the New World." It was the newly arriving Europeans following Christopher Columbus who were new in the Western Hemisphere. Should the term "America" to mean only the United States be used sparingly and should the *hemispheric* meaning of the term be the usual usage?

Differential use of adjectives, the passive as opposed to the active voice, and other syntactic and semantic usages can betray unintended, unrecognized, but nonetheless real bias. For example, in the syllabus for grades 9/10, the African climate is described as essentially hostile to human migration ("There are few jungle environments in Africa and nearly 45% of the continent consists of desert or dry steppe ... "), while that of Western Europe is described in the following terms: "Western Europe's environment exhibits great diversity in terms of physical geography and climate. Europeans have used technology to reshape their physical environment. Most of Western Europe has easy access to warm water ports. ..." Why is desert seen as a hostile environment, but not freezing cold and snow?

Perhaps the most persistent and fundamental language problem in the teaching of social studies is the use of the terms "minority," "minorities," "minority persons" or "minority groups." Although commonly used, such terms nonetheless establish in the minds of all students inaccurate perceptions of the world and, increasingly, of our own nation. If social studies are to be taught from a global perspective, many of the so-called "minorities" in America are more accurately described as part of the world's majorities, a profoundly important point for young Americans who will come to maturity in the next century.

Recommendation: The syllabi and all related support materials and locally developed curricula should be regularly reviewed to insure that the language used is accurate and reflects current scholarship. Classroom instruction must include sensitivity to and awareness of the changing legitimacy of terms, such as the shift in meaning of terms such as "third world," "Negro," and "Oriental."

Number Three:

Finding: A limited range of examples. There is a tendency to use white male examples of achievement and to leave out examples of the contributions of women and of the many men and women of other than the traditional white groups. When women and people of color are mentioned, they are often marginalized as "other" groups "also" to be studied, implying that all the remaining content must not be about them. For example: the syllabus for grade 11 notes that "Inventions ... in the 19th century were often the product of individual genius . . . , including that of lesser known, minority inventors." It recommends, under "Model Activities" on labor unionization: "Also examine the roles of women and racial/ethnic minorities at this time in labor history." Standard definitions of "achievement," too, omit the seemingly ordinary lives of people of all groups—lives which, in aggregate, help us understand the human experience of a time and place. . . .

Early in its work the *Committee agreed that to reflect a multicultural perspective, the syllabi need not attempt to provide an encyclopedic list of every contribution by every person and group. Rather, as the emphasis shifts from an information-based to a conceptual curriculum, the syllabi should offer many appropriate examples of the experiences of many people and groups.* Further, the Committee believes that it can be particularly intriguing to students to examine with care what the elements are that hold together a nation or culture in spite of what are often great differences. This surely is one of the central questions to be considered in any course in American history.

Recommendation: The syllabi and other materials should provide teachers with several examples, drawn from different peoples, as appropriate to each topic. In this way, what begins to take shape in the mind of the student is an appreciation of the broader range of contributions of many people and groups to the building of our nation and the world.

Number Four:

Finding: The visual environment of the classroom and school is a major educational element. Maps and pictures hang on classroom walls, silently sending messages all day, all year. Many of the maps used in social studies are out of date; they often portray areas only from one perspective, not unlike the famous *New Yorker* cover showing the rest of the nation as a minor place west of the Hudson. For example, a map representing North America in 1700 might give the impression that nobody lived in the areas which were home to native peoples. Similarly, photographs on walls that show only white male inventors and heroes teach their own powerful, distorted lessons.

Recommendation: The visual environments of schools should reflect multicultural perspectives. . . .

VI. Reflections on the Work of the NYS Social Studies Syllabus Review Committee

Statement
by Edmund W. Gordon and Francis Roberts
Cochairpersons

. . . As the Cochairpersons of this very challenging enterprise, we too have elected to identify a few of the currents which we have observed to flow throughout our deliberations. The Committee does not have a consensus position on these issues, but it seems that these concerns are important enough to be a part of the continuing discourse concerning the place of attention to cultural and other sources of human diversity in the social studies curriculum.

We are asked to consider how the social studies syllabi of the public schools of New York State should be modified, the better to ensure that our children understand and know about themselves, other people in their state and country, and the cultures and histories of the world in which they live. This very reasonable request and goal led us into discussions and debates concerning the nature of the canon as well as the knowledge which it enshrines. A high degree of importance attaches to the integrity of the canon, but problems arise when we consider the boundaries of the canon. Thus questions concerning the validity of various knowledge components constantly stood just beneath the surface of many of our discussions. Some of us were more comfortable with knowledge and sources that have been recognized and certified by the academy. Others repeatedly called attention to new knowledge, new sources and new voices and their claim to validity equal to that assigned to the traditional and the hegemonic. The tension between these two positions is not a new phenomenon. The history of human societies, our own nation included, is marked by debates and even wars over different conceptions of truth and views of reality. It is a measure of human progress that we have arrived at the stage of societal development that in democratic societies, these debates are verbal and written and not the subject of physical combat. However, they are nonetheless critical, in part, because in modern societies the changing conception of what it means to be an educated and intelligent person includes our capacity to entertain and understand phenomena from perspectives different from our own, on our way to arriving at wise judgments and the reconciliation of differences. Without falling into the futile debate concerning whose canon shall be taught we have elevated the question to include pedagogical problems concerning how we enable learners to respect and deal with multiple perspectives, i.e., multiple ways of seeing things and using different sources of knowledge better to understand experiences and information. This is not to argue that all information is necessarily valid. Rather, we argue that all information deserves to be understood in the context within which it has been developed. This assertion is advanced, in part, because for much of our knowledge validity is difficult to establish independent of context.

This plea for tolerance and openness in the examination of ideas and perspectives came into conflict with another set of important purposes and values. One of the long-recognized functions of the social studies is to prepare students for citizenship in support of the continuing effort at nation-building. *We recognize that nation-building, especially in so diverse a populace, requires that we give attention, not so much to our differences as to our commonalities.* Some of us feel strongly that social studies should stress the nation's common values and traditional conceptions of our history. Others of us feel that those values and conceptions have become truncated as a result of the hegemonic ascendance of cultural elements, values and world views that tend to be associated with our European ancestry alone. Thus the insistence on the inclusion of broader perspectives and non-dominant knowledge sources. But the question arises as to whether we can conjointly serve both *pluribus* and *unum*. . . .

Some of us were shocked by the depth of feelings about diverse renditions of history. Some of us who are comfortable in the belief that the history that we know is valid were offended by the assertion that much of that history is incomplete or false. Some of us who feel that the standard histories have excluded or misrepresented important players found it difficult to assert our claims dispassionately. In the views represented by some of us, it appears that much of the dominant or traditional information available to us is viewed with doubt, skepticism and distrust because it does not fit comfortably with the experiences of some, while for others, it is simply counter-intuitive. Deciding what to teach under such existential circumstances confronts us with problems of monumental complexity. Even more problematic for the teaching and learning of history and the social studies is the ease with which information, ideology and belief become commingled in the minds of people whose interests are at stake— sometimes so much that these concepts, despite their differential order, come to be interchangeable one for the other. Although we were generally in agreement that histories tend to reflect the interests and perspectives of those who write them, there was a ubiquitous undercurrent of concern for the recognition of historical and other truth.

It may well be a limited understanding of the meaning of the word 'truth' that will create the most difficulty as we seek to reconcile our search for 'truth' with our conception of education as being directed at the development of intellect and understanding. . . .

Additional Comments

By Nathan Glazer

This report is not a document that stands by itself, without interpretation. Different members of the Committee, as well as different elements of the public, will read it differently, and selectively. Probably no member of the committee accepts every part and point in the report with equal commitment, and we differ in the way we see dangers in how the report will be read, and how we would like the broad direction it sets for the development of social studies in New York State developed in detail.

The report does reject two extremes in the treatment of ethnic and racial diversity in American social studies: One is the emphasis on forceful Americanization and assimilation that characterized much of American public education during the period of the great European immigration and for some time later. The other is the parceling out of American history into a different and incompatible story for each group, generally told by a few activists and militants speaking for the group. . . .

Within the broad spectrum that remains after the extremes have been rejected, the report points out a very general direction, rather than specifies the details of a syllabus or curriculum. It continues a debate, rather than concludes it.

Even within the bounds of this broad arena of development and debate, there is one major danger I see against which we must be alert, one to which the report offers some support. This is the danger of the hypostatization of race, ethnic groups, culture, people. (To hypostatize: "to make into, or regard as, a separate and distinct substance; ... to assume a reality.") The various ethnic group, races, sub-cultures, the components of what we like to call with some exaggeration "the peoples of America," are not composed of a "distinct and separate substance." The groups we refer to when we speak of "multiculturism" are not monolithic and unchanging realities. Each is made up of different classes with different interests, each has been marked by differences created by the time of arrival of different waves under different circumstances, each has undergone various degrees of assimilation, acculturation, intermarriage, and each carries different attitudes to its past: European immigrants overwhelmingly see their assimilation to the United States, under the system of public education they experienced, as a good thing, even if their specific culture and language at the time played no role in the curriculum. Many of us recognize no identity other than American. When we speak of "multiculturism," we should be aware there are no fully distinct cultures in the United States, aside from American culture. We should not make of something labile, changeable, flexible and variable—the cultures people bring with them to the United States or develop as variants of our common American culture—something hard and definite and unchanging, something that establishes itself as a distinct and permanent element in American society and polity. That is not the way our society works, or should work. . . .

A DISSENTING COMMENT

Kenneth T. Jackson
Jacques Barzun Professor of History and the Social Sciences
Columbia University

The purpose of this Committee is a good one. Certainly, we should celebrate the cultural diversity which has made the United States almost unique among the world's nations. Certainly, we should acknowledge that heterogeneity has made this land rich and creative. Certainly, we should give our students a varied and challenging multicultural education.

Just as certainly, we should celebrate the common culture that Americans share. Unfortunately, our report seems to disparage "Anglo" conformity. Leaving aside the debatable question of whether or not we in fact have conformity (from Broadway in New York to Broadway in Los Angeles we can easily find more diversity than exists anywhere else on earth) or whether earlier immigrant groups were "required" to "shed their specific cultural differences in order to be considered Americans," I would argue that it is politically and intellectually unwise for us to attack the traditions, customs, and values which attracted immigrants to these shores in the first place. The people of the United States will recognize, even if this Committee does not, that every viable nation has to have a common culture to survive in peace. As our own document indicates, one need look no further than Yugoslavia, the Soviet Union, or Canada to see the accuracy of this proposition. We might want to add India after the events of the past two weeks. The dominant American culture might have been German or French or Chinese or Algonquin or African, but for various historical reasons the English language and British political and legal traditions prevailed. Whether or not we would have been better off if Montcalm had defeated Wolfe on the Plains of Abraham is beside the point. . . .

A better strategy for this Committee would have been to argue in a positive rather than a negative way. Because we are made up of many peoples and cultures, because all these peoples and cultures have contributed to national greatness, and because the United States has typically done a better job of integrating newcomers into its social and political fabric (with racial prejudice being a glaring and persistent exception) than other places, its educational system should reflect that experience. We have been multicultural, we are multicultural, and we hope that we will always be multicultural. Moreover, the enemies of multiculturism are not teachers, textbooks, or curricular guides, but shopping centers, fast food outlets, and situation comedies, all of which threaten to turn us into an amorphous mass.

The report highlights the notion that all cultures are created equal. This may be true in the abstract, and I have no problem with the philosophical concept. But I cannot endorse a "Declaration of Cultural Independence," which is the subtitle of our Committee report. Within any single country, one culture must be accepted as the standard. Unfortunately, our document has virtually nothing to say about the things which hold us together. . . .

SCHLESINGER'S DISSENT

A Dissenting Opinion

Arthur Schlesinger, Jr.

I agree with many of the practical recommendations in the report. It is unquestionably necessary to diversify the syllabus in order to meet the needs of a more diversified society. It is unquestionably necessary to provide for global education in an increasingly interdependent world. Our students should by all means be better acquainted with women's history, with the history of ethnic and racial minorities, with Latin American, Asian and African history. Debate, alternative interpretations, "multiple perspectives" are all essential to the educational enterprise. I welcome changes that would adapt the curriculum to these purposes. If that is what the report means by multicultural education, I am all for it.

But I fear that the report implies much more than this. The underlying philosophy of the report, as I read it, is that ethnicity is the defining experience for most Americans, that ethnic ties are permanent and indelible, that the division into ethnic groups establishes the basic structure of American society and that a main objective of public education should be the protection, strengthening, celebration and perpetuation of ethnic origins and identities. Implicit in the report is the classification of all Americans according to ethnic and racial criteria.

These propositions are assumed rather than argued in the report. They constitute an ethnic interpretation of American history that, like the economic interpretation, is valid up to a point but misleading and wrong when presented as the whole picture.

The ethnic interpretation, moreover, reverses the historic theory of America—which has been, not the preservation and sanctification of old cultures and identities, but the creation of a *new* national culture and a *new* national identity. . . .

Of course students should learn more about the rich variety of peoples and cultures that have forged this new American identity. They also should understand the curse of racism—the great failure of the American experiment, the glaring contradiction of American ideals and the still-crippling disease of American society. But we should also be alert to the danger of a society divided into distinct and immutable ethnic and racial groups, each taught to cherish its own apartness from the rest.

While I favor curricular changes that make for more inclusive interpretations of past and present, I do not believe that we should magnify ethnic and racial themes at the expense of the unifying ideals that precariously hold our highly differentiated society together. The republic has survived and grown because it has maintained a balance between *pluribus* and *unum*. The report, it seems to me, is saturated with *pluribus* and neglectful of *unum*. . . .

Obviously the reason why the United States, for all its manifest failure to live up to its own ideals, is still the most successful large multi-ethnic nation is precisely because, instead of emphasizing and perpetuating ethnic separatism, it has assimilated immigrant cultures into a new *American* culture. . . .

. . . If the ethnic subcultures had genuine vitality, they would be sufficiently instilled in children by family, church and community. It is surely not the office of the public school to promote ethnic separatism and heighten ethnic tensions.

Should public education move in this direction, it will only increase the fragmentation, resegregation and self-ghettoization of American life. The bonds of national cohesion in the republic are sufficiently fragile already. Public education should aim to strengthen those bonds, not to weaken them. . . .

What has held Americans together in the absence of a common ethnic origin has been the creation of a new American identity—a distinctive American culture based on a common language and common adherence to ideals of democracy and human rights, a culture to which many nationalities and races have made emphatic contributions in the past and will (one hopes) make emphatic contributions in the future. Our democratic ideals have been imperfectly realized, but the long labor to achieve them and to move the American experiment from exclusion to participation has been a central theme of American history. It should be a central theme of the New York social studies curriculum.

And it is important for students to understand where these democratic ideals come from. They come of course from Europe. Indeed, Europe is the *unique* source of these ideals—ideals that today empower people in every continent and to which today most of the world aspires. That is why it is so essential (in my view) to acquaint students with the western history and tradition that created our democratic ideals—and why it is so wrong to tell students of non-European origin that western ideals are not for them.

I regret the note of Europhobia that sometimes emerges in vulgar attacks on "Eurocentric" curriculums. Certainly Europe, like every other culture, has committed its share of crimes. But, unlike most cultures, it has also generated ideals that have opposed and exposed those crimes.

The report, however, plays up the crimes and plays down the ideals. Thus, when it talks about the European colonization of Africa and India, it deplores "the eradication of many varieties of traditional culture and knowledge." Like infanticide? slavery? polygamy? subjection of women? suttee? veil-wearing? foot-binding? clitorectemies? Nothing is said about the influence of European ideas of democracy, human rights, self-government, rule of law. . . .

I also am doubtful about the note occasionally sounded in the report that "students must be taught social criticism" and "see themselves as active makers and changers of culture and society" and "promote economic fairness and social justice" and "bring about change in their communities, the nation, and the world." I very much hope that, as citizens, students will do all these things, but I do not think it is the function of the schools to teach students to become reformers any more than I ever thought it the function of the schools to teach them the beauty of private enterprise and the sanctity of the status quo. I will be satisfied if we can teach children to read, write and calculate. If students understand the nature of our western democratic tradition, they will move into social criticism of their own. But let us not politicize the curriculum on behalf either of the left or of the right. . . .

REPORT OF THE NATIONAL COMMISSION ON CHILDREN

June 24, 1991

The National Commission on Children released its final report June 24, portraying children as America's poorest people and advocating a costly plan to improve their well-being. The report, "Beyond Rhetoric: A New American Agenda for Children and Families," was the result of a two-and-a-half year assessment by the blue-ribbon, bipartisan commission headed by Sen. John D. Rockefeller IV, D-W. Va. Its thirty-four members, appointed partly by President George Bush and partly by the leadership of Congress, included Gov. Bill Clinton of Arkansas, Mayor Raymond L. Flynn of Boston, two U.S. representatives (Theresa H. Esposito of North Carolina and George Miller of California), educators, children's advocates, philanthropists, business and labor leaders, and experts in child health and development.

"We are deeply disturbed that a nation so captivated by youth is leaving so many of its young behind," the commission wrote in the report's introduction. "Some adults take on the responsibilities of parenthood with little thought or planning; others shed them with equal abandon. In the halls of government, public investments in strong families and healthy, whole children are grudging and piecemeal." As expressed by Rockefeller in releasing the report, "Americans claim to love children, but these are often empty words."

Noting that one child in five lives in poverty, the commission proposed a comprehensive income security package that included a $1,000 refundable tax credit for each child under age eighteen to replace the existing personal exemption for children. If enacted, the estimated cost to the government in lost tax revenue would be $40.3 billion a year. Similar *proposals had been made by two Washington research organizations, the Progressive Policy Institute and the Urban Institute. The commission also proposed testing a program of government-insured benefits for children whose absent parents were unable to provide child support and recommended job training, child care, health insurance benefits for parents moving from welfare to work, and expanded work opportunities in the community for parents who had difficulty finding other jobs.*

Addressing concern over the high rate of dropouts from schools and ill-educated graduates, the report emphasized a need to better prepare children for school. The commission specifically recommended that spending for Head Start—which provides health, education, and nutrition services to low-income pre-school children—be expanded to $4 billion annually, up from $830 million.

The commission was unable to reach a consensus on health policy recommendations. A majority of its members called on the government and private employers to develop a universal system of health insurance coverage for pregnant women and for children through age eighteen. A nine-member minority, composed mostly of Bush appointees, proposed instead that tax incentives and deductions for health care be restructured and that families take more responsibility for adopting more healthful life styles.

The commission estimated that its recommendations would require $52-56 billion in new federal spending. "It's not easy to call for more government spending in the face of a looming federal deficit," Rockefeller acknowledged. "But we have to face reality. In the end, we're going to pay one way or the other, and prevention is less expensive. I for one would rather pay for Head Start than for prisons. I'll also take prenatal care over intensive care any day."

Although the report received a generally favorable reception for its thorough discussion of children's needs, Congress was skeptical that the added billions of dollars could be obtained. Conservatives endorsed at least limited government spending boosts and lauded the report's recognition that two-parent families provided the best environment for children. At the same time, liberals acknowledged the need for individuals to take more responsibility for their families' well-being and applauded the recognition that helping children would require new spending.

> *Following are excerpts from the executive summary of the report, "Beyond Rhetoric: A New American Agenda for Children and Families," released June 24, 1991, by the National Commission on Children:*

Most American children are healthy, happy, and secure. They belong to warm, loving families. For them, today is filled with the joys of childhood—growing, exploring, learning, and dreaming—and tomorrow is full of hope and promise. These children will become the competent and caring parents, employees, and community leaders upon whom America's future depends.

But at every age, among all races and income groups, and in communities nationwide, many children are in jeopardy. They grow up in families whose lives are in turmoil. Their parents are too stressed and too drained to provide the nurturing, structure, and security that protect children and prepare them for adulthood. Some of these children are unloved and ill tended. Others are unsafe at home and in their neighborhoods. Many are poor, and some are homeless and hungry. Often, they lack the rudiments of basic health care and a quality education. Almost always, they lack hope and dreams, a vision of what their lives can become, and the support and guidance to make it a reality. The harshness of these children's lives and their tenuous hold on tomorrow cannot be countenanced by a wealthy nation, a caring people, or a prudent society. America's future depends on these children, too.

If we measure success not just by how well most children do, but by how poorly some fare, America falls far short. One in four children is raised by just one parent. One of every five is poor. Half a million are born annually to teenage girls who are ill prepared to assume the responsibilities of parenthood. An increasing number are impaired before birth by their parents' substance abuse. Others live amid violence and exploitation, much of it fueled by a thriving drug trade. Rich and poor children alike face limited futures when their educations are inadequate and they have few opportunities for cultural enrichment and community service. Too many children at every income level lack time, attention, and guidance from parents and other caring adults. The result is often alienation, recklessness, and damaging, antisocial behavior....

The combined effects are that too many children enter adulthood without the skills or motivation to contribute to society. They are poorly equipped to reap the benefits or meet the responsibilities of parenthood, citizenship, and employment. The consequences of their problems and limitations reach far beyond their personal lives. America's future as a democratic nation, a world leader, and an economic power will depend as much on youngsters who are ill educated, alienated, or poor as on those who are more advantaged. For them, and for the nation, the years to come will be less safe, less caring, less free, unless we act....

... Members of the Commission have studied and debated the state of America's children and have come to a broad consensus on recommendations, except for those related to health care. Some disagreements remain, but it is critical that the Commission's agenda go forward to spark the public action that our nation's children deserve.

Principles for Action

... [T]he following principles form the foundation for our specific proposals for public and private sector policy and program development.

- Every American child should have the opportunity to develop to his or her full potential.
- Parents bear primary responsibility for meeting their children's physi-

cal, emotional, and intellectual needs and for providing moral guidance and direction. It is in society's best interests to support parents in
their childrearing roles, to enable them to fulfill their obligations, and
to hold them responsible for the care and support of their children.

- Children do best when they have the personal involvement and
  material support of a father and a mother and when both parents
  fulfill their responsibility to be loving providers.
- The family is and should remain society's primary institution for
  bringing children into the world and for supporting their growth and
  development throughout childhood.
- Cultural diversity is one of America's greatest riches; it must be
  respected and preserved, while at the same time ensuring that all
  children have an equal opportunity to enter the social and economic
  mainstream.
- Community institutions—schools, religious organizations, service and
  charitable organizations, and employers—have an important role in
  creating an environment that is supportive of parents and children.
- Communities have a responsibility to provide safe, secure environments for families with children.
- Society has a legitimate interest in childrearing and a moral obligation
  to intervene whenever parents who fail to meet their responsibilities
  put their children at risk.
- Preventing problems before they become crises is the most effective
  and cost-effective way to address the needs of troubled families and
  vulnerable children.
- Basic moral values are part of our national heritage and should guide
  society in its actions toward children and families.
- Effectively addressing the needs of America's children and families
  will require a significant commitment of time, leadership, and financial resources by individuals, the private sector, and government at all
  levels.

An Agenda for the 1990s

Coherent national policies for children and families will require both a
greater emphasis on family values and more effective intervention. Both
are important; neither alone is sufficient. For this reason, the Commission's recommendations are directed to the public and private sectors, and
to individuals as well as institutions. They apply to the major domains of
family life and the basic needs of children and families. Taken together,
they form a bold blueprint for strengthening families and promoting the
healthy development of all the nation's children.

Ensuring Income Security

... [T]oday's children—especially those in single-parent families—are
the poorest Americans. Failure to prevent childhood poverty and address
the economic needs of families leads to other social ills—more crime and

delinquency, more teenage childbearing, more unhealthy babies, more failure in school, more substance abuse and mental illness, more child abuse and neglect, and lower productivity by tomorrow's labor force. These problems take a dreadful toll on the individuals directly affected, and they also impose enormous costs on society, including significant expenditures for treatment of chronic health conditions and disabilities, special education, foster care, prisons, and welfare.

But it is not just poor families who struggle today to make ends meet, nor is it only poor children who suffer the consequences of economic instability. Middle-income parents also express concern about their ability to provide for their children and maintain a secure standard of living. The costs of housing, transportation, education, and health care have risen steadily since the 1970s and today consume substantially more of a typical family's income than they did 20 years ago. In recent decades, the average working family's tax burden has also risen. Combined state and local taxes, federal income tax, and the employee's share of Social Security taxes (after computing deductions and exemptions) now account for approximately 25 percent of median family income, compared to only 14 percent in 1960. As a consequence, many middle-income families need more than one paycheck to maintain a modest standard of living or just to meet their children's basic needs. Families with only one wage-earner—especially families headed by a single mother—have suffered the greatest losses and are the most economically vulnerable.

The National Commission on Children calls on the nation to develop over the coming decade a comprehensive income security plan based on fundamental American principles of work, family, and independence. Building on the Family Support Act of 1988 and recent pro-family reforms in the federal tax system, the Commission recommends six important steps:

- *We recommend the creation of a $1,000 refundable child tax credit for all children through age 18 and elimination of the personal exemption for dependent children to partially offset the costs.*
- *We strongly endorse the Earned Income Tax Credit, as recently expanded, to encourage low-income parents to enter the paid workforce and strive for economic independence.*
- *We recommend that a demonstration of suitable scale be designed and implemented to test an insured child support plan that would combine enhanced child support enforcement with a government-insured benefit when absent parents do not meet their support obligations. Contingent on positive findings from this demonstration, the Commission recommends establishment of the insured child support benefit in every state.*
- *We strongly endorse the Job Opportunities and Basic Skills Training Program (JOBS) and the provision of transitional supports and services to low-income parents moving from welfare to work.*
- *We recommend that states and localities provide community employ-*

*ment opportunities, where feasible and appropriate, for parents who
are able and willing to work but cannot find a job on their own. We do
not recommend the establishment of a major new federal employment program.*

- *We recommend that welfare be reoriented as short-term relief in
  periods of unanticipated unemployment, disability, or other economic hardship to provide a safety net to poor families with children
  who through no fault of their own would otherwise fall through the
  cracks.*

Improving Health

... The National Commission on Children did not reach consensus on
strategies for addressing the health needs of the nation's children and
pregnant women. A substantial majority of commissioners offers the
following recommendations to improve the chances that all American
children will be born healthy and grow up healthy:

- *We recommend that parents protect their children's health by
  protecting their own health and being role models for healthful
  behavior, by doing everything in their power to provide a safe home
  environment, and by seeking and advocating for essential health
  services for their children.*
- *We recommend that communities take responsibility for creating
  safe neighborhoods, supporting the development of community-based
  health education and health care programs, and sponsoring activities
  and special projects to help families gain access to needed services.*
- *We recommend that government and employers together develop a
  universal system of health insurance coverage for pregnant women
  and for children through age 18 that includes a basic level of care and
  provisions to contain costs and improve the quality of care.* A new
  system must build upon, not patch or replace, the current combination
  of employment-based and public coverage. It must ensure that adequate insurance protection is available to those who now have it
  through their employers; it must extend employer-based coverage to
  those who do not; and it must supplement employer-provided coverage
  with decent public coverage for those who are outside the work force.
  Decisions concerning care should allow for substantial autonomy and
  choice by the patient or parent in consultation with his or her medical
  practitioner. Finally, the health care system and the provision of
  health insurance must contain incentives to economize and reduce
  rapidly rising health care costs.
- *We recommend that the federal and state governments expand
  effective health care programs that provide services for underserved
  populations.* Health care will continue to be beyond the reach of many
  pregnant women and children unless the services they need are
  available in their communities. In particular, minority children, low-
  income children, children who live in geographically isolated areas,

and those whose parents are poorly educated often have difficulty getting the health care they need. For this reason, we recommend expansion of the National Health Service Corps, Community and Migrant Health Centers, the Maternal and Child Health Block Grant, and the Special Supplemental Food Program for Women, Infants, and Children (WIC).

- *We recommend that health professionals work together with professionals from other disciplines to improve the quality and comprehensiveness of health and social services, participate in publicly funded programs, and serve their communities as volunteers and resource persons.*

Minority Chapter on Health Care

Because nine commissioners had fundamental disagreements with the key recommendations presented in the majority chapter on health care, a minority chapter on health care is also included in the report of the National Commission on Children. The following is a summary of the minority chapter.

We believe that if we are to improve the health of our nation's families and children, individuals must assume responsibility for their health, and that any reform must have prevention as its key goal; the family unit is the principal health educator, and single parenthood creates significant risks for children's health; all people should be able to obtain necessary health care through a private-public partnership; health care delivery and financing schemes should constrain the rate of growth in health care expenditures; any health care reform design should promote innovation, not adversely affect economic growth and stability, and promote the delivery of high-quality, cost-effective care.

Given these principles, we recommend:

- *All programs and services for children and youth should ensure that they involve parents and respect their values, taking care not to undermine parents' authority or to diminish their important role and influence in adolescent decision making;*
- *Problems resulting from malnutrition should be addressed by combating the climate of violence, drugs and promiscuous sexual activity instead of simply increasing funding for the Special Supplemental Food Program for Women, Infants and Children (WIC);*
- *Increased support for abstinence education is recommended as a means of reducing the spread of sexually transmitted diseases (STDs) and AIDS, as well as the rate of unwed teenage pregnancies;*
- *The media and other community organizations should take seriously their role in promoting healthy behaviors on the part of parents and children, and do nothing to either glamorize or reinforce unhealthy lifestyles, such as the use of drugs, sexual promiscuity, smoking, and unhealthy dietary habits.*

Furthermore, we believe that the financing of health care in the United States will only be truly reformed by empowering consumers and permitting undistorted markets to function in medical care and insurance, and by restructuring existing tax subsidies and public programs to target those who are in greatest need. In contrast, we believe that the majority chapter's recommendation for a "play or pay" plan would be inflationary, result in substantial job losses or reduced wages, and encourage discrimination against employees with families.

As important as health care financing is to the health of families and children, we also believe that the weakening of the structure of the American family may be an even greater threat to the health of children. Solving the health problems of children will be an expensive, upwardly spiraling, and potentially fruitless quest for government if it fails at the same time to restore societal expectations for and support of the two-parent marital norm. Consequently, we believe that one of the surest practical routes to preserving the health and well-being of children is to strengthen the American family.

Increasing Educational Achievement

Despite more than a decade of education reform, America remains "a nation at risk." American students continue to lag behind their counterparts in many developed and developing nations in standardized measures of reading, math, and science. Far too many of the nation's youth drop out of school, and even among those who complete high school, a substantial number lack the basic skills and knowledge needed to get a job.

Every child in America needs an excellent education—because global competition demands a highly skilled and knowledgeable workforce, because democracy depends on a thoughtful and well-educated citizenry, and because knowledge and a love of learning are among the most precious gifts society can give to its children. Yet approximately 40 percent of the nation's children are at risk of school failure. They include children who are poor, those from minority groups, those with limited command of English, those who live in a single-parent family or with parents who are poorly educated, and those with disabling conditions. These children are less likely to enter school ready to learn—healthy, well-fed, confident, able to focus their attention and energy, and able to interact positively with adults and other children. Over the years, they are more likely to be held back, to drop out of school, and to fail to earn a high school diploma.

But even those students who enter school ready to learn and whose families have the wherewithal to support their educational progress are not guaranteed a quality education that prepares them to assume challenging roles in their communities and in the workforce. Many schools across the country lack the basic ingredients and flexibility to be lively, innovative learning centers. They often lack a common educational vision and strong leadership. They fail to set rigorous academic standards and do little to foster initiative, innovation, and creativity among teachers and staff. Many do not encourage parents to be active partners in their children's education, and some are unable to maintain order and discipline.

To ensure that every child enters school ready to learn and every school meets the educational needs of all its students, the National Commission on Children proposes five related strategies:

- *We recommend that all children, from the prenatal period through the first years of life, receive the care and support they need to enter school ready to learn—namely, good health care, nurturing environments, and experiences that enhance their development.* In particular, we urge that Head Start be available to every income-eligible child in the United States. A majority of commissioners defines full participation in Head Start as enrollment by up to 100 percent of all eligible three- and four-year-olds and up to 30 percent of eligible five-year-olds. A minority of commissioners defines full participation as enrollment by up to 80 percent of all eligible children for one year, and by up to 20 percent of eligible children for more than one year.

- *We recommend that the educational system adopt a series of fundamental reforms, including:*
  - *a rigorous and challenging academic curriculum;*
  - *measures to recruit and retain skilled teachers;*
  - *measures to improve the effectiveness of principals;*
  - *school-based management;*
  - *greater accountability by all parties responsible for the quality of education;*
  - *improvements in the school environment; and*
  - *equitable financing across school districts.*

- *We encourage states to explore school choice policies as part of an overall plan to restructure and improve public schools. School choice should only be implemented where accountability measures are specified and where the special needs of educationally disadvantaged students are addressed.* Some members of the Commission would extend the concept of school choice to include private and parochial as well as public schools. Other members of the Commission, however, are concerned that choice policies, in the absence of major steps to restructure schools and ensure every child a quality education, will further disadvantage the nation's most educationally vulnerable students, who may be overlooked in a market-driven system.

- *We recommend that all schools and communities reevaluate the services they currently offer and design creative, multidisciplinary initiatives to help children with serious and multiple needs reach their academic potential.*

- *We recommend that parents, communities, employers, and the media take mutually reinforcing steps to emphasize to young people the personal rewards and long-term benefits of academic and intellectual achievement, cultural enrichment, hard work, and perseverance.*

Preparing Adolescents for Adulthood

... Today, one in four adolescents in the United States engages in high-risk behaviors that endanger his or her own health and well-being and that of others. These 7 million young people have multiple problems that can severely limit their futures. Most have fallen behind in school, and some have already dropped out. Many engage in sexual activity, and some have experienced pregnancies or contracted sexually transmitted diseases. Many are frequent and heavy users of drugs and alcohol. Some have been arrested or have committed serious offenses. We must reach these young people early and provide them with both the means and the motivation to avoid risky, dangerous, and destructive activities that threaten their futures, their families, and their communities. Where damage has already occurred, we must also help those young people experiencing problems cope with the consequences of their actions.

Society's concern and involvement must also extend to the three-quarters of young people at low and moderate risk of serious problems. ... To help all young people successfully navigate the passage from childhood to adulthood, the National Commission on Children offers the following recommendations:

- *We recommend that individual adults, communities, and the public and private sectors take aggressive steps to ensure that all young people have access to a broad array of supports in their communities to promote healthy adolescent development and help them avoid high-risk behaviors—including school dropout, premature sexual activity, juvenile delinquency, crime and violence, and alcohol and drug abuse—that jeopardize their futures.*
- *We recommend that parents, schools, employers, and government initiate or expand efforts to introduce young people to employment and career options; to help them acquire the skills, knowledge, and experience for their chosen fields; and to link more closely the worlds of school and work.*
- *We recommend that communities create and expand opportunities for community service by young people.*

Strengthening and Supporting Families

The conditions of children's lives and their future prospects largely reflect the well-being of their families. When families are strong, stable, and loving, children have a sound basis for becoming caring and competent adults. When families are unable to give children the affection and attention they need and to provide for their material needs, children are far less likely to achieve their full potential.

The value that society places on families and the way it supports their needs have a great deal to do with how children fare. When society values children and the quality of family life, individuals, families themselves, and outside institutions are moved to make the necessary commitment and create supportive environments at home, at school, at work, and in the community. The nation's laws and public policies should therefore reflect sound family values and aim to strengthen and support families in their childrearing roles. Accordingly, the National Commission on Children offers the following recommendations to support and strengthen families:

- *We urge individuals and society to reaffirm their commitment to forming and supporting strong, stable families as the best environment for raising children.*
- *We emphasize the need for both parents to share responsibility for planning their families and delaying pregnancy until they are financially and emotionally capable of assuming the obligations of parenthood. Although decisions concerning family planning are and should continue to remain a private matter, public support for family planning services should be sustained to ensure that all families, regardless of income, can plan responsibly for parenthood.*
- *We recommend that government and all private sector employers establish family-oriented policies and practices—including family and medical leave policies, flexible work scheduling alternatives, and career sequencing—to enable employed mothers and fathers to meet their work and family responsibilities.* The majority of commissioners strongly recommends that the federal government require all employers to provide the option of a job-protected leave at the time of childbirth, adoption, and family and medical emergencies. Healthy child development depends on parents and children having adequate time together during the early months of life to form close and enduring relationships. A minority of commissioners strongly opposes such prescribed and inflexible federal mandates, which they believe all too often result in discriminatory practices in the workplace and restrict employees' choices of benefits that meet the particular needs of their families. In addition, they believe the costs of implementing such mandates often produce adverse and unintended economic consequences.
- *We recommend that government at all levels, communities, and employers continue to improve the availability, affordability, and quality of child care services for all children and families that need them.*
- *We recommend that federal, state, and local governments, in partnership with private community organizations, develop and expand community-based family support programs to provide parents with the knowledge, skills, and support they need to raise their children.*
Some commissioners are concerned that a fiscal commitment of the magnitude proposed requires careful attention to the design and evaluation of the expanded services to ensure that they produce outcomes that are beneficial to the families who need them.

Protecting Vulnerable Children and Their Families

When families are in turmoil, children are often the helpless victims of their parents' frustration and despair. They may suffer parental neglect; experience physical, emotional, or sexual abuse; or develop behavioral problems that make them difficult to care for. In the absence of adequate support and services, these children are frequently removed from their families and placed in the custody of the state. This separation from their parents, siblings, schools, and communities is shocking and painful for most children. Thousands move from one placement to another, effectively denied a permanent home and family. Many bear scars for the rest of their lives. Foster care is intended to protect children from neglect and abuse at the hands of parents and other family members, yet all too often it becomes an equally cruel form of neglect and abuse by the state.

The number of children in foster care has increased dramatically over the past several years, reversing declines in the late 1970s and early 1980s. Recent estimates project that more than half a million children will be in foster care by 1995. This increase has overwhelmed the capacity of the judicial system and every child welfare system in the country to deal sensitively and responsively to the needs of vulnerable children and their troubled families.

In part, the increasing number of children in the state's custody reflects increased reports of abuse and neglect. But it also reflects misguided public funding incentives, particularly at the federal level. Federal funding for preventive efforts to keep families together is fixed each year under the provisions of Title IV-B of the Child Welfare and Adoption Assistance Act and has barely grown in the past decade, while funding for out-of-home care is supported by Title IV-E, an open-ended entitlement that grows automatically according to need. This encourages states to place children in out-of-home care rather than to help troubled families overcome their problems and maintain custody of their children.

Marginal changes will not turn this system around. Instead, we need fundamental reform to ensure that family support and basic preventive services are available early to reduce the likelihood of family crises and lessen the need for children to be removed from their homes.

- *The National Commission on Children recommends a comprehensive community-level approach to strengthen families. We believe that early family support and the availability of preventive services will ultimately lessen the need for children to be removed from their homes. We therefore urge that programs and services for vulnerable children and their families be restructured to include three complementary approaches:*
  - *Promoting child development and healthy family functioning through locally controlled and coordinated community-based family support networks that offer access and referrals to a broad range of services, including health and mental health care, education, recreation, housing, parenting education and support, em-*

ployment and training, and substance abuse prevention and treatment.

- *Assisting families and children in need in order to strengthen and preserve families that voluntarily seek help before their problems become acute. Human service programs—including health and mental health, juvenile services, substance abuse programs, education, and economic and social supports—must collaborate to provide prevention and early intervention services that offer practical solutions to problems faced by families in crisis.*

- *Protecting abused and neglected children through more comprehensive child protective services, with a strong emphasis on efforts to keep children with their families or to provide permanent placement for those removed from their homes.* In particular, when babies are abandoned at birth and when repeated attempts to reunify older children and parents have failed, the adoption process should be streamlined to expedite placement of children in permanent, stable families.

The majority of commissioners recommends changing Title IV-B to an entitlement, making funds equally available for the provision of family preservation services and for foster care. This will eliminate any fiscal incentive for removing children from their homes unnecessarily by ensuring that states have adequate funds for prevention. A minority of commissioners believes that the current problems in child welfare are not related primarily to inadequate funding. They recommend that the relationship between Titles IV-B and IV-E be altered to allow greater flexibility in spending monies for preventive services.

Making Policies and Programs Work

All families, regardless of their resources and circumstances, need occasional support and assistance. To meet these needs, an array of public and private programs and services has developed over the last half century to promote children's health and development, encourage success in school, and protect children from abuse. Families also receive assistance and support through employment-based benefits, voluntary and community efforts, and informal networks of friends, relatives, and neighbors.

For the majority of well-functioning families with ample financial, social, and psychological resources, this mix of informal support and public and private programs is both adequate and appropriate. But families facing severe problems often need more integrated and sustained interventions delivered by skilled professionals who are able to respond early and comprehensively to a family's multiple needs.

Unfortunately, the present system of human services generally fails to meet the needs of these seriously troubled families. Service providers in separate programs serving the same family rarely confer or work to reinforce one another's efforts. Few resources are available to help families early, before their problems become too mammoth to ignore. Low salaries and poor working conditions discourage talented individuals from pursuing careers in early childhood development, child welfare, and teaching. As a result, families seeking assistance often encounter a service delivery system that is confusing, difficult to navigate, and indifferent to their concerns. For many parents and children, these obstacles appear at a time when they are least able to cope with additional stress or adversity.

Fragmentation and lack of coordination among programs and services contribute to a widespread perception of inefficiency and waste in public health and social service programs. In many cases, this perception is justified. Multiple layers of bureaucracy and extensive record-keeping and reporting requirements, developed in part to guard against misuse of public funds, have often cost more than they have saved. Familiar stories of records irretrievably lost and multiple appointments to resolve single issues further fuel public impressions of waste and incompetence in publicly administered or publicly funded programs.

To bring greater cohesion and efficiency to the delivery of public health and social services and to enhance their ability to meet the needs of severely troubled children and families, the National Commission on Children offers the following proposals:

- *We recommend a series of changes in the organization, administration, implementation, and budget of programs at all levels of government to encourage a more collaborative and comprehensive service delivery system, including:*
  - *greater coordination of child and family policies across the executive branch;*
  - *creation of a joint congressional committee on children and families to promote greater coordination and collaboration across the authorizing and appropriating committees with jurisdiction over relevant policies and programs;*
  - *decategorization of selected federal programs to bring greater cohesion and flexibility to programs for children and families;*
  - *uniform eligibility criteria and consolidated, streamlined application processes for the major federal means-tested programs and for other programs that serve the same or overlapping populations;*
  - *incentives to encourage demonstration projects and other experiments in coordination and collaboration of services at the state and local levels; and*
  - *new accountability measures that focus on enhanced child and family well-being, rather than solely on administrative procedures.*
- *We call upon the nation to increase its investment in the prevention of problems that limit individual potential and drain social resources.*
- *We recommend that salaries and training opportunities be significantly increased in the early childhood and child welfare fields, and that states and school districts with teachers' salaries below the national average bring these salaries up to the average. In every case,*

pay structures and incentives should be linked to demonstrated competence.

Creating a Moral Climate for Children

Today, too many young people seem adrift, without a steady moral compass to direct their daily behavior or to plot a thoughtful and responsible course for their lives. We see the worst manifestation of this in reports of violent and predatory behavior by adolescents in large and small communities across the nation. It is evident in lifestyles and sexual conduct that indulge personal gratification at the expense of others' safety and well-being. It is revealed as well in a culture that ranks wealth and the acquisition of material possessions above service to one's community or to the nation. It is also demonstrated in the declining voting rates of young citizens.

Much of what we saw and heard also made us worry about the public values implicit in individual words and actions and in Americans' failure to act in concert to change the conditions that harm children and undermine their families' ability to support and nurture them. As a commission on children, we could not avoid questioning the moral character of a nation that allows so many children to grow up poor, to live in unsafe dwellings and violent neighborhoods, and to lack access to basic health care and a decent education.

At least some of children's moral confusion stems from the conduct and attitudes of some prominent adults, including entertainers and athletes, corporate executives, religious leaders, and public officials, as well as from the cultural messages reflected in television programming, movies, videos, and popular music. Some of children's confusion also has roots in the behavior of fathers and mothers who lack the ability and commitment to be responsible parents. And some of it reflects the contradictions apparent in American society. In a nation with professed commitments to equal opportunity and to the protection and nurturance of the young, racism persists and a recent explosion of violence kills and maims children.

Children and adolescents need clear, consistent messages about personal conduct and public responsibility. The National Commission on Children urges public and private sector leaders, community institutions, and individual Americans to renew their commitment to the fundamental values of human dignity, character, and citizenship, and to demonstrate that commitment through individual actions and national priorities:

- *We recommend that parents be more vigilant and aggressive guardians of their children's moral development, monitoring the values to which their children are exposed, discussing conflicting messages with their children, and if necessary, limiting or precluding their children's exposure to images that parents consider offensive.*
- *We recommend that the recording industry continue and enhance its efforts to avoid distribution of inappropriate materials to children.*
- *We recommend that television producers exercise greater restraint in*

363

the content of programming for children. We further urge television stations to exercise restraint in the amount and type of advertising aired during children's programs.

- *We recommend that communities create opportunities for voluntary service by children and adults and recognize the contributions of volunteers that better the community and assist its members.*
- *We urge all Americans to renew their personal commitment to the common good and demonstrate this commitment by giving highest priority to personal actions and public policies that promote the health and well-being of the nation's children.*

Investing in America's Future

Without a vision of a better society, Americans will never be moved to act. The National Commission on Children developed such a vision over two years of sometimes painful and always moving investigation into the lives of children and families and through many months of honest and thoughtful negotiation. We envision a nation of strong and stable families, where every child has an equal opportunity to reach his or her full potential, and where public policies and personal values give highest priority to healthy, whole children. Realizing this vision will require leadership and sustained commitment, significant investments of individual time and attention, and the allocation of financial resources.

Every sector of society benefits from caring, competent, and literate citizens, and every individual has a direct stake in seeing that all children are able to develop to their full potential. The federal government cannot and should not bear sole responsibility or the full financial costs of this national effort, but it must play a significant role. Leadership and financial support must come from other sectors as well. Some of the costs of our recommendations must be borne by state and localities and by employers. Philanthropy and voluntarism must also continue to play a critical role.

Implementation of the Commission's recommendations will cost approximately $52 billion to $56 billion in new federal funds in the first year. The largest portion of this total (approximately $40 billion) is for the refundable child tax credit which offers tax relief to families raising children. Health care proposals account for another $9.1 billion. A minority of commissioners do not endorse the recommendations contained within the majority health chapter and therefore do not endorse the $9.1 billion of expenditures. Most of the remainder is for social service programs. The majority of commissioners regard all of these expenditures as necessary investments to preserve personal freedom, economic prosperity, and social harmony well into the future.

To cover the federal share of costs associated with our recommendations, the Commission offers several alternative financing options. Each is based on three general principles:

- **Deficit Neutrality.** We recognize the need to generate significant funds to cover the cost of our recommendations, rather than add to the existing federal deficit. Continuing large deficits leave middle- and low-income families vulnerable to economic downturns by limiting government's ability to cushion or counter recessions. They also limit economic growth and opportunity and restrict the nation's ability to meet new needs. Their persistence ensures that a future generation of Americans must pay this generation's bills.

- **Progressivity.** We are reluctant to add further to the taxes paid by young workers raising families, since these families have been especially hard hit by economic changes and increases in relative tax burdens in recent decades. In general, we prefer revenue sources that are progressive or that are generated on the purchase of luxury items, rather than taxes that reduce the take-home pay of low- and middle-income workers. Our income security plan recognizes the personal costs and social benefits of raising children, in part through establishment of a refundable child tax credit. We do not favor financing options that would in effect, tax away the value of the new credit.

- **Growth.** We looked for sources of revenue with the potential to grow over time. While we are confident that our recommendations will ultimately yield considerable savings, we also recognize that some of this savings will only be fully realized in later years. To achieve these long-term gains, however, we must be willing to make short-term investments.

Each financing option presents a different concept of how to generate the required funding. No commissioner endorses all of the options, but each regards at least one as a viable approach. While some commissioners oppose tax increases of any kind, others rely in varying combinations on increasing taxes on individuals and corporations and on reallocating and establishing caps on federal spending.

The National Commission on Children calls on all Americans to work together to change the conditions that jeopardize the health and well-being of so many of our youngest citizens and threaten our future as an economic power, a democratic nation, and a caring society. Our failure to act today will only defer to the next generation the rising social, moral, and financial costs of our neglect. Investing in children is no longer a luxury, but a national imperative.

INDEPENDENCE OF
YUGOSLAV REPUBLICS
June 24, 1991

The northern Yugoslav republics of Slovenia and Croatia declared their independence June 24, pushing the political disintegration of Yugoslavia a step further. The most industrially advanced and prosperous of Yugoslavia's six republics, they together accounted for nearly 7 million of the country's 24 million people.

In Croatia, home of more than half-a-million Serbs, fighting promptly broke out between Serbs and Croats in the republic's predominantly Serbian areas. Serbian rebels, backed by their national army, conducted sporadic—sometimes sustained—attacks on Croatian defense units and gained control of several cities, including historic Dubrovnik on the Aegean Sea. This confusing pattern of partly open, partly guerrilla warfare defied the European Community's repeated attempts to invoke truces and impose a peace settlement.

Frustrated by its failures, the European Community imposed economic sanctions on Yugoslavia November 8 in an attempt to cut off supplies to the national army. The United States followed suit by embargoing American exports. On November 27, the United Nations Security Council pledged to send a peacekeeping force of 10,000 soldiers to enforce a ceasefire then in effect.

Since the death of President Josip Broz Tito in 1980, the central government had been weakened by feuding among the disparate ethnic, linguistic, and religious groups that make up Yugoslavia. For instance, Croatians and Slovenes, who consider themselves the most "Europeanized" of the Yugoslav peoples, are predominantly Roman Catholic and use the Latin alphabet. Serbs, the most populous group, are principally

Eastern Orthodox and use the cyrillic script.

During his thirty-six years of undisputed Marxist rule, Tito made the Yugoslav nation function. None of his political heirs commanded the the same authority, which permitted old ethnic emnities to surface. After communism lost control of other East European states in 1989, several ex-Communist leaders in Yugoslavia's semiautonomous republics sought to win popular favor by rekindling Balkan grievances that had been suppressed but not forgotten under communism.

One such leader was Slobodan Milosevic, the president of Serbia, who espoused a strong brand of Serbian nationalism. Serbia, the biggest of the six Yugoslav republics, was an independent state from about 1830 until 1918, when the Serbs joined with the Croats and Slovenes to found the state that later became Yugoslavia. At that time, the Serbs considered themselves the dominant partner. That notion inspired Milosevic to revive the concept of a "Greater Serbia," embracing not only the Republic of Serbia with nearly 10 million people but also some 3 million Serbs and the ethnically related Montenegrins living in other republics.

Milosevic's ardor for protecting the Serbian minority in Croatia was fostered by memories from World War II. During the Nazi occupation of Yugoslavia, a Croatian puppet government put to death tens—possibly hundreds—of thousands of Serbs, gypsies, and Jews. In turn, entire villages of Croats were massacred by Serbian Chetniks, or guerrillas. Those wartime grievances were given new life in statements such as Milosevic's repeated declaration that present-day Croatia was scheming with Germany to "impose a Fourth Reich."

Until March, Milosevic had defended the Yugoslav government's authority and sought to bend it to his will. But then he openly challenged it in a way that amounted to Serbia's secession from the Yugoslav Federation. In May the crisis was deepened when Serbia refused to approve what previously had been a routine rotation of the national presidency among the leaders of the republics. On May 15 outgoing president Borisav Jovic, a Serbian, vetoed the choice of Stipe Mesic, a Croat, as his successor.

With the central government virtually ceasing to function, the Slovenia and Croatia parliaments voted to adopt declarations of independence. But the two republics held out the prospect of stopping short of full secession if all would agree to a loosely structured confederation of autonomous republics. There appeared little hope that such an arrangement could be devised as long as fighting continued between Croats and Serbs.

Residents of Macedonia, the southernmost Yugoslav republic, voted September 9 to follow Croatia and Slovenia in seeking independence. Macedonian leaders said they would prefer to retain some connection with Yugoslavia but would secede if the the government in Belgrade was not replaced by a confederation.

Following are English translations of the declarations of
independence for Slovenia and Croatia, adopted in the two
Yugoslav republics by their parliaments on June 24, 1991:

On the basis of the right of the Slovene nation to self-determination, of the principles of international law and the Constitution of the former SFRY and of the Republic of Slovenia, and on the basis of the absolute majority vote in the plebiscite held on December 23, 1990, the people of the Republic of Slovenia have decided to establish an independent state, the Republic of Slovenia, which will no longer be a part of the Socialist Federal Republic of Yugoslavia.

On the basis of an unanimous proposal of all parliamentary parties and groups of delegates and in compliance with the plebiscitary outcome, the Assembly of the Republic of Slovenia has adopted the Basic Constitutional Charter on the Sovereignty and Independence of the Republic of Slovenia at the sessions of all its chambers held on June 25, 1991.

I.

Prior to the plebiscite on sovereignty and independence, Slovenia proposed, jointly with the Republic of Croatia, a draft agreement to the other Yugoslav republics stipulating an alliance or a confederation of sovereign states, according to which the present members of the Yugoslav federation would continue to cooperate in economic, foreign policy and other spheres. The Assembly of the Republic of Slovenia called a plebiscite, in which the vast majority of the people of Slovenia voted in favor of a sovereign and independent Republic of Slovenia.

Slovenia notified the other Yugoslav republics, and the Yugoslav public, of the actions which Slovenia was required to take on the basis of the plebiscitary outcome. These messages included the Resolution of the Proposal for a Multilateral Dissolution of the Socialist Republic of Yugoslavia and other initiatives. Slovenia also proposed to Yugoslavia and the Yugoslav republics, as the constitutive entities of the federation, a bilateral dissolution, which would create two or more sovereign states, which would acknowledge each other's status as legal, international entities. Slovenia repeatedly voiced readiness to reach agreement on the arrangement of interrelations in the event of a Yugoslav confederative, or economic community, or some other suitable form of association which would benefit all its nations and citizens.

The proposal for a bilateral dissolution and the initiation of talks on new forms of relations ... was not accepted within the reasonably allotted time, except by the Republic of Croatia. The Republic of Slovenia was thus compelled to pass the Constitutional Act on the Sovereignty and Independence of the Republic of Slovenia.

II.

The Republic of Slovenia has proclaimed its sovereignty and independence and has thereby assumed effective jurisdiction over its territory.

Consequently, Slovenia seeks, as an international legal entity in the full sense of the term and in conformity with the principles of the unification of sovereign states in Europe, association with other states, membership of the Organization of the United Nations, participation in the process of CSCE, in the Council of Europe, membership of the European Community and participation with other associations of states. The sovereignty and independence of the Republic of Slovenia must be understood as a condition for entering into new integrational processes within the framework of former Yugoslavia and within the European framework. Moreover, the Republic of Slovenia will strictly adhere to the Charter of the United Nations, to the Conventions of the Council of Europe, to Helsinki Final Document, to the Declaration and other acts of the Conference on Security and Cooperation in Europe, as well as to other international treaties.

The establishment of the sovereign and independent state of the Republic of Slovenia on the basis of the right to self-determination is not an act against any political entity in Yugoslavia or any other foreign political unit. Slovenia recognizes the right to self-determination of the other republics, nations and nationalities of Yugoslavia. Slovenia wishes to exercise its right to sovereignty and association with other sovereign states in a peaceful manner, by mutual agreement, through dialogue, in line with standards of the international community, namely that future relationships on the territory of former Yugoslavia should stand on democratic principles, without changing the external and internal borders of Yugoslavia.

III.

The Republic of Slovenia as a sovereign and independent state hereby proclaims:

- that the Constitution of the Socialist Federal Republic of Yugoslavia is no longer in force on the territory of the Republic of Slovenia. The Republic of Slovenia is continuing the procedure of assuming effective rule on its territory. The procedure will be carried out gradually and in agreement with the other republics of former Yugoslavia, without encroaching on the rights of other republics;
- that it is prepared to continue negotiations regarding the possible forms of association with the states which will be constituted on the territory of former Yugoslavia. On the basis of mutual recognition, the Republic of Slovenia is prepared immediately to initiate talks in order to reach agreement on an association of sovereign states on the territory of former Yugoslavia. Within this association, the member states would be free to realize their joint economic, political, international and other interests. The achievement of such an agreement, or at least a joint declaration of the desire to reach such an agreement, would guarantee that the process of assuming authority in the newly founded states and the process of constituting an association of these

states would not cause undue conflicts. On the contrary, these processes would be mutually stimulating and would facilitate the process of self-determination in all Yugoslav nations, the achievement of the rights of the Albanians in Kosovo, the rights of national minorities and the development of democracy in the community of sovereign states on the territory of former Yugoslavia;

- that in compliance with the decisions of the Sabor of the Republic of Croatia, Slovenia recognizes the Republic of Croatia as a sovereign state and an international legal entity; she will also recognize all other Yugoslav republics which proclaim themselves sovereign states.

The mandate to the Slovene delegates in the Federal Chamber of the Assembly of SFR of Yugoslavia and the delegations of the Republic of Slovenia in the Chambers of the Republics and Provinces of the Assembly of the SFR of Yugoslavia, is terminated with the proclamation of the Declaration of Independence. The Assembly of the Republic of Slovenia elects a new 12-member delegation, which will be authorized to participate in negotiations regarding the dissolution of Yugoslavia in the Assembly of former Yugoslavia, in the solving of current issues in the transition period and in negotiations regarding the possible formation of a community of sovereign states on the basis of approval by the Assembly of the Republic of Slovenia. The Republic of Slovenia appeals to the other Yugoslav republics to delegate such authority to their respective delegations. The Assembly of the Republic of Slovenia also expects the federal institutions of the former SFRY to participate in this process.

The Assembly of the Republic of Slovenia authorizes its present Member of the Presidency of the SFR of Yugoslavia to represent the Republic of Slovenia, in the Presidency of the SFR of Yugoslavia in conformity with the guidelines of the Assembly of the Republic of Slovenia.

All issues which still remain to be resolved, such as the status of the Yugoslav National Army in the Republic of Slovenia, competencies in the sphere of international relations and the issue of the division of common property will be dealt with by special agreement to be reached by the Republic of Slovenia and the corresponding bodies of former Yugoslavia.

IV.

In the capacity of an international and legal entity, the Republic of Slovenia:

- pledges to respect all the principles of international law and, in the spirit of legal succession, the provisions of all international contracts signed by Yugoslavia and which apply to the territory of the Republic of Slovenia. In conformity with the anticipated agreement on the assumption of the rights and obligations of former Yugoslavia, the Republic of Slovenia will honor its share of international financial obligations towards other states and international organizations, and ensure the free flow of goods, services and people across its borders, as well as ensure the uninterrupted flow of transport and communications on its territory. In establishing a border with the Republic of Croatia, the state agencies of the Republic of Slovenia will seek to ensure in accordance with their mutual interests the free flow of people, goods and services;

- will endeavor to gain the approval of the international community regarding the proclamation of the sovereign and independent Republic of Slovenia and to improve economic, cultural, political, financial and other ties with the international community. Furthermore, Slovenia expects legal recognition from other countries. Slovenia also anticipates that the international community will use its influence to contribute to the shaping of the community of sovereign states on the territory of former Yugoslavia and thus contribute to the bilateral and peaceful implementation of the decision to constitute the sovereign and independent state of the Republic of Slovenia;
- expects neighboring countries to respect and further develop the level of protection of the Slovene minority, guaranteed by international conventions and bilateral agreements.

V.

The Republic of Slovenia is a state in which law and social welfare are respected, whose environment is suitable for a market economy. Slovenia pledges to observe human rights and civil liberties, the special rights of autochthonous Hungarians and Italians in the Republic of Slovenia, as well as the European achievements of industrial democracy (above all, socio-economic rights, the rights of the employed to take part in the decision-making processes and independent unions), the inviolability of property and the freedom of association in a civil society. Slovenia pledges to guarantee multiparty parliamentary democracy and local, or regional, self-rule. Slovenia guarantees that no political, or other kind of persuasion will be used as a basis for inequality or discrimination of any kind, pledges to solve all contentious internal and external issues in a peaceful, non-violent manner and to strive to improve cooperation, on an equal footing, with all nations and citizens of Europe in which people, regions, nations and states are free and equal.

DECLARATION OF THE ESTABLISHMENT OF THE SOVEREIGN AND INDEPENDENT REPUBLIC OF CROATIA

I.

Throughout its thirteen centuries of life in the land between the Adriatic Sea and the Drava and the Mura rivers, the Croatian people has maintained a consciousness of its own identity and of its right to autonomy and independence in an autonomous and sovereign Croatian state.

History has placed the Croatian people on the frontier of Eastern and Western Christianity, two often antagonistic civilizations and cultures, and on the watershed of various political, economic, and other interests; there, the Croatian people has for centuries defended its national state, and, often, at the same time, those of the nations to the west of its national borders. During these years the Croatian people was governed by its own national rulers and by the Croatian Parliament, fully independent, or in personal and contractual unions and alliances with other nations, but it has always vigilantly safeguarded its national autonomy and sovereignty. Even in the darkest moments of history, the Croatian people has retained a part of its national territory including the capital city of Zagreb, nor has it ever relinquished characteristics of Croatian national sovereignty, which, from the period of the national dynasty, have been guarded by the Croatian Parliament and the Croatian Bans, who exercised the viceroyal powers and prerogatives at those times when the Croatian Kingdom was associated with other states.

The Croatian Parliament has always maintained the tradition of Croatian historic rights and Croatian sovereignty throughout its entire 1300 year history, making the Croatian people one of the oldest nation-forming peoples in Europe.

II.

Under centralist and totalitarian system of the Socialist Federal Republic of Yugoslavia, the Republic of Croatia was unable to promote and safeguard its legitimate political, economic, cultural, and other interests. For that reason the Croatian people developed an increasing desire for disassociation from the Yugoslav federal state.

Today we are faced with attempts to disrupt the constitutional system and territorial integrity of the Republic of Croatia through acts of organized brigandage and terror directed by forces outside the Republic, seeking to prevent, moreover, the implementation of the will of the Croatian people and of all other citizens of Croatia expressed through free elections and legislated through the Constitution, and, in particular, voiced by the Referendum for Sovereignty, Independence and Autonomy of the Republic of Croatia (May 19, 1991).

The Croatian people, together with all other citizens of the Republic who consider Croatia their homeland, is determined to defend, by all possible means, the autonomy and territorial integrity of the Republic from any act of aggression.

III.

The Republic of Croatia is a democratic and social state based on the rule of law, and the paramount values of the constitutional system, i.e., freedom, equality, national equality, pursuit of peace, social justice, human rights, political pluralism, inviolability of ownership, preservation of natural and human environment, observance of laws, and a democratic, multiparty system.

The Republic of Croatia guarantees Serbs in Croatia, and other national minorities who live on its territory, all human and civil rights, and, in particular, the full right to use their national language and promote national culture, and the right of free political association.

The Republic of Croatia promotes the rights and interests of its citizens regardless of their religious preference or ethnic or racial background.

In accordance with the rules of international law, the Republic of Croatia declares to all other states and international bodies that it will totally and conscientiously fulfill all the obligations descending upon it as the legal successor to the Socialist Federal Republic of Yugoslavia on that territory of the latter which coincides with the territory of the Republic of Croatia.

IV.

According to the previous and current Constitutions of the Federal Peoples' Republic of Yugoslavia and of the Socialist Federal Republic of Yugoslavia, the Republic of Croatia has retained the right of self-determination as well as the right of disassociation.

By constituting itself an independent and sovereign state the Republic of Croatia, which heretofore has realised some of its sovereignty rights jointly with the other Republics and Autonomous Regions within the Federal Socialist Republic of Yugoslavia, hereby modifies its position and constitutional relationship with the Federal Socialist Republic of Yugoslavia, agreeing, however, to participate in some of the federal institutions and services which are of mutual interest in the course of the act of disassociation. During the process of disassociation it will be necessary to establish the rights and obligations, namely the share of the Republic of Croatia in the total movable and immovable wealth and entitlements of the Socialist Federal Republic of Yugoslavia.

By the proclamation of the Constitutional Act of Independence, the Republic of Croatia initiates the process of disassociation from the other Republics and from the Socialist Federal Republic of Yugoslavia, with the intention of completing this process in as short a time as possible and in a democratic and peaceful manner, respecting the interests of other Republics and Autonomous Regions which have been constituent parts of the Socialist Federal Republic of Yugoslavia.

By the proclamation of the Constitutional Act of Independence, the Republic of Croatia has provided a foundation for its recognition as an international-legal entity. The President and the Government of the Republic of Croatia will take the necessary steps in that direction.

By the Constitutional Act of Independence the existing borders of the Republic of Croatia have become international borders between Croatia and the other Republics and neighbouring states of the present-day Socialist Federal Republic of Yugoslavia.

Only the laws promulgated by the Croatian Parliament, and until the completion of disassociation, those federal laws not invalidated by the Parliament, have any legal power or effect on the territory of the Republic of Croatia.

Issues which cannot be immediately resolved, such as the position of the Yugoslav National Army, federal diplomatic corps, and a division of entitlements and obligations, shall be settled through separate agreements between the Republic of Croatia and other federal units of the Socialist Federal Republic of Yugoslavia in the course of the process of disassociation. In the meantime the Republic of Croatia recognizes only those federal bodies in which decisions are made on the basis of parity and consensus.

Federal bodies shall not be allowed to act on the territory of the Republic of Croatia, unless the Government of the Republic of Croatia approves temporary exceptions.

The Republic of Croatia is withdrawing its representatives to the Federal Council of the Parliament of the Socialist Federal Republic of Yugoslavia, the mandate of which has expired, and the existence of which is deemed unnecessary during the process of disassociation.

The Republic of Croatia maintains that the Council of the Republics and Regions is sufficient to provide a forum for a parliamentary discussion of the question of disassociation.

V.

The Republic of Croatia recognizes the sovereignty and international-legal status of all new states created through disassociation from the Federal Socialist Republic of Yugoslavia, within the existing borders of the Socialist Federal Republic of Yugoslavia, and within their own borders as they are defined by the current Constitution of the Federal Socialist Republic of Yugoslavia or may be agreed upon through democratic negotiations among the sovereign states.

By this Declaration of Independence and Sovereignty the Republic of Croatia does not wish to sever its relations with the other Republics, or to disrupt economic, traffic or financial relationships and transactions.

The Republic of Croatia will enter into a special contractual agreement with the Republic of Slovenia, forming an alliance of two independent, sovereign nations.

The Republic of Croatia invites the other Republics of the existing Socialist Federal Republic of Yugoslavia to form an alliance of sovereign nations under the following conditions: that there be a mutual recognition of the state of international sovereignty and territorial integrity; that there be mutual respect and acceptance of political pluralism, democracy, private ownership and a market economy; that there be respect of human and other rights of national minorities, and of other values of the civilized world; that there be readiness to treat unresolved issues between individual Republics—sovereign states—through reciprocal agreements and accords.

The Republic of Croatia maintains that an alliance of sovereign nations with the Republic of Slovenia, as well as with the other Republics, in the form of a contractual, voluntary, and mutually beneficial community, would be of advantage to all the Republics of the present-day Socialist Federal Republic of Yugoslavia, granted that mutual interests be respected according to the existing rules of international law, in particular such rules and regulations as have determined the foundation and development of the European Community, since the aforementioned rules represent a live and effective body of principles which could successfully direct the alliance of sovereign nations—until its eventual entry into the European Community—toward peace, prosperity and international acceptance.

RESIGNATION OF JUSTICE MARSHALL
FROM THE SUPREME COURT
June 27, 1991

Justice Thurgood Marshall submitted his resignation to President George Bush June 27, saying that his "advancing age and medical condition" were incompatible with the strenuous demands of being a justice of the Supreme Court. He was only five days shy of his eighty-third birthday and had served on the Court since 1967. He was its first black member and remained the only one until succeeded by Clarence Thomas. (Hearings on Clarence Thomas's Supreme Court Nomination, p. 551)

Marshall fought for the underprivileged throughout his six-decade legal career—as the mastermind of the civil rights revolution and then in the federal judiciary. As counsel for the National Association for the Advancement of Colored People (NAACP) and later the separate NAACP Legal Defense and Education Fund, he devised the litigation that abolished white-only party primary elections, barred racial covenants in private housing, and outlawed racial segregation in public schools.

President John F. Kennedy appointed Marshall to the Second U.S. Circuit Court of Appeals, on which he served until 1965 when Lyndon B. Johnson made him solicitor general, whose duty it was to represent the government before the Supreme Court. Two years later Johnson nominated Marshall to become an associate justice. The Senate confirmed him by a vote of 61 to 11, over the objection of some Southern senators who objected to his "activist" judicial temperament.

On the Court, Marshall wrote relatively few major opinions. His most important doctrinal contribution—influential though never officially adopted—was to advocate a relaxed standard for deciding whether state or federal law violated the constitutional protection of equal rights. Marshall also wrote decisions expanding free speech rights, but some of his decisions were later overturned. Despite his efforts, he never was able to persuade a majority of his fellow justices to outlaw the death penalty.

Marshall increasingly found himself a dissenter of Court decisions after chief justices Warren E. Burger and William H. Rehnquist weakened affirmative action rules and protection for criminal defendants. In his last term, Marshall was the senior member of the Court's dwindling liberal wing and often was the author of dissenting opinions—a task that fell to him after the resignation in June 1990 of his close friend and older colleague, Justice William J. Brennan, Jr.

Marshall's later dissents often revealed an acute sense of frustration with the Court's expanding conservative ideology. In the justice's final opinion, issued only hours before he announced his retirement, he bitterly assailed the majority's "radical reconstruction of the rules for overturning this Court's decisions" and added that he feared this was "but a preview of an even broader and more far-reaching assault on this Court's precedents." (Court On Murder Case Sentencing, p. 381)

At a news conference on June 28 Marshall denied press reports that the Court's shift in ideology had motivated him to resign. In his customarily gruff manner, he refused to discuss politics, individual judges, or judicial philosophy. As for his successor—who then had not been named—the retiring justice urged President Bush to pick the "best person for the job, not on the basis of race one way or another." Marshall said in his letter to Bush that his resignation would become effective "when my successor is qualified" (confirmed by the Senate).

In a letter of response, the president accepted Marshall's resignation "with deep regret" and told him that the nation "is deeply indebted to you for your long and distinguished public service."

> *Following are Justice Thurgood Marshall's letter of June 27, 1991, to President George Bush, resigning from the Supreme Court, and the president's letter of response, dated the following day:*

June 27, 1991

My Dear Mr. President:

The strenuous demands of court work and its related duties required or expected of a Justice appear at this time to be incompatible with my advancing age and medical condition.

I, therefore, retire as an Associate Justice of the Supreme Court of the United States when my successor is qualified.

Respectfully,

Thurgood Marshall

June 28, 1991

Dear Mr. Justice:

It is with deep regret that I acknowledge your letter of retirement from the Supreme Court effective at such time as a successor is qualified.

Our Nation is deeply indebted to you for your long and distinguished public service. Your courageous leadership in the fight for equal opportunity, exemplified by your brief and oral argument in the landmark case of *Brown v. Board of Education,* is a powerful example of how one person's commitment to his convictions can shape a nation's attitude on such a fundamental issue.

Your distinguished service to our country, first on the U.S. Court of Appeals for the Second Circuit, as our Nation's 33rd Solicitor General, and capped by a great career on the Supreme Court will also be long remembered.

Barbara and I wish you happiness and every blessing in your years of retirement.

Sincerely,

George Bush

COURT ON MURDER CASE SENTENCING

June 27, 1991

Overturning two of its own recent decisions, a bitterly divided Supreme Court closed its 1990-1991 term June 27 by permitting submission of evidence in a murder trial about the effects of the crime on the victim's family. The ruling applied to the sentencing stage of a trial, after a jury had found the defendant guilty.

Chief Justice William H. Rehnquist, writing for a six-member majority in the case of Payne v. Tennessee, *said the previous ban on "victim impact" evidence in capital cases had "unfairly weighted" the scales of justice toward defendants, who could introduce mitigating evidence about their own behavior and life circumstances.*

An acerbic dissent came from Justice Thurgood Marshall, who hours later announced his resignation from the Court. (Resignation of Justice Marshall from Supreme Court, p. 377) *He contended that neither the law nor the facts had changed since the two previous cases were decided. "Only the personnel of this Court did," Marshall wrote, alluding to conservative-minded appointees of presidents Ronald Reagan and George Bush. "Power, not reason, is the new currency of this Court's decisionmaking."*

"Today's decision charts an unmistakable course," Marshall wrote. It portends "an even broader and more far-reaching assault upon this Court's precedents"—including the rights of minorities, women, and the indigent—and "will squander the authority and the legitimacy of this Court as a protector of the powerless."

In a similar vein, Justice John Paul Stevens authored a separate dissent, writing that the majority had "obviously been moved by an argument that has strong political appeal but no proper place in a reasoned judicial opinion." Stevens concluded by declaring, "Today is a sad day for a great institution."

Victim's Kin Tells Jury of Loss

The case arose from the trial of Pervis T. Payne, who was convicted of stabbing to death a young woman, Charisse Christopher, and her two-year-old daughter Lacie, and attempting to kill her three-year-old son Nicholas. The incident occurred in the woman's apartment in Millington, Tennessee, in June 1987.

Nicholas's grandmother, called by the prosecution, testified that "he cries for his mom. He doesn't seem to understand why she doesn't come home." In asking for the death penalty, the prosecutor told the jury: "There is nothing you can do to ease the pain of the families involved in this case. ... But there is something that you can do for Nicholas. ... He is going to want to know what type of justice was done. ... With your verdict, you will provide the answer." Payne was sentenced to death.

The Tennessee Supreme Court upheld the conviction and sentence, rejecting the defense argument that the admission of the grandmother's remarks and the prosecutor's argument had violated Payne's Eighth Amendment rights to a fair trial, as applied in the cases of Booth v. Maryland *in 1987 and* South Carolina v. Gathers *in 1989. Both were decided by 5-4 votes. The authors of the two opinions, Justices Lewis F. Powell, Jr. (Booth) and William J. Brennan (Gathers), had since retired. Their departures brought Justices Anthony M. Kennedy and David H. Souter to the bench. Both voted with the chief justice in the* Payne *decision.*

The decision elicited concurring opinions from Justices Sandra Day O'Connor, Antonin Scalia, Kennedy, and Souter. Justices Byron A. White joined in O'Connor's concurrence, while Justice Harry A. Blackmun joined in the dissenting opinions by Stevens and Marshall.

Defense of Discarding Precedents

Rehnquist, O'Connor, and Scalia all seemed at pains to defend the decision not to abide by Booth *and* Gathers. *Rehnquist said that* stare decisis, *the legal principal of letting precedent rule, "is usually the wise policy ... [but it] is not an inexorable command. ..." The chief justice said the Court was never constrained to follow precedent "when governing decisions are unworkable or are badly reasoned." He noted thirty-three constitutional decisions the Court had overturned, in part or in whole, during the past twenty terms.*

The Booth *and* Gathers *cases were the third and fourth constitutional precedents to be overruled in the 1990-1991 term. The court struck down* Arkansas v. Sanders, *a 1979 decision limiting the ability of the police to search automobiles without search warrants; and later a portion of* Chapman v. California, *a 1967 ruling that barred the use of any coerced confession in a criminal trial, was overruled. Still another precedent was struck down the same week* Payne *was issued. In* Coleman v. Thompson, *the Court restricted the right of state prisoners to file for relief in federal courts. The decision was based not on the Constitution, though, but on the Court's interpretation of a federal habeas corpus statute.*

Following are excerpts from the majority, concurring, and dissenting opinions in the Supreme Court's ruling of Payne v. Tennessee, *June 27, 1991, permitting evidence about the impact of a murder on the victim's family to be presented to a jury as it considers whether to invoke the death penalty:*

No. 90-5721

Pervis Tyrone Payne, Petitioner *v.* Tennessee	On writ of certiorari to the Supreme Court of Tennessee, Western Division

[June 27, 1991]

CHIEF JUSTICE REHNQUIST delivered the opinion of the court.

In this case we reconsider our holdings in *Booth* v. *Maryland* (1987), and *South Carolina* v. *Gathers* (1989), that the Eighth Amendment bars the admission of victim impact evidence during the penalty phase of a capital trial.

The petitioner, Pervis Tyrone Payne, was convicted by a jury on two counts of first-degree murder and one count of assault with intent to commit murder in the first degree. He was sentenced to death for each of the murders, and to 30 years in prison for the assault.

The victims of Payne's offenses were 28-year-old Charisse Christopher, her 2-year-old daughter Lacie, and her 3-year-old son Nicholas. The three lived together in an apartment in Millington, Tennessee, across the hall from Payne's girlfriend, Bobbie Thomas. On Saturday, June 27, 1987, Payne ... entered the Christophers' apartment, and began making sexual advances towards Charisse. Charisse resisted and Payne became violent....

Inside the apartment, the police encountered a horrifying scene. Blood covered the walls and floor throughout the unit. Charisse and her children were lying on the floor in the kitchen. Nicholas, despite several wounds inflicted by a butcher knife that completely penetrated through his body from front to back, was still breathing. Miraculously, he survived....

During the sentencing phase of the trial.... The State presented the testimony of Charisse's mother, Mary Zvolanek. When asked how Nicholas had been affected by the murders of his mother and sister, she responded:

> "He cries for his mom. He doesn't seem to understand why she doesn't come home. And he cries for his sister Lacie. He comes to me many times during the week and asks me, Grandmama, do you miss my Lacie. And I tell him yes. He

says, I'm worried about my Lacie."

In arguing for the death penalty during closing argument, the prosecutor commented on the continuing effects of Nicholas' experience, stating:

"... There is nothing you can do to ease the pain of any of the families involved in this case. There is nothing you can do to ease the pain of Bernice or Carl Payne, and that's a tragedy. There is nothing you can do basically to ease the pain of Mr. and Mrs. Zvolanek, and that's a tragedy. They will have to live with it the rest of their lives. There is obviously nothing you can do for Charisse and Lacie Jo. But there is something that you can do for Nicholas.

"Somewhere down the road Nicholas is going to grow up, hopefully. He's going to want to know what happened. And he is going to know what happened to his baby sister and his mother. He is going to want to know what type of justice was done. He is going to want to know what happened. With your verdict, you will provide the answer."

In the rebuttal to Payne's closing argument, the prosecutor stated:

"You saw the videotape this morning. You saw what Nicholas Christopher will carry in his mind forever. When you talk about cruel, when you talk about atrocious, and when you talk about heinous, that picture will always come into your mind, probably throughout the rest of your lives.

"... No one will ever know about Lacie Jo because she never had the chance to grow up. Her life was taken from her at the age of two years old. So, no there won't be a high school principal to talk about Lacie Jo Christopher, and there won't be anybody to take her to her high school prom. And there won't be anybody there—there won't be her mother there or Nicholas' mother there to kiss him at night. His mother will never kiss him good night or pat him as he goes off to bed, or hold him and sing him a lullaby.

"[Petitioner's attorney] wants you to think about a good reputation, people who love the defendant and things about him. He doesn't want you to think about the people who love Charisse Christopher, her mother and daddy who loved her. The people who loved little Lacie Jo, the grandparents who are still here. The brother who mourns for her every single day and wants to know where his best little playmate is. He doesn't have anybody to watch cartoons with him, a little one. These are the things that go into why it is especially cruel, heinous, and atrocious, the burden that that child will carry forever."

The jury sentenced Payne to death on each of the murder counts.

The Supreme Court of Tennessee affirmed the conviction and sentence. The court rejected Payne's contention that the admission of the grandmother's testimony and the State's closing argument constituted prejudicial violations of his rights under the Eighth Amendment as applied in *Booth* v. *Maryland* (1987), and *South Carolina* v. *Gathers* (1989). The court characterized the grandmother's testimony as "technically irrelevant," but concluded that it "did not create a constitutionally unacceptable risk of an arbitrary imposition of the death penalty and was harmless beyond a reasonable doubt."

The court determined that the prosecutor's comments during closing argument were "relevant to [Payne's] personal responsibility and moral guilt." The court explained that "[w]hen a person deliberately picks a butcher knife out of a kitchen drawer and proceeds to stab to death a twenty-eight-year-old mother, her two and one-half year old daughter and her three and one-half year old son, in the same room, the physical and mental condition of the boy he left for dead is surely relevant in determining his 'blameworthiness.' " The court concluded that any violation of Payne's rights under *Booth* and *Gathers* "was harmless beyond a reasonable doubt."

We granted certiorari to reconsider our holdings in *Booth* and *Gathers* that the Eighth Amendment prohibits a capital sentencing jury from considering "victim impact" evidence relating to the personal characteristics of the victim and the emotional impact of the crimes on the victim's family.

In *Booth*, the defendant robbed and murdered an elderly couple. As required by a state statute, a victim impact statement was prepared based on interviews with the victims' son, daughter, son-in-law, and granddaughter. The statement, which described the personal characteristics of the victims, the emotional impact of the crimes on the family, and set forth the family members' opinions and characterizations of the crimes and the defendant, was submitted to the jury at sentencing. The jury imposed the death penalty. The conviction and sentence were affirmed on appeal by the State's highest court.

This Court held by a 5-to-4 vote that the Eighth Amendment prohibits a jury from considering a victim impact statement at the sentencing phase of a capital trial. The Court made clear that the admissibility of victim impact evidence was not to be determined on a case-by-case basis, but that such evidence was *per se* inadmissible in the sentencing phase of a capital case except to the extent that it "relate[d] directly to the circumstances of the crime." In *Gathers*, decided two years later, the Court extended the rule announced in *Booth* to statements made by a prosecutor to the sentencing jury regarding the personal qualities of the victim.

The *Booth* Court began its analysis with the observation that the capital defendant must be treated as a " 'uniquely individual human bein[g]' " (quoting *Woodson* v. *North Carolina* (1976)), and therefore the Constitution requires the jury to make an individualized determination as to whether the defendant should be executed based on the " 'character of the individual and the circumstances of the crime' " (quoting *Zant* v. *Stephens* (1983)). The Court concluded that while no prior decision of this Court had mandated that only the defendant's character and immediate characteristics of the crime may constitutionally be considered, other factors are irrelevant to the capital sentencing decision unless they have "some bearing on the defendant's 'personal responsibility and moral guilt.' " (quoting *Enmund* v. *Florida* (1982)). To the extent that victim impact evidence presents "factors about which the defendant was unaware, and that were irrelevant to the decision to kill," the Court concluded, it has nothing to do with the "blameworthiness of a particular defendant." Evidence of the victim's character, the Court observed, "could well distract the sentencing jury from its constitutionally required task [of] determining whether the death penalty is appropriate in light of the background and record of the accused and the particular circumstances of the crime." The Court concluded that, except to the extent that victim impact evidence relates "directly to the circumstances of the crime," the prosecution may not introduce such evidence at a capital sentencing hearing because "it creates an impermissible risk that the capital sentencing decision will be made in an arbitrary manner."

Booth and *Gathers* were based on two premises: that evidence relating to a particular victim or to the harm that a capital defendant causes a victim's family do not in general reflect on the defendant's "blameworthiness," and that only evidence relating to "blameworthiness" is relevant to the capital sentencing decision. However, the assessment of harm caused by the defendant as a result of the crime charged has understandably been an important concern of the criminal law, both in determining the elements of the offense and in determining the appropriate punishment. . . .

The principles which have guided criminal sentencing—as opposed to criminal liability—have varied with the times. The book of Exodus prescribes the *Lex talionis*, "An eye for an eye, a tooth for a tooth." In England and on the continent of Europe, as recently as the 18th century crimes which would be regarded as quite minor today were capital offenses. . . .

Gradually the list of crimes punishable by death diminished, and legislatures began grading the severity of crimes in accordance with the harm done by the criminal. The sentence for a given offense, rather than being precisely fixed by the legislature, was prescribed in terms of a minimum and a maximum, with the actual sentence to be decided by the judge. With the increasing importance of probation, as opposed to imprisonment, as a part of the penological process, some States such as California developed the "indeterminate sentence," where the time of incarceration was left almost entirely to the penological authorities rather than to the courts. But more recently the pendulum has swung back. The Federal Sentencing Guidelines, which went into effect in 1987, provided for very precise calibration of sentences, depending upon a number of factors. These factors relate both to the subjective guilt of the defendant and to the harm caused by his acts.

Wherever judges in recent years have had discretion to impose sentence, the consideration of the harm caused by the crime has been an important factor in the exercise of that discretion. . . . Whatever the prevailing sentencing philosophy, the sentencing authority has always been free to consider a wide range of relevant material. In the federal system, we observed that "a judge may appropriately conduct an inquiry broad in scope, largely unlimited as to the kind of information he may consider, or the source from which it may come." *United States* v. *Tucker* (1972). . . .

The Maryland statute involved in *Booth* required that the presentence report in all felony cases include a "victim impact statement" which would describe the effect of the crime on the victim and his family. Congress and most of the States have, in recent years, enacted similar legislation to enable the sentencing authority to consider information about the harm caused by the crime committed by the defendant. The evidence involved in the present case was not admitted pursuant to any such enactment, but its purpose and effect was much the same as if it had been. . . .

"We have held that a State cannot preclude the sentencer from considering 'any relevant mitigating evidence' that the defendant proffers in support of a sentence less than death." *Eddings* v. *Oklahoma* (1982). Thus we have, as the Court observed in *Booth*, required that the capital defendant be treated as a " 'uniquely individual human bein[g].' " But it was never held or even suggested in any of our cases preceding *Booth* that the defendant, entitled as he was to individualized consideration, was to receive that consideration wholly apart from the crime which he had committed. The language quoted from *Woodson* in the *Booth* opinion was not intended to describe a class of evidence that *could not* be received, but a class of evidence which *must* be received. . . . This misreading of precedent in *Booth* has, we think, unfairly weighted the scales in a capital trial; while virtually no limits are placed on the relevant mitigating evidence a capital defendant may introduce concerning his own circumstances, the State is barred from either offering "a glimpse of the life" which a defendant "chose to extinguish," or demonstrating the loss to the victim's family and to society which have resulted from the defendant's homicide.

Booth reasoned that victim impact evidence must be excluded because it would be difficult, if not impossible, for the defendant to rebut such evidence without shifting the focus of the sentencing hearing away from the defendant, thus creating a " 'mini-trial' on the victim's character." In many cases the evidence relating to the victim is already before the jury at least in part because of its relevance at the guilt phase of the trial. But even as to additional evidence admitted at the sentencing phase, the mere fact that for tactical reasons it might not be prudent for the defense to rebut victim impact evidence makes the case no different than others in which a party is faced with this sort of a dilemma. . . .

Payne echoes the concern voiced in *Booth*'s case that the admission of victim impact evidence permits a jury to find that defendants whose victims were assets to their community are more deserving of punishment than those whose victims are perceived to be less worthy. As a general matter, however, victim impact evidence is not offered to encourage comparative judgments of this kind—for instance, that the killer of a hardworking, devoted parent deserves the death penalty, but that the murderer of a reprobate does not. It is designed to show instead *each* victim's "uniqueness as an individual human being," whatever the jury might think the loss to the community resulting from his death might be. . . .

Under our constitutional system, the primary responsibility for defining crimes against state law, fixing punishments for the commission of these crimes, and establishing procedures for criminal trials rests with the States. The state laws respecting crimes, punishments, and criminal procedure are of course subject to the overriding provisions of the United States Constitution. Where the State imposes the death penalty for a particular crime, we have held that the Eighth Amendment imposes special limitations upon that process. . . . But, as we noted in *California* v. *Ramos* (1983), "[b]eyond these limitations . . . the Court has deferred to the State's choice of substantive factors relevant to the penalty determination." . . . The States remain free, in capital cases, as well as others, to devise new procedures and new remedies to meet felt needs. Victim impact evidence is simply another form or method of informing the sentencing authority about the specific harm caused by the crime in question, evidence of a general type long considered by sentencing authorities. We think the *Booth* Court was wrong in stating that this kind of evidence leads to the arbitrary imposition of the death penalty. In the majority of cases, and in this case, victim impact evidence serves entirely legitimate purposes. In the event that evidence is introduced that is so unduly prejudicial that it renders the trial fundamentally unfair, the Due Process Clause of the Fourteenth Amendment provides a mechanism for relief. . . .

We are now of the view that a State may properly conclude that for the jury to assess meaningfully the defendant's moral culpability and blameworthiness, it should have before it at the sentencing phase evidence of the specific harm caused by the defendant. . . . By turning the victim into a "faceless stranger at the penalty phase of a capital trial," *Booth* deprives the State of the full moral force of its evidence and may prevent the jury from having before it all the information necessary to determine the proper punishment for a first-degree murder.

The present case is an example of the potential for such unfairness. The capital sentencing jury heard testimony from Payne's girlfriend that they met at church, that he was affectionate, caring, kind to her children, that he was not an abuser of drugs or alcohol, and that it was inconsistent with his character to have committed the murders. Payne's parents testified that he was a good son, and a clinical psychologist testified that Payne was an extremely polite prisoner and suffered from a low IQ. None of this testimony was related to the circumstances of Payne's brutal crimes. In contrast, the only evidence of the impact of Payne's offenses during the sentencing phase was Nicholas' grandmother's description—in response to a single question—that the child misses his mother and baby sister. Payne argues that the Eighth Amendment commands that the jury's death sentence must be set aside because the jury heard this testimony. But the testimony illustrated quite poignantly some of the harm that Payne's killing had caused; there is nothing unfair about allowing the jury to bear in mind that harm at the same time as it considers the mitigating evidence introduced by the defendant. . . .

We thus hold that if the State chooses to permit the admission of victim impact evidence and prosecutorial argument on that subject, the Eighth Amendment erects no *per se* bar. A State may legitimately conclude that evidence about the victim and about the impact of the murder on the victim's family is relevant to the jury's decision as to whether or not the death penalty should be imposed. There is no reason to treat such evidence differently than other relevant evidence is treated.

Payne and his *amicus* [friends-of-the-court petitions] argue that despite these numerous infirmities in the rule created by *Booth* and *Gathers*, we should adhere to the doctrine of *stare decisis* and stop short of overruling those cases. *Stare decisis* is the preferred course because it promotes the evenhanded, predictable, and consistent development of legal principles, fosters reliance on judicial decisions, and contributes to the actual and perceived integrity of the judicial process. Adhering to precedent "is usually the wise policy, because in most matters it is more important that the applicable rule of law be settled than it be settled right." [quoting] *Burnet* v. *Coronado Oil & Gas Co.* (1932). Nevertheless, when governing decisions are unworkable or are badly reasoned, "this Court has never felt constrained to follow precedent," [quoting] *Smith* v. *Allwright* (1944). *Stare decisis* is not an inexorable command....

[T]he Court has during the past 20 Terms overruled in whole or in part 33 of its previous constitutional decisions. *Booth* and *Gathers* were decided by the narrowest of margins, over spirited dissents challenging the basic underpinnings of those decisions. They have been questioned by members of the Court in later decisions, and have defied consistent application by the lower courts.... Reconsidering these decisions now, we conclude for the reasons heretofore stated, that they were wrongly decided and should be, and now are, overruled. We accordingly affirm the judgment of the Supreme Court of Tennessee.

Affirmed.

JUSTICE O'CONNOR, with whom JUSTICE WHITE and JUSTICE KENNEDY join, concurring.

... I agree with the Court that *Booth* v. *Maryland* and *Gathers* were wrongly decided. The Eighth Amendment does not prohibit a State from choosing to admit evidence concerning a murder victim's personal characteristics or the impact of the crime on the victim's family and community. *Booth* also addressed another kind of victim impact evidence—opinions of the victim's family about the crime, the defendant, and the appropriate sentence. As the Court notes in today's decision, we do not reach this issue as no evidence of this kind was introduced at petitioner's trial. Nor do we express an opinion as to other aspects of the prosecutor's conduct. As to the victim impact evidence that was introduced, its admission did not violate the Constitution. Accordingly, I join the Court's opinion.

JUSTICE SCALIA, with whom JUSTICE O'CONNOR and JUSTICE KENNEDY join as to Part II, concurring.

I

The Court correctly observes the injustice of requiring the exclusion of relevant aggravating evidence during capital sentencing, while requiring the admission of all relevant mitigating evidence....

II

... It seems to me difficult for those who were in the majority in *Booth* to hold themselves forth as ardent apostles of *stare decisis*. That doctrine, to the extent it rests upon anything more than administrative convenience, is merely the application to judicial precedents of a more general principle that the settled practices and expectations of a democratic society should generally not be disturbed by the courts. It is hard to have a genuine regard for *stare decisis* without honoring that more general principle as well. A decision of this Court which, while not overruling a prior holding, nonetheless announces a novel rule, contrary to long and unchallenged practice, and pronounces it to be the Law of the Land—such a decision, no less than an explicit overruling, should be approached with great caution. It was, I suggest, *Booth*, and not today's decision, that compromised the fundamental values underlying the doctrine of *stare decisis*.

JUSTICE SOUTER, with whom JUSTICE KENNEDY joins, concurring.

... I fully agree with the majority's conclusion, and the opinions expressed by the dissenters in *Booth* and *Gathers*, that nothing in the Eighth Amendment's condemnation of cruel and unusual punishment would require that evidence to be excluded....

I do not, however, rest my decision to overrule wholly on the constitutional error that I see in the cases in question. I must rely as well on my further view that *Booth* sets an unworkable standard of constitutional relevance that threatens, on its own terms, to produce such arbitrary consequences and uncertainty of application as virtually to guarantee a result far diminished from the case's promise of appropriately individualized sentencing for capital defendants. These conclusions will be seen to result from the interaction of three facts. First, although *Booth* was prompted by the introduction of a systematically prepared "victim impact statement" at the sentencing phase of the trial, *Booth*'s restriction of relevant facts to what the defendant knew and considered in deciding to kill applies to any evidence, however derived or presented. Second, details of which the defendant was unaware, about the victim and survivors, will customarily be disclosed by the evidence introduced at the guilt phase of the trial. Third, the jury that determines guilt will usually determine, or make recommendations about, the imposition of capital punishment....

... If we were to require the rules of guilt-phase evidence to be changed to guarantee the full effect of *Booth*'s promise to exclude consideration of specific facts unknown to the defendant and thus supposedly without significance in morally evaluating his decision to kill, we would seriously reduce the comprehensibility of most trials by depriving jurors of those details of context that allow them to understand what is being described. If, on the other hand, we are to leave the rules of trial evidence alone, *Booth*'s objective will not be attained without requiring a separate sentencing jury to be empaneled. This would be a major imposition on the States, however, and I suppose that no one would seriously consider adding such a further requirement....

Thus, the status quo is unsatisfactory and the question is whether the case that has produced it should be overruled.... In prior cases, when this Court has confronted a wrongly decided, unworkable precedent calling for some further action by the Court, we have chosen not to compound the original error, but to overrule the precedent. . . . Following this course here not only has itself the support of precedent but of practical sense as well. Therefore, I join the Court in its partial overruling of *Booth* and *Gathers*.

JUSTICE MARSHALL, with whom JUSTICE BLACKMAN joins, dissenting.

Power, not reason, is the new currency of this Court's decisionmaking. Four Terms ago, a five-Justice majority of this Court held that "victim impact" evidence of the type at issue in this case could not constitutionally be introduced during the penalty phase of a capital trial. *Booth* v. *Maryland* (1987). By another 5-4 vote, a majority of this Court rebuffed an attack upon this ruling just two Terms ago. *South Carolina* v. *Gathers* (1989). Nevertheless, having expressly invited respondent to renew the attack, today's majority. overrules *Booth* and *Gathers* and credits the dissenting views expressed in those cases. Neither the law nor the facts supporting *Booth* and *Gathers* underwent any change in the last four years. Only the personnel of this Court did.

In dispatching *Booth* and *Gathers* to their graves, today's majority ominously suggests that an even more extensive upheaval of this Court's precedents may be in store. . . . [T]he majority declares itself free to discard any principle of constitutional liberty which was recognized or reaffirmed over the dissenting votes of four Justices and with which five or more Justices *now* disagree. The implications of this radical new exception to the doctrine of *stare decisis* are staggering. The majority today sends a clear signal that scores of established constitutional liberties are now ripe for reconsideration, thereby inviting the very type of open defiance of our precedents that the majority rewards in this case. Because I believe that this Court owes more to its constitutional precedents in general and to *Booth* and *Gathers* in particular, I dissent.

I

Speaking for the Court as then constituted, Justice Powell and Justice Brennan set out the rationale for excluding victim-impact evidence from the sentencing proceedings in a capital case. . . . As Justice [Lewis] Powell explained in *Booth*, the probative value of such evidence is always outweighed by its prejudicial effect because of its inherent capacity to draw the jury's attention away from the character of the defendant and the circumstances of the crime to such illicit considerations as the eloquence with which family members express their grief and the status of the victim in the community. I continue to find these considerations wholly persuasive. . . .

There is nothing new in the majority's discussion of the supposed deficiencies in *Booth* and *Gathers*. Every one of the arguments made by the majority can be found in the dissenting opinions filed in those two cases, and . . . each argument was convincingly answered by Justice Powell and Justice Brennan.

But contrary to the impression that one might receive from reading the majority's lengthy rehearsing of the issues addressed in *Booth* and

Gathers, the outcome of this case does not turn simply on who—the *Booth* and *Gathers* majorities or the *Booth* and *Gathers* dissenters—had the better of the argument. Justice Powell and Justice Brennan's position carried the day in those cases and became the law of the land. The real question, then, is whether today's majority has come forward with the type of extraordinary showing that this Court has historically demanded before overruling one of its precedents. In my view, the majority clearly has not made any such showing. Indeed, the striking feature of the majority's opinion is its radical assertion that it need not even try.

II

The overruling of one of this Court's precedents ought to be a matter of great moment and consequence. Although the doctrine of *stare decisis* is not an "inexorable command," this Court has repeatedly stressed that fidelity to precedent is fundamental to "a society governed by the rule of law." ... Consequently, this Court has never departed from precedent without "special justification." *Arizona* v. *Rumsey* (1984). Such justifications include the advent of "subsequent changes or development in the law" that undermine a decision's rationale; the need "to bring [a decision] into agreement with experience and with facts newly ascertained"; and a showing that a particular precedent has become a "detriment to coherence and consistency in the law."

The majority cannot seriously claim that *any* of these traditional bases for overruling a precedent applies to *Booth* or *Gathers*.... The majority does assert that *Booth* and *Gathers* "have defied consistent application by the lower courts," but the evidence that the majority proffers is so feeble that the majority cannot sincerely expect anyone to believe this claim....

This truncation of the Court's duty to stand by its own precedents is astonishing. By limiting full protection of the doctrine of *stare decisis* to "cases involving property and contract rights," the majority sends a clear signal that essentially *all* decisions implementing the personal liberties protected by the Bill of Rights and the Fourteenth Amendment are open to reexamination....

III

Today's decision charts an unmistakable course. If the majority's radical reconstruction of the rules for overturning this Court's decisions is to be taken at face value—and the majority offers us no reason why it should not—then the overruling of *Booth* and *Gathers* is but a preview of an even broader and more far-reaching assault upon this Court's precedents. Cast aside today are those condemned to face society's ultimate penalty. Tomorrow's victims may be minorities, women, or the indigent. Inevitably, this campaign to resurrect yesterday's "spirited dissents" will squander the authority and the legitimacy of this Court as a protector of the powerless.

I dissent.

JUSTICE STEVENS, with whom JUSTICE BLACKMAN joins, dissenting.

The novel rule that the Court announces today represents a dramatic departure from the principles that have governed our capital sentencing jurisprudence for decades. JUSTICE MARSHALL is properly concerned about the majority's trivialization of the doctrine of *stare decisis*. But even if *Booth* and *Gathers* had not been decided, today's decision would represent a sharp break with past decisions. Our cases provide no support whatsoever for the majority's conclusion that the prosecutor may introduce evidence that sheds no light on the defendant's guilt or moral culpability, and thus serves no purpose other than to encourage jurors to decide in favor of death rather than life on the basis of their emotions rather than their reason.

Until today our capital punishment jurisprudence has required that any decision to impose the death penalty be based solely on evidence that tends to inform the jury about the character of the offense and the character of the defendant. Evidence that serves no purpose other than to appeal to the sympathies or emotions of the jurors has never been considered admissible. Thus, if a defendant, who had murdered a convenience store clerk in cold blood in the course of an armed robbery, offered evidence unknown to him at the time of the crime about the immoral character of his victim, all would recognize immediately that the evidence was irrelevant and inadmissible. Evenhanded justice requires that the same constraint be imposed on the advocate of the death penalty.

[I omitted]

II

Today's majority has obviously been moved by an argument that has strong political appeal but no proper place in a reasoned judicial opinion. Because our decision in *Lockett* recognizes the defendant's right to introduce all mitigating evidence that may inform the jury about his character, the Court suggests that fairness requires that the State be allowed to respond with similar evidence about the *victim*. This argument is a classic non sequitur: The victim is not on trial; her character, whether good or bad, cannot therefore constitute either an aggravating or mitigating circumstance.

...Just as the defendant is entitled to introduce any relevant mitigating evidence, so the State may rebut that evidence and may designate any relevant conduct to be an aggravating factor provided that the factor is sufficiently well defined and consistently applied to cabin the sentencer's discretion.

The premise that a criminal prosecution requires an evenhanded balance between the State and the defendant is also incorrect. The Constitution grants certain rights to the criminal defendant and imposes special limitations on the State designed to protect the individual from overreaching by the disproportionately powerful State. Thus, the State must prove a defendant's guilt beyond a reasonable doubt. Rules of evidence are also weighted in the defendant's favor. For example, the prosecution generally cannot introduce evidence of the defendant's character to prove his propensity to commit a crime, but the defendant can introduce such reputation evidence to show his law-abiding nature. Even if balance were required or desirable, today's decision, by permitting both the defendant and the State to introduce irrelevant evidence for the sentencer's consideration without any guidance, surely does nothing to enhance parity in the sentencing process.

III

Victim impact evidence, as used in this case, has two flaws, both related to the Eighth Amendment's command that the punishment of death may not be meted out arbitrarily or capriciously. First, aspects of the character of the victim unforeseeable to the defendant at the time of his crime are irrelevant to the defendant's "personal responsibility and moral guilt" and therefore cannot justify a death sentence....

Second, the quantity and quality of victim impact evidence sufficient to turn a verdict of life in prison into a verdict of death is not defined until after the crime has been committed and therefore cannot possibly be applied consistently in different cases. The sentencer's unguided consideration of victim impact evidence thus conflicts with the principle central to our capital punishment jurisprudence that, "where discretion is afforded a sentencing body on a matter so grave as the determination of whether a human life should be taken or spared, that discretion must be suitably directed and limited so as to minimize the risk of wholly arbitrary and capricious action." *Gregg* v. *Georgia* (1976)....

IV

.... In the case before us today, much of what might be characterized as victim impact evidence was properly admitted during the guilt phase of the trial and, given the horrible character of this crime, may have been sufficient to justify the Tennessee Supreme Court's conclusion that the error was harmless because the jury would necessarily have imposed the death sentence even absent the error....

In reaching our decision today, however, we should not be concerned with the cases in which victim impact evidence will not make a difference. We should be concerned instead with the cases in which it will make a difference. In those cases, defendants will be sentenced arbitrarily to death on the basis of evidence that would not otherwise be admissible because it is irrelevant to the defendants' moral culpability. The Constitution's proscription against the arbitrary imposition of the death penalty must necessarily proscribe the admission of evidence that serves no purpose other than to result in such arbitrary sentences.

V

The notion that the inability to produce an ideal system of justice in which every punishment is precisely married to the defendant's blameworthiness somehow justifies a rule that completely divorces some capital sentencing determinations from moral culpability is incomprehensible to me. Also incomprehensible is the argument that such a rule is required for the jury to take into account that each murder victim is a "unique" human being. The fact that each of us is unique is a proposition so obvious that it surely requires no evidentiary support. What is not obvious, however, is the way in which the character or reputation in one case may differ from that of other possible victims. Evidence offered to prove such differences can only be intended to identify some victims as more worthy of protection than others. . . .

Given the current popularity of capital punishment in a crime-ridden society, the political appeal of arguments that assume that increasing the severity of sentences is the best cure for the cancer of crime, and the political strength of the "victims' rights" movement, I recognize that today's decision will be greeted with enthusiasm by a large number of concerned and thoughtful citizens. The great tragedy of the decision, however, is the danger that the "hydraulic pressure" of public opinion that Justice Holmes once described . . . has played a role not only in the Court's decision to hear this case, and in its decision to reach the constitutional question without pausing to consider affirming on the basis of the Tennessee Supreme Court's rationale, but even in its resolution of the constitutional issue involved. Today is a sad day for a great institution.

July

USSR AND EASTERN EUROPE
ON END OF WARSAW PACT

July 1, 1991

The Warsaw Pact, Moscow's Cold War answer to the North Atlantic Treaty Organization (NATO), was dissolved July 1 at a meeting in Prague attended by leaders of the six member countries: Bulgaria, Czechoslovakia, Hungary, Poland, Romania, and the Soviet Union. This alliance, which Moscow had imposed on its former satellite states in Eastern Europe, effectively ceased to function after those countries emerged from Soviet control in 1989, but it lingered in name until the leaders formally signed a document in the Czech capital declaring that the Treaty of Friendship, Cooperation and Mutual Assistance—the pact's formal name—would "cease to be valid." It had been in effect since its signing in Warsaw on May 14, 1955.

Albania and East Germany had also been original signers of the treaty. Albania quit in 1968 after an ideological dispute with Moscow, and East Germany resigned in 1990 upon its unification with West Germany. The Soviet leadership, realizing the futility of trying to hold the alliance together, acquiesced in its abandonment.

Vaclav Havel of Czechoslovakia, the host president, jubilantly said after the meeting: "As of noon today, the Warsaw Pact no longer exists. We are saying goodbye to an era when Europe was divided by ideological intolerance." He noted at a news conference that "Prague, once the victim of the Warsaw Pact, is the city where the Warsaw Pact is meeting its end as an instrument of the cold war." Soviet troops and tanks, acting under Warsaw Pact authority, had moved into Prague in the spring of 1968 to subdue a Czech movement for self-rule. A Hungarian uprising for freedom had similarly been smashed in 1956.

Technically the Warsaw Treaty Organization would not expire until the signatory governments ratified the protocol in the weeks ahead. The defense and foreign ministers of the six countries had met February 27 in Budapest and announced that military cooperation under the Warsaw Pact would cease. On July 1 the organization's political framework was dismantled. The related Council for Mutual Economic Assistance—the Soviet-dominated trading bloc known as Comecon—was terminated on June 28.

Gennadi I. Yanayev, the ill-fated Soviet vice president, signed the document in Prague for President Mikhail S. Gorbachev, who remained in the Soviet Union to struggle with its domestic problems. The next month Yanayev engaged in an attempt to overthrow Gorbachev. He declared himself acting president while fellow conspirators forcibly detained Gorbachev at his vacation home in the Crimea. The coup attempt failed, and Yanayev was cast out of the vice presidency in disgrace. (Failure of Soviet Coup Attempt, p. 515)

At the signing ceremony, Yanayev called on Western leaders to dismantle NATO, but he drew no support from the East European leaders. Prime Minister Jozsef Antall of Hungary said: "The rejuvenated NATO represents a warranty for European security, and the same holds true for the presence of the United States in Europe. European integration and the Atlantic alliance are very compatible."

In previous months representatives of Czechoslovakia, Hungary, and Bulgaria had visited NATO headquarters in Brussels and expressed an interest in joining the alliance. In apparent response to such requests, the NATO foreign ministers issued a statement June 6 at their meeting in Copenhagen declaring that any "coercion or intimidation" of the countries of Central and Eastern Europe would be treated as a matter of "direct and material concern" to the sixteen NATO members.

Despite his scorn for the Warsaw Pact, Havel said its demise "is not a signal for us to restrict the significance and extent of our relations with our former allies in the East Bloc. We are and we will remain not only geographic neighbors, but above all prominent partners who have something to offer each other and are linked in many ways." In a similar vein, Antall predicted that the abolition of Comecon might result in friendlier ties with Moscow. "Now that the shackles are off our hands," he said, "we can extend a friendly hand."

In addition to Havel, Yanayev, and Antall, the signers of the Prague protocol were presidents Zhelyu Zhelev of Bulgaria, Lech Walesa of Poland, and Peter Roman of Romania.

Following is the protocol for terminating the Treaty of Friendship, Cooperation and Mutual Assistance (the Warsaw Pact), translated by the government of Czechoslovakia, signed in Prague, July 1, 1991, by representatives of Bulgaria, Czechoslovakia, Hungary, Poland, Romania, and the Soviet Union:

On terminating the validity of the Treaty of Friendship, Cooperation and Mutual Assistance, signed in Warsaw on May 14, 1955, and of the protocol on extending its validity, signed in Warsaw on April 26, 1985.

The states—parties to the Treaty of Friendship, Cooperation and Mutual Assistance, signed in Warsaw on May 14, 1955,

Bearing in mind the profound changes currently under way in Europe, which are bringing to an end the era of confrontation and division of the continent,

Resolved to actively develop, in the new situation, their relations on a bilateral and, if interested, on a multilateral basis,

Recalling the significance of the joint declaration of twenty-two states, which signed the Treaty on Conventional Armed Forces in Europe, and which declared that they are no longer enemies, and that they will build new relations of partnership and cooperation,

Resolved to promote gradual transition to all-European security structures, in the spirit of the arrangements made at the Paris Summit of the Conference on Security and Cooperation in Europe in November, 1990,

Have agreed as follows:

Article 1

The Treaty of Friendship, Cooperation and Mutual Assistance, signed in Warsaw on May 14, 1955 (henceforth referred to only as the Warsaw Treaty), and the Protocol extending the validity of the Treaty of Friendship, Cooperation and Mutual Assistance, signed in Warsaw on April 26, 1985, will cease to be valid on the day this protocol enters into force.

Article 2

The parties to this Protocol declare they claim no property towards one another, arising from the Warsaw Treaty.

Article 3

1. This Protocol is subject to ratification.
2. The original of the Protocol and the ratification instruments will be retained in the archives of the government of the Czech and Slovak Federal Republic. The government of the Czech and Slovak Federal Republic will inform the other parties to this Protocol on depositing every ratification instrument.

Article 4

The Protocol will enter into force on the day when the last ratification instrument is deposited in the archives.

Done in Prague on July 1, 1991, in one copy in each of the Czech, Bulgarian, Hungarian, Polish, Romanian and Russian languages, with all versions having equal validity. The authorized copies of this Protocol will be given by the government of the Czech and Slovak Federal Republic to all other parties to this protocol.

REPORT ON LOS ANGELES
POLICE DEPARTMENT ABUSES
July 9, 1991

An investigative commission concluded in a report issued July 9 that a "significant number of officers in the LAPD [Los Angeles Police Department] . . . repetitively use excessive force against the public and persistently ignore the written guidelines of the department regarding force." Police brutality "is a national problem," said Warren M. Christopher, the commission chairman, upon releasing the report. "We have conducted our study with an awareness that it might have considerable relevance for other cities, other police departments around the country. We hope that our findings will ignite a national effort to prevent the excessive use of force by police officers."

The investigation was triggered after the release of a videotape that showed four policemen beating a black motorist, Rodney King, who had been caught after a high-speed auto chase. Eleven other Los Angeles police officers, all white, stood by and watched. This scene was recorded by a nearby resident, George Holliday, who happened to be on his balcony trying out a new video camera. He sold the two-minute tape to the Cable News Network, which broadcast it nationwide on March 5, two days after the beating occurred.

Reaction across the country was swift and nearly unanimous in condemning the beating. President George Bush called it "sickening." Many news commentators, public officials, and citizens demanded that the Los Angeles Police Department take steps to prevent such incidents. Some, particularly in Los Angeles, demanded the resignation of Daryl F. Gates, the police chief since 1978.

On April 1, Los Angeles mayor Tom Bradley established the ten-

member "independent commission" headed by Christopher to conduct "a full and fair examination" of the police force. It supplanted an internal department investigation that Gates had ordered. The commission held five public hearings, received testimony from fifty expert witnesses, interviewed more than 300 current and former police officers, examined scores of citizen complaint reports, and conducted an opinion survey of 950 officers.

Findings and Recommendations

Among other things, the commission reviewed messages transmitted during a 180-day period over the department's high-speed Mobile Digital Terminal (MDT) network that links patrol cars to headquarters and each other. The commission said it detected numerous instances of callous attitudes toward suspects, contempt for racial and ethnic minorities, and a glorification of the use of force.

The commission found police officers reluctant to inform on misconduct by their colleagues. "Virtually all of the FTOs [field training officers] interviewed stated that they would report serious police misconduct," the report said. Yet the fact that few FTOs had ever filed a complaint against a fellow officer indicated that a "code of silence" was observed throughout the force. "The department not only failed to deal with the problem group of officers but it often rewarded them with positive evaluations and promotions," the report noted.

The commission recommended that the initial psychological evaluation process for applicants focus "less on test and oral interview results and more on an analysis of past behavior." It was also suggested that veteran officers be retested every three years "to uncover both psychological and physical problems."

To counteract attitudes expressed in some of the MDT messages, the commission recommended changes in the training of new officers, noting that the current eight-hour cultural awareness curriculum was "insufficient." The report noted that officers were imbued with "an organizational culture that emphasizes crime control over crime prevention and that isolates the police from the communities and the people they serve."

The commission found that "people who wish to file complaints [against the police] face significant hurdles. Some intake officers actively discourage filing by being uncooperative or requiring long waits.... In many heavily Latino divisions, there is often no Spanish speaking officer available to take complaints."

Declaring that the current system of handling complaints against the police "does not work," the commission recommended a "civilian oversight process" under the aegis of the existing police commission, which would establish an Office of the Inspector General to track complaints and any resulting disciplinary action.

Of the structural changes proposed by the commission, the most controversial was a recommendation that the police chief serve a five-year term, renewable for only one additional term. The panel also urged *that the power to appoint the police chief be shifted to the mayor from the police commission and that the chief's civil service protection be eliminated.*

Finally, the commission recommended that Gates be replaced. After weeks of resisting widespread demands that he step down, Gates announced July 22 that he planned to retire in April 1992, provided a successor had been selected by then.

Reaction

Most police chiefs were reluctant to comment on the Rodney King incident or the commission report. However, Texas Police Chief Thomas Windham said every police department in the country could "improve with a review as thorough as the Christopher Commission did." The commission report "will cause other cities to look more closely at their police problems," commented Hubert Williams, president of the Washington-based Police Foundation and former police chief in Newark, New Jersey. "We'll see positive changes in the attitude of police officers and less tolerance by citizens."

Following are the summary and first chapter of the "Report of the Independent Commission" on the conduct of the Los Angeles Police Department, released July 9, 1991:

Summary of Report

The videotaped beating of Rodney G. King by three uniformed officers of the Los Angeles Police Department, in the presence of a sergeant and with a large group of other officers standing by, galvanized public demand for evaluation and reform of police procedures involving the use of force. In the wake of the incident and the resulting widespread outcry, the Independent Commission on the Los Angeles Police Department was created. The Commission sought to examine all aspects of the law enforcement structure in Los Angeles that might cause or contribute to the problem of excessive force. The Report is unanimous.

The King beating raised fundamental questions about the LAPD, including:

- the apparent failure to control or discipline officers with repeated complaints of excessive force
- concerns about the LAPD's "culture" and officers' attitudes toward racial and other minorities
- the difficulties the public encounters in attempting to make complaints against LAPD officers
- the role of the LAPD leadership and civilian oversight authorities in addressing or contributing to these problems

These and related questions and concerns form the basis for the Commission's work.

Los Angeles and Its Police Force

The LAPD is headed by Police Chief Daryl Gates with an executive staff currently consisting of two assistant chiefs, five deputy chiefs, and 17 commanders. The City Charter provides that the Department is ultimately under the control and oversight of the five-member civilian Board of Police Commissioners. The Office of Operations, headed by Assistant Chief Robert Vernon, accounts for approximately 84 % of the Department's personnel, including most patrol officers and detectives. The Office of Operations has 18 separate geographic areas within the City, divided among four bureaus (Central, South, West, and Valley). There are currently about 8,450 sworn police officers, augmented by more than 2,000 civilian LAPD employees.

While the overall rate of violent crime in the United States increased three and one-half times between 1960 and 1989, the rate in Los Angeles during the same period was more than twice the national average. According to 1986 data recently published by the Police Foundation, the Los Angeles police were the busiest among the officers in the nation's largest six cities. As crime rates soar, police officers must contend with more and more potential and actual violence each day. One moment officers must confront a life-threatening situation; the next they must deal with citizen problems requiring understanding and kindness. The difficulties of policing in Los Angeles are compounded by its vast geographic area and the ethnic diversity of its population. The 1990 census data reflect how enormous that diversity is: Latinos constitute 40 % of the total population; Whites 37 %; African-Americans 13 %; and Asian/Pacific Islanders and others 10 %. Of the police departments of the six largest United States cities, the LAPD has the fewest officers per resident and the fewest officers per square mile. Yet the LAPD boasts more arrests per officer than other forces. Moreover, by all accounts, the LAPD is generally efficient, sophisticated, and free of corruption.

The Problem of Excessive Force

LAPD officers exercising physical force must comply with the Department's Use of Force Policy and Guidelines, a well as California law. Both the LAPD Policy and the Penal Code require that force be reasonable; the Policy also requires that force be necessary. An officer may resort to force only where he or she faces a credible threat, and then may use only the minimum amount necessary to control the suspect.

The Commission has found that there is a significant number of LAPD officers who repetitively misuse force and persistently ignore the written policies and guidelines of the Department regarding force. The evidence obtained by the Commission shows that this group has received inadequate supervisory and management attention.

Former Assistant Chief Jesse Brewer testified that this lack of management attention and accountability is the "essence of the excessive force problem. ... We know who the bad guys are. Reputations become well known, especially to the sergeants and then of course to lieutenants and the captains in the areas. . . . But I don't see anyone bring these people up. . . ." Assistant Chief David Dotson testified that "we have failed miserably" to hold supervisors accountable for excessive force by officers under their command. Interviews with a large number of present and former LAPD officers yield similar conclusions. Senior and rank-and-file officers generally stated that a significant number of officers tended to use force excessively, that these problem officers were well known in their divisions, that the Department's efforts to control or discipline those officers were inadequate, and that their supervisors were not held accountable for excessive use of force by officers in their command.

The Commission's extensive computerized analysis of the data provided by the Department (personnel complaints, use of force reports, and reports of officer-involved shootings) shows that a significant group of problem officers poses a much higher risk of excessive force than other officers:

- Of approximately 1,800 officers against whom an allegation of excessive force or improper tactics was made from 1986 to 1990, more than 1,400 had only one or two allegations. But 183 officers had four or more allegations, 44 had six or more, 16 had eight or more, and one had 16 such allegations.
- Of nearly 6,000 officers identified as involved in use of force reports from January 1987 to March 1991, more than 4,000 had fewer than five reports each. But 63 officers had 20 or more reports each. The top 5 % of the officers (ranked by number of reports) accounted for more than 20 % of all reports. . . .

Blending the data disclosed even more troubling patterns. For example, in the years covered, one officer had 13 allegations of excessive force and improper tactics, 5 other complaint allegations, 28 use of force reports, and 1 shooting. Another had 6 excessive force/improper tactics allegations, 19 other complaint allegations, 10 use of force reports, and 3 shootings. A third officer had 7 excessive force/improper tactic allegations, 7 other complaint allegations, 27 use of force reports, and 1 shooting.

A review of personnel files of the 44 officers identified from the LAPD database who had six or more allegations of excessive force or improper tactics for the period 1986 through 1990 disclosed that the picture conveyed was often incomplete and at odds with contemporaneous comments appearing in complaint files. As a general matter, the performance evaluation reports for those problem officers were very positive, documenting every complimentary comment received and expressing optimism about the officer's progress in the Department. The performance evaluations generally did not give an accurate picture of the officers' disciplinary history, failing to record "sustained" complaints or to discuss their significance, and failing to assess the officer's judgment and contacts with the public in light of disturbing patterns of complaints.

The existence of a significant number of officers with an unacceptable and improper attitude regarding the use of force is supported by the

Commission's extensive review of computer messages sent to and from patrol cars throughout the City over the units' Mobile Digital Terminals ("MDTs"). The Commission's staff examined 182 days of MDT transmissions selected from the period from November 1989 to March 1991. Although the vast majority of messages reviewed consisted of routine police communications, there were hundreds of improper messages, including scores in which officers talked about beating suspects: "Capture him, beat him and treat him like dirt. . . ." Officers also used the communications system to express their eagerness to be involved in shooting incidents. The transmissions also make clear that some officers enjoy the excitement of a pursuit and view it as an opportunity for violence against a fleeing suspect.

The patrol car transmissions can be monitored by a field supervisor and are stored in a database where they could be (but were not) audited. That many officers would feel free to type messages about force under such circumstances suggests a serious problem with respect to excessive force. That supervisors made no effort to monitor or control those messages evidences a significant breakdown in the Department's management responsibility.

The Commission also reviewed the LAPD's investigation and discipline of the officers involved in all 83 civil lawsuits alleging excessive or improper force by LAPD officers for the period 1986 through 1990 that resulted in a settlement or judgment of more than $15,000. A majority of cases involved clear and often egregious officer misconduct resulting in serious injury or death to the victim. The LAPD's investigation of these 83 cases was deficient in many respects, and discipline against the officers involved was frequently light and often nonexistent.

While the precise size and identity of the problem group of officers cannot be specified without significant further investigation, its existence must be recognized and addressed. The LAPD has a number of tools to promote and enforce its policy that only reasonable and necessary force be used by officers. There are rewards and incentives such as promotions and pay upgrades. The discipline system exists to impose sanctions for misconduct. Officers can be reassigned. Supervisors can monitor and counsel officers under their command. Officers can be trained at the Police Academy and, more importantly, in the field, in the proper use of force.

The Commission believes that the Department has not made sufficient efforts to use those tools effectively to address the significant number of officers who appear to be using force excessively and improperly. The leadership of the LAPD must send a much clearer and more effective message that excessive force will not be tolerated and that officers and their supervisors will be evaluated to an important extent by how well they abide by and advance the Department's policy regarding use of force.

Racism and Bias

The problem of excessive force is aggravated by racism and bias within the LAPD. That nexus is sharply illustrated by the results of a survey recently taken by the LAPD of the attitudes of its sworn officers. The survey of 960 officers found that approximately one-quarter (24.5 %) of 650 officers responding agreed that "racial bias (prejudice) on the part of officers toward minority citizens currently exists and contributes to a negative interaction between police and community." More than one-quarter (27.6 %) agreed that "an officer's prejudice towards the suspect's race may lead to the use of excessive force."

The Commission's review of MDT transmissions revealed an appreciable number of disturbing and recurrent racial remarks. Some of the remarks describe minorities through animal analogies ("sounds like monkey slapping time"). Often made in the context of discussing pursuits or beating suspects, the offensive remarks cover the spectrum of racial and ethnic minorities in the City ("I would love to drive down Slauson with a flame thrower ... we would have a barbecue"; "I almost got me a Mexican last night but he dropped the dam gun too quick, lots of wit"). The officers typing the MDT messages apparently had little concern that they would be disciplined for making such remarks. Supervisors failed to monitor the messages or to impose discipline for improper remarks and were themselves frequently the source of offensive comments when in the field.

These attitudes of prejudice and intolerance are translated into unacceptable behavior in the field. Testimony from a variety of witnesses depict the LAPD as an organization with practices and procedures that are conducive to discriminatory treatment and officer misconduct directed to members of minority groups. Witnesses repeatedly told of LAPD officers verbally harassing minorities, detaining African-American and Latino men who fit certain generalized descriptions of suspects, employing unnecessarily invasive or humiliating tactics in minority neighborhoods and using excessive force. While the Commission does not purport to adjudicate the validity of any one of these numerous complaints, the intensity and frequency of them reveal a serious problem.

Bias within the LAPD is not confined to officers' treatment of the public, but is also reflected in conduct directed to fellow officers who are members of racial or ethnic minority groups. The MDT messages and other evidence suggest that minority officers are still too frequently subjected to racist slurs and comments and to discriminatory treatment within the Department. While the relative number of officers who openly make racially derogatory comments or treat minority officers in a demeaning manner is small, their attitudes and behavior have a large impact because of the failure of supervisors to enforce vigorously and consistently the Department's policies against racism. That failure conveys to minority and non-minority officers alike the message that such conduct is in practice condoned by the Department.

The LAPD has made substantial progress in hiring minorities and women since the 1981 consent decree settling discrimination lawsuits against the Department. That effort should continue, including efforts to recruit Asians and other minorities who are not covered by the consent decree. The Department's statistics show, however, that the vast majority of minority officers are concentrated in the entry level police officer ranks in the Department. More than 80 % of African-American, Latino and Asian officers hold the rank of Police Officer I-III. Many minority officers cite white dominance of managerial positions within the LAPD as one reason for the Department's continued tolerance of racially motivated language and behavior.

Bias within the LAPD is not limited to racist and ethnic prejudices but includes strongly felt bias based on gender and sexual orientation. Current LAPD policy prohibits all discrimination, including that based on sexual orientation. A tension remains, however, between the LAPD's official policy and actual practice. The Commission believes that the LAPD must act to implement fully its formal policy of nondiscrimination in the recruitment and promotion of gay and lesbian officers.

A 1987 LAPD study concluded that female officers were subjected to a double standard and subtle harassment and were not accepted as part of the working culture. As revealed in interviews of many of the officers charged with training new recruits, the problem has not abated in the last four years. Although female LAPD officers are in fact performing effectively, they are having a difficult time being accepted on a full and equal basis.

The Commission heard substantial evidence that female officers utilize a style of policing that minimizes the use of excessive force. Data examined by the Commission indicate that LAPD female officers are involved in use of excessive force at rates substantially below those of male officers. Those statistics, as confirmed by both academic studies and anecdotal evidence, also indicate that women officers perform at least as well as their male counterparts when measured by traditional standards.

The Commission believes that the Chief of Police must seek tangible ways, for example, through the use of the discipline system, to establish the principle that racism and bias based on ethnicity, gender, or sexual orientation will not be tolerated within the Department. Racism and bias cannot be eliminated without active leadership from the top. Minority and female officers must be given full and equal opportunity to assume leadership positions in the LAPD. They must be assigned on a fully nondiscriminatory basis to the more desirable, "coveted" positions and promoted on the same nondiscriminatory basis to supervisory and managerial positions.

Community Policing

The LAPD has an organizational culture that emphasizes crime control over crime prevention and that isolates the police from the communities and the people they serve. With the full support of many, the LAPD insists on aggressive detection of major crimes and a rapid, seven-minute response time to calls for service. Patrol officers are evaluated by statistical measures (for example, the number of calls handled and arrests made) and are rewarded for being "hardnosed." This style of policing produces results, but it does so at the risk of creating a siege mentality that alienates the officer from the community.

Witness after witness testified to unnecessarily aggressive confrontations between LAPD officers and citizens, particularly members of minority communities. From the statements of these citizens, as well as many present and former senior LAPD officers, it is apparent that too many LAPD patrol officers view citizens with resentment and hostility; too many treat the public with rudeness and disrespect. LAPD officers themselves seem to recognize the extent of the problem: nearly two-thirds (62.9 %) of the 650 officers who responded to the recent LAPD survey expressed the opinion that "increased interaction with the community would improve the Department's relations with citizens."

A model of community policing has gained increased acceptance in other parts of the country during the past 10 years. The community policing model places service to the public and prevention of crime as the primary role of police in society and emphasizes problem solving, with active citizen involvement in defining those matters that are important to the community, rather than arrest statistics. Officers at the patrol level are required to spend less time in their cars communicating with other officers and more time on the street communicating with citizens. Proponents of this style of policing insist that addressing the causes of crime makes police officers more effective crime-fighters, and at the same time enhances the quality of life in the neighborhood.

The LAPD made early efforts to incorporate community policing principles and has continued to experiment with those concepts. For example, the LAPD's nationally recognized DARE program has been viewed by officers and the public alike as a major achievement. The LAPD remains committed, however, to its traditional style of law enforcement with an emphasis on crime control and arrests. LAPD officers are encouraged to command and to confront, not to communicate. Community policing concepts, if successfully implemented, offer the prospect of effective crime prevention and substantially improved community relations. Although community-based policing is not a panacea for the problem of crime in society, the LAPD should carefully implement this model on a City-wide basis. This will require a fundamental change in values. The Department must recognize the merits of community involvement in matters that affect local neighborhoods, develop programs to gain an adequate understanding of what is important to particular communities, and learn to manage departmental affairs in ways that are consistent with the community views expressed. Above all, the Department must understand that it is accountable to all segments of the community.

Recruitment

Although 40 % of the candidates for admission to the Police Academy are disqualified as a result of psychological testing and background investigation, the Commission's review indicated that the initial psychological evaluation is an ineffective predictor of an applicant's tendencies toward violent behavior and that the background investigation pays too little attention to a candidate's history of violence. Experts agree that the best predictor of future behavior is previous behavior. Thus, the background investigation offers the best hope of screening out violence-prone applicants. Unfortunately, the background investigators are overworked and inadequately trained.

Improved screening of applicants is not enough. Police work modifies behavior. Many emotional and psychological problems may develop during an officer's tenure on the force. Officers may enter the force well suited psychologically for the job, but may suffer from burnout, alcohol-related problems, cynicism, or disenchantment, all of which can result in poor control over their behavior. A person's susceptibility to the behavior-modifying experiences of police work may not be revealed during even the most skilled and sophisticated psychological evaluation process. Accordingly, officers should be retested periodically to determine both psychological and physical problems. In addition, supervisors must understand their role to include training and counseling officers to cope with the problems policing can often entail, so that they may be dealt with before an officer loses control or requires disciplinary action.

Training

LAPD officer training has three phases. Each recruit spends approximately six months at the Police Academy. The new officer then spends one year on probation working with more experienced patrol officers who serve as field training officers ("FTOs"). Thereafter, all officers receive continuing training, which includes mandatory field training and daily training at roll call. The Commission believes that in each phase of the training additional emphasis is needed on the use of verbal skills rather than physical force to control potentially volatile situations and on the development of human relationship skills.

The quality of instruction at the Police Academy is generally impressive. However, at present the curriculum provides only eight hours in cultural awareness training. No more than 1-1/2 hours is devoted to any ethnic group. Substantially more training on this important topic is essential. In addition, the Academy's current Spanish language program needs to be reviewed and current deficiencies corrected. Officers with an interest in developing broader language skills should be encouraged to do so.

Upon graduation the new officer works as a "probationary officer" assigned to various field training officers. The FTOs guide new officers' first contacts with citizens and have primary responsibility for introducing the probationers to the culture and traditions of the Department. The Commission's interviews of FTOs in four representative divisions revealed that many FTOs openly perpetuate the siege mentality that alienates patrol officers from the community and pass on to their trainees confrontational attitudes and disrespect for the public. This problem is in part the result of flaws in the way FTOs are selected and trained. The hiring of a very large number of new officers in 1989, which required the use of less experienced FTOs, greatly exacerbated the problem.

Any officer promoted to Police Officer III by passing a written examination covering Department policies and procedures is eligible to serve as an FTO. At present there are no formal eligibility or disqualification criteria for the FTO position based on an applicants' disciplinary records. Fourteen of the FTOs in the four divisions the Commission studied had been promoted to FTO despite having been disciplined for use of excessive force or use of improper tactics. There also appears to be little emphasis on selecting FTOs who have an interest in training junior officers, and an FTO's training ability is given little weight in his or her evaluation.

The most influential training received by a probationer comes from the example set by his or her FTO. Virtually all of the FTOs interviewed stated that their primary objective in training probationers is to instill good "officer safety skills." While the Commission recognizes the importance of such skills in police work, the probationers' world is quickly divided into "we/they" categories, which is exacerbated by the failure to integrate any cultural awareness or sensitivity training into field training.

The Commission believes that, to become FTOs, officers should be required to pass written and oral tests designed to measure communications skills, teaching aptitude, and knowledge of Departmental policies regarding appropriate use of force, cultural sensitivity, community relations, and nondiscrimination. Officers with an aptitude for and interest in training junior officers should be encouraged by effective incentives to apply for FTO positions. In addition, the training programs for FTOs should be modified to place greater emphasis on communication skills and the appropriate use of force. Successful completion of FTO School should be required before an FTO begins teaching probationers.

Promotion, Assignment, and Other Personnel Issues

In the civil service process for promotion of officers in the LAPD, the information considered includes performance evaluations, educational and training background, and all sustained complaints. The number and nature of any not sustained complaints, however, are not considered. The Commission recommends that a summary of not sustained complaints be considered in promotion decisions, as well as in paygrade advancements and assignments to desirable positions that are discretionary within the LAPD and outside the civil service system.

This is not to say that a past complaint history, even including a sustained complaint for excessive force, should automatically bar an officer from promotion. But there should be a careful consideration of the officer's complaint history including a summary of not sustained complaints, and particularly multiple complaints with similar fact patterns.

Complaint histories should also be considered in assignment of problem officers who may be using force improperly. For example, a problem officer can be paired with an officer with excellent communications skills that may lessen the need for use of force, as opposed to a partner involved in prior incidents of force with that problem officer. Another example is assignments to the jail facilities where potential for abuse by officers with a propensity to use excessive force is high. As several incidents examined by the Commission made clear, transfer of an officer to another geographical area is not likely to address a problem of excessive force without other remedial measures such as increased supervising, training and counseling.

Since 1980 the Department has permitted police officers working in patrol to select the geographic area or division for their patrol assignment subsequent to their initial assignment after completion of probation. As a result, sergeants and patrol officers tend to remain in one division for extended periods. The Commission believes that assignment procedures should be modified to require rotation through various divisions to ensure that officers work in a wide range of police functions and varied patrol locations during their careers. Such a rotation program will increase officers' experience and also will enable the Department to deploy police patrols with greater diversity throughout the City.

Under the current promotion system officers generally must leave patrol to advance within the Department. Notwithstanding the importance of the patrol function, therefore, the better officers are encouraged to abandon patrol. To give patrol increased emphasis and to retain good, experienced officers, the LAPD should increase rewards and incentives for patrol officers.

Personnel Complaints and Officer Discipline

No area of police operations received more adverse comment during the Commission's public hearings than the Department's handling of complaints against LAPD officers, particularly allegations involving the use of excessive force. Statistics make the public's frustration understandable. Of the 2,152 citizen allegations of excessive force from 1986 through 1990, only 42 were sustained.

All personnel complaints are reviewed by a captain in the LAPD's Internal Affairs Division ("IAD") to determine whether the complaint will be investigated by IAD or the charged officer's division. Generally IAD investigates only a few cases because of limited resources. Wherever investigated, the matter is initially adjudicated by the charged officer's division commanding officer, with a review by the area and bureau commanders.

The Commission has found that the complaint system is skewed against complainants. People who wish to file complaints face significant hurdles. Some intake officers actively discourage filing by being uncooperative or requiring long waits before completing a complaint form. In many heavily Latino divisions, there is often no Spanish speaking officer available to take complaints.

Division investigations are frequently inadequate. Based on a review of more than 700 complaint investigation files, the Commission found many deficiencies. For example, in a number of complaint files the Commission reviewed, there was no indication that the investigators had attempted to identify or locate independent witnesses or, if identified, to interview them. IAD investigations, on the whole, were of a higher quality than the division investigations. Although the LAPD has a special "officer involved shooting team," the Commission also found serious flaws in the investigation of shooting cases. Officers are frequently interviewed as a group, and statements are often not recorded until the completion of a "pre-interview."

The process for complaint adjudication is also flawed. First, there is no uniform basis for categorizing witnesses as "independent" or "non-involved" as opposed to "involved," although that distinction can determine whether a complaint is "not sustained" or "sustained." Some commanding officers also evaluate witnesses' credibility in inconsistent and biased ways that improperly favor the officer. Moreover, even when excessive force complaints are sustained, the punishment is more lenient than it should be. As explained by one deputy chief, there is greater punishment for conduct that embarrasses the Department (such as theft or drug use) than for conduct that reflects improper treatment of citizens. Statistical data also support the inference that the Department treats excessive force violations more leniently than it treats other types of officer misconduct.

Perhaps the greatest single barrier to the effective investigation and adjudication of complaints is the officers' unwritten code of silence: an officer does not provide adverse information against a fellow officer. While loyalty and support are necessary qualities, they cannot justify the violation of an officer's public responsibilities to ensure compliance with the law, including LAPD regulations.

A major overhaul of the disciplinary system is necessary to correct these problems. The Commission recommends creation of the Office of the Inspector General within the Police Commission with responsibility to oversee the disciplinary process and to participate in the adjudication and punishment of the most serious cases. The Police Commission should be responsible for overseeing the complaint intake process. Citizens must believe they can lodge complaints that will be investigated and determined fairly. All complaints relating to excessive force (including improper tactics) should be investigated by IAD, rather than at the involved officer's division, and should be subject to periodic audits by the Inspector General. While the Chief of Police should remain the one primarily responsible for imposing discipline in individual cases, the Police Commission should set guidelines as a matter of policy and hold the Chief accountable for following them.

Structural Issues

Although the City Charter assigns the Police Commission ultimate control over Department policies, its authority over the Department and the Chief of Police is illusory. Structural and operational constraints greatly weaken the Police Commission's power to hold the Chief accountable and therefore its ability to perform its management responsibilities, including effective oversight. Real power and authority reside in the Chief.

The Chief of Police is the general manager and chief administrative officer of the Police Department. The Police Commission selects the Chief from among top competitors in a civil service examination administered by the Personnel Department. Candidates from outside the Department are disadvantaged by City Charter provisions and seniority rules.

The Chief's civil service status largely protects him or her from disciplinary action or discharge by giving him a "substantial property right" in his job and declaring that he cannot be suspended or removed except for "good and sufficient cause" based upon an act or omission occurring within the prior year. In addition, recently enacted Charter Amendment 5 empowers the City Council to review and override the actions of the City's commissions, including the Police Commission.

The Police Commission's staff is headed by the Commanding Officer, Commission Operations, a sworn LAPD officer chosen by the Police Commissioners, who normally serves in that post for two to three years. Because the Police Commission depends heavily on the Commanding Officer to review information received from the Department and to identify issues, it must also rely on his willingness to criticize his superior officers. However, he lacks the requisite independence because his future transfer and promotion are at the discretion of the Chief of Police, and he is part of the Chief's command structure as well as being answerable to the Police Commission.

The Police Commission receives summaries, prepared by the Department, of disciplinary actions against sworn officers, but cannot itself impose discipline. The summaries are brief and often late, making it impossible for the Police Commission to monitor systematically the discipline imposed by the Chief in use of force and other cases.

The Commission believes that the Department should continue to be under the general oversight and control of a five-member, part-time citizen Police Commission. Commissioners' compensation should be increased substantially. They should serve a maximum of five years with staggered terms. The Police Commission's independent staff should be increased by adding civilian employees, including management auditors, computer systems data analysts, and investigators with law enforcement experience. It is vital that the Police Commission's staff be placed under the control of an independent civilian Chief of Staff, a general manager level employee.

The Chief of Police must be more responsive to the Police Commission and the City's elected leadership, but also must be protected against improper political influences. To achieve this balance, the Chief should serve a five-year term, renewable at the discretion of the Police Commission for one additional five-year term. The selection, tenure, discipline, and removal of the Chief should be exempted from existing civil service provisions. The Chief should be appointed by the Mayor, with advice from the Police Commission and the consent of the City Council after an open competition. The Police Commission should have the authority to terminate the Chief prior to the expiration of the first or second five-year term, but the final decision to terminate should require the concurrence of the Mayor and be subject to a reversal by vote of two-thirds of the City Council.

Implementation

Full implementation of this Report will require action by the Mayor, the City Council, the Police Commission, the Police Department, and ultimately the voters. To monitor the progress of reform, the City Council should require reports on implementation at six month intervals from the Mayor, the Council's own Human Resources and Labor Relations Committee, the Police Commission, and the Police Department. The Commission should reconvene in six months to assess the implementation of its recommendations and to report to the public.

Chief Gates has served the LAPD and the City 42 years, the past 13 years as Chief of Police. He has achieved a noteworthy record of public service in a stressful and demanding profession. For the reasons set forth in support of the recommendation that the Chief of Police be limited to two five-year terms, the Commission believes that commencement of a transition in that office is now appropriate. The Commission also believes that the interests of harmony and healing would be served if the Police Commission is now reconstituted with members not identified with the recent controversy involving the Chief.

More than any other factor, the attitude and actions of the leaders of the Police Department and other City agencies will determine whether the recommendations of this Report are adopted. To make genuine progress on issues relating to excessive force, racism and bias, leadership must avoid sending mixed signals. We urge those leaders to give priority to stopping the use of excessive force and curbing racism and bias and thereby to bring the LAPD to a new level of excellence and esteem throughout Los Angeles.

Chapter One:
The Rodney King Beating and the Questions It Has Raised

Rodney G. King—March 3, 1991

Rarely has the work of an amateur photographer so captured the nation's attention as did the dramatic and disturbing scene recorded by George Holliday's video camera in the early morning of March 3, 1991—the morning Rodney G. King, a 25-year-old African-American, was beaten by three uniformed officers of the Los Angeles Police Department while a sergeant and a large group of LAPD, California Highway patrol, and Los Angeles Unified School District officers stood by. The Holliday tape showed the officers clubbing King with 56 baton strokes and kicking him in the head and body. Within days, television stations across the country broadcast and rebroadcast the tape, provoking a public outcry against police abuse.

This Commission is not responsible for determining the culpability of the officers involved in the King incident; that is properly in the hands of the courts. Nevertheless, the King incident is described here in some detail because it was that event that led to the creation of this Commission, and because in many respects the King beating raises most of the issues we consider.

The Pursuit

California Highway Patrol Officers Melanie Singer and Timothy Singer first observed King's white Hyundai at approximately 12:40 a.m. on Sunday morning, March 3, 1991, in the Pacoima area of the northeastern San Fernando Valley in Los Angeles. King's vehicle was approaching from the rear of the CHP vehicle at a high speed as the Singers drove westbound on the Interstate 210 freeway. King was driving, accompanied by two passengers, both of whom were also African-Americans. King passed the patrol car and then slowed. The CHP unit left the freeway and immediately reentered to pace King's vehicle, which had resumed traveling at a high speed.

The CHP officers reported that King's vehicle "was traveling at 110 to 115 m.p.h. (using the #1, 2 and 3 lanes)." (Some have questioned whether a Hyundai is capable of being driven in excess of 100 m.p.h.) The CHP unit activated its emergency lights and siren. King slowed somewhat, but failed to stop. Instead, he left the freeway and continued through a stop sign at the bottom of the ramp at approximately 50 m.p.h. King drove westbound at a high speed (estimated at 80 m.p.h.), reportedly running a red light. One passenger in King's car, Bryant Allen, reportedly urged King to slow down and pull over. The other passenger, Freddie Helms, said he was asleep during the entire chase. (Helms subsequently died in an unrelated traffic accident.)

LAPD patrol car unit 16A23, assigned to Officers Laurence M. Powell and Timothy Wind, joined the pursuit as the LAPD's primary pursuit car. A Los Angeles Unified School District Police squad car which was in the area also joined the pursuit.

King apparently stopped at a red light at the corner of Osborne Street and Foothill Boulevard in Lakeview Terrace. When the light turned green, King pulled through the intersection and came to a stop. The time was 12:50 a.m. An LAPD unit, probably 16A23, radioed a "Code 6"—indicating that the chase had concluded.

Arrival of Additional LAPD Units

Following the Code 6 broadcast from the field, the LAPD Radio Transmission Operator (RTO) reported the Code 6 and "cleared" the broadcast frequencies so that units in other divisions monitoring the pursuit could return to normal transmissions. Approximately 60 seconds later, an unknown voice reported to the RTO, "... Foothill and Osborne, there appears to be sufficient units here." At 12:50:50 a.m., the RTO broadcast a "Code 4." According to the LAPD manual, a Code 4 notifies all units that "additional assistance is not needed at the scene" and indicates that all units not at the scene "shall return to their assigned patrol area."

In all, 11 additional LAPD units (including one helicopter) with 21 officers arrived at the end-of-pursuit scene. At least 12 of the officers arrived following the Code 4 broadcast. A number of these officers had no convincing explanation for why they went to the scene after the Code 4 broadcast. For example, five of the officers were at Foothill Station doing paperwork at the end of their shift when they heard the pursuit broadcast on the radio. The five took two separate cars, joined the pursuit, and continued to its termination after the Code 4. One of these officers told District Attorney investigators that he proceeded to the scene after the Code 4 "to see what was happening."

Officers Theodore J. Briseno and Rolando Solano heard a radio call of the CHP pursuit and were heading toward the pursuit when they were designated the LAPD's secondary pursuit car. They then heard that the pursuing units were Code 6, saw flashing police lights off in the distance, and proceeded to the scene. As they parked, King was beginning to get out of his car in response to directions from officers at the site. Sergeant Stacey Koon also arrived at the scene as the pursuit ended. Sergeant Koon was an assigned field supervisor responsible for monitoring the activities of Foothill officers.

Beating and Arrest

Disputed Events Before the Holliday Video. At the termination of the pursuit, CHP Officer Timothy Singer, following "felony stop" procedures, used a loudspeaker to order all occupants out of King's car. Passengers Allen and Helms exited the car on the right-hand side. According to Koon and Powell, King initially refused to comply with the order to leave his car. Both stated that when he finally did leave the car, he did not follow directions, reentered the car, and then came back out.

In a statement to the press on March 6, 1991, King insisted he had followed orders to exit the car. Passenger Allen told investigators that King responded to the initial command, but neglected to unbuckle his seat belt, thus requiring him to sit down again to undo it before actually leaving the car.

CHP Officer Melanie Singer told District Attorney investigators that she began to approach King intending to perform a "felony kneeling" procedure to take him into custody. However, the LAPD sergeant told her to stay back, "that they [the LAPD] would handle it."

When King first stepped out of the car, Koon said he "felt threatened, but felt enough confidence in his officers to take care of the situation." Koon described King as big and muscular. (The arrest report lists King as 6'3" tall, weighing 225 pounds.) He said he believed King was "disoriented and unbalanced" and under the influence of PCP.

After he left the car, King was ordered to lie flat on the ground. According to Koon and Powell, King responded by getting down on all fours, slapping the ground, and refusing to lie down. Powell said he tried to force King to the ground, but King rose up and almost knocked him off his feet.

Use of the Taser

Koon ordered the officers to "stand clear." King was still on the ground. Koon fired the Taser electric stun gun once, and then again. Koon subsequently reported that King did not respond to either firing. Powell's arrest report states that the Taser "temporarily halt[ed] deft's [King's] attack," and Solano stated that the Taser appeared to affect King at first because the suspect shook and yelled for almost five seconds.

Beating with Batons: Events on the Holliday Video

As George Holliday's videotape begins, King is on the ground. He rose and moved toward Powell. Solano termed it a "lunge," and said it was in the direction of Koon. It is not possible to tell from the videotape if King's movement is intended as an attack or simply an effort to get away. Taser wires can be seen coming from King's body.

As King moved forward, Powell struck King with his baton. The blow hit King's head, and he went down immediately. Powell hit King several additional times with his baton. The videotape shows Briseno moving in to try to stop Powell from swinging, and Powell then backing up. Koon reportedly yelled "that's enough." King then rose to his knees; Powell and Wind continued to hit King with their batons while he was on the ground. King was struck again and again.

Koon acknowledged that he ordered the baton blows, directing Powell and Wind to hit King with "power strokes." According to Koon, Powell and Wind used "bursts of power strokes, then backed off."

Notwithstanding the repeated "power strokes" with the batons, the tape shows that King apparently continued to try to get up. Koon ordered the officers to "hit his joints, hit his wrists, hit his elbows, hit his knees, hit his ankles." Powell said he tried to strike King only in the arms and legs.

Finally, after 56 baton blows and six kicks, five or six officers swarmed in and placed King in both handcuffs and cordcuffs restraining his arms and legs. King was dragged on his stomach to the side of the road to await arrival of a rescue ambulance.

King's Passengers

Bryant Allen and Freddie Helms both complied with officers' commands at the end of the pursuit to exit the Hyundai and to lie flat on the ground, in the so-called "prone-out" position. They were immediately handcuffed. A School District police officer had his gun drawn on the two of them as they lay on the ground on the passenger side of the car.

Passengers Allen and Helms both heard screams from King, but could not see any of the beating because of their positions on the right side of the car. They were ordered not to look and to keep their heads on the ground. According to Helms, when he raised his head to get it out of the dirt, he was kicked in the side and hit in the head with a baton, drawing blood. Helms was treated at Huntington Memorial Hospital the next morning. Allen alleged he was kicked several times. After King had been handcuffed, Allen and Helms were pulled to their feet, taken to CHP squad cars, asked for identification, checked by computer, and released on the scene.

Racial References During the Incident

The officers involved in the use of force, as well as those who witnessed the incident, denied that any racial epithets or slurs were used. King told reporters in March 1991 that he heard "a little bit of yelling," but that "they beat me so bad I would not pay attention to what they were saying." By early May 1991, however, King, through his attorney Steven Lerman, maintained that officers repeatedly screamed racial slurs during the incident.

On May 7, 1991, Los Angeles public television station KCET broadcast an "enhanced audio" version of George Holliday's videotape. According to KCET, the enhanced video indicates that as King is being beaten, an officer is yelling "nigger, hands behind your back—your back." An audio enhancement done for the Los Angeles County District Attorney's Office, on the other hand, was described as "inconclusive."

Post-Arrest Events

King was taken by rescue ambulance to Pacifica Hospital of the Valley for emergency treatment. Wind and Officer Susan Clemmer rode with King in the ambulance. King received 20 stitches, including five on the inside of his mouth, and was then transferred to the jail ward at County-USC Medical Center. Medical records indicate that King had a broken cheekbone and a broken right ankle. In his negligence claim filed with the City, King alleged he had suffered "11 skull fractures, permanent brain damage, broken [bones and teeth] kidney damage [and] emotional and physical trauma."

Blood and urine samples taken from King five hours after his arrest showed that his blood-alcohol level was 0.075 %, indicating that at the time of his arrest, he was over the level (0.08 %) at which one can be presumed intoxicated under California law. The tests also showed "traces" of marijuana (26 ng/ml), but no indication of PCP or any other illegal drug.

King was booked for evading arrest and held for four days. He was released on Wednesday, March 6, after prosecutors determined there was insufficient evidence to prosecute him.

Inaccurate Reports After the King Beating

Following the King beating, Powell prepared the Department's standard form arrest report. Powell described his use of the baton and King's alleged resistance:

> Deft recovered almost immediately [from the effects of the Taser] and resumed his hostile charge in our direction. Ofcr Wind and I drew our batons to defend against deft's attack and struck him several times in the arm and leg areas to incapacitate him. Deft. continued resisting kicking and swinging his arms at us. We finally kicked deft down and he was subdued by several ofcrs using the swarm technique.

Powell's report of the incident is inconsistent with the scenes captured on the Holliday videotape in terms of the number and location of baton blows, as well as in the description of King's "resistance."

King's injuries and medical treatment ("MT"") were also described in the arrest report: "Deft was MT'd for abrasions and contusions on his face, arms, legs and torso areas." In his daily sergeant's log report, Koon included a similar description of King's injuries: "Several facial cuts due to contact with asphalt. Of a minor nature. A split inner lip. Suspect oblivious to pain."

The Department's Reaction to Attempts to Report the King Incident

Both video cameraman George Holliday and Paul King, Rodney's brother, attempted to report the apparent police abuse of Rodney King.

Paul King

Paul King was awakened by Rodney King's passenger, Bryant Allen, on Sunday, March 3, at approximately 4:00 a.m., and told that his brother Rodney had been beaten and arrested by the police. Allen also said someone might have videotaped the incident. On Monday morning, Paul King went to the Foothill station to complain about the treatment of his brother.

The officer at the front desk told Paul King he would have to wait. After waiting and then growing impatient, Paul King returned to the front desk as a sergeant came out from the back of the station. Paul King said he wanted to make a complaint about his brother; the sergeant took Paul King back to a detective's interview room.

According to Paul King, the sergeant went in and out of the interview room several times during the 40 minutes Paul King was there, spending approximately half of that time out of the room. The sergeant states that he left the room once for about 30 minutes to find the arrest report and to attempt to locate a use of force report, which is required after any LAPD officer uses force more severe than a "firm grip." Paul King specifically asked about the procedures for making a complaint and advised the sergeant that a videotape of the incident existed.

According to Paul King, the sergeant began by asking whether he had ever been in trouble. Paul King responded that he was there to talk about Rodney King, not himself. The sergeant recalls discussing the public perception of and reaction to police officers in general in an effort to make Paul King feel more comfortable.

The sergeant told Paul King that he would check the logs and said something to the effect that an investigation was going on. In response to Paul King's inquiry as to what was being investigated, the sergeant told him that Rodney King was in "big trouble," that he had been caught in a high-speed chase going 100 m.p.h. or so and that, according to the reported ground for the arrest, Rodney King had put someone's life in danger, possibly a police officer.

The sergeant told Paul King that he should try to find the video, and that the video could be of help. The sergeant did not at any time fill out a personnel complaint form. According to Paul King, when he left Foothill Station "I knew I hadn't made a complaint."

The sergeant told the Commission staff he followed the usual procedures when conducting the Paul King interview. The sergeant explained that when an individual makes a general complaint of police misconduct without specific details, he conducts a preliminary investigation. If that investigation reveals facts that, if true, would warrant discipline, a personnel complaint is prepared. If no complaint is prepared, the information he gathers is written down and passed along to his superior officers. Based on the general information he received from Paul King, the sergeant reported in his daily log that no further action was necessary, pending completion and evaluation of the use of force report or receipt of additional evidence such as the videotape.

George Holliday

George Holliday reported that he called the Foothill Station on Monday, March 4, intending to offer his videotape to the police. Holliday informed the desk officer who answered the call that he had witnessed an incident involving a motorist who had been beaten by LAPD officers. Holliday said he inquired as to the condition of the motorist and was told that "we [the LAPD] do not release information like that."

According to Holliday, the desk officer made no attempt to learn any details of the event Holliday witnessed. No personnel complaint was generated as a result of his call. Holliday said he did not inform the Foothill officer that he had videotaped the beating.

Confronted with what he viewed as disinterest on the part of the LAPD, Holliday made arrangements with Los Angeles television station KTLA to broadcast the videotape on Monday evening. The following day the tape received national exposure on the Cable News Network, and thereafter was reported widely in the media.

The LAPD Officers at the Scene

Twenty-three LAPD officers responded to the scene of the Rodney King incident. Four LAPD officers—Sergeant Koon and Officers Powell, Briseno, and Wind—were directly involved in the use of force and have been indicted on felony charges, including assault with a deadly weapon. Koon and Powell are also charged with submission of a false police report. Two of the LAPD officers were in a helicopter overhead. Ten other LAPD officers were actually present on the ground during some portion of the beating. Seven other LAPD officers merely drove by the scene or otherwise did not directly witness the use of force. Four uniformed officers from two other law enforcement agencies—the California Highway Patrol and the Los Angeles Unified School District—were also at the scene.

The ages of these 23 LAPD officers ranged from 23 to 48 years. Their experience varied from 10 days to 29 years since graduation from the

Police Academy. In the group were one African-American male, one African-American female, four Latino males, two white females, and 15 white males. Four of the 10 LAPD bystanders were field training officers responsible for supervising "probationary" officers in their first year after graduation from the Police Academy.

Earlier that evening during roll call, a training session on use of the baton had been conducted in the parking lot of the Foothill Station. Both Powell and Wind participated in that session.

Because of the pending criminal trial of the four indicted officers, the Commission's access to their personnel files was restricted by court order. Based on published reports and public documents, however, it appears that three of the four indicted officers had been named in prior complaints for excessive force. Public records confirm that one officer had been suspended for 66 days in 1987 for kicking and hitting a Latino suspect with a baton. This officer was also the subject of a 1985 excessive force complaint, corroborated by a witness who came forward with information to the Commission, that had been rejected by the LAPD as "not sustained." According to press reports, another officer had been suspended for five days in 1986 for failing to report his use of force against a suspect following a vehicle pursuit and foot chase. (The suspect's excessive force complaint against the officer was held "not sustained" by the LAPD.) A third indicted officer was the subject of a 1986 "not sustained" complaint for excessive force against a handcuffed suspect. Since the King incident, that officer has been sued by a citizen who alleges that the officer broke his arm by hitting him with a baton in 1989.

The Official Response to the Rodney King Incident

The Rodney King beating was televised on March 4 on local Los Angeles station KTLA. The public reaction was immediate and overwhelming. Telephone calls expressing outrage at Rodney King's treatment flooded the Mayor's Office, the Police Department, and the media. The strong negative reaction included expressions of shock by some that such an incident could occur in Los Angeles, given the LAPD's national reputation for professional policing.

Immediately after the Holliday video was televised, Police Chief Daryl Gates stated that the tape was "shocking," but that he would withhold judgment on the behavior of the officers until the incident could be investigated. Chief Gates also described the incident as an aberration and expressed his hope that the public would not judge the entire Department on this one case. Mayor Tom Bradley said he was "shocked and outraged" by the incident and emphasized that "this is something we cannot, and will not tolerate."

By March 6, the Federal Bureau of Investigation, the Los Angeles District Attorney's Office, and the Los Angeles Police Department's Internal Affairs Division had begun investigations. The Police Commission, the civilian panel that oversees the Police Department, also began an inquiry.

On March 27, Chief Gates announced a "10-Point Plan" (included in Appendix I) in response to the Rodney King beating, stating that "there must be a thorough and diligent search for any underlying reasons why those officers engaged in such lawlessness." In addition, Chief Gates made several personnel changes in the command structure at the Valley Bureau and Foothill Division, the area where the King beating occurred. The Valley Bureau commander was reassigned to LAPD headquarters and an African-American officer was made commander of patrol officers at the Foothill Division. The Foothill Division Commanding Officer, Captain Tim McBride, remained in his position.

Four officers were indicted by the District Attorney's office on criminal charges: Sergeant Stacey Koon and Officers Laurence Powell, Timothy Wind, and Theodore Briseno. Wind, a first-year officer still on probation, has been fired; the other three officers face administrative hearings in which the Department is seeking their dismissal. The District Attorney's office did not seek indictments against the 17 LAPD officers who were at the scene and did not attempt to prevent the beating or report it to their superiors. The District Attorney, however, referred the matter of the bystanders to the United States Attorney for an assessment of whether federal civil rights laws were violated. To date, the United States Attorney has taken no action against the bystanders. The Department has transferred most of the bystander officers to other divisions within the City, and disciplinary action is pending against some of the bystanders. The watch commander (a lieutenant) was also transferred from Foothill Division.

The CHP has disciplined its officers present at the King beating, as well as their superiors in the chain of command. CHP Officers Timothy and Melanie Singer received written reprimands for failing to report the excessive use of force in sufficient detail. The sergeant who was their immediate supervisor was suspended for 10 days for his delay in informing his supervising lieutenant of the King beating. The CHP lieutenant was demoted to sergeant for failing to initiate an investigation of the incident. The Los Angeles School District terminated its officers who were at the scene.

Computer and Radio Transmissions

Computer and radio messages transmitted among officers immediately after the beating raised additional concerns that the King beating was part of a larger pattern of police abuse. Shortly before the King beating, Powell's and Wind's patrol unit transmitted the computer message that an earlier domestic dispute between an African-American couple was "right out of 'Gorillas in the Mist'," a reference to a motion picture about the study of gorillas in Africa.

The initial report of the beating came at 12:56 a.m., when Koon's unit reported to the Watch Commander's desk at Foothill Station, "You just had a big time use of force . . . tased and beat the suspect of CHP pursuit, Big Time." The station responded at 12:57 a.m., "Oh well . . . I'm sure the lizard didn't deserve it . . . HAHA I'll let them know OK."

Whoever was operating the Watch Commander's MDT did "let them know." At 12:57 a.m., the message went out from the station: "They just tased and beat the susp up big time in the pursuit." At 1:07 a.m., a further message said: "CHP chasing ... failing to yield ... passed A23 [Powell's and Wind's car] ... they became primary then went C6 [Code 6] ... got 415 [disturbance call] ... then tased, then beat ... basic stuff really."

In response to a request from the scene for assistance for a "victim of a beating," the LAPD dispatcher called the Los Angeles Fire Department for a rescue ambulance:

P.D.: ... Foothill & Osborne. In the valley dude *(Fire Department dispatcher laughs)* and like he got beat up.

F.D.: *(laugh)* wait *(laugh)*.

P.D.: We are on scene.

F.D.: Hold, hold on, give me the address again.

P.D.: Foothill & Osborne, he pissed us off, so I guess he needs an ambulance now.

F.D.: Oh, Osborne. Little attitude adjustment?

P.D.: Yeah, we had to chase him.

F.D.: OH!

P.D.: CHP and us, I think that kind of irritated us a little.

F.D.: Why would you want to do that for?

P.D.: *(laughter)* should know better than run, they are going to pay a price when they do that.

F.D.: What type of incident would you say this is.

P.D.: It's a ... it's a ... battery, he got beat up.

Powell's and Wind's unit transmitted the word "oops" at 1:12 a.m. to foot patrol officers working the Sunland Tujunga area of Foothill Division, who were not at the scene of the beating. The following exchange then occurred during the next five minutes:

"Oops, what?"

[From Powell/Wind] "I haven't beaten anyone this bad in a long time."

"Oh not again ... why for you do that ... I thought you agreed to chill out for a while. What did he do?"

[From Powell/Wind] "I think he was dusted ... many broken bones later after the pursuit."

At Pacifica Hospital, where King was taken for initial treatment, nurses reported that the officers who accompanied King (who included Wind) openly joked and bragged about the number of times King had been hit.

The Public Response

As noted above, public reaction to the King beating, and in particular to the degree and duration of the force used, was clear: the officers' conduct as depicted in the videotape was denounced as intolerable. Public outrage focused not simply on the fact that the officers involved used more than 50 "power strokes" with their batons and kicks to Rodney King's head and body in an open, public location, but also on the presence at the scene of a sergeant, who failed to control the situation, and a large number of other officers, none of whom attempted to intervene.

Moreover, the videotape and subsequently reported computer communications provoked concern that the beating was an example of widespread, racially motivated "street justice" administered by some in the LAPD, and reinforced the belief, particularly held by some members of Los Angeles' minority communities, that excessive use of force by the LAPD is common.

That view is shared by many outside Los Angeles' minority communities. A *Los Angeles Times* poll conducted on March 7-8, 1991, found that nearly two-thirds (63 %) of the respondents in the City of Los Angeles, including a majority of whites, said that they believed incidents of police brutality involving the LAPD are "common." The same question asked two weeks later produced comparable results, with 68 % of all respondents (59 % of whites, 87 % of African-Americans, and 80 % of Latinos) stating that incidents of LAPD brutality were either "very common" or "fairly common." A similar, although somewhat less dramatic perception concerning the LAPD's excessive use of force was found a year before the King beating. More than half (53 %) of those from the City of Los Angeles who responded to a February 1990 *Times* poll stated that there was at least some police brutality within the City. In contrast, only 37 % of the Orange County respondents believed there was some police brutality in their area.

The Aftermath of the Beating: Questions That Demand Answers

The Rodney King beating gave immediate rise to myriad questions about the Los Angeles Police Department. Concerns were voiced about the openness of the officers' conduct; the presence of a sergeant who failed to control and indeed directed the violence; the puzzling convergence of so many officers at the end-of-pursuit location after the Code 4 broadcast that no assistance was needed; the number of officers who stood by during the beating and failed to report it afterwards; and the radio comments and computer transmissions before and after the incident that suggested a possible racial motivation and a ready acceptance of excessive force as "basic stuff" by LAPD officers.

More fundamental questions quickly arose as well:

- concerns about the LAPD's "culture" and officers' attitudes toward racial and other minorities
- the apparent failure to control or discipline officers with repeated complaints of excessive force
- the accuracy with which arrest and use of force reports are completed
- the inability to screen out applicants to the LAPD with psychological profiles indicating a propensity to violence
- the possibility that "street justice" is regularly meted out by LAPD officers after a pursuit or chase
- the disparity between the training received at the Police Academy and the way the LAPD operates in the field

- the difficulties the public encounters in attempting to make complaints against LAPD officers
- the role of the LAPD leadership and civilian oversight authorities in addressing or contributing to these problems

These and related questions and concerns form the basis for the Commission's work.

NEW PLEAS AND CHARGES
IN IRAN-CONTRA CASES
July 9 and September 6, 1991

Alan D. Fiers, Jr., a former official of the Central Intelligence Agency (CIA), admitted to a federal court July 9 that he misled Congress in an attempt to cover up his agency's involvement in secretly selling arms to Iran and illegally diverting payments to Nicaraguan contras (guerrillas). His admissions in court papers filed in Washington, D.C., also implicated other CIA and Reagan administration officials.

Fiers's account of Iran-contra dealings, while not mentioning former CIA deputy director Robert M. Gates, nevertheless caused the Senate Intelligence Committee to delay its approval of Gates's nomination to become CIA director until it questioned him further on his knowledge of the illegal activities. In the mid-1980s Gates was directly over Clair E. George, who was Fiers's immediate superior. Fiers said that George ordered him not to tell Congress what they both knew about contra supply operations. (Senate Hearings on Gates as CIA Director, p. 651)

Fiers's testimony gave a boost to Iran-contra prosecutors, whose conviction of Lt. Col. Oliver L. North was undermined by a federal appeals court ruling. Consequently, the case against him had to be abandoned. Lawrence E. Walsh, the independent counsel who headed the prosecution staff, had predicted in the spring that the entire inquiry—then under way for more than four years—would be finished by the fall. But on July 11 he told a news conference that information from Fiers had opened new leads and left him unable to say how long the investigation might continue. (Appeals Court Ruling on North Conviction, Historic Documents of 1990, p. 491; Dismissal of Iran-Contra Changes Against Oliver North, p. 617)

In exchange for his cooperation, Fiers was permitted to plead guilty to two misdemeanor charges of withholding information from Congress. U.S. District Court Judge Aubrey E. Robinson, Jr., ordered Fiers released without bail and deferred sentencing until Fiers underwent further questioning by a prosecution team, which hoped to use his information to obtain other convictions.

As chief of the CIA's Central American operations from October 1984 through November 1986, Fiers worked directly with North and reported to George. Fiers said that before the Iran-contra deal was publicly disclosed in the fall of 1986, he heard about it from North and promptly informed George—who appeared to know about it already. Both he and George denied that knowledge in a congressional committee briefing. On another occasion, Fiers said, George directed him to falsely testify to another congressional committee that he did not know whether an arms-carrying plane shot down over Nicaragua was on a CIA mission.

Charges Against George

On September 6 a federal grand jury in Washington indicted George on counts of committing perjury, withholding information from Congress, and obstructing congressional and grand jury investigations of Iran-contra matters. Six days later George pleaded not guilty, and his attorney requested access to thousands of classified documents and related court papers from two earlier Iran-contra cases. Prosecutors protested that the request was an attempt to prevent a trial from taking place.

Those secret documents and sealed pleadings were from the trials of North and Joseph F. Fernandez, a former CIA station chief in Costa Rica. Both cases involved bitter fights over the use of classified documents. Prosecutors were forced to drop two main charges against North on the eve of his trial in 1989 when intelligence agencies refused to disclose certain documents. The case against Fernandez was dismissed that year by a federal judge when Attorney General Dick Thornburgh refused to release classified information the judge had ruled relevant to the defense.

Abrams Pleads Guilty

Former assistant secretary of state Elliott Abrams, an outspoken advocate of arming the contras, was mentioned prominently in the Fiers document but was not directly accused of lying to Congress. However, on October 7 Abrams pleaded guilty in Judge Robinson's court to two misdemeanor charges of withholding information from Congress. The charges, relating to Abrams's testimony to Congress on October 10 and 14, 1986, were filed just days before the statute of limitations expired. After a full five years had elapsed, such charges would not have been permitted.

The guilty pleas did not make clear whether Abrams was aware of the Iran-contra operation as it developed. He had denied to Congress that he was. Prosecutors said in legal papers that Abrams frequently discussed highly sensitive issues with North and Fiers. At the time, Abrams was head of the Restricted Interagency Group, a panel that coordinated the Reagan administration's Central American policy among officials at the White House, State Department, CIA, and Pentagon. But he told Congress he had scant knowledge about contra supply operations.

Following are the prosecution's court statement for the factual basis of obtaining two guilty pleas from CIA official Alan D. Fiers, Jr., on July 9, 1991, on charges of withholding information from Congress in the Iran-contra investigation; and a ten-count federal grand jury indictment returned September 6, 1991, against Clair E. George, Fiers's supervisor at the CIA, charging him with perjury, withholding information from Congress, and obstructing a congressional and grand jury investigation of Iran-contra matters:

Criminal No. 91-396

United States of America
v.
Alan D. Fiers, Jr., Defendant.

Violations: 2 U.S.C. § 192

[July 9, 1991]

GOVERNMENT'S STATEMENT OF THE FACTUAL BASIS FOR THE GUILTY PLEA

Count One

From October 1984 through November 25, 1986, ALAN D. FIERS, JR., was the Chief of the Central Intelligence Agency's ("CIA") Central American Task Force, which managed CIA operations in Central America. MR. FIERS worked closely with Lt. Col. Oliver L. North on Central American issues and, in particular, on matters relating to the activity of the Nicaraguan resistance fighters, known as the Contras.

During the period from October 1984 until November 25, 1986, Lt. Col. North was detailed by the United States Marine Corps to the National Security Council ("NSC") staff, where, among other things, Lt. Col. North engaged in certain activities with respect to the Contras, counter-terrorism, and a United States initiative involving the sale of arms to elements in Iran.

Beginning with the overthrow of the Shah of Iran on or about January 16, 1979, and the seizure of the United States Embassy in Iran and its staff on November 4, 1979, relations between the United States Government and the Government of Iran were characterized by mutual hostility and tension. At all times relevant to this Information, the United States Government imposed an embargo on shipments of arms to Iran. In January 1984 the Secretary of State designated Iran a sponsor of international terrorism and, thereafter, the United States Government actively urged its allies not to permit the shipment of arms to Iran, in part because of its sponsorship of international terrorism and the continuation of the Iran-Iraq war.

Despite the embargo on arms shipments to Iran and the effort to urge United States allies not to permit Iranian arms shipments, a United States Government initiative involving sales of arms to elements in Iran and efforts to obtain the release of American citizens held hostage in Lebanon was undertaken in the latter part of 1985 and continued in 1986. Millions of dollars from the proceeds of arms sales to Iran were generated and secretly used for various purposes, including the purchase and delivery of military weapons and supplies for the Contras. The use of proceeds from these arms sales to assist the Contras became known as "the diversion."

During the early Spring of 1986, Lt. Col. North told ALAN D. FIERS, JR., that Israel was selling weapons to Iran and "kicking dollars into the Contras' pot."

Shortly after receiving this information from Lt. Col. North, ALAN D. FIERS, JR., told his superior, the Chief of the CIA's Latin American Division, of North's revelation. Shortly after this conversation, the Chief of the Latin American Division was routinely reassigned and the new Chief of the Latin American Division (hereinafter referred to as C/LAD #2) began his duties in the Spring of 1986.

By late Summer of 1986, Lt. Col. North told ALAN D. FIERS, JR., that the United States was selling arms to Iran and using proceeds from the sales to aid the Contras. MR. FIERS reported this information to his superior, C/LAD #2. C/LAD #2 instructed MR. FIERS to report this information immediately to Clair E. George, the CIA's Deputy Director for Operations.

Shortly thereafter, MR. FIERS informed Mr. George that Lt. Col. North had told him that the United States was selling arms to Iran and using proceeds from the sales to assist the Contras. Mr. George informed MR. FIERS that, "Now you [Fiers] are one of a handful of people who know this."

On November 25, 1986, President Reagan held a press conference and announced that on November 21, 1986, he had become concerned about whether his national security apparatus had provided him with a complete factual record with respect to the implementation of his policy toward Iran. President Reagan stated that he had directed Attorney General Edwin Meese III to review the matter. President Reagan introduced Attorney General Meese and asked him to brief the media on his preliminary findings. Attorney General Meese described arms transactions to Iran involving the United States and stated that the preliminary inquiry revealed that proceeds from those arms transactions had been deposited in bank accounts under the control of the Contras.

Later that day, ALAN D. FIERS JR., and Assistant Secretary of State for Inter-American Affairs Elliott Abrams appeared before the United States Senate Select Committee on Intelligence to give it a briefing on Nicaragua.

During the briefing, but prior to addressing specific questions on Nicaragua, Committee members asked about the revelation by Attorney General Meese regarding the diversion. Assistant Secretary of State Abrams and the defendant, ALAN D. FIERS, JR., were asked to comment on events of the day.

After Assistant Secretary of State Abrams explained his lack of knowledge of the diversion prior to the November 25, 1986 press conference, MR. FIERS expressed his purported lack of knowledge by stating:

> [MR. FIERS]: No, I don't have anything to add to it except to add the footnote that the Agency was in the same boat, and *the first I knew of it was on CNN today*, and *that that is the first that I know that the Agency knew of it at that point in time.*

* * *

[SENATOR EAGLETON]: Back to you, Mr. Abrams. Are you speaking for the sum totality of the State Department or are you speaking just of your own personal knowledge? As to who knew what and when they knew it.

[MR. ABRAMS]: Well, I am speaking for the State Department. That is, that I think that I can say with some degree of confidence that the Secretary and others who would be expected to know if I knew, or maybe even if I didn't know, were not aware that money was going into this. I think it is—you know, I haven't asked everybody individually, but I am pretty certain in saying that there was nobody in the Department of State who knew about this Iranian business.

[SENATOR EAGLETON]: All right. How about, Mr. Fiers, you said the Agency—could you give the same all encompassing answer with respect to the Agency?

[Mr. Fiers]: Yeah. *Everyone that I have talked to in the Agency, and that goes—over time, I am fairly confident didn't know that this was going on. I certainly know that people* below me and *immediately above me didn't.*

Count Two

ALAN D. FIERS, JR., was aware generally from November 1984 through November 25, 1986, that Lt. Col. North was actively involved in coordinating lethal assistance for the Contras. During this period, the United States Government, and specifically the CIA, was prohibited by the Boland Amendment from providing lethal assistance to the Contras. MR. FIERS coordinated the Central American Task Force's activities with Lt.

Col. North's to facilitate North's efforts to provide Contra assistance. MR. FIERS endeavored, however, to keep the Task Force's activities within his understanding of the scope of the Boland Amendment.

MR. FIERS became aware by February 1986 that Lt. Col. North was involved specifically in coordinating flights carrying lethal supplies to the Contras from Ilopango air base in El Salvador. He learned this from Lt. Col. North and from his interactions with two individuals involved in the resupply operation: Richard Gadd and Felix Rodriguez.

MR. FIERS met Mr. Gadd in February 1986 at Charley's, a restaurant in McLean, Virginia. The meeting had been arranged by Richard Secord, at the suggestion of Lt. Col. North. At this meeting, Mr. Gadd described the C-7 airplanes that would be used by the operation to deliver supplies to the Contras. Mr. Gadd also told MR. FIERS that, in addition to his operations as a contractor of the Department of State's Nicaraguan Humanitarian Assistance Office ("NHAO"), he had also arranged for aerial deliveries of lethal supplies for the Contras to Central America.

MR. FIERS had a confrontation with Mr. Rodriguez at Ilopango air base in February 1986. MR. FIERS had become aware of Mr. Rodriguez' involvement in NHAO operations from Lt. Col. North and from intelligence reports. The confrontation occurred because Mr. Rodriguez had authorized a resupply flight that would have compromised United States Government objectives in the region. Mr. Rodriguez informed MR. FIERS that Lt. Col. North had authorized the flight. MR. FIERS spoke to Lt. Col. North by telephone in Mr. Rodriguez' presence and told Lt. Col. North that the flight would have to be cancelled. Later in the call, Lt. Col. North spoke to Mr. Rodriguez in Mr. Fiers' presence and told Mr. Rodriguez to cancel the flight.

MR. FIERS became aware during March and April 1986 that the planes managed by Mr. Gadd were carrying lethal supplies to the Contras. MR. FIERS also was aware that in April 1986 a Southern Air Transport L-100 airplane used for NHAO deliveries had been used to drop lethal supplies to Contra forces operating in southern Nicaragua. Lt. Col. North had informed MR. FIERS of the potential for such a delivery before the L-100 drop took place.

On August 12, 1986, Mr. Fiers attended a meeting in the office of Donald P. Gregg, national security advisor to Vice President Bush, in which Mr. Rodriguez' complaints about the lethal resupply operation were discussed. Several other United States Government officials attended the meeting, including Lt. Col. Robert L. Earl, a Marine officer detailed to the NSC staff under Lt. Col. North, and the United States Ambassador to El Salvador, Edwin G. Corr.

At this meeting, the resupply activity at Ilopango was discussed. Ambassador Corr said that Mr. Rodriguez had been instrumental in this activity because of his personal friendship with the commander of Ilopango air base. MR. FIERS stated that the CIA was not interested in using the resupply assets at Ilopango once the CIA was authorized to provide lethal assistance to the Contras. MR. FIERS told Lt. Col. Earl that

Lt. Col. North should be informed promptly about this meeting.

On October 5, 1986, one of the resupply operation's planes was shot down over Nicaragua. The plane carried arms and ammunition. The only survivor of the crash was Eugene Hasenfus, an American citizen. MR. FIERS learned of the crash on October 6, 1986. After the downing, but before October 10, 1986, MR. FIERS had a secure telephone conversation with Lt. Col. North regarding the downed plane. MR. FIERS asked Lt. Col. North whether the downed aircraft was Lt. Col. North's. Lt. Col. North told MR. FIERS that the plane was part of his operation, and that the operation was being dismantled.

During a press conference in Managua, Nicaragua, on October 9, 1986, Mr. Hasenfus, then in Nicaraguan custody, stated that he had made ten trips to supply the Contras and had worked with Max Gomez and Ramon Medina, who he alleged were CIA employees. Mr. Hasenfus stated that Mr. Gomez and Mr. Medina oversaw housing for the crews, transportation, refueling and flight plans. That same day, the United States Senate Committee on Foreign Relations and the United States House of Representatives Permanent Select Committee on Intelligence requested briefings from CIA officials on the circumstances surrounding the downed plane.

On October 9, 1986, MR. FIERS and Mr. George met to discuss briefing the committees. MR. FIERS and Mr. George agreed that Mr. George would read an opening statement prepared by the Central American Task Force, and that MR. FIERS would answer more specific questions, if necessary. MR. FIERS told Mr. George that the CIA would have to acknowledge that Felix Rodriguez was the "Max Gomez" named by Mr. Hasenfus because MR. FIERS knew that to be a fact. MR. FIERS also told Mr. George that they should describe how the NHAO operation at Ilopango metamorphosed into the lethal resupply operation.

Mr. George informed MR. FIERS that neither topic would be discussed. Mr. George stated that the CIA was still gathering information about Mr. Rodriguez and that, therefore, the Agency did not know conclusively who Mr. Rodriguez was. Mr. George also stated that he wanted to avoid giving the level of detail suggested by MR. FIERS about the genesis of the lethal resupply program. Mr. George told MR. FIERS that the information should not be disclosed because it would "put the spotlight" on the Administration and thus reveal Lt. Col. North's involvement in the operation. MR. FIERS acquiesced to Mr. George's plan and had a draft of Mr. George's opening statement revised to delete the information identified by Mr. George as troublesome.

On October 14, 1986, Mr. George and MR. FIERS, accompanied by Assistant Secretary of State Abrams, testified before the House Permanent Select Committee on Intelligence, during which the following exchange occurred on the matter of the downed plane:

[MR. CHAIRMAN]: You don't know whose airplane that was?

[MR. GEORGE]: I have no idea. I read—except what I read in the paper.

[MR. CHAIRMAN]: I understand, but you don't know?

[MR. FIERS]: *No, we do not know.*

[MR. CHAIRMAN]: There are a number of planes that take off there to supply the Contras regularly. You don't know who they are?

[MR. FIERS]: We know what the planes are by type, we knew, for example, there were two C-123s and two C-7 cargoes. . . . We knew in some cases much less frequently that they were flying down the pacific air corridors into southern Nicaragua for the purposes of resupply, but as to who was flying the flights and *who was behind them we do not know.*

[MR. CHAIRMAN]: And you still don't?

[MR. FIERS]: *No.*

Respectfully submitted,
LAWRENCE E. WALSH
Independent Counsel

<u>Criminal No. 91-0521</u>

United States of America v. Clair E. George, Defendant.	Violations: 18 U.S.C. § 1503, § 1505, § 1001, § 1621, § 1623

[September 8, 1991]

Count One
Introduction

1. At all times relevant to this Indictment, the Central Intelligence Agency ("CIA") was the principal United States Government agency responsible for the collection of foreign intelligence and the conduct of covert and foreign intelligence operations. From July 1984 through December 1987, the defendant, CLAIR E. GEORGE, was the Deputy Director for Operations at the CIA. As Deputy Director for Operations, the defendant, CLAIR E. GEORGE, supervised the worldwide intelligence activities of the CIA in the areas of covert action, intelligence collection and counterintelligence.

Central America

2. At all times relevant to this Indictment, the Nicaraguan democratic resistance, also known as the Contras, were insurgents engaged in military and paramilitary operations in Nicaragua.

3. From in or about December 1981 until on or about October 11, 1984, the United States Government, acting principally through the CIA, pursuant to written Presidential findings, provided the Contras with financial support, arms and military equipment, as well as supervision and

instruction, tactical and other advice, coordination, intelligence and direction.

4. On October 12, 1984, Public Law 98-473 was enacted and expressly prohibited funds available to the CIA, as well as to certain other agencies and entities of the United States, from being obligated or expended in support of military or paramilitary operations in Nicaragua, stating in relevant part:

> During fiscal year 1985 no funds available to the Central Intelligence Agency, the Department of Defense, or any other agency or entity of the United States involved in intelligence activities may be obligated or expended for the purpose of which would have the effect of supporting, directly or indirectly, military or paramilitary operations in Nicaragua by any nation, group, organization, movement, or individual.

This provision of law was commonly known as the "Boland Amendment." Subject to certain modifications discussed hereafter, the Boland Amendment remained in effect until October 1986.

5. After enactment of the Boland Amendment and continuing into 1986, certain private individuals, including American citizens, provided financial support and supplied arms, military equipment and logistical support to the Contras. Within the CIA, these individuals became known as the "private benefactors."

6. On August 12, 1985, Congress modified the Boland Amendment by approving $27 million for humanitarian assistance to the Contras.

7. By an executive order signed August 29, 1985, President Reagan created the Nicaraguan Humanitarian Assistance Office ("NHAO") in the United States Department of State for the purpose of administering the appropriated $27 million for humanitarian assistance to the Contras.

8. At all times relevant to this Indictment until November 25, 1986, Oliver L. North was a Lieutenant Colonel in the United States Marine Corps detailed to the National Security Council ("NSC") staff, where he held the position of Deputy Director, Political-Military Affairs. Among other things, Lt. Col. North helped coordinate the activities of private benefactors in supplying weapons and other lethal equipment to the Contras. Between November 1984 and November 1986, Lt. Col. North was actively engaged in raising funds for and providing arms and materiel to the Contras. Lt. Col. North worked with retired Air Force Maj. Gen. Richard V. Secord, among others, in providing assistance to the Contras.

9. From November 1984 until November 1986, Lt. Col. North had direct contact on a number of occasions with the defendant, CLAIR E. GEORGE, on Contra-related issues.

10. In early 1986, NHAO used the Ilopango air base in El Salvador for transshipment of humanitarian supplies to the Contras.

11. In late 1985 and early 1986, Lt. Col. North used persons and facilities associated with NHAO operations at Ilopango air base in El Salvador to assist in the deliveries of lethal equipment to the Contras by private benefactors.

12. Felix Rodriguez, using the alias Max Gomez, began assisting and

coordinating Contra resupply flights from Ilopango air base in El Salvador in early 1986. Felix Rodriguez had been recruited by Lt. Col. North in the Fall of 1985 to assist the portion of the Contra resupply effort to be based at Ilopango air base. When NHAO used Ilopango air base in January and February 1986, Felix Rodriguez helped coordinate the delivery of humanitarian supplies to the Contras. Additionally, Mr. Rodriguez assisted the private effort based out of Ilopango to deliver lethal and non-lethal materiel to the Contras.

13. During 1986, President Reagan requested that the United States Congress appropriate $100 million for support to the Contras. As of October 14, 1986, the United States Congress had not completed the enactment of this legislation.

14. From on or about October 9, 1984, through 1987, Alan D. Fiers, Jr., was the Chief of the Central American Task Force in the CIA.

15. The Central American Task Force was the headquarters element that managed CIA operations in Central America.

16. Although the Central American Task Force was a component of the Latin American Division of the CIA, Alan D. Fiers, Jr., as Chief of the Central American Task Force, had direct access to William J. Casey, Director of Central Intelligence, and to the defendant, CLAIR E. GEORGE, Deputy Director for Operations of the CIA, on important matters regarding Central America, particularly Contra-related issues.

Iran

17. Beginning with the overthrow of the Shah of Iran on or about January 16, 1979, and the seizure of the United States Embassy in Iran and its staff on November 4, 1979, relations between the United States Government and the Government of Iran were characterized by mutual hostility and tension. At all times relevant to this Indictment, the United States Government imposed an embargo on shipments of arms to Iran. In January 1984, the Secretary of State designated Iran as a sponsor of international terrorism and, thereafter, the United States Government actively urged its allies not to permit the shipment of arms to Iran, in part because of its sponsorship of international terrorism and the continuation of the Iran-Iraq war.

18. In 1985 President Reagan secretly authorized Israel to transfer United States-supplied weapons to Iran to facilitate the release of American citizens held hostage in Lebanon. On January 17, 1986, President Reagan signed a finding authorizing further arms sales to Iran.

19. On January 20, 1986, the defendant, CLAIR E. GEORGE, attended a meeting in the Situation Room of the White House. The purpose of the meeting was to prepare to implement the January 17, 1986, finding, which directed the CIA in part

> to facilitate efforts by third parties and third countries to establish contact with moderate elements within and outside the Government of Iran by providing these elements with arms, equipment and related materiel in order to enhance the credibility of these elements in their effort to achieve a more pro-U.S. government in Iran. . . .

The goal of these efforts was, among other things, to obtain the release of American citizens held hostage in Lebanon. These activities formed part of what became known as the "Iran initiative." The January 17, 1986, finding instructed the Director of Central Intelligence "to refrain from reporting this Finding to the Congress as provided in Section 501 of the National Security Act of 1947, as amended, until I [President Reagan] otherwise direct."

20. In addition to the defendant, CLAIR E. GEORGE, the meeting was attended by the Assistant to the President for National Security Affairs, Vice Admiral John M. Poindexter; Lt. Col. North; the Deputy Chief of the CIA's Near East Division, Thomas A. Twetten; the General Counsel for the CIA, Stanley Sporkin; and retired Maj. Gen. Richard V. Secord.

21. During the January 20, 1986, meeting, retired Maj. Gen. Secord was introduced to the defendant, CLAIR E. GEORGE, as a consultant to the NSC. At the meeting, the defendant, CLAIR E. GEORGE, designated Thomas A. Twetten as the CIA operations officer who would respond to the NSC's day-to-day requirements for the "Iran initiative," and Admiral Poindexter designated Lt. Col. North as the NSC operations officer for the "Iran initiative."

22. Shortly after learning that retired Maj. Gen. Secord was participating in the "Iran initiative," the defendant, CLAIR E. GEORGE, spoke separately with Admiral Poindexter and Director of Central Intelligence William J. Casey. The defendant, CLAIR E. GEORGE, told Admiral Poindexter and Director Casey about concerns stemming from allegations that retired Maj. Gen. Secord had been associated with Edwin Wilson, a former CIA employee who had been convicted of several federal felonies.

23. On or about January 25, 1986, Lt. Col. North delivered to the CIA a document entitled "Notional Timeline for Operation Recovery" ("Timeline"). The Timeline indicated that a person named "Copp" (1) would assist the CIA in the packing and shipment of 4,508 TOW missiles from the United States to Iran; (2) possessed an account through which funds payable to the CIA for the purchase and transport of these missiles would pass, and to which the CIA could bill its expenses for the transportation of these missiles; and (3) would travel to Israel to survey a point at which a "Copp a/c [aircraft]" would transfer missiles to an "Israeli 'sterile' a/c piloted by Copp crew" prior to the missiles' arrival in Iran. The defendant, CLAIR E. GEORGE, was aware that the name "Copp," as used in the Timeline, was an alias for retired Maj. Gen. Secord.

24. On or about January 25, 1986, the defendant, CLAIR E. GEORGE, was given a copy of the Timeline, which the defendant, CLAIR E. GEORGE, kept in a safe located in his office at the CIA. Because of the extreme sensitivity of the "Timeline," the copy that the defendant, CLAIR E. GEORGE, kept in his safe was the only official CIA copy of the document.

25. On or about January 25, 1986, Thomas A. Twetten met with the defendant, CLAIR E. GEORGE, and discussed the contents of the Timeline.

26. During 1986, pursuant to the "Iran initiative," HAWK missile spare parts and approximately 1,500 TOW missiles were caused to be delivered to Iran by the United States Government through the CIA and retired Maj. Gen. Secord.

27. The United States Congress was not notified of the "Iran initiative" until November 1986.

The Shoot-Down

28. On October 5, 1986, while Congressional authorization for $100 million Contra aid awaited final action, a C-123K aircraft was shot down over Nicaragua carrying supplies, including arms, to the Contras inside Nicaragua. Three crewmen, William H. Cooper, Wallace Sawyer, Jr., and a Latin male, were killed; Eugene Hasenfus, the sole survivor, was captured by the Nicaraguans.

29. During a press conference in Managua, Nicaragua, on October 9, 1986, Eugene Hasenfus, then in Nicaraguan custody, stated that he had made ten trips to supply the Contras and had worked with Max Gomez and Ramon Medina, whom he alleged were CIA employees. Mr. Hasenfus stated that Gomez and Medina oversaw housing for the crews, transportation, refueling and flight plans.

30. On October 10, 1986, in an article entitled "Fliers' Network Shares Old CIA Links," the *Washington Post* reported that unnamed sources speculated that the flight of the C-123K aircraft shot down in Nicaragua on October 5, 1986, might have been financed by Saudi Arabian officials, possibly through retired Maj. Gen. Richard V. Secord.

Congressional Inquiries

31. On October 9, 1986, the United States Senate Committee on Foreign Relations requested a briefing from CIA officials on the circumstances surrounding the downed resupply plane. Also on October 9, 1986, the United States House of Representatives Permanent Select Committee on Intelligence requested a briefing on the downed aircraft and the lethal resupply operation of which it was a part.

32. During the morning of October 9, 1986, the defendant, CLAIR E. GEORGE, instructed Alan D. Fiers, Jr., to prepare an opening statement to be read the following day at the briefing of the United States Senate Committee on Foreign Relations. Mr. Fiers drafted an opening statement that contained a paragraph describing the use of the Ilopango air base in El Salvador by NHAO in early 1986 to facilitate the delivery of the humanitarian supplies to the Contras.

33. Later on October 9, 1986, Alan D. Fiers, Jr., met with the defendant, CLAIR E. GEORGE, to discuss what information was to be provided to the Congressional committees investigating the circumstances surrounding the downed aircraft and the resupply operation of which it was a part.

34. During the course of the meeting, the defendant, CLAIR E. GEORGE, told Alan D. Fiers, Jr., that certain facts were not to be conveyed to the Congressional committees because they would lead to

further Congressional inquiry that would "turn the spotlight" on the Administration and thus reveal the role of Lt. Col. North in the Contra resupply effort.

35. The defendant, CLAIR E. GEORGE, directed Alan D. Fiers, Jr., to remove the portion of the draft opening statement regarding NHAO's use of the Ilopango air base for Contra resupply.

36. Prior to the United States Senate Committee on Foreign Relations briefing on October 10, 1986, Alan D. Fiers, Jr., told the defendant, CLAIR E. GEORGE, that they must admit at the briefing that "Max Gomez" was an alias for Felix Rodriguez because Mr. Fiers knew that for a fact.

37. The defendant, CLAIR E. GEORGE, told Alan D. Fiers, Jr., that the response to any question regarding Max Gomez' true identity would be that the CIA was still checking into the matter.

REFUSAL TO ADJUST
1990 CENSUS COUNT
July 15, 1991

In congressional testimony July 15, Secretary of Commerce Robert A. Mosbacher announced that the government would not adjust the 1990 census to correct its undercount. The Census Bureau had reported April 18 that a special postcensus survey of 170,000 households indicated that approximately 5 million people—2.1 percent of the total—had eluded the censustakers.

The official U.S. census count finding of 248.7 million people not only understated the total population but distorted the true size of the nation's racial minorities and Hispanics. The undercount appeared disproportionately large among those groups, especially in cities. Even so, Americans identifying themselves with those groups accounted for nearly 30 percent of the population—more than ever before.

Although "deeply troubled" by the minority-skewed results, Mosbacher found "the evidence in support of an adjustment to be inconclusive and unconvincing." On this matter, he overruled the recommendations of Census Director Barbara E. Bryant and the majority members of an in-house advisory panel.

In his appearance before the House Subcommittee on Census and Population, Mosbacher acknowledged that possibly two-thirds of the nation's people lived in areas where an adjustment might improve the accuracy of the census. But the secretary said that in low-population areas "the adjusted figures become increasingly unreliable." In that situation, Mosbacher added, "we cannot proceed on unstable ground in such an important matter of public policy."

At issue were the reapportionment of congressional and state legisla-

tive seats and the annual distribution of federal funds that are tied to census-based formulas. An adjustment made in accordance with the postcensus survey would have cost Pennsylvania and Wisconsin one congressional seat each and added one each to Arizona and California.

Mosbacher's decision drew protests from several large cities and states, minority groups, and many Democrats in Congress. Much of the undercount occurred in traditional Democratic bastions, the inner cities. Mayors Raymond Flynn of Boston, president of the United States Conference of Mayors, and David N. Dinkins of New York called Mosbacher's decision politically motivated. Mosbacher denied the allegation. As expressed in his congressional testimony, he was "deeply concerned that adjustment would open the door to political tampering with the census in the future."

Suit Filed to Require Adjustment

The question of adjusting the census had arisen in response to complaints from New York and several other cities that they had been cheated by an undercount in the 1980 census. The Census Bureau agreed in 1987 to plan a special survey as a cross-check and possible correction for the 1990 census. The Commerce Department scuttled the plan, but the cities sued to reinstate it.

The plaintiffs included the cities of Chicago, Cleveland, Denver, Houston, Inglewood (California), Los Angeles, New York, Oakland, Pasadena, Philadelphia, San Antonio, and San Francisco; Broward and Dade counties in Florida; the states of California, Florida, New Jersey, New York, and Texas; the U.S. Conference of Mayors, the League of United Latin American Citizens, the National League of Cities, the National Association for the Advancement of Colored People, and several individuals.

As the case progressed in federal district court in New York City, all parties agreed that the census would adhere to a special agreement under which the department promised an all-out effort to count as many people as possible and then evaluate the results. The evaluation performed by the Census Bureau yielded the 5 million undercount figure. A later assessment by the General Accounting Office (GAO), an investigative arm of Congress, said that as many as 9.7 million people might not have been counted. The GAO further said that a sampling of census returns indicated that they were marred by nearly 26 million errors.

California Attempts to Get Data

In California, Assembly Speaker Willie L. Brown, a Democrat, sued in federal court to obtain adjustment data from the Commerce Department for use in California's legislative redistricting. On August 20 a U.S. district court judge in Sacramento ordered the data released under terms of the Freedom of Information Act. The U.S. Court of Appeals for the Ninth Circuit, in San Francisco, approved the ruling, but the U.S. Supreme Court held on September 10 that the department was not required to release the data until a full hearing had taken place before the circuit court.

The Democratic leadership in Congress declined to push for legislation directing the Census Bureau to use the adjustment data. But in October Congress passed a bill requiring the National Academy of Sciences to conduct a three-year study on how the next census, in 2000, could be made more accurate.

Following is the statement Secretary of Commerce Robert A. Mosbacher issued July 15, 1991, to the Census and Population Subcommittee of the House Post Office and Civil Service Committee, rejecting an adjustment of the 1990 census:

Reaching a decision on the adjustment of the 1990 census has been among the most difficult decisions I have ever made. There are strong equity arguments both for and against adjustment. But most importantly, the census counts are the basis for the political representation of every American, in every state, county, city, and block across the country.

If we change the counts by a computerized, statistical process, we abandon a two hundred year tradition of how we actually count people. Before we take a step of that magnitude, we must be certain that it would make the census better and distribution of the population more accurate. After a thorough review, I find the evidence in support of an adjustment to be inconclusive and unconvincing. Therefore, I have decided that the 1990 census counts should not be changed by a statistical adjustment.

The 1990 census is one of the two best censuses ever taken in this country. We located about 98 percent of all the people living in the United States as well as U.S. military personnel living overseas, which is an extraordinary feat given the size, diversity and mobility of our population. But I am sad to report that despite the most aggressive outreach program in our nation's history, census participation and coverage was lower than average among certain segments of our population. Based on our estimates, Blacks appear to have been undercounted in the 1990 census by 4.8%, Hispanics by 5.2%, Asian-Pacific Islanders by 3.1%, and American Indians by 5.0%, while non-Blacks appear to have been undercounted by 1.7%.

I am deeply troubled by this problem of differential participation and undercount of minorities, and I regret that an adjustment does not address this phenomenon without adversely affecting the integrity of the census. Ultimately, I had to make the decision which was fairest for all Americans.

The 1990 census is not the vehicle to address the equity concerns raised by the undercount. Nonetheless, I am today requesting that the Census Bureau incorporate, as appropriate, information gleaned from the Post-Enumeration Survey into its intercensal estimates of the population. We should also seek other avenues for the Bush Administration and Congress to work together and address the impact of the differential undercount of minorities on federal programs.

In reaching the decision not to adjust the census, I have benefited from frank and open discussions of the full range of issues with my staff, with senior professionals from the Economics and Statistics Administration and the Census Bureau, with my Inspector General, and with statisticians and other experts. Throughout these discussions, there was a wide range of professional opinion and honest disagreement. The Department has tried to make the process leading to this decision as open as possible. In that spirit, we will provide the full record of the basis for our decision as soon as it is available.

In reaching the decision, I looked to statistical science for the evidence on whether the adjusted estimates were more accurate than the census count. As I am not a statistician, I relied on the advice of the Director of the Census Bureau, the Associate Director for the Decennial Census and other career Bureau officials, and the Under Secretary for Economic Affairs and Administrator of the Economics and Statistics Administration. I was also fortunate to have the independent counsel of the eight members of my Special Advisory Panel. These eight experts and their dedicated staffs gave generously of their time and expertise, and I am grateful to them.

There was a diversity of opinion among my advisors. The Special Advisory Panel split evenly as to whether there was convincing evidence that the adjusted counts were more accurate. There was also disagreement among the professionals in the Commerce Department, which includes the Economics and Statistics Administration and the Census Bureau. This compounded the difficulty of the decision for me. Ultimately, I was compelled to conclude that we cannot proceed on unstable ground in such an important matter of public policy.

The experts have raised some fundamental questions about an adjustment. The Post-Enumeration Survey, which was designed to allow us to find people we had missed, also missed important segments of the population. The models used to infer populations across the nation depended heavily on assumptions, and the results changed in important ways when the assumptions changed. These problems don't disqualify the adjustment automatically—they mean we won't get a perfect count from an adjustment. The question is whether we will get better estimates of the population. But what does better mean?

First, we have to look at various levels of geography—whether the counts are better at national, state, local, and block levels. Secondly, we have to determine both whether the actual count is better and whether the share of states and cities within the total population is better. The paradox is that in attempting to make the actual count more accurate by an adjustment, we might be making the shares less accurate. The shares are very important because they determine how many congressional seats each state gets, how political representation is allocated within states, and how large a "slice of the pie" of federal funds goes to each city and state. Any upward adjustment of one share necessarily means a downward adjustment of another. Because there is a loser for every winner, we need solid ground to stand on in making any changes. I do not find solid enough ground to proceed with an adjustment.

To make comparisons between the accuracy of the census and the adjusted numbers, various types of statistical tests are used. There is general agreement that at the national level, the adjusted counts are better, though independent analysis shows that adjusted counts, too, suffer from serious flaws. Below the national level, however, the experts disagree with respect to the accuracy of the shares measured from an adjustment. The classical statistical tests of whether accuracy is improved by an adjustment at state and local levels show mixed results and depend critically on assessments of the amount of statistical variation in the survey. Some question the validity of these tests, and many believe more work is necessary before we are sure of the conclusions.

Based on the measurements so far completed, the Census Bureau estimated that the proportional share of about 29 states would be made more accurate and about 21 states would be made less accurate by adjustment. Looking at cities, the census appears more accurate in 11 of the 23 metropolitan areas with 500,000 or more persons: Phoenix, Washington, D.C., Jacksonville, Chicago, Baltimore, New York City, Memphis, Dallas, El Paso, Houston and San Antonio. Many large cities would appear to be less accurately treated under an adjustment. While these analyses indicate that more people live in jurisdictions where the adjusted counts appear more accurate, one third of the population lives in areas where the census appears more accurate. As the population units get smaller, including small and medium sized cities, the adjusted figures become increasingly unreliable. When the Census Bureau made allowances for plausible estimates of factors not yet measured, these comparisons shifted toward favoring the accuracy of the census enumeration. Using this test, 28 or 29 states were estimated to be made less accurate if the adjustment were to be used.

What all these tests show, and no one disputes, is that the adjusted figures for some localities will be an improvement and for others the census counts will be better. While we know that some will fare better and some will fare worse under an adjustment, we don't really know how much better or how much worse. If the scientists cannot agree on these issues, how can we expect the losing cities and states as well as the American public to accept this change?

The evidence also raises questions about the stability of adjustment procedures. To calculate a nationwide adjustment from the survey, a series of statistical models are used which depend on simplifying assumptions. Changes in these assumptions result in different population estimates. Consider the results of two possible adjustment methods that were released by the Census Bureau on June 13, 1991. The technical differences are small, but the differences in results are significant. The apportionment of the House of Representatives under the selected scheme moved two seats relative to the apportionment implied by the census, whereas the modified method moved only one seat. One expert found that among five reasonable alternative methods of calculating adjustments, none of the resulting apportionments of the House were the same, and eleven different states either lost or gained a seat in at least one of the five methods.

I recognize that the formulas for apportioning the House are responsive to small changes and some sensitivity should be expected. What is unsettling, however, is that the choice of the adjustment method selected by Bureau officials can make a difference in apportionment, and the political outcome of that choice can be known in advance. I am confident that political considerations played no role in the Census Bureau's choice of an adjustment model for the 1990 census. I am deeply concerned, however, that adjustment would open the door to political tampering with the census in the future. The outcome of the enumeration process cannot be directly affected in such a way.

My concerns about adjustment are compounded by the problems an adjustment might cause in the redistricting process, which is contentious and litigious enough without an adjustment. An adjusted set of numbers will certainly disrupt the political process and may create paralysis in the states that are working on redistricting or have completed it. Some people claim that they will be denied their rightful political representation without an adjustment. Those claims assume that the distribution of the population is improved by an adjustment. This conclusion is not warranted based on the evidence available.

I also have serious concerns about the effect an adjustment might have on future censuses. I am worried that an adjustment would remove the incentive of states and localities to join in the effort to get a full and complete count. The Census Bureau relies heavily on the active support of state and local leaders to encourage census participation in their communities. Because census counts are the basis for political representation and federal funding allocations, communities have a vital interest in achieving the highest possible participation rates. If civic leaders and local officials believe that an adjustment will rectify the failures in the census, they will be hard pressed to justify putting census outreach programs above the many other needs clamoring for their limited resources. Without the partnership of states and cities in creating public awareness and a sense of involvement in the census, the result is likely to be a further decline in participation.

In looking at the record of public comment on this issue, I am struck by the fact that many civic leaders are under the mistaken impression that an adjustment will fix a particular problem they have identified—for example, specific housing units or group quarters that they believe we missed. It does not do so. It is not a recount. What an adjustment would do is add over 6 million unidentified people to the census by duplicating the records of people already counted in the census while subtracting over 900,000 people who were actually identified and counted. The decisions about which places gain people and which lose people are based on statistical conclusions drawn from the sample survey. The additions and deletions in any particular community are often based largely on data gathered from communities in other states.

The procedures that would be used to adjust the census are at the forefront of statistical methodology. Such research deserves and requires careful professional scrutiny before it is used to affect the allocation of political representation. Since the results of the evaluation studies of the survey were made available, several mistakes have been found which altered the certainty of some of the conclusions drawn by my advisors. The analysis continues, and new findings are likely. I am concerned that if an adjustment were made, it would be made on the basis of research conclusions that may well be reversed in the next several months.

It is important that research on this problem continue. We will also continue the open discussion of the quality of the census and the survey and will release additional data so that independent experts can analyze it. We must also look forward to the next census. Planning for the year 2000 has begun. A public advisory committee on the next census has been established and by early fall I will announce the membership of that committee. I have instructed the Census Bureau's Year 2000 task force to consider all options for the next census, including methods for achieving sound adjustment techniques.

I give my heartfelt thanks to the many people who have devoted so much time and energy to this enterprise. The staff at the Census Bureau have demonstrated their professionalism at every turn through the last two difficult years. They executed a fine census and an excellent survey and then condensed a challenging research program into a few short months. I am deeply grateful for their help. Let me reiterate my sincere thanks to the Special Advisory Panel for their substantial contribution. The staff at the Department, especially those in the Economics and Statistics Administration, also deserve praise.

With this difficult decision behind us, we will commit ourselves anew to finding sound, fair and acceptable ways to continue to improve the census process. We welcome the leadership of Congress and other public officials, community groups, and technical experts in maximizing the effectiveness and minimizing the difficulties of the year 2000 census.

LONDON ECONOMIC SUMMIT
July 17, 1991

Meeting in London July 17 with leaders of the world's major industrial democracies, Soviet president Mikhail S. Gorbachev described plans in his country for a monumental shift from communism to a market economy. His hosts—the leaders of Britain, Canada, France, Germany, Italy, Japan, and the United States (the so-called Group of Seven or G-7)—expressed support and promised technical aid, but they withheld financial assistance. The influential London magazine, The Economist, *wryly observed that the Soviet leader "was greeted with more respect than beggars usually receive at the tables of rich men." Gorbachev said he was nevertheless pleased with the "unprecedented political dialogue." It was the first time any Soviet leader had been invited to an annual economic summit of Western leaders.*

Scarcely more than a month after his return, a group of hard-line Communist officials and generals attempted to seize control of the Kremlin, unseat Gorbachev, and scuttle all recent political and economic reforms. The failure of the coup unleashed a reformist reaction that swept away the Communist party and accelerated economic change. This, in turn, prompted more generous offers of assistance from the Group of Seven than had been put forth at the London summit. (Failure of Soviet Coup Attempt, p. 515, Plans for Restructuring the Soviet Union, p. 531)

While in London, Gorbachev and President George Bush announced an agreement on the Strategic Arms Reduction Treaty (START), which the two countries had negotiated since 1982. They signed it July 31 in Moscow. (Decisions to Reduce U.S.-Soviet Nuclear Weaponry, p. 475) *If ratified by legislative bodies in both countries, the treaty would be the first to reduce, rather than merely limit, the number of strategic warheads in the nuclear arsenals of both countries. "This is a historic day for the United States and for East-West relations," Bush told reporters at the American ambassador's residence after the agreement was announced.*

The long-sought resolution to the remaining treaty questions had been arrived at earlier that day during a "working lunch" by Bush and Gorbachev. Bush denied there was any "linkage" between the agreement and economic assistance and told reporters that "it wasn't a set deal." When asked, "Who caved? Who gave in?" Bush replied, "There was compromise on all sides, and it's in the best interest of the United States, and I hope that the Soviet people feel it's in the best interest of the Soviet people."

Division Over Soviet Aid

The Group of Seven leaders responded to Gorbachev's presentations by offering him a plan designed as a first step toward making the Soviet Union, in his words, "an organic part of the world economic space." They proposed to give the Soviet Union "a special association" with the International Monetary Fund (IMF) and the World Bank, thus enabling it to receive technical assistance on how to create and operate a market economy. But the plan stopped short of allowing Moscow to borrow money from either the IMF or the World Bank. The aid package included some direct forms of assistance from the seven countries and a promise of continued consultations with their leaders and financial ministers. British prime minister John Major told reporters that technical help would be provided in such areas as energy, conversion of defense industries, food distribution, nuclear safety, and transportation.

The G-7 leaders were divided over the amount and kind of aid to offer Gorbachev. Chancellor Helmut Kohl of West Germany, President François Mitterand of France, and Prime Minister Giulo of Italy were reported to have argued for generous funding. Prime Minister Kaifu of Japan apparently spoke for the "hard-nosed group"—the United States, Britain, Canada, and Japan—when he said that "under the present circumstances, given the present situation in the Soviet Union, financial support would not be effective." This bloc of nations questioned whether the Soviet Union had the ability to put large infusions of foreign capital to good use. Some said the Soviet Union might possess the ability to bail itself out by better utilizing its gold reserves and vast national resources, while others contended that high Soviet defense spending should be drastically cut before the country receives Western aid.

Group of Seven Agenda

Before Gorbachev's arrival, the Group of Seven took strong positions on several international issues. In a series of lengthy declarations, the leaders warned Iraq that "severe measures" would be taken if it failed to dismantle nuclear, chemical, and biological warfare programs; backed diplomatic moves undertaken by the United States aimed at bringing peace to the Middle East region; and supported an international arms registry, under the auspices of the United Nations, to track the sales of conventional weapons.

Noting signs of global economic recovery, the Group of Seven endorsed fiscal and monetary policies that "provide the basis for lower real interest rates." The leaders said they were committed to ending the Uruguay Round of trade talks, which were deadlocked in meetings in Geneva, Switzerland, over the issue of agricultural subsidies. At last year's economic summit in Houston, Texas, President Bush had sought to break the logjam by asking the other nations to open their markets to cheaper farm products grown in the United States and Third World countries. Prime Minister Major said the Group of Seven might call a special session to rescue the Uruguay Round if the negotiators failed to complete their work by the end of the year. (Houston Economic Summit Conference, Historic Documents of 1990, p. 467)

Following are excerpts from the London Economic Summit declarations issued July 16 and 17, 1991, and excerpts from a news conference with President George Bush and Soviet president Mikhail Gorbachev:

LONDON ECONOMIC SUMMIT DECLARATION ON CONVENTIONAL ARMS TRANSFERS AND NUCLEAR, BIOLOGICAL, AND CHEMICAL WEAPONS PROLIFERATION

1. At our meeting in Houston last year, we, the Heads of State and Government and the representatives of the European Community, underlined the threats to international security posed by the proliferation of nuclear, biological and chemical weapons and of associated missile delivery systems. The Gulf crisis has highlighted the dangers posed by the unchecked spread of these weapons and by excessive holdings of conventional weapons. The responsibility to prevent the re-emergence of such dangers is to be shared by both arms suppliers and recipient countries as well as the international community as a whole. As is clear from the various initiatives which several of us have proposed jointly and individually, we are each determined to tackle, in appropriate fora, these dangers both in the Middle East and elsewhere.

Conventional Arms Transfers

2. We accept that many states depend on arms imports to assure a reasonable level of security and the inherent right of self-defence is recognised in the United Nations Charter. Tensions will persist in international relations so long as underlying conflicts of interest are not tackled and resolved. But the Gulf conflict showed the way in which peace and

stability can be undermined when a country is able to acquire a massive arsenal that goes far beyond the needs of self defence and threatens its neighbours. We are determined to ensure such abuse should not happen again. We believe that progress can be made if all states apply the three principles of transparency, consultation and action.

3. The principle of *transparency* should be extended to international transfers of conventional weapons and associated military technology. As a step in this direction we support the proposal for a universal register of arms transfers under the auspices of the United Nations, and will work for its early adoption. Such a register would alert the international community to an attempt by a state to build up holdings of conventional weapons beyond a reasonable level. Information should be provided by all states on a regular basis after transfers have taken place. We also urge greater openness about overall holdings of conventional weapons. We believe the provision of such data, and a procedure for seeking clarification, would be a valuable confidence and security building measure.

4. The principle of *consultation* should now be strengthened through the rapid implementation of recent initiatives for discussions among leading arms exporters with the aim of agreeing on a common approach to the guidelines which are applied in the transfer of conventional weapons. We welcome the recent opening of discussions on this subject. These include the encouraging talks in Paris among the Permanent Members of the United Nations Security Council on 8/9 July; as well as ongoing discussions within the framework of the European Community and its Member States. Each of us will continue to play a constructive part in this important process, in these and other appropriate fora.

5. The principle of *action* requires all of us to take steps to prevent the building up of disproportionate arsenals. To that end all countries should refrain from arms transfers which would be destabilising or would exacerbate existing tensions. Special restraint should be exercised in the transfer of advanced technology weapons and in sales to countries and areas of particular concern. A special effort should be made to define sensitive items and production capacity for advanced weapons, to the transfer of which similar restraints could be applied. All states should take steps to ensure that these criteria are strictly enforced. We intend to give these issues our continuing close attention.

6. Iraqi aggression and the ensuing Gulf war illustrate the huge costs to the international community of military conflict. We believe that moderation in the level of military expenditure is a key aspect of sound economic policy and good government. While all countries are struggling with competing claims on scarce resources, excessive spending on arms of all kinds diverts resources from the overriding need to tackle economic development. It can also build up large debts without creating the means by which these may be serviced. We note with favour the recent report issued by the United Nations Development Programme (UNDP) and the recent decisions by several donor countries to take account of military expenditure where it is disproportionate when setting up aid programmes

and encourage all other donor countries to take similar action. We welcome the attention which the Managing Director of the International Monetary Fund (IMF) and the President of the World Bank have recently given to excessive military spending, in the context of reducing unproductive public expenditure.

Non-Proliferation

7. We are deeply concerned about the proliferation of nuclear, biological and chemical weapons and missile delivery systems. We are determined to combat this menace by strengthening and expanding the non-proliferation regimes.

8. Iraq must fully abide by Security Council Resolution 687, which sets out requirements for the destruction, removal or rendering harmless under international supervision of its nuclear, biological, and chemical warfare and missile capabilities; as well as for verification and long-term monitoring to ensure that Iraq's capability for such weapon systems is not developed in the future. Consistent with the relevant UN resolutions, we will provide every assistance to the United Nations Special Commission and the International Atomic Energy Agency (IAEA) so that they can fully carry out their tasks.

9. In the nuclear field, we:

- Reaffirm our will to work to establish the widest possible consensus in favour of an equitable and stable non-proliferation regime based on a balance between nuclear non-proliferation and the development of peaceful uses of nuclear energy;
- Reaffirm the importance of the nuclear Non-Proliferation Treaty (NPT) and call on all other non-signatory states to subscribe to this agreement;
- Call on all non-nuclear weapon states to submit all their nuclear activities to IAEA safeguards, which are the cornerstone of the international non-proliferation regime;
- Urge all supplier states to adopt and implement the Nuclear Suppliers Group guidelines.

We welcome the decision of Brazil and Argentina to conclude a full-scope safeguard agreement with the IAEA and to take steps to bring the Treaty of Tlatelolco into force, as well as the accession of South Africa to the NPT.

10. Each of us will also work to achieve:

- Our common purpose of maintaining and reinforcing the NPT regime beyond 1995;
- A strengthened and improved IAEA safeguards system;
- New measures in the Nuclear Suppliers Group to ensure adequate export controls on dual-use items.

11. We anticipate that the Biological Weapons Review Conference in September will succeed in strengthening implementation of the conven-

tion's existing provisions by reinforcing and extending its confidence-building measures and exploring the scope for effective verification measures. Each of us will encourage accession to the convention by other states and urge all parties strictly to fulfill their obligations under the convention. We each believe that a successful Review Conference leading to strengthened implementation of the BWC, would make an important contribution to preventing the proliferation of biological weapons.

12. The successful negotiation of a strong, comprehensive, and effectively verifiable convention banning chemical weapons, to which all states subscribe, is the best way to prevent the spread of chemical weapons. We welcome recent announcements by the United States which we believe will contribute to the swift conclusion of such a convention. We hope that the negotiation will be successfully concluded as soon as possible. . . .

13. We must also strengthen controls on exports which could contribute to the proliferation of biological and chemical weapons. We welcome the measures taken by members of the Australia Group and by other states on the control of exports of chemical weapons precursors and related equipment. We seek to achieve increasingly close convergence of practice between all exporting states. We urge all states to support these efforts.

14. Our aim is a total and effective ban on chemical and biological weapons. Use of such weapons is an outrage against humanity. In the event that a state uses such weapons each of us agrees to give immediate consideration to imposing severe measures against it both in the UN Security Council and elsewhere.

15. The spread of missile delivery systems has added a new dimension of instability to international security in many regions of the world. As the founders of the Missile Technology Control Regime (MTCR), we welcome its extension to many other states in the last two years. We endorse the joint appeal issued at the Tokyo MTCR meeting in March 1991 for all countries to adopt these guidelines. These are not intended to inhibit cooperation in the use of space for peaceful and scientific purposes.

16. We can make an important contribution to reducing the dangers of proliferation and conventional arms transfers. Our efforts and consultations on these issues, including with other supplier countries, will be continued in all appropriate fora so as to establish a new climate of global restraint. We will only succeed if others, including recipient countries, support us and if the international community unites in a new effort to remove these threats which can imperil the safety of all our peoples.

LONDON ECONOMIC SUMMIT POLITICAL DECLARATION: STRENGTHENING THE INTERNATIONAL ORDER

1. We, the leaders of our seven countries and the representatives of the European Community, renew our firm commitment to the ideal of a

peaceful, just, democratic and prosperous world. The international community faces enormous challenges. But there is also reason for hope. We must reinforce the multilateral approach to the solution of common problems and work to strengthen the international system of which the United Nations, based on its Charter, remains so central a part. We call on the leaders of other nations to join us in that cause.

2. It is a matter for hope and encouragement that the United Nations Security Council, with the backing of the international community, showed during the Gulf crisis that it could fulfil its role of acting to restore international peace and security and to resolve conflict. With the East-West confrontation of the last four decades behind us, the international community must now build on this new spirit of cooperation not only in the Middle East but wherever danger and conflict threaten or other challenges must be met.

3. We believe the conditions now exist for the United Nations to fulfil completely the promise and the vision of its founders. A revitalised United Nations will have a central role in strengthening the international order. We commit ourselves to making the UN stronger, more efficient and more effective in order to protect human rights, to maintain peace and security for all and to deter aggression. We will make preventive diplomacy a top priority to help avert future conflicts by making clear to potential aggressors the consequences of their actions. The UN's role in peacekeeping should be reinforced and we are prepared to support this strongly.

4. We note that the urgent and overwhelming nature of the humanitarian problem in Iraq caused by violent oppression by the Government required exceptional action by the international community, following UNSCR 688. We urge the UN and its affiliated agencies to be ready to consider similar action in the future if the circumstances require it. The international community cannot stand idly by in cases where widespread human suffering from famine, war, oppression, refugee flows, disease or flood reaches urgent and overwhelming proportions.

5. The recent tragedies in Bangladesh, Iraq and the Horn of Africa demonstrate the need to reinforce UN relief in coping with emergencies. We call on all Member States to respond to the Secretary General's appeal for voluntary contributions. We would like to see moves to strengthen the coordination, and to accelerate the effective delivery, of all UN relief for major disasters. Such initiatives, as part of an overall effort to make the UN more effective could include:

(a) the designation of a high level official, answerable only to the United Nations Secretary-General, who would be responsible for directing a prompt and well-integrated international response to emergencies, and for coordinating the relevant UN appeals; and

(b) improvement in the arrangements whereby resources from within the UN system and support from donor countries and NGOs can be mobilised to meet urgent humanitarian needs in time of crisis.

The United Nations would then be able to take the early action that has sometimes been missing in the past. The United Nations should also make full use of its early warning capacity to alert the international community to coming crises and to work on the preparation of contingency plans, to include the question of prior earmarking of resources and material that would be available to meet these contingencies.

6. Since we last met the world has witnessed the invasion, occupation and subsequent liberation of Kuwait. The overwhelming response of the international community in reversing the forcible annexation of one small nation was evidence of the widespread preference for

- taking collective measures against threats to the peace and to suppress aggression
- settling disputes peacefully
- upholding the rule of law and
- protecting human rights.

These principles are essential to the civilised conduct of relations between states.

7. We express our support for what the countries of the Gulf and their neighbours are doing to ensure their security in future. We intend to maintain sanctions against Iraq until all the relevant resolutions of the Security Council have been implemented in full and the people of Iraq, as well as their neighbours, can live without fear of intimidation, repression or attack. As for the Iraqi people, they deserve the opportunity to choose their leadership openly and democratically. We look forward to the forthcoming elections in Kuwait and to an improvement of the human rights situation there and in the region.

8. We attach overriding importance to the launching of a process designed to bring comprehensive, just and lasting peace between Israel and her Arab neighbours, including the Palestinians. Such a peace should be based on UNSCRs 242 and 338 and the principle of territory for peace. We support the concept of a peace conference starting parallel and direct negotiations between Israel and representative Palestinians on the one hand and Israel and the Arab states on the other. We confirm our continuing support for the current American initiative to advance the peace process, which we believe offers the best hope of progress towards a settlement. We urge all the parties to the dispute to adopt reciprocal and balanced confidence-building measures and to show the flexibility necessary to allow a peace conference to be convened on the basis set out in this initiative. In that connection we believe that the Arab boycott should be suspended as should the Israeli policy of building settlements in the occupied territories.

9. We take note with satisfaction of the prospects opened by the restoration of security in Lebanon. We continue to support efforts by the Lebanese authorities to achieve the implementation of the Taif process, which will lead to the departure of all foreign forces and the holding of free elections.

10. We express our willingness to support the development of economic cooperation among the countries of the Middle East on the basis of liberal

policies designed to encourage the repatriation of capital, an increase in investment and a decrease in obstacles to trade. Such policies should be accompanied by comprehensive long-term efforts to bring about more stability for the Middle East and the Mediterranean.

11. We welcome the further substantial progress in reform, both political and economic, achieved in the countries of Central and Eastern Europe during the last year and recognise that these gains will need to be maintained through a difficult period of economic transition, including through regional initiatives. We have a strong interest in the success of market reforms and democracy in Central and Eastern Europe and we commit ourselves to full support for these reforms. We also take note of the progress of Albania towards joining the democratic community of nations.

12. Our support for the process of fundamental reform in the Soviet Union remains as strong as ever. We believe that new thinking in Soviet foreign policy, which has done so much to reduce East/West tension and strengthen the multilateral peace and security system, should be applied on a global basis. We hope that this new spirit of international co-operation will be as fully reflected in Asia as in Europe. We welcome efforts to create a new union, based on consent not coercion, which genuinely responds to the wishes of the peoples of the Soviet Union. The scale of this undertaking is enormous: an open and democratic Soviet Union able to play its full part in building stability and trust in the world. We reiterate our commitment to working with the Soviet Union to support their efforts to create an open society, a pluralistic democracy and a market economy. We hope the negotiations between the U.S.S.R. and the elected governments of the Baltic countries will resolve their future democratically and in accordance with the legitimate aspirations of the people.

13. It is for the peoples of Yugoslavia themselves to decide upon their future. However the situation in Yugoslavia continues to cause great concern. Military force and bloodshed cannot lead to a lasting settlement and will only put at risk wider stability. We call for a halt to violence, the deactivation and return of military forces to barracks and a permanent ceasefire. We urge all parties to comply with the provisions of the Brioni agreement as it stands. We welcome the efforts of the European Community and its member states in assisting in the resolution of the Yugoslav crisis. We therefore support the dispatch of EC monitors to Yugoslavia, within the framework of the CSCE emergency mechanism. We will do whatever we can, with others in the international community, to encourage and support the process of dialogue and negotiation in accordance with the principles enshrined in the Helsinki Final Act and the Paris Charter for a new Europe, in particular respect for human rights, including rights of minorities and the right of peoples to self-determination in conformity with the Charter of the United Nations and with the relevant norms of international law, including those relating to territorial integrity of states. The normalisation of the present situation will allow us to contribute to

the indispensable economic recovery of the country.

14. We welcome the positive developments in South Africa, where the legislative pillars of apartheid have at last been dismantled. We hope that these important steps will be followed by the de facto elimination of apartheid and improvement in the situation of the most impoverished among the population of South Africa. We hope that negotiations on a new Constitution leading to non-racial democracy will begin shortly and will not be disrupted by the tragic upsurge of violence. All parties must do all that is in their power to resolve the problem of violence. We are concerned that the foundation for a new non-racial South Africa will be undermined by mounting social problems and declining economic prospects for the majority of the population, which have contributed to the violence. There is an urgent need to restore growth to the economy to help reduce inequalities of wealth and opportunity. South Africa needs to pursue new economic, investment and other policies that permit normal access to all sources of foreign borrowing. In addition to its own domestic efforts, South Africa also needs the help of the international community, especially in those areas where the majority have long suffered deprivation: education, health, housing and social welfare. We will direct our aid for these purposes.

15. Finally, we look for further strengthening of the international order by continued vigorous efforts to deter terrorism and hostage taking. We call for the immediate and unconditional release of all hostages wherever they may be held and for an accounting of all persons taken hostage who may have died while being held. We welcome the undertakings given by governments with an influence over hostage holders to work for the release of hostages and urge them to intensify their efforts to this end. We extend our sympathy to the friends and relations of those held. We reaffirm our condemnation of all forms of terrorism. We will work together to deter and combat terrorism by all possible means within the framework of international law and national legislation, particularly in the fields of international civil aviation security and the marking of plastic explosives for the purpose of detection.

16. This forum continues to provide an invaluable opportunity for representatives from Europe, Japan and North America to discuss the critical challenges of the coming years. But we cannot succeed alone. We call on the leaders of the other nations to join us in our efforts to make a practical and sustained contribution to the cause of peace, security, freedom and the rule of law, which are the preconditions for trying to bring about greater justice and prosperity throughout the world.

LONDON ECONOMIC SUMMIT ECONOMIC DECLARATION: BUILDING WORLD PARTNERSHIP

1. We, the Heads of State and Government of the seven major industrial democracies and the representatives of the European Community, met in

London for our seventeenth annual Summit.

2. The spread of freedom and democracy which we celebrated at Houston has gathered pace over the last year. Together the international community has overcome a major threat to world peace in the Gulf. But new challenges and new opportunities confront us.

3. We seek to build world partnership, based on common values, and to strengthen the international order. Our aim is to underpin democracy, human rights, the rule of law and sound economic management, which together provide the key to prosperity. To achieve this aim, we will promote a truly multilateral system, which is secure and adaptable and in which responsibility is shared widely and equitably. Central to our aim is the need for a stronger, more effective UN system, and for greater attention to the proliferation and transfer of weapons.

Economic Policy

4. Over the last year, some of our economies have maintained good growth, while most have slowed down and some gone into recession. But a global recession has been avoided. The uncertainty created by the Gulf crisis is behind us. We welcome the fact that there are now increasing signs of economic recovery. Progress has been made too in reducing the largest trade and current account imbalances.

5. Our shared objectives are a sustained recovery and price stability. To this end, we are determined to maintain, including through our economic policy coordination process, the medium-term strategy endorsed by earlier Summits. This strategy has contained inflationary expectations and created the conditions for sustainable growth and new jobs.

6. We therefore commit ourselves to implement fiscal and monetary policies, which, while reflecting the different situations in our countries, provide the basis for lower real interest rates. In this connection, continued progress in reducing budget deficits is essential. This, together with the efforts being made to reduce impediments to private saving, will help generate the increase in global savings needed to meet demands for investment. We also welcome the close cooperation on exchange markets and the work to improve the functioning of the international monetary system.

7. We will also, with the help of the Organisation for Economic Co-operation and Development (OECD) and other institutions, pursue reforms to improve economic efficiency and thus the potential for growth. These include:

a) greater competition in our economies, including regulatory reform. This can enhance consumer choice, reduce prices and ease burdens on business

b) greater transparency, elimination or enhanced discipline in subsidies that have distorting effects, since such subsidies lead to inefficient allocation of resources and inflate public expenditure

c) improved education and training, to enhance the skills and improve the opportunities of those both in and out of employment, as well as policies contributing to greater flexibility in the employment system

d) a more efficient public sector, for example through higher standards of management and including possibilities for privatisation and contracting out

e) the wide and rapid diffusion of advances in science and technology.

f) essential investment, both private and public, in infrastructure.

8. We will encourage work nationally and internationally to develop cost-effective economic instruments for protecting the environment, such as taxes, charges and tradeable permits.

International Trade

9. No issue has more far-reaching implications for the future prospects of the world economy than the successful conclusion of the Uruguay Round. It will stimulate non-inflationary growth by bolstering confidence, reversing protectionism and increasing trade flows. It will be essential to encourage the integration of developing countries and Central and East European nations into the multilateral trading system. All these benefits will be lost if we cannot conclude the Round.

10. We therefore commit ourselves to an ambitious, global and balanced package of results from the Round, with the widest possible participation by both developed and developing countries. The aim of all contracting parties should be to complete the Round before the end of 1991. We shall each remain personally involved in this process, ready to intervene with one another if differences can only be resolved at the highest level.

11. To achieve our objectives, sustained progress will be needed in the negotiations at Geneva in all areas over the rest of this year. The principal requirement is to move forward urgently in the following areas taken together:

a) market access, where it is necessary, in particular, to cut tariff peaks for some products while moving to zero tariffs for others, as part of a substantial reduction of tariffs and parallel action against non-tariff barriers

b) agriculture, where a framework must be decided upon to provide for specific binding commitments in domestic support, market access and export competition, so that substantial progressive reductions of support and protection may be agreed in each area, taking into account non-trade concerns

c) services, where accord on a general agreement on trade in services should be reinforced by substantial and binding initial commitments to reduce or remove existing restrictions on services trade and not to impose new ones

d) intellectual property, where clear and enforceable rules and obligations to protect all property rights are necessary to encourage investment and the spread of technology.

12. Progress on these issues will encourage final agreement in areas already close to conclusion, such as textiles, tropical products, safeguards and dispute settlement. Agreement to an improved dispute settlement mechanism should lead to a commitment to operate only under the multilateral rules. Taken all together, these and the other elements of the negotiations, including GATT rule-making, should amount to the substantial, wide-ranging package which we seek.

13. We will seek to ensure that regional integration is compatible with the multilateral trading system.

14. As we noted at Houston, a successful outcome of the Uruguay Round will also call for the institutional reinforcement of the multilateral trading system. The concept of an international trade organisation should be addressed in this context.

15. Open markets help to create the resources needed to protect the environment. We therefore commend the OECD's pioneering work in ensuring that trade and environment policies are mutually supporting. We look to the General Agreement on Tariffs and Trade (GATT) to define how trade measures can properly be used for environmental purposes.

16. We are convinced that OECD members must overcome in the near future and, in any case, by the end of the year, remaining obstacles to an agreement on reducing the distortions that result from the use of subsidised export credits and of tied aid credits. We welcome the initiative of the OECD in studying export credit premium systems and structures and look forward to an early report.

Energy

17. As the Gulf crisis showed, the supply and price of oil remain vulnerable to political shocks, which disturb the world economy. But these shocks have been contained by the effective operation of the market, by the welcome increase in supplies by certain oil-exporting countries and by the actions co-ordinated by the International Energy Agency (IEA), particularly the use of stocks. We are committed to strengthen the IEA's emergency preparedness and its supporting measures. Since the crisis has led to improved relations between producers and consumers, contacts among all market participants could be further developed to promote communication, transparency and the efficient working of market forces.

18. We will work to secure stable worldwide energy supplies, to remove barriers to energy trade and investment, to encourage high environmental and safety standards and to promote international cooperation on research and development in all these areas. We will also seek to improve energy efficiency and to price energy from all sources so as to reflect costs fully, including environmental costs.

19. In this context, nuclear power generation contributes to diversifying energy sources and reducing greenhouse gas emissions. In developing nuclear power as an economic energy source, it is essential to achieve and maintain the highest available standards of safety, including in waste management, and to encourage co-operation to this end throughout the

world. The safety situation in Central and Eastern Europe and the Soviet Union deserves particular attention. This is an urgent problem and we call upon the international community to develop an effective means of coordinating its response.

20. The commercial development of renewable energy sources and their integration with general energy systems should also be encouraged, because of the advantages these sources offer for environmental protection and energy security.

21. We all intend to take a full part in the initiative of the European Community for the establishment of a European Energy Charter on the basis of equal rights and obligations of signatory countries. The aim is to promote free and undistorted energy trade, to enhance security of supply, to protect the environment and to assist economic reform in Central and East European countries and the Soviet Union, especially by creating an open, non-discriminatory regime for commercial energy investment.

Central and Eastern Europe

22. We salute the courage and determination of the countries of Central and Eastern Europe in building democracy and moving to market economies, despite formidable obstacles. We welcome the spread of political and economic reform throughout the region. These changes are of great historical importance. Bulgaria and Romania are now following the pioneering advances of Poland, Hungary and Czechoslovakia. Albania is emerging from its long isolation.

23. Recognising that successful reform depends principally on the continuing efforts of the countries concerned, we renew our own firm commitment to support their reform efforts, to forge closer ties with them and to encourage their integration into the international economic system. Regional initiatives reinforce our ability to cooperate.

24. All the Central and East European countries except Albania are now members of the International Monetary Fund (IMF) and the World Bank. We welcome the steps being taken by those countries that are implementing IMF-supported programmes of macro-economic stabilisation. It is crucial that these programmes are complemented by structural reforms, such as privatising and restructuring state-owned enterprises, increasing competition and strengthening property rights. We welcome the establishment of the European Bank for Reconstruction and Development (EBRD), which has a mandate to foster the transition to open, market-oriented economies and to promote private initiative in Central and East European countries committed to democracy.

25. A favourable environment for private investment, both foreign and domestic, is crucial for sustained growth and for avoiding dependence on external assistance from governments. In this respect, technical assistance from our private sectors and governments, the European Community and international institutions should concentrate on helping this essential market-based transformation. In this context, we emphasise the impor-

tance of integrating environmental considerations into the economic restructuring process in Central and Eastern Europe.

26. Expanding markets for their exports are vital for the Central and East European countries. We welcome the substantial increases already made in exports to market economies and we undertake to improve further their access to our markets for their products and services, including in areas such as steel, textiles and agricultural produce. In this context, we welcome the progress made in negotiating Association Agreements between the European Community and Poland, Hungary and Czechoslovakia, as well as the Presidential Trade Enhancement Initiative announced by the United States, all of which will be in accordance with GATT principles. We will support the work of the OECD to identify restrictions to East/West trade and to facilitate their removal.

27. The Group of Twenty-four (G24) process, inaugurated by the Arch Summit and chaired by the European Commission, has mobilised $31 billion in bilateral support for these countries, including balance of payments finance to underpin IMF-supported programmes. Such programmes are in place for Poland, Hungary and Czechoslovakia. We welcome the contributions already made for Bulgaria and Romania. We are intensifying the G24 coordination process and we reaffirm our shared willingness to play our fair part in the global assistance effort.

The Soviet Union

28. We support the moves towards political and economic transformation in the Soviet Union and are ready to assist the integration of the Soviet Union into the world economy.

29. Reform to develop the market economy is essential to create incentives for change and enable the Soviet people to mobilise their own substantial natural and human resources. A clear and agreed framework within which the centre and the republics exercise their respective responsibilities is fundamental for the success of political and economic reform.

30. We have invited President Gorbachev to meet us for a discussion of reform policies and their implementation, as well as ways in which we can encourage this process.

31. We commend the IMF, World Bank, OECD and EBRD for their study of the Soviet economy produced, in close consultation with the European Commission, in response to the request we made at Houston. This study sets out many of the elements necessary for successful economic reform, which include fiscal and monetary discipline and creating the framework of a market economy.

32. We are sensitive to the overall political context in which reforms are being conducted, including the "New Thinking" in Soviet foreign policy around the world. We are sensitive also to the importance of shifting resources from military to civilian use.

33. We are concerned about the deterioration of the Soviet economy, which creates severe hardship not only within the Soviet Union but also

for the countries of Central and Eastern Europe.

The Middle East

34. Many countries have suffered economically as a result of the Gulf crisis. We welcome the success of the Gulf Crisis Financial Co-ordination Group in mobilising nearly $16 billion of assistance for those countries suffering the most direct economic impact of the Gulf crisis and urge all donors to complete disbursements rapidly. Extensive assistance is being provided by Summit participants for the Mediterranean and the Middle East, as well as by the IMF and World Bank.

35. We believe that enhanced economic co-operation in this area, on the basis of the principles of non-discrimination and open trade, could help repair the damage and reinforce political stability. We welcome the plans of major oil exporting countries for providing financial assistance to others in the region and their decision to establish a Gulf Development Fund. We support closer links between the international financial institutions and Arab and other donors. We believe this would encourage necessary economic reforms, promote efficient use of financial flows, foster private sector investment, stimulate trade liberalisation and facilitate joint projects e.g. in water management, which would draw on our technical skills and expertise.

Developing Countries and Debt

36. Developing countries are playing an increasingly constructive role in the international economic system, including the Uruguay Round. Many have introduced radical policy reforms and are adopting the following principles:

   a) respect for human rights and for the law, which encourages individuals to contribute to development;
   b) democratic pluralism and open systems of administration, accountable to the public;
   c) sound, market-based economic policies to sustain development and bring people out of poverty.

We commend these countries and urge others to follow their example. Good governance not only promotes development at home, but helps to attract external finance and investment from all sources.

37. Our steadfast commitment to helping developing countries, in conjunction with a durable non-inflationary recovery of our economies and the opening of our markets, will be the most effective way we have of enhancing prosperity in the developing world.

38. Many of these countries, especially the poorest, need our financial and technical assistance to buttress their own development endeavors. Additional aid efforts are required, to enhance both the quantity and the quality of our support for priority development issues. These include alleviating poverty, improving health, education and training and enhancing the environmental quality of our aid. We endorse the increasing

attention being given to population issues in devising strategies for sustainable progress.

39. Africa deserves our special attention. Progress by African governments towards sound economic policies, democracy and accountability is improving their prospects for growth. This is being helped by our continued support, focused on stimulating development of the private sector, encouraging regional integration, providing concessional flows and reducing debt burdens. The Special Programme of Assistance for Africa, coordinated by the World Bank and providing support for economic reform in over 20 African countries, is proving its worth. We will provide humanitarian assistance to those parts of Africa facing severe famine and encourage the reform of United Nations structures in order to make this assistance more effective. We will also work to help the countries concerned remove the underlying causes of famine and other emergencies, whether these are natural or provoked by civil strife.

40. In the Asia-Pacific region, many economies, including members of the Association of South-East Asian Nations (ASEAN) and the Asia-Pacific Economic Co-operation (APEC), continue to achieve dynamic growth. We welcome the efforts by those economies of the region which are assuming new international responsibilities. Other Asian countries, which are strengthening their reform efforts, continue to need external assistance.

41. In Latin America we are encouraged by the progress being made in carrying out genuine economic reforms and by developments in regional integration. We welcome the continuing discussions on the Multilateral Investment Fund, under the Enterprise for the Americas Initiative which, together with other efforts, is helping to create the right climate for direct investment, freer trade and a reversal of capital flight.

42. We recognize with satisfaction the progress being made under the strengthened debt strategy. Some countries have already benefited from the combination of strong adjustment with commercial bank debt reduction or equivalent measures. We encourage other countries with heavy debts to banks to negotiate similar packages.

43. We note:

a) The agreement reached by the Paris Club on debt reduction or equivalent measures for Poland and Egypt, which should be treated as exceptional cases;

b) the Paris Club's continued examination of the special situation of some lower middle-income countries on a case by case basis.

44. The poorest, most indebted countries need very special terms. We agree on the need for additional debt relief measures, on a case by case basis, for these countries, going well beyond the relief already granted under Toronto terms. We therefore call on the Paris Club to continue its discussions on how these measures can best be implemented promptly.

45. We recognize the need for appropriate new financial flows to developing countries. We believe the appropriate way to avoid unsustain-

able levels of debt is for developing countries to adopt strengthened policies to attract direct investment and the return of flight capital.

46. We note the key role of the IMF, whose resources should be strengthened by the early implementation of the quota increase under the Ninth General Review and the associated Third Amendment to the Articles of Agreement.

Environment

47. The international community will face formidable environmental challenges in the coming decade. Managing the environment continues to be a priority issue for us. Our economic policies should ensure that the use of this planet's resources is sustainable and safeguards the interests of both present and future generations. Growing market economies can best mobilize the means for protecting the environment, while democratic systems ensure proper accountability.

48. Environmental considerations should be integrated into the full range of government policies, in a way which reflects their economic costs. We support the valuable work in this field being undertaken by the OECD. This includes the systematic review of member countries' environmental performance and the development of environmental indicators for use in decision-making.

49. Internationally, we must develop a co-operative approach for tackling environmental issues. Industrial countries should set an example and thus encourage developing countries and Central and East European nations to play their part. Co-operation is also required on regional problems. In this context, we welcome the consensus reached on the Environmental Protocol of the Antarctic Treaty, aimed at reinforcing the environmental preservation of this continent. We note the good progress of the Sahara and Sahel Observatory as well as the Budapest Environmental Centre.

50. The UN Conference on Environment and Development (UNCED) in June 1992 will be a landmark event. It will mark the climax of many international environmental negotiations. We commit ourselves to work for a successful Conference and to give the necessary political impetus to its preparation.

51. We aim to achieve the following by the time of UNCED:—

a) an effective framework convention on climate change, containing appropriate commitments and addressing all sources and sinks for greenhouse gases. We will seek to expedite work on implementing protocols to reinforce the convention. All participants should be committed to design and implement concrete strategies to limit net emissions of greenhouse gases, with measures to facilitate adaptation. Significant actions by industrial countries will encourage the participation of developing and East European countries, which is essential to the negotiations.

b) agreement on principles for the management, conservation and sustainable development of all types of forest, leading to a framework convention. This should be in a form both acceptable to the developing countries where tropical forests grow and consistent with the objective of a global forest convention or agreement which we set at Houston.

52. We will seek to promote, in the context of UNCED:—

a) mobilization of financial resources to help developing countries tackle environmental problems. We support the use of existing mechanisms for this purpose, in particular the Global Environment Facility (GEF). The GEF could become the comprehensive funding mechanism to help developing countries meet their obligations under the new environmental conventions.

b) encouragement of an improved flow of beneficial technology to developing countries, making use of commercial mechanisms.

c) a comprehensive approach to the oceans, including regional seas. The environmental and economic importance of oceans and seas means that they must be protected and sustainably managed.

d) further development of international law of the environment, drawing inter alia on the results of the Siena Forum.

e) the reinforcement of international institutions concerned with the environment, including the United Nations Environment Programme (UNEP), for the decade ahead.

53. We support the negotiation, under the auspices of UNEP, of an acceptable framework convention of biodiversity, if possible to be concluded next year. It should concentrate on protecting ecosystems, particularly in species-rich areas, without impeding positive developments in biotechnology.

54. We remain concerned about the destruction of tropical forests. We welcome the progress made in developing the pilot programme for the conservation of the Brazilian tropical forest, which has been prepared by the Government of Brazil in consultation with the World Bank and the European Commission, in response to the offer of co-operation extended following the Houston Summit. We call for further urgent work under the auspices of the World Bank, in co-operation with the European Commission, in the framework of appropriate policies and with careful attention to economic, technical and social issues. We will financially support the implementation of the preliminary stage of the pilot programme utilising all potential sources, including the private sector, non-governmental organisations, the multilateral development banks, and the Global Environmental Facility. When details of the programme have been resolved, we will consider supplementing these resources with bilateral assistance, so that progress can be made on the ground. We believe that good progress with this project will have a beneficial impact on the treatment of forests at UNCED. We also welcome the spread of debt for nature exchanges, with an emphasis on forests.

55. The burning oil wells and polluted seas in the Gulf have shown that we need greater international capacity to prevent and respond to environmental disasters. All international and regional agreements for this purpose, including those of the International Maritime Organisation (IMO), should be fully implemented. We welcome the decision by UNEP to establish an experimental centre for urgent environmental assistance. In the light of the recent storm damage in Bangladesh, we encourage the work on flood alleviation under the auspices of the World Bank, which we called for at the Arch Summit.

56. Living marine resources threatened by over-fishing and other harmful practices should be protected by the implementation of measures in accordance with international law. We urge control of marine pollution and compliance with the regimes established by regional fisheries organisations through effective monitoring and enforcement measures.

57. We call for greater efforts in co-operation in environmental science and technology, in particular:—

a) scientific research into the global climate, including satellite monitoring and ocean observation. All countries, including developing countries, should be involved in this research effort. We welcome the development of information services for users of earth observation data since the Houston Summit.

b) the development and diffusion of energy and environment technologies, including proposals for innovative technology programmes.

Drugs

58. We note with satisfaction progress made in this field since our Houston meeting, notably the entry into force of the 1988 United Nations Convention Against Illicit Traffic in Narcotic Drugs and Psychiatric [Psychotropic] Substances. We welcome the formation of the United Nations International Drugs Control Programme (UNDCP).

59. We will increase our efforts to reduce the demand for drugs as a part of overall anti-drug action programmes. We maintain our efforts to combat the scourge of cocaine and will match these by increased attention to heroin, still the principal hard drug in Europe and Asia. Enhanced co-operation is needed both to reduce production of heroin in Asia and to check its flow into Europe. Political changes in Central and Eastern Europe and the opening of frontiers there have increased the threat of drug misuse and facilitated illicit trafficking, but have also given greater scope for concerted Europe-wide action against drugs.

60. We applaud the efforts of the "Dublin Group" of European, North American and Asian governments to focus attention and resources on the problems of narcotics production and trafficking.

61. We commend the achievements of the task-forces initiated by previous Summits and supported by an increasing number of countries:—

a) We urge all countries to take part in the international fight against money laundering and to cooperate with the activities of the Financial Action Task Force (FATF). We strongly support the agreement on a mutual evaluation process of each participating country's progress in implementing the FATF recommendations on money laundering. We endorse the recommendation of the FATF that it should operate on a continuing basis with a secretariat supplied by the OECD.

b) We welcome the report of the Chemical Action Task Force (CATF) and endorse the measures it recommends for countering chemical diversion, building on the 1988 UN Convention against drug trafficking. We look forward to the special meeting in Asia, concentrating on heroin, and the CATF meeting due in March 1992, which should consider the institutional future of this work.

62. We are concerned to improve the capacity of law enforcement agencies to target illicit drug movements without hindering the legitimate circulation of persons and goods. We invite the Customs Cooperation Council to strengthen its cooperation with associations of international traders and carriers for this purpose and to produce a report before our next Summit.

Migration

63. Migration has made and can make a valuable contribution to economic and social development, under appropriate conditions, although there is a growing concern about worldwide migratory pressures, which are due to a variety of political, social and economic factors. We welcome the increased attention being given these issues by the OECD and may wish to return to them at a future Summit.

Next Meeting

64. We have accepted an invitation from Chancellor Kohl to hold our next Summit in Munich, Germany in July 1992.

BUSH'S NEWS CONFERENCE WITH GORBACHEV IN LONDON

President Bush. Well, may I say that it was a pleasure to have President Gorbachev in this Embassy. We've made a good deal of progress, and we will—he might have something to say about how much progress. But from the standpoint of the United States and the economic front and the arms front, we are very pleased with this meeting.

And once again, Mikhail, welcome, sir. I'm delighted to see you and your top people here.

President Gorbachev. Mr. President, it was very short, and that's because of the circumstances. In fact, we didn't have a lot of time at our disposal, but we used it very well and very productively, and we were able to talk about quite a few things. Again, there's not much time for the press conference, and maybe later you will be able to satisfy yourselves as far as what happens at our subsequent meeting.

Now, what I wanted to say was, in view of the fact that we were told that all of the issues are solved on the START treaty, we, with the President of the United States, have agreed to finalize everything in Geneva, and we will give commensurate instructions so that we could then sign that treaty. And this connection—there's also the issue of the visit of the President of the United States to the Soviet Union.

Once again, I've invited the President to come to the Soviet Union on a visit at the very end of July, and I hope that everything is clear now about the visit—the visit will take place. The Soviet people, all of us will be ready to give our hospitality to the President of the United States and, I also hope, to Mrs. Bush and to all those who will accompany him to Moscow. Welcome, Mr. President, to Moscow, and welcome all of you to Moscow.

And the last point: The President and I have had a discussion within the framework of what is happening in the context of this unique meeting with the G-7. And we are pleased with the kind of discussion that has taken place on those issues. So, I'm through, too.

President Bush. May I simply say that we accept with pleasure President Gorbachev's invitation. I hope we can get a lot done. And we've already accomplished a lot in treaty negotiations.

The goal, of course, is an economic goal. We'd be cooperatively working with President Gorbachev and, I would say, the rest of the G-7 and the rest of the world in integrating the Soviet economy into the rest of the world's economies. It's a big problem, a big project, but I pledge to him my interest and our efforts to do just exactly that.

But thank you, Mikhail, for your invitation. And before you change your mind, we accept with pleasure. [*Laughter*]

President Gorbachev. Well, I think that over the years of our cooperation you have seen, Mr. President, that we are true to our word in all those things: in working together, in accommodating you, your interests, and the interests both of ourselves and of our partners—particularly the United States.

I think that we have to say that the President and I have very limited time and so will not be able to answer all the questions that you would like to ask. After the meeting with the G-7, maybe then I will be able to answer all of your questions.

Soviet-U.S. Relations

Q. Does this mean you have a START treaty ready to sign now, and you are going to Moscow, and everything is on the line? Who caved? Who gave in?

President Bush. Helen [Helen Thomas, United Press International] always asks the questions where there has to be a winner or a loser or somebody continuing to fight each other; that's the way it is. There was compromise on all sides, and it's in the best interest of the United States, and I hope that the Soviet people feel it's in the best interest of the Soviet people.

Q. Well, does that mean that you will not build a new missile?

President Gorbachev. Let me say, I share what the President has just said. We will not be able to succeed either today or tomorrow in building new international relations, new international security, in achieving a balance of interest in the world if we try to achieve advantage and if we try to win. We have to move reciprocally towards each other in the interests of both our peoples, and I hope very much that the meeting that will take place in Moscow will be in the interest of all mankind, of all those who will be able to now breathe more quietly and to say that we have moved further away from the threat of nuclear war. So, it's our common victory, and I think that all those who have worked toward this important step—they really deserve a lot of credit.

Q. About G-7, what do you see as the strong position—strong points of the Gorbachev proposal?

President Bush. I think it would be unwise and inhospitable for me to start talking about the G-7 and what might happen to it until Mr. Gorbachev has a chance to come to this meeting hosted by John Major. That's the first point.

Secondly, leave out any communication between the two of us, let me simply say that in terms of our luncheon, I am convinced, as I have been, that President Gorbachev is determined to continue with economic reform. They face difficult problems. I'll be candid with you—we face difficult problems at home in a budgetary sense. But all in all, I would leave anything coming out of the G-7 until after the President has had a chance to discuss this with the other seven leaders.

Q. President Gorbachev—

President Gorbachev. Thank you, ladies and gentlemen.

President Bush. Are we finished? [*Laughter*]

Q. There's been talk during this summit of political support and technical assistance—

President Gorbachev. We have discussed with the President.

Q. Is that enough for you to take home in terms of economic aid, or are you looking for a bundle of cash here? [*Laughter*]

President Gorbachev. Well, that's my general answer. [*Laughter*]

President Bush. I've learned something about how to handle all these guys. This is good news.

Q. What's the date—pin it down?

President Bush. Well, we're pinning it down, but I'd say the very end of July.

Q. How long will the summit be?

President Bush. Oh, 2 or 3 days, but that's up to our host.

Q. Will you actually sign it then?

President Bush. We're trying.

Q. Was President Gorbachev helpful to you on the Mideast? Was he helpful to you?

President Bush. Very much. He continues to be.

DECISIONS TO REDUCE
U.S.-SOVIET NUCLEAR WEAPONRY
July 31, September 17, and October 5, 1991

Meeting in Moscow for their fourth summit conference, Presidents George Bush of the United States and Mikhail S. Gorbachev of the Soviet Union on July 31 signed the first arms treaty that would actually reduce the number of strategic nuclear weapons in the arsenals of the two powers. Previous U.S.-Soviet nuclear agreements placed limits on testing, development, and deployment of the weapons but did not reduce the existing inventories of either side.

The Moscow summit meeting took place less than three weeks before an attempted coup d'état, during which Gorbachev was held captive for two days. (Failure of Soviet Coup Attempt, p. 515) The takeover attempt, coupled with a threatened disintegration of the Soviet Union, left Washington unsure which political factions might gain control over Soviet nuclear weapons. That situation prompted Bush to push for further disarmament. To entice Gorbachev to follow his lead, Bush announced September 27 that the United States would cut its array of nuclear weapons far deeper than the Moscow treaty required. Within days, the Soviet Union responded with its own wide-ranging reductions in nuclear arms.

The Strategic Arms Reduction Treaty, known as START, had been nearly ten years in the making. For more than a year, American and Soviet officials had appeared close to agreement on the treaty's provisions. But it was not until July 17, at the Group of Seven economic summit in London, that Bush and Gorbachev announced they were ready to sign. (London Economic Summit, p. 451) The way was cleared by an agreement the two sides had reached June 1 on their interpretation of a treaty to reduce conventional forces in Europe. The two leaders had signed that treaty in Paris in November 1990, but disagreements quickly arose over Moscow's attempts to exclude certain categories of weapons and Bush declined to send the treaty to the Senate for ratification. Meeting in Lisbon on June 1, Secretary of State James A. Baker III and Soviet foreign minister Aleksandr A. Bessmertnykh said the differences had been resolved.

For decades, deployment of U.S. nuclear weapons in Europe had been viewed as necessary to deter any attack by large Soviet conventional— nonnuclear—forces. By cutting many categories of nonnuclear weapons in Europe, the conventional forces treaty reduced that threat, making it extremely difficult for either the West or the Soviet Union to launch a land offensive in Europe.

Key START Provisions

START applied to long-range nuclear weapons, including sea-launched cruise missiles and the bombs and attack missiles carried by heavy bombers. Within seven years the treaty would reduce the number of Soviet ballistic missile warheads by about 50 percent and U.S. warheads by about 35 percent. The United States and the Soviet Union, under terms of the treaty, would still possess nuclear arsenals about as large as when strategic arms reduction talks began in 1982. However, the additional reductions announced separately by Bush and Gorbachev in September and October would deplete the two arsenals even more.

Cuts Beyond Treaty Requirements

In a televised address to the nation, Bush announced September 27 that the United States would remove short-range nuclear weapons from bases in Europe and Asia, and from all naval vessels. He also announced that U.S. long-range bombers would no longer be kept on ready-alert status. Bush said that a Soviet invasion of Europe was "no longer a realistic threat," and "we now have an unparalleled opportunity to change the nuclear posture of both the United States and the Soviet Union."

Gorbachev responded to Bush's dramatic gesture by announcing in Moscow on October 5 that the Soviet Union would exceed the START requirements and within seven years reduce its number of strategic nuclear weapons to 5,000—1,000 below the treaty's ceiling—and destroy all tactical nuclear ammunition and missiles. He also said Soviet troop strength would be trimmed from 3.7 million to 3.0 million.

The Soviet Union's dire need for economic aid accounted for its willingness to conclude arms-reduction agreements. Many experts detected a tacit understanding that Moscow would yield on arms issues to win favor for Western economic assistance. On July 30, the first day of the summit, Bush said he would ask Congress to grant preferred tariff terms, known as "most-favored nation" status, to the Soviet Union. Congress was seen as almost certain to approve the president's request, thus putting the Soviet Union on a par with America's other trading partners.

Some seven weeks earlier the Soviet parliament had lifted virtually all restrictions on the right of Soviet citizens to emigrate or travel abroad. Congress, concerned about the plight of Soviet Jews, passed legislation in 1989 forbidding "most-favored nation" status for the Soviet Union until it, by law, permitted freer emigration. The Soviet emigration law was enacted over powerful protests by Communist hardliners who opposed political and economic reforms.

Uncertainty in the Soviet Union

The Moscow summit took place amid increasing difficulties in the relationships between the Soviet Union's central authority and its constituent republics. Bush made clear his commitment to Gorbachev. Speaking at St. George's Hall at the Kremlin July 30, he praised Gorbachev for "instituting reforms that changed the world." Bush added that the Soviet leader had won America's "respect and admiration for his vision and courage in replacing old orthodoxy."

Bush also met with the elected president of the Russian republic, Boris N. Yeltsin. When the summit ended Bush traveled to Kiev in the Ukraine to address that republic's parliament, saying that the United States would "not try to pick winners and losers in political competition between republics or between republics and the center."

The Ukraine, having declared its independence, announced October 22 that it would create an army of 400,000 troops and take control of the nuclear weapons on its soil. Ukranian leaders said they would give up the weapons eventually, but only after negotiations in which it would participate as an independent nation. (End of the Soviet Union and Gorbachev's Rule, p. 785)

Following are remarks by Presidents George Bush and Mikhail S. Gorbachev at the signing of the Strategic Arms Reduction Treaty in Moscow, July 31, 1991; a White House Fact Sheet on the treaty, issued the same day; excerpts from Bush's televised address from the White House on September 27 announcing further reductions in U.S. nuclear weaponry; and Gorbachev's televised response October 5:

GORBACHEV AND BUSH AT SIGNING CEREMONY

President Gorbachev. Mr. President, ladies and gentlemen, comrades. In a few moments the President of the United States and I will put our signatures under the treaty on the reduction of strategic offensive arms. This completes many years of efforts that required hard work and patience on the part of government leaders, diplomats, and military officials. They required will, courage, and the rejection of outdated perceptions of each other. They required trust.

This is also a beginning—the beginning of voluntary reduction of the nuclear arsenals of the U.S.S.R. and the United States, a process with unprecedented scope and objectives. It is an event of global significance, for we are imparting to the dismantling of the infrastructure of fear that has ruled the world, a momentum which is so powerful that it will be hard to stop.

In both countries we face the complex process of the ratification of the new treaty. There will be critics. Here in Moscow some will point to our unilateral concessions, while in Washington there will be talk about concessions made to the Soviet Union. Some will say the new treaty does not really fulfill the promise of a peace dividend since considerable resources will be required to destroy the missiles. And if the missiles are not destroyed, critics will say they're obsolete and must be replaced with new ones, and that will be even more expensive.

Sharp criticism is to be expected also from those who want to see faster and more ambitious steps toward abolishing nuclear weapons. In other words, the treaty will have to be defended. I'm sure we have achieved the best that is now possible and that is required to continue progress.

Tremendous work has been done and unique experience has been gained of cooperating in this enormously complex area. It is important that there is a growing realization of the absurdity of overarmament now that the world has started to move toward an era of economic interdependence, and that the information revolution is making the indivisibility of the world ever more evident.

But the policymakers have to bear in mind that as we move toward that era we will have to make new, immense efforts to remove the dangers inherited from the past and newly emerging dangers, to overcome various physical, intellectual, and psychological obstacles. Normal human thinking will have to replace the kind of militarized political thinking that has taken root in the minds of men. That will take time. A new conceptual foundation of security will be a great help. Doctrines of war fighting must be abandoned in favor of concepts of preventing war. Plans calling for a crushing defeat of the perceived enemy must be replaced with joint projects of mutual stability and defense sufficiency.

The document before us marks a moral achievement [and] major breakthrough in our country's thinking and behavior. Our next goal is to make full use of this breakthrough to make disarmament an irreversible process. So, as we give credit to what has been achieved, let us express our appreciation to those who have contributed to this treaty—their talent and their intellectual and numerous resources—and let us get down to work again for the sake of our own and global security.

Mr. President, we can congratulate each other. We can congratulate the Soviet and American people and the world community on the conclusion of this agreement.

Thank you.

President Bush. Thank you, Mr. President. To President Gorbachev and members of the Soviet Government, and all the honored guests here: May I salute you.

The treaty that we sign today is a most complicated one—the most complicated of contracts governing the most serious of concerns. Its 700 pages stand as a monument to several generations of U.S. and Soviet negotiators, to their tireless efforts to carve out common ground from a thicket of contentious issues—and it represents a major step forward for our mutual security and the cause of world peace.

And may I, too, thank everybody who worked on this treaty—the military, State Department arms control negotiators—really on both sides. And I would like to say that many are here today; some, like my predecessor, President Reagan, is not here. But I think all of us recognize that there are many who are not in this room that deserve an awful lot of credit on both the Soviet side and the United States side.

The START treaty vindicates an approach to arms control that guided us for almost a decade: the belief that we could do more than merely halt the growth of our nuclear arsenals. We could seek more than limits on the number of arms. In our talks we sought stabilizing reductions in our strategic arsenals.

START makes that a reality. In a historic first for arms control, we will actually reduce U.S. and Soviet strategic nuclear arsenals. But reductions alone are not enough. So, START requires even deeper cuts of the most dangerous and destabilizing weapons.

The agreement itself is exceedingly complex, but the central idea at the heart of this treaty can be put simply: Stabilizing reductions in our strategic nuclear forces reduce the risk of war.

But these promises to reduce arms levels cannot automatically guarantee success. Just as important are the treaty's monitoring mechanisms so we know that the commitments made are being translated into real security. In this area, START builds on the experience of earlier agreements—but goes far beyond them in provisions to ensure that we can verify this treaty effectively.

Mr. President, in the warming relations between our nations, this treaty stands as both cause and consequence. Many times during the START talks, reaching agreement seemed all but impossible. In the end, the progress that we made in the past year's time—progress in easing tensions and ending the cold war—changed the atmosphere at the negotiating table, and paved the way for START's success.

Neither side won unilateral advantage over the other. Both sides committed themselves instead to achieving a strong, effective treaty—and securing the mutual stability that a good agreement would provide.

Mr. President, by reducing arms, we reverse a half-century of steadily growing strategic arsenals. But more than that, we take a significant step forward in dispelling a half-century of mistrust. By building trust, we pave a path to peace.

We sign the START treaty as testament to the new relationship emerging between our two countries—in the promise of further progress toward lasting peace.

Thank you very much.

WHITE HOUSE FACT SHEET

Today, the United States and the Soviet Union signed the Strategic Arms Reduction Treaty. This treaty marks the first agreement between the two countries in which the number of deployed strategic nuclear weapons will actually be reduced. Reductions will take place over a period of 7 years, and will result in parity between the strategic nuclear forces of the two sides at levels approximately 30 percent below currently deployed forces. Deeper cuts are required in the most dangerous and destabilizing systems.

START provisions are designed to strengthen strategic stability at lower levels and to encourage the restructuring of strategic forces in ways that make them more stable and less threatening. The treaty includes a wide variety of very demanding verification measures designed to ensure compliance and build confidence.

Central Limits

The treaty sets equal ceilings on the number of strategic nuclear forces that can be deployed by either side. In addition, the treaty establishes an equal ceiling on ballistic missile throw-weight (a measure of overall capability for ballistic missiles). Each side is limited to no more than:

- 1600 strategic nuclear delivery vehicles (deployed intercontinental ballistic missiles [ICBM's], submarine launched ballistic missiles [SLBM's], and heavy bombers), a limit that is 36 percent below the Soviet level declared in September 1990 and 29 percent below the U.S. level.
- 6000 total accountable warheads, about 41 percent below the current Soviet level and 43 percent below the current U.S. level.
- 4900 accountable warheads deployed on ICBM's or SLBM's, about 48 percent below the current Soviet level and 40 percent below the current U.S. level.
- 1540 accountable warheads deployed on 154 heavy ICBM's, a 50 percent reduction in current Soviet forces. The U.S. has no heavy ICBM's.
- 1100 accountable warheads deployed on mobile ICBM's.
- Aggregate throw-weight of deployed ICBM's and SLBM's equal to about 54 percent of the current Soviet aggregate throw-weight.

Ballistic Missile Warhead Accountability

The treaty uses detailed counting rules to ensure the accurate accounting of the number of warheads attributed to each type of ballistic missile.

- Each deployed ballistic missile warhead counts as 1 under the 4900 ceiling and 1 under the 6000 overall warhead ceiling.
- Each side is allowed 10 on-site inspections each year to verify that deployed ballistic missiles contain no more warheads than the number that is attributed to them under the treaty.

Downloading Ballistic Missile Warheads

The treaty also allows for a reduction in the number of warheads on certain ballistic missiles, which will help the sides transition their existing forces to the new regime. Such downloading is permitted in a carefully structured and limited fashion.

- The U.S. may download its three-warhead Minuteman III ICBM by either one or two warheads. The Soviet Union has already downloaded it's [sic] seven warhead SS-N-18 SLBM by four warheads.
- In addition, each side may download up to 500 warheads on two other existing types of ballistic missiles, as long as the total number of warheads removed from downloaded missiles does not exceed 1250 at any one time.

New Types

The treaty places constraints on the characteristics of new types of ballistic missiles to ensure the accuracy of counting rules and prevent undercounting of missile warheads.

- The number of warheads attributed to a new type of ballistic missile must be no less than the number determined by dividing 40 percent of the missile's total throw-weight by the weight of the lightest RV tested on that missile.
- The throw-weight attributed to a new type must be no less than the missile's throw-weight capability at specified reference ranges (11,000 km for ICBM's and 9,500 km for SLBM's).

Heavy ICBM's

START places significant restrictions on the Soviet SS-18 heavy ICBM.

- A 50-percent reduction in the number of Soviet SS-18 ICBM's; a total reduction of 154 of these Soviet missiles.
- New types of heavy ICBM's are banned.
- Downloading of heavy ICBM's is banned.
- Heavy SLBM's and heavy mobile ICBM's are banned.
- Heavy ICBM's will be reduced on a more stringent schedule than other strategic arms.

Mobile ICBM's

Because mobile missiles are more difficult to verify than other types of ballistic missiles, START incorporates a number of special restrictions and notifications with regard to these missiles. These measures will significantly improve our confidence that START will be effectively verifiable.

- Nondeployed mobile missiles and nondeployed mobile launchers are numerically and geographically limited so as to limit the possibility for reload and refire.
- The verification regime includes continuous monitoring of mobile ICBM production, restrictions on movements, on-site inspections, and cooperative measures to improve the effectiveness of national technical means of intelligence collection.

Heavy Bombers

Because heavy bombers are stabilizing strategic systems (e.g., they are less capable of a short-warning attack than ballistic missiles), START counting rules for weapons on bombers are different than those for ballistic missile warheads.

- Each heavy bomber counts as one strategic nuclear delivery vehicle.
- Each heavy bomber equipped to carry only short-range missiles or gravity bombs is counted as one warhead under the 6000 limit.
- Each U.S. heavy bomber equipped to carry long-range nuclear ALCM's (up to a maximum of 150 bombers) is counted as 10 warheads even though it may be equipped to carry up to 20 ALCM's.
- A similar discount applies to Soviet heavy bombers equipped to carry long range nuclear ALCM's. Each such Soviet heavy bomber (up to a maximum of 180) is counted as 8 warheads even though it may be equipped to carry up to 16 ALCM's.
- Any heavy bomber equipped for long-range nuclear ALCM's deployed in excess of 150 for the U.S. or 180 for the Soviet Union will be accountable by the number of ALCM's the heavy bomber is actually equipped to carry.

Verification Regime

Building on recent arms control agreements, START includes extensive and unprecedented verification provisions. This comprehensive verification regime greatly reduces the likelihood that violations would go undetected.

- START bans the encryption and encapsulation of telemetric information and other forms of information denial on flight tests of ballistic missiles. However, strictly limited exemptions to this ban are granted sufficient to protect the flight-testing of sensitive research projects.
- START allows 12 different types of onsite inspections and requires roughly 60 different types of notifications covering production, testing, movement, deployment, and destruction of strategic offensive arms.

Treaty Duration

START will have a duration of 15 years, unless it is superseded by a subsequent agreement. If the sides agree, the treaty may be extended for successive 5-year periods beyond the 15 years.

Noncircumvention and Third Countries

START prohibits the transfer of strategic offensive arms to third countries, except that the treaty will not interfere with existing patterns of cooperation. In addition, the treaty prohibits the permanent basing of strategic offensive arms outside the national territory of each side.

Air-Launched Cruise Missiles (ALCM's)

START does not directly count or limit ALCM's. ALCM's are limited indirectly through their association with heavy bombers.

- Only nuclear-armed ALCM's with a range in excess of 600 km are covered by START.
- Long-range, conventionally armed ALCM's that are distinguishable from nuclear-armed ALCM's are not affected.
- Long-range nuclear-armed ALCM's may not be located at air bases for heavy bombers not accountable as being equipped for such ALCM's.
- Multiple warhead long-range nuclear ALCM's are banned.

Sea Launched Cruise Missiles (SLCM's)

SLCM's are not constrained by the treaty. However, each side has made a politically binding declaration as to its plans for the deployment of nuclear-armed SLCM's. Conventionally-armed SLCM's are not subject to such a declaration.

- Each side will make an annual declaration of the maximum number of nuclear-armed SLCM's with a range greater than 600 km that it plans to deploy for each of the following 5 years.
- This number will not be greater than 880 long-range nuclear-armed SLCM's.
- In addition, as a confidence building measure, nuclear-armed SLCM's with a range of 300-600 km will be the subject of a confidential annual data exchange.

Backfire Bomber

The Soviet Backfire bomber is not constrained by the treaty. However, the Soviet side has made a politically binding declaration that it will not deploy more than 800 air force and 200 naval Backfire bombers, and that these bombers will not be given intercontinental capability.

Other Background

The START agreement consists of the treaty document itself and a number of associated documents. Together they total more than 700 pages. The treaty was signed in a public ceremony by Presidents Bush and Gorbachev in St. Vladimir's Hall in the Kremlin. The associated documents were signed in a private ceremony at Novo Ogaryevo, President Gorbachev's weekend dacha. Seven of these documents were signed by

Presidents Bush and Gorbachev. Three associated agreements were signed by Secretary Baker and Foreign Minister Bessmertnykh. In addition, the START negotiators, Ambassadors Brooks and Nazarkin, exchanged seven letters related to START in a separate event at the Soviet Ministry of Foreign Affairs in Moscow.

Magnitude of START—Accountable Reductions

Following is the aggregate data from the Memorandum of Understanding, based upon agreed counting rules in START. (Because of those counting rules, the number of heavy bomber weapons actually deployed may be higher than the number shown in the aggregate.) This data is effective as of September 1990 and will be updated at entry into force:

	United States	Soviet Union
Delivery Vehicles	2,246	2,500
Warheads	10,563	10,271
Ballistic Missile Warheads.	8,210	9,416
Heavy ICBM's/Warheads.	None	308/3080
Throw-weight (metric tons).	2,361.3	6,626.3

As a result of the treaty, the above values will be reduced by the following percentages:

	United States	Soviet Union
Delivery Vehicles.	29 percent	36 percent
Warheads	43 percent	41 percent
Ballistic Missile Warheads.	40 percent	48 percent
Heavy ICBM's/Warheads.	None	50 percent
Throw-weight (metric tons).	None	46 percent

BUSH'S ADDRESS

Good evening. Tonight I'd like to speak with you about our future and the future of the generations to come. The world has changed at a fantastic pace, with each day writing a fresh page of history before yesterday's ink is even dried. And most recently, we've seen the peoples of the Soviet Union turn to democracy and freedom and discard a system of government based on oppression and fear.

Like the East Europeans before them, they face the daunting challenge of building fresh political structures based on human rights, democratic principles and market economies. Their task is far from easy and far from over. They will need our help, and they will get it.

But these dramatic changes challenge our nation as well. Our country has always stood for freedom and democracy, and when the newly elected leaders of Eastern Europe grappled with forming their new governments, they looked to the United States; they looked to American democratic principles in building their own free societies. Even the leaders of the

U.S.S.R. republics are reading "The Federalist" papers, written by America's founders, to find new ideas and inspiration.

Today, America must lead again as it always has, as only it can. And we will. We must also provide the inspiration for lasting peace, and we will do that, too. We can now take steps in response to these dramatic developments, steps that can help the Soviet peoples in their quest for peace and prosperity.

More importantly, we can now take steps to make the world a less dangerous place than ever before in the nuclear age. A year ago I described a new strategy for American defenses, reflecting the world's changing security environment. That strategy shifted our focus away from the fear that preoccupied us for 40 years, the prospect of a global confrontation. Instead, it concentrated more on regional conflicts, such as the one we just faced in the Persian Gulf. I spelled out a strategic concept, guided by the need to maintain the forces required to exercise forward presence in key areas, to respond effectively in crises, to maintain a credible nuclear deterrent, and to retain the national capacity to rebuild our forces, should that be needed.

We are now moving to reshape the U.S. military to reflect that concept. The new base force will be smaller by half a million than today's military, with fewer Army divisions, Air Force wings, Navy ships and strategic nuclear forces. This new force will be versatile, able to respond around the world to challenges, old and new.

As I just mentioned, the changes that allowed us to adjust our security strategy a year ago have greatly accelerated. The prospect of a Soviet invasion into Western Europe, launched with little or no warning, is no longer a realistic threat. The Warsaw Pact has crumbled. In the Soviet Union, the advocates of democracy triumphed over a coup that would have restored the old system of repression. The reformers are now starting to fashion their own futures, moving even faster toward democracy's horizon.

New leaders in the Kremlin and the republics are now questioning the need for their huge nuclear arsenal. The Soviet nuclear stockpile now seems less an instrument of national security and more of a burden. As a result, we now have an unparalleled opportunity to change the nuclear posture of both the United States and the Soviet Union.

If we and the Soviet leaders take the right steps, some on our own, some on their own, some together, we can dramatically shrink the arsenal of the world's nuclear weapons. We can more effectively discourage the spread of nuclear weapons. We can rely more on defensive measures [and] on our strategic relationship. We can enhance stability and actually reduce the risk of nuclear war.

Now is the time to seize this opportunity. After careful study and consultations with my senior advisers, and after considering valuable counsel from [British] Prime Minister [John] Major, [French] President [François] Mitterrand, [German] Chancellor [Helmut] Kohl and other allied leaders, I am announcing today a series of sweeping initiatives affecting every aspect of our nuclear forces on land, on ships and on aircraft.

I met again today with our Joint Chiefs of Staff, and I can tell you, they wholeheartedly endorse each of these steps. I'll begin with the category in which we will make the most fundamental change in nuclear forces in over 40 years: non-strategic or theater weapons.

Last year, I canceled U.S. plans to modernize our ground-launched theater nuclear weapons. Later, our NATO allies joined us in announcing that the alliance would propose the mutual elimination of all nuclear artillery shells from Europe as soon as short-range nuclear forces negotiations began with the Soviets.

But starting these talks now would only perpetuate these systems while we engage in lengthy negotiations. Last month's events not only permit but indeed demand swifter, bolder action. I am therefore directing that the United States eliminate its entire worldwide inventory of ground-launched, short-range—that is, theater—nuclear weapons. We will bring home and destroy all of our nuclear artillery shells and short-range ballistic missile warheads.

We will of course ensure that we preserve an effective air-delivered nuclear capability in Europe. That's essential to NATO's security. In turn, I have asked the Soviets to go down this road with us, to destroy their entire inventory of ground-launched theater nuclear weapons, not only their nuclear artillery and nuclear warheads for short-range ballistic missiles but also the theater systems the U.S. no longer has, systems like nuclear warheads for air defense missiles and nuclear land mines.

Recognizing further the major changes in the international military landscape, the United States will withdraw all tactical nuclear weapons from its surface ships and attack submarines, as well as those nuclear weapons associated with our land-based naval aircraft. This means removing all nuclear Tomahawk cruise missiles from U.S. ships and submarines, as well as nuclear bombs aboard aircraft carriers.

The bottom line is that under normal circumstances, our ships will not carry tactical nuclear weapons. Many of these land- and sea-based warheads will be dismantled and destroyed. Those remaining will be secured in central areas where they would be available if necessary in a future crisis.

Again, there is every reason for the Soviet Union to match our actions by removing all tactical nuclear weapons from its ships and attack submarines by withdrawing nuclear weapons for land-based naval aircraft and by destroying many of them and consolidating what remains at central locations.

I urge them to do so.

No category of nuclear weapons has received more attention than those in our strategic arsenals. The Strategic Arms Reduction Treaty, START, which [Soviet] President [Mikhail S.] Gorbachev and I signed last July, was the culmination of almost a decade's work. It calls for substantial stabilizing reductions and effective verification.

Prompt ratification by both parties is essential. But I also believe the time is right to use START as a springboard to achieve additional stabilizing changes. First, to further reduce tensions, I'm directing that all United States' strategic bombers immediately stand down from their alert posture. As a comparable gesture, I call upon the Soviet Union to confine its mobile missiles to their garrisons, where they will be safer and more secure.

Second, the United States will immediately stand down from alert all intercontinental ballistic missiles [ICBMs] scheduled for deactivation under START. Rather than waiting for the treaty's reduction plan to run its full seven-year course, we will accelerate elimination of these systems once START is ratified. I call upon the Soviet Union to do the same.

Third, I am terminating the development of the mobile Peacekeeper ICBM as well as the mobile portions of the small ICBM program. The small single-warhead ICBM will be our only remaining ICBM modernization program, and I call upon the Soviets to terminate any and all programs for future ICBMs with more than one warhead and to limit ICBM modernization to one type of single-warhead missile, just as we have done.

And fourth, I am canceling the current program to build a replacement for the nuclear short-range attack missile for our strategic bombers.

And fifth, as a result of the strategic nuclear weapons adjustments that I've just outlined, the United States will streamline its command and control procedures, allowing us to more effectively manage our strategic nuclear forces.

As the system works now, the Navy commands the submarine part of our strategic deterrent while the Air Force commands the bomber and land-based elements. But as we reduce our strategic forces, the operational command structure must be as direct as possible, and I therefore approve the recommendation of [Defense] Secretary [Dick] Cheney and the Joint Chiefs to consolidate operational command of these forces into a U.S. strategic command under one commander, with participation from both services.

Since the 1970s the most vulnerable and unstable part of the U.S. and Soviet nuclear forces has been intercontinental missiles with more than one warhead. Both sides have these ICBMs in fixed silos in the ground where they are more vulnerable than missiles on submarines. I propose that the U.S. and the Soviet Union seek early agreement to eliminate from their inventories all ICBMs with multiple warheads. After developing a timetable acceptable to both sides we could rapidly move to modify or eliminate these systems under procedures already established in the START agreement.

In short, such an action would take away the single most unstable part of our nuclear arsenals.

But there is more to do. The United States and the Soviet Union are not the only nations with ballistic missiles. Some 15 nations have them now and in less than a decade, that number could grow to 20.

The recent conflict in the Persian Gulf demonstrates in no uncertain terms that the time has come for strong action on this growing threat to world peace. Accordingly, I am calling on the Soviet leadership to join us in taking immediate, concrete steps to permit the limited deployment of non-nuclear defenses to protect against limited ballistic missile strikes, what-ever their source, without undermining the credibility of existing deterrent forces.

And we will intensify our effort to curb nuclear and missile proliferation. These two efforts will be mutually reinforcing. To foster cooperation, the United States soon will propose additional initiatives in the area of ballistic missile early warning.

And finally, let me discuss yet another opportunity for cooperation that can make our world safer. During last month's attempted coup in Moscow, many Americans asked me if I thought Soviet nuclear weapons were under adequate control. I do not believe that America was at increased risk of nuclear attack during those tense days. But I do believe more can be done to ensure the safe handling and dismantling of Soviet nuclear weapons.

And therefore I propose that we begin discussions with the Soviet Union to explore cooperation in three areas: First, we should explore joint technical cooperation on the safe and environmentally responsible storage, transportation, dismantling and destruction of nuclear warheads; second, we should discuss existing arrangements for the physical security and safety of nuclear weapons, and how these might be enhanced; third, we should discuss nuclear command and control arrangements, and how these might be improved to provide more protection against the unauthorized or accidental use of nuclear weapons. . . .

GORBACHEV'S RESPONSE

A week ago, U.S. President George Bush put forward an important initiative on nuclear weapons.

This initiative confirms that new thinking has been widely supported by the world community. George Bush's proposals continue the drive started in Reykjavik. This is my opinion. I know that Boris Yeltsin and leaders of other republics share this opinion.

In this statement, I will announce our reciprocal steps and counter-measures.

First. The following steps will be made as regards tactical nuclear weapons:

All nuclear artillery ammunition and nuclear warheads for tactical missiles will be destroyed.

Nuclear warheads of anti-aircraft missiles will be removed from the army and stored in central bases. Part of them will be destroyed. All nuclear mines will be eliminated.

All tactical nuclear weapons will be removed from surface ships and multi-purpose submarines. These weapons, as well as weapons from ground-based naval aviation will be stored. Part of them will be destroyed.

Thus, the Soviet Union and the United States are taking reciprocal radical measures leading to the elimination of tactical weapons.

Moreover, we propose that the United States remove on a reciprocal basis from the Navy and destroy tactical nuclear weapons. Also on a reciprocal basis, we could remove from active units of front tactical aviation all nuclear ammunition bombs and aircraft missiles and store them.

The Soviet Union urges other nuclear powers to join these far-reaching Soviet-U.S. measures as regards tactical weapons.

Point No. 2, I support—just like the President of the United States of America—the earliest possible ratification of the START treaty, and this will be put on the agenda of the first session of the new Supreme Soviet. Considering the unilateral measures taken by the United States and declared by President Bush concerning tactical nuclear weapons, we will take the following steps:

Our heavy bombers, just like the American heavy bombers, will not be on operational duty. Instead, their nuclear weapons will be stationed at depots, at garrisons. Modified nuclear short-range missiles for Soviet heavy bombers will not be designed any further. Mobile compact-size I.C.B.M.'s will stop being designed in the Soviet Union, the plan of it will be discontinued. Where the intercontinental ballistic missiles are based on railroads, the number of launchers will be kept at the current figures, and such missiles will not be modernized. This is to say that mobile I.C.B.M.'s with MIRV warheads, individually targeted warheads, will not be enhanced in number in this country. All our railway-based intercontinental ballistic missiles will be kept at their permanent bases, as our reciprocal step will remove from operational duty 503 I.C.B.M.'s, including 134 I.C.B.M.'s with MIRV warheads.

We have removed from operational duty three nuclear submarines which in between them carry 44 launchers. We are also removing another three nuclear submarines that contain 48 missile launchers.

Point No. 3. We have made a decision on deeper cuts in the strategic offensive weapons than the provisions contained in the START treaty provide for. As a result, after the seven-year period of the cuts program, the number of strategic nuclear warheads will be not 6,000 units as provided for in the treaty, but 5,000 units.

Naturally, we would welcome a similar approach should such approach be displayed by the United States of America. We propose to the United States immediately upon the ratification of the Start treaty to embark on intensive negotiations on further radical reductions of the strategic offensive weapons, approximately to halve them.

We are prepared to consider proposals from the United States of American on non-nuclear anti-missile defense systems. We also suggest that the United States consider the possibility of setting joint systems for warning against a nuclear missile attack with elements based in space and on land.

Point No. 4. We declare that as of today we have imposed a unilateral moratorium on nuclear tests for the period of one year. We're hoping that this example will be followed by the other nuclear powers, and in this way a road will be opened up for earliest and complete cessation of all nuclear tests.

We also want to agree with the United States on a controllable cessation of the production of all fissionable materials which are used for the manufacturing of weapons.

No. 5. We hereby stress readiness to embark on a specific dialogue with the United States on the elaboration of safe and ecologically responsible technologies for the storage and transportation of nuclear warheads and on the methods of utilization of nuclear warheads and nuclear charges, and to design jointly measures to enhance nuclear safety.

To increase control over nuclear weapons, we bring under one operational command all the strategic nuclear weapons. We include the strategic defense systems in just one single arm of the armed forces.

Point No. 6. We're hoping that in the long run the efforts of the Soviet Union and of the United States of America will be joined in an active manner by the other nuclear powers. And I believe that it is time that a joint statement be made by all the nuclear powers on the non-use of—on the non-first use of nuclear weapons.

The Soviet Union has for a long period of time abided by this principle of non-first use of nuclear weapons. And it is my conviction that this step—a similar step by the United States of America would make a major impact.

Point No. 7. It is with a feeling of satisfaction that we received the statement made by the United States of America that they are going to cut their armed forces by half a million. We, for our part, are planning to reduce our armed forces by 700,000 personnel.

In conclusion, I would like to emphasize the following. By acting in this manner unilaterally or reciprocally or by way of negotiations, we are firmly and steadily taking forward the process of disarmament and thus reaching for the goal that was declared in 1986: the goal of building a more stable and more secure world and a nuclear-free world.

SENATE DEBATE ON
WOMEN IN COMBAT
July 31, 1991

Mindful that American military units in the Persian Gulf included nearly 35,000 women, Congress returned to the question of whether women should be assigned to combat duty. In previous years the lawmakers had been vehemently opposed to this action, but in 1991 they lifted a ban on women combat pilots and commissioned a high-level study on whether women should be allowed to enter battle in additional ways.

Compared with the usual glacial pace of congressional action, legislation clearing the way for women to fight in the skies moved through the House and Senate in a political blitzkrieg. Proponents began their effort May 8 by winning approval from the House Armed Services Committee— and later the full House—for a provision in the annual defense authorization bill to repeal a 1948 law that barred the assignment of women to air warfare.

On July 31, despite objections by the Senate Armed Services Committee, a broad-based coalition of Democrats and Republicans, placed a similar amendment in the Senate version of the defense bill. However, the new legislation stopped short of directing that women be added to combat air crews. It permitted but did not require the Pentagon to issue such an order. Other longtime prohibitions against women serving in combat ground forces or warships remained unchanged.

Public opinion polls cited in the debate indicated that Americans generally held conflicting emotions on the question. The amendment's principal sponsors, Sens. Edward M. Kennedy, D-Mass., and William V. Roth, Jr., D-Del., cast their arguments in terms of providing equal opportunity to women in the armed forces.

Persian War Impetus for Change

Female military officers had long argued that their career prospects were limited by their inability to serve in combat units. This argument gained momentum from laudatory reports on the performance of servicewomen, including those who flew helicopters and airplanes in combat conditions during the Persian Gulf War. (Prelude and Onset of War with Iraq, p. 15) *"They flew behind enemy lines and transported troops into enemy territory," Roth told the Senate. "We owe our victory, in part, to the superb performance of the women pilots."*

The military operations in the war subtly highlighted aspects of modern warfare that undermined traditional reasons for barring women from some combat roles. In the cockpit, especially, technology had reduced the significance of men's superior physical strength. "Today's aircraft is a great equalizer," Roth said. The fighting also underscored the dangers that face all military personnel in war zones—even those well behind the front lines—from terrorists, bombs, missiles, and chemical weapons.

According to Defense Department accounts, eleven U.S. servicewomen were killed during Operation Desert Storm, five of them from enemy action. The other six, plus two others during the preceding military buildup in the region, died as a result of accidents. In addition, during the fighting two women soldiers were captured by the Iraqis and briefly held as prisoners of war.

Repeal of Bar to Women Combat Fliers

Sen. Sam Nunn, D-Ga., the committee chairman, and its senior Republican member, Sen. John W. Warner of Virginia, urged the Senate to reject the Kennedy-Roth amendment and instead authorize a presidential commission of fifteen experts to study issues involved in assigning women to combat, including the effect on unit morale, the cost of required changes in equipment and quarters, and whether it would render unconstitutional the draft registration law, which applies only to men. The commission would submit its recommendations by November 15, 1992, and the president would send them with his own to Congress one month later.

Sens. John Glenn, D-Ohio, and John McCain, R-Ariz., two former fighter pilots, cautioned against haste in repealing the combat-exclusion law for female fliers. The debate was "all too driven by emotions and far too little driven by national security requirements," McCain said. He contended that, unlike pilots, who are officers, "the overwhelming majority of enlisted women in the Army and Marine Corps do not wish to be in combat." Only about one-half of 1 percent of the 227,000 women in military service were aviators.

The Senate opted not to choose between repealing the exclusion law and setting up a study commission, and instead approved both measures. By a 30-69 vote it rejected the Armed Services Committee's effort to kill the repeal amendment, and then on a 96-3 vote approved the commission proposal.

Following are excerpts from the Congressional Record *of July 31, 1991, of that day's Senate debate on amendments to repeal a law barring women fliers from combat duty and to commission a study on the assignment of servicewomen to combat:*

Mr. Roth. Mr. President, the amendment which Senator Kennedy and I will propose later is not about gender, but about excellence. It is not about women pilots flying combat missions, but about the best pilots flying combat missions.

The readiness and preparedness of our military defense is a serious matter. When our Nation's future is at stake—and the future of free nations is at stake—we want the most skilled and seasoned men and women on the job.

Make no mistake—military excellence must be our first priority. Our Secretary of Defense must have the greatest flexibility and maneuverability to marshall the forces at his command. We want the best and brightest pilots in the air, not on the ground. We want the best person in the cockpit of a Stealth fighter or a B-1 bomber—not the second best.

Mr. President, America is with us on this issue. A Newsweek poll released just this week shows that 63 percent of Americans favor allowing women to fly combat aircraft. The American people know that what is good for our military defense is also good for the country. And what is good for the country is excellence, readiness, preparedness, strength, and flexibility.

Forty years ago Congress imposed a rule which now prevents women from serving as combat pilots. This congressional restriction is as old and outdated in today's military as a World War II propeller plane.

Flexibility is impeded and excellence is shortchanged because of this artificial barrier. Our Secretary of Defense needs to have the flexibility to make intelligent decisions about who should fly these fighter aircraft.

Leaving an antiquated barrier in place—when it impairs the maximum effectiveness of our armed services—makes no sense at all. Adm. William Lawrence, the president of the Association of Naval Aviators and a past Chief of Naval Personnel, summed up the problem succinctly when he wrote the following:

> The principle problem which must be solved is that the 1948 law which governs the role of women in the military had become totally outmoded and inappropriate as the roles and numbers of women have been expanded over the past 40 years.

Congress should wake up and lift the ban—and let the Pentagon do its job.

The amendment before us today would remove this outdated law. Our legislation gives the Secretary of Defense maximum flexibility to fill the job with the best-qualified person.

The Department of Defense has underscored its desire to assume this authority and has supported the intent of our legislation. I quote Pentagon spokesman Pete Williams, who said:

> ... The Department welcomes this legislation, because it gives the Department of Defense the authority to decide where the line should be drawn, rather than having Congress set the limits on the role of women in combat.

Individual ability and individual skill—not gender—must determine who flies these high performance planes. And with today's technology, the only true distinctions are skill, performance, speed, reflexes, nerves, guts, and brains. These are the qualities we want when the critical moment arises.

Today's aircraft is a great equalizer, as our women pilots have said. Technology has enabled women to compete on a level playing field. These changes can no longer be ignored. Our military needs pilots who have, in the words of writer Tom Wolfe, the "right stuff"—and many of our women pilots do indeed have the right stuff.

Our goal is very simple, Mr. President: to lift artificial barriers where they are no longer needed. We do not instruct the Pentagon to hire women as combat pilots. We leave these decisions in the hands of the professionals, not the politicians. . . .

The Senate Armed Services Committee—instead of adopting my proposal—has called for a study commission. We do not need a commission to study the issue. A commission will not tell us anything we do not already know about the performance of women pilots in battle.

Women have proven themselves—the documentation is clear and well documented. The best arguments are performance, experience, and aptitude—and women military pilots have come through with flying colors on all three counts.

For anyone who thinks we need more studies, more evidence, I say, look at the record. Women have been pulling G's in high performance aircraft for over 15 years now. Women aviators train our male combat pilots. They test the newest generation aircraft. They fly the space shuttle. Women pilots test FA-18s and C-27s. They fly transport planes and refueling planes, they fly AWACS and helicopters. In fact, women have flown just about every plane that the Pentagon has built in the past three decades. There is no question about their performance, or their experience, in this regard.

But women have proven themselves not only in the instructor's seat and in the test pilot's seat, but in battle conditions and in the line of fire. Their aptitude and ability may have been proven here at home—but their courage and mettle were proven in the skies over Saudi Arabia, Kuwait, and Iraq. . . .

Our women pilots showed cool thinking and competence as Army helicopter pilots, Air Force AWACS pilots, and Navy surveillance pilots in Operation Desert Storm. They flew behind enemy lines and transported troops into enemy territory. Some of them flew ahead of the ground assault into Iraq. We owe our victory, in part, to the superb performance of these women pilots.

The bottom line is clear, Mr. President. Women are already involved in just about every aspect of high performance flight. They have proven themselves steadily and consistently over the years, and they have served with great distinction as part of Operation Desert Storm. Frankly, the verdict is in.

Our women military pilots are an exciting new generation of aviators. They are smart, articulate, and professional. They are commanders of squadrons and test pilots of advanced fighter aircraft. They are trainers at our best air combat schools.

They are the kind of dedicated pilots who earned their pilot's license before they got their driver's license. Many of these young women entered the military with the express purpose of flying fighter aircraft—of being the top guns of their profession. Their male counterparts have attested to their ability and competence.

For example, Capt. Thomas J. Bernsen of the Patuxent Naval Air Station was recently quoted in the Washington Post as saying, "These are exceptional ladies . . . they blew out on top of the guys to wind up coming here. . . . I'd put them up against any man, anywhere."

I have had the opportunity to talk with many of these women, and let me tell you, they are an inspiration. You might expect them to talk about equality or career advancement, but that has not been the case. These women talk about serving America to the best of their ability. They talk about what our military defense should look like—why readiness and flexibility are so important now and in the future.

Many of these women are distinguished war veterans. They know the risks they have already taken, the risks they will take in the future. . . .

Mr. Nunn. Mr. President, I ask unanimous consent that there be 3 hours for debate to be controlled by the sponsors of the amendments. There will be one amendment offered by Senators Roth and Kennedy and one amendment offered by Senators Glenn and McCain. . . .

Mr. Warner. . . . It has been hoped that Senators Roth and Kennedy would come forward with their amendment. The amendment just offered by Senator Glenn on behalf of himself, Mr. McCain, Mr. Nunn, and myself would be in the nature of a substitute. But for various reasons, that is not being done at this time.

I wish to indicate that as these two debates are debated in this one time agreement, it is very clear to this Senator, and I believe to my three colleagues on the second amendment, that we intend to oppose clearly the amendment by the Senator from Delaware and the Senator from Massachusetts. I see some conflict between the two amendments should the Senate adopt both amendments.

During the course of the debate, I urge my colleagues to listen carefully because I think there is a clear distinction between the two amendments, and this Senator intends not only to debate against the amendment offered by the distinguished Senators from Massachusetts and Delaware, but also to vote against it. I will so urge my colleagues at the appropriate time.

Women feel they have considerably more to contribute in the military than they are currently permitted to do.... They are willing to allow changes to be made that are based on proven performance and need. They just don't want ridiculous artificial barriers to be placed in their path.

Mr. President, it is time to remove the barrier.

Mr. Kennedy. ... The Armed Forces claim that they are an equal opportunity employer, and they are, partly. They have made great strides in opening up all branches of the service to racial minorities.

But the same cannot be said with regard to sex discrimination, because archaic statutes still in the books deny equal opportunity to women.

Barriers based on sex discrimination are coming down in every part of our society. The Armed Forces should be no exception. Women should be allowed to play a full role in our national defense, free of any arbitrary and discriminatory restrictions. The only fair and proper test of a woman's role is not gender but ability to do the job.

The 1948 law that limited the role of women in the regular armed services contained three parts: First it limited the total number of women in the armed services. Second, it put a ceiling at the lieutenant colonel level, commander in the Navy, on the highest rank women could achieve. Third, it barred women from serving aboard combat aircraft in the Air Force and Navy, as well as combat ships in the Navy.

The Army does not have to contend with a statutory exclusion. The Army prohibitions on women in combat are contained entirely in service regulations, which are adapted to changing times without the enactment of legislation. The Marine Corps addresses the issue of women in ground combat in the same way as the Army—through regulation.

Ironically, the most complex questions about the exclusion of women from combat are related to the Army, not the Air Force or the Navy. Yet it is the Air Force and the Navy that have to contend with statutory exclusions that make worthwhile and essential reforms impossible.

During the late 1960s, Congress repealed the first two restrictions contained in the 1948 law. The time has come to remove the last of these statutory prohibitions on the role of women in the military. It has become an embarrassing anachronism. The changing nature of modern warfare means that old distinctions are obsolete.

The dangers now extend well behind the front lines. As we saw in the Persian Gulf war, military personnel well behind the lines can be killed or wounded. At the same time, the infusion of advanced electronic and computer technology into modern weapons has changed many phases of warfare from a test of physical strength to a test of technical skill.

In the gulf war, the technological abilities of our personnel were as important to our victory as their physical strength and courage. There is virtually universal consensus that the women who served in Operation Desert Storm did an outstanding job, including jobs that were, for all practical purposes, combat jobs. They faced hostile fire; they flew into enemy territory, they suffered death, injury, and were captured as prisoners of war; they lived in conditions of extreme hardship, and they performed tasks requiring physical strength and stamina.

In short, to quote Secretary of Defense Dick Cheney, women members of our Armed Forces "were every bit as professional as their male colleagues." This performance comes as no surprise. Women have been proving themselves in the military for many years. The real surprise is that the outstanding performance of women in the military and the changing nature of modern warfare has not led the Congress to repeal the statutory restrictions on women in combat roles before now.

These laws are bad for women, because they deny them an equal opportunity for service and advancement in the military. Over the past two decades, the Pentagon has informally narrowed the scope of the combat exclusion laws. But as the Department's manpower chief testified before the Senate Armed Services Committee last month, DOD [Department of Defense] has reached the point where further expansion of the opportunities for women in the military is difficult unless we lift the combat exclusions. And the combat exclusion laws are bad for men because they place an inequitable portion of the burdens of military duty on male service members. Combat positions in all services often call for military personnel to be away from their families for extended periods, to risk death and injury, and to live under hardship conditions. Because women are barred from these positions, the men must take up the slack and bear a disproportionate share of these hardships.

The combat exclusion laws are bad for our nation's security because they deny the military the opportunity to put the best personnel by virtue of training and skills in the most important positions. Today, if the best person for a combat position is a woman, she will not get the job.

The amendment that Senators Roth, McConnell, Bingaman, Leahy, and I are offering is a sensible first step toward changing the combat exclusion laws. It repeals only the laws barring women from serving in combat aircraft in the Navy and the Air Force. It does nothing more. Our amendment does not require the Air Force and Navy to open a single combat position to women fliers. It only gives the Secretary of the Air Force and the Navy the same authority that the Secretary of the Army has had since 1948 to assign women to all combat positions.

Our amendment does not direct the military to lower its standards. Each service determines the qualifications necessary for performance of each assignment. Repeal of the statutory exclusions for air combat will not require that women be placed in jobs for which they are not qualified. It will not require that any standards be lowered to increase numbers of women. The fact is, women already meet the very demanding standard to fly high performance combat aircraft. They test combat aircraft. They train combat pilots.

It is ludicrous for Congress to bar them from flying in combat in the planes they have tested and with the officers they have trained.

Our amendment does not open ground combat positions to women. Women in the Army and the Marine Corps are not barred from ground combat by law but by Pentagon regulations. These regulations will remain unchanged by repeal of the combat exclusion laws for pilots.

Finally, our amendment does not make women eligible for a military draft. There is no draft now, and there is none in sight. Congress retains full control over the terms of any future draft law.

The amendment does not change the Pentagon policies barring women from ground combat, and it is preposterous to suggest that the change proposed by this amendment would cause the Supreme Court to reverse its past decision upholding draft registration only for men.

The issue is not whether women should be in combat. They already are. Thousands of women served ably and courageously in the Persian Gulf war. The real issue is whether women are entitled to serve in all military positions for which they are qualified.

The issue is not whether women should be shot at. They already are—five women died from enemy fire during the gulf war. The real issue is whether women can shoot back.

The issue is not whether women should fly high-performance aircraft. They already do. Women serve as instructors for combat pilots. The real issue is whether we select our pilots based on ability or on gender.

It is an embarrassment to Congress and an injustice to every woman in the Armed Forces that we retain these foolish restrictions on the statute books, and I urge the Senate to repeal them.

Mr. Glenn. . . . [As] the sponsors of our amendment, Senators McCain, Warner, Nunn, and myself oppose the Roth-Kennedy amendment. We will vote against it. We urge our colleagues to vote against it. . . .

Mr. President, the arguments in favor of our amendment we believe greatly strengthen the committee's provision establishing a commission to study and report on the assignment of women in our military services. Our amendment basically would authorize a Presidential commission, along with that of the Secretary of Defense, to temporarily waive combat exclusion laws, all of them—combat exclusion laws and policies, whatever they may be, so that women may be assigned during this period to combat roles in the air, at sea, on the ground, on a test basis.

This would allow the commission to evaluate the performance of women in these roles and make appropriate recommendations to us on the basis of some real analysis. This will be a very broad look at the whole thing, not just the narrow focus on pilots, and women in the military. It would take a look at the pilots, women in the military, take a look at all the other functions, all the MOS's [military occupation specialties] in the military, evaluate the performance of women in these roles, and then make appropriate recommendations to us on the basis of that kind of an analysis. It would be very broad but it would be temporary until the commission finishes up its deliberations and reports back to us, and one very important part is it does not prejudge any direction.

It says that basically the Department of Defense is charged with the military security of this Nation of ours and they can run these tests and analyses, see where we can open up the areas without disturbing combat efficiency into the future, and what roles women could perform and perform in an excellent fashion just as my distinguished colleague from Delaware says he favors doing.

I favor the same thing. But I want to do it on a more studied basis, and with some data other than just us standing upon the floor and saying what people can do.

So, Mr. President, our amendment is a much broader and much more positive step than the amendment offered by my colleague from Delaware, and supported by the Senator from Massachusetts, which would only open combat aircraft to women. That affects less than one-half of 1 percent of the 227,000 women in our military services.

Our amendment on the other hand would let all of our women in uniform participate on a test basis in all combat roles for which they wish to compete. It is very broad. Our amendment would say to all military women that we are looking for positive ways to improve their opportunities while at the same time being conscious of the effects such as the potential of subjecting women to involuntary assignments to ground combat assault roles on the same basis as men—I repeat, involuntary assignments or requiring women to register for the draft and to be drafted on the same basis as men, in the future as necessary.

Mr. President, I believe we all acknowledge, I certainly do, the outstanding contributions made to our national defense by women serving in our Armed Forces. Despite laws and DOD policies that restrict their assignments from certain combat skills and positions, and today women in the military serve in many extremely demanding roles—combat support, combat service support, which has already been noted here, which put them in the positions of actual combat during the Persian Gulf [War], and some lost their lives—some of these roles expose women to the risk of death in combat. Most recently women have performed under those conditions in the Persian Gulf conflict.

So our interest in expanding the role of women in our military services is understandable and it is laudable. However, assigning women to combat skills and positions does raise some very basic questions about the future shape and structure of the Armed Forces that cannot be answered by merely saying we just open all our selected combat skills and positions to women or by shoveling such decisions to the Secretary of Defense.

I believe Congress should accept this responsibility in this regard, should make such decisions openly, deliberately but after a full examination of all the available facts. We must neither continue the current combat restriction laws and policies for invalid reasons nor repeal such laws or policies without full understanding of the meaning of such action.

Mr. President, we had a hearing on this issue on June 18 of this year. At that hearing defense witnesses indicated that the administration would not make any substantive changes to its policies on the utilization of women even if the current assignment restrictions in law are repelled. Other witnesses testified on the other hand that women should be provided the same opportunities as men to serve in any skill or position in the Armed Forces and the women should share the same responsibilities for national defense as men with all that implies.

These responsibilities would include being subject to draft registration, being subject to involuntary assignment after being drafted into combat during military service, and being subject to conscription during periods when conscription may be authorized by law. On the other hand, other witnesses testified that women should not be placed in any combat role whatsoever, none at all.

Mr. President, it was evident from the very wide range of strongly held views heard by the committee at that hearing, and the many crucial questions that were left unanswered, that substantially more study is required before we can act conclusively on the overall future role of women in the Armed Forces. And that includes all women in the Armed Forces, not just pilots. For example, we do not know at this point what the implications would be of opening some or all combat positions to women with regard to questions such as—let me just run through some of the things that came to mind or that we asked questions about during that hearing.

For instance, if we decided to open any combat assignments to women, should assignments of women to these positions be voluntary? Or should women be compelled to serve in combat assignments regardless of their personal desires in the same manner that men can be assigned involuntarily to combat positions? Should women be required to register, be subject to the draft on the same basis as men if women are to have the same opportunity as men to compete for all skills and positions in the military? If current combat exclusion laws are repealed but the military services retain the discretion to prescribe combat assignment restrictions for women what affect will this have on the constitutionality of the male only registration and service requirements of the Military Selective Service Act?

What are the physical requirements for each combat skill or position, including the full implications of gender norming? Those are practices where women are given lesser tests or tests that are less physically demanding, and allowed to assume positions for which their male counterparts would have to have a higher physical capability.

What are the full implications of gender norming where there are physical requirements and men and women are treated alike? What is the impact of pregnancy and child care on assignment policies for military personnel? What is the practical effect of opening combat skills and positions to women on unit morale and cohesion?

If current combat exclusion laws and policies are repealed, would the present policy under which only males may be involuntarily assigned to combat skills and positions be sustainable?

What would be the impact of required changes in quarters, weapons, training, and the resultant costs of changes?

What would be the practical rate at which any required changes can be made in an era of severely constrained defense budgets?

Mr. President, the other aspect the Commission would help us with is on what the American people think about all of this.

A recent Newsweek poll, as an example, indicates to me that there is considerable uncertainty in the American public about just how far we should go in opening combat jobs for women, and which jobs should be opened up.

The general conclusion of the poll was that, although the majority of Americans think women should be placed in combat positions if they so desire, they should be placed in those positions only if they want to.

And here are the questions and answers to that poll:

One: Do you think women in the Armed Forces should get combat assignments?

That was the question in the Newsweek poll.

Fifty-three percent of those polled said "only if the women want them." Twenty-six percent said that such assignments should be made on the same basis as for men. Eighteen percent said women should never be assigned to combat jobs.

So if you go by that poll, we have about one-fourth of those polled who think women should bear the same responsibility as men in combat.

Second question: If women were allowed to get combat assignments, are you very or somewhat concerned about the following:

Eighty-nine percent say they were concerned about mothers leaving small children at home. Seventy-six percent said they were concerned about putting a pregnant woman's fetus at risk. Sixty-four percent said they were concerned about women becoming pregnant and having to be replaced from their combat unit. Fifty-three percent said they were concerned about women being able to perform at the same level as men. Thirty-eight percent said they were concerned that men will fight less well because women are present.

These responses should not be taken as a basis for action here on the Senate floor, but I think these responses do indicate more than a small amount of concern in the American public about assigning women in combat roles, and that is what we propose for the Commission to take into consideration.

The third question that they had on the Newsweek poll was: If a draft became necessary, should young women be required to participate?

Fifty percent said "yes." Forty-seven percent said "no."

At the same time, should mothers on active duty be able to refuse assignment?

Fifty-four percent said "yes." Forty percent said "no".

Finally, the question: Would allowing women to serve in combat roles be an advantage or burden to the military?

Twenty percent said it would be a burden in combat support roles, and women already serve in those roles now. Some 70 percent of the military occupation specialty are open to women right now.

Thirty percent said it would be a burden in jet fighter pilot roles, where women do not currently serve in these roles.

Thirty-three percent said it would be a burden on Navy warships.

Women do not currently serve on these ships.

Fifty-one percent said it would be a burden for women to serve in the infantry. Women do not currently serve in the infantry.

What do we conclude from the polls?

The results of the poll tell me that the American public is concerned about the roles of women in our military. I think they instinctively believe, as I do, that women can do more jobs in the military than women are currently allowed to do. At the same time, I think they are as concerned as we are, as we approach this issue, that we ensure the bottom line of what a military is supposed to be for, and that is to deter war—hopefully, by having such a strong force, that war never comes—and if war comes, to fight and win at the least cost in American lives. That is the bottom line—combat capability. Or if we do not have that same capability, we stand to lose more American lives in combat. . . .

Mr. President, in order to get conclusive answers to the questions I have posed, and to address the public concerns captured so well in the poll that I have just described, the committee approved a provision that would require the President to appoint a commission to study and report, then, on the assignment of women in military.

The formation of this committee responds to our interest in providing more opportunities for women in the military, and our amendment reinforces this interest. We look at the whole spectrum of jobs clear across the military. We do not limit it just to the narrow focus of pilots in the military. We say that the commission should look at every job in the military and see if it can be opened up. If they determine that, then we would move in that direction.

Under our provision, the military services can, for the very first time, place women in all combat roles on a test basis to help an independent commission develop recommendations for us based on empirical analysis.

I believe that is a very positive first step toward making the kinds of changes that responsibly address our desire for providing more opportunities for women in our military service. It is a much more broad approach than the amendment proposed by the distinguished Senator from Delaware.

Mr. President, as spelled out in the committee report, the commission would consist of 15 members, Presidential commission, who have distinguished themselves in the public sector, the private sector, who have had significant experience in matters, such as scholarly inquiry into social, cultural matters affecting the workplace; constitutional and other law; the effects of medical and physiological factors on job performance; military personnel management, and service in the Armed Forces in land, air, and sea combat environments.

The commission would be required to submit its report to the President by November 15, 1992, and the President would be required to submit his comments and recommendations on the report to the Congress by December 15, 1992.

The commission would be required to make specific recommendations with regard to whether existing law and policies governing the assignment of women in the military should be retained, modified, or repealed; what roles women should have in the military, including what, if any, roles women should have in combat; what transition process is appropriate, if women are to be given the opportunity to be assigned to combat positions in the military; and whether special conditions and different standards should apply to women that apply to men performing similar roles in the military.

Mr. Glenn. Mr. President . . . let me address some of the questions about assignment of women in the military.

This is the first question: What is wrong with the Roth-Kennedy amendment that would allow military women to fly combat aircraft when they have proven themselves in other aircraft?

I feel that the Roth-Kennedy amendment gets the cart before the horse. We really do not have the empirical analyses right now that indicates how women perform in combat aircraft. For example, no women have completed the Navy's Top Gun or the Air Force Red Flag air combat evaluations. Our amendment would open that up. We would not prohibit that. We would say that can be done. Let the women participate in these and other sea and ground training evaluations.

The Roth-Kennedy amendment would set up two classes of women in the military, as we see it. For example, a woman officer who is an aviator would be allowed to be assigned to an operational aircraft carrier. On the other hand, a woman petty officer just as interested in her career advancement as anyone else, but a woman officer who works on the very aircraft that the woman officer flies would be prohibited from being assigned to the same aircraft carrier. So the status is changed only for a tiny fraction of women officers who constitute less than one-half of 1 percent of all women in the military.

I think a very broad approach of all women in all assignments in the military having that assessed makes more sense.

The Roth-Kennedy amendment would change the focus of the Commission that the committee proposes to make a broad policy review focus on the assignment of all women in the military to a much narrower focus on the implementation of the assignment only of women officer aviators to combat aircraft.

Our amendment strengthens the Commission by giving it the authority and tools to gather information and develop empirical analyses that we could use as the basis for making judgments then on the assignment policy for all women in the military and not just a small percentage of women.

The second question: Why should we not repeal the combat exclusion laws and leave the policies governing the assignment of women in the military up to DOD?

I think we have a responsibility in Congress to take a broader view than just to saying it to the Pentagon. We have a responsibility for manning our Armed Forces in peace and war. We make those decisions in the Congress. Congress has exercised this responsibility in the past and in determining that women should not be assigned in direct combat assault roles.

Now we may want to change that. But we do not know the implications of such action without looking at this very carefully and with regard to questions such as:

If we decide to open any combat assignments to women, should assignments of women to these positions be voluntary or should women be compelled to serve in combat assignments, regardless of their personal desires, in the same manner that men can be assigned involuntarily to combat positions?

Should women be required to register and be subject to the draft on the same basis as men if women have the same opportunity as men to compete for all skills and positions in the military?

If current combat exclusion laws are repealed, but the military services retain the discretion to prescribe combat assignment restrictions for women, what effect will this have on the constitutionality of the male-only registration and service requirements of the Military Selective Service Act?

And once again, what are the physical requirements for each combat skill or position, including the full implications of gender norming that I discussed earlier?

What is the impact of pregnancy and child care on assignment policies for military personnel?

What is the practical effect of opening combat skills and positions to women on unit morale and cohesion?

If current combat exclusion laws and policies are repealed, would the present policy under which only males may be involuntarily assigned to combat skills and positions be sustainable?

One little thought, I take it by some people, what would be the impact to the required changes in quarters, weapons training, and the resultant costs of such changes?

What would be the practical rate at which any required changes can be made in an era of severely constrained defense budgets?

Another question: Why should we not repeal the combat exclusion laws and let the Commission do its work at the same time?

Repeal of the combat exclusion laws at the same time we are forming a Commission to make recommendation on whether such laws should be retained, modified, or repealed, we feel gets the cart before the horse. We should not prejudge the outcome of the Commission's work.

We are looking not just for a short-term panacea; we are looking for the long-term solution and policies for women in the military across the board, not just the narrow focus of pilots.

There is no national security need to rush to judgment on this issue. We should have the full benefit of well-developed facts and analyses before we act to modify or repeal the existing combat exclusion laws.

Mr. President, we are not trying to delay this. We are just trying to make these changes—which will be very major changes in our military—on the best studied basis that we can make those decisions.

Another question: Why does the committee oppose equal opportunity for women in the military?

I respond by saying the committee does not oppose equal opportunity for women in the military.

By its action, the committee has set out on a course to objectively determine how equal opportunity for all women in the military should be improved, for all women, all officers, all enlisted, everyone in the military, not just the narrow focus of pilots.

Repealing the combat exclusion laws has symbolic appeal, but the reality is that DOD would not make any substantive changes to its policies, as DOD witnesses have testified.

A well documented study could lead to the opening up of more opportunities for women, because we would be in a better position to advocate affirmative changes with regard to the roles of women in the military.

And just one more question: Why should we have another study on the assignment of women when this matter has been studied to death, as we have been told?

The facts are that there are no substantive, comprehensive studies on the assignment of women in the military that are current. There are no evaluations on the assignment of women in combat assault roles, because there are no women assigned to such roles. For example, although women fly a variety of aircraft, including high performance jet aircraft, I think we would be on firmer grounds for making changes if they had gone through changes if they had gone through some of the Navy Top Gun exercises or Red Flag Air Force combat evaluations.

The commission the committee proposes would allow such evaluations to be conducted in a training environment. The Congress can then decide this issue on the basis of facts and analyses rather than instinct. . . .

Mr. McCain. . . . . The real focus of this debate is how we should address the future role of women in combat. It is how we should take the national security aspects of this issue into full consideration, because the purpose of the military is first to defend this Nation's vital security interests throughout the globe, and only second to ensure equality.

I do not mean these purposes are mutually exclusive. We can achieve both purposes, Mr. President, but only if we address this issue in a measured, mature, and analytical fashion. Other nations have had experiences that we should look at, including the nation of Israel, and many have reached a different conclusion than the proponents of this amendment.

We all recognize the clear and compelling need to ensure equality in our society. At the same time, we must also listen to our military leadership. They expressed their views in a hearing which was conducted by Senator Glenn in the Manpower and Personnel Subcommittee of the Armed Services Committee on June 18. I would like to read a few quotes that our senior military officers provided during that hearing.

Gen. Carl Vuono, the highest ranking officer in the U.S. Army, said:

...Should you change (the law) and open up all those positions to women soldiers, then they would be involuntarily assigned to those positions ... it would seem to me then that you would open up the registration for the draft.

Admiral Kelso, the highest ranking officer in the Navy, said:

...I think you'll ... find the Navy's enlisted community as well as its officer community in the female ranks divided on this issue. We have a fitness standard and the standard is different for males and females.

The Assistant Secretary of Defense for Manpower and Personnel said:

...Some can perceive as an inequity to some women officers, that under the current House language ... women officers who are aviators (would be) assigned to aircraft carriers as part of the air wing but not, for example, as part of the air wing staff (or) as part of the ship's company. And frankly, this strikes me—and I know it strikes many—as a real inconsistency.

Former Marine Commandant Robert Barrow, one of our great national American heroes, said:

Please, Congress of the United States, you keep this responsibility; you draw the line, don't pass it to DOD ... you put it into law, they put it in policy. Policy can change at whim.... They change the policy to fit the pressure....

Gen. Alfred Gray, the Commandant of the Marine Corps said:

I see no need to change the law or the exclusion policy at this time ... your Commandant would be against that.

General McPeak, Chief of Staff of the Air Force, said:

I find great comfort in the law. I would like it to stay on the books personally.

Adm. Frank Kelso also said:

As I said, it's my personal view that the law should remain as it stands.

And again, General Vuono said:

I do not believe you should change the law. You should keep it the way it is.

Mr. President, I am not saying these individuals are correct, nor am I saying they are incorrect. But their statements, and the other results of that hearing, clearly show that we do not have a national consensus on this issue....

Before I conclude, Mr. President, let me talk about Israel. I do not think there is a nation that is more admired for its valiant struggle for independence and freedom than the State of Israel, at least by this Member. Israel has had to utilize all of its national resources to the maximum time after time. Ever since its birth as a nation, Israel has been required to have its entire population ready to go on wartime footing at a moment's notice.

Yet, the record of Israel in dealing with women in combat is often misunderstood. The popular conception is that Israeli women fight alongside men as equals. The truth is that, although Israel drafts both men and women for military service, Israel has excluded women from combat units since 1950. I think it is important to point out that while female soldiers fought alongside their male colleagues in Israel's war of liberation in 1948, this created many problems, and Israeli women were never again sent into battle.

Edward Luttwak describes the true state of affairs when he says women are integrated into the Israeli military at many levels and conduct most of the training. Women also serve in the Mossad, Israel's counterterrorist force. "But women are excluded," he notes, "from infantry and combat experience based on pragmatic experience of over 40 years." I might also note they are also barred from flying combat aircraft, or serving on ships in combat. It would be well for us, during our deliberations, to consider what the experience of another nation has been over 40 years of combat. . . .

Mr. Warner. . . . The Roth-Kennedy amendment states as follows: "The Secretary of the Army may prescribe the conditions under which female members of the Army may be assigned to duty in aircraft that are engaged in combat missions." That is in one section.

When we go to a second section which is parallel, and it addresses the "Secretary of the Air Force may prescribe," they are independent sections.

The problem that I can foresee is having once been a secretary of a military department myself, the discretion is reposed in a service Secretary. One may decide to do it; the other may not. Where does that leave this critical issue? That would be my first question.

The second is, Why did the authors of the amendment give just a discretionary authority to these Secretaries? Why did they not put in the word that the Secretary of the Army "shall" prescribe, because I think those following this debate are of the impression that you are moving this a step forward where, in reality, you are doing little more than reposing in two service secretaries the discretion, whereas the Glenn amendment, of which I am a co-sponsor, in section D makes it clear that the Secretary of Defense shall have this authority, thereby obviating one Secretary agreeing to try and another Secretary declining. . . .

Mr. Kennedy. Mr. President, I will answer that in the following way. This amendment eliminates the statutory prohibition that currently exists in the laws that prohibits the Secretaries to be able to permit women in aircraft in the Navy and the Army and the Air Force. That is effectively what this amendment does.

What we also permit is the discretion, which exists with regard to the Army and also exists with regard to the service Secretaries in terms of the Secretaries making the determination as to the suitability of the various combat requirements. That makes it completely consistent with regard to this aspect, the combat air, to what has been done with regard to the Army. . . .

Mr. Warner. Mr. President, where in this amendment is the protection against one Secretary exercising the authority and the other Secretary doing nothing? That is the question. . . .

Mr. Kennedy. Mr. President, let me ask a question. The Senator [Warner] was a Secretary of the Navy. Is the Senator going to urge if this is successful, that they permit them in the Navy for combat air? . . .

Mr. Warner. Mr. President, I would urge the Secretary of the Navy to abide by discretion exercised by a commission after they go through a series of findings of fact. If I was Secretary, I would urge the Secretary of Defense, under the Glenn amendment, to allow the Secretary to go in and make very selective experiments, to try and develop a body of evidence for the commission. . . .

Mr. Kennedy. . . . . I listened with interest to Senator McCain talk about the position of the various secretaries of Defense with reference to people in combat. Secretary Cheney was asked:

> Question: Secretary Cheney, the Defense Advisory Committee on Women in the Service has recommended that the combat exclusion for women be eliminated. And recently, the House Armed Services Committee has recommended that women be allowed to fly Navy and Air Force combat aircraft.
> Could you tell us your reactions to these recommendations?
> Answer: We welcome all legislation that gives the Secretary of Defense greater flexibility to manage the Department.

No rejection, no comment that we do not believe that they are prepared to fill that job. That is the Secretary of Defense.

> Question: I am sure you are aware that the Army and Marine Corps have expressed opposition to removal of the combat exclusion for women. Indeed, General Gray, Commandant of the Marine Corps, has been vehement in his opposition. Would you favor two services, the Navy and Air Force, allowing women to go into combat and two prohibiting them?
> Answer: I would expect the Department of Defense to issue policy guidance that would ensure consistency, but not necessarily identical practices, among the services.

Here he has two opportunities to reject this. . .and what he is indicating, certainly anyone can conclude, is that it is going to be the judgment that we want to repeal the archaic laws, and that the Secretary of Defense is prepared to move forward. . . .

In January 1990, the British opened seagoing positions on combat ships of the British Royal Navy. Women in Canada and Denmark are trained as fighter pilots.

Ironically, the United States Air Force has trained Danish women fighter pilots but will not train United States women pilots to fly fighter aircraft. Five NATO nations have no combat exclusion laws: Canada, Denmark, Luxembourg, Norway, Portugal. In addition, Greece, Netherlands, and Turkey have no statutory restrictions, although they do have selected policies.

All our allies are effectively ahead of us. A wonderful thing we find is that we train Danish fighter pilots, and we cannot train our own. Mr. President, the reports and the analyses of their performance really have been done.

Just briefly, Mr. President, I hear that old chestnut brought out about the draft and we do not have a draft at the present time. What you are talking about in terms of the combat arms and flying combat planes is that they are all volunteers, number one. . . .

I have not heard, until we started talking about this amendment, how we are going to go back to the draft. We just do not have it. It is a phony argument. It is a red herring argument. . . .

Mr. McCain. First of all, let me try to educate my colleague from Massachusetts. There seem to be some glaring gaps in his knowledge of what the laws of this country are.

We do have draft laws on the books. I might say to my friend from Massachusetts that although it might be many years since he was 18, a young man who turns 18 in this country still has to register for the draft. We do have standby draft laws. While the Senator from Massachusetts may have believed for many years that we do not need a strong national defense, and may not believe we will ever again be involved in a war, many of us feel differently. There are many of us who believe there has to be a standby draft, and that no action of this kind can ignore the laws on the books today so I say to my friend who believes there is no draft, there are draft laws on the books and every eighteen-year-old male has to register. . . .

Mr. Roth. . . . I would just like to point out some of these questions that have been raised.

One is, why now? Let us wait for a commission. Well, as I said already, Secretary Cheney, himself, has assured me that he does not oppose this legislation. So what he is saying, in effect, is that he sees no reason to postpone action on it.

What about women in ground combat? Some have raised that specter, that fear, that the Kennedy and Roth amendment will lead women down the slippery slope into the trenches of ground combat. That is an unfounded fear, and it is an unnecessary fear. Our amendment is surgical, precise, circumscribed, and only germane to the role of women combat aviators; nothing more, nothing less. We are not establishing a dangerous precedent here.

Legal experts agree that lifting the combat aircraft restriction will not mean a dramatic change in the woman's role in the military.

They raise a question about unit cohesion and bonding. Just let me point out that something like 35,000 women served in the Persian Gulf, and military leader after military leader including Mr. Cheney, have said women pilots are successful members of aircraft crews. . . .

We think there is no substitute for eliminating the Roth-Kennedy amendment, because we are eliminating a legal obstacle that the hearings and others have shown to be no longer necessary, and are an impediment in providing the best military security for this Nation. . . .

Mr. Nunn. Mr. President, I rise in support of the Glenn-McCain-Nunn-Warner amendment. . . .

The major difference between the committee approach and the Roth-Kennedy approach is that under the committee approach, including the Glenn amendment which I hope we will agree to on the floor, we will not preempt the work of the commission. We do not arbitrarily create different categories of women in the military.

The Roth-Kennedy provision affects less than one-half of 1 percent of the women in the military and ignores the remaining 99.6 percent. One-half percent is affected under that proposal and the others are ignored. It ignores service at sea. It basically says if you fly aircraft as a woman, you can fly on the carrier, but in any other assignment you are still barred by law.

The approach we are advocating here today recognizes all women in the military are currently restricted from assignment to direct combat assault roles. And the appropriate way to determine what changes in law or policy are appropriate would be to allow the waiver of all of these restrictions during the time the commission is conducting its study.

This approach is fair to all the women in the military and does not single out a very tiny segment of officers for special treatment. Most important, we will have the results of the commission deliberation and have the results of these tests, before we make our final judgment about what the law should be....

Mrs. Kassebaum. Mr. President, I have some questions I would like to ask because I personally am a bit confused by some of the debate that I have heard....

It was my understanding that all we were doing was just repealing the statute that barred women from combat in the Air Force and Navy.

Mr. Roth. ...Under the Roth-Kennedy amendment all we are doing is deleting that part of the code which prohibits women from being assigned to combat duty in the Air Force and the Navy.

Mrs. Kassebaum. Mr. President, then I would ask, this is not saying women will be automatically in combat?

Mr. Roth. That is absolutely correct.

Mrs. Kassebaum. This is merely saying, is this correct, then, that it will be up to the armed services to make that decision?

Mr. Roth. Absolutely. Each of the services will have the freedom, the flexibility to do whatever they think is best.

Mrs. Kassebaum. Mr. President, it seems to me the Army has been able to do that for some period of time. It seems to me to make sense simply to say that this should be a decision that would be made by the armed services. I always believed that is where that decision should lie.

Women have been in combat areas in many of our wars. Women pilots flew troops into combat areas in World War II. How we define combat area today is something else I think is a decision that has to be made by those in authority to determine how women can best serve. But I, frankly, think it should be left to those who are in the best position to know, and that is the armed services themselves....

It seems to me to make sense to repeal the statutory ban and let the armed services make the decisions themselves.

Mr. McCain. ... in response to the Senator's questions, the Glenn amendment waives the combat exclusion. It allows the Secretary of Defense to waive the prohibition against women serving in combat roles, and allows the Secretary of Defense to experiment while the commission is sitting and place women in various combat roles. . . .

Mr. Simpson. Mr. President, I thank the Senator from Delaware, and I was particularly impressed with the remarks of my friend from Kansas. I think Senator Kassebaum stated it very clearly. This has been good, and both proposals have merit. I specifically rise to speak in favor of the Kennedy-Roth proposal. I represent a State which is known as the "Equality State." I am not going to give one of those Chamber pitches, but we were the first Government in the Western World to give women the right to vote. That was in 1869. A long time ago.

I have been in the infantry. I served for 2 years. I was very honored to do that. I did not think so when I was there, but it was a great growing-up experience. I firmly believe that women should be given the opportunity to serve in certain areas depending upon their capabilities and demonstrated skills. I think that decision should be up to the Secretary of Defense. It is his charge, his mission, to decide who should go where and in what capacity.

I happen to have been in command of an 81-millimeter mortar platoon. This is not intended in any way to be a sexist statement—but, I do not really think there are many women who can haul a base plated of a 81-millimeter mortar unless they are making them out of a different substance than when I served.

What I am saying is, we must give women in the armed services every opportunity. That is what I am trying to do, and that is what most of us are trying to do, commensurate with their physical abilities and the mission of the outfit in which they serve.

These other issues like quartering can be worked out in a sensible way. But the real issue is whether women should have every possible avenue open to them that is there. I believe so, and it should be done in a way which does not injure the mission of the United States in the protection of our country, as defined by the Secretary of Defense. I thank the Chair.

The Presiding Officer. Who yields time?

Mr. Nunn. Mr. President, if I could get 1 minute from the managers.

Mr. Glenn. I yield 1 minute.

Mr. Nunn. Mr. President . . . I suggest, unless someone has a compelling thought that is as yet undisclosed, we go ahead and vote on these two amendments. . . .

August

FAILURE OF SOVIET COUP ATTEMPT
August 19-24, 1991

The world was startled August 19 by the announcement that Soviet president Mikhail S. Gorbachev was ill and had been relieved of his authority. The message, which was released at about 6 a.m. in Moscow by the news agency Tass, went on to say that Vice President Gennardi I. Yanayev had assumed Gorbachev's duties as well as the title of acting president on behalf of a self-appointed State Committee for the State of Emergency.

The committee included Yanayev, Prime Minister Valentin S. Pavlov, Defense Minister Dmitri T. Yazov, Interior Minister Boris K. Pugo, and KGB chairman Vladimir A. Kryuchkov. They and other coup leaders were identified as hard-line Communists who strongly opposed a pending treaty that would formalize a newly negotiated power-sharing arrangement between the Kremlin and nine Soviet republics. Gorbachev was scheduled to return from his vacation in the Crimea and sign the treaty the next day. Instead, he, his wife Raisa, and their daughter Irina were being held captive at their seaside cottage.

About twelve hours after the announcement, several of the coup leaders held a televised news conference to defend their ouster of Gorbachev and assumption of power. Yanayev contended that over the years Gorbachev had become "very tired and needs some time to get his health back."

Many Soviet citizens were dismayed by the turn of events and clearly disbelieved the explanation. That night in Moscow and Leningrad tens and possibly hundreds of thousands took to the streets in open defiance of the curfew the new regime had imposed. Armored columns and troops moved into Moscow but their presence angered rather than cowed the protesters, who retaliated with rocks and fire bombs. Three young civilians were crushed to death by army tanks.

Yeltsin Rallies Resistance

The nerve center of protest activity was the Russian Federation Building, a massive white structure a mile or so from the Kremlin where the republic's parliament held its sessions. Boris N. Yeltsin, president of the Russian republic, also maintained offices there. Yeltsin, the Soviet Union's foremost advocate of democratic reforms, set aside his rivalry with Gorbachev to demand that the ousted leader be returned to power. Yeltsin's outspoken opposition to the junta rallied the people's resistance.

The coup leaders had closed independent newspapers and taken over the state's broadcast facilities, but Yeltsin's pleas for a general strike and civil disobedience were beamed back to Soviet listeners by foreign broadcasts. Inexplicably, telephone communications remained intact, enabling Yeltsin to solicit support from foreign leaders, including President George Bush, who called the coup an "illegal" act and offered Yeltsin words of encouragement.

At Yeltsin's urging, some Russian soldiers defected and placed tanks and armored vehicles outside the Russian Federation Building to defend against an expected attempt by the junta to arrest or murder him. In a moment of high drama and personal courage, Yeltsin mounted one of the vehicles and denounced the new men in the Kremlin.

On the second day of the standoff between a defiant Yeltsin and the Kremlin, some leaders of other Soviet republics overcame their initial wariness and declared that the coup was an illegal usurpation of power. Aleksy II, patriarch of the Russian Orthodox Church, also questioned the junta's legitimacy and called on Soviet soldiers to use great restraint in their encounters with civilian protesters.

Coup Leaders Capitulate

As the opposition grew, the coup crumbled. Gorbachev arrived unannounced at Vnukovo Airport outside Moscow early August 22 and remained publicly silent until his news conference later that day. Yeltsin meanwhile told the Russian parliament that the "group of adventurists who tried to seize power has been arrested" and that Gorbachev was back in office. At the news conference, a somber Gorbachev described his three-day ordeal that began "on the 18th of August at 10 minutes to 5" when "I was told by the head of my guard that people were demanding to see me." A group of conspirators whom he did not identify presented him with a demand that he resign. Unable to reason with them, he summarized his response as, "To hell with you."

Though thirty-two loyal and armed bodyguards remained with the Gorbachevs, they did not attempt a breakout because they presumed that the captors had more firepower. Fearful for his life, Gorbachev made a secret tape in the hope that it could be smuggled out to inform the world of what really occurred. To his surprise, some bodyguards were able to rig up an old radio and receive foreign broadcasts, thereby keeping his party informed that the coup had created open protests. That news raised Gorbachev's spirits and reinforced his will to resist.

On August 21 some members of the junta went to the Crimea to talk directly to Gorbachev. They included Yazov, Kryuchkov, and Anatoly I. Lukyanov, chairman of the Soviet parliament and one of Gorbachev's oldest friends, whom some considered the mastermind of the conspiracy. Gorbachev said that his bodyguards seized the visitors upon their arrival. In the meantime, Gen. Aleksandr Rutskoi, vice president of the Russian republic, was leading an armed party to the Crimea to free Gorbachev. On August 22 Rutskoi's soldiers rushed the villa, but they met no opposition. By then the leading members of the coup had been arrested, except for Pugo, who committed suicide, and Pavlov, who had been hospitalized for hypertension.

Gorbachev offered more details about his confinement in a long memoir published in late October as an English-language book, The August Coup. *In it he strongly denied rumors that he was not the victim of the coup but its mastermind—that he promoted it as a means of eliminating right-wing opposition to his economic and political reforms. Regardless of his role in the coup, its failure was to present him with that opportunity. It discredited the Communist party and compelled Gorbachev to resign as its leader. Moreover, the union treaty that had triggered the coup was promptly ratified.* (Gorbachev's Resignation From Communist Party, p. 527, Plans for Restructuring the Soviet Union, p. 531)

> *Following are excerpts from Russian president Boris N. Yeltsin's speech to the Russian parliament saying the coup had collapsed and from Soviet president Mikhail S. Gorbachev's news conference describing his captivity, both on August 22; and Yeltsin's eulogy August 24 for the three men who died in Moscow street confrontations with army tanks, as recorded and translated by the Associated Press and Foreign Broadcast Information Service:*

YELTSIN'S SPEECH

Dear Muscovites, dear Russians, compatriots:

Last night, major events occurred.... The group of adventurists who tried to seize power has been arrested. The attempt to change the direction of the development of our country, to cast it into the abyss of violence and lawlessness, has failed. On the third day, the anti-people, anti-constitutional rebellion was eliminated.

During the extremely short existence of the Dictatorship of the Eight, it became exceedingly clear what would await the country and its citizens if the putschists won victory and seized power. From the first minutes of the dictatorship, brute force was the main means of carrying out the anti-people policy.... A malicious attempt was made to smother freedom and democracy, to revive the wolf law of a totalitarian system; within a few hours the country was drowned in a sea of lies, starting with the imaginary illness of the deposed president....

Yes, within a few hours *glasnost* had been trampled on. Even during the days of Stalinism there was none of the rigid censorship introduced by the putschists....

During those days and nights, many thousands of Muscovites demonstrated steadfastness, citizenship and heroism. It was they who halted the advance of reaction and inflicted a crushing blow against it.... Your weapon was the enormous will to defend the ideals of freedom, democracy and human worth.... I express profound gratitude to the thousands of servicemen and personnel of the law enforcement bodies, the security bodies and the true patriots of Russia who came to its aid in its hour of destiny. The active stance of the inhabitants of many cities and villages of the country ... of people of various ages and professions, men and women, played an inestimable role in breaking the mutiny. The miners, the church and others had a large say in the defense of the sovereign rights of Russia.

Our joint efforts have been crowned with success, and a major victory over the forces of reaction has been won. The activities of the so-called Committee for the State of Emergency were in flagrant contradiction not only with the laws, the constitution and the declaration of the state sovereignty of the republics, but also with elementary moral norms....

A most grave state crime has been committed, and the criminals—traitors to the motherland—must be handed over to the courts. ... Retribution for what has been perpetrated must follow, and not for the sake of vengeance, but for the sake of the highest human justice so that such a thing should never be repeated in our country.

All of us have to draw serious lessons from the past. Once again we have seen how fragile freedom is in our society, and how vulnerable democracy and glasnost are. Once again we have seen that the reforms being carried out in the country have not yet become irreversible....

This is a lesson for us all, including the country's president—Gorbachev. At the same time, it has again been shown how great are the powers of the people. The political course of Russia, the honor and virtue of its highest bodies of authority, of its leadership, were defended by unarmed, peaceful citizens. It is symbolic that among those who became the defense of the constitution, the law, and human worth, there were a great many young people. This means that the future course of this reform is ensured.

The past days make it necessary to draw a number of conclusions: Today, the lagging of reforms in the center behind the transformation in the republics is extremely dangerous. The putsch has shown once again that the union structures remain conservative, impermissibly cumbersome, and they work first and foremost on an each-for-himself basis. At any moment they will seek to restore their dictatorship over the republics. Their immediate and resolute transformation is necessary.

The formation of a government of national accord can no longer be postponed. It should be mobile, effective, rationally structured, and the republics forming the union should have the decisive word in its formation. Adjustments in the matter of the union treaty are also necessary. The coup d'etat disrupted its signing, but it is impermissible to postpone this procedure for an indefinite period.

At the same time, Russia, but not it alone, has become convinced that some of the articles of the last version of the treaty have proven, bluntly, to be weak, and they have to be corrected. And, of course, on the other hand, this document should take account of the experience we have acquired over these past three black days.

Life has again shown us that Russia cannot feel itself secure without its own national guard ... [and] we intend to adopt a more principled stand with regard to ensuring the economic sovereignty of Russia. The Russian republic must have a full-blown economy, and yesterday a decree was signed transferring union property on the territory of Russia to the jurisdiction of Russia, all enterprises.

The days of rule by the notorious committee showed that the mass media were extremely vulnerable. In the very shortest time, it is essential to adopt resolute measures to strengthen the mass media system in the republic. The stability of freedom of speech is a most important condition of progress in Russian society. The appropriate decree has been drawn up and was signed last night. Other measures are also being prepared. . . .

Support for the illegal and anti-constitutional actions on the part of whoever carried them out cannot remain unpunished. Yesterday, the Russian parliament instructed me to conduct a reorganization of staff in those regions where the leaders supported the illegal Committee for the State of Emergency. Even before, those people were, in effect, in a state of cold war with the leadership of Russia. Now they must leave their jobs. The decree on their dismissal was signed last night.

Esteemed fellow citizens, the situation in the country is getting back to normal. The shameful days of the appearance of the gang of high-ranking adventurists is receding into the past, but too high a price has been paid for this—the irreplaceable loss of human life, of people killed during the putsch, huge losses in the economy. Still, the main thing is that the coup failed. The country is emerging from the crisis foisted upon it. The forces that organized [the coup] are historically doomed, and first and foremost because the people have already made their choice and do not intend to reject it. The people have already freed themselves from the fear of former years.

In the name of national unity, I call on all my fellow citizens to embark on creative work directed at the regeneration and renewal of Russia. For the victory of democracy over reaction, and as always in Russia, in conclusion: Hoorah! Hoorah!

GORBACHEV'S NEWS CONFERENCE

Today's press conference is taking place after events which more than anything I hope are not repeated, and that similar press conferences on this topic will not have to take place.

We made it through. As I want to be accurate—did we make [it] all the way through or not—yes we did—the most difficult test in all the years in the reformation of our society since 1985.

We faced a real, without any exaggeration, anti-constitutional coup organized by reactionary forces, which appeared to be in the leadership, in the very center of the leadership, people which I advanced, believed in and trusted, who appeared to be not only the participants but the organizers of this coup, against the president, against the constitution, against perestroika and against democracy.

On Aug. 18, 10 minutes to 5 p.m., my head guard told me that a group of people had arrived demanding a meeting with me. I told them that I was not expecting anybody, had invited nobody, and that nobody notified me in advance. . . .

I decided to clarify who sent them here, and as far as I had [available] all sorts of communications [at my disposal]—ordinary, governmental, strategic and satellite—I was working in my office, picked up the one telephone, it didn't work. I lifted the second, the third, the fourth, the fifth—nothing. Then I tried the house phone and realized nothing worked and I was cut off. . . .

Then I went to another place, called the family, my wife, daughter, and said that an event had taken place. I didn't need any new information, I knew that a very serious event was going on, that they would either blackmail me or there would be attempts to arrest me or take me away somewhere. Basically, anything could happen.

I told Raisa Maximovna and Irina Anatoleyevna [Gorbachev's wife and daughter] that if we talk about the main thing, about politics, the course of politics, that I will stick to my position to the end and that I would not step back, not under any pressure, blackmail or threats. I would neither change nor take up new positions.

All the family—I thought it was important to tell them, you understand why—because I realized that anything could happen, especially to the members of my family. This we also know. The family told me that I, this should be my decision and that [they] would go with me through this to the end. This was the end of our conversation.

Then I went to invite them, but by that time they had already come in, they didn't stand on ceremony, with the head of the presidential apparatus [chief of staff Valery] Boldin, ahead of them. They gave the president an ultimatum: to transfer all power to the vice president.

I told them that before I answered, I wanted to know who had sent them, what committee. They said the State Committee for the State of the Emergency in the country. Who created it? I didn't create it, the Supreme Soviet didn't create it.

They told me that people had already united and they needed a presidential decree, either you issue this decree and stay here or transfer your powers to the vice president. They said the situation in the country was such, that it was nearing catastrophe, and that we should take measures, a state of emergency, other measures won't do, we shouldn't daydream anymore. . . .

I told them that I knew the situation in the country better than anyone, politically, economically, and the life of people and all the difficulties they were facing, and that we had come to the phase where we need to do everything as fast and decisive as we can to live better.

I told them that I was always an opponent of such methods, not only because of political and moral reasons, but because in the history of our country they have always led to the death of hundreds, thousands and millions of deaths. And we need to get away from that, and to refuse it forever. If we do differently, we are not behaving like ourselves, and everything that we started we'll have to bury forever. We should agree that we are going in a bloody circle.

Then I told them that you and those who sent you are adventurists, you will kill yourselves, but the hell with you, it's your problem, do what you want to do, but you will also kill the country, everything that we are doing. . . .

Only those who want to commit suicide can now suggest to lead a totalitarian regime in the country.

They demanded that I resign. You won't get that from me, not one or the other. Tell that to the people who sent you here.

Well, after that everything developed according to the logic of confrontation. Full isolation from land and sea. Thirty-two security people stayed with me, to the end, as they say, they decided to stay. They divided up all the spheres of defense, including my family, divided all the locations, and decided to stand until the end.

When it became known . . . they said I was ill, seriously, and that in general, I understood, that I was not capable of returning to a normal life, then it became clear to me that what would follow was that reality would soon be synchronized to this statement.

This is why—it was understood the same way by security—decision was taken to refuse all ordered food and live on only what we already had at hand. I was sure, I was positive, and absolutely calm, although I was struck to the bones and indignant with the political blindness and irresponsibility of these criminals.

It won't last long, and it won't succeed. Basically, that's how it was. Seventy-two hours of total isolation and struggle. I think everything was done to psychologically break the president down. It is difficult, it's also difficult to talk about it here. Every day, morning and evening, I put forth demands, and passed them on.

The demands were that communications of the president be re-established, that a plane was sent immediately to take me to Moscow, back to work, and after the [Yanayev] press conference, I added to the demands that they publish the refutation of this announcement made in front of you about the condition of my health. . . .

. . . I want to tell you that I, all of us, have indeed seen the truth, that these six years in this country that we have gone through have not been wasted. And with difficulty, and often painfully, we have looked for the path to move forward. This society—and now we can now speak about this—has rejected the putchists. They turned out to be isolated. They weren't able to direct the army, the army made contact with the people, and nothing could be done about it. It became clear to them that they failed.

The republics took a negative position, and here I want to pay tribute and put in first place the principled position of our Russian parliament, Russian deputies, Russian government officials, and the outstanding role of the president of Russia, Boris Nikolayevich Yeltsin [applause]. I have to say that we also have to pay tribute to the principled positions of Muscovites and Leningraders, as well as people from many other regions. . . .

Basically, when it became clear, when Russia, its leadership, the republics and the people took such an irreconcilable position, that the army didn't go, they began to look for an exit in panic. They told me that the group of conspirators have arrived in the Crimea on the presidential plane, to talk to the president and to take him to Moscow. When they arrived, I said to put them in the house, detain them, and tell them my demands: I won't talk to any of them until all the governmental communications are reestablished. . . . So the communications were turned back on, and I began to speak with the country. I spoke first with Boris Nikolayevich Yeltsin. I called [Kazakh President Nursultan] Nazarbayev, [Ukraine President Leonid] Kravchuk, [Byelorussian President Nikolai] Dementei, [Uzbek President Islam] Karimov. . . . I started to work. I gave [Soviet Chief of Staff Gen. Mikhail] Moiseyev orders to take over the leadership of Defense Ministry, and he was also summoned from the Crimea and taken there. I gave troops orders to go back immediately to the places where they were located, to their barracks, and to announce that Yazov will be dismissed and arrested. All that was done. . . . Basically I started calling to the most important points, to block everything at once. Because everything was still dangerous and they could have destroyed me on my way [to Moscow] or anywhere. I decided not to go until—then they told me that the plane of the Russian delegation was coming and I said I would receive them first of all. I got in touch with [Civil Aviation Minister Boris] Panyukov, with Moiseyev and told them to land not in Simferopol, which would have meant they would get to me in three hours, but at the military airport where I usually land. Then I gave the orders to meet them there, to organize the transport to bring them here. So the work started. The delegation arrived, we all sat down, came to great understanding. I think what we had suffered through has contributed not only to our experience but also to our understanding, the difference between a united democratic force and a divided one. . . .

Then I had to issue more instructions. Then [Communist Party Deputy General Secretary Vladimir] Ivanskho and [Supreme Soviet speaker Anatoly] Lukyanov arrived separately—they didn't give them transport—and I received them. I didn't receive the conspirators, I didn't see them, and I don't want to see them. We put them into different planes, brought them to Moscow, and getting off the plane they were arrested and interned. I gave an order to the Kremlin not to let anyone in who cooperated with that "Commandant." And so forth, that is, so to say, the work has begun. I planned a meeting tomorrow with the leaders of the nine republics that signed the [Union] treaty—who worked out the treaty and prepared it to be signed.

Tomorrow we will meet and we should discuss everything. These were hard lessons, for me it has been the most difficult, it's simply a hard trauma for me. I think that tomorrow we will come close to discussing, seriously thinking about and developing the positions on the main questions of moving forward and what new steps to take. We have to think about this, we have to see not only the great sorrow that occurred, but also we have to see what an enormous chance this event opened up to us, how it showed the true position of the people. In conversations with foreign leaders, the leaders of foreign governments, they all drew attention to this fact, that the position of the people and the army showed that the Soviet Union has already gone through changes that were irreversible. For that reason they hope will take advantage of all opportunities, and they all said that they will cooperate with us, and that this cooperation should take more active forms, more decisive ones. . . .

About the decisions that were made: I issued a decree that annulled the decrees. . . . [I]t looked like they could destroy or do anything . . . to my family, to me, to everyone who was with me, and tell [the people] that the president has such and such a position. Moreover, they could say that they were acting on orders from him. For that reason, at the [Emergency Committee] press conference I saw all this craftiness, though a primitive one, crude. As one of the comrades in the Russian Federation said, "They can't even do this properly, like the other things they do."

I decided to immediately make four tapes . . . and we started to look for channels whom we could trust to send them. Here is the tape, one of them [holds up a tape], the others may appear because they have, in any case, gone. The doctor wrote his opinion, several copies, and we gave them out, I distributed them so that the people knew the actual state of the condition of the health of the president. And I finally put forward the first four points in written form, I wrote some things by hand so that people could see that it was I who wrote it . . . and I signed it.

Point One: The fact that [Vice President Gennady] Yanayev took over the responsibilities of president on the pretext of my illness and inability to fulfill responsibilities is a deception of the people, and given this, can only be considered a governmental coup.

Point Two: This means that all the actions that followed are illegal. Neither the president nor the Congress of People's Deputies delegated such responsibility to Yanayev.

Point Three: I ask to tell [parliament speaker Anatoly] Lukyanov my demand to immediately convene a meeting of the Supreme Soviet and the Congress of People's Deputies to consider the situation that emerged. They and only they, having considered the emerging situation, have the right to solve the problems of taking and putting into effect necessary government measures.

Point Four: I demand immediately to freeze the actions of the State Committee of the State of Emergency until the Supreme Soviet or the Congress of People's Deputies pass the aforementioned decisions.

The continuation of these actions, the further escalation of the measures taken by the State Committee for the State of Emergency, could turn out to be a tragedy for all the peoples, to exacerbate the situation and even completely destroy the concensual work of the center and the republics that has already begun to find a way out of the crisis.

[Remark: When was the document written? The 20th?] Yes, the 20th.... The prosecutor's office, the prosecutor of the Russian Federation, reported to me that yesterday he began criminal proceedings, and we agreed that the group should include both Russian and Soviet investigators.

Temporary decisions were adopted in cases where in certain agencies [where] people could not be trusted, not even for a single day. Tomorrow when we meet with the leaders of the republics, we'll start to think over the disposition of forces among other problems, that's the most important thing, so that the authorities acted, and the consensual actions built a momentum. We cannot lose. We have a program, we have to move and solve the problems, this is the most important thing. But enough for the introduction.

YELTSIN'S EULOGY

Dear relatives and loved ones of Dmitri Komar, Vladimir Usov and Iliya Krichevsky, dear fellow countrymen and Muscovites:

Today many millions of Muscovites, the whole of Russia, are parting with our heroes, with our defenders, with our saviors. Of course, we are not parting with their names forever, because from now on their names are sacred names for Russia, for all the people of our long-suffering Russia.

When television and radio reported about the coup on Monday, the hearts of millions and millions of mothers and fathers trembled most of all, because they were scared for their children. Because it was young people, it was our children, who more than anyone else rushed to defend Russia's honor, its freedom, its independence and its democracy, to defend its Parliament. Yes, from now on, this square, on which a battle raged for three days, on which tens of thousands of Muscovites kept vigil, will be called the Square of Free Russia.

The enemy is cruel, and, of course, bloodthirsty, especially when he knows that if he loses no one will take him in. All the participants, all the main participants of the putsch, are arrested. Criminal proceedings have been started against them, and I am sure that they will be made to answer for everything. But even today, how cynical the words of arrested [former KGB chief Vladimir] Kryuchkov sound, the man who yesterday said that if he could do it over again he would have started a little faster and more energetically, and that the most important thing was to behead Russia. This entire plot, and we must understand this very clearly, was aimed in the first place against Russia, its parliament, its government, its president. But all of Russia stood up to its defense: Moscow, Leningrad, the Urals, the Far East, the Kuzbass, practically all regions of the republic, although there were some regions which immediately put up banners and slogans expressing loyalty to the Extraordinary Committee. These officials already have been dismissed from their posts. And the prosecutor's office is considering their cases.

But we cannot resurrect those who died at the walls of our White House. We pay tribute to their courage, those who have become Heroes of the Soviet Union in death. I bow down to the mothers and fathers of Dmitri, Volodya and Iliya, and I express to them by deep condolences, and to all their relatives and loved ones. Forgive me, your president, that I could not defend, could not save, your sons.

In this day of Russia's national mourning, we of course need to strengthen our unity to energetically act further. We have cleared ourselves a path, our deceased heroes have helped us to do so. This is a difficult day for us, a hard day, but it could have been even worse, because the enemies are already like cockroaches in a bottle, trying to eat each other, they are pointing fingers at each other, asking who played a more important role in the plot, revealing to each other the lists of people they wanted to kill first, second, third, fourth.

Only the first 12 victims in these lists [apparently referring to members of the Russian government] were designated to be killed at 6 p.m. on Aug. 19 during the storming of the House of Soviets [Russian Parliament building]. So it was not in vain the Muscovites were here, defending the honor of Russia.

It was a difficult loss, and the memory of it will be with us forever. For that reason, our heroes, sleep peacefully and let the earth be soft for you.

GORBACHEV'S RESIGNATION FROM COMMUNIST PARTY

August 24, 1991

Soviet president Mikhail S. Gorbachev resigned August 24 as head of the discredited Communist party. His dramatic gesture was interpreted as a desperate attempt to stabilize his political authority in the aftermath of a coup attempt engineered by his trusted colleagues in the party. (Failure of Soviet Coup Attempt, p. 515)

Speaking to the Russian republic's parliament the previous day, Gorbachev was repeatedly heckled for defending the party. Saying that it was unfair to blame all Communists for the coup attempt, he warned against "anti-Communist hysteria." Moreover, the Soviet leader said he wanted no "witch hunt" for collaborators of the coup leaders.

Even as Gorbachev spoke, party offices and newspapers were being closed throughout the Russian republic on orders of its president, Boris N. Yeltsin, and several local governments. In a number of provincial cities, large crowds unimpeded by local authorities tore down statues of Lenin, communism's founder. A few days later his namesake city, Leningrad, reverted to its original name St. Petersburg.

With the political ground shifting beneath him, Gorbachev changed course and said in a statement carried the next day by the Tass news agency, "I don't think it is possible for me to fulfill the functions of general secretary of the Communist Party of the Soviet Union, and I'm relinquishing the corresponding powers." Gorbachev further said that the Central Committee, whose 300 members made up the inner circle of the party, "should make the difficult but honest decision to disband itself." The Communist parties of the various Soviet republics and local party organizations, he added, "will decide their own fate."

Although Gorbachev did not formally disband or resign from the party, he issued two decrees on August 24 that all but spelled its demise. Gorbachev ordered that the Soviet parliament take charge of all Communist party property until its future could be decided "in strict compliance with Soviet and republican law." He also barred the party's activities in the military services, security forces, and all agencies of government.

The Communist party, founded in 1920 by the Bolshevik victors in the Russian Revolution and the following civil war, was a pervasive and powerful presence in the Soviet Union for seven decades. Its firm—often harsh—hold on the people lessened after Gorbachev came to power in 1985 and attempted to revitalize a sagging national economy by infusing it with Western practices and lifting many political restrictions.

This opening up of a hitherto closed society created divisions in the party. Gorbachev wavered in his positions as he sought to maintain a delicate balance between faster-moving reformers on the left and a fearful old guard on the right. The depth of those divisions was apparent when the Communist party held its 28th Congress in Moscow in July 1990. It closed in such discord that Yeltsin, Gorbachev's populist rival, left the party to direct the growing political opposition. (Documents from the 28th Communist Congress, Historic Documents of 1990, p. 439)

As the party's leading political and economic reformer, Yeltsin was expelled from its ruling Politburo in 1987. Though still nominally a Communist, he was a virtual outsider, uninhibited about exposing the privileged position of the party's elite. He won a devoted following and in 1989 was elected to the new Congress of People's Deputies—the Soviet parliament—despite an all-out effort by the party's leadership to defeat him. (Remarks on Soviet Election and Perestroika, Historic Documents of 1989, p. 173)

In June 1991, Yeltsin was elected to the newly created presidency of the Russian federation, which includes about half of the people and three-fourths of the territory in the Soviet Union. He thus became Russia's first popularly elected leader in history and was in a position to challenge much of Gorbachev's authority, which he often did.

The situation led to the negotiation of a power-sharing agreement between Gorbachev and the presidents of nine Soviet republics, restructuring the Soviet government. Old-line Communists who viewed the pact as a threat to party dominance and their own privileges plotted to seize control of the government before a treaty could be signed formalizing the agreement. The failure of their coup took the Soviet Communist party to the point of extinction.

On November 7, Revolution Day brought none of the usual festivities marking the Bolshevik overthrow of the czarist government in 1917. In past years, the Communist hierarchy reviewed grandiose military parades in Red Square as millions watched. In Moscow, the once-familiar hammer-and-sickle banners of the revolution were glimpsed only amid a few furtive clusters of unrepentant Communists who had ventured into the streets.

Following is Soviet president Mikhail S. Gorbachev's state-
ment of August 24, 1991, in translation from the Tass news
agency, declaring his resignation as secretary general of the
Communist party in the Soviet Union:

The secretariat [and] the Politburo failed to stand against the coup d'etat, the Central Committee proved unable to take a resolute position of condemnation and opposition to the coup, it didn't urge Communists to fight against the suppression of constitutional legality. Members of the party leadership were among the conspirators, a number of party committees and mass media organs supported the actions of the state criminals. This put millions of Communists into an ambiguous position. Many party members refused to collaborate with the conspirators, [they] condemned the coup and joined the fight against it. Nobody has a moral right to blame all Communists indiscriminately, and I, as President, consider it my duty to defend them as citizens from unsubstantiated accusations.

In this situation, the Communist Party Central Committee should take the difficult but honest decision to dissolve itself. The republic Communist parties and local party organizations will decide their own fate.

I don't think it's possible for me to continue to fulfill the functions of general secretary of the Communist Party of the Soviet Union, and I'm relinquishing the corresponding powers. I believe that democratic-minded Communists loyal to constitutional lawfulness, to the course of renewal of society, will stand up for creation on a new basis of a party capable of joining in the ongoing radical democratic transformations along with all progressive forces in the interests of the working people.

Mr. Roth addressed the Chair.

The Presiding Officer. The Senator from Delaware is recognized.

Mr. Roth. Mr. President, I will only say to my distinguished friend and colleague from Virginia, we are hopeful that he and his colleagues will change their minds as the debate continues this afternoon. We, of course, are very hopeful that a majority of the Senate, like in the House of Representatives, will support our amendment.

Mr. President, as I was saying before the unanimous-consent request was agreed upon, excellence in our military forces means many things. It means dedication during long hours and it means quiet pride in accomplishments that go unnoticed. It means getting the best training you can because you might save someone's life, or the lives of an entire aircrew. It means knowing the ins and outs of the newest technology—how to use it, how not to abuse it.

There is certain spirit of resolve, of alertness, of intelligence, and of patriotism that I associate with excellence in our armed services. And I can tell you that the women pilots who I have spoken with exemplify that spirit.

Whether they can meet the performance standards will be up to their superiors. But they certainly should have the opportunity to compete—if that is their choice—and to give us their best.

The amendment we bring here today does not perform major surgery on the composition of our armed services. Instead, I liken it to pinpoint laser surgery—this amendment is very precise. We simply remove the congressionally imposed restriction which prevents women from flying combat aircraft—and give the Defense Department the authority to determine how best to use women aviators.

Legal experts agree that lifting the restriction will not mean a dramatic change for women's roles in the military. Like the surgical strike weapons used in Operation Desert Storm, our amendment has a specific intent and a specific mission—it is designed to hit the target.

We have looked at an area where women have proven themselves beyond a doubt, and where technology has equalized opportunity. We have looked at an area where the Pentagon has expressed a need which has merit and value. And we have found that action is appropriate and called for. This amendment is not only the right action, but the right action at the right time.

America agrees with us, Mr. President. The people have expressed their conviction that women combat pilots would be an asset to our military defense. They have shown a sophisticated understanding of the substantive difference between women as combat aviators and women in other combat roles. The public's perceptions have caught up with the changes that have occurred, and the people see women pilots as ready and capable professionals—a true asset to our military.

As always, Vice Admiral Lawrence has stated the problem eloquently. He has written:

PLANS FOR RESTRUCTURING THE SOVIET UNION

August 26 and September 2, 1991

After a failed coup attempt in August, Soviet leadership was in a crisis. President Mikhail S. Gorbachev emerged from three days of captivity bodily unharmed but politically wounded. The subsequent collapse of the Communist party crumbled his political base and strengthened the fifteen Soviet republics' demands for more power or outright independence. (Failure of Soviet Coup Attempt, p. 515, and Gorbachev's Resignation from Communist Party, p. 527)

In the spring the central government and nine republics had hammered out a treaty to bring about a fuller measure of power-sharing, but the coup's plotters struck before it could be signed. Strengthened by the recent upheaval, politicians from the various republics increased their demands; instead of a federation of semiautonomous republics, which the so-called union treaty sought to establish, they began advocating a commonwealth of independent states.

Appealing to the nation not to split apart, Gorbachev on August 26 sought support for the power-sharing treaty by proposing that national elections be held within six months of its signing—letting the voters choose a Soviet president for the first time. He conceded in an address to the Supreme Soviet parliamentary body that the Kremlin's old dominant relationship with the republics could not be sustained, but argued for devising an arrangement that stopped short of giving them outright independence.

Gorbachev's audience—some 500 delegates who sit between full sessions of the Congress of the People's Deputies—was not persuaded. Speaker after speaker arose during the nationally televised session to assert his republic's right to greater autonomy than the treaty provided. Many of them also criticized Gorbachev for taking into his cabinet the old-line Communist foes of reforms who later turned out to be coup makers.

The Soviet leader insisted that he had acted in a spirit of compromise to prevent the possibility of bloodshed. Then to the legislators' applause, he added, "There will be no more compromises ..."

Congress Approves Emergency Plan

The Supreme Soviet called its parent body, the Congress of the People's Deputies, into special session September 2. As the congress opened, the deputies were stunned by a proposal concluded only hours before by Gorbachev and leaders of ten Soviet republics asking that all central power be turned over to them until a new union treaty could be negotiated. The congress, which in March 1989 became the Soviet Union's first freely elected legislature and had since held the nation's highest constitutional authority, was in effect being asked to cease functioning.

Many of the 1,780 attending deputies were dismayed and outraged at the leaders' request for emergency powers but acquiesced after two days of debate in which Gorbachev and his chief rival, Russian republic president Boris N. Yeltsin, worked together to apply heavy political pressure to forge a favorable vote. President Nursultan A. Nazarbayev of the large Kazakh republic was a prime figure in negotiating the proposal and introduced it in the congress. The plan's backers argued that such a drastic measure was needed to avert political chaos and possibly civil war—such as had beset Yugoslavia. (Independence of Yugoslav Republics, p. 367) *They joined with Gorbachev in declaring that the Soviet Union was "on the brink of catastrophe" and in need of coordinated direction. Gorbachev threatened to resign if the plan was defeated.*

The required two-thirds majority was attained only on a third vote held September 5. The new law created an interim ruling structure consisting of a State Council, Legislative Council, and Economic Council. Gorbachev and the republic presidents would form the first council, and a small group of appointees from the same republics would fill the other two. The functions and procedures of the State Council, by far the most important of the three, were left for its new members to determine.

Differences Among Soviet Republics

The ten republics participating in the plan were Armenia, Azerbaijan, Byelorussia, Kazakhstan, Kirghizia, Russia, Tadzhikistan, Turkmenia, the Ukraine, and Uzbekistan. All but Armenia were parties to the original, unsigned union treaty. Georgia sent observers to the negotiations but did not accept the plan. Moldavia, on the Romanian border, did not participate, nor did the Baltic republics of Latvia, Lithuania, and Estonia, which had declared their independence. However, Latvia and Estonia continued to send deputies to the congress.

All fifteen republics had asserted some degree of independence—eight of them (including Latvia and Estonia) following the Soviet coup attempt. But aside from the Baltic states, whose governments received foreign diplomatic recognition, it appeared uncertain how far the others would push toward a complete break with the Soviet Union. (U.S. on Renewing Diplomatic Ties with Baltic States, p. 545)

Ukraine Balks at Economic Pact

While the republics' task of negotiating with the central government may have been made easier by its post-coup weakness, achieving agreement among the independent-minded republics was more difficult than ever. In October the Ukraine, the Soviet Union's agricultural heartland, refused to sign an economic pact for a free-market association that Russia had persuaded eight other republics and the central government to sign.

"History has given us a chance to be an independent nation, and we do not want to continue to be a colony," Ivan Pliusch, first deputy chairman of the Ukrainian Parliament, explained on Ukrainian television October 17. In response, Vice President Aleksandr Rutskoi of the Russian republic said, "I do not know if the Ukraine will survive without Russia, but I definitely know that Russia will survive without the Ukraine."

On November 1 Yeltsin won overwhelming support from the Russian parliament for drastic free-market reforms within the republic that also cut off Russian financing for key Soviet ministries. These reforms set the economic pace for most of the other republics to which Russia is joined by the free-market association. On November 17 Yeltsin issued a set of economic decrees that asserted even fuller domination over the sinking Soviet economy.

Gorbachev, in an apparent move to strengthen the central government's credibility and to retain its control of foreign affairs, on November 19 reappointed the popular Eduard S. Shevardnadze to the post of foreign minister. The principal architect of Gorbachev's policy of friendship with the West, Shevardnadze had unexpectedly resigned that post in December 1990, warning that "dictatorship is coming" from the old guard that had increasingly begun to surround Gorbachev. The coup attempt in August made Shevardnadze's warning appear prophetic and enhanced his standing with reformers.

> *Following are excerpts from English translations of Soviet president Mikhail S. Gorbachev's speech to the Supreme Soviet in Moscow on August 26, 1991, urging the republics to sign a power-sharing treaty with the central government, and from a proposal submitted by Gorbachev and ten republic presidents to the Congress of the People's Deputies on September 2 requesting emergency powers until a new treaty could be negotiated:*

GORBACHEV'S SPEECH

... First of all, I support the decision taken by the U.S.S.R. Supreme Soviet to convene an extraordinary Congress of the People's Deputies of the U.S.S.R. because the problem itself—and all that we lived through in that time, in those days—and the decisions that we need to make on all of that, is in fact the prerogative of the Congress.

That's the first thing. I submit to your consideration a proposal to invite to the Congress deputies of the R.F.S.F.R. [Russian Federation] Supreme Soviet and representatives of the parliaments of other republics.

In the days before the Congress I would like to ask the people's deputies to have a detailed discussion and to think over all that has happened to us, and why it happened to us, and what lessons need to be learned from it [to discuss it in] commissions and committees, as well as in [parliamentary] factions, and at the session and in the chambers. It's up to you to decide where to discuss it.

I'm not talking about philosophizing on this, but rather about specific political and practical actions and decisions which would be based on precise and uncompromising analysis of all that we have lived through. Naturally, in these days before the Congress we are not going to just sit with our hands folded. In fact we are already acting. I am speaking about submitting to the Supreme Soviet [the question] of confidence in the Cabinet of Ministers, which failed to fulfill its constitutional role in those days. And some of its members turned out to be direct participants in this anti-constitutional coup.

Decrees have been issued on removing the party from the army, law enforcement organs and other state services. The main [figures] in the army, KGB and Interior Ministry who actively supported the conspirators in implementing their plans have been removed from their posts. New people have been appointed to key posts in those organs. The U.S.S.R. and R.F.S.F.R. prosecutors offices are together investigating the actions of the coup organizers.

You are familiar with my statement in which I resigned my duties as general secretary of the Communist Party of the Soviet Union and suggested that the Central Committee of the party should dissolve itself. Naturally, similar measures that intend to stabilize the situation in the country and to prevent an explosion of revanchism will continue until the Congress convenes.

This line will be firmly pursued....

The coup did not break out unexpectedly, out of the blue. Its forerunners were hysterical publications by the rightists in the press and at Central Committee plena and provocative statements by some generals, including from the rostrum of the Congress of People's Deputies and the open sabotage of many perestroika-related decisions by party-state structures.

In other words, the conspiracy was ripening. There was more than enough justification to take urgent measures to defend the constitutional order. However, it was not done even though it was not left without attention or evaluation. It was rebuffed in various organs including the press, at the plenum, here in the Supreme Soviet. And yet instead of decisive actions, liberalism and indulgence were shown. In the first place, I refer to myself.

But this is a lesson of the first order, so to speak. There is a more important cause, or reason, which made possible this attempt against democracy, the attempt to turn the country back to totalitarianism by force. This reason is a lack of decisiveness and consistency in carrying out democratic reforms, especially in those structures where the coup was growing. It's not only my fault, but the fault of all of us, the Supreme Soviet of the U.S.S.R., the leading organs of the party, the government.

Our good intentions, our well-formulated goals and plans were largely not fulfilled because we failed to change the old mechanism of power. I have in mind the state apparatus, which has remained basically unchanged, and the tolerance toward those workers, including those people in ruling positions who remained true to Stalinism and everything connected to it. Or at least to post-Stalinism.

We hesitated for a long time and have not yet really started decisive democratic changes in the economy. And that reflected on the socio-economic situation in the country. It's no secret that the conspirators wanted to take advantage of the difficulties in the life of the entire population. These are all real facts of our life; people are carrying a burden of great problems. The living standards are slipping, there is no personal safety, criminal elements are rampaging and they rule the show in many places even now.

The reason for what happened is a lack of agreement, coordination in the actions of democratic, truly perestroika forces, whatever shade they were. We and people who were in effect adherents of the same goals were separated and sometimes they managed to lead us into positions on different sides of the political barricades. Here, at plenums on other occasions, I said that we would make our greatest gift to those who oppose the new course and transformations in our country if we, adherents of democracy ... clash head-to-head or get bogged down in political fighting.

Insufficient political foresight and responsibility for our common cause was telling, however. Here I mean for the democrats. The armed forces proved to be under no appropriate constitutional control. The army is a separate subject. Indeed, the conspirators failed to carry out the criminal plot to the end and throw the army against its own people.

There were two major miscalculations made by the conspirators. They thought that our people could be manipulated, sent like a herd here and there. I apologize for this phrase, but this is what they must have thought. But the country is not the same anymore. That's their main miscalculation. Since the country is not the same and the people are not the same, the army is not the same, either, because it is a part of the people....

... And yet, it turned out to be possible to move troops, tanks and other armored vehicles into the streets of Moscow and Leningrad without confirmation by the supreme legislative body of the country. It's a fact, and that means not everything is right in our mechanisms.

The clearly needed reform of the KGB was not carried out. Of course, KGB officers provide the defense of state borders, defend state interests with the help of intelligence and counter-intelligence. That's what the committee ought to do. However, at the same time, even in conditions of deep democratic transformations in society, it still continued in some parts to be a mechanism for political struggle.

I, as president, bear the greatest share of responsibility for the failure of the Supreme Soviet mechanism to work, that many members of the Cabinet of Ministers were shamefully helpless and cowardly in the face of the conspiracy, that three organizations having armed forces were headed by people capable of the coup. I am saying this because I have thought and reconsidered much in these days. I have made my conclusions from this entire tragedy that happened.

They say that I have come back to a different country. I agree with this. I can add to it; a man came back to a different country who looks upon every-thing—the past, today, and future prospects—with different eyes. In any case, I will not allow any hesitation or delays in implementing reforms as long as I am president. There will be no more compromises with those with whom it is impossible and impermissible to seek compromise. [Applause]

I take it that your applause means that you understand that there were times in the past when compromises should not have been made. But my main wish is that whatever we do may be kept within a democratic framework and without blood. And this, perhaps, is [why I made compro-mises] when decisive measures were needed to prevent the entire country being plunged into a sea of blood.

There is another reason which made the process of reform so tortuous and had a bad effect on peoples' lives. It is the delay in eliminating the party monopoly on power, eliminating party bureaucratic structures largely preserved since the previous regime. We remember the exhausting struggle at plena with those who tried to block democratic transformations in every possible way.

The old system was undermined, disorganized, but continued to hold as much as it could and prevented forward movement. While talking about it, I think it is a matter of principle to separate millions of rank-and-file party members from the party bureaucracy. I have been saying this since the first days I was able to speak. It was my confidence in the millions of ordinary party members that gave me hope for the possibility of the party's radical transformation from a Stalinist into a modern, democratic organization. The coup obliterated this hope. That is why, as you know, I resigned my duties as general secretary and suggested that the Central Committee makes a decision to dissolve.

And yet, despite all those reasons which made the conspiracy possible, it was doomed from the start. It turned out that the last six years were not in vain. The country and the people were changed beyond recognition. Democratic forces, even though they are not well organized, grew up. They may not be in complete agreement with each other, but together with all the people they gave a decisive rebuff to the conspirators. This conclusion is directly linked with trying to understand why the conspirators were in such a hurry to carry out their plan. I can say with deep conviction that they realized that delay would mean their death because such processes such as the nine-plus-one Novo-Ogarevo [the proposed Union Treaty] emerged.

Let's be honest, not just at Central Committee plena but also in the Supreme Soviet, they did not fully accept this process. There were many questions asked. Let's be entirely honest and say everything on this day, because we [lawmakers] did it [held back the Union Treaty] with the country standing behind us.

So they had to hurry because of the Novo-Ogarevo process, the forthcoming signing of the Union Treaty, the inevitable and already on-going transition to a market, and this seven-plus-one international meeting making the integration of our economy into the world economy possible.

The coup d'etat was foiled, crushed. I would like once again to express my unending gratitude to the hundreds of thousands of Muscovites who went out in the streets, looking fearlessly into the barrels of automatic weapons and tank cannons. They defended freedom and legality. Boris Nikolayevich Yeltsin and the Russian parliament, the people of Leningrad and their leaders, Kiev, the position taken by the people of other republics played a very important role in foiling the conspiracy.

However much they tried to dress up their appeals—make them most attractive, most people-oriented—the people did not accept what they wanted to do. This happened in the most difficult situation, with people really wishing for decisive transformations but not in this manner.

But the bare fact that the conspiracy was possible shows that we are only halfway down the road and must take the most urgent and reliable measures to set up guarantees for constitutional legality.

What should we do now?

First, I think the most important thing is an immediate resumption of the signing of the Union Treaty. The conspirators managed to disrupt the planned signing. . . .

After the meeting on Aug. 23 with leaders of nine republics, which was held on the second day after I came back, it was proposed that the Treaty should be signed. We must take a specific position on republics that are unwilling to sign the Union Treaty.

They must be given the right of independent choice. Immediately after the Union Treaty is signed, negotiations must be started with those who wish to leave the union. Preparations for this can be started now. This agreement must include guarantees for safeguarding human rights irrespective of nationality, the question of compensation to those citizens who are unwilling to remain outside the union and move, the question of military infrastructure which must be kept on their territory for some time determined by the agreement. Considering the vital interest of all 15 republics in retaining economic ties, we must begin to work on an economic agreement and do it without delay. [Applause]

Third, some issues of governing the country in the period before a new constitution is put into effect must be resolved at once. Circumstances make us act without waiting for its adoption. Even before the general election, we must settle such important issues as the election by the forthcoming Congress of Peoples Deputies of a vice president of the country. We must consult very carefully about it.

At the meeting with republic leaders on the 23rd a proposal was put forward to have an authoritative organ that could make decisions on all important issues of government on the union territory.

Such a constitutional organ as a Security Council was proposed. It is possible if leaders of republics that decided to sign the Union Treaty become its members as well as Comrades Yakovlev, [Vadim] Bakatin, Primakov, Sobchak and Popov, Revenko, who has become the chief of staff of the U.S.S.R. president.

We need to form a Cabinet of Ministers on the basis of agreement with republic leaders. Meanwhile, for day-to-day government of the country, I have decided to form a committee headed by Comrade Silayev. You are familiar with this decree.

Fourth, the conspirators would have been unable to carry out their plans if the Supreme Soviet of the U.S.S.R. and its chairman had firmly and decisively stood in their way. The events demanded an immediate convening of the Supreme Soviet. Russia did it at once. It played a huge role in opposition to the putsch. The union Supreme Soviet failed to realize its constitutional authority at this moment. Where was the presidium? Where were the deputies? Why didn't they rush to their place immediately? All of this must be thought of. Look deeply into yourselves. We must learn all the lessons, not only morally and politically. We need a special provision if such a situation occurs. Everyone must be there in the capital without any telegrams or invitations.

Such a provision must be made in the constitution or another document. In the days left before the Congress I suggest we think seriously about who should become chairman of the U.S.S.R. Supreme Soviet. As always, I am ready for consultations, but especially now. Here and with republics we must ensure that no opinion is unheard.

We must be sure that these people will do their business as required by the circumstances.

Fifth, we must evaluate the situation and design and establish reliable constitutional, public control over the activities of the armed forces and law enforcement.

Deep changes will be needed here—everything should be done immediately, within the framework of preparing the military reform law or maybe separating the issue, solving it so that later it becomes a component of the military reform law.

We need to conduct the reform of the Committee for State Security (KGB). In my decree on the appointment of Comrade Bakatin as chairman of the committee, there is a point instructing him to submit his proposals on reorganizing the entire system immediately. An impenetrable shield must be erected to the use of security organs for anti-constitutional purposes. I will sign a decree on the subordination of KGB border guards to the Defense Ministry.

Apparently it is necessary to suspend the law on the KGB and work out a new concept of state security. On its basis [we can] quickly and reasonably reform the appropriate structures.

Sixth, on economic measures: The former line of gradual movement along the path of reforms in conditions of radical change in the situation in the country needs to be reconsidered. I am coming to this conclusion. Let's discuss it together at the forthcoming Congress and work out measures on major issues of economic policy taking into account the fact that we are now in a different time. . . .

I think our measures should include firstly, removing all obstacles artificially erected by those structures on the way towards the market. That is [give] full freedom to entrepreneurship, removing monopolies, dictate from above, forcible methods, creating basic market institutions.
We need:

- Decisive transferal of the emphasis in governing the economy and the responsibility for resolving economic issues to republics, with the union retaining legislative control for regulating a single economic space.
- To return to the idea of an inter-republican economic meeting.
- Decisive reduction of the budget deficit and budget expenditures, strengthening the ruble and normalization of money circulation.
- Remove all obstacles to giving land to all those who want to work on it. And we have land already. But that's not the main thing. We must make sure that the land reform gets a second wind. Our support is necessary. We must decide these things in the fall and winter. Now, of course, we must gather the crops and store them. . . .
- A decisive acceleration of reorganization of foreign economic and monetary relations, convertibility of the ruble, efficient use of credits and other economic assistance which the West is giving us and which it is prepared to increase. Judging by conversations I have had with all major leaders, they confirm that the way the country and the people looked during those days convinced them that the Soviet Union has embarked on the way of final and irreversible reforms, and they realized the need for cooperation, its strengthening and broadening.
- Ridding social policies of demagogy, groundless promises, unfulfillable programs. We must get rid of economic populism. [We must concentrate] our attention on basic issues of social protection during the transition to the market—job placement, maintaining living standards especially of low-income people, housing, etc. The problems of food and power and fuel are especially difficult. Proposals on these matters have been prepared by all republics.

We must solve this issue and prevent disruption of food supplies and provide fuel and power during autumn and winter. Even now I would like to ... appeal to all peasants and all people who live on the land, all miners, oil and gas industry workers, power industry workers, to be at their jobs to the end and do everything possible to resolve these major issues. ...

Seventh: Immediately after the Union Treaty is signed [we must] begin the election campaign to elect all union organs, including the president. ...

I think that the Supreme Soviet will ensure that legality, law and order exist. All those who took part in the conspiracy must get all that they deserve under the law. But on the other hand we, and I think all people, are against [senseless revenge]. That's it. I have finished.

UNION PROPOSALS

As a result of the coup on Aug. 19-21 this year, the process of forming new union relations between the sovereign states broke down. This brought the country to the brink of catastrophe.

The situation that has emerged in the country since the putsch, if it runs out of control, could bring unpredictable consequences inside the country and in relations with foreign states. We state that the failure of the coup and victory of democratic forces have delivered a serious blow to reactionary forces and to everything that had been hindering the process of democratic change.

Thus, a historic chance has been created to speed up reform and renovation of the country. In these conditions, legally elected leaders of the country—the president of the country, presidents and chairmen of the Supreme Soviets [legislatures] of the republics—agree on the following measures for a transitional period until a new constitution is adopted and new organs of power are elected. ... All republics that wish to, should:

1. Work out and sign a Treaty of the Union of Sovereign States in which each of them will independently determine the form of its participation in the union.
2. Appeal to all republics, irrespective of the status they have declared ... to immediately conclude an economic agreement for cooperation ... and accelerated implementation of radical economic reform.
3. Create for the transitional period a Council of Representatives of People's Deputies on the principle of equal representation from union republics—20 people's deputies delegated by each republic's Supreme Soviet to decide upon matters of general principle.
4. Set up a State Council consisting of the Soviet president and top state officials of the republics to coordinate foreign and internal issues that concern common interests among the republics.
5. Set up an Interim Inter-Republic Economic Committee consisting of representatives of all the republics, on parity basis, to coordinate economic management and ... reform.

The draft constitution, when ready, should be considered and approved by republic legislatures and finally approved at a congress of plenipotentiary representatives of union republics.

6. Sign an agreement on defense—on the principles of collective security—to preserve united armed forces and military-strategic space [and] to carry out radical military reforms in the armed forces, KGB, Interior Ministry and prosecutor's office of the U.S.S.R., taking into account the republics' interests [and confirming] strict observation of all international agreements and obligations of the Soviet Union, including the question of arms cuts and control as well as foreign economic obligations.

7. Adopt a declaration granting rights and freedoms of citizens, irrespective of their nationality, place of residence, party membership or political views, as well as the rights of national minorities.

8. Ask the Congress of People's Deputies of the U.S.S.R. to support applications of the union republics to the United Nations to recognize them as subjects of international law and to consider their membership in this organization.

September

U.S. ON RENEWING DIPLOMATIC TIES WITH BALTIC STATES

September 2, 1991

President George Bush announced September 2 that the United States was ready to establish diplomatic relations with Lithuania, Latvia, and Estonia—thereby formally recognizing their secession from a deteriorating Soviet empire. The three Baltic states had reasserted the sovereign status they held before the Soviet Union seized and forcibly annexed them in 1940. The United States had condemned the annexation as illegal and continued to recognize them technically as independent states but withdrew its diplomats from their capitals after the Soviet takeover.

Lithuania declared independence in March 1990. Latvia and Estonia took preliminary steps toward secession the same year but, aware of Moscow's resistance to Lithuania's breakaway attempt, did not fully assert their independence until August 20-21—immediately following an abortive coup in the Soviet Union that left President Mikhail S. Gorbachev weak and the central government in disarray. (Lithuanian Declaration of Independence, Historic Documents of 1990, p. 183, and Failure of Soviet Coup Attempt, p. 515)

Bush delayed his announcement several days, fearing it might add to Gorbachev's problems. U.S. officials hoped that the Soviet leader would ease tensions by openly acknowledging the Baltic states' independence. Gorbachev had veered in that direction by saying in an interview September 1 that he would accept their newly declared status if "this is the ultimate will and intention of the people." Russians formed sizable minority populations in all three republics, and Gorbachev's remark seemed to suggest that their interests had not been taken into account. Bush apparently felt that the remark offered him a sufficient opening to act; the next day at his Maine vacation home he told an impromptu news conference that the United States "is now prepared to establish diplomatic relations" with Latvia, Lithuania, and Estonia and "do whatever it can to assist in the completion of the current process of making Baltic independence a reality." But he held little hope that the United States would offer any sizable amount of economic assistance, which all three countries were seeking.

By this time nearly thirty other nations and the Russian Federation—the dominant Soviet republic—had already extended formal recognition to the Baltic countries. Officials in the three countries welcomed Bush's announcement but, according to press reports, Lithuanian spokesmen also expressed irritation that it had not come sooner. President Vytautis Lansbergis of Lithuania issued no public response.

The previous year Lansbergis had criticized the United States for not supporting Lithuania when it came under heavy pressure from Moscow not to break away. In January 1991, at a time when Gorbachev seemed to be especially influenced by old-line Communists, Soviet paratroops and tanks moved into the Lithuanian capital of Vilnius. They briefly besieged the parliament building, killing fifteen unarmed civilian defenders. The crackdown evoked protests from Washington, but formal recognition of the new Lithuanian government was not forthcoming.

Lithuania's defiance of Moscow created a dilemma for Western democracies, especially the United States. For decades Congress had ritually passed resolutions condemning the Soviet occupation of the "captive nations." But cheers for Lithuania's bold stand were muted by its timing. By insisting on immediate secession, Lithuania exposed Gorbachev's difficulties with other restive Soviet republics before he was prepared to deal with them. Bush, having thrown his support to Gorbachev at the Malta summit meeting in December 1989, had an enormous stake in the Soviet leader's success. He initially warned Gorbachev not to intervene in the Baltics, but as the situation waxed and waned Bush said little and adopted what amounted to a hands-off approach.

Following are excerpts from President George Bush's news conference September 2, 1991, at his home in Kennebunkport, Maine, in which he announced that the United States would renew diplomatic relations with Lithuania, Latvia, and Estonia:

PRESIDENT BUSH: . . . The Baltic peoples of Estonia, Latvia and Lithuania, and their democratically elected governments, have declared their independence and are moving now to control their own national territories and their own destinies. The United States has always supported the independence of the Baltic States, and is now prepared immediately to establish diplomatic relations with their governments.

The United States is also prepared to do whatever it can to assist in the completion of the current process of making Baltic independence a factual reality. To facilitate this, I'll be sending the deputy assistant secretary of State, Mr. [Curtis W.] Kamman, to the Baltics. We also understand the enormous challenges that lie ahead for the Soviet people in meeting their own food and energy needs particularly, and beginning true economic reform. And therefore I'm sending Under Secretary of Agriculture [Richard T.] Crowder with an experts' mission to survey with Soviet and republic officials their critical food requirements for the coming winter, particularly in those republics that are likely to be in great need. And, in a month, a presidential mission led by Secretary of Agriculture Madigan —Ed Madigan—will bring a delegation of senior private-sector and government officials to the U.S.S.R. to seek solutions to a winter food problem, if we determine that one exists, and to continue our long-term efforts to help the Soviet Union and the Soviet people resolve problems in food distribution.

I've also asked Secretary of State Jim Baker, and our AID [Agency for International Development] administrator, Mr. [Ronald W.] Roskens, to work with Project Hope to augment and extend my presidential initiative on medical assistance to the U.S.S.R. through the end of 1992. We intend to work closely with Soviet and republic officials in both of these efforts. This morning I talked with the presidents of Estonia and Latvia, as I did to Mr. [Vytautus] Landsbergis of Lithuania a couple of days ago, to tell him of this official position now being taken by the United States of America. . . .

Q: What does today's action signify to the independence movements of the other republics? Does it offer the guarantee that when they declare their independence that the United States will also recognize them?

P: Well, what we'll do is look at each case on a case-by-case basis, but I think more important than what we might do down the road is what apparently is happening there in agreement between the center and the republics, and that is that each shall determine its own future. The Baltics, of course, are quite different. We never, as you know, recognized their incorporation in the first place. So there are some technical difficulties as we go along.

But I think this is very good news that they're willing to sort it out, and we'll look at it obviously on a case-by-case basis. We got to know first what kind of relationship these republics want to have with the center before we can jump way ahead and say what we're going to do in each case.

Q: Mr. President, you delayed recognizing the Baltic countries, we are given to understand, because of the role of the United States as a superpower and because of your desire not to undercut Mikhail Gorbachev. What are the criteria now that you have decided this is the time to do this? Have you talked with someone in the Soviet Union? Are you satisfied with what the Russian Parliament is doing?

P: Well, I think it's all moving in the right direction. I thought that Gorbachev's statement yesterday, for example, which was heralded around the world as recognizing the right of the Baltics to be free, whether that's a proper interpretation or not—that was a good statement. And we have been quietly asserting to him for a long time that the best thing he could do in terms of relationships with the United States is to free the Baltic States. And we've been working hard on that.

And so it's taking a final decision three or four more days than somebody else. But in the sweep of history I think we will be proved correct in taking just a few days to see if we can't effect change within the Soviet Union. And I'm very pleased at the two developments I talked to you today about. . . .

Q: You called for the Baltics to become independent as soon as possible. Gorbachev in his public statements seemed very vague about how cumbersome this constitutional process will be, how long it will take. Has he given you any assurances in private about some of the practical and legal dynamics and complications at work here?

P: Not in the last couple of weeks . . . but I've been into that with him in great detail in terms of what he says are the constitutional constraints, if you will. In spite of all that, my urging is to anybody with authority in the Soviet Union, is turn the Baltics loose now, free, clear—and, yes, there's going to have to be some negotiation between the center and between the states, because there's an overlapping of resource responsibility, where does the energy come from, how do the steel imports go from one of the Baltics into the center. There's a lot of—and there's, you know, control of one's own territory.

One of the things that we have felt was necessary before full recognition has been control of the territory. And yet, as you see these Soviet troops leaving and you hear statements out of the Soviet Union that give you encouragement, then we feel that they are in a much better position to control their own territory totally. There are still, as you point out, some details to be worked out, however.

Q: And do you think that he thinks at this point that this is a fait accompli, that this is going to happen, probably sooner rather than later?

P: I have nothing that would be definitive on that for you, nothing that could cause me to make such a statement, about what he thinks.

Q: What about your belief in the matter?

P: Well, my belief is that it's inexorable, this quest for freedom and independence on the part of the Baltics. It's going to be a fait accompli—and it's pretty close to it now with the recognition of these different states and with the statements out of Moscow. But, no, I don't think that process can be reversed if that's your question. . . .

Q: What about economic aid to the Baltics, Mr. President? Now that you're recognizing their independence, these countries are going to have a hard time economically. Are you going to step in with some money?

P: I think it's a little premature to say what we will or won't do. I'm sending somebody over there to survey the scene. We'll be in close touch with these leaders. And there's an awful lot of people who want aid and are entitled to aid. We are limited in what we can do. I'm not about to forget Eastern Europe. It's all very exciting what's happening in the Baltic States and in the republics and in Moscow, but it's also very important that

Czechoslovakia and Hungary and Poland succeed. And we have a commitment to them in terms of aid—and I'm not about to forget it.

And so we've got to sort all of this out. But clearly we will be in a listening mode, and hopefully we can be constructive partners as these countries move toward the independence they so richly deserve and achieve the independence they so richly deserve. . . .

HEARINGS ON CLARENCE THOMAS'S SUPREME COURT NOMINATION

September 10-13 and October 11 and 15, 1991

On July 1 President George Bush nominated Clarence Thomas, a forty-three-year-old black judge from the U.S. Court of Appeals for the District of Columbia, to succeed retiring Justice Thurgood Marshall on the Supreme Court. (Resignation of Justice Marshall from the Supreme Court, p. 377) *After prolonged hearings marked by emotion-packed charges of sexual harassment and racism, the Senate on October 15 approved the nomination 52-48. It was the closest Supreme Court confirmation vote in more than a century.*

While Thomas's judicial record was scant, his speeches, writings, and prior government service pointed to a pronounced conservative ideology. The president's choice of Thomas to replace the Court's most outspoken liberal was destined to incur strong Democratic opposition. Thomas fit into the Court's prevailing philosophy as fixed by the four conservative appointees of President Ronald Reagan and the elevation of William H. Rehinquist to chief justice.

Interest groups that pushed the Senate to reject the Supreme Court nomination of conservative jurist Robert H. Bork in 1987 began organizing a campaign against the nomination of Thomas. (Bork Confirmation Battle, Historic Documents of 1987, p. 717) *Abortion rights groups, especially, thought the stakes were higher this time because the Supreme Court had since retreated from its 1973 landmark decision* Roe v. Wade *that legalized abortion nationwide, and they feared the Court was likely to reverse it. The National Organization of Women quickly expressed its opposition to the nomination.*

Thomas presented a dilemma for civil rights groups. Sidney Hook, executive director of the National Association for the Advancement of Colored People (NAACP), said it was important to have a black person on the Court but added that the NAACP wanted someone "who embodies many of the attributes Justice Marshall so ably articulated." Jesse Jackson noted that Thomas had benefited from affirmative action but opposed it in favor of self-help and individual initiative. Civil rights groups faulted Thomas's handling of minority complaints when he was chairman of Reagan's Equal Employment Opportunity Commission (EEOC) from 1982 to 1989.

The NAACP, AFL-CIO, Leadership Conference on Civil Rights, and eighteen of the nineteen black members of Congress opposed the nomination. The American Bar Association gave Thomas a mixed rating in judging his fitness for the job. A majority on the ABA's evaluation committee found him "qualified," but none gave him the highest rating of "well qualified."

For a Supreme Court appointee, Thomas's judicial experience was relatively brief. After graduation from Yale Law School, he was an assistant from 1974 to 1977 to Missouri attorney general John C. Danforth, his political mentor. Then, after two years as an attorney for the Monsanto Company, Thomas went to Washington as legislative assistant to Danforth, who had meanwhile been elected to the Senate. In 1981 President Reagan named Thomas assistant secretary of education for civil rights and the next year made him EEOC chairman. He served in that post until 1989 when Bush placed him on the U.S. Court of Appeals for the District of Columbia.

Hearings on Judicial Philosophy

In five days of questioning by the Senate Judiciary Committee, beginning September 10, Thomas refused to declare a position on abortion, disavowed many of his provocative writings, and generally left committee members with few clues as to his constitutional philosophy. Instead, the nominee sounded his own themes, often referring to his impoverished childhood in Pin Point, Georgia, and portraying himself as a champion of civil rights in a conservative administration.

The committee's majority Democrats often expressed their frustration at not being able to pin down his views. On one occasion, Sen. Howell Heflin, D-Ala., asked in exasperation: "What is the real Clarence Thomas like? What would the real Clarence Thomas do on the Supreme Court?" He replied: "I am the real Clarence Thomas, and I have attempted to bring that person here.... I am simply different from what people painted me to be."

On September 27, the committee deadlocked 7-7 on whether to recommend confirmation. The vote split along party lines except for Dennis DeConcini, D-Ariz., who sided with the committee's six Republicans in support of Thomas. But before the Senate could vote on confirmation October 8, as scheduled, a startling new development threw doubt on the outcome.

Anita Hill's Sexual Harassment Charges

The news media reported that the committee had learned of a sexual harassment allegation against Thomas but never pursued it or made it public. Thomas's accuser was Anita Hill, a black law professor at the University of Oklahoma. She told investigators looking into the nominee's background that he sexually harassed her when she worked for him as an attorney-adviser—first at the Department of Education and then at the EEOC. Committee leaders contended that the matter had not been made public because Hill sought confidentiality.

She broke her public silence at a news conference October 7 in Norman, Oklahoma, defending her accusations and saying that the committee gave them scant notice. The charge raised fundamental questions about Thomas's character—the one attribute that the White House and his Senate supporters had played up. When Bush nominated Thomas, he spoke of Thomas's boyhood poverty and called him "a model for all Americans."

Faced with a wave of angry protests, especially from women and women's groups, the Senate delayed the vote and ordered an investigation of Hill's allegations. A Washington Post-ABC News poll conducted the day of her news conference found that 87 percent of those questioned had heard about the accusations and that 63 percent said that, if true, Thomas should not be confirmed. Under pressure, the committee took the unusual step of reopening the hearings, beginning October 11.

That extraordinary hearing resumed in the Senate Caucus Room with a moving declaration of innocence by Thomas. For the next seven hours Hill meticulously recounted to the committee and a national television audience her story of how Thomas humiliated her by making lewd comments. Under questioning, she gave graphic details of Thomas's sexually oriented statements. Asked why, if offended by this harassment, she moved with Thomas from the Department of Education to the EEOC. Hill said, "I needed the job," noting that she was twenty-five at the time and perhaps had not made the best decision.

Thomas's Denial; "Lynching" Countercharge

After nightfall, Thomas was back on the stand with his own accusations. "This is a circus. It's a national disgrace. And from my standpoint, as a black American," he said, "it is a high-tech lynching for uppity blacks who in any way deign to think for themselves." Thomas said the message was "that unless you kowtow to an old order, this is what will happen to you. You will be lynched, destroyed, caricatured by a committee of the U.S. Senate rather than hung from a tree."

He returned to the witness stand the next day for another round of testimony, denying Hill's claim of sexual impropriety and refusing to submit to questions about his private life. On the third day, the committee heard supporting testimony for both Thomas and Hill. President Bush expressed confidence in the embattled nominee, saying that

Thomas had made "a very, very powerful and convincing statement. This decent and honorable man had been smeared."

Several political analysts observed that Thomas's "lynching" references had caused his detractors to ease their questioning lest the voting public accept his self-depiction as a victim of race. Women's groups in particular contended that committee Democrats were far gentler in their questioning of Thomas than Republicans were with Hill. Sens. Orrin G. Hatch, R-Utah, and Arlen Specter, R-Pa., portrayed Hill as a fantasizer or fabricator. Although Hill's lawyers announced on October 13 that she had passed a lie-detector test, Republican members dismissed it as the result of her "delusion" and the fallibility of the testing device.

Two days later, eleven Democrats—mostly Southerners—cast their votes with the Republican minority to confirm Thomas; only two Republicans voted against him. Thomas joined the Supreme Court on October 23 immediately following a private swearing-in ceremony in the Court chambers.

Following are excerpts from Senate Judiciary Committee hearings September 10-13, 1991, on the nomination of Judge Clarence Thomas to become a Supreme Court justice, and from Senate debate October 11 and 15, 1991, on the nomination. (The bracketed headings have been added by Congressional Quarterly to highlight the organization of the text):

SEPTEMBER 10 HEARING

THOMAS: Mr. Chairman, Sen. [Strom] Thurmond, members of the committee: I am humbled and honored to have been nominated by President Bush to be an associate justice of the Supreme Court of the United States. I would like to thank the committee, especially you, Chairman [Joseph R.] Biden [Jr.], for your extraordinary fairness throughout this process, and I would like to thank each of you and so many of your colleagues here in the Senate for taking the time to visit with me.

There are not enough words to express my deep gratitude and appreciation to Sen. [John C.] Danforth, who gave me my first job out of Yale Law School. I have never forgotten the terms of his offer to me: more work for less pay than anyone in the country could offer. Believe me, he delivered on his promise, especially the less pay.

I appreciate his wise counsel and his example over the years, and his tireless efforts on my behalf during the confirmation process.

And I would like to thank Sens. [Christopher S.] Bond, [Sam] Nunn, [Wyche] Fowler [Jr.], [John W.] Warner, and [Charles S.] Robb, for taking the time to introduce me today.

Much has been written about my family and me over the past 10 weeks. Through all that has happened throughout our lives and through all adversity, we have grown closer, and our love for each other has grown stronger and deeper. I hope these hearings will help to show more clearly who this person Clarence Thomas is and what really makes me tick.

My earliest memories, as alluded to earlier, are those of Pin Point, Ga., a life far removed in space and time from this room, this day and this moment. As kids, we caught minnows in the creeks, fiddler crabs in the marshes; we played with plovers and skipped shells across the water. It was a world so vastly different from all this.

In 1955, my brother and I went to live with my mother in Savannah. We lived in one room in a tenement. We shared a kitchen with other tenants, and we had a common bathroom in the back yard which was unworkable and unusable. It was hard, but it was all we had and all there was.

Our mother only earned $20 every two weeks as a maid, not enough to take care of us. So she arranged for us to live with our grandparents later in 1955. Imagine, if you will, two little boys with all their belongings in two grocery bags. Our grandparents were two great and wonderful people who loved us dearly. I wish they were sitting here today. Sitting here so they could see that all their efforts, their hard work were not in vain, and so that they could see that hard work and strong values can make for a better life.

I am grateful that my mother and my sister could be here. Unfortunately, my brother could not be.

I attended segregated parochial schools and later attended a seminary near Savannah. The nuns gave us hope and belief in ourselves when society didn't. They reinforced the importance of religious beliefs in our personal lives. Sister Mary Virgilius, my eighth-grade teacher, and the other nuns were unyielding in their expectations that we use all of our talents, no matter what the rest of the world said or did.

After high school, I left Savannah and attended Immaculate Conception Seminary, then Holy Cross College. I attended Yale Law School. Yale had opened its doors, its heart, its conscience to recruit and admit minority students. I benefited from this effort.

My career is as has been delineated today. I was an assistant attorney general in the state of Missouri. I was an attorney in the corporate law department of Monsanto Co. I joined Sen. Danforth's staff here in the Senate, was an assistant secretary in the Department of Education, chairman of EEOC [Equal Employment Oppurtunity Commission], and since 1990 a judge on the U.S. Court of Appeals for the District of Columbia Circuit.

But for the efforts of so many others who have gone before me, I would not be here today. It would be unimaginable. Only by standing on their shoulders could I be here. At each turn in my life, each obstacle confronted, each fork in the road, someone came along to help.

I remember, for example, in 1974 after I completed law school I had no money, no place to live. Mrs. Margaret Bush Wilson, who would later become chairperson of the NAACP, allowed me to live at her house. She provided me not only with room and board, but advice, counsel and guidance.

As I left her house that summer, I asked her, "How much do I owe you?" Her response was, "Just along the way, help someone who is in your position." I have tried to live by my promise to her to do just that, to help others.

So many others gave their lives, their blood, their talents. But for them, I would not be here. Justice [Thurgood] Marshall, whose seat I have been nominated to fill, is one of those who had the courage and the intellect. He is one of the great architects of the legal battles to open doors that seemed so hopelessly and permanently sealed, and to knock down barriers that seemed so insurmountable to those of us in the Pin Point, Georgias of the world.

The civil rights movement, [the] Rev. Martin Luther King and the SCLC [Southern Christian Leadership Conference], Roy Wilkins and the NAACP, Whitney Young and the Urban League, Fannie Lou Hamer, Rosa Parks and Dorothy Hite, they changed society and made it reach out and affirmatively help. I have benefited greatly from their efforts. But for them, there would have been no road to travel.

My grandparents always said there would be more opportunities for us. I can still hear my grandfather, "Y'all goin' have mo' of a chance than me," and he was right. He felt that if others sacrificed and created opportunities for us, we had an obligation to work hard, to be decent citizens, to be fair and good people, and he was right.

You see, Mr. Chairman, my grandparents grew up and lived their lives in an era of blatant segregation and overt discrimination. Their sense of fairness was molded in a crucible of unfairness. I watched as my grandfather was called "boy." I watched as my grandmother suffered the indignity of being denied the use of a bathroom. But through it all they remained fair, decent, good people. Fair in spite of the terrible contradictions in our country.

They were hard-working, productive people who always gave back to others. They gave produce from the farm, fuel oil from the fuel-oil truck. They bought groceries for those who were without, and they never lost sight of the promise of a better tomorrow. I follow in their footsteps, and I have always tried to give back.

Over the years I have grown and matured. I have learned to listen carefully, carefully to other points of views and to others, to think through problems recognizing that there are no easy answers to difficult problems, to think deeply about those who will be affected by the decisions that I make and the decisions made by others. But I have always carried in my heart the world, the life, the people, the values of my youth, the values of my grandparents and my neighbors, the values of people who believed so very deeply in this country in spite of all the contradictions.

It is my hope that when these hearings are completed that this committee will conclude that I am an honest, decent, fair person. I believe that the obligations and responsibilities of a judge, in essence, involve just such basic values. A judge must be fair and impartial. A judge must not bring to his job, to the court, the baggage of preconceived notions, of ideology, and certainly not an agenda. And the judge must get the decision right. Because when all is said and done, the little guy, the average person, the people of Pin Point, the real people of America will be affected not only by what we as judges do, but by the way we do our jobs.

If confirmed by the Senate, I pledge that I will preserve and protect our Constitution and carry with me the values of my heritage: fairness, integrity, open-mindedness, honesty and hard work.

[Thoughts on Natural Law]

JUDICIARY COMMITTEE CHAIRMAN BIDEN, D-DEL.: And, as I said at the outset, there is good natural law, if you will, and bad natural law in terms of informing the Constitution, and there is a whole new school of thought in America that would like very much to use natural law to lower the protections for individuals in the zone of personal privacy—and I will speak to those later—and who want to heighten the protection for businesses and corporations.

Now, one of those people is a Professor Macedo, a fine, first-class scholar at Harvard University. Another is Mr. Epstein, a professor at the University of Chicago. And, in the speech you gave in 1987 to the Pacific Research Institute, you said, and I quote: "I find attractive the arguments of scholars such as Stephen Macedo, who defend an activist Supreme Court that would—not could, would—strike down laws restricting property rights."

My question is a very simple one, Judge. What exactly do you find attractive about the arguments of Professor Macedo and other scholars like him?

THOMAS: Senator, again, it has been quite some time since I have read Professor Macedo and others. That was, I believe, 1987 or 1988. My interest in the whole area was as a political philosophy. My interest was in reassessing and demonstrating a sense that we understood what our Founding Fathers were thinking when they used phrases such as "all men are created equal," and what that meant for our form of government.

I found Macedo interesting and his arguments interesting, as I remembered. Again, it has been quite some time. But I don't believe that in my writings I have indicated that we should have an activist Supreme Court or that we should have any form of activism on the Supreme Court. Again, I found his arguments interesting, and I was not talking particularly of natural law, Mr. Chairman, in the context of adjudication.

BIDEN: I am not quite sure I understand your answer, Judge. You indicated that you find the arguments—not interesting—attractive, and you explicitly say one of the things you find attractive—I am quoting from you: "I find attractive the arguments of scholars such as Stephen Macedo, who defend an activist Supreme Court that would strike down laws resisting property rights."

Now, it would seem to me what you were talking about is you find attractive the fact that they are activists and they would like to strike down existing laws that impact on restricting the use of property rights because, you know, that is what they write about.

THOMAS: Well, let me clarify something. I think it is important,

Mr. Chairman.

BIDEN: Please.

THOMAS: As I indicated, I believe, or attempted to allude to in my confirmation to the Court of Appeals, I don't see a role for the use of natural law in constitutional adjudication. My interest in exploring natural law and natural rights was purely in the context of political theory. I was interested in that. There were debates that I had with individuals, and I pursued that on a part-time basis. I was an agency chairman.

BIDEN: Well, Judge, in preparing for these hearings, some suggested that might be your answer. So I went back through some of your writings and speeches to see if I misread them. And, quite frankly, I find it hard to square your speeches, which I will discuss with you in a minute, with what you are telling me today.

Just let me read some of your quotes. In a speech before the Federalist Society at the University of Virginia, in a variation of that speech that you published in the Harvard Journal of Law and Policy, you praised the first Justice [John] Harlan's opinion in *Plessy v. Ferguson,* and you said: "Implicit reliance on political first principles was implicit rather than explicit, as is generally appropriate for the Court's opinions. He gives us a foundation for interpreting not only cases involving race, but the entire Constitution in the scheme of protecting rights." You went on to say, "Harlan's opinion provides one of our best examples of natural law and higher law jurisprudence."

Then you say, "The higher law background of the American government, whether explicitly appealed to or not, provides the only firm basis for a just and wise constitutional decision."

Judge, what I would like to know is, I find it hard to understand how you can say what you are now saying, that natural law was only a—you were only talking about the philosophy in a general philosophic sense, and not how it informed or impacted upon constitutional interpretation.

THOMAS: Well, let me attempt to clarify. That, in fact, though, was my approach. I was interested in the political theory standpoint. I was not interested in constitutional adjudication. I was not at the time adjudicating cases. But with respect to the background, I think that we can both agree that the founders of our country, or at least some of the drafters of our Constitution and our declaration, believed in natural rights. And my point was simply that in understanding overall our constitutional government, that it was important that we understood how they believed—or what they believed in natural law or natural rights.

BIDEN: For what purpose, Judge?

THOMAS: My purpose was this, in looking at this entire area: The question for me was from a political theory standpoint. You and I are sitting here in Washington, D.C., with Abraham Lincoln or with Frederick Douglass, and from a theory, how do we get out of slavery? There is no constitutional amendment. There is no provision in the Constitution. But by what theory? Repeatedly Lincoln referred to the notion that all men are created equal. And that was my attraction to, or beginning of my attraction to, this approach. But I did not—I would maintain that I did not feel that natural rights or natural law has a basis or has a use in constitutional adjudication.

My interest in this area started with the notion, with a simple question: How do you end slavery? By what theory do you end slavery? After you end slavery, by what theory do you protect the right of someone who was a former slave or someone like my grandfather, for example, to enjoy the fruits of his or her labor?

At no point did I—or do I—believe that the approach of natural law or that natural rights has a role in constitutional adjudication. I attempted to make that plain or to allude to that in my confirmation to the Court of Appeals. And I think that that is the position that I take here.

[Rights of Women]

BIDEN: Now, Judge, in your view, does the liberty clause of the 14th Amendment protect the right of women to decide for themselves in certain instances whether or not to terminate pregnancy?

THOMAS: Senator, first of all, let me look at that in the context other than with natural law principles.

BIDEN: Let's forget about natural law for a minute.

THOMAS: My view is that there is a right to privacy in the 14th Amendment.

BIDEN: Well, Judge, does that right to privacy in the liberty clause of the 14th Amendment protect the right of a woman to decide for herself in certain instances whether or not to terminate a pregnancy?

THOMAS: Senator, I think that the Supreme Court has made clear that the issue of marital privacy is protected, that the State cannot infringe on that without a compelling interest, and the Supreme Court, of course, in the case of *Roe v. Wade* has found an interest in the woman's right to—as a fundamental interest—a woman's right to terminate a pregnancy. I do not think that at this time that I could maintain my impartiality as a member of the judiciary and comment on that specific case.

BIDEN: Well, let's try it another way, Judge. I don't want to ask you to comment specifically on Roe there. What I am trying to get at, there are two schools of thought out there. There is a gentleman like Professor Michael Moore of the University of Pennsylvania and Mr. Louis Lehrman of the Heritage Foundation who both think natural law philosophy informs their view, and they conclude one who strongly supports a woman's right and the other one who strongly opposes a woman's right to terminate a pregnancy.

Then there are those who say that, no, this should be left strictly to the legislative bodies, not for the courts to interpret, and they fall into the school of thought represented by John Hart Healy and former Judge Robert H. Bork, for example, who say the court has nothing to do with that.

Now, let me ask you this: Where does the decision lie? Does it lie with the court? For example, you quote, with admiration, Mr. Lehrman's article. Mr. Lehrman's article was on natural law and—I forget the exact title here. Let me find it. "Natural Law and the Right to Life." And you say when you are speaking at a gathering that you think that that is a superb application of natural law. You say, "It is a splendid example of applying natural law."

Now, what did you mean by that?

THOMAS: Well, let me go back to, I guess, my first comment to you when we were discussing natural law—I think that is important—and then come back to the question of the due process analysis.

The speech that I was giving there was before the Heritage Foundation. Again, as I indicated earlier, my interest was civil rights and slavery. What I was attempting to do in the beginning of that speech was to make clear to a conservative audience that blacks who were Republicans—and the issues that affected blacks—were being addressed and being dealt with by conservatives in what I considered a less-than-acceptable manner.

. . . The second point that I wanted to make to them was that they had, based on what I thought was an appropriate approach, they had an obligation just as conservatives to be more open and more aggressive on civil rights enforcement. What I thought would be the best way to approach that would be using the underlying concept of our Constitution that we were all created equal.

I felt that conservatives would be skeptical about the notion of natural law. I was using that as the underlying approach. I felt that they would be conservative and that they would not—or be skeptical about that concept. I was speaking in the Lou Lehrman Auditorium of the Heritage Foundation. I thought that if I demonstrated that one of their own accepted at least the concept of natural rights, that they would be more apt to accept that concept as an underlying principle for being more aggressive on civil rights. My whole interest was civil rights enforcement.

[Privacy Decisions]

BIDEN: Well, Judge, let me conclude this round by saying that—picking up that context, that you were a part of the Reagan administration. In 1986, as a member of the administration, you were part of what has been referred to here, the administration's Working Group on the Family.

This group put out what I think can only be characterized as a controversial report. And you sign that report, which recommends more state regulation of the family than is now allowed under the law. That report concludes that the Supreme Court's privacy decisions for the last 20 years are fatally flawed and should be corrected.

Judge, did you read this report before it was released?

THOMAS: Well, let me explain to you how working groups work in the domestic policy context—or the way that they worked in the [Reagan] administration. Normally what would happen is that there would be a number of informal meetings. At those meetings, you would express your—there would be some discussion around the table. My interest was in low-income families. I transmitted—after several meetings—transmitted to the head of that working group, my views on the low-income family and the need to address the problems of low-income families in the report.

The report, as it normally works in these working groups in domestic policy, the report is not finalized, nor is it a team effort in drafting. You are submitted your document. That document is then, as far as I know, it may be sent around or may not be sent around. But there is no signature required on those.

BIDEN: Did you ever read the report, Judge?

THOMAS: The section that I read was on the family. I was only interested in whether they included my comments on the low-income family....

BIDEN: Well, let me conclude. This is the last thing I will ask you. This report, which is only 67 pages long, of which your report is part of—and I acknowledge your suggesting, telling us that you did not read the report before or after, and your part was only a small part of this. But in this report, take my word for it, it says that one of these fatally flawed decisions—and they explicitly pick out one—is *Moore v. City of East Cleveland*, where the city of East Cleveland said a grandmother raising two grandchildren who are cousins and not brothers is violating the zoning law and therefore has to do one of two things: move out of the neighborhood or tell one of her grandchildren to leave.

As you know, that case, I believe, was appealed to the Supreme Court, that grandmother, and the court said, "Hey, no, she has an absolute right of privacy to be able to have two of those grandchildren, even though they are cousins, to live with her and no zoning law can tell her otherwise."

Now, this report says, explicitly it says, that the city of East Cleveland and other cities should be able to pass such laws if they want and they should be upheld. And if we can't get them upheld, then we should change the court. That is what this report says. And they say that the cities and states should be able to establish norms of a traditional family.

If you will give me the benefit of the doubt that I am telling you the truth and accurately characterizing the report on that point, do you agree with what I suggested to you is the conclusion of that report in the section you have not read?

THOMAS: I have heard recently that that was the conclusion, but I would like to make a point there. I think—and I think the Supreme Court's rulings in the privacy area support—that the notion of family is one of the most personal and most private relationships that we have in our country. If I had, of course, known that that section was in the report before it became final, of course I would have expressed my concerns.

[Marbury v. Madison]

THURMOND, R-S.C.: ... Judge Thomas, *Marbury v. Madison* is a famous Supreme Court decision. It provides the basis of the Supreme Court's authority to interpret the Constitution and issue decisions which are binding on both the executive and legislative branches. Would you briefly discuss your views on this authority?

THOMAS: Senator, I think it is important to recognize—and we all do recognize—that *Marbury v. Madison* is the underpinning of our current judicial system, that the courts do decide and do the cases in the constitutional area, and it is certainly an approach that we have grown accustomed to and around which our institutions, our legal institutions, have grown.

THURMOND: Judge Thomas, the 10th Amendment to the Constitution provides that all powers are reserved to the states or the people if not specifically delegated to the federal government. What is your general view about the proper relationship between the federal and state governments, and do you believe that there has been a substantial increase in federal authority over the last few decades?

THOMAS: Senator, I think that it is clear that our country has grown and expanded in very important ways. Through the commerce clause, for example, there has been growth in the national scope of our government. Through the 14th Amendment, there has been application of our Bill of Rights, or portions, to the state governments. Through the growth in communications and travel, of course, we are more nationalized than we were in the past.

I think what the Court has attempted to do is to preserve in a way as best it possibly could, the autonomy of the state governments, but at the same time recognize the growth and expansion and the natural growth and expansion of our national government.

[Sex Discrimination]

SEN. EDWARD M. KENNEDY, D-MASS.: ... Let me move to another subject area, and this is referring to an article about you in the Atlantic Monthly in 1987. You said that hiring disparities could be due to cultural differences between men and women. This is the article "A Question of Fairness," by Juan Williams.

That article states that you said that it could be that women are generally unprepared to do certain kinds of work by their own choice, it could be that women choose to have babies instead of going to medical school. Do you still think that that explains the underrepresentation of women in so many jobs in our economy today?

THOMAS: I think, and I think it is important to state this unequivocally, and I have said this unequivocally in speech after speech. There is discrimination. There is sex discrimination in our society. My only point in discussing statistics is that I don't think any of us can say that we have all the answers as to why there are statistical disparities. For example, if I sit here and I were to look at the statistics in this city, say with the example of number of blacks, I couldn't—and compare the number of blacks that are on that side of the table, for example. I cannot automatically conclude that that is a result of discrimination. There could be other reasons that should be explored that aren't necessarily discriminatory reasons.

I am not justifying discrimination, nor would I shy away from it. But when we use statistics, I think that we need to be careful with those disparities.

KENNEDY: Very little I could differ with you on the comment. But I was really driving at a different point, and that is whether you consider [that] women are generally unprepared to do certain kinds of work by their own choice; it could be that women choose babies instead of going to medical school.

Let me just move on to your comments about Thomas Sowell, an author whose work you respect and many—whose ideas you have stated that you agree with. Mr. Sowell wrote a book called the "Civil Rights Rhetoric: A Reality." You reviewed that book for the Lincoln Review in 1988 as part of a review of the works of Thomas Sowell, and in particular you praised Mr. Sowell's discussion, Chapter 5 of his book, entitled "A Special Case of Women," and you called it a much needed anecdote to cliches about women's earnings and professional status.

Mr. Sowell explains that women are paid 59 percent of what men receive for the same work by saying that women are typically not educated as often in such highly paid fields as mathematics, science and engineering, nor attracted to physically taxing and well-paid fields, such as construction work, lumberjacking and coal mining, and the like.

As a matter of fact, there were no women employed in the coal mine industry in 1973. In 1980, after the federal government had begun an effort to enforce antidiscrimination laws, 3,300 women were working in coal mines.

Does that surprise you at all?

THOMAS: If there is discrimination, it doesn't surprise me. There were lots of places I think in our society. You know, I used to when I—I can remember in my own classrooms looking around and realizing that seven or eight of the top 10 students in my classroom in grammar school were the smartest students and wondering at that age: If eight of the 10 of them are the brightest, then why aren't there women doctors and why aren't there women lawyers?

But the point that I was making with respect to Professor Sowell again is a statistical one. There is a difference between the problem that, say, a 16-year-old or 18-year-old minority kid, female, in this city or in Savannah or across the country, who is about to—who has dropped out of high school—there is a difference between the problems of that child or that student than there is for someone who has a Ph.D. or someone who has a college degree.

And I thought that it would be more appropriate, again referring back to the programs that you talked about, that we talked about earlier, in looking at how to solve these problems that you disaggregate the problems and you be more specific instead of lumping it all into one set of statistics.

SEPTEMBER 11 HEARING

REP. HOWARD M. METZENBAUM, D-OHIO: . . . Your statement yesterday in support of the right to privacy does not tell us anything about whether you believe that the Constitution protects a woman's right to choose to terminate her pregnancy. I fear that you, like other nominees before the committee, could assure us that you support a fundamental right to privacy but could also decline to find that a woman's right to choose is protected by the Constitution. If that happens soon, there could be nowhere for many women to go for a safe and legal abortion.

I must ask you to tell us here and now whether you believe that the Constitution protects a woman's right to choose to terminate her pregnancy, and I am not asking you as to how you would vote in connection with any case before the court.

THOMAS: . . . I am afraid, though, on your final question, Senator, that it is important for any of us who are judges, in areas that are very deeply contested, in areas where I think we all understand and are sensitive to both sides of a very difficult debate, that for a judge—and as I said yesterday, for us who are judges, we have to look ourselves in the mirror and say, Are we impartial or will we be perceived to be impartial? I think that to take a position would undermine my ability to be impartial, and I have attempted to avoid that in all areas of my life after I became a judge. And I think it is important.

I can assure you—and I know, I understand your concern that people come here and they might tell you A and then do B. But I have no agenda. I have tried to wrestle with every difficult case that has come before me. I don't have an ideology to take to the court to do all sorts of things. I am there to take the cases that come before me and to do the fairest, most open-minded, decent job that I can as a judge. And I am afraid that to begin to answer questions about what my specific position is in these contested areas would greatly—or leave the impression that I prejudged this issue.

METZENBAUM: Having said that, Judge, I will just repeat the question. Do you believe—I am not asking you to prejudge the case. I am just asking you whether you believe that the Constitution protects a woman's right to choose to terminate her pregnancy.

THOMAS: Senator, as I noted yesterday, and I think we all feel strongly in this country about our privacy—I do—I believe the Constitution protects the right to privacy. And I have no reason or agenda to prejudge the issue or to predispose to rule one way or the other on the issue of abortion, which is a difficult issue.

METZENBAUM: I am not asking you to prejudge it. Just as you can respond—and I will get into some of the questions to which you responded yesterday, both from Sens. Thurmond, Hatch and Biden about matters that might come before the court. You certainly can express an opinion as to whether or not you believe that a woman has a right to choose to terminate her pregnancy without indicating how you expect to vote in any particular case. And I am asking you to do that.

THOMAS: Senator, I think to do that would seriously compromise my ability to sit on a case of that importance and involving that important issue.

METZENBAUM: Let us proceed. Judge Thomas, in 1990, I chaired a committee hearing on the Freedom of Choice Act, where we heard from women who were maimed by back-alley abortionists. Prior to the *Roe* decision, only wealthy women could be sure of having access to safe abortions. Poor [and] middle-class women were forced to unsafe back alleys, if they needed an abortion. It was a very heart-rending hearing.

Frankly, I am terrified that if we turn the clock back on legal abortion services, women will once again be forced to resort to brutal and illegal abortions, the kinds of abortions where coat hangers are substitutes for surgical instruments.

The consequences of Roe's demise are so horrifying to me and to millions of American women and men that I want to ask you once again, of appealing to your sense of compassion, whether or not you believe the Constitution protects a woman's right to an abortion.

THOMAS: Senator, the prospect—and I guess as a kid we heard the hushed whispers about illegal abortions and individuals performing them in less than safe environments, but they were whispers. It would, of course, if a woman is subjected to the agony of an environment like that, on a personal level, certainly, I am very, very pained by that. I think any of us would be. I would not want to see people subjected to torture of that nature.

I think it is important to me, though, on the issue, the question that you asked me, as difficult as it is for me to anticipate or to want to see that kind of illegal activity, I think it would undermine my ability to sit in an impartial way on an important case like that.

[Conversion on Natural Law?]

SEN. ALAN K. SIMPSON, R-WYO.: . . . I might ask you, then, to set the record straight: Is it accurate to say that on the day of Sept. 10, 1991, was that the day on which Clarence Thomas "changed" his views or had a conversion or sprinted from his previous record on natural law? Or were those the views you explained so well and ones that you have held for some period of time?

THOMAS: Senator, I have been consistent on this issue of natural law. As I indicated, my interest in the area resulted from an interest in finding a common theme and finding a theme that could rekindle and strengthen enforcement of civil rights, and ask the basic or answer a basic question of how do you get rid of slavery, how do you end it.

Our founders, the drafters of the 13th, 14th Amendments, abolitionists, believed in natural law, but they reduced it to positive law. The positive law is our Constitution. And when we look at constitutional adjudication, we look to that document. We may want to know, and I think it is important at times to understand, what the drafters believed they were doing as a part of our history and tradition in some of the provisions such as the liberty component of the due process clause of the 14th Amendment. But we don't make an independent search or an independent reference to some notion or a notion of natural law.

That is the point that I tried to make, and there was no follow-up question, as I remember it, at my confirmation to the Court of Appeals. But that has been a consistent point. We look at natural law beliefs of the founders as a background to our Constitution.

SIMPSON: Have you seen anything come up at this hearing thus far that is really anything different, much different than what happened when we confirmed you for the Circuit Court, other than the fact that you have remained absolutely silent as those out there decided to distort these issues?

THOMAS: Well, I think the one difference, Senator, of course is that I am a sitting federal judge now. When I came before this committee the last time, I was a policy-maker. I was someone who had taken policy positions, and those questions and concerns were raised of me as chairman of EEOC.

Today I am a sitting federal judge, and I find myself in a much different posture. It is a different role. I have no occasion to make policy speeches, have no occasion to speculate about policy in our government or to be a part of that policy debate. And I believe at my last confirmation, much of that debate or those debates were explored in the hearings.

Today I have refrained from it, from those debates, primarily because, as I have said before, engaging in such policy debate, particularly in public, I think undermines the impartiality of a federal judge. Taking strong positions on issues that are of some controversy in our society when there are viewpoints on both sides undermines your ability.

My Dallas Cowboys, for example, played the Redskins on Monday night, and I am totally convinced that every referee in those games is a Redskins fan. But none would admit to it.

I think that in something as simple as that, even though we have strong views about who should win, something as simple as that, we would want to feel that the referees—and judges are, to a large extent, referees—are fair and impartial, even when we don't agree with the calls.

[The Equal Protection Clause]

SEN. DENNIS DeCONCINI, D-ARIZ.: Judge Thomas, I would like to pursue the equal protection clause, the 14th Amendment and how it relates to discrimination. As you so well know, but for purposes of clarity, the 14th Amendment prohibits a state from depriving a person of life, liberty or property, without due process of law or equal protection of those laws.

The equal protection clause provides the primary constitutional protection against laws that discriminate on the basis of gender. And as we also know from previous hearings, there are three tests. There is the rational relationship test, which is the most lenient of those tests. There is the intermediate scrutiny test or a heightened test, which has been used in gender cases. And then there is the scrutiny test, which has been used in race and national origin.

Judge Thomas, there has been much discussion already regarding reliance on natural law. Unfortunately, natural law has been invoked historically, or maybe it is fortunate, depending on how you define it, but it goes back a long time that my staff was able to dig out.

For example, in 1873, in the *Bradwell v. Illinois* case, the Supreme Court denied a woman a license to practice law, arguing the following: "Civil law, as well as nature herself, has always recognized a wide difference in the respective spheres and destinies of man and woman. The natural and proper delicacy which belong to the female sex evidently unfits it for many of the occupations of civil life. The paramount destiny and mission of women is to fulfill the noble and benign office of wife and mother. This is the law of the Creator."

Now, I know you went on with Sen. Kennedy at some length about your position on natural law, which I did review this morning, and I welcome some clarification that you have given. But with the *Bradwell* case, we see that those justices applied natural law.

I know that you stated that your duty would be to uphold the Constitution and not a natural law philosophy, but I would like to just clarify for the record, do you disagree with the justices' decisions that were held back in 1873 in the *Bradwell* case?

THOMAS: Senator, I do.

DeCONCINI: Thank you. That is really all I want to know, because I want to be very clear, based on your statements to Sen. Kennedy, that you do not have any lingering thoughts that stare decisis, or what have you, dating back to a clear case where natural law was used poses any problems to you.

THOMAS: No.

DeCONCINI: Thank you.

When you were nominated, Judge Thomas, to the Court of Appeals, I submitted written questions, because of time constraints and other things that prohibited me from coming to those hearings at any length and waiting my turn to ask you questions, to comment on the Court's approach to the Equal Protection Clause. We also discussed this before these hearings when you were in to see me, and I told you I would address you with some questions and some thought on that.

In response to my written questions, your partial response was, "Though I do not have a fully developed constitutional philosophy, I have no personal reservations about applying the three standards as an appellate court judge in cases which might come before me."

Now that you have been on the court for 18 months and may soon be making decisions on important equal protection cases on the highest court of the land, let me ask you if you have developed a constitutional philosophy regarding the court's three-tier approach to the equal protection cases.

THOMAS: Senator, I have no reason and had no reason to question or to disagree with the three-tier approach. Of course, the rational basis test being the least structured or least strict of the tests, the heightened scrutiny test, which has been used in the area of gender and alienage and legitimacy, and the strict scrutiny test, which has been used in the area of fundamental rights and race, Senator, I think that those tests attempt in our society to demonstrate the concern that we have for classifications that could infringe on fundamental rights, and I believe that underlying, when we move away just from the legalese—and I do accept this structure of the three-tier test—when we move away from it, at bottom what we are talking about is are we going to allow people to be treated in arbitrary ways, either because of their gender or because of their race, are we going to defer to classifications based on gender or race, and what the court is attempting to do in an important way is to say no, we are going to look at those classifications.

DeCONCINI: Thank you, Judge Thomas. That is helpful, and I guess it goes without saying, but I am going to say it anyway, you have no agenda or hidden belief or anything else regarding the present position that the Supreme Court has taken with these three tiers on equal protection as they relate to gender or any other minority or class that it may be applied to.

THOMAS: Senator, I think it is important for judges not to have agendas or to have strong ideology or ideological views. That is baggage, I think, that you take to the court or you take as a judge.

It is important for us, and I believe one of the justices, whose name I cannot recall right now, spoke about having to strip down, like a runner, to eliminate agendas, to eliminate ideologies, and when one becomes a judge, it is an amazing process, because that is precisely what you start doing. You start putting the speeches away, you start putting the policy statements away. You begin to decline forming opinions in important areas that could come before your court, because you want to be stripped down like a runner. So, I have no agenda, Senator.

[Hispanic Concerns]

DeCONCINI: Judge Thomas, I want to go into some areas that deal with Hispanic concerns. As a former chairman of the Equal Employment Opportunity Commission, you were responsible [for]—and I am sure you are familiar with—the 1983 charge study—you weren't responsible, but I am sure you are familiar with it, or I hope you are—titled "Analysis of the EEOC Service by Hispanics in the United States," which was conducted by the EEOC-appointed task force. That task force concluded that the needs of Hispanics were not being adequately addressed by the EEOC.

At the time, the task force indicated a need to improve EEOC's record of investigations of Hispanic charges and to increase outreach and education efforts within the Hispanic community.

Now, as the commissioner, what programs did you initiate to improve the accessibility of the EEOC within the Hispanic community?

THOMAS: Senator, when I arrived at EEOC, one of the first concerns among many—believe me, there were many—with which I met was that EEOC was underserving the Hispanic community; for example, in Los Angeles and certainly in your home state.

There were a number of hearings, some of which I participated in, across the country in various major cities discussing the problem and what the probable or possible responses could be. A number of the, I think, concerns were that the national origin charges were low. The problem there, of course, is that not all of the charges which we received from Hispanic employees or Hispanic-Americans are national origin charges. They go across the line. They can involve age; they can involve gender discrimination also.

A number of the things that we did included opening offices in predominantly Hispanic communities—satellite offices. That was a part of our expanded presence program. I made sure that we developed public service announcements that were bilingual. I installed a 1-800 number at EEOC so that the agency could be accessible. We developed posters that were bilingual. We took all of our documents, our brochures, and translated them into Spanish.

The effort was to make sure that we reached out, that we included, and also in areas where we had—there was a significant Hispanic population— we made every effort to see to it that the top managers and the investigators spoke Spanish. Again, the effort, the overall effort was to reach out, and that was consistent with the recommendations.

I might also add that during the major part of my tenure, two of our five commissioners were also Hispanic. So there was considerable interest on my part, on their part, and, indeed, the commission's part, in being of greater service to Hispanic-Americans.

DeCONCINI: Judge, an interim result of a study conducted by the National Council of La Raza indicates that since the 1983 task force study, the situation at EEOC with regard to Hispanics has not improved. While the Hispanic population in the United States has grown in the last decade from 6 percent of the total U.S. population in 1980 to over 9 percent of the total population today, the percentage of the EEOC total charge caseloads filed by Hispanics was only 4.15 percent.

Given your efforts to improve the EEOC record with regard to Hispanics since 1983, how do you account for the disproportionate[ly] small number of charges filed by Hispanics?

THOMAS: Again, Senator, I have and had the very same concern that we were underserving—or that EEOC during my tenure and when I arrived there—was underserving the Hispanic community. I don't know how the numbers were arrived at. To my knowledge, the agency does not keep data in areas that do not involve national origin charges by national origin. So I don't know, for example, whether we are looking at numbers reflecting only the national origin charges as opposed to other areas.

I can say this: That we made every effort during my tenure to change the commission's accessibility to Hispanic-Americans, to individuals across this country. That was the purpose for our expanded presence program, for our satellite offices, for our educational programs, all of which were started during my tenure. Our outreach efforts were all designed so that we are not sitting in our offices waiting for people to come in, but we actually go to them.

Sometimes it is frustrating because they don't all work, but it certainly was not because of a lack of trying.

[Right to Life]

SEN. PATRICK J. LEAHY, D-VT.: Well, let me make sure that I understand. Is it your testimony here today and yesterday that you do not endorse the Louis Lehrman article to the extent that it argues under the natural law principles of the Declaration of Independence, a fetus has an inalienable right to life in the moment of conception? Is that your testimony?

THOMAS: I do not—my testimony is that, with respect to those issues, the issues involved or implicated in the issue of abortion, I do not believe that Mr. Lehrman's application of natural law is appropriate.

LEAHY: Had you read that article before you praised it?

THOMAS: I think I skimmed it, Senator. My interest, again, was in the fact that he used the notion or the concept of natural law, and my idea was to import that notion to something that I was very interested in.

LEAHY: When you gave the speech, which was in 1987, as I recall the testimony, did you understand that the consequences of Mr. Lehrman's position was not that just that *Roe v. Wade* should be overturned, but that abortion, even in cases of rape and incest, should be banned in every state of the Union? Did you understand that to be the position that he was taking in that article?

THOMAS: Senator, until recently, in reflecting on it, I did not know, I could not recall the entire content of that article until I read recent articles about it. Again, my interest was very, very limited. . . .

LEAHY: Well, let's just go, then, to Mr. Lehrman's positions. Under his theory of natural law, that would criminalize every abortion in this country. Do you understand that to be his position? I am not asking whether it is yours, but do you understand that to be his position in that article?

THOMAS: Again, I would have to reread the article, Senator. I understand the criticisms that you have of the article, but my point to you here today, as well as in other questioning concerning this article, is that I did not adopt or import anything more from this article than the use of this one notion of natural law. . . .

LEAHY: Judge, you were in law school at the time *Roe v. Wade* was decided. That was 17 or 18 years ago. I would assume—well, let me back up this way. You would accept, would you not, that in the last generation *Roe v. Wade* is certainly one of the more important cases to be decided by the U.S. Supreme Court?

THOMAS: I would accept that it has certainly been one of the more important, as well as one that has been one of the more highly publicized and debated cases.

LEAHY: So, I would assume that it would be safe to assume that when that came down, you were in law school, recent case law is oft discussed, that *Roe v. Wade* would have been discussed in the law school while you were there?

THOMAS: The case that I remember being discussed most during my early part of law school was I believe in my small group with Thomas Emerson, may have been *Griswold,* since he argued that, and we may have touched on *Roe v. Wade* at some point and debated that, but let me add one point to that.

Because I was a married student and I worked, I did not spend a lot of time around the law school doing what the other students enjoyed so much, and that is debating all the current cases and all of the slip opinions. My schedule was such that I went to classes and generally went to work and went home.

LEAHY: Judge Thomas, I was a married law student who also worked, but I also found at least between classes that we did discuss some of the law, and I am sure you are not suggesting that there wasn't any discussion at any time of *Roe v. Wade?*

THOMAS: Senator, I cannot remember personally engaging in those discussions.

SEPTEMBER 12 HEARING

HERB KOHL, D-WIS.: Judge Thomas, I would like to ask you why you want this job.

THOMAS: Senator, being nominated to the Supreme Court of the United States is one of the highest callings in our country. It is an opportunity. It is an entrustment, an entrusting of responsibility by the people of this country, by this body, to make some of the most difficult and important decisions in our country.

It is an opportunity to serve, to give back. That has been something that has been important to me. And I believe Senator, that I can make a contribution, that I can bring something different to the court, that I can walk in the shoes of the people who are affected by what the court does.

You know, on my current court [U.S. Court of Appeals for the District of Columbia Circuit], I have occasion to look out the window that faces C Street, and there are converted buses that bring in the criminal defendants to our criminal justice system, busload after busload. And you look out, and you say to yourself, and I say to myself almost every day, but for the grace of God there go I.

So you feel that you have the same fate, or could have, as those individuals. So I can walk in their shoes, and I can bring something different to the court. And I think it is a tremendous responsibility, and it is a humbling responsibility; and it is one that, if confirmed, I will carry out to the best of my ability.

[Preparation for Testimony]

KOHL: All right. Judge, I would like to come back to a question about preparation. When I was running for the Senate, I worked with people who helped prepare me for debates, so in my mind there is nothing wrong with getting some advice and help in preparing for this hearing, but I would like to ask you some questions about the process.

When you were holding practice sessions, did your advisers ever critique you about responses to questions in the substantive way? Did they say, for example, "you should soften that answer," or "don't answer that question; just say that you can't prejudge an issue that may come before the court?"

THOMAS: Senator, the answer to that is unequivocally no. I set down ground rules at the very beginning that they were there simply to ask me and to hear me respond to questions that have been traditionally asked before this committee in other hearings and to determine whether or not my response was clear, just to critique me as to how it sounded to them, not to myself, but not to tell me whether it was right or wrong or too little or too much.

KOHL: Good. Judge Thomas, most Americans believe that the Supreme Court should have a fierce independence. Do you see any problem in terms of the system of checks and balances and separation of powers in having members of the executive branch detailed to assist in the confirmation of a member to the Supreme Court? Do you think that such assistance creates an appearance of impropriety because it blurs the lines between the branches of government?

THOMAS: Senator, the process of confirmation, as you can imagine, is a difficult one. The last 10 weeks have involved my answering countless questions, responding to significant document requests that I personally could not respond to, and information that was contained in the executive branch.

Traditionally, individuals in the executive branch have assisted, but, again, there I made it clear what my rules were. They were to do nothing more than provide me with information such as case law, documents that I needed to prepare myself at my request. They in no way did anything more than provide that information.

For example, they would be more in the order of what I would have my law clerk do, provide me with the material that I need.

KOHL: But it is said in The New York Times—were they misquoted— that there were mock sessions between you and people from that branch, during which questions were asked and answers were given. That is entirely different from what you just said.

THOMAS: To my knowledge, there was one individual from the—there were a number of individuals from the executive branch, that is right. I thought you were talking about the individuals who assisted me with the documents, not the individuals in mock sessions.

KOHL: No, no. We are talking about the whole process, the preparation, the involvement, the fact that the executive branch and you have been working together on this nomination in all the various ways, including preparation for this hearing. And I am asking you not whether or not you have the right to do it. You do. I am asking whether or not that blurs the separations that are supposed to exist as between the branches of government.

THOMAS: I am sorry I was not responsive. I think that there would certainly be no more conflict than one would have when a clerk from your staff argues before you in the subsequent years. I do not think there would be, Senator. I can see the concern, but I do not think that there would be at all. . . .

[Criticism of Congress]

KOHL: Judge Thomas, you have had some harsh things to say about Congress, and so have I and so have most of the American people. But unlike most of the American people, you have worked in the Congress. In fact, you have worked in the executive, legislative and the judicial branches. I would like to ask you a few questions about your experience in these areas.

In a 1988 speech at Wake Forest [University], you said that legislators did "browbeat, threaten and harass agency heads." In the Wake Forest speech and in another 1988 speech . . . you said that Congress was, and I quote, "a coalition of elites which failed to be a deliberative body, which legislates for the common or the public interest," and that Congress was "no longer primarily a deliberative or even a lawmaking body."

So, Judge Thomas, why would a man like you, with strongly held ideas about public policy, ever want to work in this branch of government, the courts, where you have an obligation to uphold the bad laws that you say Congress makes?

THOMAS: First, let me go back to the position that I was in as a member of the executive branch. As I indicated yesterday, there is tension between the two branches, and particularly in the oversight process. I felt, as the head of an agency [the Equal Employment Opportunity Commission (EEOC)] who had been called to the Hill on a number of occasions in some very difficult circumstances, that particularly some of the staffers went too far in micromanaging the agency and made it very, very difficult.

I think that the legislative role of Congress, as well as the oversight roles of Congress, are very, very important. It is a little easier to see, when you are not the object of an oversight hearing.

In my current job, our role is to determine the intent of Congress. I believe that I have done that fairly and impartially. I have stated very clearly that my job is not to engage in a policy debate with Congress. I am out of that role. I am not in the political branch. I am in the neutral branch, and my job is to remain neutral.

When I was in the political branch, I think I fought the policy-making battles, and I am sure that individuals on this side have some—

KOHL: That is all right. I just want to go back and quote to you what you said, and do you remember saying it, is it true, do you believe it? You said that "Congress was a coalition of elites which failed to be a deliberative body that legislates for the common good or the public interest," and you said that "Congress was no longer primarily a deliberative or even a lawmaking body." Is that how you feel?

THOMAS: Today?

KOHL: Today. Here, sitting before 14 of us who are going to vote.

THOMAS: I can't, Senator, remember the total context of that, but I think I said that, and I think I said it in the context of saying that Congress was at its best when it was legislating on great moral issues. Now, I could be wrong. I think I have turned over 138 speeches, and I can't remember the details of all of them, but I did say, and I do remember saying that Congress was at its best when it was deliberating the great moral issues of our time, such as, for example, our involvement in the Persian Gulf conflict.

KOHL: All right. Finally, Judge, with respect to all the things that you have said and written in the past and the things that you have asked us to discount today—I am thinking also about the meeting we had in my office when you said that we should for the most part forget about what we have read and written about you, that the real Judge Thomas will come out at the hearings. My question is: Why is it inappropriate for us to make an evaluation of your candidacy based upon all the things that you have written and said, particularly in view of the fact that you have been on the court for only 16 months? If we are going to make an informed judgment on behalf of the American people, why are not your policy positions important? How are we supposed to make a judgment on you?

THOMAS: Senator, I think that I have turned over in responding to requests, as a result, I think 32,000 pages of documents. I have spent the last decade in the government. I think that the material is there. I think that a fair reading of my record is a reading which indicates that I am one person who has attempted to be involved and attempted to do some good, who did not hide, who did not sneak away from the problems, who tried to grapple with them, who tried to take them head-on, and who tried to make a difference. I think the record is relevant, but I think it has to be understood that when I was in the executive branch, I was in the executive branch. I am a member of the judiciary, and I think a fair question from me to you is to see whether or not my policy positions have tainted my role as a judge. . . .

KOHL: . . . I guess the question I am asking is whether or not you would have us—in your opening statement, for example, for the most part what it said is that you are an example of a person who has pulled himself up by the bootstraps, who is a good, honest, decent, hard-working, effective, intelligent man—which you are in spades. And I think to an extent that troubles me somewhat. Your hearing has been a continuation of that kind of an experience and a past and a history and an encouragement for us to judge you on. And I think that we and the American people, Judge Thomas, should be given the full opportunity to judge you on the whole range of your life experiences, which does include the things that you have said and written and done, just like it does for the rest of us.

When I ran for office, I wasn't able to say don't consider this or don't consider that. The voters wouldn't allow that. And they consider everything I have done, everything I have said. And I think that that is the way the process should work in a democracy. And to the extent that you think I am exaggerating, I would be interested in your response, and then I am finished.

THOMAS: Senator, I think that if this were an oversight hearing and I could go back and discuss all the policies and tell you that, yes, it is relevant to me going back and running my agency, running the agency that I have been asked to run or permitted to run.

When one becomes a judge, the role changes, the roles change. That is why it is different. You are no longer involved in those battles. You are no longer running an agency. You are no longer making policy. You are a judge. It is hard to explain, perhaps, but you strive—rather than looking for policy positions, you strive for impartiality. You begin to strip down from those policy positions. You begin to walk away from that constant development of new policies. You have to rule on cases as an impartial judge. And I think that is the important message that I am trying to send to you; that, yes, my whole record is relevant, but remember that that was as a policy-maker not as a judge....

[Right to Privacy]

BIDEN: Now, do you agree that the right to marital and family privacy is a fundamental liberty?

THOMAS: Yes.

BIDEN: Let me ask you a second question. You have written a great deal about the rights of individuals as opposed to groups, that human rights, natural rights, positive law rights apply to individuals not to groups. And in fairness to you, you have done it almost always in the context of talking about civil rights as opposed to civil liberties. That doesn't mean exclusive of civil liberties, but you have made your point about affirmative action, I mean quotas and other things, through that mechanism.

Now, am I correct in presuming that you believe that the right of privacy and the right to make decisions about procreation extend to single individuals as well as married couples, the right of privacy?

THOMAS: The privacy, the kind of intimate privacy that we are talking about, I think—

BIDEN: The right about specifically procreation.

THOMAS: Yes, procreation that we are talking about, I think the court extended in *Eisenstadt v. Baird* to non-married individuals.

BIDEN: Well, that is a very skillful answer, Judge. Judge [David H.] Souter—and I was not fully prepared when he gave me the answer. I am now. Judge Souter waltzed away from that by pointing out it was an equal protection case. So that I want to know from you, do single individuals, not married couples alone, have a right of privacy residing in the 14th Amendment liberty clause?

THOMAS: Senator, the courts have never decided that, and I don't know of a case that has decided that explicit point. *Eisenstadt* was, of course, decided as an equal protection case and—

BIDEN: Not alone, but go on.

THOMAS: My answer to you is I cannot sit here and decide that. I don't know—

BIDEN: Judge, why can't you? That case is an old case. I know of no challenge before the court on the use of contraceptives by an individual. I can see no reasonable prospect there is going to be any challenge. And, Judge, are you telling me that may come before you? Is that the argument you are going to give me?

THOMAS: Well, I am saying that I think that for a judge to sit here without the benefit of arguments and briefs, et cetera, and without the benefit of precedent, I don't think anyone could decide that.

BIDEN: Well, Judge, I think that is the most unartful dodge that I have heard. . . .

SEPTEMBER 13 HEARING

ARLEN SPECTER, R-PA.: Judge Thomas, before the break I had been discussing with you affirmative action, to gauge your own thinking as you have moved in favor of flexible standards and goals to bring against it, against the backdrop of deciding cases, and I had asked you about the pros and cons on having a remedy for a category which I classified as affirmative action for future certain discrimination victims. . . . I want to come to the Yale Law School admission, and not to personalize it with you, but take Professor Steven Carter, who is an African-American, a distinguished professor now at Yale, Yale being a very good law school. Professor Carter has just written a book, "Affirmative Action Baby," and he says flat out that he enjoyed the benefits of racial preference.

Let's assume, although it may not apply to Professor Carter, that somebody who comes to Yale, an African-American, a product of inferior elementary school, high school and college, but has the potential, why shouldn't Yale give a preference? You in your testimony, in response to my question, oppose a preference. But why shouldn't the law school like Yale give a preference, to give that person an opportunity to blossom fully, even though on the test scores at the moment that African-American doesn't measure up quite to the white person he has displaced?

THOMAS: Senator, I guess the difference that we have there is perhaps semantics, but let me explain to you what I have supported and what we argued for when I was in school, and that was that schools like Yale or other schools across the country should look at how far a person has come as a part of the total person, that you can look at kids who had gone to elite schools or had the finest family background and professional parents, or you could take a kid from the inner-city who did not have all those advantages, but had done very, very well, and assess whether, one, the fact that this kid has done so well against the odds, is that an indication of what kind of person this is or how good that kid can be, is that an indication of how much drive that person has, how much stick-to-itivity that person has.

I think that during that era, those of us who were then the beneficiaries of what were called preferential treatment programs, I think that was the exact terminology that, it was an effort to determine whether kids had been disadvantaged, had socioeconomic disadvantages, had done very, very well in other endeavors against those odds, and I think that the law schools, that the colleges involved attempted to determine: are these kids, with all those disadvantages, qualified to compete with these kids who have had all the advantages.

That is a difficult, subjective determination, but I thought that it was one that was appropriately made. One of the aspects of that is that the kids could come from any background of disadvantage. The kid could be a white kid from Appalachia, could be a Cajun from Louisiana, or could be a black kid or Hispanic kid from the inner-cities or from the barrios, but I defended that sort of a program then and I would defend it today.

SPECTER: Judge Thomas, what you are just saying, though, is a preference implicit, if I understand you correctly, is the fact that the kid, as you put him, has come a long way, does not at that precise moment, going into Yale, have as good a record as another person. Take an African-American who has come a long way, come from a disadvantaged circumstance, at the moment of critical judgment, that applicant, an African-American, does not have as good a record as a white student, but would you then give him the preference, do I understand you correctly?

THOMAS: What I said is that kid, particularly with the socioeconomic background, I think the law school—we all make that determination, how much drive does this person have. You know, we hear in playing sports, sometimes you hear coaches talk about it's not the size of the dog, it's the size of the fight in the dog. I think that the point that I am attempting to make is that Yale or other schools try to make that subjective determination about the total person, and I thought that was appropriate. I think there are other individuals like myself, when we hire, we look for more than just the person who has had all the advantages. We look for people who have had some of the disadvantages and have overcome those odds. I think it is very important.

SPECTER: Judge, I hear you very close to my position, but what I believe I am hearing is that you are in favor of affirmative action preference, at least in that context.

THOMAS: I think I have said that.

SPECTER: Well, I haven't understood it from all your writings. . . . If a preference there, Judge Thomas, if a preference there for the disadvantaged kid, as you put it, who has come a long way, but he can't quite measure up at that moment, why not a preference in employment?

THOMAS: I think, again, Senator, I have looked at education as a chance to become prepared. I have in my thinking personally—and I am talking totally from a policy standpoint—that education was that chance to be prepared to go on in life. It was an opportunity to gain opportunities.

For example, when we have our programs, even the ones that I established at EEOC, the effort was to give training, to bring kids in, to bring individuals in and give them an opportunity to prepare themselves, not in a way that I thought was offensive or in a way that was strictly based on race, but, rather, based on a number of criteria, a number of factors, including how far that person had come. I think that is important, and I think that you can measure a person by how far that person has come and by what that person has overcome to get there.

SPECTER: Judge Thomas, that is fine for those of us who have gone to Yale, but what about the African-American youngster who doesn't have an educational background and is fighting for a job, and you have a case like *Crowson v. Richmond* [*City of Richmond v. J. A. Croson Co.*], which upset a minority set-aside, and after that happened, the Philadelphia Plan was one of the first in the country to move ahead with affirmative action. You should see the figures taking an immediate nose-dive in African-American young people.

So, that if you have a Judge Thomas or a Professor Carter, who comes to Yale Law in that context, that is fine for their next step ahead. But if you have someone who is a 10th-grade dropout and is struggling to get a job in a trade union in Philadelphia or in New York in the case we talked about, why not give that person a preference, because of the discrimination which has affected that person in his schooling, where that person has the potential to be ultimately as good as, if not better than the white applicant who he displaces?

THOMAS: Senator, of course, you do have the question that I have indicated, and I don't think that the cases necessarily break down that way. They don't make the distinction subjectively that way. I believe it just strictly says it doesn't say that this kid has to come from a disadvantaged background, it doesn't say that the kid has to have had problems in life. It is race-specific, and I think we all know that all disadvantaged people aren't black and all black people aren't disadvantaged.

The question is whether or not you are going to pinpoint your policy on people with disadvantages, or are you simply going to do it by race. That is a difficult question. I was the first to admit that. It is one that needed constructive debate and discussion. But I don't think there is a person in this country who cares more about what happens to kids who are left out. What I have tried to offer and what I have tried to say, from the first days I entered the executive branch, was that we need to look at all avenues of inclusion.

You talk about education. In this day and age of mandatory education up to the 12th grade, I think we should ask ourselves a rhetorical question, why is it that a kid who completes 12 years of mandatory education can't function in our society. That is particularly detrimental to minorities. We know it, and we know that there is a tremendous correlation between education and the ability to live well in this society, as well as to be employed and to have a good life in this society.

SPECTER: Judge Thomas, I accept and applaud your sincerity, and I agree that there are disadvantaged people who are not in minorities. But focusing on minorities for just a moment, because that is the central problem, when you talk about the lack of educational opportunity for African-Americans, it is true across this country, and that is why it seems to me that the logic that you accept on a preference to get into Yale Law School ought to be applied as a preference to get a job in New York City, where the [union] local discriminated, or Philadelphia where the Philadelphia Plan had been put into operation, where there is good reason to conclude that that person has the potential to succeed.

BIDEN: Before I yield to the Senator from Alabama, a point of clarification. Did you say, Judge, that affirmative action preference programs are all right as long as they are not based on race?

THOMAS: I said that from a policy standpoint I agreed with affirmative action policies that focused on disadvantaged minorities and disadvantaged individuals in our society.

BIDEN: For example—

THOMAS: I am not commenting on the legality or the constitutionality. I have not visited it from that standpoint, Senator. . . .

[Personal Background]

HOWELL HEFLIN, D-ALA.: . . . I started talking about your biographical, that you were in an enigma or a good deal of uncertainty or changing times and changing, and during these hearings I think you have maybe surprised some people with your position, for example, on the fact you don't think natural law ought to be used as a method of constitutional adjudication, that you support, in effect, public housing, that you believe that multiple languages ought to be used and we ought not to have an English-only approach in governmental activities and schools. You found a right of privacy. You seem to have an adherence to the present methodology in deciding cases on separation of church and state. You have expressed some ideas that would indicate you believe that the Constitution evolves and develops, as issues change, and certainly in your own office, it is subject to the idea that you did follow some affirmative action, which brings us to the question of what is the real Clarence Thomas like or what will the real Clarence Thomas do on the Supreme Court, if he is confirmed.

Some believe you are a closet liberal, and some, on the other hand, believe you are part of the right-wing extreme group. Can you give us any answer as to what the real Clarence Thomas is like today?

THOMAS: Senator, I think that during the past 10 weeks, people have written and formed conclusions about me, and that has gotten to be a part of this process. I think they are free to do that. But it reminds me of the story that I heard about Judge [Clement F.] Haynsworth during his ill-fated nomination and confirmation process in which he was reading about himself in the morning paper, and having read the story, he looks up and says to his wife, "You know, I don't like this Haynsworth guy either."

HEFLIN: I thought it was otherwise; that his wife said that.

THOMAS: Well, either way, it works.

The point is, though, Senator, that people form conclusions. The one aspect of a lot of the publicity that I did like was that my friends from as far back as my college years—and I mean my friends, not people who have claimed to be friends—have pointed out the continuity and consistency, the growth and development. That has been one of the most touching aspects and rewarding aspects of the past 10 weeks in reading and hearing.

But those conclusions that people form about you were not—about me, were not the real Clarence Thomas. I am the real Clarence Thomas, and I have attempted to bring that person here and to show you who he was, not just snippets from speeches or snippets from articles. The person you see is Clarence Thomas. I don't know that I would call myself an enigma. I am just Clarence Thomas. And I have tried to be fair and tried to be what I said in my opening statement. And I try to do what my grandfather said, stand up for what I believe in. There has been that measure of independence.

But, by and large, the point is I am just simply different from what people painted me to be. And the person you have before you today is the person who was in those Army fatigues, combat boots, who has grown older, wiser, but no less concerned about the same problems.

PAUL SIMON, D-ILL.: One of the questions that we face is: What really makes Judge Thomas tick? That is really what Sen. Heflin's questions were approaching.

When you told the story about Judge Haynsworth saying to his wife, "I don't like this Judge Haynsworth guy," if we were to vote in this committee on whether we like this Clarence Thomas guy, it would be unanimous that we like Clarence Thomas. That is not the question that we have to face. It is where you are going.

When you told about being a student at Holy Cross, I would feel comfortable voting for that student for the Supreme Court. And then in describing yourself, you said, "Then we thought we really could change the world"—making it past tense.

Some of us still think we can change the world. Maybe not in huge giant steps, but in little steps. And you are going to a place where you are going to change the world for a lot of people.

The people on the Supreme Court who voted for *Dred Scott* [*v. Sandford*] changed the world. The people who voted for *Plessy v. Ferguson* changed the world for a lot of people. The people who voted in the *Brown* [*v. Board of Education*] decision, *Roe v. Wade*, changed the world.

Members of the Supreme Court who voted on the *Croson* decision that Sen. Specter referred to, the set-aside, the Richmond decision, have denied the right, the opportunity for a great many people. They have changed the world for a lot of people.

The *Wards Cove* [*v. Atonio*] decision changed the world for a lot of people, people of—again, quoting Sen. Specter, "that 10th grade dropout." And that is, I guess, the person that I am concerned about.

Frankly, a person with Clarence Thomas' ability is going to make out all right. Whether you get confirmed or not confirmed, you are going to do very well. That 10th-grade dropout may not do well.

We all bring something of a philosophy to our jobs, and Sen. [Alan K.] Simpson [R-Wyo.] perhaps partially answered this question with his quotation from that interview, the bottom line. But what is the political philosophy, what is the judicial philosophy you bring to the United States Supreme Court?

THOMAS: Senator, when I spoke earlier about changing the world, I think I would distinguish between the way that as a youth you feel that you can go out and take on everything tomorrow morning and get it all accomplished tomorrow morning. At some point I think you realize that you have to take a step back and begin to approach it more—not so much in a rush or impatiently, but persistently. And if there was one lesson that I learned during that period, it was the difference between impatience and persistence, the difference between being upset and being committed to something.

So today I didn't suggest or mean to suggest by using the past tense that we felt that we could make a difference, or that we could change the world, that we can't do that today or have an impact today. I indicated earlier that I felt that if I were confirmed by this body and were fortunate to be on the Supreme Court that I could make a difference. And I also indicated that the same person that was at Holy Cross with the same feelings, a little older and a little wiser, is sitting before you.

There was a time when in law school—and I was asked why I went to law school. But there was a time actually before I went to law school that I didn't think there was any reason to go to law school. There was no further reason to prepare, to be ready to make some of the changes in society. There was a time when many of us didn't feel that working through the system, as we called it, was worthwhile.

So at some point we had to make the decision that if we prepared ourselves—and as Abraham Lincoln said, I paraphrase it, I will prepare myself and when the time comes I will be ready. What will you be ready for? I don't know exactly, or didn't know. With respect to my own approach, though, I tried to be persistent about preparing to make a difference.

As far as overall philosophy, Senator, as a judge I think that the approach that I have taken has been one of starting with the legislation or the document before me. It has been one to arrive at the intent of this body in statutory construction and certainly in broader analysis to not certainly impose my own point of view, but to be honest, intellectually honest and honest as a person in doing my job. I have done that.

But there is something that you point to also that goes beyond that, and

I think this is either the third or the fourth time I have appeared before you for confirmation. And the something that you have been interested in is this, and I took it to heart—perhaps you don't remember it, but in my job, my current position on the Court of Appeals, one of the things that I always attempt to do is to make sure that in that isolation that I don't lose contact with the real world and the real people—the people who work in the building, the people who are around the building, the people who have to be involved with that building, the people who are the neighborhood, the real people outside. Because our world as an appellate judge is a cloistered world, and that has been an important part of my life, to not lose contact.

OCTOBER 11 HEARING

BIDEN: We are here today to hold open hearings on Professor Anita Hill's allegations concerning Judge Thomas. This committee's handling of her charges has been criticized. . . .

Some have asked: How could you have the United States Senate vote on Judge Thomas' nomination and leave senators in the dark about Professor Hill's charges?

To this I answer: How can you expect us to have forced Professor Hill against her will into the blinding light which you see here today?

But I'm deeply sorry that our actions in this respect have been seen by many across this country as a sign that this committee does not take the charge of sexual harassment seriously. We emphatically do.

Sexual harassment of working women is an issue of national concern. But that said, let me make clear that this is not—I emphasize: this is not— a hearing about the extent and nature of sexual harassment in America. That question is for a different sort of meeting, of this or any other committee.

This is a hearing convened for a specific purpose: to air specific allegations against one specific individual, allegations which may be true or may not be true.

Whichever may be the case, this hearing has not been convened to investigate the widespread problem, and it is indisputably widespread, the widespread problem of sexual harassment in this country.

*   *   *

Perhaps 14 men sitting here today cannot understand these things fully. I know there are many people watching today who suspect we never will understand. But fairness means doing our best to understand, no matter what we do or do not believe about the specific charges, that we are going to listen as closely as we can to these charges.

Fairness also means that Judge Thomas must be given a full and fair opportunity to confront these charges against him, to respond fully, to tell his side of the story, to be given the benefit of the doubt.

SEN. STROM THURMOND, R-S.C., ranking member: Both Judge Thomas and Professor Hill find themselves in the unenviable position of having to discuss very personal matters in a very public forum.

I want to assure them at the outset that they will be dealt with fairly. This will be an exceedingly uncomfortable process for us all, but a great deal hangs in the balance, and our duty is clear: We must find the truth.

*   *   *

In conclusion I want to comment briefly about the allegations that have been raised by Professor Hill. The alleged harassment she describes took place some 10 years ago. During that time, she continued to initiate contact with Judge Thomas, in an apparently friendly manner. In addition, Professor Hill chose to publicize her allegations the day before the full Senate would have voted to confirm Judge Thomas.

While I fully intend to maintain an open mind during today's testimony, I must say that the timing of these statements raises a tremendous number of questions which must be dealt with. And I can assure all the witnesses that we shall be unstinting in our effort to ascertain the truth.

THOMAS: As excruciatingly difficult as the last two weeks have been, I welcome the opportunity to clear my name today. No one other than my wife and Sen. [John C.] Danforth [R-Mo.], to whom I read this statement at 6:30 a.m., has seen or heard the statement. No handlers, no advisers.

The first I learned of the allegations by Professor Anita Hill was on Sept. 25, 1991, when the FBI came to my home to investigate her allegations. When informed by the FBI agent of the nature of the allegations and the person making them, I was shocked, surprised, hurt and enormously saddened. I have not been the same since that day.

For almost a decade, my responsibilities included enforcing the rights of victims of sexual harassment. As a boss, as a friend and as a human being, I was proud that I have never had such an allegation leveled against me, even as I sought to promote women and minorities into non-traditional jobs.

In addition, several of my friends who are women have confided in me about the horror of harassment, on the job or elsewhere. I thought I really understood the anguish, the fears, the doubts, the seriousness of the matter. But since Sept. 25, I have suffered immensely as these very serious charges were leveled against me. I have been racking my brains and eating my insides out trying to think of what I could have said or done to Anita Hill to lead her to allege that I was interested in her in more than a professional way and that I talked with her about pornographic or X-rated films.

Contrary to some press reports, I categorically denied all of the allegations and denied that I ever attempted to date Anita Hill when first interviewed by the FBI. I strongly reaffirm that denial.

Let me describe my relationship with Anita Hill. In 1981, after I went to the Department of Education as an assistant secretary in the Office of

Civil Rights, one of my closest friends from both college and law schools, Gil Hardy, brought Anita Hill to my attention. As I remember, he indicated that she was dissatisfied with her law firm and wanted to work in government. Based primarily, if not solely, on Gil's recommendation, I hired Anita Hill.

During my tenure at the Department of Education, Anita Hill was an attorney-adviser who worked directly with me. She worked on special projects as well as day-to-day matters. As I recall, she was one of two professionals working directly with me at the time. As a result, we worked closely on numerous matters.

I recalled being pleased with her work product and the professional, but cordial, relationship which we enjoyed at work. I also recall engaging in discussions about politics and current events.

Upon my nomination to become chairman of the Equal Employment Opportunity Commission [EEOC], Anita Hill, to the best of my recollection, assisted me in the nomination and confirmation process. After my confirmation, she and Diane Holt, then my secretary, joined me at EEOC.

I do not recall that there was any question or doubt that she would become a special assistant to me at EEOC, although as a career employee, she retained the option of remaining at the Department of Education.

At EEOC our relationship was more distant, and our contacts less frequent, as a result of the increased size of my personal staff and the dramatic increase and diversity of my day-to-day responsibilities.

Upon reflection, I recall that she seemed to have had some difficulty adjusting to this change in her role. In any case, our relationship remained both cordial and professional. At no time did I become aware, either directly or indirectly, that she felt I had said or done anything to change the cordial nature of our relationship.

I detected nothing from her, or from my staff, or from Gil Hardy, our mutual friend, with whom I maintained regular contact.

I am certain that had any statement or conduct on my part been brought to my attention, I would remember it clearly because of the nature and seriousness of such conduct, as well as my adamant opposition to sex discrimination and sexual harassment.

But there were no such statements.

[Hill's Teaching Job]

In the spring of 1983, Mr. Charles Coffey contacted me to speak at the law school at Oral Roberts University in Tulsa, Okla. Anita Hill, who is from Oklahoma, accompanied me on that trip. It was not unusual that individuals on my staff would travel with me occasionally.

Anita Hill accompanied me on that trip primarily because this was an opportunity to combine business and a visit to her home.

As I recall, during our visit at Oral Roberts University, Mr. Coffey mentioned to me the possibility of approaching Anita Hill to join the faculty at Oral Roberts University Law School.

I encouraged him to do so and noted to him, as I recall, that Anita Hill would do well in teaching. I recommended her highly, and she eventually was offered a teaching position.

Although I did not see Anita Hill often after she left EEOC, I did see her on one or two subsequent visits to Tulsa [Okla.] and on one visit, I believe she drove me to the airport.

I also occasionally received telephone calls from her. She would speak directly with me or with my secretary, Diane Holt. Since Anita Hill and Diane Holt had been with me at the Department of Education, they were fairly close personally, and I believe they occasionally socialized together.

I would also hear about her through Linda Jackson, then Linda Lambert, whom both Anita Hill and I met at the Department of Education, and I would hear of her from my friend Gil.

Throughout the time that Anita Hill worked with me, I treated her as I treated my other special assistants. I tried to treat them all cordially, professionally and respectfully. And I tried to support them in their endeavors and be interested in and supportive of their success. I had no reason or basis to believe my relationship with Anita Hill was anything but this way until the FBI visited me a little more than two weeks ago.

I find it particularly troubling that she never raised any hint that she was uncomfortable with me. She did not raise or mention it when considering moving with me to EEOC from the Department of Education. And she never raised it with me when she left EEOC and was moving on in her life. And to my fullest knowledge, she did not speak to any other women working with or around me who would feel comfortable enough to raise it with me, especially Diane Holt, to whom she seemed closest on my personal staff. Nor did she raise it with mutual friends such as Linda Jackson and Gil Hardy.

[Cordial Relationship]

This is a person I have helped at every turn in the road since we met. She seemed to appreciate the continued cordial relationship we had since day one. She sought my advice and counsel, as did virtually all of the members of my personal staff.

During my tenure in the executive branch, as a manager, as a policy-maker and as a person, I have adamantly condemned sex harassment. There is no member of this committee or this Senate who feels stronger about sex harassment than I do. As a manager, I made every effort to take swift and decisive action when sex harassment raised or reared its ugly head.

The fact that I feel so very strongly about sex harassment and spoke loudly about it at EEOC has made these allegations doubly hard on me. I cannot imagine anything that I said or did to Anita Hill that could have been mistaken for sexual harassment. But with that said, if there is anything that I have said that has been misconstrued by Anita Hill or anyone else to be sexual harassment, then I can say that I am so very sorry, and I wish I had known. If I did know, I would have stopped immediately, and I would not, as I've done over the past two weeks, had to tear away at myself trying to think of what I could possibly have done.

But I have not said or done the things that Anita Hill has alleged. God has gotten me through the days since Sept. 25, and he is my judge.

Mr. Chairman, something has happened to me in the dark days that have followed since the FBI agents informed me about these allegations. And the days have grown darker as this very serious, very explosive and very sensitive allegation, or these sensitive allegations were selectively leaked in a distorted way to the media over the past weekend.

As if the confidential allegations themselves were not enough, this apparently calculated public disclosure has caused me, my family and my friends enormous pain and great harm.

I have never, in all my life, felt such hurt, such pain, such agony.

My family and I have been done a grave and irreparable injustice. During the past two weeks, I lost the belief that if I did my best all would work out. I called upon the strength that helped me get here from Pin Point[, Ga.] And it was all sapped out of me.

It was sapped out of me because Anita Hill was a person I considered a friend, whom I admired and thought I had treated fairly and with the utmost respect.

Perhaps I could have been—better weathered this if it was from someone else. But here was someone I truly felt I had done my best with.

Though I am, by no means, a perfect person—no means—I have not done what she has alleged. And I still don't know what I could possibly have done to cause her to make these allegations.

When I stood next to the president in Kennebunkport, [Maine,] being nominated to the Supreme Court of the United States, that was a high honor. But as I sit here before you, 103 days later, that honor has been crushed.

From the very beginning, charges were leveled against me from the shadows—charges of drug abuse, anti-Semitism, wife beating, drug use by family members, that I was a quota appointment, confirmation conversion and much, much more. And now, this.

["Enough is Enough"]

I have complied with the rules. I responded to a document request that produced over 30,000 pages of documents. And I have testified for five full days under oath.

I have endured this ordeal for 103 days. Reporters sneaking into my garage to examine books that I read. Reporters and interest groups swarming over divorce papers, looking for dirt. Unnamed people starting preposterous and damaging rumors. Calls all over the country specifically requesting dirt.

This is not American. This is Kafkaesque. It has got to stop. It must stop for the benefit of future nominees and our country. Enough is enough.

I am not going to allow myself to be further humiliated in order to be confirmed. I am here specifically to respond to allegations of sex harassment in the workplace. I am not here to be further humiliated by this committee or anyone else, or to put my private life on display for prurient interests or other reasons.

I will not allow this committee or anyone else to probe into my private life.

This is not what America is all about. To ask me to do that would be to ask me to go beyond fundamental fairness.

Yesterday, I called my mother. She was confined to her bed, unable to work and unable to stop crying. Enough is enough.

Mr. Chairman, in my 43 years on this earth, I have been able with the help of others and with the help of God to defy poverty, avoid prison, overcome segregation, bigotry, racism and obtain one of the finest educations available in this country.

But I have not been able to overcome this process. This is worse than any obstacle or anything that I have ever faced. Throughout my life I have been energized by the expectation and the hope that in this country I would be treated fairly in all endeavors. When there was segregation, I hoped there would be fairness one day, or someday. When there was bigotry and prejudice, I hoped that there would be tolerance and understanding—someday.

Mr. Chairman, I am proud of my life. Proud of what I have done and what I've accomplished, proud of my family. And this process, this process, is trying to destroy it all.

No job is worth what I've been through—no job. No horror in my life has been so debilitating. Confirm me if you want. Don't confirm me if you are so led. But let this process end. Let me and my family regain our lives.

[Too High a Price]

I never asked to be nominated. It was an honor. Little did I know the price, but it is too high.

I enjoy and appreciate my current position, and I am comfortable with the prospect of returning to my work as a judge on the U.S. Court of Appeals for the D.C. Circuit and to my friends there. Each of these positions is public service, and I have given at the office.

I want my life and my family's life back, and I want them returned expeditiously.

I have experienced the exhilaration of new heights from the moment I was called to Kennebunkport by the president to have lunch, and he nominated me. That was the high point. At that time I was told, eye to eye, that, Clarence, you made it this far on merit; the rest is going to be politics. And it surely has been.

There have been other highs. The outpouring of support from my friends of longstanding, a bonding like I have never experienced with my old boss, Sen. Danforth. The wonderful support of those who have worked with me. There have been prayers said for my family and me by people I know and people I will never meet, prayers that were heard, and that sustained not only me but also my wife and my entire family.

Instead of understanding and appreciating the great honor bestowed upon me, I find myself here today defending my name, my integrity, because somehow select portions of confidential documents dealing with this matter were leaked to the public.

Mr. Chairman, I am a victim of this process. My name has been harmed. My integrity has been harmed. My character has been harmed. My family has been harmed. My friends have been harmed. There is nothing this committee, this body or this country can do to give me my good name back. Nothing.

I will not provide the rope for my own lynching or for further humiliation. I am not going to engage in discussions, nor will I submit to roving questions, of what goes on in the most intimate parts of my private life or the sanctity of my bedroom. These are the most intimate parts of my privacy, and they will remain just that: private.

* * *

ANITA HILL: My name is Anita F. Hill, and I am a professor of law at the University of Oklahoma. I was born on a farm in Okmulgee County, Okla., in 1956. I am the youngest of 13 children.

I had my early education in Okmulgee County. My father, Albert Hill, is a farmer in that area. My mother's name is Irma Hill. She is also a farmer and a housewife.

My childhood was one of a lot of hard work and not much money, but it was one of solid family affection as represented by my parents. I was reared in a religious atmosphere in the Baptist faith, and I have been a member of the Antioch Baptist Church in Tulsa, Okla., since 1983. It is a very warm part of my life at the present time.

For my undergraduate work, I went to Oklahoma State University and graduated from there in 1977.... I graduated from the university with academic honors and proceeded to the Yale Law School, where I received my J.D. degree in 1980.

Upon graduation from law school, I became a practicing lawyer with the Washington, D.C., firm of Wald, Hardraker & Ross. In 1981, I was introduced to now-Judge Thomas by a mutual friend.

Judge Thomas told me that he was anticipating a political appointment, and he asked if I would be interested in working with him.

He was in fact appointed as assistant secretary of Education for civil rights. After he was, after he had taken that post, he asked if I would become his assistant, and I accepted that position.

In my early period there, I had two major projects. The first was an article I wrote for Judge Thomas' signature on the education of minority students. The second was the organization of a seminar on high-risk students, which was abandoned because Judge Thomas transferred to the EEOC, where he became the chairman of that office.

During this period at the Department of Education my working relationship with Judge Thomas was positive. I had a good deal of responsibility and independence. I thought he respected my work and that he trusted my judgment.

[Alleged Harassment]

After approximately three months of working there, he asked me to go out socially with him. What happened next, and telling the world about it, are the two most difficult things—experiences of my life.

It is only after a great deal of agonizing consideration and sleepless— number of—great number of sleepless nights that I am able to talk of these unpleasant matters to anyone but my close friends.

I declined the invitation to go out socially with him and explained to him that I thought it would jeopardize at—what at the time I considered to be a very good working relationship. I had a normal social life with other men outside the office. I believe then, as now, that having a social relationship with a person who was supervising my work would be ill-advised. I was very uncomfortable with the idea and told him so.

I thought that by saying no and explaining my reasons, my employer would abandon his social suggestions. However, to my regret, in the following few weeks, he continued to ask me out on several occasions.

He pressed me to justify my reasons for saying no to him. These incidents took place in his office or mine. They were in the form of private conversations, which not—would not have been overheard by anyone else.

My working relationship became even more strained when Judge Thomas began to use work situations to discuss sex. On these occasions he would call me into his office for a course on education issues and projects, or he might suggest that because of the time pressures of his schedule we go to lunch to a government cafeteria.

After a brief discussion of work, he would turn the conversation to a discussion of sexual matters. His conversations were very vivid. He spoke about acts that he had seen in pornographic films involving such matters as women having sex with animals and films showing group sex or rape scenes.

He talked about pornographic materials depicting individuals with large penises or large breasts involving various sex acts. On several occasions, Thomas told me graphically of his own sexual prowess.

Because I was extremely uncomfortable talking about sex with him at all, and particularly in such a graphic way, I told him that I did not want to talk about this subject. I would also try to change the subject to education matters or to non-sexual personal matters, such as his background or his beliefs.

My efforts to change the subject were rarely successful.

Throughout the period of these conversations, he also from time to time asked me for social engagements. My reaction to these conversations was to avoid them by eliminating opportunities for us to engage in extended conversations.

This was difficult because, at the time, I was his only assistant at the office of education—or the Office for Civil Rights. During the latter part of my time at the Department of Education, the social pressures, and any conversation of his offensive behavior, ended. I began both to believe and hope that our working relationship could be a proper, cordial and professional one.

[Changing Jobs Together]

When Judge Thomas was made chair of the EEOC, I needed to face the question of whether to go with him. I was asked to do so, and I did.

The work itself was interesting, and at that time it appeared that the sexual overtures which had so troubled me had ended.

I also faced the realistic fact that I had no alternative job. While I might have gone back to private practice, perhaps in my old firm or at another, I was dedicated to civil rights work, and my first choice was to be in that field. Moreover, at that time, the Department of Education itself was a dubious venture. President [Ronald] Reagan was seeking to abolish the entire department.

For my first months at the EEOC where I continued to be an assistant to Judge Thomas, there were no sexual conversations or overtures. However, during the fall and winter of 1982, these began again. The comments were random and ranged from pressing me about why I didn't go out with him to remarks about my personal appearance. I remember his saying that some day I would have to tell him the real reason that I wouldn't go out with him.

He began to show displeasure in his tone and voice and his demeanor and his continued pressure for an explanation. He commented on what I was wearing in terms of whether it made me more or less sexually attractive. The incidents occurred in his inner office at the EEOC.

One of the oddest episodes I remember was an occasion in which Thomas was drinking a Coke in his office. He got up from the table at which we were working, went over to his desk to get the Coke, looked at the can and asked, "Who has put pubic hair on my Coke?"

On other occasions, he referred to the size of his own penis as being larger than normal, and he also spoke on some occasions of the pleasures he had given to women with oral sex. At this point, late 1982, I began to feel severe stress on the job. I began to be concerned that Clarence Thomas might take out his anger with me by degrading me or not giving me important assignments. I also thought that he might find an excuse for dismissing me. In January of 1983, I began looking for another job. I was handicapped because I feared that if he found out, he might make it difficult for me to find other employment, and I might be dismissed from the job I had. Another factor that made my search more difficult was that there was a period—this was during a period—of a hiring freeze in the government.

In February 1983 I was hospitalized for five days on an emergency basis for acute stomach pain, which I attributed to stress on the job. Once out of the hospital I became more committed to find other employment and sought further to minimize my contact with Thomas. This became easier when Allison Duncan became office director, because most of my work was then funneled through her, and I had contact with Clarence Thomas mostly in staff meetings.

In the spring of 1983, an opportunity to teach at Oral Roberts University opened up. I participated in a seminar, taught an afternoon session in a seminar at Oral Roberts University. The dean of the university saw me teaching and inquired as to whether I would be interested in further pursuing a career in teaching beginning at Oral Roberts University. I agreed to take the job, in large part because of my desire to escape the pressures I felt at the EEOC due to Judge Thomas.

When I informed him that I was leaving in July, I recall that his response was that now I would no longer have an excuse for not going out with him. I told him that I still preferred not to do so. At some time after that meeting, he asked if he could take me to dinner at the end of the term. When I declined, he assured me that the dinner was a professional courtesy only and not a social invitation. I reluctantly agreed to accept that invitation but only if it was at the very end of a working day.

On, as I recall, the last day of my employment at the EEOC in the summer of 1983, I did have dinner with Clarence Thomas. We went directly from work to a restaurant near the office. We talked about the work I had done, both at Education and at the EEOC. He told me that he was pleased with all of it except for an article and speech that I had done for him while we were at the Office for Civil Rights. Finally he made a comment that I will vividly remember. He said that if I ever told anyone of his behavior that it would ruin his career. This was not an apology, nor was it an explanation. That was his last remark about the possibility of our going out or reference to his behavior.

[Continued Contacts]

In July of 1983 I left the Washington, D.C., area, and I've had minimal contacts with Judge Clarence Thomas since. I am of course aware from the press that some questions have been raised about conversations I had with Judge Clarence Thomas after I left the EEOC. From 1983 until today, I have seen Judge Thomas only twice. On one occasion I needed to get a reference from him, and on another, he made a public appearance in Tulsa. On one occasion he called me at home, and we had an inconsequential conversation. On one occasion he called me without reaching me, and I returned the call without reaching him, and nothing came of it.

I have, on at least three occasions, been asked to act as a conduit to him for others. I knew his secretary, Diane Holt. We had worked together at both EEOC and Education. There were occasions on which I spoke to her, and on some of these occasions, undoubtedly, I passed on some casual comment to then-Chairman Thomas.

There were a series of calls in the first three months of 1985 occasioned by a group in Tulsa, which wished to have a civil rights conference. They wanted Judge Thomas to be the speaker and enlisted my assistance for this purpose. I did call in January and February, to no effect, and finally suggested to the person directly involved, Susan Cahall, that she put the matter into her own hands and call directly. She did so in March of 1985.

In connection with that March invitation, Miss Cahall wanted conference materials for the seminar, and some research was needed. I was asked to try to get the information and did attempt to do so. There was another call about a possible conference in July of 1985.

In August of 1987 I was in Washington, D.C., and I did call Diane Holt. In the course of this conversation, she asked me how long I was going to be in town, and I told her. It is recorded in the message as Aug. 15. It was in fact Aug. 20. She told me about Judge Thomas' marriage, and I did say congratulate him.

It is only after a great deal of agonizing consideration that I am able to talk of these unpleasant matters to anyone except my closest friends. As I've said before, these last few days have been very trying and very hard for me, and it hasn't just been the last few days this week.

It has actually been over a month now that I have been under the strain of this issue.

Telling the world is the most difficult experience of my life, but it is very close to having to live through the experience that occasioned this meeting. I may have used poor judgment early on in my relationship with this issue. I was aware, however, that telling at any point in my career could adversely affect my future career, and I did not want, early on, to burn all the bridges to the EEOC.

As I said, I may have used poor judgment. Perhaps I should have taken angry or even militant steps, both when I was in the agency or after I left it. But I must confess to the world that the course that I took seemed the better, as well as the easier, approach.

I declined any comment to newspapers, but later, when Senate staff asked me about these matters, I felt I had a duty to report. I have no personal vendetta against Clarence Thomas. I seek only to provide the committee with information which it may regard as relevant.

It would have been more comfortable to remain silent. It took no initiative to inform anyone—I took no initiative to inform anyone. But when I was asked by a representative of this committee to report my experience, I felt that I had to tell the truth. I could not keep silent.

[Questioning Hill]

BIDEN: Can you describe to us how it was that you came to move over to the EEOC with Judge Thomas?

HILL: Well, my understanding, I did not have much notice that Judge Thomas was moving over to the EEOC.

My understanding from him at that time was that I could go with him to the EEOC, that I did not have, since I was his special assistant, that I did not have a position at the office for education, but that I was welcome to go to the EEOC with him.

It was a very tough decision because this behavior had occurred. However, at the time that I went to the EEOC, there was a period prior to the time we went to the EEOC, there was a period where the incidents had ceased.

And so after some consideration of the job opportunities in the area, as well as the fact that I was not assured that my job at Education was going to be protected, I made a decision to move to the EEOC.

BIDEN: Were you not assured of that because you were a political appointee? Or were you not assured of it because—tell me why you felt you weren't assured of that?

HILL: Well, there were two reasons, really. One, I was a special assistant of a political appointee, and therefore I assumed and I was told that that position may not continue to exist. I didn't know who was going to be taking over the position. I had not been interviewed to become the special assistant of the new individual. I assumed that they would want to hire their own, as Judge Thomas had done.

In addition, the Department of Education at that time was scheduled to be abolished. There had been a lot of talk about it, and at that time it was truly considered to be on its way out. And so, for a second reason, I could not be certain that I would have a position there.

BIDEN: Professor, you've testified that you had regular contact with Judge Thomas at the Department of Education and you've just described the extent of your contact with Judge Thomas at EEOC. And you've described your professional interaction with him.

Now, I must ask you now to describe once again and more fully the behavior that you have alleged he engaged in while your boss, which you say went beyond the professional conventions and were unwelcome to you.

Now, I know these are difficult to discuss. But you must understand that we have to ask you about them.

Professor, did some of the attempts at conversation that you have described in your opening statement occur in your office or in his office?

HILL: Some occurred in his office. Some comments were made in mine. Most often they were in his office.

BIDEN: Did all of the behavior that you have described to us in your written statement to the committee and your oral statement now and what you have said to the FBI—did all of that behavior take place at work?

HILL: Yes, it did.

BIDEN: Now, I'd like you to go back—

HILL: Let me clarify that. If you're including a luncheon during the weekday to be at work, yes.

BIDEN: Well, I'm just trying to determine—it was in what you describe and you believe to be part of the workday?

HILL: Yes.

BIDEN: Now, I have to ask you, where did each of these events occur? If you can, to the best of your ability, I'd like you to recount for us where each of the allegations that you have mentioned in your opening statement—each of the incidences—occurred, physically where they occurred.

HILL: Well, I remember two occasions—these incidents occurred at lunch.

BIDEN: Do you remember which of those incidences were at lunch, judge—I mean, professor?

HILL:—in a cafeteria.

BIDEN: Let me ask this as an antecedent question. Were you always alone when the alleged conversations would begin or the alleged statements by Judge Thomas would begin?

HILL: Well, when the incidents occurred in the cafeterias, we were not alone. There were other people in the cafeterias, but because of the way the tables were set—or there were few individuals who were in the immediate area of the conversation.

BIDEN: Those incidents that occurred other than in the cafeteria, those incidents occurred in his office, can you tell me what incidents occurred in his office, can you tell me which incidents occurred, of the ones you've described to us, occurred in his office?

HILL: Well, I recall specifically that the incident about the Coke can occurred in his office at the EEOC.

BIDEN: And what was that incident again?

HILL: The incident with regard to the Coke can that's spelled out in my statement.

BIDEN: Would you describe it once again for me, please.

HILL: The incident involved his going to his desk, getting up from a work table, going to his desk, looking at this can, and saying, who put pubic hair on my Coke.

BIDEN: Was anyone else in his office at the time?

HILL: No.

BIDEN: Was the door closed?

HILL: I don't recall.

BIDEN: Are there any other incidents that occurred in his office with just—in his office, period?

HILL: There is—I recall at least one instance in his office at the EEOC where he discussed some pornographic material, or he brought up the substance or the content of pornographic material.

BIDEN: Again, it's difficult, but for the record, what substance did he bring up in this instance in his—at EEOC in his office? What was the content of what he said?

HILL: This was a reference to an individual who had a very large penis. And he used the name that he had been referred to in the pornographic material.

BIDEN: Do you recall what it was?

HILL: Yes, I do. The name that was referred to was Long Dong Silver.

BIDEN: Were you—were you working on any matter in that context? You just were called into the office. Do you remember what the circumstance was of your being in the office on that occasion?

HILL: Very often, I went in to report on memos that I had read. I'm sure that that's why I was in the office.

What happened generally was that I would write a note to Clarence Thomas, and he would call me in to talk about what I had written to him, and I believe that's what happened on that occasion.

[The Pornographic Films]

BIDEN: Can you tell the committee what was the most embarrassing of all the incidents that you have alleged?

HILL: I think the one that was the most embarrassing was his discussion of pornography involving these women with large breasts and engaged in a variety of sex with different people or animals. That was the thing that embarrassed me the most and made me feel the most humiliated.

BIDEN: If you can, in his words, not yours, in his words, can you tell us what on that occasion he said to you. You have described the essence of the conversation. In order for us to determine—well, can you tell us in his words, what he said.

HILL: I really cannot quote him verbatim. I can remember something like, you really ought to see these films that I've seen or this material that I've seen. This woman has this kind of breast, or breasts that measure this size. And they've got here in there with all kinds of things, she's doing all kinds of different sex acts, and you know, that kind of—those were the kinds of words, where he expressed his enjoyment of it and seemed to try to encourage me to enjoy that kind of material as well.

BIDEN: Did he indicate why he thought you should see this material?

HILL: No.

BIDEN: Why do you think—what was your reaction? Why did you think he was saying these things to you?

HILL: Well, coupled with the pressure about going out with him, I felt that implicit in this discussion about sex was the offer to have sex with him, not just to go out with him. There was never any explicit thing about going out to dinner or going to a particular concert or movie, it was, we ought to go out. And given his other conversations, I took that to mean, we ought to have sex or we ought to look at these pornographic movies together.

BIDEN: Professor, at your press conference—one of your press conferences—you said that the issues you raised about Judge Thomas, you referred to it as an ugly issue. Is that how you viewed these conversations?

HILL: Yes, they were very ugly. They were very dirty; they were disgusting.

SPECTER: But I was just saying about the importance of the court, where there should be a feeling of confidence and of fairness of decisions. Parties can take unfavorable decisions if they think they're being treated fairly.

I think this hearing is very important to the Senate, and to this committee, because by 20-20 hindsight we should have done this before. And obviously it's of critical importance to Judge Thomas and you, whose reputations and careers are on the line.

It's not easy to go back to events which happened almost a decade ago to find out what happened. Very, very difficult to do.

I would start, Professor Hill, with one of your more recent statements, at least according to a man by the name of Carlton Stewart, who says that he met you in August of this year, ran into you at the American Bar Association in Atlanta, where Professor Hill stated to me, in the presence of Stanley Grayson, quote, how great Clarence's nomination was and how much he deserved it, unquote.

"We went on to discuss Judge Thomas and our tenure at EEOC, for an additional 30 minutes or so." There was no mention of sexual harassment or anything negative about Judge Thomas stated during that conversation. And there is a statement from Stanley Grayson corroborating what Carlton Stewart has said.

My question is, did Mr. Stewart accurately state what happened with you at that meeting?

HILL: As I recall, at that meeting, I did see Carlton Stewart, and we did discuss the nomination. Carlton Stewart was very excited about the nomination, and said, I believe that those are his words, how great it was that Clarence Thomas had been nominated.

I only said that it was a great opportunity for Clarence Thomas. I did not say that it was a good thing, that this nomination was a good thing.

I might add that I have spoken with newspaper reporters and have gone on record as saying that I have some doubts and some questions about the nomination. I, however, in that conversation, where I was faced with an individual who was elated about the probability of his friend being on the Supreme Court, I did not want to insult him or argue with him at that time about the issue. So I was very passive in the conversation.

SPECTER: Professor Hill, you testified that you drew an inference that Judge Thomas might want you to look at pornographic films, but you told the FBI specifically that he never asked you to watch the films, is that correct?

HILL: He never said, let's go to my apartment and watch films or go to my house and watch films. He did say, you ought to see this material.

SPECTER: But when you testify that, as I wrote it down, "we ought to look at pornographic movies together," that was an expression of what was in your mind—

HILL: That was the inference that I drew, yes, with his pressing me for social engagements, yes.

SPECTER: That's something he might have wanted you to do, but the fact is, flatly, he never asked you to look at pornographic movies with him.

HILL: With him? No, he did not.

[The FBI Report]

SPECTER: Thank you, Mr. Chairman.

Professor Hill, now that you have read the FBI report—now that you have read the FBI report, you can see that it contains no reference to any mention of Judge Thomas' private parts or sexual prowess or size, etc. And my question would be, on something that is as important as it is in your written testimony and in your responses to Sen. Biden, why didn't you tell the FBI about that?

HILL: Senator, in paragraph 2 on page 2 of the report, it says that he liked to discuss specific sex acts and frequency of sex. And I am not sure what that—what all that summarizes, but his sexual prowess, his sexual preferences, could have—

SPECTER: Which line are you referring to, Professor?

HILL: The very last line in paragraph 2 of page 2.

SPECTER: Well, that says, quote—and this is not too bad; I can read it—Thomas liked to discuss specific sex acts and frequency of sex, closed quote.

Now, are you saying, in response to my question as to why you didn't tell the FBI about the size of his private parts and his sexual prowess and Long John Silver that that information was comprehended within the statement, quote, Thomas liked to discuss specific acts and frequency of sex?

HILL: I am not saying that that information was included in that. I don't know that it was. I don't believe that I even mentioned the latter information to the FBI agent. And I could only respond again that, at the time of the investigation, I tried to cooperate as fully as I could to recall information that—to answer the questions that they asked.

SPECTER: Professor Hill, you said that you took it to mean that Judge Thomas wanted to have sex with you, but in fact, he never did ask you to have sex, correct?

HILL: No, he did not ask me to have sex. He did continually pressure me to go out with him—continually. And he would not accept my explanation as one being valid.

SPECTER: Professor Hill, the next subject I want to take up with you involves the kind of strong language which you say Judge Thomas used in a very unique setting, where there you have the chairman of the EEOC, the nation's chief law enforcement officer on sexual harassment, and here you have a lawyer who's an expert in this field, later goes on to teach civil rights and has a dedication to making sure that women are not discriminated against. And if you take the single issue of discrimination against women, the chairman of the EEOC has a more important role on that question even than a Supreme Court justice. A Supreme Court justice is a more important position overall but if you focus just on sexual harassment.

And the testimony that you have described here today depicts a circumstance where the chairman of the EEOC is blatant, as you describe it. And my question is, understanding the fact that you're 25 and that you're shortly out of law school and the pressures that exist in this world, and I know about it to a fair extent—I used to be a district attorney, and I know about sexual harassment and discrimination against women—and I think I have some sensitivity on that.

But even considering all of that, given your own expert standing, and the fact that here you have the chief law enforcement officer of the country on this subject, and the whole purpose of the civil rights laws being perverted right in the office of the chairman with one of his own female subordinates, what went through your mind, if anything, on whether you ought to come forward at that stage? Because if you had, you'd have stopped this man from being head of EEOC, perhaps for another decade.

What went on through your mind? I know you decided not to make a complaint, but did you give that any consideration? And if so, how could you allow this kind of reprehensible conduct to go on right in the headquarters without doing something about it?

HILL: Well, it was a very trying and difficult decision for me not to say anything further. I can only say that when I made the decision to just withdraw from the situation and not press a claim or charge against him, that I may have shirked a duty, a responsibility that I had.

And to that extent, I confess that I am very sorry that I did not do something or say something. But at the time that was my best judgment. Maybe it was a poor judgment, but it wasn't a dishonest, and it wasn't a completely unreasonable choice that I made, given the circumstances.

THOMAS REBUTTAL

[Later that evening, Clarence Thomas returned to the hearing room to address the charges against him and to answer additional questions.]

THOMAS: Senator, I would like to start by saying unequivocally, uncategorically, that I deny each and every single allegation against me today that suggested in any way that I had conversations of a sexual nature or about pornographic material with Anita Hill, that I ever attempted to date her, that I ever had any personal sexual interest in her or that I in any way ever harassed her.

The second, and I think more important, point: I think that this today is a travesty. I think that it is disgusting. I think that this hearing should never occur in America. This is a case in which this sleaze, this dirt was searched for by staffers of members of this committee, was then leaked to the media, and this committee and this body validated it and displayed it at prime time over our entire nation.

How would any member on this committee, any person in this room or any person in this country would like sleaze said about him or her in this fashion? Or this dirt dredged up and this gossip and these lies displayed in this manner, how would any person like it?

The Supreme Court is not worth it. No job is worth it. I am not here for that. I am here for my name, my family, my life and my integrity. I think something is dreadfully wrong with this country when any person, any person in this free country would be subjected to this.

This is not a closed room. There was an FBI investigation. This is not an opportunity to talk about difficult matters privately or in a closed environment. This is a circus. It's a national disgrace.

And from my standpoint, as a black American, it is a high-tech lynching for uppity blacks who in any way deign to think for themselves, to do for themselves, to have different ideas, and it is a message that unless you kowtow to an old order, this is what will happen to you. You will be lynched, destroyed, caricatured by a committee of the U.S. Senate rather than hung from a tree.

HEFLIN: All right, sir, I'll reserve an exception, as we used to say.

Now, you, I suppose, have heard Professor Hill, Miss Hill, Anita F. Hill, testify today.

THOMAS: No, I haven't.

HEFLIN: You didn't listen?

THOMAS: No, I didn't. I've heard enough lies.

HEFLIN: You didn't listen to her testimony?

THOMAS: No, I didn't.

HEFLIN: On television?

THOMAS: No, J didn't; I've heard enough lies. The day is not a day that in my opinion is high among the days in our country; this is a travesty. You've spent the entire day destroying what it has taken me 43 years to build and providing a forum for that.

HEFLIN: Well, Judge Thomas, you know, we have a responsibility, too. I have nothing to do with Anita Hill coming here and testifying. We're trying to get to the bottom of this, and if she is lying, then I think you can help us prove that she was lying.

THOMAS: Senator, I am incapable of proving the negative. It did not occur.

HEFLIN: Well, if it did not occur, I think you are in a position, with certainly your ability to testify to, in effect, try to eliminate it from people's minds.

THOMAS: Senator, I didn't create it in people's minds. This matter was investigated by the Federal Bureau of Investigation in a confidential way. It was then leaked last weekend to the media. I did not do that. And how many members of this committee would like to have the same scurrilous, uncorroborated allegations made about him and then leaked to national newspapers and then be drawn and dragged before a national forum of this nature to discuss those allegations that should have been resolved in a confidential way?

HEFLIN: Well, I certainly appreciate your attitude towards leaks. I happen to serve on the Senate Ethics Committee, and it's been a sieve.

THOMAS: Well, but it didn't leak on me. This leaked on me, and it is drowning my life, my career and my integrity. And you can't give it back to me, and this committee can't give it back to me, and this Senate can't give it back to me. You have robbed me of something that can never be restored.

DeCONCINI: I know exactly how you feel.

HEFLIN: Judge Thomas, one of the aspects of this is that she could be living in a fantasy world. I don't know. We're just trying to get to the bottom of all these facts. But if you didn't listen and didn't see her testify, I think you put yourself in an unusual position. You in effect are defending yourself, and basically some of us want to be fair to you, fair to her; but if you didn't listen to what she said today, then that puts it somewhat in a more difficult task to find out what the actual facts are relative to this matter.

THOMAS: The facts keep changing, Senator. When the FBI visited me, the statements to this committee and the questions were one thing, the FBI's subsequent questions were another thing, and the statements today as I received summaries of them were another thing.

It is not my fault that the facts change. What I have said to you is categorical, that any allegations that I engaged in any conduct involving sexual activity, pornographic movies, attempted to date her, any allegations, I deny. It is not true.

So the facts can change, but my denial does not. Miss Hill was treated in a way that all of my special assistants were treated—cordial, professional, respectful.

HEFLIN: Judge, if you're on the bench, and you approach a case where you appear to have a closed mind and that you are only right, doesn't it raise issues of judicial temperament?

THOMAS: Senator, there is a big difference between approaching a case objectively and watching yourself being lynched. There is no comparison whatsoever.

HATCH: How do you feel right now, Judge, after what you've been through?

THOMAS: Senator, as I indicated this morning, it just isn't worth it. The nomination isn't worth it; being on the Supreme Court isn't worth it. There is no amount of money that is worth it; there is no amount of money that can restore my name. Being an associate justice of the Supreme Court will never replace what I've been robbed of. And I wouldn't recommend that anyone go through it.

This has been an enormously difficult experience. But I don't think that that's the worst of it. I'm 43 years old, and if I'm not confirmed, I'm still the youngest member of the U.S. Court of Appeals for the D.C. Circuit. I'll go on. I'll go back to my life of talking to my neighbors and cutting my grass and getting a Big Mac at McDonalds and driving my car, seeing my kid play football. I'll live. I'll have my life back. And all this hurt has brought my family and I closer, my wife and I, my mother. But that isn't— so there's no pity for me. I think the country has been hurt by this process. I think we are destroying our country; we are destroying our institutions. And I think it's a sad day when the U.S. Senate can be used by interest groups and hatemongers and people who are interested in digging up dirt to destroy other people, and who will stop at no tactics, when they can use our great institutions for their own political ends. We have gone far beyond McCarthyism. This is far more dangerous than McCarthyism. At least McCarthy was elected. . . .

OCTOBER 15 SENATE DEBATE

SEN. ROBERT C. BYRD, D-W.VA.: I believe Anita Hill. I believe what she said. I watched her on that screen, intensely. And I replayed as I have already said her appearance and her statement.

I did not see on that face the knotted brow of Satanic revenge. I did not see a face that was contorted with hate. I did not hear a voice that was tremulous with passion.

I saw a face of a woman, one of 13 in a family of Southern blacks who grew up on the farm and who belonged to the church, who belongs to the church today, and who was evidently reared by religious parents.

We all saw them as they came into the hearing room. The aging father, the kind mother, hugging their daughter, giving her succor and comfort in her hour of trial.

I saw an individual who did not flinch, who showed no nervousness, who spoke calmly throughout, dispassionately, and who answered difficult questions. Some thought there were inconsistencies, but a careful reading of the exact language of the questions that were put to her can at least in one case, and perhaps in others, explain the apparent—the appearance of an inconsistency in what she was saying in response to that question.

I won't go into details here. But it is very easy to charge an inconsistency in asking questions. But I thought that Anita Hill was thoughtful, reflective and truthful.

That was my impression.

Aside from believing Anita Hill, I was offended by Judge Thomas' stonewalling the committee. He said he wanted to come back before the committee and clear his name. That's what I heard. He wanted to clear his name. He was given the opportunity to clear his name. But he didn't even listen to the principal witness—the only witness against him. He said he didn't listen to it. He was tired of lies. What kind of judicial temperament does that demonstrate? He didn't listen to it.

What senator can imagine that if he was the object of scrutiny in that situation that he would not have listened to this witness so that he would know how to respond, how to defend himself, how to clear his name. But instead of that, came back and said he didn't even listen.

He set up a wall when he did that, because it made it extremely difficult for members of the committee to ask him what did you think about this or that that she said. He wanted to clear his name.

I know that hindsight is great, and I would imagine that most of the members of that committee wished they had asked for a week's delay. That should have been done. That's gone. Much of this could have been avoided with a week's delay and by calling in the two persons—principal persons here—talking with them in private. But again, that's water over the dam. We have only what happened—the circumstances to deal with—and he asked to come back to clear his name. I was extremely disappointed and astonished, as a matter of fact, when he came back and said he hadn't listened—hadn't listened to Anita Hill.

Well, by refusing to watch her testimony, he put up a wall between himself and the committee. How could the committee question him? How could the committee learn the truth if the accused refused to even hear the charges? What does this say about the conduct of a judge? He is a judge, now—a circuit court of appeals judge. What does this say about him? The conduct of a judge—a man whose primary function in his professional life is to listen to the evidence, listen to both sides—whether plaintiff or defendant in a civil case or prosecutor and the accused in a criminal case.

I had substantial doubts after this episode about the judicial temperament of Judge Thomas—doubts that I did not have prior to this weekend's hearings. How can we have confidence if he is confirmed that he will be an objective judge, willing to decide cases based on the evidence presented, if the one case that has mattered most to him in his lifetime—he shut his eyes and closed his ears, and closed his mind and didn't even watch—the sworn testimony of Anita Hill? She was testifying under oath.

He professed to want nothing more than to clear his name. And yet he could not be bothered to even hear what the allegations were from the person who is making the allegation.

Another reason why I shall vote against Judge Thomas: He not only effectively stonewalled the committee, he just in the main made his speeches before the committee. He made his own defense by charging that the committee proceedings were a "high-tech lynching of uppity blacks."

Now, Mr. President, in my judgment that was an attempt to shift the ground. That was an attempt to fire the prejudices of race hatred, shift it to a matter involving race. And I frankly was offended by his injection of racism into these hearings. It was a diversionary tactic intended to divert both the committee's and the American public's attention away from the issue at hand, the issue being: Which one is telling the truth? I was offended by that.

HATCH: And I am telling you and everybody in this country and everybody that listens, or everybody that sees this or reads this, that Clarence Thomas is an honorable, decent, wonderful man, and I think if you look at the fact—he said that at one point he was so poor he'd had a divorce, was in the midst of a divorce, he sold his only car to help keep his son in school.

And that doesn't sound like a man on the prowl or a person that doesn't have good values to me. He has tremendous values, and everybody, everybody who has worked with Clarence Thomas or knows Clarence Thomas or has a relationship socially with Clarence Thomas, knows he's a good man. Everybody except this one woman. And some others who did not come forth, one or two, and I think would not come forth. And rightly so. This man is a decent human being whose life has been wronged and really hurt and, frankly, because of a process that broke down because of at least one dishonest person who sits in this body, the greatest deliberative body in the world, only 100 people.

And his life, though not ruined by any stretch of the imagination, has been severely harmed.

Now, it seems to me that all of that lifetime and all of that service to the federal government and all of the good things that he's done should not be swept away because of one substantiated [sic] set of allegations that really don't stand up, that were 10 years old, nine years and nine months after the statute of limitations expired on the charges.

That's why we have statute of limitations: so we stop people from bringing up charges afterward; so they have to bring them within a reasonable time or eat them; so that they have to live within that statute and get these charges made so that the problems can be corrected; so that if the individual doesn't realize that he or she is committing sexual harassment, they can be informed of it and changes can be made, and life changes can be made, and recompense can be brought.

SEN. PATRICK J. LEAHY, D-VT.: The president sent us a nominee who is not prepared for a seat on the court. He has asked us to confirm Judge Thomas on the basis of his character. His nomination was a political calculation that, notwithstanding the lack of his qualifications, it would be politically difficult to oppose. I disagree.

I voted against Judge Thomas because, after reviewing his record and listening to his testimony, I was left with too many unanswered questions.

As I've discussed in detail in my previous statements, I was troubled by his lack of expertise in constitutional issues, by his disturbing flight from his record, by his extraordinary comment that he never discussed *Roe v. Wade*, or the one that he didn't even watch his accuser, by his unwillingness to answer legitimate questions and by his unwillingness to clarify a troubling record and the fundamental right to privacy.

I urge my colleagues to go back to Sept. 10 to look at the whole record to put this in context.

The fact that he pulled himself up by his bootstraps, succeeded in a hostile world, is not enough. Not for elevation to the Supreme Court, not for a lifetime appointment that could last unto the third decade of the next century, not to be a final arbiter of our Constitution and our Bill of Rights.

This weekend, Judge Thomas talked about his loss of privacy, of government intruding into his private life. He said he wanted his privacy back. I only hope that if he's confirmed as a Supreme Court justice, he remembers how important the right of privacy is to women in this country.

THURMOND: Before I go any further, Mr. President, I'd like to commend our distinguished chairman, Sen. Biden, for his fairness under extremely difficult circumstances. He has a tough job, but he has done it fairly and with respect for all concerned.

Now for the facts of Miss Anita Hill. Mr. President, this is a woman not one of us knows personally and whose background has not been investigated for anywhere close to 100 days. The allegations she has raised are the most serious kind, and the behavior she describes was hateful and disgusting. Yet her testimony has provided us with many more questions than answers.

If this behavior did take place, why did she wait 10 years—I repeat, 10 long years—to bring this charge? Why did she not bring it up to investigators or even to the media during Judge Thomas' four previous confirmation hearings? If she was being harassed while working for Clarence Thomas at the Department of Education, why did she follow him—I repeat—follow him to the EEOC? Why would she continue to subject herself to these unwelcome advances? Not one of desperation for a job. For, contrary to what she told this committee, she could have easily kept her job at the Department of Education.

In addition, Professor Hill was and is an attorney. She must have been well aware there was legal redress available to her if she was being harassed. Especially as an employee of the agency responsible for enforcing civil rights protection, Professor Hill must have been aware of the procedures for bringing such a charge and for keeping contemporaneous records of such treatment. Why did she not bring charges against this man if he was harassing her?

After leaving the Washington area, why did Professor Hill maintain a cordial relationship with a man who treated her so badly that she had to be hospitalized for stress? Why would she telephone Clarence Thomas just to say hello, or even more, resolved to congratulate him on his marriage?

Professor Hill's statements and actions are not congruent. The Judiciary Committee is not capable of discerning her clear motive for Professor Hill to tell an untruth, but I believe that is what has occurred.

* * *

Mr. President, a great injustice has been committed here. The good name of a good man has been tarnished. I do not believe Judge Thomas is capable of the kind of behavior Professor Hill described to this committee, and I do not believe that Professor Hill is telling the truth.

... We cannot restore to him his peace of mind or his belief in the fairness of this system. However, we can dismiss these charges against him for what they are: baseless, incredible, inconsistent and simply unbelievable.

Mr. President, Judge Thomas will be an outstanding justice of the United States Supreme Court. As I have said on many occasions, his background provides him with the ability to fulfill his responsibilities in an outstanding manner. And he should be confirmed.

DANFORTH: Mr. President, it is the position of this senator that the process that we have just seen is clearly wrong. It is wrong for Clarence Thomas, and it is wrong for the United States. It must be stopped. The business of interest groups fanning out through the country, digging up dirt on a nominee; the business of leaks of confidential documents put out to members of the press; the idea that absolutely anything goes, if necessary to stop a nominee for the Supreme Court of the United States—this whole process must be ended.

We in the Senate have the power to encourage the process or we have the power to stop it. We have the power by the vote that we are about to cast to say to our country that the strategy of digging up dirt, the strategy of throwing dirt, the strategy of leaking confidential reports does not work.

Mr. President, I speak to those senators who find the choice before us to be a difficult choice, who find it to be a close call whether to vote for or against the nomination of Clarence Thomas.

The New York Times today took the position that in the case of a close call, it should be resolved against the nominee. I believe that if that is the rule, that we follow that the burden of proof shifts to the nominee where charges are made, then the result of that will be to encourage just such a situation to be replicated again and again and again in the future.

The reason the burden against the accuser must be very heavy in a case such as this is to discourage exactly the kind of process that we have seen particularly during the next 10 days.

Mr. President, Clarence Thomas can survive without confirmation by the United States Senate. But if we vote against Clarence Thomas, we reward a process which is clearly wrong. And for that reason, not for the sake of Clarence Thomas, not for the sake of the Supreme Court, but for the sake of the basic American standard of decency and fairness, I ask senators to vote for the confirmation of Clarence Thomas.

SEN. JIM EXON, D-NEB.: After carefully listening to both Thomas and Hill, this one member of the eventual jury of 100 feels both appear believable, but one seemingly is lying under oath, a criminal offense of perjury. Unfortunately, after the hearing, it is difficult, if not impossible, for me to determine what the facts or truths are. I suspect that this might be the opinion of many who listened to the recently concluded hearings.

Both of the principals in the controversy have been hurt, and I feel deeply and personally for both. Judge Thomas was forthright in his denial, and that impressed me. Professor Hill was equally forthright in what I interpreted as a difficult disclosure on her part. If her detailed statements of alleged sexual harassment are accurate, it does not take just a woman to understand her anguish. Indeed, regardless of the eventual outcome of this matter, the controversy has clearly been beneficial in its significant contributions to necessary changes and understanding in the workplace.

Unfortunately, in my view, the hearings of the past few days have not produced any overall conclusive facts or definitive truths on the charges by Hill or the firm denials by Thomas.

The key and central issue here, though, is not what is in the best interests of either of the two antagonists. We cannot ignore what is fair or not fair to the individuals, nor the harm to either that our eventual decision will bring. But even more important than that is how our decision will affect the future. To assail the process or attempt to punish individuals or institutions which one might conclude in retrospect should have acted differently evades and tends to place out of focus the real object of the process, as painful as it is for all.

We must concentrate now on the all-encompassing issue as to whether or not Clarence Thomas should be confirmed for a lifetime appointment to the highest court in the land. On October 4, I supported the nomination on the floor on the basis of my knowledge at that time. Among other things, I stated that I felt Judge Thomas met the test of judicial temperament.

But now, Mr. President, it is decision-making time, and we cannot punt.

In conclusion, I have deliberated over this position and studied it for hours and hours, for days. There have been swings, pro and con, as I watched the hearings for solid conclusions that never materialized. Unlike [what] some might believe, there has been no pressure on me from any source other than my determination to do what was best and right under the circumstances.

There has developed in my mind no clear-cut correct choice, more a mixture of concerns and doubts. How best do we conclude this whole unhappy chapter?

Notwithstanding my reservations as to the nominee, I intend to vote for confirmation, but without enthusiasm. It is my hope that, if confirmed, Judge Thomas will be a better justice because of this ordeal.

* * *

MAJORITY LEADER GEORGE J. MITCHELL, D-MAINE: Mr. President and members of the Senate, this year marks the 200th anniversary of the Bill of Rights, the most eloquent and compelling statement of the limits on government and of the rights of individuals against the power of government ever devised, adopted or enforced. As elected officials, members of the Senate are sworn to uphold the Constitution of which those rights are an integral part.

Ultimately, however, in our system it is the Supreme Court which is the arbiter of the Constitution. That's why one of our most important responsibilities is to advise and consent on those nominated by the president to serve on the Supreme Court.

It's been said often in recent weeks, including today, that a high level of controversy over Supreme Court nominees is new to our history—but that's not true. Nominations to the Supreme Court have often been contentious. In June of 1968, the last time a Democratic president nominated someone to the Supreme Court, President [Lyndon B.] Johnson nominated Associate Justice [Abe] Fortas to be chief justice of the [United States]. On the very same day that the nomination was made, 19 Republican senators issued the following statement—and I quote:

"It is the strongly held view of the undersigned that the next chief justice of the United States and any nominee for vacancies on the Supreme Court should be selected by the newly elected president after the people have expressed themselves in the elections. We will, therefore, because of the above principle, and with absolutely no reflection on any individuals involved, vote against confirming any Supreme Court nomination of the incumbent president."

In the nomination now before us, our Republican colleagues have repeatedly said that 100 days to consider it is too long. But the last time the situation was reversed, they wanted a delay of seven months to even begin consideration of the nomination. The hearings on the Fortas nomination were stormy. Some senators shouted at the nominee, demanding that he answer questions about specific cases decided by the Supreme Court.

Of course, the opponents didn't want a delay, they wanted to defeat the nomination—and they did. Even though a majority of senators favored the nomination, a minority of senators defeated the nomination by a filibuster for a reason that had nothing to do with the nominee's qualifications. In the process, as they searched for ammunition to use against the nominee, they uncovered some financial dealings which ultimately led to his resignation from the Supreme Court.

I cite this history to put the current issue into some perspective and to rebut the view repeated so often in recent days that controversy over Supreme Court nominees is a recent phenomenon. It is not.

That does not justify the process in this or any other case. Just the opposite. The fact that it's been going on for so long is more, not less, reason to review the whole process. How can we responsibly consider those nominated by the president and do it in a way that is both perceived as and is in fact fair, fair to our obligation under the Constitution and fair to those involved in the process.

We must confront and respond to that question in a way better than we have in the past.

In 1980 the Republican National Convention adopted a platform which called for the appointment of judges committed to the pro-life position on abortion. Since 1980, in honoring that commitment, Presidents [Ronald] Reagan and Bush have established as a litmus test for a potential nominee to the Supreme Court that person's position on abortion. The president opposes a woman's right of choice. In order to have any hope of being nominated to the Supreme Court, so must any potential nominee.

The president selects nominees because of their views, not despite them. That is his privilege. It is the reward of election to the presidency. He is answerable for the quality of his choices only to the voters and to history.

But, by the same token, the Senate is not required to be a rubber stamp, to approve any nomination simply because it's been made by a president. It is illogical and untenable to suggest that the president has the right to select someone because of that person's views and then to say that the Senate has no right to reject that person because of those very same views.

Throughout the hearings, Judge Thomas repeatedly invoked his personal background of deprivation and segregation as a reason why he should be confirmed. Personal background and personal achievement undoubtedly say a great deal about character; they should be given great weight in the nomination process. But while invoking his early personal life as a reason for his confirmation, Judge Thomas repeatedly asked the committee to ignore much of what he said and wrote in the more than 10 years of his adult life in public service. He said that in preparing for service on the court, he would be like a runner stripping down for a race. He asked us to believe that his early experience shaped him but that much of his recent experience left him untouched.

Every nominee who comes to the Senate with a record will face questions about earlier statements and writings that may be inconsistent with more recent views. There's nothing unusual about that. The views of anyone in public life evolve, and statements made a decade ago may not reflect the current belief.

But this is the first nominee I can recall who asked just the opposite, that we consider his early experience but ignore his recent views. We should consider his early experience; we should also consider his recent views.

*   *   *

In summary, over and over again, Judge Thomas at his hearings denied, repudiated, abandoned his thoughts, his words, his views of the past decade; over and over again he now says that he didn't mean what he said, he didn't mean what he wrote in the 10 years that he served both the Reagan and Bush administrations.

So we're faced with a nominee who has an extensive public record but who has run from that record, a nominee who asks the Senate to make a leap of faith that defies common sense and reason.

Of all the things that have been said about the nominee, the least believable was President Bush's statement that race was not a factor at all in the nomination and that Judge Thomas is the best qualified person in America to be on the Supreme Court. Both statements are obviously untrue. Race clearly was a factor in the nomination. That's no reason to reject it; diversity on the court is desirable, and in an institution which so directly affects the lives of Americans, having someone who had to overcome racism and poverty is desirable. No, race is not the issue. Qualification is, specifically the nominee's lack of qualifications.

Judge Thomas is not the best-qualified American to be on the Supreme Court, as claimed by the president. Judge Thomas is not the best-qualified African-American to be on the Supreme Court. There are many, many superbly qualified African-Americans, men and women, who could serve with distinction on the Supreme Court.

A recent analysis by the Alliance for Justice indicates that Judge Thomas received the lowest rating by the American Bar Association of the last 23 nominees to the Supreme Court, going all the way back to 1955. Let me repeat that: Since 1955, there have been 23 nominees to the Supreme Court, each of them rated by the American Bar Association. Judge Thomas received the lowest ratings of any of the 23.

The hearing revealed a nominee willing to say whatever was necessary to win confirmation. It's worked. There will be the votes to confirm him to the Supreme Court, but mine will not be among them.

A Senate hearing is intended to focus on legislation and broad issues of policy. That's what they usually do. But a hearing is not a good place to protect anyone's rights or to deal at all with matters of such sensitivity.

Hearings are poorly suited to determining specific questions of fact, of truth and falsehood.

Perhaps something good may yet come from this terrible episode: If the national debate which it has generated leads to changed attitudes, leads to a process where serious charges can be evaluated in a more fair and less controversial way, to a society where the words of women have the same weight as the words of men, to a society where the workplace will finally be free of all discrimination, whether by race, by sex or in any other form. . . .

SEN. JOHN C. DANFORTH, R-Mo.: The situation before us is as follows. Sometime earlier this month, prompted by apparently repeated inquiries from Senate staff, Miss Anita Hill made a written statement making certain allegations about Judge Clarence Thomas.

Those allegations were subsequently investigated by the Federal Bureau of Investigation. The investigative report was then delivered to the chairman and to the ranking member of the Judiciary Committee.

They, in turn, briefed the majority leader and the minority leader of the Senate.

[Judiciary Committee Chairman Joseph R. Biden Jr., D-Del.] tells me that he then briefed each of the Democratic members of the Senate on the content of that report. As a result of those briefings—and I am told that during the briefings a copy of the FBI report was present, and that if members did not actually look at it, they had a right to look at it—as a result of those briefings it was determined by each of the members of the Judiciary Committee that the FBI report did not contain any basis for further action, that no further investigation was necessary and that no delay was necessary.

That was the stated position of the members of the Judiciary Committee.

Having failed to win any response from the Judiciary Committee, having failed to have the vote put off—and incidentally, I am told that as a matter of right, any member of the committee could have put off the committee vote for one week—having failed that, someone violated the rules of the Senate.

Someone released into the public domain an FBI report or the contents, selected contents, it would appear, of an FBI report. That was done the weekend before today's scheduled vote on the Thomas nomination.

It became, as many might have predicted, the lead item on each of the network news programs on Sunday. It became the front-page headline of the newspapers on Monday.

It has generated a tremendous rush of activity by various organizations opposed to the Thomas nomination. I am told two different times that various people who work at EEOC [Equal Employment Opportunity Commission] have been flooded with phone calls from people who have identified themselves as being with the organization, People for the American Way, asking for the dirt on Clarence Thomas.

This whole confirmation process has been turned into the worst kind of sleazy political campaign, with no effort spared to assassinate the character of Clarence Thomas. Staff members, interest group representatives, fanning out over the country, trying to drum up whatever they can to attack this person's character.

The allegations, of course, have been called into question. Today, Clarence Thomas issued a sworn statement categorically denying the charges that have been made against him.

Today, I released upstairs in the press gallery excerpts from the telephone logs of Clarence Thomas. Those excerpts from the telephone logs of Clarence Thomas indicate that on 11 separate occasions since Miss Hill left the employ of the EEOC, she took the initiative of telephoning Clarence Thomas.

The first entry on the telephone log, Jan. 31, 1984, written in the handwriting of Clarence Thomas' secretary at EEOC, says, Anita Hill, 11:50, just called to say hello. Sorry she didn't get to see you last week.

Another one of the entries. This one Aug. 4, 1987, Anita Hill, and then there's a phone number, time, 4 o'clock. Message: In town until 8:15, presumably Aug. 15. Wanted to congratulate you on marriage.

Now, these are the phone messages of the person who has accused Clarence Thomas of harassing her on the job.

Then we have the statement of a lawyer and former co-worker at EEOC, who reported that he had seen Ms. Hill at the American Bar Association Convention in August, and that she said, isn't it great that Clarence has been nominated for the Supreme Court? And this same person has come forward, and she's made certain statements, and those statements were investigated by the FBI, and that investigation was turned over to the Judiciary Committee, and the Judiciary Committee said: no basis for action.

And then, someone went public.

Now, Mr. President, what's the reason for the secrecy of FBI reports? What is the reason for Senate rules providing that FBI reports are not supposed to be released to the public? What is the reason why a senator who releases an FBI report can be expelled from the United States Senate?

The reason is that it is manifestly unfair to an individual to release an FBI report, and that's what happened here. And you talk about unfairness. What is more unfair than to have a person's character called into question as the lead item on the network news. What is more unfair to an individual than to have senator after senator go on the floor and say, oh, we don't know enough.

Why? It satisfied the Judiciary Committee. Yes, they read the reports and said no further action. Let's keep this ball in play. We need delay. We need more time for the People for the American Way to make their phone calls, digging up the dirt.

We need the interest groups to have more time to gin up their opposition. There's blood in the water. We need more time for the sharks to gather around the body of Clarence Thomas.

Oh, we need a delay.

The Judiciary Committee, when they said it doesn't warrant further action, they blew it, it is said. I don't think so at all.

One hundred days ago today, Clarence Thomas was nominated for the Supreme Court of the United States, for 100 days the interest groups and their lawyers and various staff members of the Senate have combed over the record of Clarence Thomas. For 100 days they have examined footnotes and law review articles to question him about, sentences and articles taken out of context, speeches from—made in a political context, which are then analyzed and criticized before the Judiciary Committee;

100 days this has gone on.

And people say, oh, no, wait, we need more. We need more time. That's a tactic, Mr. President.

I've been asked by the press, I have been asked by the press today, why not delay? Why not delay? One hundred days isn't enough. The Judiciary Committee's word for it isn't enough. Why not delay? Why not keep this circus—and I use that word in the Roman context—why not keep this circus going?

The lions aren't satisfied yet. Why not just have a delay? And my answer throughout the day has been, I don't think there should be a delay. Because all of the relevant evidence is before us now. The charge of Ms. Hill, the response to the charge by Clarence Thomas denying the allegation of Ms. Hill. It is not as though at some future time after some appropriate hearing the skies will miraculously open. The clouds will dissipate. And we will know the answer to these charges.

I am quite sure that if we have a delay, no matter how long that delay would be, people would say: Well, we need another delay. We still have doubts. Or she proved her point. Or he proved his point.

The questions will still exist. People say, clear the clouds away. There's a cloud of doubt. Well, we can't do anything while the cloud of doubt exists.

Mr. President, the cloud of doubt was created by a violation of the rules of the United States Senate. Think about voting down the nomination of Clarence Thomas solely on the basis of a violation of Senate rules. Think about voting down the nomination of Clarence Thomas solely because an FBI report was distributed to the media illegally.

Talk about scandal! That is scandal.

So Mr. President, I have said to the press, and I have said to some of my dear friends in the Senate today, I don't think there should be a delay. This poor guy has been tortured enough. And at the end of the delay, they're going to continue at it. And at the end of the delay, they're going to say, wait, there's somebody else. There's something else. Let's have another delay.

I have said, in my opinion, a delay would serve no purpose whatever. And that's how I feel about it.

But Mr. President, it's not my call. At least in my mind it's not my call. Because the person who I respect so greatly, and a person I love dearly, said to me on the phone, they have taken from me what I have worked 43 years to create. They have taken from me what I have taken 43 years to build: my reputation.

And he said I want to clear my name.

I don't know that it's possible; I doubt it. Because I think, as I've said, that it will just be another delay for the sharks. And that at the end, they'll say, oh, we need more.

But we need a lot of time, a lot of witnesses, a lot of lions. But Clarence Thomas said to me on the phone, I have to clear my name. I have to restore what they have taken from me. I have to appear before the appropriate forum and clear my name.

So for 100 days I've been the spokesman for this person, Clarence Thomas. And on this 100th day, I act as the spokesman again, with great pain and great anger at an injustice which is being perpetrated on him.

And I ask for a delay. And Mr. President, not a delay to torture him. A delay I would say of one day, some would say you can't do it in one day, two days. To bring her here, to bring him here, to do whatever else they want to do. And then to have a vote at a time certain, 6 p.m., next Thursday, this coming Thursday, two days from now.

Now that is reasonable. I think it's unfair. But it is certainly reasonable from the standpoint of any reasonable person.

That is the proposition, Mr. President, that I am asked to put to the United States Senate. Forty-eight hours, in a proper forum, for Clarence Thomas to try to clear his name.

[After negotiations with other leaders, Senate Majority Leader George J. Mitchell, D-Maine, announced an agreement to postpone the vote until Tuesday, Oct. 15. He then explained the delay to the Senate.]

MITCHELL: Mr. President, I believe that the delay just agreed upon with respect to the vote on this nomination is important and appropriate. The events of the past weekend have created a circumstance in which many senators believe, and have stated, that there should be a delay in the vote so that the issues now publicly raised can be publicly and fairly resolved. I share that view. I believe there should be a delay.

I believe that it's necessary in fairness to all concerned. It's important that senators and the American people understand how we have come to this situation.

On the evening of Sept. 25, two weeks ago tomorrow, Sen. Biden, the chairman of the Judiciary Committee, and Sen. [Strom] Thurmond [S.C.], the ranking Republican member of the committee, requested a meeting with the minority leader, Sen. [Bob] Dole [R-Kan.], and myself, the majority leader. In that meeting they described to us the nature of the statement made by Professor Anita [F.] Hill and Judge Thomas' denial of those assertions. Professor Hill had requested two things: first, that the information she provided in the form of a sworn statement be made available to members of the Senate Judiciary Committee; and, secondly, that it not be made available to anyone else because of her concern for the protection of her identity.

Sen. Biden indicated to me that he intended to comply with that request, that he would make the information available to the Democratic members of the committee and would not make it available beyond that, in accordance with Professor Hill's request.

Two days later, the committee voted and recommended that the matter be sent to the Senate. The vote in the committee was 7-7.

To my knowledge, at that time there had been compliance with Professor Hill's request, both with respect to making the information available to members of the committee prior to their vote and not making it available beyond that. Following that, the committee acted.

I then discussed the matter with Sen. Dole and with many other involved senators. As a result of those discussions, I then proposed to the Senate that there be four days for debate on the nomination, those four days being last Thursday and Friday, yesterday and today, and that at 6 p.m. today, following four days of debate, the Senate vote on the nomination. That was approved by unanimous consent. Each of the 100 senators agreed to that procedure. No one objected.

As we all know—but it bears repeating because there has been some misunderstanding among the American people—once the Senate has agreed to set a vote by unanimous consent, that is, with the approval of each and every one of the 100 senators, the only way the Senate can change that time is with the agreement of each of the 100 senators.

Last evening and throughout the day today and until just now I've been discussing this matter with a number of senators, Democrats and Republicans, in an effort to obtain agreement on the best way to proceed in this matter. The contradictions between the statements of Professor Hill and Judge Thomas have not been resolved; indeed, with the information now available to us, those conflicts cannot be resolved this evening, the time for which the vote was set under the unanimous consent agreement.

The situation that confronted us, therefore, that unless the Senate now agreed otherwise, we face the vote this evening on a nomination with serious and highly controversial and unresolved charges and denials having been made publicly, simply because the Senate had previously agreed to set a vote at this time. . . .

I believe the delay now approved is important to the integrity of the Senate, to the integrity of the confirmation process, to the integrity of the Supreme Court and, not least, to the integrity of those who find themselves deeply involved in this matter.

It is most unfortunate that we have been placed in this situation. But events which are unpredictable, unplanned and unfortunate can and frequently do intervene to cause a change in the plans of human beings. That has now occurred in this matter, in my judgment. . . .

MINORITY LEADER BOB DOLE, R-KAN.: Mr. President, I certainly—I don't quarrel with anything in the majority leader's statement—I think it's accurate, it's factual, it certainly indicates what's happened to date. I think there are some who would have rolled the dice at 6 p.m. There are some who felt—I'm talking about some on my side of the aisle that when the chips were down, there would be enough votes for confirmation this evening.

But none of those who were making those statements were the nominee. And so it seemed to me that it was a gamble that should not be taken.

In addition, there was a serious allegation, and, notwithstanding our best efforts through affidavits, phone logs and other things, to take care of that allegation, there are still some questions that remain.

But I would certainly hope that people would not misinterpret or misjudge what we've just agreed to. I've heard some of the comments—oh, this means the nomination is in trouble. Some have already predicted its demise, some are hopeful.

But I have enough faith in many of my colleagues, in this case on the other side of the aisle, that I've talked to personally the past several hours who are prepared to vote for Judge Thomas' confirmation but who told me they thought there should be a further investigation. And I'm not certain that I disagree with them. This is a very important vote.

And I have enough confidence in the judgment of the 16 to 18 senators who've indicated they may support Judge Thomas on the Democratic side that in my view, by agreeing to the extension— longer than we wanted— we've strengthened the chances of his nomination.

Over the years I've been a fairly good vote-counter, and I couldn't put together 50 votes at 6 o'clock. And, as I said earlier, the bottom line in our business is how many votes do you have. If you don't have the majority, don't have enough, you're out of business.

Now, I know the senator from Delaware, Sen. Biden, and the senator from South Carolina, Sen. Thurmond, and other members of the Judiciary Committee and Sen. Danforth have been talking about the scope, when the hearings will start, how many witnesses may be called, the order of witnesses and all those things that I think should be determined by the distinguished senator from South Carolina and the distinguished senator from Delaware rather than the leadership. This is a Judiciary Committee determination.

And someone asked the question: Well, what about next Tuesday at 6 o'clock? I think it's fair to say the leaders hope that that's it. And if the investigation goes as everybody believes it will go, it probably will be out.

And finally I would say that this is a test for Clarence Thomas. It's a test of his character. And I believe he's up to the test. He's indicated that, as much to Sen. Danforth. . . . But I would say to those, even those who are violently opposed to his nomination, that Clarence Thomas is a human being, too, and he has certain rights that should be protected, much as Miss Hill has certain rights that should be protected.

As Clarence Thomas indicated earlier today, he wanted to clear his name. It's important to him, it's important to his mother, it's important to his sister, it's important to his family, it's important to the people who came here to testify on his behalf, and it's important to us as an institution not to overreach and to make certain that he'll be treated fairly—because he's the one who's been accused, he's the one who's on trial in effect between now and next Tuesday. In my view he's been on trial by some for 100 days.

And so I just ask my colleagues, particularly those who have indicated they're favorably disposed to the nomination, to continue that open mind and that impression of Clarence Thomas, because as a Republican leader I have a couple of responsibilities, one to make certain there is a fair disposition of this matter. When I say fair disposition, I mean fair to everyone, including the nominee. Sometimes the nominee is forgotten. I happen to think he's a decent person.

And I guess from the standpoint of politics, to try to make certain that Clarence Thomas is confirmed—he's President Bush's nominee; we believe he deserves to be confirmed; we believe there should be bipartisan support. And I believe there will be bipartisan support. Without it, it's over. . . . And I'm willing to stand here and predict, unless there's some bombshell out there that I haven't heard about, that on next Tuesday Clarence Thomas will be confirmed by a good margin, by a bipartisan margin.

BIDEN: . . . I want to make two points. It was not until Monday, September the 23, after the hearing was over, on Friday the 20th, that we were able to get permission from Professor Hill even to have the FBI look at this matter. We have honored and continue to honor every request Professor Hill made to me as chairman of the committee. Understandably, this is an incredibly difficult thing for her to do. Understandably, for the previous 11 days or 12 days—11 days—the 12th of September, the first day being the first time Professor Hill's concerns were made known to the committee and made known to me.

From that point on, it's understandable how difficult it was for Professor Hill to reach the point where she agreed to allow me to have the FBI investigate and the nominee be made aware of the charges.

At that point what happened was that, having honored her request, we continue to honor her request, which was that no one, no one, in the United States Senate be made aware of her allegations beyond the members of the committee, unless we were able to guarantee that her name would never be mentioned and that no one would ever know, a guarantee that could not—and, I would add, should not—have been made.

So consequently the committee was unable to move on any further with the investigation beyond what the FBI had done. But that all changed on Monday when Professor Hill went public, authorizing, directly and indirectly, the committee and the Senate to look further into her allegations.

It is a difficult thing for Professor Hill and a difficult thing for the nominee, and a dilemma in balancing each of their rights. But the one point I want to make is the first balance that took place was the balance between the right of the institution to know and the right of Professor Hill to determine whether the institution should know.

I took her charges seriously, as we did on the committee, but we also took her request not to have anyone outside the committee be aware of this seriously. And one of the reasons why we've spent so much time in conference these last two days is because after she had gone public, we continued to take the matter seriously and continued to work toward undoing the unanimous consent request.

So, Mr. President, once we were given clearance—and now have been given clearance, as of Monday given clearance by Professor Hill—to proceed, the Senate is going to do just that. In consultation for many hours with the ranking Republican member, with the leadership on the Republican side as well as Sen. Danforth, who has a keen interest in all of this, we have agreed upon a procedure that would allow the committee to begin possibly as early as Friday, holding public hearings. I want to make it clear to everyone involved in this—this will be public, all of it will be public, number one.

Number one, people who say they have something to offer—and even those who don't say they have anything to offer but have spoken to this issue, on the alleged harassment—will be subpoenaed by the committee, because we are going to ventilate this subject, to give both Professor Hill the opportunity to make her case in full and give the nominee his opportunity to state his defense in full.

It is my hope and expectation that a thorough hearing, continued investigation and hearing, can be completed and that we will vote on Tuesday night at 6 o'clock.

Well, let me conclude by suggesting once again, the nominee has the right to be confronted by his accusers. So any accusation against any nominee before any committee which I chair that is not able to be made public to the nominee, will not be made known to the Senate unless the individual wishes to do it all by themselves. Then it's known to the nominee. This is not a star chamber.

But, on the other hand, it is incredibly difficult, assuming for the moment that Professor Hill is telling the truth, in cases relating to harassment, in cases relating to sexual violence, in cases where women have been victimized—I have spent too many hours, had too many hearings, spent too much of my professional career dealing with that subject as chairman of the Judiciary Committee not to know that it's incredibly difficult, incredibly difficult, for an alleged victim to come forward without worrying about whether they will be victimized by the system.

So it is explainable, in my view,—it is not dispositive—that Professor Hill was unwilling to let me use her name or make the allegations known even to the nominee in the beginning and to the Senate later.

But it is also not dispositive, absent the ability of the nominee to be able to come before the committee under oath and present his denial and any rebuttal. This is not going to be an easy hearing, this is not going to be easy to conduct, this is not going to be easy for the members of the committee nor Professor Hill nor the nominee. It is uncomfortable for everyone. But it must be done, because we cannot fail to take seriously such a charge, but we cannot fail to conclude that the charge is correct without the evidence being presented and the nominee having an opportunity to rebut. . . .

I expect that the members of the committee, Democrat and Republican alike, will operate in good faith in an attempt to give the nominee every opportunity to make his case and issue and put forward a rebuttal.

But we are entitled to know—the allegation is serious, harassment is serious—and it warrants us looking further into it. I thank the chair, thank my colleagues.

DISMISSAL OF IRAN-CONTRA CHARGES AGAINST OLIVER NORTH
September 16, 1991

The prosecution of former National Security Council aide Lt. Col. Oliver L. North came to an end September 16 after nearly five years of legal battle when a federal judge dismissed the two remaining verdicts against him for his role in the Iran-contra scandal. North was found guilty in May 1989 by a U.S. District Court jury in Washington, D.C., on three felony charges arising from thorough investigations into the secret sale of arms to Iran and the illegal diversion of proceeds from the sale to Nicaraguan guerrillas (contras).

North was convicted of deceiving Congress about the arms sales, illegally accepting a home security system as a gift, and altering and destroying government documents. The trial judge, Gerhard A. Gesell, fined North $150,000 and ordered him to perform 1,200 hours of community service in lieu of a jail sentence. (Sentencing of Oliver North, Historic Documents of 1989, p. 391)

But a three-member panel of the U.S. Court of Appeals for the District of Columbia struck down the third conviction and ordered the judge to conduct an inquiry to determine if the other two had been tainted by testimony North gave Congress during nationally televised hearings in July 1987. In compelling North to testify, Congress had granted him limited immunity—protection against prosecution for what he said at the hearings. Only evidence obtained elsewhere could be used to prosecute him.

The appeals court panel, splitting 2-1, ruled that Gesell had to conduct a witness-by-witness, line-by-line review of the trial testimony to determine if any of the sixty-seven witnesses had been influenced by what North told Congress. (Appeals Court Ruling on North Conviction, Historic

Documents of 1990, p. 491)

In making this determination, Gesell on September 14 questioned Robert McFarlane, a key government witness at the trial. As national security adviser in the mid-1980s, McFarlane was North's immediate superior. McFarlane surprised the prosecution by stating that his trial testimony had been colored by what North told Congress.

Lawrence E. Walsh, the independent counsel in charge of Iran-contra prosecutions, returned to court two days later and agreed to drop the case. The matter was formally disposed of in a matter of minutes by the two sets of opposing lawyers appearing before the judge.

North Asserts Total Exoneration

Ouside the courtroom North asserted that he had been "totally exonerated." President George Bush observed at a news conference that "the system of justice is working." In Congress, Senate Republican leader Bob Dole of Kansas said—as he had on previous occasions—that it was time for the Iran-contra prosecutions to cease.

In contrast, the New York Times *derided North's contention that he was exonerated. In an editorial, the newspaper commented: "It's as though Ernesto Miranda had claimed that the Supreme Court gave him a character reference when it threw out his famous confession to crimes because the police had not read him his rights." In congressional testimony, North had admitted instances of lawbreaking.*

North was not the highest-ranking official to be prosecuted by Walsh's legal team, but he was a central figure in the Iran-contra operations and his case had fully captured the public's attention. His appearance at televised congressional hearings transfixed the nation. A decorated Marine lieutenant colonel, North wore his uniform to the witness stand and defiantly asserted that his work had been solely in the nation's best interests. Soon afterward he was in demand as a speaker, commanding high fees.

In his book Under Fire: An American Story, *published in October 1991, North contended that "President Reagan knew everything" about arms-for-hostages dealings. Reagan had denied knowledge of what was happening. Various legal trials of Iran-contra participants had left unclear what role, if any, was played by the most senior officials in the Reagan administration, including Reagan and his vice president, George Bush.*

The prosecution reached into the White House offices of McFarlane and his successor as national security adviser, John M. Poindexter. McFarlane pleaded guilty in March 1988 to four misdemeanor charges and drew a $20,000 fine and two years' probation in lieu of prison. Poindexter, who took over North's supervision from McFarlane, was convicted in April 1990 on five counts of lying to, obstructing, and conspiring to obstruct Congress and sentenced to six months in prison.

Poindexter Conviction Overturned

However, on November 15 the same appeals court panel that set aside North's convictions dismissed Poindexter's outright. Like North,

Poindexter had testified before Congress under a grant of limited immunity. This time, though, the panel's 2-1 majority dropped the charges against Poindexter rather than having the trial court determine if the evidence was tainted. The dissenting appellate judge, Abner J. Mikva, protested that "this court changed the standards the special prosecutor had to meet [in the North case]; today, we refuse to let him try to meet them."

While losing the North and Poindexter cases, Walsh obtained a guilty plea July 9 from Alan D. Fiers, Jr., a former head of the Central Intelligence Agency's Central American Task Force, for withholding Iran-contra information from Congress. The prosecution later obtained federal grand jury indictments against Fiers's former CIA boss, Clair E. George. On November 9 Elliott Abrams, former assistant secretary of state for Latin America, who worked closely with North, pleaded guilty to withholding information from Congress. He drew two years' probation. (New Pleas and Charges in Iran-contra Cases, p. 429)

Other Iran-contra Prosecutions

Two other Iran-contra defendants, Richard V. Secord and Albert Hakim, each drew sentences of two years' probation plus fines upon entering guilty pleas in November 1989 to various charges. Secord, a retired air force major general, served as North's chief operative in the arms deal and contra resupply network; Hakim, a businessman, managed the network's finances. Thomas G. Clines, a former CIA agent and partner of Secord and Hakim, was convicted in September 1990 on four felony tax charges and sentenced to sixteen months in prison but appealed.

Still other defendants were Carl R. Channell and Richard R. Miller, both of whom drew two years' probation. Channel, a fundraiser, pleaded guilty in April 1987 to a tax fraud charge; Miller, head of a Washington public relations firm, pleaded guilty in May 1987 to conspiring to supply the contras with military equipment financed by tax-deductible contributions.

Following is a transcript of the hearing before Judge Gerhard A. Gesell in U.S. District Court for the District of Columbia, September 16, 1991, at which remaining charges against Oliver L. North were dismissed:

The Deputy Clerk: Criminal Number 88-80. United States of America versus Oliver L. North. Mr. Walsh, Mr. Bromwich, Mr. Rothfelt and Mr. Gillen for the government. Mr. Sullivan, Mr. Simon, Miss Seligman and Mr. Cline for the defendant.

The Court: Well, Mr. Walsh, I have your motion.

Mr. Walsh: Yes, Sir.

The Court: And I guess all that remains is to find out whether the defendant opposes it in any way.

Mr. Walsh: I'll give them an opportunity.

The Court: I take it, Mr. Sullivan, it's not opposed?

Mr. Sullivan: Unopposed, Your Honor.

The Court: I will sign it. And this terminates the case.

I will say to you, Judge Walsh, and Mr. Sullivan and all concerned, that the temptation on the court to comment about this experience is simply overwhelming but my common sense tells me the best thing to do is to say nothing. So I am not going to make any comment on this disposition one way or the other.

Mr. Walsh: Your Honor, I appreciate that and now that the case is over and we're no longer before you and I don't think I have any other matters before you I would simply like to congratulate Mr. Sullivan and Mr. Simon and their team on their exceptional advocacy and to thank Your Honor and your chambers for the many courtesies and to say that I had hoped that this would somehow produce an opportunity for a commentary because my feeling is that in the long record of this case there should be room for a paragraph as to Your Honor's exceptional devotion and the intuitiveness and the perception of which you led us through 102 pre-trial motions and brought this case to a conclusion in spite of the—its own complexity and also in spite of the great difficulties in dealing with classified information and indeed you opened our eyes to that conflict which is still going on, and at least on behalf of my office, and I speak for the government, I should like to thank you.

The Court: Well, you're very kind. I simply did what I felt my job required and I was assisted greatly by your office as well as by counsel for Colonel North.

These proceedings are adjourned.

Mr. Walsh: Thank you.

(Proceedings concluded at 9:35 A.M.)

CLIFFORD AND BCCI
BANKING SCANDAL
September 11, 1991

Vigorously denying any wrongdoing, Clark M. Clifford—sometimes referred to as a "superlawyer" and the ultimate Washington insider—defended his reputation September 11 before a House Banking Committee inquiry. The eighty-four-year-old Clifford and Robert Altman, his forty-four-year-old law and banking partner, were questioned about their involvement with the discredited Bank of Credit and Commerce International (BCCI).

Clifford appeared voluntarily to answer questions for the first time in public about his role as chairman of First American Bankshares, Inc., the Washington area's largest bank holding company. He had assumed the position nine years earlier, at the age of seventy-five.

Counsel to President Harry S. Truman, secretary of defense in the Johnson administration, and adviser to other Democratic presidents, Clifford had enjoyed a towering reputation and a thriving legal practice as head of a prestigious law firm. Now, in the twilight of his career, his activities, as well as Altman's, were being investigated by federal authorities and at least one grand jury. Asked if he regretted having become a banker, Clifford replied, "Maybe I should have stuck with the law."

Altman, who served for nine years as president of First American Bankshares, possessed none of the storied background of Clifford but attracted media attention mostly because of his wife, television actress Lynda Carter. For twenty years Altman had been associated with Clifford in the practice of law and in banking. According to press reports, both men had been forced out of their posts at First American in August 1991 by the Federal Reserve Board. However, no formal charges had been filed against either.

BCCI's Mystery Role

A central issue was whether Clifford and Altman knowingly misled federal regulators by repeatedly asserting that BCCI did not own or control the bank they headed. But the Federal Reserve Board disclosed in January 1991 that it believed BCCI held a secret controlling interest in First American Bankshares.

Arab-owned and Pakistani-run, BCCI had been chartered in Luxembourg and the Cayman Islands. Because of allegations of widespread money laundering and fraud, BCCI had been shut down in July 1991 by regulators in seven countries. In the United States, the closures were followed by federal and state indictments against several BCCI officials for fraud and racketeering. The Federal Reserve imposed a $200 million fine on the bank. Clifford and Altman forcefully contended to an openly skeptical committee that they, like the federal regulators, had been deceived.

Clifford's law firm, Clifford & Warnke, represented both BCCI and First American Bankshares. In the committee hearings, Altman and Clifford denied that they had been engaged in conflicts of interest. But, as an attorney for a group of Middle Eastern investors, in 1982 Clifford assured authorities that neither BCCI nor anyone else would possess a hidden interest in his bank. Nine years later, however, the Federal Reserve Board disclosed that it now believed the "investors" were front men for BCCI.

Profitable Stock Deal

Confidence in Clifford and Altman was shaken in May 1991 when details were disclosed by the Federal Reserve Board of a stock deal from which Clifford and Altman made a profit of at least $9.8 million in nineteen months, according to press reports. The Federal Reserve Board said the stock deal was arranged entirely by BCCI.

The two men bought the stock in First American Bankshares with a loan from BCCI. The shares became available after BCCI arranged for a First American stockholder to waive his right to buy them at a special insider's price. Nineteen months later, BCCI found a buyer willing to pay nearly three times as much for the stock, which was now owned by Clifford and Altman. The buyer was a money-lender from Beirut, Lebanon; his purchase of the stock was financed by a shadowy BCCI affiliate.

Questioning by members of the House Banking Committee concentrated on whether BCCI secretly owned and controlled First American Bankshares, whether the profits Clifford and Altman realized in the stock transaction were manipulated by BCCI, and whether as lawyers and bankers they engaged in conflicts of interest.

Several committee members, both Democrats and Republicans, found it incredulous that Clifford and Altman said they knew little of BCCI's operations. "Many of us find it difficult to believe that the chairman of the board and the president of a major Washington bank, especially men of your stature and reputation in the business world, didn't really know who was controlling your bank," said Rep. Carroll Hubbard, Jr., D-Ky. Similarly, Rep. Rose Mary Oakar, D-Ohio, told Clifford and Altman that it was "preposterous . . . that you did not know for the entire time BCCI owned First American."

Following are excerpts from the opening statement of Clark Clifford to the House Banking Committee, September 11, 1991, and from questioning that followed about the relationship of First American Bankshares to the Bank of Credit and Commerce International, as recorded by Reuter Transcript Reports:

Clark Clifford: Thank you, Mr. Chairman [Rep. Henry B. Gonzalez, D-Texas].

We appreciate the invitation that you and Mr. [Rep. Chambers P.] Wylie [R-Pa.] extended to us to appear before your committee. We come voluntarily. And we come in the hope that we may be able to be of some assistance to the committee as you meet your legislative responsibility.

We bring another side to this problem, and we present it because we believe it will be helpful to you to know the other side of this particular situation.

From the time that the Federal Reserve first announced in January that they were conducting an investigation, we have cooperated at every stage with our government. We appeared before the Fed for lengthy examination there before their counsel, took days.

We have appeared before a federal grand jury here in Washington. That took days on the part of each of us.

We appeared in New York before the staff of Mr. [U.S. Attorney Robert] Morgenthau. That also took days.

We have answered every question that has been asked us.

Now the reasons we have done that is because our consciences are clear. And we are here today because we voluntarily choose. Under the law we might have avoided. We chose not to avoid it.

We choose to come before you so we can tell you what has happened in this phase of the matter that could bring us into the case, and it's been mentioned before that we are experienced professional men. What could bring us into the case, persuade us of the legitimacy of the actions, and have us continue through the process.

For nine years we have operated First American Bank. I have been chairman of the board. I want to explain how that occurred so that you all will understand.

As I listened to each of you gentlemen, I understand your attitude. I have also read all of the pieces about BCCI. I understand all the charges that are made.

And yet, as far as we are concerned, we are not involved in that. We have not been guilty of not only any legal infraction, we have not been guilty of any misconduct. I'm not even conscious of being guilty of any impropriety upon our part.

Now, this comes as a surprise to many of you as I listen to you. But it is our hope that as we speak to you, that you will begin to understand not only our participation but how this operation from abroad could conduct itself in such a manner that it could escape the surveillance of the law.

Now, I recognize as I listen to you gentlemen, we have a formidable task in persuading many of you of our innocence in this. But I approach it willingly. I approach it with a desire to have this hearing.

Each of you, at some time in your career, has been attacked. And you've recognized the difficulty with how you respond to the attack. You don't own a newspaper through which you can speak, and neither do we. You don't have persons who will rise to your defense, and neither do we.

The whole atmosphere of the public, all of the proceedings that have taken place, all would be against us. And yet, we appear here so that you can hear our side. And I suggest to you that it is my deep conviction that when you have heard us, you will at least in some way have a different attitude. . . .

And let me say it is of such vital importance to me, because many of you are lawyers, and I've been a practicing lawyer for 63 years. And in all that time, there has never been a cloud placed against my name until now. And this gives me some opportunity to attempt to remove that cloud in addition to meeting the much more important responsibility of helping you men with your legislative responsibility. . . .

In December of 1977, a former client of ours, Bertram Lance, whom we had represented at the request of President Carter when he had a problem with the banking committee in the Senate, he called and said that he had a friend from abroad that he would like to bring in to meet me just on a social basis.

He brought in a man called Agha Hasan Abedi. I had never heard of him before. He was a man of quiet demeanor. He spoke intelligently. His English was perfect. He was Pakistani. He was a banker. He was a man of considerable charm. Nothing about him that was entrepreneurial or promoting in his conduct.

We had a visit together. It was a very pleasant visit, and came to nothing.

Then in the weeks that followed I learned that Mr. Abedi and Mr. Lance and others were interested in acquiring an interest in a rather obscure bank holding company in Washington named Financial General Bankshares.

After awhile four individuals had acquired each an interest of approximately 4 1/2 percent.

They were just under the 5 percent limitation. And when the information came to the attention [of] Financial General that these four individuals—they were Arabs—had acquired a total of 18 percent. That gave them deep concern that possibly this might be the beginning of a takeover move.

They go to the SEC [Securities Exchange Commission] with the information. First the Financial General called in very experienced counsel from New York and filed a suit against these four individuals, and they include BCCI, which was in the process of acquiring the stock, as they said, in behalf of the individuals. They included Mr. Abedi as one of the defendants also in the case.

Shortly thereafter, the SEC started an investigation to determine whether these four individuals might constitute a group. It began to appear to them that possibly it did constitute a group. . . .

Now, I might say that as the matter developed at that particular time, the question would naturally occur to you men, Now, here is BCCI; we have accepted them as a client; now how would we at that particular time in the light of all that we know now, why would we have accepted BCCI, now known as the Bank of Crimes and Criminals?

Well, I ask, if you will, to go back 13 years with me and see if you could open your mind to what might have existed 13 years ago. So in come now Mr. Abedi and some of his associates and they seek our assistance and they employ us because the litigation had been filed. Now, what do we find about this BCCI at that time?

In the first place, what impressed us was that the Bank of America owned 30 percent of the stock of BCCI and had from the beginning. The Bank of America at the time was not only the largest bank in the United States, but I think perhaps the most highly regarded. And the fact that the Bank of America had looked at BCCI and had decided to invest and gain a 30 percent in our minds placed an imprimatur of approval upon that operation.

A second interesting development that occurred that was there was at that particular time, there appeared an article in *The Economist* magazine in Great Britain, a highly accepted magazine, and let me read a sentence or two at that time. It says—it was devoted to the Bank of Credit and Commerce:

"The Bank of Credit and Commerce International, BCCI, is the fastest growing bank in London since the early 1970s. The man with all the answers is Agha Hasan Abedi, founder and president of the bank. He is highly regarded in the banking world. The Bank of England is prepared to vouch for him. He made his reputation building up the second largest bank in his home country Pakistan. When it was nationalized, he pulled out to start afresh, taking a lot of his top management with him.". . .

But I am attempting to give you some feel of what is the situation that existed at that time. This is what we learned.

The only one criticism in all our different contacts that we heard about BCCI was some banks looked with some concern upon the fact that they did not have one strong central regulator. That would be of great interest, of course, to this committee, because you're going to want to face up to that as you look at legislation.

But most of the banks in this country did business with them, but there were some who were concerned about that one particular item.

When these men came in, and we got to know them, I came not only to believe what they were saying, but I respected them. They carried through on commitments to us. When they told us something and we looked into it, it proved to be true. And so they made a very favorable impression on us.

And what they told us was that they were engaged in acquiring stock in this company, Financial General Bankshares, because they believed that it had a great future.

Now, one important individual through the story is a Saudi Arabian named Sheikh Kamal Adham. He was a very important businessman. He was related by marriage to the king of Saudi Arabia. He is still today one of the leading businessmen in Saudi Arabia. And he was part of the group that we became acquainted with during this particular time.

And they said that we wished to acquire this stock. It first came to the attention of these men when a letter was written by a local official in the Saudi Arabian embassy to Kamal Adham saying he'd been reading in the paper about this bank holding company named Financial General that was splitting into cliques and groups and warring tribal constituents among shareholders.

And he'd looked into it, this man had, and thought Kamal Adham should look into it. Apparently the Saudi Arabian embassy here served to a certain extent as financial adviser to prominent men back in Saudi Arabia.

Kamal Adham then turns to Abedi. Abedi's head of the BCCI bank. Abedi was the investment adviser to a substantial number of very prominent and wealthy Arabs. That was one of his main functions. He had gotten his original financing to start his bank from Arabs, and they had been exceedingly generous in that regard.

So that we were then informed by Kamal Adham and by Mr. Abedi, and occasionally as we met others of the investors, that they had become interested in this stock. The word after Abedi had investigated it, he concluded it would be an excellent buy; that they had a splendid charter. And he was right in that, because they were the only bank holding company east of the Mississippi that was granted the right to operate in more than one state. . . .

And that appealed to these foreign investors. So we understood what the situation was, and complied with their wish that we represent them.

Now, as the matter developed, the question came about who were these different investors. We'd already checked carefully into BCCI and found that they constituted a respectable, creditable operation.

Now we wanted to find out more about the investors, and we did find out quite a lot about them. When the time came, and we had ultimately closed a deal with Financial General and had ended the litigation and had agreed to purchase all the stock for cash, we then went before the Federal Reserve for a hearing. We had been before all the state also.

Discussing the matter with the Fed, we learned a good deal about the investors. We got information of our own and passed it on to the Fed.

Let me refer to a kind of compendium of the information that we obtained about them, because not only was it important to us that our bank client, BCCI, be a respectable client, but it was important to us that these investors be respectable people. The whole arrangement was a matter of importance to us. . . .

Finally the day came, I knew it—I sensed it was coming sometime—in London when Abedi and Kamal Adham said, Mr. Clifford, we want you to come in and take over the operation of First American Bankshares, and the eight banks that they own. We've come to know you. We know that you can go out and get the best banking talent. But we want somebody to head it up. We would like you to be chairman of the board.

Now, this is very personal. I was 75 years old at the time. I had been practicing law for over 50 years. The routine practice had been interesting to me, but there was nothing particularly exciting going on at the time, and this offer was a challenge to me.

I was well, I was strong, I was vigorous. I had friends who'd retired and the story I got from them was a pretty sad one. I had a former head of General Electric tell me one time, I saw him in Florida, I said, how do you like being retired, and he shook his head sadly, and he said, you know there's one thing, you wouldn't realize it, but he says, being retired ruins your weekends.

Well, it was a curious weekend. Every day is kind of a weekend, and when you've worked all your life and suddenly to retire, there isn't anything. I've worked all my life; that's what my life's been, just work. And it's kept me alive, and kept me able, and I hope able, and kept me vigorous.

I didn't want to retire. I didn't want to just sit on the porch and rock and wait to die. And I said, here's a challenge. This is a real test. I wonder if I could do this. I wonder if I could take this obscure company and build it into something important and big and impressive. . . .

What I wanted to do is buy stock in my own company. It's so customary in this country for top officials to own stock in their own company. They're given stock options. If you want to attract a top officer, you wouldn't think of coming unless he was going to participate in the stock.

So this was my idea. I got the impression from reading stories that they thought I was acquiring stock in some other company. It was my own company, the one that I'd put so much of myself into to build. And I said, when the time came, I'd like to acquire some stock.

I thought they might say, well, we'll get the shareholders to contribute stock to you. But nobody suggested that. Or we might have some kind of a stock dividend plan; nobody suggested that.

But what they did come up with was an idea that was appealing. They said, when the time comes for us to offer new stock rights to our shareholders, if there is any rights left over that are not subscribed over, you can come in, Mr. Clifford and Mr. Altman, and acquire stock at the same price as the shareholders.

I said, all right, that sounds right. The bylaws of CCAH—that's the top holding company of First American—provided for that very arrangement.

So in 1986, when we had a very large stock offering of $150 million. It was not fully subscribed, so that gave me the chance to come in and acquire $9 million worth of the stock, and Mr. Altman half. I won't keep referring to him, because he got half of what I did at the time.

We bought it at the same price as the other shareholders. We bought it under the bylaws of the company. We got the consent of the other directors of the CCAH.

Just to be sure, we got it in writing, so it would be there in the record. So we acquired that first holding of stock....

Our New York counsel advised us that under the circumstances, particularly at my age, because this was 1986, and I was 80 then, they said, Mr. Clifford, let's see if we can't make a loan with a non-recourse note. It doesn't make any sense for you at your age to enter into a situation where you acquire a rather substantial debt, and then it's left to your estate. Your expectancy is very problematical, and I understood that.

So they tried to work all that out with the French people, and they had some ideas that weren't appealing at all. They wanted a big payment on their loan at the very beginning, which didn't appeal to us.

When our New York firm was unable to work out the firm with BAII I then spoke to Mr. Abedi and said, we would like to borrow the money to pay for the stock that you know that Mr. Altman and I are acquiring, and we're acquiring it at book. And it seems to me that the value is there. And I think you'd be totally protected if you were to lend us the money based on the value of the stock.

He said, that would not bother me at all. I have no qualms about it. I know the stock. I know the number of inquiries that I get from others, from other shareholders. Is there any stock for sale? He says, I have no trouble with that. I'd be glad to make that kind of loan.

So we borrowed the money at that time to pay for the stock. I borrowed mine; Altman borrowed his. And we gave the notes which were executed by the New York firm and by their own counsel over in London.

Then one year later, we made another offering, a smaller offering, and we wished to participate then as shareholders, because we had certain rights and we had become shareholders.

And on that second loan I borrowed $2 million and Altman borrowed $1 million, again from BCCI, under the same circumstances.

All during this time, First American was getting stronger and stronger and more valuable. So in 1988, the market in bank stocks was strong, strong in this country, strong worldwide, and we said at that time we think that with the very substantial interest amounts we're carrying, because before we made the second loan we had to pay off out of our funds close to a million dollars in interest to get the second loan.

And by that time Abedi had become ill. We talked to the number two man, Mr. Naqvi. He said—fact is, I wrote him a letter in February of 1988—and said, we would like to sell something in the neighborhood of half our stock.

In conversations that I'd had with Naqvi after that, he said, what do you expect to get for it? I said, we would like to get for our stock what is the going rate now in this country, because there's a lot of interest in bank stocks, and they're selling for 2 1/4 times book, 2 1/2 times book, even some banks were selling for three times book at the time.

So I said, if we could get 2 1/2 times book, we would be pleased with it.

About a month went by, and he advised us that he has found a purchaser, and the purchaser would pay the price that they'd agreed on, 2.6 times book. That was perfectly satisfactory.

We received the price of $6,800 per share for the stock. Now, sometime in that same period prior to that, there had been a very substantial purchase of stock . . . and they had paid $6,100 per share for the stock.

So what we were getting for ours was in that general neighborhood. The book had increased since they had brought theirs. So it was in the general neighborhood of that particular transaction.

So the deal was closed. The purchase price was funded to us. We paid off all the loans that we had made to BCCI. We paid off all their interest. BCCI charged me a commission of a million and a half for making the sale, and they charged Mr. Altman $750,000 for making the sale.

And that was the conclusion of that, and we still own the balance of the stock. I still own about 2,000 shares, and he still owns around 1,000 shares, something of that kind.

But we continued to have confidence in First American, so in '89 we subscribed again as shareholders, because we feel that the value is there.

Now, in an interesting way, and again, there is a certain irony here, all this took place after all these years of the work that we put in to First American. We did not go into it on a basis of it being a money-making opportunity. That was not it. I've explained to you why I really went into it as a test of myself.

We waited four years before getting into a stock situation.

Now, the value that we had brought to the investors was exceedingly substantial. They put in about $200 million into the company at the beginning, then in various stock offerings they'd put in another $300 million, so they put in something around $500 million; it may have exceeded that some.

We felt that at the time that we were in the process of making the sale of our stock, that the value of First American had grown from the half a billion that they'd put into it to over a billion dollars in value. . . .

At no time did BCCI exert any control whatsoever over First American. At no time did they ever make an effort to do it. Because Abedi and Kamal Adham, who still continued in charge of the proceeding, were the ones who made the agreement with me that I was to have total responsibility and total authority.

So at no time has any decision been made for First American by BCCI.

You have my word for it. I give you my word under oath. At no time did we turn to them, for a decision. We were always willing to hear anybody, if anyone—if Abedi had a suggestion, if Kamal Adham had a suggestion, if any shareholder had a suggestion, we were always glad to hear from them. . . .

I would not under any circumstances jeopardize the reputation that I've built up with such care during 63 years of the law practice to go into any matter and jeopardize that reputation. I did not need any earnings from it. I've had a successful law practice all these years. I've invested conservatively. My wife is here. I've taken care of her and the three daughters comfortably. They will never have to worry.

I wasn't in this to try and make some money. Later on, when we built it up, I saw no reason why these wealthy investors should not compensate us for what we had done in building up the value of their company, but that wasn't the reason that I went into it. I went into it to test myself.

What we learned, I believe, as we watched all this, and what the committee will have to go into perhaps is, in BCCI there were really two banks. There was this outside facade thing. That's the one we dealt with. In all these years, we didn't encounter a single suspicious circumstance. And I think the reason is because they had that second inside bank, and there's the one that was engaged in what we've read about so much in the paper all during that particular time.

Were we deceived? Apparently we were deceived. I don't know that it's any comfort, but the Bank of England was deceived. Year after year the Bank of England had the right to go in any time.

They conducted their examinations at routine intervals, and the Bank of England didn't act until July 5, 1991.

They had a former prime minister on their payroll, Lord Callahan, for years. He was totally and completely nonplussed when the story broke.

They had the same auditor, Price Waterhouse, all those years.

Year after year after year Price Waterhouse gives them a certificate at the end of the year, and finds nothing wrong with the operations of BCCI. Recently I saw where Price Waterhouse had given them a report covering the years 1987, 1988, 1989, and they attached that British expression, they say, we find all accounts true and correct. That was that.

So they were deceived. Up and down the line, it's been embarrassing to former President Jimmy Carter. He got to know Mr. Abedi well. They travelled together a good deal, particularly in Africa. They had a joint interest in trying to raise the level of society, particularly the health of the underprivileged there at that particular time. . . .

My judgment is questionable. I guess I should have learned it some way. I've been in this business a long time; it's been a very active life; you learn a good deal from government. I guess I should have some way sensed it. I did not.

Gonzalez: . . . Our purpose is not to try to impeach a witness; we're not a prosecutorial body; we're not a judicial body. I think, Mr. Clifford, you stated fairly well there at the end what the main underlying basic objectives of a legislative committee such as this one are and should be. . . .

However, reluctantly as some of us have been, and anguished to see prominent people of your status involved, it does add to the rather sad and very tragic history that we have been seeing develop on this level for the last five-six years.

I think if there's any conclusion I were to draw, it'd be, Mr. Clifford, that in your zeal to accept the challenge, and then depart from the traditional profession, you might have forgotten that old law school saying.

That the law is a jealous mistress. But so is financing; so is banking. So that in attempting to satisfy that challenge, which I can understand, and particularly as you relate it, at what point in your life, I can see where judgments could be clouded. . . .

Altman: It is true that in connection with our involvement here, we did at times wear different hats.

I suppose that is not uncommon given complicated financial transactions, but we did, we were counsel to the company. We also served in management positions, and what that suggests is that there is a need to be particularly sensitive to any conflicts that may arise.

I might say that I am unaware of any conflicts that did arise. At all times we acted in the best interests of 1st American, to protect the interests of that bank, and to ensure that it remained a sound institution.

You made a reference in that regard to our obtaining loans. The loans we obtained to purchase the stock of course were not loans that we obtained from 1st American. Those loans were financed by BCCI and of course were repaid to BCCI.

In so far as our sensitivity to these issues, I think I addressed in my opening statement this morning, we did not shut our eyes or become insensitive to the kinds of issues that are now being explored in these hearings.

When we received indications, even though we thought that they were probably unfounded, we investigated them and we pursued them rather vigorously. So I don't think that it would be fair or accurate to suggest that we closed our eyes to these matters.

We looked into them, we talked to our shareholders, we talked to the senior management of BCCI. We talked to the counsel representing Mr. Awan as to his comments. We talked to auditors. At not [sic] time did we get any confirmation of these allegations.

Everyone we talked to indicated to us that the allegations were untrue, and of course we didn't have access to the books and records of the company of, that is, of BCCI. . . .

Gonzalez: Let me put it this way: why should it be unfair to the American public to conclude or believe, given the many direct and indirect relationships with BCCI and their stockholders, that your objectivity, of both of you, was somewhat affected, and that good judgment was thereby clouded in doing business with BCCI and their stockholders? . . . [T]o any objective reader or member of the general American public, would you not believe that there would tend to be a skepticism as to how prudent you were in exercising your judgment, both as a member of the board of trustees of a bank, as well as the legal counsel for that bank in your relationship with this international bank.

Clifford: I have not been conscious of any conflict of interest, Mr.

Chairman. We served in a capacity. Let's take first as chairman of the board. I started right in at the very beginning, back in May, 1982, with the company, and learned the position, learned all of the facts regarding the banks, and a very important part of me went into that particular endeavor.

Now, when I took that position, we had already been involved for some four years in representing the parties that were involved in it. So we had an excellent background of knowledge. We had all of the facts in it.

So, for instance, when the old Financial General became First American, and we became counsel, we had a background that really no other lawyers would have had, and that background was very useful to us. And we started in at once, and over nine years the firm really became the legal department for First American.

And we grew up with it, as a small company, as it got larger. So we know that well.

Now, it was not much of a transition from serving in that capacity to moving over and becoming chairman. In fact, it might well be argued that from the knowledge that I gained in our legal work for the company that that was of advantage and some help to me in serving as chairman.

I was very close to the board in this instance. We brought in men that I had known and worked with for many years, and these men were men of good judgment and value. . . .

Wylie: Mr. Clifford, I must follow up on what the chairman said about skepticism, and I wouldn't say anything behind your back that I wouldn't say to you personally. But a reporter asked here this morning what I thought about your testimony, and I said that I thought you did extremely well, your presentation was most impressive, sir—and I mean that. I said for me, though it did not pass the so called straight face test.

To say you represented all the persons involved in the acquisition of First American Bank by BCCI, collected millions of dollars in fees, made money on business transactions, and did not know what the boss was doing is a little bit hard for me to believe.

And I'm sorry. I think that you knew or should have known of the goings-on between BCCI and First American. . . .

Rep. Frank Annunzio, D-Ill.: BCCI had a very close association with the First American Corporation, one of the First American holding companies. It is my understanding that BCCI had accounts at First American New York.

Mr. Altman, as president of First American Corporation, did you examine those accounts in relation to the BCCI money laundering indictments and convictions? Did you order a review of the operations of those accounts? Did you check whether any banks owned by First American Corporation had BCCI accounts?

Altman: The answer to your question, and I'm happy to address it and would like to expand on it—the short answer to your question is yes, we absolutely did. . . .

Rep. Carroll Hubbard, Jr., D-Ky.: Many of us find it difficult to believe that the chairman of the board and the president of a major

Washington bank, especially men of your stature and reputation in the business world, didn't really know who was controlling your bank.

Mr. Altman, there are reports that you regularly submitted financial information to BCCI, so that the bank could evaluate First American's condition. Is that accurate?

Altman: It is.

Rep. Hubbard: Why did you do that?

Altman: Mr. Hubbard, when we went through the regulatory proceedings, it was explained to all parties that BCCI had a continuing role. BCCI's continuing role was, as we have described, they were a communications link for us to communicate with the shareholders ... communicating with people scattered in the Middle East.

And secondly, they were the investment adviser. There were other relationships as well that were disclosed.

In our Federal Reserve application it specifically says that it's contemplated that BCCI is going to continue to provide these services.

Hubbard: Why would they provide these services?

Robert Altman: In this case, as—

Hubbard: As a good friend, or did they have control?

Altman: I'm sorry?

Hubbard: Was it a friendship relationship, or was it control of First American that caused them to advise you periodically?

Altman: There was no control relationship, sir. No, that is not what led to our dealings with BCCI. As I say, we disclosed in our written application and in oral discussions that there was going to be a continuing relationship.

The investors here were people of very substantial means.

Several of them were rulers, or members of ruling families, who were making an investment. They were passive. It seemed quite normal for us that they would have someone who would follow the progress of that investment.

And BCCI was expressly designated to have that function. In the tender offer document, which was distributed to the world when the company was bought, it states expressly in that document about this role of BCCI. So everybody knew that BCCI had this role.

Now, in that regard, for us to provide financial reports on the health and progress of First American we always understood would be consistent with that understanding. . . .

Hubbard: BCCI approved tens of millions of dollars in loans to both of you, Mr. Altman and Mr. Clifford? The proceeds of these loans were used to buy stock in First American's holding company. Are these correct? Did BCCI approve loans to both of you, just yes or no?

Clifford: We discussed that this morning, if I remember correctly. There were two instances, one in '86, and one in '87, in which Mr. Altman and I each made a loan from BCCI to buy First American stock.

Hubbard: Would this not represent a conflict of interest?

Clifford: It did not—I do not know what conflict of interest?

Hubbard: Mr. Altman, would you answer that?

Altman: I would agree. I see no conflict of interest.

Rep. Bill McCollum, R-Fla.: Mr. Clifford, throughout your testimony and Mr. Altman's, you have given us all an indication that you were innocent of knowledge of any reason to be suspicious of the investors in First American and CCAH, that they were all outstanding individuals, their reputation was impeccable. . . . I am concerned . . . why a reasonable, well-versed person like yourself would not be suspicious of some of these folks, when I consider the fact that you've been secretary of defense, and you've had all these positions of knowledge in world affairs, I'm sure you must have known that Sheikh Adham, who was the principal organizer of these investors, as I understand it, and the main person, the first person on the list of those accused by the Federal Reserve of having been a nominee of BCCI and having had a cozy relationship, and having actually been a proxy for BCCI in the acquisition of First American, I'm sure you must have known that Sheikh Adham was implicated very strongly back in the '70s in the scandal involving Boeing, and was accused at that time of receiving bribes of substantial amounts in the airplane scandal of that era, which was really your era.

Were you not aware that Sheikh Adham was a suspicious character from that period, and didn't that concern you at all in all of the dealings that you have had with him, particularly with regard to this matter of the acquisition of First American?

Clifford: I had no prior information about Kamal Adham. Some time later I learned that for some period of time he had been head of Saudi Arabian intelligence, and I learned from others that in that regard, our intelligence operations had a very high opinion of him. They felt he cooperated exceedingly well with the United States.

So what I heard about Kamal Adham was commendatory rather than critical.

Rep. Rosemary Oakar, D-Ohio: I find it almost preposterous to believe, and I want to believe you, I really do, for many reasons, but I find it almost preposterous to believe that given your close relationship . . . with BCCI . . . that you did [not] know that for the entire time BCCI owned First American. . . . How is it that you could be so closely related to BCCI as attorney, as individuals getting astounding lines of credit and loans and God knows what, and how it is that you didn't know that they were essentially running First American.

That to me is what you have not quite convinced me of. And I'm not a jury or anything, but Mr. Chairman if they could respond to that, I'd really appreciate it.

Clifford: I think you've touched on a matter that is important for me to comment on.

There are two types of control in this banking operation. Mr. Taylor, the Fed, commented on it some time ago. He said one type of control is control of stock. Another type of control is control of the management of a company.

There's a great distinction between the two. Now we had no way of knowing if you please that BCCI had secretly acquired stock in First American. I don't know of anybody else who knew about it.

None of the regulators knew about it. They didn't acquire it out in the open market. They acquired it secretly, apparently, if we can believe what some of the reports say. . . .

Now as far as their controling the operations of First American, which is really the important factor, I know that they did not control First American. From the day we took it over in May, 1982, they had no control whatsoever of First American. We made literally hundreds of decisions during the nine years that we controlled First American. At no time did they make any one of those decisions. . . .

Oakar: And they had no influence on your decisions?

Clifford: We would discuss matters with them from time to time, but we ended up using our judgment. We might get their opinion on something, particularly if it pertained to a foreign field.

When the time came, after we consulted with them and others, and a decision was made, the board of directors and I made it, and I so swear. . . .

Rep. Bruce F. Vento, D-Minn.: So you knew what their views were, what would please them, what their concerns were, and you attempted to try and respond to that, thinking that you were responding to the shareholders. Is that correct?

Clifford: See, the shareholders turned the responsibility of monitoring this investment over to Mr. Abedi and Kamal Adham.

And we understood that, so we reported to them, rather than going around to report to 14 other individual shareholders scattered all through the Persian Gulf. . . .

Rep. Charles E. Schumer, D-N.Y.: I guess the first thing I'd say, particularly directed to you, Mr. Clifford is, this is the first time we've met, and I can now see why you were so persuasive to presidents and financial moguls and everybody else. Because your presentation was made with intelligence and elegance and was to the point.

And after hearing your presentation I guess I could say to you that my heart wants to believe you, my head says no. There is just too much, there is just too great a nexus between BCCI and First American to believe that, I mean you want to call it one type of control versus another type of control to believe that the two weren't inextricably linked, that anyone who walked around with their eyes open would know it. Anyone who wanted to see it would see it.

The thing I find puzzling about your presentation here is it seems to me backwards. Your strong suit is not that you didn't know that BCCI controlled this institution. Your strong suit is whoever controlled it, that First American didn't do anything at least that's been able to be found by anybody, anything wrong.

And I'm sort of puzzled by why you are hanging your hat on something that seems so implausible. And that is that BCCI and First American were so—were separate institutions protected by you, even though you had loans to BCCI, your firm represented BCCI. When the proxies came in, you mentioned the proxies came into you, they came through BCCI. Everywhere you look you can't separate the two. . . .

Clifford: Mr. Chairman I've read with great interest the report that you got out. I found it exceedingly valuable. You used a word that intrigued me. You're "mystified" by this. Let me suggest to you—I am mystified by the actions of BCCI.

What did BCCI have in mind? Why did they accumulate the stock that they did in secret, and possibly illegally? What were they going to do with it? I don't know. I am mystified by that. Because here they accumulate stock in their vault, and the concern is, that the first time anybody learns about it, they're in the deepest trouble they've ever been in. I don't understand what they were up to. They started something. They never finished the closure of it. . . .

ACCESS GRANTED TO DEAD SEA SCROLLS

September 22, 1991

A brief announcement September 22 from the Huntington Library in San Marino, California, created a furor among scholars engaged in a bitter dispute over access to the Dead Sea Scrolls. The big research library said in a press release that it possessed photographic copies of the actual scrolls in Jerusalem, and would permit all qualified scholars to study them.

Access to these ancient writings, which include some of the oldest known biblical texts, has been tightly controlled by a small group of eminent scriptural researchers. After nearly four decades of translating and publishing these documents, which cast new light on the formative period of Christianity and modern Judaism, the job was only about half-done. Several outsiders were irritated at the slow pace at which the material was being published.

The scrolls consist mostly of texts from the Hebrew Bible and manuals of worship and discipline used by a community of ascetic Jews identified with the Essene sect of Judaism, who lived at Qumran, a remote site west of the Dead Sea. The community became extinct in the first century. Its members had placed their sacred scrolls in nearby caves, apparently for safekeeping. Some 800 of these rolled-up documents—many of them in fragments—were discovered between 1947 and 1956 by nomadic Bedouins in what was then Jordan.

Jordanian authorities moved the scrolls to the Palestine Archaeological Museum in East Jerusalem, and in 1953 vested access to an appointed editing team of scholars headed by Roland de Vaux, a French Catholic priest of the Ećole Biblique. After Israel seized East Jerusalem during the Six Day War of 1967, thereby acquiring the scrolls, it retained the same editing team. Only years later did it have any Jewish members. As the original members died or retired, their work tended to be passed to favored assistants.

The Huntington Library's announcement touched off a heated debate in academia over questions of access to research material, ownership of "intellectual property," and scholarly ethics. Eugene Ulrich, professor of Hebrew scriptures at the University of Notre Dame and a general editor of the scrolls, was quoted in the Washington Post as saying: "I understand all the frustrations, and most are absolutely fair. But many of us have devoted much of our lives to staring at little scraps of ancient Hebrew. Would it be fair now for others to rush in and publish some of the most interesting work, leaving us again with scraps?"

Among those applauding the library's decision was Lawrence H. Schiffman, professor of Hebrew and Judaic Studies at New York University. He said most scholars would regard those who make such material available as "Robin Hoods stealing from the academically privileged to give to those hungry for the knowledge secreted in these texts."

The Israel Antiquities Authority, which maintains the scrolls at the Rockefeller Museum in Jerusalem, initially threatened to take legal action against the library but instead invited the main participants in the controversy to a conference in Jerusalem to negotiate a compromise agreement.

In the meantime, Professor Emanuel Tov of Hebrew University in Jerusalem, one of the chief editors of the scrolls, told a meeting of the Society for Biblical Literature in Kansas City on November 26 that the Israel Antiquities Authority had removed the last restrictions on scholarly study of the scrolls.

The Huntington Library's photographs of the Dead Sea Scrolls were made in 1980 for the Ancient Biblical Manuscript Center in Claremont, California, on behalf of its president and founder, the late Elizabeth Hay Bechtel. After a dispute with officials at the center, she gave a duplicate set of photographic copies—about 3,000 negatives on spools of microfilm—to the library. They became its property upon her death in 1987. Other sets were held by Hebrew Union College in Cincinnati, and by the Center for Postgraduate Hebrew Studies at Oxford University.

Two California scholars, Drs. Robert H. Eisenman at California State University and James M. Robinson of Claremont Graduate School, said they had been given photographic copies of the scrolls, which would be published by the Biblical Archaeology Society in a two-volume book. Even before the Huntington Library acted, two scholars at Hebrew Union College said that, with the aid of a computer and certain available material, they were making a reproduction of the scrolls for publication.

*Following is the press release from the Huntington Library
at San Marino, California, September 22, 1991, announcing
that its photographic copies of the Dead Sea Scrolls would
become available for study by all qualified scholars:*

The Huntington Library in San Marino, California, which has been the repository for the last 10 years of some 3,000 master photographic negatives of all the Dead Sea Scrolls, will permit access to them without restriction to qualified scholars throughout the world, it was announced today by Library Director William A. Moffett.

"This action should bring an unprecedented openness into Scrolls research by making possible a new era of cooperation on the part of biblical scholars specializing in this field," Moffett predicted. Heretofore, access to the Scrolls has been limited to a small group of scholars responsible for translating and publishing the documents. Other scholars are concerned that much of the material is still not available.

The Dead Sea Scrolls, believed written between 200 BC and AD 68, were discovered in 1947 in caves in what is now the Israeli-occupied West Bank. The scrolls provide information on the development of Judaism and Christianity and are a link between the teachings of Jesus and an ascetic Jewish cult called the Essenes.

The Huntington's collection consists of some 3,000 photographs taken of original fragments of the Dead Sea Scrolls. It also includes duplicates made of the photographic archives at the Rockefeller Museum and the Shrine of the Book in Jerusalem, including photographs taken in the early years after the initial Scroll discoveries and before the fading and deterioration that has subsequently affected some of the fragments. The collection is believed to include all of the so-called Dead Sea Scrolls in official repositories, including both unpublished and published manuscripts.

The collection is one of the finest and most extensive anywhere, according to Moffett. The photographs were made following the highest archival and technical standards in a series of trips to Israel beginning in 1980 by Robert Schlosser, the Huntington's chief photographer and a widely respected practitioner of the art of documentary photography. Schlosser was contracted to do the work as a freelancer by the late philanthropist Elizabeth Hay Bechtel who in 1980 was president and founder of the Ancient Biblical Manuscript Center in Claremont, California.

The Huntington Library, founded in 1919 by railroad magnate Henry E. Huntington, is one of the world's foremost research libraries. It has extensive collections of rare books, photographs, and manuscripts that draw more than 1,800 research scholars from all over the world each year. The Library is one branch of a three-part institution that includes world-renowned art collections and botanical gardens.

Academics unable to come to San Marino can request the Scrolls microfilm through interlibrary loan.

FINAL AGREEMENT ON
ALASKAN OIL SPILL DAMAGES
September 30, 1991

A settlement of federal and state lawsuits against the Exxon Corpora-
tion over the 1989 Alaskan oil spill was submitted to the U.S. District
Court in Anchorage on September 30 and approved eight days later by
Judge J. Russel Holland. The before-trial agreement fixed Exxon's
liability to the United States and state of Alaska at about $1 billion.
Although the settlement ended government claims in regard to the
company's responsibility for the biggest oil spill ever to occur in Ameri-
can waters, Exxon still faced some 250 private claims alleging oil-related
damages to property and fishing. (Congressional Hearing on Alaskan Oil
Spill, Historic Documents of 1989, p. 225)

The Exxon tanker Valdez *ran aground on Bligh Reef in Prince William*
Sound during the night of March 23-24, 1989, spilling 11 million gallons
of crude oil from the ship's ruptured cargo tanks. The oil fouled waters
critical to an extensive range of marine and plant life, and ultimately
coated more than 1,200 miles of shoreline, according to a comprehensive
report issued in March 1991 by the National Oceanic and Atmospheric
Administration in Washington, D.C.

Under terms of the settlement, Exxon agreed to pay $900 million in
civil damages and possibly an additional $100 million if more damages
were detected. The payments would be spread over a ten-year period and
made to a trust fund to be administered by three state and three federal
officials. Felony charges against the president of Exxon (Lawrence G.
Rawl) and the president of its subsidiary Exxon Shipping Company
(Augustus Elmer) were dropped when the two executives pleaded guilty
to misdemeanor charges of violating environmental laws. The two compa-

nies agreed to pay fines and restitution payments totaling $125 million within thirty days.

An earlier agreement had been rejected the previous spring by both Judge Holland and the state legislature. It had been personally negotiated by Gov. Walter J. Hickel and called for $100 million in criminal penalties. Holland said the amount was too low; the lawmakers were persuaded by private plaintiffs that the agreement was detrimental to their lawsuits.

The new agreement did not require the legislature's approval. Hickel, who signed the document on behalf of the state, said it overcame the objections of the plaintiffs by allowing them access to resource-damage data gathered by government scientists—which the earlier agreement had denied them.

"Over the past two-and-a-half years the Exxon Valdez spill has divided Alaskans," the governor said on October 8. "The settlement is a good one, and I appreciate Judge Holland's decision to accept it and let it go forward.... I believe the whole ... episode sends a clear signal to industry that care of the environment is definitely a cost of doing business."

Several environmental organizations called the settlement too lenient on Exxon. Justice Department officials disagreed. Charles De Monaco, assistant chief of the department's environmental crimes section, said the new agreement brought Exxon's total cleanup costs to $3.5 billion. "There is no question that Exxon has paid dearly for this oil spill," he said.

James Neal, an Exxon attorney, noted that his company had engaged in a cleanup effort since shortly after the spill and contended that it was "a good corporate citizen." He blamed the disaster on the tanker's captain, Joseph L. Hazelwood, who had abandoned the ship's bridge in violation of company policy as the vessel navigated a treacherous passage en route to open sea. In March 1990, a state court jury found Hazelwood guilty of a single charge of negligence—a misdemeanor—and acquitted him on three other charges, including one of operating a ship while intoxicated.

> *Following are excerpts from the agreement and consent decree submitted September 30, 1991, to the U.S. District Court in Anchorage, Alaska, and later approved, in which the United States and the state of Alaska settled their lawsuits against the Exxon Corporation over the 1989 Alaskan oil spill:*

AGREEMENT AND CONSENT DECREE

This Agreement and Consent Decree (the "Agreement") is made and entered into by the United States of America and the State of Alaska

("State") (collectively referred to as the "Governments"), Exxon Corporation and Exxon Shipping Company ("Exxon Shipping") (collectively
referred to, together with the T/V EXXON VALDEZ, as "Exxon") and
Exxon Pipeline Company ("Exxon Pipeline")....

[1-6 omitted]

Effect of Entry of Decree by Court

7. Upon approval and entry of this Agreement by the District Court, this
Agreement and Consent Decree shall constitute a final judgment between
the Governments [of the United States and Alaska] and Exxon and Exxon
Pipeline in accordance with its terms.

Payment Terms

8. Exxon shall pay to the Governments pursuant to this Agreement a
total of $900 million....

[9 omitted]

10. As agreed to between the Governments, without any consultation
with or participation by Exxon or Exxon Pipeline, the amounts paid under
Paragraphs 8 or 9 shall be applied by the Governments solely for the
following purposes: (1) to reimburse the United States and the Senate for
response and clean-up costs incurred by either of them on or before
December 31, 1990 in connection with the Oil Spill; (2) to reimburse the
United States and the State for natural resource damages assessment costs
(including costs of injury studies, economic damages studies, and restoration planning) incurred by either of them on or before March 12, 1991 in
connection with the Oil Spill; (3) to reimburse the State for attorneys fees,
experts' fees, and other costs (collectively, "Litigation Costs") incurred by
it on or before March 12, 1991 in connection with litigation arising from
the Oil Spill; (4) to reimburse the United States and the State for response
and clean-up costs incurred by either of them after December 31, 1990 in
connection with the Oil Spill; and (5) to reimburse or pay costs incurred by
the United States or the State or both after March 12, 1991 to assess injury
resulting from the Oil Spill and to plan, implement, and monitor the
restoration, rehabilitation, or replacement of Natural Resources, natural
resource services, or archaeological sites and artifacts injured, lost, or
destroyed as a result of the Oil Spill, or the acquisition of equivalent
resources or services; and (6) to reimburse the State for reasonable
Litigation Costs incurred by it after March 12, 1991. The aggregate
amount allocated for United States past response and clean-up costs and
damage assessment costs shall not exceed $67 million, and the aggregate
amount allocated for State past response and clean-up costs, damage
assessment costs, and, Litigation Costs incurred on or before March 12,
1991 shall not exceed $75 million. The amounts allocated for State
Litigation Costs incurred after March 12, 1991 shall not exceed $1 million
per month....

Commitment by Exxon to Continue Clean-up

11. (a) Exxon shall continue clean-up work relating to the Oil Spill after the Effect Date, as directed by and in accordance with the directions of the Federal On-Scene Coordinator ("FOSC"), subject to prior approval by the FOSC of the costs of work directed by the FOSC. After the Effective Date, Exxon shall also perform any additional clean-up work directed by the State On-Scene Coordinator ("State OSC") that does not interfere or affirmatively conflict with work directed by the FOSC or with federal law, in accordance with the directions of, and subject to prior approval of costs by, the State OSC.... Exxon should have no liability to any person or entity, including the Governments, by reason of undertaking clean-up work performed in accordance with directions of the FOSC or the State OSC.

(b) Upon Final Approval, Exxon shall have no further obligations with respect to clean-up of the Oil Spill except as set forth in this Agreement....

[12 omitted]

Releases and Covenants
Not to Sue by the Governments

13. Effective upon Final Approval, the Governments release and covenant not to sue or to file any administrative claim against Exxon with respect to [the Oil Spill]....

(a) claims by either Government to enforce this Agreement....

(b) claims by the State for tax revenues which would have been or would be collected under existing AS 43.75 (Fisheries Business Tax) but for the Oil Spill....

(c) exclusively private claims, if any, by Alaska Native Villages and individual Alaska Natives ... seeking damages for private harms to Native subsistence well being, community, culture, tradition and way of life resulting from the Oil Spill....

(d) exclusively private claims, if any, by Alaska Native Corporations, other than claims for Natural Resource Damages, seeking damages for private harms resulting from injuries caused by the Oil Spill to lands in which a Native Corporation holds any present right, title, or interest ... lost or diminished land values, for preservation, protection and restoration of archaeological or cultural resources and archaeological sites found on the lands described in this subparagraph, for private harms resulting from injuries to Natural Resources found on lands described in this subparagraph, for impairment of riparian or littoral rights, if any, and any other claims that are available to Alaska Native Corporations as private landowners; provided, however, that such claims shall not include any claims based upon injuries to tidelands or submerged lands.

14. Effective upon Final Approval, except insofar as Exxon Pipeline is liable to the Governments, or either of them, for claims relating to or

arising from the Oil Spill as a result of its ownership interest in, participation in, or responsibility for Alyeska, each of the Governments provides to Exxon Pipeline covenants not to sue identical to the covenants not to sue provided to Exxon in Paragraph 13. This paragraph shall not be construed as a release or covenant not to sue given by either Government to Alyeska [Alyeska Pipeline Service Company].

15. Effective upon the Effective Date, each of the Governments covenants not to sue any present or former director, officer, or employee of Exxon or Exxon Pipeline with respect to any and all civil claims ... provided, however, that if any such present or former director, officer, or employee brings any action against the Governments, or either of them, for any claim whatsoever arising from or relating to the Oil Spill ... this covenant not to sue shall be null and void with respect to the director, officer, or employee bringing such action. ...

[16 omitted]
Reopener For Unknown Injury

17. Notwithstanding any other provision of this Agreement, between September 1, 2002, and September 1, 2006, Exxon shall pay to the Governments such additional sums as are required for the performance of restoration projects in Prince William Sound and other areas affected by the Oil Spill to restore one or more populations, habitats, or species which, as a result of the Oil Spill, have suffered a substantial loss or substantial decline in the areas affected by the Oil Spill; provided, however, that for a restoration project to qualify for payment under this paragraph the project must meet the following requirements:

(a) the cost of a restoration project must not be grossly disproportionate to the magnitude of the benefits anticipated from the remediation; and

(b) the injury to the affected population, habitat, or species could not reasonably have been known nor could it reasonably have been anticipated by any Trustee from any information in the possession of or reasonably available to any Trustee on the Effective Date.

18. The amount to be paid by Exxon for the restoration projects referred to in Paragraph 17 shall not exceed $100,000,000.

19. The Governments shall file with Exxon, 90 days before demanding any payment pursuant to Paragraph 17, detailed plans for all such restoration projects, together with a statement of all amounts they claim should be paid under Paragraph 17 and all information upon which they relied in the preparation of the restoration plan and the accompanying cost statement.

Releases and Covenants Not To Sue by Exxon and Exxon Pipeline

20. Effective upon Final Approval, Exxon and Exxon Pipeline release, and covenant not to sue or to file any administrative claim against, each of

the Governments and their employees with respect to any and all claims. . . . This paragraph shall not be construed as a release or covenant not to sue given by Alyeska (including its shareholders and owner companies other than Exxon Pipeline) to the Governments.

Trans-Alaska Pipeline Liability Fund

21. The release in Paragraph 20 shall not be construed to bar any claim by Exxon against the TAPL [Trans-Alaska Pipeline Liability] Fund relating to or arising from the Oil Spill. If the TAPL Fund asserts any claims against the Governments that are based upon subrogation rights arising from any monies paid to Exxon or Exxon Pipeline by the TAPL Fund, Exxon agrees to indemnify and hold the Governments harmless from any liability that they have to the TAPL Fund based on such claims.

Provisions Pertaining to Alyeska

22. Effective upon Final Approval, the Governments release and covenant not to sue Alyeska with respect to all claims for Natural Resource Damages and with respect to all other claims for damages for injury to Natural Resources, whether asserted or not, that either may have against Alyeska relating to or arising from the Oil Spill. If Alyeska asserts claims against the Governments, or either of them, that are based upon third party contribution or subrogation rights . . . arising from any liability of or settlement payment by Alyeska to Exxon or Exxon Pipeline . . . Exxon shall indemnify and hold the Governments harmless from any liability that the Governments have to Alyeska based on such claims.

23. In order to resolve as completely as practicable all civil claims of the Governments arising from the Oil Spill against all Exxon Defendants, including Exxon Pipeline (which has a 20.34% participation in Alyeska), and in consideration of Exxon's obligations hereunder, the Governments agree that if either recovers any amount from Alyeska for any claim of any kind relating to or arising from the Oil Spill (such as asserted in the State Court Action against Alyeska), each Government so recovering shall instruct Alyeska to pay to Exxon, and shall take other reasonable steps to ensure that Exxon receives, 20.34% of the amount due to that Government from Alyeska.

24. Exxon and Exxon Pipeline agree that, if Alyeska receives any amount from the Governments for any claim of any kind relating to or arising from the Oil Spill, except for an amount indemnified by Exxon under Paragraph 22 or 25, Exxon and/or Exxon Pipeline shall promptly pay to the Government against which judgment is entered 20.34% of such amount.

25. If Alyeska successfully asserts claims, if any, against the Governments, or either of them, that are based upon Alyeska's own damages or losses, or upon third party contribution or subrogation rights, or other theories of recovery over, arising from Alyeska's liability to persons other than Exxon or Exxon Pipeline relating to the Oil Spill, Exxon shall indemnify the Governments for any sums paid by either of them to

Alyeska based on such claims; provided that the Governments shall assert in good faith all defenses the Governments may have to such claims by Alyeska, and provided further that no indemnity shall be provided under this paragraph if the Governments refuse a good faith proposal for a monetary settlement of such claims agreed to by Exxon and Alyeska, under which Alyeska shall fully release the Governments in exchange for a payment by or other consideration from Exxon, on behalf of the Governments, to Alyeska.

Third Party Litigation

26. (a) Except as provided in subparagraph (b) of this paragraph, if any person or entity not a party to this Agreement ("Third Party") asserts a claim relating to or arising from the Oil Spill in any present or future litigation against Exxon or Exxon Pipeline and the Governments, or against Exxon or Exxon Pipeline and either the United States or the State, each of the sued Parties ("Sued Parties") shall be responsible for and will pay its share of liability, if any, as determined by the proportional allocation of liability contained in any final judgment in favor of such Third Party....

(b) If any person or entity, other than the TAPL Fund or Alyeska, asserts claims against the Governments arising from any liability of or payment by said person or entity to Exxon or Exxon Pipeline... the foregoing indemnity (i) shall not be enforceable with respect to any amount in excess of value actually received by Exxon or Exxon Pipeline, and (ii) shall be enforceable only if the Governments assert in good faith all defenses they may have to such claims.

27. Neither Exxon nor Exxon Pipeline shall assert any right of contribution or indemnity against either Government in any action relating to or arising form the Oil Spill where that respective Government is not a party. Neither Government shall assert any right of contribution or indemnity against Exxon or Exxon Pipeline in any action relating to or arising from the Oil Spill where Exxon and Exxon Pipeline, respectively, are not parties, except that either Government may assert against Exxon the rights to indemnification as expressly provided in Paragraphs 21, 22, and 25.

28. Any liability which Exxon incurs as a result of a suit by a Third Party, as described in Paragraphs 26 or 27, shall not be attributable to or serve to reduce the payments required to be paid by Exxon pursuant to Paragraph 8 or any additional payment required under Paragraph 17....

[29-31 omitted]

Reservations of Rights

32. This Agreement does not constitute an admission of fact or law, or of any liability, by any Party to this Agreement. Except as expressly stated in this Agreement, each Party reserves against all persons or entities all rights, claims, or defenses available to it relating to or arising from the Oil

Spill. Nothing in this Agreement, however, is intended to affect legally the claims, if any, of any person or entity not a Party to this Agreement.

33. Nothing in this Agreement creates, nor shall it be construed as creating, any claim in favor of any person not a Party to this Agreement.

34. Nothing in this Agreement shall prevent or impair the Governments from providing program assistance or funding to those not signatories to this Agreement under the programs of their agencies pursuant to legislative authorization or appropriation.

35. Nothing in this Agreement shall affect or impair any existing contract between Exxon or Exxon Pipeline and any entity of either Government, including without limitation the agreement between Exxon and the Environmental Protection Agency dated December 21, 1990, relating to joint conduct of bioremediation studies. . . .

[36-40 omitted]

October

SENATE HEARINGS ON GATES'S NOMINATION AS CIA DIRECTOR

October 1-3, 1991

Senate hearings on President George Bush's choice of Robert M. Gates to direct the Central Intelligence Agency (CIA) unveiled the presence of internal feuds and exposed the nominee to attack from former colleagues in an agency once renowned for its secrecy. Gates's public testimony before the Senate Intelligence Committee on October 1 and 2, followed by his rebuttal October 3, highlighted three weeks of confirmation hearings. They opened September 16 after a summer's delay because of new questions about Gates's role, if any, in the Iran-contra scandal during Ronald Reagan's presidency.

Gates seemed to dispel those questions this time—something he was unable to do when Reagan nominated him for the same job in 1987. Gates, then the CIA's deputy director, withdrew his nomination before the Senate voted. When Bush succeeded Reagan in 1989, he named Gates assistant to the president and deputy national security adviser. On May 14, 1991, Bush nominated Gates to replace William H. Webster, the retiring director of central intelligence.

The one overriding concern in 1991, as in 1987, was how much Gates knew about the illegal diversion of funds to Nicaraguan guerrillas (contras) from secret sales of U.S. arms to Iran in the mid-1980s. In light of a new development in Iran-contra prosecutions, Gates was asked to clarify statements he had made to Congress in 1986 and 1987 that he knew virtually nothing of the diversion until it was publicly announced in November 1986.

On July 9, 1991, Alan D. Fiers, Jr., a former CIA operative in Central America, pleaded guilty to unlawfully withholding information from

Congress by saying he had no prior knowledge of the diversion. Fiers told prosecutors that he passed the information on to two superiors in August 1986. The superiors were Clair E. George and William J. Casey, then the CIA director. Casey later died; George was indicted September 6 on ten counts of lying to Congress and obstructing Iran-contra investigations. (New Pleas and Charges in Iran-contra Cases, p. 429)

While Fiers did not mention Gates, the admissions raised new questions about how the CIA's deputy director at the time could know so little about the operation if George, his immediate subordinate, and Casey, his immediate superior, were aware of the covert operation. However, the Senate hearings produced no irrefutable evidence that Gates deceived Congress—or slanted intelligence solely to suit the policy agenda of the Reagan administration, as was charged by some former colleagues and subordinates in the CIA.

Committee Approval Despite Questions

Gates won the Senate Intelligence Committee's endorsement by an 11-4 vote October 18. Its chairman, David L. Boren, D-Okla., and Sen. Sam Nunn, D-Ga., the influential chairman of the Senate Armed Services Committee, had been outspoken in their support of Gates, splintering Democratic opposition. Boren argued that the new director would "immediately have to plunge into the process of radically changing the intelligence community" in light of the Soviet Union's disintegration and U.S. budgetary constraints, and "this is no time to bring in a new director from the outside."

But critics said Gates's long relationship with the CIA and its spotty record under Casey in the 1980s made Gates uniquely unqualified to oversee such a massive change. Sen. Bill Bradley, D-N.J., a leader of the opposition, contended that "his management of CIA analysts left a legacy of doubt that would be hard to overcome."

Bradley alluded to testimony that Gates had tailored intelligence information to suit the policy agenda of the Reagan administration. This allegation had come from Melvin A. Goodman, a former CIA division chief in Soviet affairs; Harold P. Ford, a forty-year veteran of the agency, and Jennifer L. Glaudemans, a former CIA Soviet analyst. Gates denied that he had done so and received supporting testimony from Graham Fuller of the Rand Corporation, formerly a national intelligence officer.

Senate Confirmation and Swearing-in

On November 5, after two days of debate, the Senate voted 64-31 for confirmation; all forty-two voting Republicans were joined by twenty-two Democrats to form the required two-thirds majority. One week later Gates was sworn into office at a White House ceremony attended by President Bush, himself a former CIA director. Gates, at age forty-nine, became the fourteenth person to hold that position since it was created in 1946, and the first to rise through the CIA ranks.

In contrast to Casey, who had served in the Office of Strategic

Services—the World War II predecessor of the CIA which was known for cloak-and-dagger operations—Gates noted in Senate hearings that he had come up through the desk-oriented analysis branch of the agency. "For good or ill, I've been in the bureaucracy my entire career, twenty-five years," he remarked. While some might find his background inhibiting, Gates added, he believed bureaucracy provided safeguards against excessive or illegal action. He promised to continue procedures instituted by Webster to prevent a recurrence of scandals such as Iran-contra.

Following are excerpts from testimony October 1-3, 1991, at Senate Intelligence Committee confirmation hearings on Robert M. Gates to become director of central intelligence. (The bracketed headings have been added by Congressional Quarterly to highlight the organization of the text.):

GOODMAN TESTIMONY

For too long the CIA has hidden behind a veil of secrecy—not to protect legitimate assets or legitimate secrets, but to protect its reputation. I feel this has complicated our efforts, the CIA's efforts, to recruit the best brains in the country. And I also feel that it has created a public perception of the CIA's disregard for law, morality and public disclosure.

I must say that there has been some confusion with regard to the circumstances of my departure from the CIA, and I'm going to take a few minutes to develop that.

In 1985 I was told privately by the director of my office that Bob Gates had ordered my removal from my managerial position in SOVA [Office of Soviet Analysis]. I was not the only one to be removed; there were three of us. One was considered too soft on Soviet-Third World relations. One was considered to have too bleak a view on the Soviet economy. And one was considered too apologetic on Soviet-American relations and arms control issues.

Why did I leave? Why did I leave the CIA? I left because of politicization. And I must state at the outset that I agree with [former deputy director of central intelligence] John McMahon, that the integrity and the objectivity of intelligence is central to the mission of CIA.

Second, I would like to say at the outset that I agree with Bob Gates that slanting intelligence would transgress the single deepest ethical, cultural principle of the CIA. Indeed, I would argue that the CIA was constructed to protect analytical independence.

And I certainly agree with the acting director of CIA, Dick Kerr, who has stated that the agency's strength is its ability to produce intelligence that represents the entire intelligence community.

Indeed, it is because intelligence data is subject to interpretation, and because policy departments have their own intelligence bureaus and their own policy agendas, that the CIA was established as the one place where objective analysis could be done without fear or favor.

Moreover, I strongly believe that any effort to subvert the process of independent analysis, that is politicization, can lead to the loss of life, as in Vietnam, to national embarrassment, as in the Bay of Pigs, and to national tragedy, as in Iran-contra.

Now I can understand the country's desire to put Iran-contra in the background. And I can certainly understand the Congress' desire to put Iran-contra in the background. But it should never be forgotten that the actions and the policies of very few people in government, including the CIA, led to the sale of arms to the same Iranians who held U.S. diplomats hostage for more than a year, and were linked—and we know this from intelligence sources—were linked to the murder of more than 200 Marines in Lebanon, the savage bombing of the U.S. Embassy in Beirut, and the death of a good friend, Bob Ames.

I can assure you I won't forget, and my colleagues at CIA and the National War College, who sacrificed their lives for this country will never forget Iran-contra.

One additional point before I begin. I have never said, I have never claimed, and I will never write that Gates politicized all issues that the Directorate of Intelligence [DI] had to deal with. Bob Gates is correct with regard to the fine work of some of my former colleagues on such issues as the Philippines, Lebanon and Soviet strategic forces. These issues were not targets of [former CIA Director William J.] Casey's politicization, and therefore, they may have been protected from efforts to corrupt the intelligence process.

There were two primary targets for politicization—first, nearly all intelligence issues connected to covert action—that is, the operational commitments that Casey had made regarding Iran, Nicaragua and Afghanistan. All those issues were politicized. The second area concerned Casey's other major concern—his world view of the Soviet Union. That is, the Soviet Union as the source of all U.S. problems in the international arena. Casey seized on every opportunity to exaggerate the Soviet threat. This included the case for Soviet involvement in the papal plot, international terrorism and Soviet-Third World relations, my own area of specialization. All of those issues were politicized. Gates' role in this activity was to corrupt the process and the ethics of intelligence on all of these issues. He was Casey's filter in the Directorate of Intelligence. He protected Casey's equity in these issues. And as the memo calling for the bombing of Nicaragua showed, he pandered to Casey's agenda.

There were other memos of this type that maybe you have not seen. I remember one calling for the bombing of Libya, to quote, change the map of the region, unquote. Gates' other contribution was to ignore and suppress signs of the Soviet strategic retreat, including the collapse of the Soviet empire, even the Soviet Union itself.

[Slanted Analysis]

I'm going to start with my first charge, the use of the Directorate of Operations to slant Directorate of Intelligence analysis. I will be making a very important charge, and I know it's a very serious charge. I believe that the CIA was responsible for providing the NSC [National Security Council] and even the president with misleading and false information on a sensitive issue.

As you well know, George Cave, from the Directorate of Operations, joined [former national security adviser] Robert C. McFarlane on the trip to Iran in 1986. Upon return, he was allowed or encouraged to do several things. One, he sent a typescript memo to the White House regarding Iranian politics. This memo was never coordinated in the Directorate of Intelligence. The memo argued for the fact that there was a moderate faction in Iran that wanted to establish contacts with the United States.

Two, he sent Directorate of Operations reporting, along with the PDB—that is, the President's Daily Brief—to the president. These reports, in terms of their message, were at variance with the views of the Directorate of Intelligence and the senior analyst on Iran with regard to whether or not there was a moderate faction in Iran.

Three, he was allowed to brief the NSC on the basis of these reports. He was given a special channel to the White House and the NSC. Also I might add that the NIO [national intelligence officer] for counterterrorism, Charlie Allen, sent a memo to the NSC that said that moderates were eager for improved relations with the United States and that they were in sufficient charge to carry this policy out.

Five [sic], the NIO for counterterrorism briefed the NSC on Iranian attitudes towards the United States. Again, the analysts of the Directorate of Intelligence were not consulted.

Now, all the activity I've cited thus far was not coordinated within the Directorate of Intelligence. It was at variance with the views of the Directorate of Intelligence and with the entire intelligence community, especially with regard to the existence of moderate factions in Iran wanting contacts with the United States.

I believe—this is my opinion—that this was a conscious attempt to provide uncoordinated information to the NSC and even the president in support of operational activities, and that this effort had devastating consequences.

This activity also violated the ethics of the intelligence community, and it may mean that when President [Ronald] Reagan said he thought he was dealing with a moderate Iranian faction with interest in dealing with the United States, he was acting on the basis of false CIA analysis.

So a question remains. Was the president himself a victim of CIA misinformation or even disinformation?

[Intelligence on Iran]

Now I want to deal with my third charge regarding intelligence on Iran, which I believe involved every instrument of politicization. Let me introduce this subject by providing some context.

From 1981 to 1985, the director of intelligence, that is, the analysts in the office of Soviet affairs and the analysts in the Near Eastern office, developed rather strong analytical positions on several key issues: Iran's support for terrorism was significant; Iran's political scene did not include a moderate faction seeking ties with the United States; that the Soviet position in Iran was in decline; and that Soviet arms sales were declining significantly.

I might add that in 1986 there were no Soviet arms deliveries to Iran.

The important point about all of this is that all of this analysis was based on very strong evidence. Now, one thing is certain and can be documented: The CIA changed its analytical position on all of these views during a very important period. We're talking about mid-May 1985, before the delivery of Hawk missiles to Iran.

I think it's also important that the views were changed without a strong evidentiary base and over the protests of the senior analysts, particularly in SOVA.

I find it's also interesting that in 1986, after the disclosure of many of these events associated with Iran-contra, the CIA then reverted to the old line it had consistently established from 1981 to 1985.

[Personnel Policy]

I would like to add two points, however, on the issue of personnel policy. Each example of politicization—and I know this firsthand from dealing in the Directorate of Intelligence—led to a great deal of self-censorship by the analysts. The perception was, by many good analysts—senior analysts—that certain evidence was going to be ignored by the seventh floor if it did not suit a certain seventh-floor policy agenda. And I think this self-censorship gets into the insidious nature of politicization.

I want to just point out one other issue. We lost a lot of good senior people in the Directorate of Intelligence because of this activity. I think we lost our best people. Some of our best people are working now for other intelligence agencies. I've already circulated a list to this committee of the tremendous seniority of Soviet analysts up to 1985 in the Office of Soviet Analysis, and the very inexperienced analysts and managers who now work there.

I think this exodus of analysts is important. I think the fact that there is almost an analytical diaspora out there throughout Washington and the academic community is very important. These are people who were fed up. These were people who felt an ethical dilemma. I know each one of them. I've talked to every one of them. I think there's a waste of government resources in the fact that this has happened.

Let me tell you about one anecdote of someone who has stayed behind— who is still there. One day he wrote a piece that apparently attracted a great deal of anger of the management of the Office of Soviet Analysis. This was recent. This was in the last year. He was called in by his supervisor, and I quote, You know, this isn't a democracy we're running here. Your job is to know the message the office wants and make sure the analysts get it right, unquote.

This kind of thing is what gets people to leave the CIA. This is the kind of event that leads to loss of very good people, very experienced people, very senior people.

Now, what are the implications of all of this? Frankly, I find this history distasteful. I don't want anyone on this committee to think that I get any satisfaction whatsoever out of bringing any of this to you. I might add that I did not come to the committee. The committee came to me.

[Intelligence Judgments]

Now, the fact has been expressed here by some that Gates lacked strategic vision in his own area of expertise, that he missed the strategic retreat of the Soviet Union, the collapse of the Soviet Union. Now that's important, and I'm not gainsaying that. That's very important.

The fact that Gates was more often wrong than right, especially when he substituted his judgment for the view of his analyst, is also important. The fact that policy-makers miss data, they miss trends, they missed analysis on trends that led to missing an historic opportunity with the Soviet Union and certainly led to the sad venture in Iran, of course that's important.

But what I think is most important and most offensive, is that Casey and Gates arrogated to themselves the power to make intelligence judgments. That they had contempt for a process designed to allow independent analysis. That they damaged the integrity of that process and the credibility of the CIA, where I've spent 24 years. That they ignored the long-established ethics and morality of an intelligence officer, and that even the president of the United States was given misleading analysis and uncoordinated views.

Frankly, I worry about the signal that would be sent in returning Gates to the environment he created. I worry about the effect this would have on the standards of others back at the Central Intelligence Agency—to be led by someone so lacking in vision, integrity and courage.

FULLER TESTIMONY

Serious charges have been raised against Bob Gates, especially those of Mel Goodman. While I know and respect Mel Goodman as a very knowledgeable and experienced Soviet analyst, in all frankness, I do not readily recognize the Bob Gates described in his testimony.

I am indeed disturbed at hearing the specific and worrisome accusations that he levels against Gates. But I find that when he talks on those incidents of which I am personally familiar, his account, in my opinion, contains serious distortions in content and in the manner of telling.

In brief, I do not believe that during my five years' tenure at the National Intelligence Council I witnessed anything that I would call improprieties in the conduct of estimative work by Bob Gates. I have no direct knowledge of his leadership of the DI, which has figured in so much of the testimony. But I do know that within the confines of the NIC [National Intelligence Council] and the national intelligence estimates, I have not seen Gates engaged in anything that can loosely be called politicization of intelligence.

[The Casey Tenure]

Mr. Chairman, I feel it's important to impart at least a little flavor of the Casey tenure at CIA. Again, I can only speak of it from the vantage point of estimative work at the NIC. Casey was a man of huge intellect and far-ranging interests. I think he's well-known to most of you in many different capacities. He had a geostrategic mind if there ever was one. It was at once his source of brilliant strength and greatest weakness.

Casey had a broad sense of global politics and the interrelationships of things. He could usually think of 10 more implications of any international event than the average analyst could. He read widely, and his NIOs had to run to keep up with his restless mind and flow of various hypotheses. He was an unabashed cold warrior and tended to view all events in terms of their impact on the struggle with the Soviet Union, apart from other regional implications.

Now, Mr. Goodman I think has suggested what I think is a slight parody of Casey's views on these things. I do not think Casey viewed as all evils emanating from the Soviet Union or from the Soviet empire. He certainly was willing to blame them for a very healthy proportion of what went on in the world, but his major strategic concern was what world events anywhere in the globe meant to the American-Soviet confrontation. That was his particular focus: How does it affect the American-Soviet balance, Western-Soviet balance?

While I shared a deep suspicion of Soviet motives and ambitions with Bill Casey, I often disagreed with him sharply on his interpretation of many issues where he was inclined to overstate the Soviet role or the Soviet ability to influence things. This was especially true in the Middle East, where I constantly pointed out to him that the Syrians and the Iranians and the Libyans and others had ample reason to want to do many nefarious things on their own, without much help from the Soviet Union. But the fact remained that the Soviet Union did give very, very considerable assistance to both Syria and Libya in pursuing those goals.

[Not a Faceless Bureaucrat]

Now, Bob Gates may be a skillful staffer who has served a number of different bosses well, but he, too, is not a faceless bureaucrat. He is immensely intelligent, has a superb grasp of substance. He is a quick study, and he fully understands the relationship between policy and intelligence. He was indeed able to keep pace with Casey's own geopolitical instincts, but he was also able to tone down some of Casey's more far-fetched hypotheses in discussions that were held in which I have been personally present.

Where Casey did not always hide what he hoped intelligence might indicate, Gates was always fully aware of the requirements of analytic procedure and the validity of independent analysis from everything I saw within the NIC. I cannot speak to charges leveled about Gates' handling of research within the DI, but he was certainly respectful of the process in the work of the NIC. Gates did share a hard-line view but a very well-informed view of the Soviet Union, independent of Casey.

The international situation at that time, I would argue, perhaps justified a fairly hard-line view in any case. The world was very different in 1980 to 1985, prior to [Soviet President Mikhail S.] Gorbachev, than it has been in the stunning years that we have witnessed following the Gorbachev tenure.

I say also that I believe SOVA was in part aggrieved because perhaps a non-Soviet NIO had tampered with their work, which most other NIO's did not do, leaving matters to Soviet specialists to duke it out among themselves. But, I too had some credentials and much experience in Soviet affairs that may have been resented. I have no idea. It may have been due to my being an outsider. But I had, quote, swerved, unquote, from the solid SOVA line on Iran, as many of these SOVA analysts have mentioned.

Yet I do believe that it can only be through the relentless examination of various new hypotheses and counter-hypotheses that the intelligence community will ever have a chance to get at the elusive truths of forecasting the unknowable.... SOVA analysts, some of them, have chosen to cast this issue in terms of right and wrong, truth vs. politicization. Their own internal frustrations seem to have caused them to reject out of hand this line of analysis that was not stated as a certitude on my part, but only as a distinct and serious strategic possibility that the U.S. government must be watchful for.

The argument instead has been presented now as to serving either Casey or serving Gates or serving the White House. I have not even been given the courtesy of simply being called wrong, but rather portrayed as someone else's instrument in the struggle against SOVA. Whether the application of the word "wrong" is appropriate in any case is questionable, when one speaks of the warning function in intelligence. The Soviet Union, in effect, did not have the field day in Iran that I was concerned it might have, but that's also because the Iranian regime did not move toward collapse and dismemberment in that year that many of us were concerned could happen.

[Plenty of Fires]

No, in the end the barn did not burn down, but there were plenty of fires raging in the region, and people were playing with matches in the barn. Even the possibility of this major calamity for American interests seems not to have been acknowledged by SOVA analysts.

Well, Mr. Chairman, the next estimate on Iran, in February '86, is commonly touted to have reversed itself, showing what an anomaly the previous May '85 estimate had been. And it's referred to as having admitted its earlier error.

Now, I find this an extraordinary interpretation. The later estimate we did about from May to February—what, nine months?—took note, and this was revisiting the Iranian memo, took note that the disturbing negative trends suggesting the Iranian regime might be foundering now seems to have receded and that the Iranian regime had in fact weathered the year better than most Iranian analysts had felt—and that includes CIA Iranian analysts—and that it had moved toward a stronger footing.

I submit, Mr. Chairman, that if going back in retrospect and recognizing that some of our concerns had not been borne out represents admission of an error or saying that, gee, we had been wrong all along, then I think the system is skewed. It is imperative that we look back at estimates and say what was fulfilled and was not fulfilled among our major concerns. That same February estimate also said that the Soviet Union still could make major gains in Iran under one of any six conditions that were then set forth. And the SOVA analysts agreed to those conditions.

Throughout these controversies, Mr. Chairman, Gates never told me what to say, he never winked at me or otherwise attempted to dictate the outcomes of these estimates. He had his views and they were very well-known to me. Mr. Casey had his views and they were very well-known to me. I had my own views on a whole range of issues, and they were well-known to the NISA [national intelligence security analysis] community and in our regular monthly brainstorming sessions that were designed to make sense of the morass of Middle East politics.

I think anyone who knew me from that period would testify that we were exhaustive and exhausting in arguing issues first one way, then another, devil's advocating and probing the meaning of regional events.

[Relying on Intuition]

Does absence of evidence, absence of evidence mean that something is not there, or it has not happened?

How much should we rely on intuition, judgment and experience in appraising the likelihood of events or motives, or the issue of who benefits from an event? This dilemma can never be solved.

SOVA seems to have clung to the idea that the sweeping force of, quote, no evidence means that we don't think it happened, which is a safe and perhaps appropriate position for a junior analyst.

But is a more experienced analyst or manager wrong to examine other considerations even in the absence of evidence that we may never collect?

In the estimative business, in any case, we are always, always, Mr. Chairman, talking about intuitions, judgments, gut feelings and experience. We are writing estimates precisely because we do not know, and there will never be enough evidence to enable us, to be sure.

Analysts love to say that it is, quote, too early to make a judgment, but the policy-maker has to make a judgment, and right now, dammit. What are we analysts paid for anyway? they will say. If the evidence was that clear, of course we wouldn't need an estimate.

Estimates are judgments. They are based on slim and sometimes no evidence. Of course we want evidence, but when we have only a tiny sliver of evidence, is that all that we go on? Or do we use our intellects to try to glean the remaining 95 percent of an unknown construct of which we have only one tiny part?

The SOVA charges seem to talk with undue certainty about evidence ignored.

I submit, Mr. Chairman, that the dilemma of evidence and judgments can never be appropriately and fully resolved. Both are essential, but judgment still goes on in the absence of evidence.

And so, too, this role of the senior manager. This is an insoluble question that we are faced with. It is not a black and white, or good and evil, or right or wrong question.

There is a hidden supposition in much of the analysts' complaints that senior people should stay the hell out of their analyses.

I respect their concern, but here, again, we have a trade-off. Is wisdom couched exclusively at the lower levels of analysis with the hard facts, quote, unquote. Or does it reside perhaps nearer the top, with senior, experienced officials who have seen much of the world and a lot of politics, and, indeed, some of whom may also have their own agendas as well?

I suspect that there are a whole lot of different things going on here rather than a systematic attempt to distort and politicize intelligence.

I think Bob Gates is too intelligent for that, for there is no quicker death for an intelligence officer than manipulation, willful and deliberate manipulation and distortion of facts.

No DCI can afford to go down in history as one who manipulated or distorted intelligence. That fact, through Irangate, has destroyed the reputation of the remarkable intellectual figure that Bill Casey was.

But in the trenches of analysis and policy over the years, mistakes do get made. We have all made them. God knows, I have made mistakes in my own judgments, and I will probably go on to make more in the future. Yet I have not personally experienced anything that I would call true politicization of estimates, in my personal experience, even by Casey.

As I said, I have taken a lot of flak off Casey, I know his views, I have argued strenuously with him and knew where he was coming from and where he wanted to go. That was his prerogative. It was my job to do what I was paid for and not to do his bidding.

Nor do I think that politicization accurately or fairly describes the Gates that I worked with for five years—whatever failings, harshness, insensitivities or analytical misjudgments he, too, may be guilty of in this period.

FORD TESTIMONY

I have some very difficult things to say today, but I feel I must say them.

In brief, my message is that I think Robert Gates should not be confirmed as director of central intelligence.

This is a difficult task for me, in part because though semi-retired I'm still an employee of the CIA on part-time contract. This is also a very painful task for me. It is painful to be negative about someone who has been my colleague, a relationship that was cooperative throughout where there was no bad blood whatsoever between us.

Moreover, as my supervisor, Bob Gates was good to me and awarded me increased responsibilities. Furthermore, he is extremely able and has clearly had unique experience in both the production of intelligence and its use by the country's top decision-makers.

It's also painful to have to differ with my good friend Graham Fuller. I see things differently, I see Bob Gates differently, as I will spell out.

For me, with respect to Mr. Gates, this is a case of divided loyalties, conflicting loyalties. As an indebted colleague, I should loyally support his candidacy. But I also have loyalties to the agency and to our country's need to have DCIs of the finest caliber and makeup possible.

[Skewing of Intelligence]

Discerning what is the skewing of intelligence and what is not is a tricky business. But from my four decades of experience in and around intelligence, I think I can help the committee thread its way through the differing kinds of pressure which Bob Gates did or did not bring on intelligence analysis.

It is my view that many of his pressures were justified as he sought to sharpen analysis and its usefulness to decision-makers; secondly, that some of the pressures he brought on analysis simply reflected differing professional judgments, and that some of the allegations that he skewed intelligence doubtless have arisen from an analyst whose pride was damaged by his revisions.

Thirdly, however, as I am prepared to discuss at greater length, it is my view based on documents that have been released in the last few days, on testimonies that have been given to this committee of late and on the confidence of many CIA officers whose ability and character I respect, that other of Bob Gates' pressures have gone beyond professional bounds and clearly constitute a skewing of intelligence—not in the fields of military and strategic issues, but chiefly concerning Soviet political matters and the Soviets the third—and the Third World.

With respect to the latter, I would interject, events have provided that the Soviets have, for some years, been definitely lessening their commitments in Asia, Africa and Latin America, thus validating the earlier judgments that SOVA made, not those that Bob Gates and his supporters did.

I would also add that the skewing of intelligence and the purging of dissident DDI analysts, as we've already heard today, goes considerably beyond the four particular issues this committee happens to be focusing on.

It isn't wholly across the board, but there are many more than just four issues.

In my view, that 1985 estimate on Iran was not an estimate in the usual sense. A national intelligence estimate presents the data, all the data on all sides, and then draws what seem to be the most likely patterns and the most likely future.

If an NIE [national intelligence estimate] or SNIE goes on to talk about, well, it's possible that the Soviets might do this, the worst case that they might do this, it clearly says so.

This 1985 estimate was a worst-case paper, clearly, but it did not clue the reader that it was, and therefore the readers could misjudge it, thinking this is the way things were going to be, not this is the way things might be if the Soviets did their damndest.

More important, that 1985 estimate skewed—had significant policy consequences. As the Congress' Iran-contra report and the Tower report both indicate, that estimate directly fed White House interest and enthusiasm with respect to reversing the then-boycott of U.S. arms to Iran.

Again as [the agency's director of Soviet analysis] Doug MacEachin said in his memo to Dick Kerr of January 1987, later national intelligence estimates backed off from the 1985 estimate's stress on the Soviet threat to Iran. I differ with Graham. I think no one can read these without drawing that same conclusion. They softened that view. Why? Because it became more clear that the level of Soviet military support to Iran had been dropping precipitously for some years.

[The Need for Intuition]

Many will share my view that Bob Gates has often depended too much on his own individual analytic judgments and has ignored or scorned the views of others whose assessments did not accord with his own.

I agree completely with Graham about the need for intuition, and we don't just stick to what reports and absolute evidence we have; but the question is, whose imagination and whose initiative and how senior are they, and do they insist that that be bought by their juniors, or is it plainly labeled as a "best guess"?

One of the things that I admired with Director Casey was that he urged all of us in the NIC, all of us NIOs and officers there, to give him think papers. We got a new idea about something, we want to question conventional wisdom, there's an outside chance that, a worse case that—all these things were carefully so labeled. They went to him alone.

Now often I think he probably did other things with them, took them downtown and so on, which is not always good.

But I think the opportunity to do that is, was correct, and should remain correct, and were I running that shop now I would want that to happen.

But it's one thing to have intuition and so on and another thing to present that to the reader, that this is a national intelligence estimate and this is the way it is, rather than this is the way I and somebody else think it might be, or I and some other senior person think it might be, but we've conned the others into silence.

My view that Bob Gates has ignored or scorned the views of others whose assessments did not accord with his own would be OK if he were uniquely all-seeing.

The trouble is he has not been. Most importantly, he has been dead wrong on the central analytic target of the past few years—the outlook for change, or not, in the fortunes of the U.S.S.R. and the Soviet-European bloc.

He was wrong in presenting the Soviet threat to Iran in 1985 as a true NIE and then telling the Senate Foreign Relations Committee two years later that those things still applied.

I think Bob Gates was overly certain earlier that the Soviets ran or were in charge of international terrorism. He certainly was overly certain that the sky would fall if we didn't bomb Nicaragua, to say nothing of the wisdom of such a recommended course of action.

The U.S.A. deserves a DCI whose analytic batting average is better than that, especially if that DCI tends to force his views on CIA and the intelligence community and especially at a time when U.S. intelligence and U.S. policy face a far more complex world than the one we have known.

GLAUDEMANS TESTIMONY

While commentators have characterized much of the 1980s as a search for simple answers, I do not believe that you, or members and policy-makers of the executive branch, deserved simple analysis. You are entitled to a realistic appraisal of Soviet policy, one that exposed limitations as well as the threats. I know of no one in SOVA or elsewhere in the agency who refused or would refuse to examine any given intelligence question, provided they were allowed to do so without prejudice.

But the atmosphere in SOVA, as I believe has been confirmed by other witnesses, was politically charged. We were all keenly aware of what Mr. Gates and the DCI were saying publicly about Soviet foreign policy in the Third World, most of which was at variance with intelligence.

Not only could we feel Mr. Gates' contempt, we could sense his party line. No one in SOVA was a Soviet apologist, but the atmosphere that was created over there, and the label that that—just the existence of that label made it extremely difficult to work in.

Because he was so public in his views, I believe Mr. Gates had a special obligation to uphold and protect the independence of CIA's analysis. His objectivity never came through.

The means by which politicization occurred is not readily documented. There is little paper to evidence the continual and subtle pressures applied to analysts to make them comply. Because it is virtually impossible to collect a paper trail, evidence quickly becomes one person's word against another. But let me suggest to you that politicization is like fog. Though you cannot hold it in your hand or nail it to the wall, it is real; it does exist. And it does affect people's behavior.

I believe it is the pervasiveness of people's perception that analysis was and still is politicized as a result of Mr. Gates' influence and the accumulation over time of incidents where it is charged to have occurred that lends tremendous credibility to your concerns here today.

No one is accusing Mr. Gates of politicizing every Soviet issue that came across his desk, but I do believe there are sufficient instances of politicization to raise serious doubts.

I know many analysts out at Langley [Virginia, CIA headquarters] are pleading, and pleading largely to you, to set a higher standard of excellence and integrity.

Thus the questions are: How many instances of politicization are acceptable? Is the detrimental impact that it has on the integrity and the health of an institution acceptable? And if it's not acceptable, do you want the problem solved by the person who is believed to have been responsible for creating it in the first place?

I had no less fun flying my computer terminal in search of an understanding of Soviet policy than an F-18 pilot has flying his aircraft. And I got no less thrill out of finding the right words that would put [one] on the cutting edge of analysis than a test pilot had pushing the envelope. That's really how I felt about my job.

[Privilege of Serving "My Country"]

For me, it was the greatest privilege to work for the U.S. government and to serve my country in the capacity as an analyst. In order to be so privileged, I consented to an extensive and intrusive personal background investigation. I submitted to psychological examinations and interviews. And twice I took and passed the polygraph examination.

After these procedures were completed and when the agency hired me, I believed I entered into a type of social contract with the CIA. I became obligated to protect sources and methods, and I became obligated to do my best as an analyst. But I also believe that the CIA had an obligation to me.

They were obligated to uphold and protect my mission as an analyst who was responsible for providing independent analysis. I waited for 3½ years for somebody in a position of authority to do just that.

GATES TESTIMONY

I've watched and listened and read with some dismay as well as some pain and anger during recent days the discussion here of slanting intelligence. I am saddened that these proceedings, except by happenstance, have not shined a brighter and deserving light on the many hundreds of extraordinarily capable, talented analysts, who work so hard, day-in and day-out, in providing first-rate and absolutely honest intelligence to our government.

These dedicated people of great integrity are owed a huge debt of gratitude by the American people for their service, and I think what we need to face here is that we're talking about how to make something that is good even better.

One cannot but be discouraged by allegations of politicization so easily made compared to the effort, specificity and evidence required to disprove them. Today you will get from me, at length, specifics and evidence and documents, in refutation of the allegations.

Again and again, inspector general reports and studies by the directorate's product-evaluation staff found pockets of perceptions of politicization, more often in the Soviet office than elsewhere, but searched in vain for evidence of slanting in our products.

Evidence of politicization was always elusive, but the perception was always a worry. I'd ask analysts when I would go down into their work spaces to talk with them if their work had been distorted. Ironically many felt this happened more often at the branch and division chief level, where their drafts were first reviewed, than higher up.

But the answer was virtually always no. But they had heard that that had happened for sure in the next branch over.

So I'd go over there, and I'd get the same answer.

I must say that I regret that this seems to lie, somewhat at least, behind the views of my old friend and admired colleague, Mr. Ford, whose testimony seems to suggest that he seems to have no complaint with me on areas where we work together directly but that he had been persuaded by negative comments from others. And that saddens me.

No manager could or can afford to forget the possibility of politicization because the perceptions themselves can affect morale and analytical courage. And so we worked hard at emphasizing integrity, investigating rumors and reassuring analysts that they were right to be sensitive to the issues.

Repeatedly, we told them, tell it like it is. Don't sugarcoat the pill.

I believe there are several causes for this perception of politicization. It's usually greater, for example, whenever people up the line have strong views on substance, and I must say in the history of [the] CIA that happens more often than not.

When major changes in draft analysis come out of a review process, it is understandable that analysts would be more inclined to blame them on an external source such as political pressure, than on weaknesses in their own analysis or exposition.

No analyst who considers himself or herself to be the best-informed person on a subject likes to be challenged. Analysts like to write on the subjects they like in the ways they like, and to be told that your specific subject, or the way that you present it, is irrelevant to policy-makers, or is not persuasive, is hard to swallow.

It was for me as an analyst, and it continues to be for analysts.

The much-maligned review process takes the analysis of a single individual, challenges assumptions, asks questions and hopefully scrubs out the biases of the analysts, as well as all others at all levels, thus turning the draft of an individual into the official view of the Central Intelligence Agency or the intelligence community.

The process can be rough-and-tumble. Most analysts do well in the give-and-take. But some do not. And some see in this process political pressure, and that's why we're here today.

I appreciate the opportunity this morning to respond to allegations that have been made about slanting intelligence. The issue goes to the fundamental ethic and the basic culture of intelligence.

I grew up in that culture. I made that ethic, the primacy of honest, objective analysis, my own. It was an extension of the values that I brought with me when I came to Washington, especially the part about telling it like it is, and with the bark off.

Thus, it is deeply disturbing to me to hear attacks not just on my integrity, but by implication, on that of many analysts, managers and leaders in CIA, in the intelligence community.

Moreover, it ignores the many instances where we published assessments unwelcome to the Reagan administration in areas such as arms control, strategic forces, Lebanon and countless others even more controversial and contentious than the Soviets in the Third World. . . .

[Objectivity and Integrity]

The principles I set out in January 1982 continue to be the principles I believe should guide our work. My top priority today would be the same as it was then, to produce the best quality intelligence available anywhere.

And that, of course, must rest first of all on a foundation of objectivity and integrity.

Before addressing specific allegations of slanted intelligence, I want to speak about the subject area on which most of the allegations are focused, the relatively narrow area of Soviet policy in the Third World.

And I might add, that part of the Soviet office from which nearly all of the allegations before this committee emanate. CIA's work on this subject in the 1970s, in my view, and in the view of many policy-makers in the Nixon, Ford and Carter administrations had been flabby. CIA's analysts missed the likelihood and significance in 1975 of the massive Soviet supply of military hardware to Angola, where it was married up with tens of thousands of Cuban soldiers. The agency missed similar developments in Ethiopia in 1977 and failed to foresee the invasion of Afghanistan in 1979. They downplayed the Soviet role in the flow of arms through Cuba to Central America.

They obscured, in the 1970s and early 1980s, the reality that the Soviets were prepared to put at risk their relationship with the United States rather than forgo opportunities in the Third World. As one agency evaluation made clear, instruments of Soviet foreign policy such as covert action and disinformation were dealt with only in passing, and the seamy side of Soviet activity, such as assassination or support for terrorism were avoided.

The need for more rigorous work was evident. Surveys of users of intelligence suggested it was our weakest area.

[Integrity Was Preserved]

In sum, Mr. Chairman, a careful review of the actual record of what was published and sent to policy-makers demonstrates that the integrity of the process was preserved. We were wrong at times, but our judgments were honest and unaffected by a desire to please or slant.

Our review process wasn't easy, but it was far from closed. It was rigorous, but it was fair. People who wanted to be heard were heard.

I was demanding and blunt, probably sometimes too much so. I had and have strong views. But as both Mr. MacEachin and Mr. Fuller said yesterday, I'm open to argumentation, and there was a lot of that. And I never distorted intelligence to support policy or to please a policy-maker.

Nevertheless, what has emerged in these hearings is clear evidence that the perception of politicization in some areas remains real and must be addressed by the next director. What is needed then is a set of measures to ensure that the integrity of the process is protected; that one or another person's views do not inhibit the diversity of analysis, and that analysts need not play it safe with upper management through self-censorship, and yet, to accomplish these objectives while maintaining and further improving the quality and intellectual toughness of the product.

To change an atmosphere, a tone, is a tall order. And in the real world, probably never perfectly attainable. Even so, there are measures that can be taken.

First, if confirmed, I would candidly and quickly address these issues for all analysts. I would stress the importance of integrity and objectivity of the product, the importance of ensuring that divergent views are heard and conveyed to the policy-maker, and emphasize to all managers that analysts are to be encouraged to speak their minds openly and that there should be incentives for doing this.

In short, we should try to codify that professional ethic Mr. MacEachin described and make it part of our daily work.

In this connection I would also tell all agency employees that my door is open to those with concerns about this and other issues, and that I intend to reach out to them as well.

I also would ask for a restoration of collegiality [and] civility that acknowledges that honest people can and will disagree and that we must not attribute base motives when disagreements are involved.

Second, all managers—I believe all managers of analysis should have as a part of their own performance evaluation an appraisal of how well they encourage the above principles and values in their organizations, their openness to alternative views, and their willingness to support their analysts up the line once they've approved the analysis themselves.

Third, if confirmed, I would direct the office of the statutory inspector general to pay special attention to problems of analytical process, and to serve as a focal point for analysts and analytical managers concerned about process and the integrity of the product.

Fourth, I believe issues relating to integrity of analysis, relationships with policy-makers and managing different points of view, should be made a part of every training course for analysts and their managers.

Fifth, this committee and its House counterpart for the past decade have focused especially on budget and clandestine activities. I encourage the committees to consider re-establishing something like their old analysis and production subcommittee that can focus oversight on the analytic process.

This also could help the DCI better deal with analytical problems such as you've heard in the last few days.

Sixth, if confirmed, I would ask the president's foreign intelligence advisory board for its help and ideas in this area.

Seventh, if confirmed, I would consider creation of an analysis council of retired former senior officers that could advise the DDI and DDCI [deputy director of central intelligence] and the deputy director for intelligence about the problems we are discussing; suggest possible additional remedies; and perhaps serve also as ombudsman to hear and evaluate analyst complaints and concerns.

Eighth, and finally: If confirmed, I would solicit from the analysts and the managers of analysis themselves their own ideas on how to rebuild morale, ensure integrity and independence, how to avoid self-censorship and deal with the perceptions of politicization.

If confirmed, I would expect to report to both Intelligence committees on implementation of these and related measures when Congress returns in January.

Mr. Chairman, I thank you and the committee for your patience. But the allegations of slanting intelligence are so insidious, and the integrity of analysis so central to our work that I felt it imperative to deal with the allegations in detail this morning and to set forth my ideas for dealing with the perceptions problem and its potentially corrosive effect.

The proof that the integrity of analysis was preserved is in the quality of the people that produced the assessments, and in the documents themselves. The nearly 2,500 major assessments and estimates produced while I was DDI and deputy DCI.

I am fully prepared to stake my reputation and integrity on the body of that work. I was, and am, proud of it, and proud to have been associated with the people who produced it.

Mr. Chairman, in closing, let me just say I have been gratified by the strong support in front of this committee by Adm. [Bobby R.] Inman and John McMahon, two of our country's most senior and esteemed intelligence professionals. Both addressed the issue of politicization, and fully endorsed my integrity and honesty in that process. And virtually all of the allegations concerned here took place at a time when one or the other was present.

They also affirmed my ability and qualifications to lead the intelligence community. Most important, President Bush, with whom I have worked so closely during these revolutionary times, has spoken publicly and repeatedly of his confidence in my integrity and my ability to lead the CIA and the intelligence community.

This uncommon relationship between us, and his expectations having himself been director, offer a unique opportunity to remake American intelligence, and to do so while preserving and promoting the integrity of the intelligence process and a strong and positive relationship with the Congress. Thank you.

UN COMMISSIONER ON REFUGEE RESETTLEMENT
October 7, 1991

During the 1980s the world refugee population doubled to approximately 15 million and then surged to as many as 18 million in 1991, constituting the largest body of displaced persons since World War II. Sadako Ogata of Japan, the United Nations high commissioner for refugees, told a UN committee October 7 that "the largest and fastest refugee exodus" resulted from the Persian Gulf War. However, she said that among the 1.5 million Iraqis who fled in fear of their lives, all but 500,000 had been returned to their homes and all but 70,000 to their country. While extolling the work of the High Commission for Refugees, the agency she heads, Ogata said in an address to its executive committee that the global task of protecting and resettling refugees would require more coordination by the United Nations and many countries.

The following month, in an address to the UN's social and humanitarian committee, Ogata said she was exploring new sources of income to supplement the agency's $980 million outlay in 1991. Anticipated new sources of financing would include loans from the World Bank and regional development banks to meet the costs of returning about 2 million refugees in Africa, Asia, and Central America to the homes from which they had been driven by war, terrorism, and famine.

Decades of civil warfare came to a halt in Ethiopia during 1991, opening the door for the return of 250,000 refugees from the northern province of Eritrea who had retreated into neighboring Sudan. In addition, approximately 400,000 Somalis moved into Ethiopia to escape civil war in their own country.

Other repatriation efforts by the UN agency in Africa included 600,000

Liberians, 500,000 Rwandans, and 300,000 Angolans—all driven from their homelands by civil strife. The agency also helped to return from exile nearly 40,000 South Africans who escaped their country for political reasons during the apartheid years.

In Asia, 350,000 Cambodian refugees awaited repatriation under a UN peace plan for that war-ravaged country. The biggest group resettlement task of all would be needed if rebel fighters reach an agreement with the Kabal government to end the guerrilla warfare in Afghanistan, thereby making possible the return of 4 million Afghans who took refuge in neighboring Pakistan and Iran.

In El Salvador, an impending settlement of a decade-old conflict between the government and leftist guerrillas enabled tens of thousands of Salvadoran exiles to return to their country.

> *Following are excerpts from the address by Sadako Ogata, United Nations high commissioner for refugees, to the agency's executive committee October 7, 1991, outlining efforts to deal with the world refugee problem:*

. . . In the Persian Gulf, we have witnessed the largest and fastest refugee exodus in recent times. Less than five months after 1.5 million Iraqis fled their homes, all but some 70,000 are back. Some have been able to return to their homes, others—numbering some 500,000—are back in their country but still displaced. A swift and volatile exodus has been followed by an equally fast but fragile return.

In the Horn of Africa, massive humanitarian operations have had to substitute for more constructive, economic and social development efforts. Continuing conflicts, timid democratisation and tenuous peace initiatives make that region a mixture of hope and concern.

In Europe, the free movements of people that only recently were seen as the harbinger of political change in the East have now become the source of deep concern—sometimes fears—in the West. Growing numbers of asylum-seekers have stretched existing procedures and practices to their limits and put the institution of asylum to test. On the other hand, the countries in Eastern Europe which not so long ago were producers of refugees are now receiving them. . . .

1991 has been a year marked, not only by exodus but also by new opportunities for returns. Last month, I signed an agreement with the Government of South Africa, paving the way for a UNHCR [United Nations High Commissioner for Refugees] presence in South Africa and the safe return of exiles.

Right now, we are standing in the wings ready to repatriate Western Saharans to participate in the referendum on the future of the Territory.

In Cambodia, as the lead agency for voluntary repatriation, we are accelerating our preparations to keep pace with the rapid and positive political developments. But further action is hampered by inadequate response to the Secretary-General's appeal last year on behalf of UNHCR for US$33 million needed for preparatory arrangements. I must take this opportunity to urge governments strongly to make immediate and generous contributions.

Some solutions are going almost unnoticed. In Central America, for instance, refugees have been returning home in large numbers, thanks to regional peace initiatives.... During my trip to Central America later this month, I shall be closing the last refugee camp for Nicaraguans in Costa Rica.

We are establishing a presence in Eritrea as a prelude to significant returns from Sudan. The peace agreement in Angola makes it realistic to plan for the return of 300,000 refugees early next year. Negotiations are continuing for a lasting solution to the Rwandese refugee problem. A Tripartite Commission, composed of Burundi, Tanzania and UNHCR, is planning for the return of some 94,000 refugees to Burundi. Tripartite discussions between Laos, Thailand and UNHCR are expected to lead to the voluntary return of some 55,000 Laotians over the next few years, while returns to Vietnam now exceed 13,000.

The outflow from Vietnam has subsided considerably, with the notable exception of arrivals to Hong Kong. However, the stalemate in finding a dignified and humane solution to those determined not to be refugees has hampered further progress. Consultations on this important subject are continuing and I am hopeful that a consensus can be reached soon so that all those who have not qualified as refugees can return home in safety and dignity.

In Afghanistan, notwithstanding the security situation, some 200,000 refugees have returned from Pakistan this year. Likewise, despite continuing insecurity, Liberian refugees are returning to their country. I do hope that political initiatives will lead to more orderly solutions to this problem which is weighing heavily on the countries neighbouring Liberia.

New refugee emergencies, actual repatriation operations or prospective return movements, as well as on-going care and maintenance programmes, have created the highest ever UNHCR programme requirements. At the end of last year, we expected total expenditure in 1991 to be at the level of some US$560 million. Today, the projected total needs for 1991 amount to US$982.5 million. A year of unprecedented needs has been matched by an equally unprecedented response. As of today, donors have made available US$785 million in voluntary contributions. I am deeply thankful for this support. I see it not only as a sign of confidence in UNHCR but also as a clear commitment on the part of the international community to participate in an effort of solidarity and burden-sharing to alleviate the plight and promote solutions for the some 17 million refugees under our care. The contribution of the countries of asylum to this international effort is immeasurable.

Greater support brings with it greater expectations and greater demands. I am acutely conscious that our performance must measure up to the confidence which the international community has placed in us. You will appreciate, Mr. Chairman, the strains on a bureaucracy that in the course of fifteen months has had three High Commissioners and, within a period of eighteen months, has gone through a retrenchment exercise followed by around 60% increase in activity. The administrative and management requirements to respond to the record needs this past year have been staggering.

I have been impressed by the tolerance, patience and commitment of UNHCR staff and their families during these turbulent times. Many of them risk their personal safety in difficult field situations. Some have paid dearly for it. Mr. Chairman, I should like to record a special tribute to six Somali and Ethiopian colleagues who lost their lives during the recent upheavals in their countries. There is no doubt that UNHCR's effectiveness depends heavily on the commitment and contributions of a motivated staff guided by a competent group of senior managers at the appropriate level. . . . I am eminently aware of the legitimate concerns in areas of staff welfare and job satisfaction. There are a range of personnel issues that need to be addressed but which have gone unattended as we have concentrated on meeting the demands of an exceptional year. I am determined to take a comprehensive look at these issues in the coming months.

Mr. Chairman, as the 40th Anniversary Year of UNHCR draws to a close, issues of migration and refugees have become an increasingly important and essential component in formulating a more open and just world order. The ending of the Cold War has placed before us new challenges. On the one hand, there are risks of further displacement as nationalistic, ethnic and religious tensions flare up. On the other hand, there are immense opportunities for solutions in the changing climate of multilaterism. At the same time, stagnant refugee situations of Afghans, Mozambicans and Liberians, fester, eroding human dignity and impeding regional peace. At this time, I believe that UNHCR must chart a forward-looking strategy which focusses on prevention and solutions and addresses the totality of the refugee problem from exodus and relief to return and reintegration. My strategic plan has three aims.

My *first* aim is to improve UNHCR's emergency preparedness and response mechanism. . . . The proposals presented to you at this session will not only enable UNHCR to respond to refugee emergencies, but can contribute also to a UN system-wide emergency response in case of large and complex humanitarian disasters. . . . Let me simply reiterate that, based on our recent experience in the Persian Gulf area and the Horn of Africa, I see a clear need for an arrangement that fully utilises the political and humanitarian potential of the UN while assuring a coordinated operational response to complex emergencies. The goal of coordination should be to facilitate cooperation and not to add to the bureaucratic layer of control. It should be based on a standby arrangement for funds, personnel and equipment and should be supported by a standing inter-agency secretariat.

In responding to emergencies we must not forget those who are the most vulnerable, in other words the women and children. With the example of the Coordinator for Refugee Women to inspire us, I intend to appoint a Coordinator for Refugee Children as soon as possible, thanks to the support of the Government of Norway. In the past few years we have developed some useful policy guidelines on refugee women and children but it is painfully obvious that the Office still has a long way to go in translating the policies into systematic, concrete action....

Another vulnerable, yet overlooked, element in emergencies, as much as in on-going refugee situations, is the environment. Economising on refugee assistance in the short term may be prohibitively costly on the environment in the long run. The impact of large numbers of refugees on the environment in Malawi and Pakistan are but two examples. We need to give greater consideration to environmental issues in our assistance activities. Degradation of the environment may lead to displacement, and displacement may cause further degradation of the environment. Conversely, sustainable development may reduce displacement. I hope that next year's UNCED Conference in Rio de Janeiro will pay attention to the link between population movements, the environment and development.

My *second* goal is to pursue every opportunity for voluntary repatriation. In a world where most refugees are confined to over-crowded, makeshift camps in conditions as dismal—if not more dismal—than the situation they have fled, the right to return to one's homeland must be given as much recognition as the right to seek asylum abroad. Renewed confidence in the ability of the United Nations to tackle global challenges is opening up new prospects for peace around the world. The prevention and solution of refugee problems is inextricably linked to these peace-building and peace-keeping efforts. I see 1992 as the year for voluntary repatriation.

It is very encouraging that the prospects for the return of many refugees seem brighter today than in the past. But I am concerned about the kind of life to which they are expected to go back. In July this year I visited Ethiopia, and met many of the Ethiopians who had come back from Somalia. They had come home to escape fighting in Somalia and found themselves hungry and homeless on return. They are back, but in the absence of prospects, the question is: for how long? Is the problem of displacement simply going to be shifted from one side of the border to the other? Are we going to be confronted with returnee emergencies just as we are now facing refugee emergencies? And at what cost to the fragile process of peace in these countries?

The country of origin must accept responsibility for its own citizens—both in terms of conditions which avert forced exile and also which promote voluntary return. However, large scale repatriation can only succeed if there is a concerted international effort to create proper conditions for return. Most of the countries to which refugees are returning or will return have been devastated by war. They already have large numbers of internally displaced persons, and little or no capacity to reabsorb those who left. Returning refugees can only be properly reintegrated if there are comprehensive programmes for political, economic, and social construction or reconstruction. As such, ensuring the success of voluntary repatriation goes beyond the mandate or resources of UNHCR alone. UNHCR's short-term relief and aid to returnees must be complemented by and integrated with the national development efforts for the entire population. UNHCR is not a development agency but I am determined to act as a catalyst, sensitising, encouraging, cooperating with development organisations, donors and, most of all, the countries concerned.

I am optimistic that the concept of returnee aid and development will attract much interest and support. Firstly, the country of origin would have a clear stake in seeing its citizens return and, in the process, act as a dynamo for local, regional or national development efforts. Secondly, I trust that development organisations and lending institutions will see an interest in contributing to humanitarian solutions which might provide more stability for long-term economic development. Thirdly, donors would wish to see their resources directed towards consolidation of lasting solutions rather than protracted care and maintenance programmes in countries of asylum. . . .

My *third* objective is to promote solutions through preventive measures at the source of the problem. The first step in this approach must be to define who is in need of international protection. The Working Group on Solutions and Protection has helped to clarify some of the issues. But it is important for the international community to arrive at a clear and agreed understanding of who deserves international protection. People leave their homes not because they want to, but because they have to. Refugees flee to save their lives, economic migrants to improve the prospects of life. A better understanding of the different reasons that drive people to move will help to identify the ways in which outflows could possibly be prevented. I should clarify that I define prevention not as building barriers to stop people moving but as removing or reducing the factors which force displacement.

The root causes of refugee flows are ultimately related to political conflict and violation of human rights. When people feel their lives and liberties are secure, they have no reason to seek asylum elsewhere. The responsibility as well as the capacity for addressing these root causes lies with governments and bodies other than UNHCR. But I firmly believe that UNHCR must promote and assist such a course. We must be prepared not only to switch resources as necessary from the country of asylum to the country of origin but also to develop the necessary tools for effective action to avoid refugee flows. Among these tools are: *one:* closer cooperation with human rights bodies and participation in wider early warning activities. *Two:* developing country of origin data base. We have already started work on it. Not only will it help develop action to avoid outflows but will also help us to provide advice on refugee status determination, the application of cessation clauses and the "safe country" concept. *Three:* closer contacts with development and lending institutions. *Four:* promotion of mass communication campaigns to address the expectations and misconceptions of those seeking to move. We are about to launch a new mass communication strategy in Europe, capitalizing on our experience from Vietnam.

In fact, many of these tools have been tested in Southeast Asia under the Comprehensive Plan for Action. They have been refined and reapplied in our approach to the problem in Albania. I see them as important elements in any strategy to address potential or actual population movements in Europe.

At our June meeting, I said that an important preventive measure must be to respond to the needs of the internally displaced. Their plight is as compelling as that of those who cross national frontiers. The problem, however, goes beyond the capacity of any one agency. What is needed is a coordinated and concerted response from the UN system. . . . UNHCR's experience, past and present, on behalf of internally displaced persons could serve as useful models for such concerted efforts. The . . . operation in El Salvador could also offer interesting pioneering lessons in this regard. In my view, respect for national sovereignty should not restrict but should rather be reconciled with the protection and assistance needs of the internally displaced. We must build on principles of humanitarian law, human rights and refugee law to develop a legal framework and operational guidelines for humanitarian access to those in need.

In developing our strategy on prevention and solutions, let me emphasize that UNHCR should not and will not abrogate its responsibility to promote a liberal asylum policy. At a time when respect for human rights and the rule of law are gaining universal ground, I would like to see a greater emphasis—and acceptance—of UNHCR's supervisory protection role in favour of refugees. With this aim in mind, we have begun a review of our resources and structures in Europe, so that new policy priorities can be established and necessary changes introduced to assure efficiency and effectiveness. It should be underlined that in attempting to restructure our existing resources, we are determined to do our utmost to avoid incurring additional costs.

In this context, I believe it is crucial for UNHCR to develop a higher public profile. An effective public information strategy is an essential tool for protection. Public opinion and public policy are shaped by mass media and statements by policy makers. I am deeply concerned to sense a rising xenophobic mood in various countries, and I strongly urge all leaders to use their power and influence to combat these dangerous trends. On its part, UNHCR must contribute to a more informed and credible public debate by providing reliable facts and figures. Thus, we have already begun work within UNHCR to help improve our reporting on refugee statistics. . . .

UNHCR was created 40 years ago in 1951 at the height of the East West confrontation in order to protect and assist those fleeing totalitarian persecution. Eventually the desire of people to move across borders to enjoy freer and better opportunities forced the repressive regimes in Eastern Europe to change. The crumbling of the Berlin Wall on 9th November 1989 was one of the most significant events symbolising the end of the Cold War. The one lesson we can learn from the past is that building walls is no answer against those who feel compelled to flee. The answer should be to build bridges—between West and East, North and South, allowing democracy, human rights and prosperity to spread. As we meet in the 40th anniversary year, I commit UNHCR to a course that will lead to a more open and just world order in which many refugees will find their way back home and no one would be forced to flee.

NAVY APOLOGY FOR ACCUSING SAILOR IN *IOWA* EXPLOSION

October 17, 1991

The U.S. Navy formally admitted October 17 that it had conducted a flawed inquiry into the April 19, 1989, gunpowder explosion aboard the battleship Iowa *and apologized for implicating Clayton M. Hartwig, one of the forty-seven victims. Adm. Frank B. Kelso II, chief of naval operations, said at a Pentagon news briefing that the Navy lacked "clear and convincing" proof that Hartwig was to blame for the accident and that its cause may never be known.*

Hartwig and the other sailors died when the blast ripped through a gun turret during practice firing of the warship's mammoth sixteen-inch guns in the Atlantic Ocean. The Navy reported September 17, 1989, that "irrefutable facts" and circumstantial evidence pointed to an act of suicidal sabotage by Clayton, a twenty-four-year-old gunner's mate, who was the turret's gun captain. (Navy's Report on the USS Iowa *Explosion, Historic Documents of 1989, p. 517)*

Relatives of the deceased sailors, the press, and members of Congress questioned the Navy's report from the time it was issued. The Senate Armed Services Committee directed the General Accounting Office to review the investigation. The agency enlisted government scientists at Sandia National Laboratories in New Mexico, who determined that the explosion could have been set off accidentally by the improper use of a hydraulic ram to load gunpowder into the weapon. (GAO Report Challenging Navy's Iowa *Findings, Historic Documents of 1990, p. 319)*

The Navy initially rejected the Sandia finding but later concurred after conducting similar tests of its own at committee insistence, thus reopening the investigation. Rear Adm. Richard L. Milligan, who super-

vised the Navy's inquiry, had said there could be no explanation for an accidental explosion. Navy investigators then deduced that someone caused the explosion, and "most probably" it was Hartwig. He was portrayed as moody, lovelorn, and suicidal in a psychological profile prepared by the FBI at the Navy's request after his death.

Admiral Kelso, announcing his endorsement of a new investigative report at the news briefing, read a statement extending "my sincere regrets" to Hartwig's family. His apology was also expressed in a letter delivered to Hartwig's parents in Cleveland, Ohio. His sister, Kathleen Kubicina, who led a public campaign to clear Hartwig's name, was quoted as saying: "I feel a whole lot better now that my brother can finally rest in peace." Several lawsuits had been filed against the Navy by families of sailors killed in the Iowa explosion, including a $40 million suit by the Hartwig family for "intentional and negligent infliction of emotional distress."

Kelso refused to comment on the pending litigation. The admiral also apologized to the other bereaved families "that such a long period has passed" without "a certain answer" as to the cause of the accident. As for Hartwig, he said: "There is no clear and convincing proof of the cause of the Iowa explosion, and the Navy will not imply that a deceased individual is to blame for his own death or the deaths of others without such clear and convincing proof."

Asked if the new report exonerated Hartwig, Kelso answered: "I suppose you could interpret it that way, yes." But in response to further questioning, he said the Navy did not rule out the possibility of sabotage. He said that "despite the Sandia theory and two years of subsequent testing, a substantial body of scientific and expert evidence . . . continues to support the initial investigation that no plausible accidental cause can be established." Nevertheless, "The opinion that the explosion on board USS Iowa . . . resulted from a wrongful intentional act is not supported by the evidence."

Kelso characterized the initial investigation as an honest attempt to determine the cause of the accident and indicated he did not expect to punish anyone involved in it. However, he said the Navy would require a higher standard of proof in future investigations.

Following is a statement by Adm. Frank B. Kelso II, chief of naval operations, at a Pentagon news briefing October 17, 1991, on the Navy's investigation of the fatal explosion on board the battleship Iowa in 1989, and excerpts from an official transcript of subsequent questions and answers:

Good afternoon. I'll make a statement on the USS Iowa investigation. This statement is my endorsement on the investigation report.

The investigation of the explosion in turret two on board the Iowa has been the most extensive ever conducted by the Navy. This unprecedented effort has consumed more than two years, during which thousands of scientific tests and experiments, and hundreds of thousands of man-hours have been expended in an attempt to discover the cause of the tragedy, and to ensure the safety of 16-inch guns. The professionalism and dedication of the scientists, technicians, and supporting teams assisting the Navy and Sandia National Laboratories, has been extraordinary. Their respective reports reflect a tremendous application of effort and intellect that has gone into this investigation.

A review of the process under which the initial investigation was conducted has led to important changes in the Navy procedures applicable to major incidents. Although a more formal investigative forum was available at the time of the Iowa explosion, it was not used. As a consequence of the Iowa experience, the Secretary has issued guidance that requires more formal procedures to be used in major incidents. These changes include requirements for a hearing or formal Board of Inquiry, and a higher, clear and convincing standard of proof when the intentional acts of a deceased member are called into question.

The initial Iowa investigation stated the opinion that the explosion in turret two resulted from a wrongful, intentional act. Based on all evidence available at the time, two factors led to the Navy's conclusion that intentional human intervention caused the explosion. Extensive laboratory and operational testing did not identify a plausible cause of the accident.

Second, microscopic traces of material believed to be foreign to the gun turret environment were found trapped in the projectile's rotating band.

At the time we released our initial investigation on September 7, 1989, we stated that future technical testing might result in changes or modifications to these findings and opinions. Ten months later, independent tests by Sandia National Laboratories, using sub-scale modeling under laboratory conditions, suggested that a possible accidental explosion might result from a high speed, compressive over-ram of the gun propellant powder. That discovery led to a re-evaluation of the Iowa explosion.

On 24 May 1990, Navy personnel from the Navel Surface Warfare Center, Dahlgren, Virginia, working with technical experts from Sandia, produced an explosive reaction using a full scale drop test fixture. The Iowa investigation was reopened to pursue this new evidence, and further testing and evaluation resulted in technical reports developed by Sandia and the Naval Sea Systems Command.

The Navy suspended firing of all 16-inch guns after the 24 May explosion reaction, and returned the 16-inch guns to service only after addressing the two crucial components of the Sandia theory—the possible presence of a small number of powder grains in the tear layer of the powder bags; and the potential compressive force that might be focused on those few grains during a high speed powder ram.

All 16-inch powder bags worldwide were inspected. Those found to have a small number of grains in the trim layer were removed from inventory. Additionally, recertification of the gun crews and a color-coded system to delineate clearly the slow speed ram position provide additional safeguards to prevent an accidental high speed powder ram. These steps eliminated the possibility of a reaction in the 16-inch guns as postulated.

During Desert Shield/Desert Storm Operations, USS Wisconsin and Missouri successfully fired 1,182 16-inch rounds under combat conditions without incident.

There is one conclusion we can draw with confidence. Our battleship 16-inch guns and their ammunition are safe to fire. This is a critically important result of our efforts. It's an assurance we owe to all our sailors, their families, and the American people.

Despite all the efforts that have gone into the Iowa investigation, however, my final conclusion is that there's no certain answer to the question of what caused the tragedy. The Sandia theory affected the foundation upon which the intentional act opinion rested by producing, at least experimentally, a possible accidental cause of the explosion. When tested under operational conditions, however, the probability of a Sandia-type reaction was found to be lower than what initial sub-scale laboratory tests had suggested. The significance of the Sandia theory to the decision-making process is that despite an enormously dedicated scientific effort, the theories relevant to the Iowa explosion cannot be proved or disproved with absolute certainty.

Considering all the evidence now available, the opinion that the explosion on board USS Iowa on 19 April 1989 resulted from a wrongful, intentional act, is not conclusively established by the evidence. Neither an intentional act nor an accidental cause can be proven or dismissed, given the limits of science and the dynamics of the blast and its aftermath. Without clear and convincing proof, an opinion—no matter how equivo-cally stated—that an individual may have intentionally brought about his own death and the deaths of 46 of his shipmates, is inappropriate.

Accordingly, the opinion that the explosion resulted from a wrongful, intentional act, is disproved. The exact cause of the explosion is unknown.

The initial investigation was an honest attempt to weigh impartially all the evidence as existed at the time. And indeed, despite the Sandia theory and almost two years of subsequent testing, a substantial body of scientific and expert evidence and analysis continue to support the initial investiga-tion finding that no plausible accidental cause can be established. How-ever, the initial investigation could not, and did not state conclusively that Gunners Mate Clayton Hartwig caused the blast.

Because there is no conclusive proof to support either theory, the final, official Navy position on the cause of the Iowa explosion is that the exact cause cannot be determined.

The initial investigation contained a qualified opinion that implicated GM2 [gunner's mate second-class] Clayton M. Hartwig, USN, and that opinion was interpreted by many as a conclusive finding of wrongdoing. For this, on behalf of the U.S. Navy, I extend my sincere regrets to the family of GM2 Hartwig. There is no clear and convincing proof of the cause of the Iowa explosion, and the Navy will not imply that a deceased individual is to blame for his own death or the deaths of others without such clear and convincing proof.

I also apologize to all the families of those who died on board USS Iowa, that such a long period has passed, and despite all efforts, no certain answer regarding the cause of this terrible tragedy can be found.

That ends my statement. I'll now take your questions.

Q: Admiral, Admiral Richard D. Milligan in his report insisted that he had to come up with a conclusion because Navy procedures required such a finding, and that he was convinced that it was the truth. What is Admiral Milligan's position now?

A: I've talked to Admiral Milligan. I can't speculate as to how he sees it now, Susanne. I see it this way—I have a different set of evidence than he had, and we changed the rules of the investigation, as I read in my statement. We have to have clear and convincing evidence in order to implicate anyone. The total of the testing that's been done since then gives you a different view of the accident. So I can't speculate as to how he would see it now. He can only speculate as to how he saw it then, I think.

Q: Are you saying that the Navy will not be able to come to such conclusion again, that you're making institutional changes that will require. . . .

A: We're making a major institutional change in how we investigate such an accident. In the future, an accident such as this, and we've used it three times since the Iowa investigation, we would require a three-man formal Board of Inquiry. The rules of evidence are different, more formal procedures to do that. The rules of evidence he was working under were a preponderance of evidence. We're now saying it's got to be clear and convincing in order to do so.

Q: The circumstances that the Sandia test set up were not determined to be in existence in turret two, was that correct? In other words, they stated that a high speed over-ram is what caused that. Since you haven't replicated that, what does that say about what really happened there?

A: What I'm saying is, Carl, I don't think we'll ever know. We did small-scale experiments based on Sandia's theory, and then we did actual gun experiments based on Sandia's theory. We absolutely proved that if the powder is rammed at slow speed, that you'll have no reaction. There is some probability that if it goes at the highest speed, that you could have a reaction. There is no evidence that the rammer was moving at a high speed. But I cannot, and Sandia's position is that they cannot prove at the time this explosion occurred, that we can't conclusively prove the speed at which the rammer was going. All the evidence I can see tends to give you the impression it was in slow speed.

Q: Admiral Kelso, what is the nature of the apology that's been conveyed to the Hartwig family this morning?

A: I provided the Hartwig family a letter. Admiral Doug Katz went out to present the letter to the Hartwig family, and to express my regrets and apology.

Q: Are you apologizing for the interpretation of the report blaming Clayton Hartwig, or are you apologizing for the conclusion that. . . .

A: I am regretting this incident. I am apologizing for the burden it has caused this family to bear.

Q: Admiral, since you have not been able to find a conclusive reason for the Iowa accident, and you have not been able to replicate the Sandia theory, how can you say any more now than you could have before, that the battleship 16-inch guns are safe to operate?

A: Because we've done an enormous amount of testing during this period of time to try to replicate Sandia's theory. Of all that testing, if you operate the powder ram in the slow speed position, we have not been able to make anything happen to cause an explosion. So if the gun is operated properly, it's a safe gun.

We've operated this type of gun for 90 years, and this is the only incident that I'm aware of that occurred where you had a cold gun: By that I mean the gun had not been fired previously, and had a accident on it. So it's a quite unusual tragedy.

Q: Is your decision today made any easier by the fact that the 16-inch guns are being mothballed?

A: No, I don't think so. I had to make that decision before we fired them in the Persian Gulf, and we had enough information then that I felt that I could make the decision that they could be fired safely then, and history proved that to be true.

Q: The earlier report indicated some criticism of inadequate training and manning of the Iowa. Has that changed with this new evidence?

A: Before I allowed them to fire the guns again, I made sure that each of the ships had the proper training and procedures. As I told you, we inspected all the powder to make sure it was in good shape, and that all the crews were prepared to do that.

Q: Admiral, there are a number of law suits pending on this case that have been filed by the families of the seamen who were killed. What impact do you think the statements you've made today will have on those?

A: Obviously, you're right. There are law suits in litigation, and I don't think I can comment on those, in the sense that they are in litigation, we'll have to let the procedure determine what the outcome is.

Q: Admiral, does your apology extend not only to the families and to the Hartwig family, but also to those individual sailors, Kendall Truitt is one that comes to mind. Another one is David Smith, who feel that they, themselves, were punished as a result of the Navy's investigation and conclusions.

A: We did not accuse Kendall Truitt of anything in the investigation, or the other gent. The accident occurred. Obviously, I'm very sorry that it ever occurred. It was a terrible, terrific tragedy that we had. I regret to anyone, and I'm sorry for anyone's personal grief or personal anguish over that. . . .

Q: Admiral, does this report exonerate Hartwig of causing the explosion?

A: I suppose you could interpret it that way, yes. I'm saying we did not have clear and convincing evidence that Clayton Hartwig caused this accident.

Q: So the Navy no longer believes that he most probably caused it?

A: What I read here is what I believe. I cannot tell you how it was caused, so I cannot blame it on Clayton Hartwig. I don't have clear and convincing evidence of that.

Q: Do you rule out any kind of human intervention?

A: No, I cannot rule out that there could have been a human intervention. It is one of the possible causes of this accident. But I can't describe for you in any convincing way as to how it took place.

Q: In other words, the first theory is almost as plausible now as the second theory, because you really don't have ...

A: I don't have proof, Carl. I don't think we'll ever know. If the evidence existed to provide conclusive proof in the aftermath of trying to take care of the deceased and all, it was unintentionally lost, and I don't know that it ever existed to do that. I don't believe, unless somebody comes forward with some evidence that we don't have now, I don't believe there's anything to continue to investigate that's going to give us an answer here.

Q: Admiral, this statement, however, isn't really inconsistent with the September 7th statement, that Hartwig most probably did it.

A: I'm not saying anybody most probably did it. I'm saying we don't know how it happened.

Q: In our [news] business, when we make mistakes this big, we are forced to apologize, and usually pay some money to the people. Do you think that's ...

A: I told you, there's a case in litigation. I can't comment on the litigation.

Q: What do you think, overall, the Navy handling of this whole incident has done to morale within the Navy—not just the crews of battleships, but morale in general?

A: I'm sure there are a lot of people who want to see this, what I've said today about, that both enlisted and officers throughout the Navy. My general belief is the morale in the Navy is very good. We all look upon this as a great tragedy.

One thing that I think we should all remember is what a great job the crew of the Iowa did to take this ship to sea after this accident, to take it on a six month cruise to the Mediterranean, and from all reports I had, they did a tremendous job. I think that speaks quite highly of the morale and dedication and discipline of the young people we have in the Navy today.

Q: Admiral, the test that caused you to reopen your investigation last year was done by Sandia at the request of the GAO [General Accounting Office], at the request of Congress, which acted at the request of Hartwig's family. If Kathy Kubocina and Hartwig's family hadn't raised cane [sic] in the wake of your initial investigation, would the Navy still be standing by its original conclusion?

A: I can't speculate on that. All I can tell you is what I'm telling you today, based on what evidence is available to me since that period of time.

Q: I'm a little confused on what the apology is for. Are you making an apology for the use of the words that Hartwig most probably did this? Or are you making the apology for the conclusion that others drew?

A: I'm making an apology for the fact that we drew the conclusion that Hartwig did this, and many considered it was conclusive that he did. Admiral Milligan originally said it was the most probable. So I'm very sorry that happened.

Q: You say making an apology for the conclusion we drew from it? Or that you . . .

A: Some people drew the conclusion for . . . No, not you, from anybody who drew that conclusion. . . .

Q: You said that even without that evidence that you shouldn't be blaming an individual without clear and conclusive proof, but certainly you did, didn't you?

A: We have changed our procedures now to make sure that we carry out a more formal investigation in the future for an incident of this magnitude.

Q: Let me try one more time then. Even without any new evidence, should the Navy have done, on September 7, 1989, what they did?

A: I cannot speculate. I have to make a decision now based on a different set of evidence, on a different set of circumstances. All I can give you is my interpretation and my explanation. . . .

Q: . . .[W]as there in fact a rush to judgment, or some pressure or requirement that there be a conclusion back in September?

A: I don't think there was any rush to judgment conclusion. I don't know, I wasn't there at the time. I'm sure there was a lot of pressure to make a decision—there always is in a case like this. I doubt that had an influence on what the judgment was.

Q: You would characterize that initial investigation as somewhat less, as shoddy?

A: No, I don't characterize it as shoddy. We had additional information based on the Sandia theory that caused us to do more investigation. I would be willing to do, if there was any other good information to tell me where to go, to do it again.

Q: Are you formally doing away with the one person investigation?

A: No. There are a lot of types of investigations where people are not killed, or something like that, that are not the nature of this accident. I'm saying we would look at the cases where we had people deceased, where there's a major accident, that we would go immediately to a formal investigation.

Q: When you have an investigation of this magnitude in the future, are you doing anything to make them more independent, so they come out from the aegis of Navy commands, would they have a wide berth to investigate without outside pressure from Navy higher-ups? Are you doing anything in that regard?

A: I'm not sure I understand the question.

Q: There's an implication that there may have been some pressures from above to rush through a judgment. Are you doing anything institutionally from within to . . .

A: I'm sorry for the length of time it's taken to come to the conclusion I've come to, but nobody could accuse me of rushing! (Laughter) I wanted to try very hard to make sure that I came to the best possible conclusion I can of this incident for both you and the American people.

Q: Admiral, you still haven't done one thing. That is, you still haven't told the Hartwigs, unless you've done something off-stage that we haven't seen, to say to them, your son definitely was not a murderer. We are sorry.

A: I provided the Hartwigs a letter of apology by Admiral Katz this morning.

Q: Which said?

A: Which said that I regretted what happened, that I regretted the burden that the family had had to bear. I apologized for the burden the family had had to bear.

Q: But all you're saying is you raised your standard of proof to clear and convincing proof. By inference, although you won't say so, that you shouldn't have accused him based on the evidence you had.

A: I am saying so. I'm saying that we're sorry that Clayton Hartwig was accused of this incident when we didn't have clear and convincing evidence.

Q: Do you have evidence that he'd most probably done it?

A: I don't know. What I'm telling you, from all the facts I know today, exactly what I said. I don't know exactly what caused the accident. I can't tell you if it was an intervention that I can't describe or an accident that I can't describe.

Q: I realize you've got an institutional burden on you, but isn't any good institution eventually capable of really doing a 180-degree turn, and isn't this an example of that?

A: I think I'm doing that.

Q: No, you're not.

A: Well, I feel that I am.

Q: Admiral, has the Navy retracted the accusation that Hartwig was a homosexual? The conclusion that that had to do, as well, was that presumed in what you're describing in your apology?

A: The Navy never accused Clayton Hartwig of being a homosexual.

Q: (Inaudible)

A: There were leaks that did. We tried to find out where the leaks came from, and there was an investigation done, and we could not conclusively find that out.

Q: That was part of the theory that was presented, that was presented here in this room as part of the theory. All I'm asking is, has that evaluation been relooked at, and specifically, does that accusation stand or not stand? And has that been discussed ...

A: I am not accusing him, nor do I think he was or have any evidence that he was....

Q: How was it that the Navy found evidence of a bomb that nobody else could find? Sandia couldn't find it, the FBI couldn't find it, but the Navy found it. How do you think that happened?

A: Well, as far as the information that's available to me as to what was there to describe that there was some device in the room. There's a difference of opinion between experienced and qualified people who do chemical analysis as to whether there is evidence of foreign material that you wouldn't expect in turret two, or whether there isn't evidence in turret two. I came to the conclusion, after reviewing the two, that it's not clear and conclusive, that it was different. There is a difference of opinion between people—on that issue.

Q: As you noted, the initial finding led to the Iowa being put back in service very quickly, and the other battleships certified as safe. Do you think the pressure to get these warships back on-line and in service, may have skewed the investigation and led to a conclusion that could not have been accurate?

A: I don't think so. I don't think any of us would dare let them use those guns if we didn't think they were safe to use.

Q: The Sandia Laboratories, I think a fair reading of the Sandia report finds the Navy wrong on three counts. One, that the iron particles that were found in the gun were evidence of a device being placed there. Second, that a high speed over-ram could not have occurred. They said wrong again. Third, that gun powder could not explode accidentally—I should say nitrocellulose propellant. They said wrong again. Do you accept those findings as contradicting the Navy's reports? Do you believe the Navy is still right? Or are you somewhere in the middle?

A: What I said. Sandia said they could not prove whether the ram was in a high or slow speed position. It was inconclusive. They said they could not prove whether there was either a device or there was not a device in it. Sandia said they agreed with the Navy that the gun powder was safe, that there was no instability in the gun powder.

Q: The Sandia report did come up with that the pellets could fracture and that they could ignite by themselves. Is there something wrong with the Navy's ...

A: No, they did not say that. They said they had to be under, in fact we proved that they have to be under pressure in order to ignite. In other words, the ram has to be traveling at a higher speed than is used to ram powder into the gun barrel.

Q: Could the Navy's technical people have found that out? Did they have the capability, or did they just not ...

A: The Navy's technical people worked with Sandia throughout this investigation, and most of the testing, all of the testing within the 16-inch guns were done by the Navy....

Q: Will your formal board include any non-Navy, that is independent people?

A: The formal board normally is a board of three officers, and they normally would be naval officers.

Q: If anything ...

A: We did not change the procedure for setting up a formal Board of Inquiry. It still would be three officers.

Q: In deciding to apologize publicly to the Hartwig family and others, did Navy lawyers or DoD lawyers consult with you over whether this might have some impact on Navy liability in the lawsuits?

A: Certainly I've talked to lawyers about what I'm going to say and what we're saying. That would be a normal procedure in any investigation, that I would consult with lawyers.

Q: Did any party urge you not to issue the apology?

A: No. . . .

Q: How hard, a question that civilians have a hard time grasping, how hard was it for you to get up here and make this apology today, and for the Navy as an institution to, as you said, do a 180-degree turn on this?

A: I think I'm doing what had to be done. It might have been hard, but that's part of the job. I feel it was the right thing to do.

Q: Was the reluctance to do this kind of responsible for the long time it took for the apology?

A: No, I don't think the reluctance, it was getting the investigations finished, being able to have the time to look them over, see what was said. I spent a lot of hours listening to the people from Sandia and from the Naval Sea Systems Command, asking them questions, looking at the mock-ups. I talked to the forensic pathologists and people like that. It takes time to put that together.

Q: Can you put a price tag on this entire investigation?

A: About $25 million. . . .

Q: Admiral, is any disciplinary action contemplated, or has any been taken against any of the people involved in the initial investigation?

A: As I said, I have reviewed all the investigations. I did not see in my review of it, that anybody had done anything but try to find out with the best information available to them what had happened, to do so. As I say, we've changed the rules of evidence to ensure that we look at it on a higher standard of proof in the future, to try to make sure we would not have that again.

Press: Thank you, Admiral.

POLITICAL SETTLEMENT
IN CAMBODIAN CONFLICT
October 23, 1991

Cambodia's warring factions signed a peace accord in Paris on October 23, promising relief for a land ravaged by two decades of internal strife, foreign occupation, mass murder, and famine. The agreement—brokered by the United States, the Soviet Union, and China—imposed an immediate cease-fire in Cambodia's thirteen-year-old civil war and authorized the use of a United Nations peacekeeping force to supervise disarmament of combatants and help prepare for free elections in 1993. Until then the existing Cambodian government, three opposition groups, and the UN would share in governing the country.

"What makes the case of Cambodia so extraordinary—and its claim for international support so compelling," said Secretary of State James A. Baker III, "is the magnitude of the suffering its people have endured." In a similar vein, French president François Mitterrand said, "A dark page of history has been turned." By some estimates, as many as 1 million Cambodians died at the hands of their countrymen—fanatical communist guerrillas known as the Khmer Rouge and supported by China. In 1975 they seized power from a U.S.-backed general, Lon Nol, and undertook a brutal campaign to reorder society along extreme Maoist lines. Typically, they forced city dwellers to the countryside for indoctrination programs involving harsh labor. Many died from beatings, starvation, and neglect. Large numbers of the educated and merchant classes were killed outright.

Vietnam, which was backed by the Soviet Union, nervously eyed China's influence in next-door Cambodia. In 1978 the Vietnamese army invaded Cambodia and drove the Khmer Rouge from power. In January

1979 Hanoi installed a puppet government, but remnants of the Khmer Rouge and two smaller armed groups carried on a guerrilla war with the Hanoi government and denied it effective control over large areas of the countryside. Under pressure from the United States and China, the three opposition groups formed a so-called coalition government in exile, but they never overcame their distrust of one another.

Return of Prince Sihanouk

The nominal head of this coalition was Prince Norodom Sihanouk—a central figure in Cambodian politics since 1941, when the ruling French leadership chose him at age eighteen to succeed his grandfather as king. Far from being the compliant monarch the French sought, Sihanouk engineered a successful drive for independence, which came in 1945. In 1955 Sihanouk abdicated in favor of his father and became prime minister.

During the 1960s Sihanouk tried to prevent Cambodia from being drawn into the Vietnam War. He angered Washington by feigning ignorance of the Viet Cong, the North Vietnamese guerrillas who oper- ated in border areas of Cambodia in order to attack South Vietnam. In 1970 American warplanes began bombing those areas of Cambodia. That year, while Sihanouk was on a visit to Moscow, Gen. Lon Nol staged a coup in Phnom Penh and deposed him. Five years later, the Khmer Rouge ousted Lon Nol's government and placed Sihanouk under house arrest. Freed when the Vietnamese army drove out the Khmer Rouge in 1978, Sihanouk then went into exile, bitterly denouncing both the Khmer Rouge and the Vietnamese occupation.

In 1987 Sihanouk stepped down as head of the opposition coalition and pursued his own peace objectives. He and Prime Minister Hun Sen of the Vietnamese-backed government met in Paris for a series of peace talks that ended inconclusively. By then Hanoi's position in Cambodia had been weakened by the Soviet Union's growing inability to continue its economic and military support of Vietnam.

Hanoi's Troop Withdrawal

Hanoi announced in April 1989 that all its troops would leave Cambo- dia by the end of September even if no agreement was reached. Following another round of uneventful peace talks among the warring Cambodian factions, the five permanent members of the United Nations Security Council—the United States, Soviet Union, China, Britain, and France—drafted a peace plan in 1990 calling for a UN administration to run the country until elections could be held.

A temporary cease-fire went into effect in May 1991, and soon afterward the Cambodian government and the opposition groups agreed to disband 70 percent of their military forces. During the summer China and Vietnam patched up their longstanding quarrels, giving the peace process new momentum. During talks in New York in September, the rival Cambodian parties removed the last big barrier to a peace pact by agreeing to a compromise system for elections—a system of proportional representation that would allow each faction parliamentary seats based on its share of the popular vote.

Final Agreement

The formal signing of the peace documents was conducted in Paris on October 23 by representatives of the opposition groups, the Cambodian goverment, and nineteen foreign guarantors of the pact. The agreement was spelled out in three documents. The first was on "a comprehensive political settlement," accompanied by detailed operational annexes. The second guaranteed Cambodian sovereignty, independence, and neutrality. The third committed the signatory nations to aid the country's reconstruction.

In return for Hanoi's support of the Cambodian agreement, Secretary Baker announced on the day of the signing that the United States would seek a gradual restoration of relations with Vietnam. Baker said similar ties would be developed with Cambodia and Laos. He also announced that an American trade embargo on Cambodian goods would be lifted and a trade liaison office would be opened in Phnom Penh.

Reaction to Agreements

The peace pact drew praise in the press and from politicians on several continents. However, the New York Times—among others—noted that the agreement "allows Pol Pot's gang of murderers to return to Phnom Penh in what is supposed to be a limited way." Many Cambodians also expressed their displeasure about the Khmer Rouge's participation in the new government.

The Khmer Rouge vowed to remain in the Supreme National Council, as the interim ruling coalition was called. However, its role was soon cast into doubt. Sihanouk received a joyous welcome from throngs of Cambodians upon his return from exile in November. Within a week the Vietnamese-installed government unexpectedly declared him interim president until elections could be held in 1993, clearly indicating an alliance with some of government's former foes in an effort to foil the Khmer Rouge. Sihanouk later announced that he wanted to bring to trial senior members of the Khmer Rouge on genocide charges.

As 1991 ended the durability of the peace process was still uncertain, as Cambodians swarmed into Phnom Penh streets December 21 to protest the return of two Khmer Rouge officials. The government responded by warning other leaders of that organization to stay out of the country because it could not guarantee their safety.

> *Following are "An Agreement on a Comprehensive Political Settlement of the Cambodia Conflict," excerpts from accompanying annexes to the document, plus a separate "Agreement Concerning the Sovereignty, Independence, Territorial Integrity and Involability, Neutrality and National Unity of Cambodia," signed in Paris on October 23,*

1991, by representatives of the participating government and principal Cambodian factions:

AGREEMENT ON A COMPREHENSIVE POLITICAL SETTLEMENT OF THE CAMBODIA CONFLICT

Part I
Arrangements During the Transitional Period

Section I
Transitional Period
Article 1

For the purposes of this Agreement, the transitional period shall commence with the entry into force of this Agreement and terminate when the constituent assembly elected through free and fair elections, organized and certified by the United Nations, has approved the constitution and transformed itself into a legislative assembly, and thereafter a new government has been created.

Section II
United Nations Transitional Authority in Cambodia
Article 2

(1) The Signatories invite the United Nations Security Council to establish a United Nations Transitional Authority in Cambodia (hereinafter referred to a "UNTAC") with civilian and military components under the direct responsibility of the Secretary-General of the United Nations. For this purpose the Secretary-General will designate a Special Representative to act on his behalf.

(2) The Signatories further invite the United Nations Security Council to provide UNTAC with the mandate set forth in this Agreement and to keep its implementation under continuing review through periodic reports submitted by the Secretary-General.

Section III
Supreme National Council
Article 3

The Supreme National Council (hereinafter referred to as "the SNC") is the unique legitimate body and source of authority in which, throughout the transitional period, the sovereignty, independence and unity of Cambodia are enshrined.

Article 4

The members of the SNC shall be committed to the holding of free and fair elections organized and conducted by the United Nations as the basis for forming a new and legitimate Government.

Article 5

The SNC shall, throughout the transitional period, represent Cambodia externally and occupy the seat of Cambodia at the United Nations, in the United Nations specialized agencies, and in other international institutions and international conferences.

Article 6

The SNC hereby delegates to the United Nations all powers necessary to ensure the implementation of this Agreement, as described in annex 1.

In order to ensure a neutral political environment conducive to free and general elections, administrative agencies, bodies and offices which could directly influence the outcome of elections will be placed under direct United Nations supervision or control. In that context, special attention will be given to foreign affairs, national defence, finance, public security and information. To reflect the importance of these subjects, UNTAC needs to exercise such control as is necessary to ensure the strict neutrality of the bodies responsible for them. The United Nations, in consultation with the SNC, will identify which agencies, bodies and offices could continue to operate in order to ensure normal day-to-day life in the country.

Article 7

The relationship between the SNC, UNTAC and existing administrative structures is set forth in annex 1.

Section IV
Withdrawal of foreign forces and its verification
Article 8

Immediately upon entry into force of this Agreement, any foreign forces, advisers, and military personnel remaining in Cambodia, together with their weapons, ammunition, and equipment, shall be withdrawn from Cambodia and not be returned. Such withdrawal and non-return will be subject to UNTAC verification in accordance with annex 2.

Section V
Cease-fire and cessation of outside military assistance
Article 9

The cease-fire shall take effect at the time this Agreement enters into force. All forces shall immediately disengage and refrain from all hostilities and from any deployment, movement or action which would extend the territory they control or which might lead to renewed fighting.

The Signatories hereby invite the Security Council of the United Nations to request the Secretary-General to provide good offices to assist in this process until such time as the military component of UNTAC is in position to supervise, monitor and verify it.

Article 10

Upon entry into force of this Agreement, there shall be an immediate cessation of all outside military assistance to all Cambodian Parties.

Article 11

The objectives of military arrangements during the transitional period shall be to stabilize the security situation and build confidence among the parties to the conflict, so as to reinforce the purposes of this Agreement and to prevent the risks of a return to warfare.

Detailed provisions regarding UNTAC's supervision, monitoring, and verification of the cease-fire and related measures, including verification of the withdrawal of foreign forces and the regrouping, cantonment and ultimate disposition of all Cambodian forces and their weapons during the transitional period are set forth in annex 1, section C, and annex 2.

Part II
Elections

Article 12

The Cambodian people shall have the right to determine their own political future through the free and fair election of a constituent assembly, which will draft and approve a new Cambodian Constitution in accordance with Article 23 and transform itself into a legislative assembly, which will create the new Cambodian Government. This election will be held under United Nations auspices in a neutral political environment with full respect for the national sovereignty of Cambodia.

Article 13

UNTAC shall be responsible for the organization and conduct of these elections based on the provisions of annex 1, section D, and annex 3.

Article 14

All Signatories commit themselves to respect the results of these elections once certified as free and fair by the United Nations.

Part III
Human Rights

Article 15

1. All persons in Cambodia and all Cambodian refugees and displaced persons shall enjoy the rights and freedoms embodied in the Universal Declaration of Human Rights and other relevant international human rights instruments.

2. To this end,

(a) Cambodia undertakes:

—to ensure respect for and observance of human rights and fundamental freedoms in Cambodia;

—to support the right of all Cambodian citizens to undertake activities which would promote and protect human rights and fundamental freedoms;

—to take effective measures to ensure that the policies and practices of the past shall never be allowed to return;

—to adhere to relevant international human rights instruments;

(b) the other Signatories to this Agreement undertake to promote and encourage respect for and observance of human rights and fundamental freedoms in Cambodia as embodied in the relevant international instruments and the relevant resolutions of the United Nations General Assembly, in order, in particular, to prevent the recurrence of human rights abuses.

Article 16

UNTAC shall be responsible during the transitional period for fostering an environment in which respect for human rights shall be ensured, based on the provisions of annex 1, section E.

Article 17

After the end of the transitional period, the United Nations Commission on Human Rights should continue to monitor closely the human rights situation in Cambodia, including, if necessary, by the appointment of a Special Rapporteur who would report his findings annually to the Commission and to the General Assembly.

Part IV
International Guarantees

Article 18

Cambodia undertakes to maintain, preserve and defend, and the other Signatories undertake to recognize and respect, the sovereignty, independence, territorial integrity and inviolability, neutrality and national unity of Cambodia, as set forth in a separate Agreement.

Part V
Refugees and Displaced Persons

Article 19

Upon entry into force of this Agreement, every effort will be made to create in Cambodia political, economic and social conditions conducive to the voluntary return and harmonious integration of Cambodian refugees and displaced persons.

Article 20

(1) Cambodian refugees and displaced persons, located outside Cambodia, shall have the right to return to Cambodia and to live in safety, security and dignity, free from intimidation or coercion of any kind.

(2) The Signatories request the Secretary-General of the United Nations to facilitate the repatriation in safety and dignity of Cambodian refugees and displaced persons, as an integral part of the comprehensive political settlement and under the overall authority of the Special Representative of the Secretary-General, in accordance with the guidelines and principles on the repatriation of refugees and displaced persons as set forth in annex 4.

Part VI
Release of Prisoners of War and Civilian Internees

Article 21

The release of all prisoners of war and civilian internees shall be accomplished at the earliest possible date under the direction of the International Committee of the Red Cross (ICRC) in co-ordination with the Special Representative of the Secretary-General, with the assistance, as necessary, of other appropriate international humanitarian organizations and the Signatories.

Article 22

The expression "civilian internees" refers to all persons who are not prisoners of war and who, having contributed in any way whatsoever to the armed or political struggle, have been arrested or detained by any of the parties by virtue of their contribution thereto.

Part VII
Principles for a New Constitution for Cambodia

Article 23

Basic principles, including those regarding human rights and fundamental freedoms as well as regarding Cambodia's status of neutrality, which the new Cambodian Constitution will incorporate, are set forth in annex 5.

Part VIII
Rehabilitation and Reconstruction

Article 24

The Signatories urge the international community to provide economic and financial support for the rehabilitation and reconstruction of Cambodia, as provided in a separate declaration.

Part IX
Final Provisions

Article 25

The Signatories shall, in good faith and in a spirit of co-operation, resolve through peaceful means any disputes with respect to the implementation of this Agreement.

Article 26

The Signatories request other States, international organizations and other bodies to co-operate and assist in the implementation of this Agreement and in the fulfilment by UNTAC of its mandate.

Article 27

The Signatories shall provide their full co-operation to the United Nations to ensure the implementation of its mandate, including by the provision of privileges and immunities, and by facilitating freedom of movement and communication within and through their respective territories.

In carrying out its mandate, UNTAC shall exercise due respect for the sovereignty of all States neighbouring Cambodia.

Article 28

(1) The Signatories shall comply in good faith with all obligations undertaken in this Agreement and shall extend full co-operation to the United Nations, including the provision of the information which UNTAC requires in the fulfilment of its mandate.

(2) The signature on behalf of Cambodia by the members of the SNC shall commit all Cambodian parties and armed forces to the provisions of this Agreement.

Article 29

Without prejudice to the prerogatives of the Security Council of the United Nations, and upon the request of the Secretary-General, the two Co-Chairmen of the Paris Conference on Cambodia, in the event of a violation or threat of violation of this Agreement, will immediately undertake appropriate consultations, including with members of the Paris Conference on Cambodia, with a view to taking appropriate steps to ensure respect for these commitments.

Article 30

This Agreement shall enter into force upon signature.

Article 31

This Agreement shall remain open for accession by all States. The instruments of accession shall be deposited with the Governments of the French Republic and the Republic of Indonesia. For each State acceding to the Agreement it shall enter into force on the date of deposit of its instruments of accession. Acceding States shall be bound by the same obligations as the signatories.

Article 32

The originals of this Agreement, of which the Chinese, English, French, Khmer and Russian texts are equally authentic, shall be deposited with the Governments of the French Republic and the Republic of Indonesia, which shall transmit certified true copies to the Governments of the other States participating in the Paris Conference on Cambodia, as well as the Secretary-General of the United Nations.

IN WITNESS WHEREOF the undersigned Plenipotentiaries, being duly authorized thereto, have signed this Agreement.

DONE at Paris this twenty-third day of October, one thousand nine hundred and ninety one.

Annex 1
UNTAC mandate

Section A. General procedures

1. In accordance with article 6 of the Agreement, UNTAC will exercise the powers necessary to ensure the implementation of this Agreement, including those relating to the organization and conduct of free and fair elections and the relevant aspects of the administration of Cambodia.

2. The following mechanism will be used to resolve all issues relating to the implementation of this Agreement which may arise between the Secretary-General's Special Representative and the Supreme National Council (SNC):

(a) The SNC offers advice to UNTAC, which will comply with this advice provided there is a consensus among the members of the SNC and provided this advice is consistent with the objectives of the present Agreement;

(b) If there is no consensus among the members of the SNC despite every endeavour of its President, H.R.H. Samdech NORODOM SIHA-NOUK, the President will be entitled to make the decision on what advice to offer to UNTAC, taking fully into account the views expressed in the SNC. UNTAC will comply with the advice provided it is consistent with the objectives of the present Agreement;

(c) If H.R.H. Samdech NORODOM SIHANOUK, President of the SNC, the legitimate representative of Cambodian sovereignty, is not, for whatever reason, in a position to make such a decision, his power of decision will transfer to the Secretary-General's Special Representative. The Special Representative will make the final decision, taking fully into account the views expressed in the SNC;

(d) Any power to act regarding the implementation of this Agreement conferred upon the SNC by the Agreement will be exercised by consensus or, failing such consensus, by its President in accordance with the procedure set out above. In the event that H.R.H. Samdech NORODOM SIHANOUK, President of the SNC, the legitimate representative of Cambodian sovereignty, is not, for whatever reason, in a position to act, his power to act will transfer to the Secretary-General's Special Representative who may take the necessary action;

(e) In all cases, the Secretary-General's Special Representative will determine whether advice or action of the SNC is consistent with the present Agreement.

3. The Secretary-General's Special Representative or his delegate will attend the meetings of the SNC and of any subsidiary body which might be established by it and give its members all necessary information on the decisions taken by UNTAC.

Section B. Civil administration

1. ... [A]ll administrative agencies, bodies and offices acting in the field of foreign affairs, national defence, finance, public security and information will be placed under the direct control of UNTAC, which will exercise it as necessary to ensure strict neutrality. In this respect, the Secretary-General's Special Representative will determine what is necessary and may issue directives to the above-mentioned administrative agencies, bodies and offices. Such directives may be issued to and will bind all Cambodian Parties.

2. ... [T]he Secretary-General's Special Representative, in consultation with the SNC, will determine which other administrative agencies, bodies and offices could directly influence the outcome of elections. These administrative agencies, bodies and offices will be placed under direct supervision or control of UNTAC and will comply with any guidance provided by it.

3. ... [T]he Secretary-General's Special Representative, in consultation with the SNC, will identify which administrative agencies, bodies, and offices could continue to operate in order to ensure normal day-to-day life in Cambodia, if necessary, under such supervision by UNTAC as it considers necessary.

4. ... [T]he authority of the Secretary-General's Special Representative will include the power to:

(a) Install in administrative agencies, bodies and offices of all the Cambodian Parties, United Nations personnel who will have unrestricted access to all administrative operations and information;

(b) Require the reassignment or removal of any personnel of such administrative agencies, bodies and offices.

5. (a) ... [T]he Special Representative of the Secretary-General will determine, after consultation with the Cambodian Parties, those civil police necessary to perform law enforcement in Cambodia....

(b) All civil police will operate under UNTAC supervision or control.... In consultation with the SNC, UNTAC will supervise other law enforcement and judicial processes throughout Cambodia to the extent necessary....

Section C. Military functions

1. UNTAC will supervise, monitor and verify the withdrawal of foreign

forces, the cease-fire and related measures in accordance with annex 2, including:

(a) Verification of the withdrawal from Cambodia of all categories of foreign forces, advisers and military personnel and their weapons, ammunition and equipment, and their non-return to Cambodia;

(b) Liaison with neighbouring Governments over any developments in or near their territory that could endanger the implementation of this Agreement;

(c) Monitoring the cessation of outside military assistance to all Cambodian Parties;

(d) Locating and confiscating caches of weapons and military supplies throughout the country;

(e) Assisting with clearing mines and undertaking training programmes in mine clearance and a mine awareness programme among the Cambodian people.

[2-5 omitted]

Section D. Elections

1. UNTAC will organize and conduct the election referred to in Part II of this Agreement in accordance with this section and annex 3.

2. UNTAC may consult with the SNC regarding the organization and conduct of the electoral process.

3. In the exercise of its responsibilities in relation to the electoral process, the specific authority of UNTAC will include the following:

(a) The establishment, in consultation with the SNC, of a system of laws, procedures and administrative measures necessary for the holding of a free and fair election in Cambodia, including the adoption of an electoral law and of a code of conduct regulating participation in the election in a manner consistent with respect for human rights and prohibiting coercion or financial inducement in order to influence voter preference;

(b) The suspension or abrogation, in consultation with the SNC, of provisions of existing laws which could defeat the objects and purposes of this Agreement;

(c) The design and implementation of a voter education programme . . . ;

(d) The design and implementation of a system of voter registration . . . to ensure that eligible voters have the opportunity to register and the subsequent preparation of verified voter registration lists;

(e) The design and implementation of a system of registration of political parties and lists of candidates;

(f) Ensuring fair access to the media, including press, television and radio, for all political parties contesting in the election;

(g) The adoption and implementation of measures to monitor and facilitate the participation of Cambodians in the elections, the political campaign, and the balloting procedures;

(h) The design and implementation of a system of balloting and polling, to ensure that registered voters have the opportunity to vote;

(i) The establishment, in consultation with the SNC, of co-ordinated arrangements to facilitate the presence of foreign observers wishing to observe the campaign and voting;

(j) Overall direction of polling and the vote count;

(k) The identification and investigation of complaints of electoral irregularities, and the taking of appropriate corrective action;

(l) Determining whether or not the election was free and fair and, if so, certification of the list of persons duly elected. . . .

Annex 2
Withdrawal, cease-fire and related measures

Article I
Cease-fire

1. All Cambodian Parties (hereinafter referred to as "the Parties") agree to observe a comprehensive cease-fire on land and water and in the air. This cease-fire will be implemented in two phases. During the first phase, the cease-fire will be observed with the assistance of the Secretary-General of the United Nations through his good offices. During the second phase, which should commence as soon as possible, the cease-fire will be supervised, monitored and verified by UNTAC. The Commander of the military component of UNTAC, in consultation with the Parties, shall determine the exact time and date at which the second phase will commence. This date will be set at least four weeks in advance of its coming into effect.

2. The Parties undertake that, upon the signing of this Agreement, they will observe a cease-fire and will order their armed forces immediately to disengage and refrain from all hostilities and any deployment, movement or action that would extend the territory they control or that might lead to a resumption of fighting, pending the commencement of the second phase. . . .

[3 omitted]

4. Immediately upon his arrival in Cambodia, and not later than four weeks before the beginning of the second phase, the Commander of the military component of UNTAC will, in consultation with the Parties, finalize UNTAC's plan for the regroupment and cantonment of the forces of the Parties and for the storage of their arms, ammunition and equipment. . . .

[5 and 6 omitted]

Article II
Liaison system and Mixed Military Working Group

A Mixed Military Working Group (MMWG) will be established with a view to resolving any problems that may arise in the observance of the cease-fire. It will be chaired by the most senior United Nations military officer in Cambodia or his representative. Each party agrees to designate an officer of the rank of brigadier or equivalent to serve on the MMWG. Its composition, method of operation and meeting places will be determined by the most senior United Nations military officer in consultation with the Parties. Similar liaison arrangements will be made at lower military command levels to resolve practical problems on the ground.

[Articles III and IV omitted]

Article V
Ultimate disposition of the forces of the Parties and of their arms, ammunition and equipment

1. In order to reinforce the objectives of a comprehensive political settlement, minimize the risks of a return to warfare, stabilize the security situation and build confidence among the Parties to the conflict, all Parties agree to undertake a phased and balanced process of demobilization of at least 70 per cent of their military forces. This process shall be undertaken in accordance with a detailed plan to be drawn up by UNTAC.... It should be completed prior to the end of the process of registration for the elections and on a date to be determined by the Special Representative of the Secretary-General.

2. The Cambodian Parties hereby commit themselves to demobilize all their remaining forces before or shortly after the elections and, to the extent that full demobilization is unattainable, to respect and abide by whatever decision the newly elected government that emerges in accordance with Article 12 of this Agreement takes with regard to the incorporation of parts or all of those forces into a new national army....

3. UNTAC will assist, as required, with the reintegration into civilian life of the forces demobilized prior to the elections....

Article VI
Verification of withdrawal from Cambodia and non-return of all categories of foreign forces

1. UNTAC shall be provided, no later than two weeks before the commencement of the second phase of the cease-fire, with detailed information in writing regarding the withdrawal of foreign forces....

[2 omitted]

3. Upon confirmation of the presence of any foreign forces, UNTAC will immediately deploy military personnel with the foreign forces and accompany them until they have withdrawn from Cambodian territory. UNTAC will also establish checkpoints on withdrawal routes, border crossing points and airfields to verify the withdrawal and ensure the non-return of all categories of foreign forces.

4. The Mixed Military Working Group (MMWG) ... will assist UNTAC in fulfilling the above-mentioned tasks.

Article VII
Cessation of outside military assistance to all Cambodian Parties

1. All parties undertake, from the time of the signing of this Agreement, not to obtain or seek any outside military assistance, including weapons,

ammunition and military equipment from outside sources.

2. The Signatories whose territory is adjacent to Cambodia, namely, the Governments of the Lao People's Democratic Republic, the Kingdom of Thailand and the Socialist Republic of Vietnam, undertake to:

(a) Prevent the territories of their respective States, including land territory, territorial sea and air space, from being used for the purpose of providing any form of military assistance to any of the Cambodian Parties. Resupply of such items as food, water, clothing and medical supplies through their territories will be allowed, but shall . . . be subject to UNTAC supervision upon arrival in Cambodia;

(b) Provide written confirmation to the Commander of the military component of UNTAC, not later than four weeks after the second phase of the cease-fire begins, that no forces, arms, ammunition or military equipment of any of the Cambodian Parties are present on their territories;

(c) Receive an UNTAC liaison officer in each of their capitals and designate an officer of the rank of colonel or equivalent, not later than four weeks after the beginning of the second phase of the cease-fire, in order to assist UNTAC in investigating, with due respect for their sovereignty, any complaints that activities are taking place on their territories that are contrary to the provisions of the comprehensive political settlement.

3. . . . Immediately after the second phase of the cease-fire begins, UNTAC will take the following practical measures:

(a) Establish check-points along the routes and at selected locations along the Cambodian side of the border and at airfields inside Cambodia;

(b) Patrol the coastal and inland waterways of Cambodia;

(c) Maintain mobile teams at strategic locations within Cambodia to patrol and investigate allegations of supply of arms to any of the Parties.

[Article VIII omitted]

Article IX
Unexploded ordnance devices

1. Soon after arrival in Cambodia, the military component of UNTAC shall ensure, as a first step, that all known mine-fields are clearly marked.

2. The Parties agree that, after completion of the regroupment and cantonment processes in accordance with Article III of the present annex, they will make available mine-clearing teams which, under the supervision and control of UNTAC military personnel, will leave the cantonment areas in order to assist in removing, disarming or deactivating remaining unexploded ordnance devices. Those mines or objects which cannot be removed, disarmed or deactivated will be clearly marked in accordance with a system to be devised by the military component of UNTAC.

3. UNTAC shall:

(a) Conduct a mass public education programme in the recognition and avoidance of explosive devices;

(b) Train Cambodian volunteers to dispose of unexploded ordnance devices;

(c) provide emergency first-aid training to Cambodian volunteers.

Article X
Investigation of violations

1. After the beginning of the second phase, upon receipt of any information or complaint from one of the Parties relating to a possible case of non-compliance with any of the provisions of the present annex or related provisions, UNTAC will undertake an investigation in the manner which it deems appropriate. Where the investigation takes place in response to a complaint by one of the Parties, that party will be required to make personnel available to accompany the UNTAC investigators. The results of such investigation will be conveyed by UNTAC to the complaining Party and the Party complained against, and if necessary to the SNC.

2. UNTAC will also carry out investigations on its own initiative in other cases when it has reason to believe or suspect that a violation of this annex or related provisions may be taking place.

Article XI
Release of prisoners of war

The military component of UNTAC will provide assistance as required to the International Committee of the Red Cross in the latter's discharge of its functions relating to the release of prisoners of war.

Article XII
Repatriation and resettlement of displaced Cambodians

The military component of UNTAC will provide assistance as necessary in the repatriation of Cambodian refugees and displaced persons carried out in accordance with articles 19 and 20 of this Agreement, in particular in the clearing of mines from repatriation routes, reception centres and resettlement areas, as well as in the protection of the reception centres.

Annex 3
Elections

1. The constituent assembly referred to in article 12 of the Agreement shall consist of 120 members. Within three months from the date of the election, it shall complete its tasks of drafting and adopting a new Cambodian Constitution and transform itself into a legislative assembly which will form a new Cambodian Government.

2. The election referred to in Article 12 of the Agreement will be held throughout Cambodia on a provincial basis in accordance with a system of proportional representation on the basis of lists of candidates put forward by political parties.

3. All Cambodians, including those who at the time of signature of this Agreement are Cambodian refugees and displaced persons, will have the same rights, freedoms and opportunities to take part in the electoral process.

4. Every person who has reached the age of eighteen at the time of application to register, or who turns eighteen during the registration period, and who either was born in Cambodia or is the child of a person born in Cambodia, will be eligible to vote in the election.

5. Political parties may be formed by any group of five thousand registered voters. Party platforms shall be consistent with the principles and objectives of the Agreement on a comprehensive political settlement.

6. Party affiliation will be required in order to stand for election to the constituent assembly. Political parties will present lists of candidates standing for election on their behalf, who will be registered voters.

7. Political parties and candidates will be registered in order to stand for election. UNTAC will confirm that political parties and candidates meet the established criteria in order to qualify for participation in the election. Adherence to a Code of Conduct established by UNTAC in consultation with the SNC will be a condition for such participation.

8. Voting will be by secret ballot, with provision made to assist those who are disabled or who cannot read or write.

9. The freedoms of speech, assembly and movement will be fully respected. All registered political parties will enjoy fair access to the media, including the press, television and radio.

Annex 4
Repatriation of Cambodian refugees
and displaced persons
Part I
Introduction

1. As part of the comprehensive political settlement, every assistance will need to be given to Cambodian refugees and displaced persons as well as to countries of temporary refuge and the country of origin in order to facilitate the voluntary return of all Cambodian refugees and displaced persons in a peaceful and orderly manner. It must also be ensured that there would be no residual problems for the countries of temporary refuge. The country of origin with responsibility towards its own people will accept their return as conditions become conducive.

Part II
Conditions Conducive to the Return
of Refugees and Displaced Persons
[2-3 omitted]

4. There must be full respect for the human rights and fundamental freedoms of all Cambodians, including those of the repatriated refugees and displaced persons, in recognition of their entitlement to live in peace and security, free from intimidation and coercion of any kind. These rights would include, *inter alia*, freedom of movement within Cambodia, the choice of domicile and employment, and the right to property. . . .
[5-7 omitted]

Part III
Operational Factors

8. Consistent with respect for principles of national sovereignty in the countries of temporary refuge and origin, and in close co-operation with the countries of temporary refuge and origin, full access by the Office of the United Nations High Commissioner for Refugees (UNHCR), ICRC and other relevant international agencies should be guaranteed to all Cambodian refugees and displaced persons, with a view to the agencies undertaking the census, tracing, medical assistance, food distribution and other activities vital to the discharge of their mandate and operational responsibilities; such access should also be provided in Cambodia to enable the relevant international organizations to carry out their traditional monitoring as well as operational responsibilities.

[9-11 omitted]

12. Those responsibilities for organizing and supervising the repatriation operation will need to ensure that conditions of security are created for the movement of the refugees and displaced persons. In this respect, it is imperative that appropriate border crossing points and routes be designated and cleared of mines and other hazards.

13. The international community should contribute generously to the financial requirements of the repatriation operation.

Annex 5
Principles for a new constitution for Cambodia

1. The constitution will be the supreme law of the land. It may be amended only by a designated process involving legislative approval, popular referendum, or both.

2. Cambodia's tragic recent history requires special measures to assure protection of human rights. Therefore, the constitution will contain a declaration of fundamental rights, including the rights to life, personal liberty, security, freedom of movement, freedom of religion, assembly and association including political parties and trade unions, due process and equality before the law, protection from arbitrary deprivation of property or deprivation of private property without just compensation, and freedom from racial, ethnic, religious or sexual discrimination. It will prohibit the retroactive application of criminal law. The declaration will be consistent with the provisions of the Universal Declaration of Human Rights and other relevant international instruments. Aggrieved individuals will be entitled to have the courts adjudicate and enforce these rights.

3. The constitution will declare Cambodia's status as a sovereign, independent and neutral State, and the national unity of the Cambodian people.

4. The constitution will state that Cambodia will follow a system of liberal democracy, on the basis of pluralism. It will provide for periodic and genuine elections. It will provide for the right to vote and to be elected by universal and equal suffrage. It will provide for voting by secret ballot,

with a requirement that electoral procedures provide a full and fair opportunity to organize and participate in the electoral process.

5. An independent judiciary will be established, empowered to enforce the rights provided under the constitution.

6. The constitution will be adopted by a two-thirds majority of the members of the constituent assembly.

AGREEMENT CONCERNING THE SOVEREIGNTY, INDEPENDENCE, TERRITORIAL INTEGRITY AND INVIOLABILITY, NEUTRALITY AND NATIONAL UNITY OF CAMBODIA

Article 1

1. Cambodia hereby solemnly undertakes to maintain, preserve and defend its sovereignty, independence, territorial integrity and inviolability, neutrality, and national unity; the perpetual neutrality of Cambodia shall be proclaimed and enshrined in the Cambodian constitution to be adopted after free and fair elections.

2. To this end, Cambodia undertakes:

(a) To refrain from any action that might impair the sovereignty, independence and territorial integrity and inviolability of other States;

(b) To refrain from entering into any military alliances or other military agreements with other States that would be inconsistent with its neutrality, without prejudice to Cambodia's right to acquire the necessary military equipment, arms, munitions and assistance to enable it to exercise its inherent right of self-defence and to maintain law and order;

(c) To refrain from interference in any form whatsoever, whether direct or indirect, in the internal affairs of other States;

(d) To terminate treaties and agreements that are incompatible with its sovereignty, independence, territorial integrity and inviolability, neutrality, and national unity;

(e) To refrain from the threat or use of force against the territorial integrity or political independence of any State, or in any other manner inconsistent with the purposes of the United Nations;

(f) To settle all disputes with other States by peaceful means;

(g) To refrain from using its territory or the territories of other States to impair the sovereignty, independence, and territorial integrity and inviolability of other States;

(h) To refrain from permitting the introduction or stationing of foreign forces, including military personnel, in any form whatsoever, in Cambodia, and to prevent the establishment or maintenance of foreign military bases, strong points or facilities in Cambodia, except pursuant to United Nations authorization for the implementation of the comprehensive political settlement.

Article 2

1. The other parties to this Agreement hereby solemnly undertake to recognize and to respect in every way the sovereignty, independence, territorial integrity and inviolability, neutrality and national unity of Cambodia.

2. To this end, they undertake:

(a) To refrain from entering into any military alliances or other military agreements with Cambodia that would be inconsistent with Cambodia's neutrality, without prejudice to Cambodia's right to acquire the necessary military equipment, arms, munitions and assistance to enable it to exercise its inherent right of self-defence and to maintain law and order;

(b) To refrain from interference in any form whatsoever, whether direct or indirect, in the internal affairs of Cambodia;

(c) To refrain from the threat or use of force against the territorial integrity or political independence of Cambodia, or in any other manner inconsistent with the purposes of the United Nations;

(d) To settle all disputes with Cambodia by peaceful means;

(e) To refrain from using their territories or the territories of other States to impair the sovereignty, independence, territorial integrity and inviolability, neutrality and national unity of Cambodia;

(f) To refrain from using the territory of Cambodia to impair the sovereignty, independence and territorial integrity and inviolability of other States;

(g) To refrain from the introduction or stationing of foreign forces, including military personnel, in any form whatsoever, in Cambodia and from establishing or maintaining military bases, strong points or facilities in Cambodia, except pursuant to United Nations authorization for the implementation of the comprehensive political settlement.

Article 3

1. All persons in Cambodia shall enjoy the rights and freedoms embodied in the Universal Declaration of Human Rights and other relevant international human rights instruments.

2. To this end,

(a) Cambodia undertakes:

—to ensure respect for and observance of human rights and fundamental freedoms in Cambodia;

—to support the right of all Cambodian citizens to undertake activities that would promote and protect human rights and fundamental freedoms;

—to take effective measures to ensure that the policies and practices of the past shall never be allowed to return;

—to adhere to relevant international human rights instruments;

(b) The other parties to this Agreement undertake to promote and encourage respect for and observance of human rights and fundamental freedoms in Cambodia as embodied in the relevant international instruments in order, in particular, to prevent the recurrence of human rights abuses.

3. The United Nations Commission on Human Rights should continue to monitor closely the human rights situation in Cambodia, including, if necessary, by the appointment of a Special Rapporteur who would report his findings annually to the Commission and to the General Assembly.

Article 4

The parties to this Agreement call upon all other States to recognize and respect in every way the sovereignty, independence, territorial integrity and inviolability, neutrality and national unity of Cambodia and to refrain from any action inconsistent with these principles or with other provisions of this Agreement.

Article 5

1. In the event of a violation or threat of violation of the sovereignty, independence, territorial integrity and inviolability, neutrality or national unity of Cambodia, or of any of the other commitments herein, the parties to this Agreement undertake to consult immediately with a view to adopting all appropriate steps to ensure respect for these commitments and resolving any such violations through peaceful means.

2. Such steps may include, *inter alia*, reference of the matter to the Security Council of the United Nations or recourse to the means for the peaceful settlement of disputes referred to in Article 33 of the Charter of the United Nations.

3. The parties to this Agreement may also call upon the assistance of the co-chairmen of the Paris Conference on Cambodia.

4. In the event of serious violations of human rights in Cambodia, they will call upon the competent organs of the United Nations to take such other steps as are appropriate for the prevention and suppression of such violations in accordance with the relevant international instruments.

Article 6

This Agreement shall enter into force upon signature.

Article 7

This Agreement shall remain open for accession by all States. The instruments of accession shall be deposited with the Governments of the French Republic and the Republic of Indonesia. For each State acceding to this Agreement, it shall enter into force on the date of deposit of its instrument of accession. . . .

[Article 8 omitted]

SENATOR KENNEDY'S APOLOGY FOR FAULTS IN HIS PRIVATE LIFE
October 25, 1991

To a Massachusetts audience, Sen. Edward M. Kennedy confessed to "faults in the conduct of my private life" and acknowledged being "painfully aware that criticism directed against me in recent months involves more than honest disagreement with my positions, or the usual criticism from the far right." His apology came in a speech October 25 at the John F. Kennedy School of Government at Harvard University, commemorating the twenty-fifth anniversary of the school named for the late president, the senator's older brother.

The senator's remarks were perceived as an attempt to overcome complaints that personal notoriety—especially his identity with a rape case involving his nephew, William Kennedy Smith—had reduced his effectiveness as a lawmaker and as an outspoken Democratic liberal. Smith was acquitted of the rape charge, but the case had not been decided when Kennedy spoke.

During Senate Judiciary Committee hearings earlier that month on Anita Hill's sexual harassment accusations against Supreme Court nominee Clarence Thomas, Kennedy—a committee member—said very little. (Confirmation of Supreme Court Justice Clarence Thomas, p. 551) The press attributed Kennedy's unusual reticence to fear that he would draw attention—and ridicule—to unfavorable stories of his own relations with women. After the Thomas hearings adjourned, a national Gallup Poll gave Kennedy a 22 percent approval rating, the lowest rating of any member of the committee. The Washington Post *reported that Kennedy's friends and close advisers long had urged him to speak out about his damaged personal reputation and publicly vow to change his habits.*

While conceding unspecified "faults" and "shortcomings" in his personal life, the senator stopped short of directly pledging to change it. "I cannot promise you that I will fulfill every expectation, even my own," he said, looking over his audience and into a bank of television cameras. "But I do pledge my commitment ... to the core values that for two centuries have made this Commonwealth a force for economic justice, for progress and compassion." He spoke to a generally sympathetic audience of about 800 at the school.

Kennedy said, "As I approach my 60th birthday, I am determined to give all I have to advance the causes for which I have stood for almost a third of a century." He was first elected to the Senate in 1964, taking a seat that John Kennedy had used to propel himself to the presidency in 1960. The president's assassination in 1963 was followed in 1968 by the slaying of another brother, Robert, a senator from New York seeking the Democratic presidential nomination. The oldest Kennedy brother, Joseph Jr., had died during World War II.

Edward, the surviving brother, appeared destined for a serious run at the presidency until he was involved in an accident in 1969. A car he was driving plunged off a bridge on Chappaquiddick Island, Massachusetts, causing the drowning death of a young woman passenger. He later pleaded guilty to leaving the scene of the accident. At that time he asked Massachusetts voters to help him decide whether to remain in office. They reelected him to the Senate the following year, and again in 1976, 1982, and 1988. But lingering questions about the accident blemished his national political ambitions.

Over the years a number of incidents involving alcohol or women kept Kennedy's name in the tabloids. In March 1991 his name was prominent in the news accounts of the rape charge against William Smith. The incident occurred at the Kennedy family's winter estate in Palm Beach, Florida. The accuser claimed she had encountered Smith, Kennedy, and his son at a late-night bar.

Kennedy, testifying as a defense witness at the trial, said that he had gone to the bar because a family gathering that weekend had brought back troubling memories of deceased kin and left him unable to sleep. His testimony appeared to draw sympathy in the courtroom and elicited press speculation that it may have influenced the jurors in their decision to acquit Smith.

Following are excerpts from Sen. Edward M. Kennedy's speech at the John F. Kennedy School of Government at Harvard University, October 25, 1991:

... Some of the anger of recent days, the powerful public reaction to the final phase of the Thomas hearings, reflects the pain of a new idea still being born—the idea of a society where sex discrimination is ended, and sexual harassment is unacceptable—the idea of an America where the majority who are women are truly and finally equal citizens.

We are told that in other nations, people watching the Thomas hearings could not understand what the fuss was all about. By that measure at least, America is different—and I believe better.

Whatever any of us may feel about the outcome of the confirmation vote—and as you know, I have strong feelings—it is a mark of our progress that here in this nation, the charges raised by Anita Hill had to be taken seriously.

With women, as with minorities, we are seeking to end the endless ages of injustice. So we should not be surprised that the passage is often stormy. Few worthwhile changes come quietly or on a gentle breeze. Yet it is also clear that when the storm comes, there are some who cannot resist a ride on the winds of fear—and others who even seek to fan them.

The success of David Duke [Republican gubernatorial candidate] in Louisiana is the latest case in point. He has taken off the white sheet, but his appeal is fundamentally the same. It is racism in a business suit. And while the denunciations now pour forth from the White House, there is also a deeper, more disturbing truth here.

David Duke is the logical, inevitable, and shameful extension of a politics that has increasingly appealed to our worst instincts. What is happening in Louisiana is a louder unmodulated echo of what has happened already on the national stage. Those who have sown the seeds of racism are reaping the whirlwind of a nation increasingly divided against itself. We must not now—we must not ever—permit the principle of equal justice to be sacrificed on the altar of negative politics.

Civil rights is the unfinished business of America. It is wrong, deeply wrong, for any Administration, let alone the Party of Abraham Lincoln, to rub salt in the nation's wounds on race.

Yet for many months, the civil rights bill that Senator [John C.] Danforth [R-Mo.] and I have been urging in the Senate was denounced as a quota bill—which it is not, and never was.

Fortunately, for our bill and for the country, the Administration has now relented. To his credit, President Bush has rejected the counsel of those who would keep the quota code word in their arsenal of racial resentment. The agreement we reached last night is a well-earned victory for civil rights—and a well-deserved defeat for those who would misuse race as a political weapon. . . .

. . . We must not betray our country and our conscience by retreating in our own day and generation from the hard, long and historic work of achieving equal rights for all Americans. I gave my maiden speech in the United States Senate on the Civil Rights Act of 1964, and that is a battle we must keep on waging, a battle I will never walk away from.

America will not be America if it is a society of unequal parts, oppressed and advantaged, powerful and exploited. At the most fundamental level, this country will fail, if we do not succeed in bringing down the barriers of race and sex and prejudice.

President Kennedy was ready to lose re-election, if he had to, for the cause of civil rights. Now, let us reaffirm his belief, that "This nation, for all its hopes and boasts, will not be fully free "... until all its citizens are free."....

If we are to revive and prosper, if we are to prepare for the 21st Century, if we are to have schools that teach, and health care that heals, and business that competes, we must stop clawing at each other for petty advantage and start asking one another what sacrifices of narrow self-interest we must make and share, in order to advance the greater public good.

Many of our problems at home and in the larger world are also opportunities. In this state they are especially urgent—and also especially promising. Vital issues that have been among my own highest priorities in the Senate are coming to the fore. Jobs and schools and health are increasingly at the center of concern about the direction of our country and our role in a dramatically changing world. Most of all for Massachusetts, we must focus on the transition to the new high-tech economy in which our state is well-positioned to excel, and which holds such high potential for our future.

Clearly, the temper and pressures of this period demand new energy from all of us, and renewed resolve. But the New Deal, the New Frontier and the Great Society are not the end of American social history. Our day will come again, and we must keep the faith until it dawns.

I say all this, understanding that no one has a monopoly on truth or virtue. But individual faults and frailties are no excuse to give in—and no exemption from the common obligation to give of ourselves.

I feel a special obligation to those who share my hopes for this state and nation, who in the past have given me their help—and often even their hearts. My views on issues have made some people angry over the years— and frankly, I accept that as the price of fighting hard for my beliefs. But I am painfully aware that the criticism directed at me in recent months involves far more than honest disagreement with my positions, or the usual criticism from the far right. It also involves the disappointment of friends and many others who rely on me to fight the good fight.

To them I say: I recognize my own shortcomings—the faults in the conduct of my private life. I realize that I alone am responsible for them, and I am the one who must confront them. Today, more than ever before, I believe that each of us as individuals must not only struggle to make a better world, but to make ourselves better too. And in this life, those endeavors are never finished.

In my own life, I have been given many gifts. I have been blessed with extraordinary parents. I have also been blessed with extraordinary brothers and sisters—and their children and my own. In the next generation's sense of public service, I take considerable pride.

Not least, unlike my brothers, I have been given length of years and time. And as I approach my 60th birthday, I am determined to give all that I have to advance the causes for which I have stood for almost a third of a century.

Above all, whether the odds are in my favor or against me, I will continue to stand up, in good times and in seasons of adversity, for the people who sent me to the Senate in the first place, nearly thirty years ago.

So I say to my fellow citizens of Massachusetts—you have supported me in many of the great battles of our time, and you have sustained me in the worst moments. You have permitted me to take positions with which you have sometimes differed.

I cannot promise you that I will fulfill every expectation, even my own. But I do pledge my commitment, unchanged and unwavering, to the core values that for two centuries have made this Commonwealth a force for economic justice, for progress and compassion.

In short, I will continue to fight the good fight. I will continue to see issues in the way I have always sought to see them—not as numbers and words, but as individuals and families with worries and dreams— firefighters in Lowell, elderly citizens at the senior center in Agawam, nurses at the community health center in Roxbury, students at U Mass working to make it through college—women and men from the Berkshires to Boston to the Cape who earn a living, try to save a little money, hope to buy a home and build a future for their children.

Twenty-five years ago, when this Institute of Politics began, the wish that many of us had was that it would help raise the quality and renew the purposes of the public arena. We need that today more than ever. We must resist disillusionment, the tendency of politics to be cautious and cynical. We must not turn aside from tough and essential challenges.

I remember the words of one of the founders of this Institute, who visited it and cherished it when it was just a small frame house on Mount Auburn Street. As Jacqueline Kennedy said, "John Kennedy believed so strongly that one's aim should not just be the most comfortable life possible—but that we should all do something to right the wrongs we see."

Many years later, that is still my belief. It is the belief that helped bring this Institute of Politics into being. And it is a belief that can sustain the efforts we each must make, now and in the years ahead, to make our country better.

MADRID CONFERENCE ON
MIDEAST PEACE
October 30 and 31, 1991

For the first time ever, Israelis and Palestinians October 30 sat down together publicly and officially to hold peace talks. At issue was finding a way to share the homeland they both call their own. They were joined at the Madrid conference by delegates from Syria, Lebanon, and Jordan— and initially by presidents George Bush of the United States and Mikhail S. Gorbachev of the Soviet Union, the conference's co-sponsoring nations.

"We come to Madrid on a mission of hope—to begin work on a just, lasting, and comprehensive settlement to the conflict in the Middle East," Bush said in his opening address in Spain's ornate Royal Palace. While cautioning that "no one mistake the magnitude of this challenge," he said "no one should assume that the opportunity before us to make peace will remain if we fail to seize the moment."

The "opportunity" was created by a U.S.-led military victory over Iraq in the Persian Gulf War and Gorbachev's friendship with the West, which had removed Moscow as a superpower rival of the United States in the Middle East. In March, at the end of the war, and on subsequent occasions the president spoke of promoting a Middle East peace settlement. (Bush on War Victory and Mideast Peace Plans, p. 121) Since then Secretary of State James A. Baker III had made eight trips to that region to persuade the principal parties to negotiate their disputes.

To Arab governments, Bush and Baker sought to portray the United States as as an "honest broker" without a pro-Israel bias. In September, Bush succeeded in postponing until 1992 congressional consideration of $10 billion in U.S. loan guarantees to help Israel absorb new emigrants. He told a news conference September 12 that he opposed immediate

719

passage of the legislation because "we're close to being able to convene a peace conference" and "nothing should be done that might interfere with this prospect." In a gesture to Israel, Bush urged the United Nations General Assembly on September 23 to repeal a 1975 resolution equating Zionism with racism; the resolution was repealed December 16.

Moscow's contribution to the conference was essentially negative. It had ceased to be Syria's military supplier and patron, leaving Syrian president Hafez al Assad in need of improving relations with the United States. With apparent reluctance, the Syrian leader sent representatives to the conference.

Particular significance was attached to the presence of official observers from Saudi Arabia. Western diplomats said it marked the first time that senior Saudi officials had consented to attend a meeting also attended by an Israeli prime minister. The Saudi delegation included a member of the royal family, Prince Bandar bin Sultan, the kingdom's ambassador to Washington, who was credited with a behind-the-scenes role of persuading Syria to attend.

Choosing the Palestine Delegation

The Palestinians' presence at the conference resulted from long pre-conference bargaining sessions between Shamir and Baker. Never before had Israel agreed to negotiate directly with a group of Palestinians that publicly said it represented national aspirations. But Shamir insisted that it include no members of the Palestine Liberation Organization, no Palestinians from East Jerusalem—which Israel had annexed—and none living outside of the occupied territories.

Those who were chosen formed a joint delegation with Jordanians and went to Madrid under heavy guard. They had received threats from the leaders of several militant Palestinian organizations that had met in Iran in October. At the head of the joint delegation was Dr. Haidar Abdul Shafi, a Palestinian scholar, whose opening address was lauded in the Western press for its moderation.

His tone was in marked contrast to many of the Arab-Israeli exchanges. On one occasion, Shamir labeled Syria "one of the most oppressive, tyrannical regimes in the world." Syrian foreign minister Farouk al-Sharaa responded by waving a poster from the 1940s depicting Shamir as a terrorist sought by British authorities, who then controlled Palestine.

Despite the rancor, Syria and Israel agreed later to hold follow-up talks on Syria's demand that Israel relinquish the Golan Heights, which it captured from Syria in the 1967 Arab-Israeli war. The Israelis additionally consented to hold talks with the Jordanian-Palestinian team on its demand for a Palestinian autonomy—possibly a separate state—in the West Bank and Gaza, which Israel also gained in the 1967 war.

Follow-up Talks in Washington

Talks resumed in Washington December 10 after a week's delay in the Israeli delegation's arrival. The Israeli team's delaying tactics empha-

sized the reluctance of Shamir's government to exchange territory for Arab recognition of Israel's sovereignty—"land for peace." Only one Arab government, Egypt, had extended such recognition—as a result of Israel's return of the Sinai Peninsula to Egypt under terms of the 1978 Camp David Accords.

Another problem in the Washington talks arose over the Palestine delegation. At U.S. urging Israel had agreed to negotiate directly and separately with Syria, Lebanon, and a joint Jordanian-Palestinian delegation. But once in Washington, the Palestinians insisted on meeting separately with the Israeli team, predictably provoking Israeli objections. After six working days devoted mostly to the restatement of stale demands and procedural squabbles, the Washington talks were recessed until mid-January 1992.

Following are excerpts from addresses delivered October 20-31, 1991, at the Middle East Peace Conference in Madrid by President George Bush, Soviet president Mikhail S. Gorbachev, Israeli prime minister Yitzhak Shamir, and Habar Abdul Shafi, head of the joint Jordanian-Palestinian delegation:

BUSH'S ADDRESS

... We come to Madrid on a mission of hope—to begin work on a just, lasting, and comprehensive settlement to the conflict in the Middle East....

Our objective must be clear and straightforward. It is not simply to end the state of war in the Middle East and replace it with a state of non-belligerency. This is not enough; this would not last. Rather, we seek peace—real peace—and by real peace I mean treaties, security, diplomatic relations, economic relations, trade, investment, cultural exchange, even tourism....

Let no one mistake the magnitude of this challenge. The struggle we seek to end has a long and painful history. Every life lost—every outrage, every act of violence—is etched deep in the hearts and history of the people of this region. Theirs is a history that weighs heavily against hope. And yet history need not be man's master.

I expect that some will say that what I am suggesting is impossible. But think back. Who back in 1945 would have thought that France and Germany, bitter rivals for nearly a century, would become allies in the aftermath of World War II? And who, 2 years ago, would have predicted that the Berlin Wall would come down? And who in the early 1960s would have believed that the Cold War would come to a peaceful end, replaced by cooperation—exemplified by the fact that the United States and the Soviet Union are here today not as rivals but as partners, as Prime Minister Gonzalez pointed out.

No, peace in the Middle East need not be a dream. Peace is possible. The Egyptian-Israeli Peace Treaty is striking proof that former adversaries can make and sustain peace. And, moreover, parties in the Middle East have respected agreements not only in the Sinai but on the Golan Heights as well.

The fact that we are all gathered here today for the first time attests to a new potential for peace. Each of us has taken an important step toward real peace by meeting here in Madrid. All the formulas on paper, all the pious declarations in the world won't bring peace if there is no practical mechanism for moving ahead.

Peace will only come as the result of direct negotiations, compromise, give-and-take. Peace cannot be imposed from the outside by the United States or anyone else. While we will continue to do everything possible to help the parties overcome obstacles, peace must come from within.

We come here to Madrid as realists. We do not expect peace to be negotiated in a day, or a week, or a month, or even a year. It will take time; indeed, it should take time—time for parties so long at war to learn to talk to one another, to listen to one another. Time to heal old wounds and build trust. In this quest, time need not be the enemy of progress.

What we envision is a process of direct negotiations proceeding along two tracks: one between Israel and the Arab states, the other between Israel and the Palestinians. Negotiations are to be conducted on the basis of UN Security Council Resolutions 242 and 338.

The real work will not happen here in the plenary session but in direct bilateral negotiations. This conference cannot impose a settlement on the participants or veto agreements, and, just as important, the conference can only be reconvened with the consent of every participant. Progress is in the hands of the parties who must live with the consequences.

Soon after the bilateral talks commence, parties will convene as well to organize multilateral negotiations. These will focus on issues that cross national boundaries and are common to the region: arms control, water, refugee concerns, economic development. Progress in these forums is not intended as a substitute for what must be decided in the bilateral talks; to the contrary, progress in the multilateral issues can help create an atmosphere in which long-standing bilateral disputes can more easily be settled.

For Israel and the Palestinians, a framework already exists for diplomacy. Negotiations will be conducted in phases, beginning with talks on interim self-government arrangements. We aim to reach agreement within 1 year. And once agreed, interim self-government arrangements will last for 5 years; beginning the third year, negotiations will commence on permanent status. No one can say with any precision what the end result will be; in our view, something must be developed, something acceptable to Israel, the Palestinians, and Jordan that gives the Palestinian people meaningful control over their own lives and fate and provides for the acceptance and security of Israel....

... Real peace—lasting peace—must be based upon security for all states and peoples, including Israel. For too long, the Israeli people have lived in fear, surrounded by an unaccepting Arab world. Now is the ideal moment for the Arab world to demonstrate that attitudes have changed, that the Arab world is willing to live in peace with Israel and make allowances for Israel's reasonable security needs.

We know that peace must also be based on fairness. In the absence of fairness, there will be no legitimacy—no stability. This applies above all to the Palestinian people, many of whom have known turmoil and frustration above all else. Israel now has an opportunity to demonstrate that it is willing to enter into a new relationship with its Palestinian neighbors, one predicated upon mutual respect and cooperation.

Throughout the Middle East, we seek a stable and enduring settlement. We've not defined what this means; indeed, I make these points with no map showing where the final borders are to be drawn. Nevertheless, we believe territorial compromise is essential for peace. Boundaries should reflect the quality of both security and political arrangements. The United States is prepared to accept whatever the parties themselves find acceptable....

I want to say something about the role of the United States of America. We played an active role in making this conference possible; both the Secretary of State, Jim Baker, and I will play an active role in helping the process succeed. Toward this end, we've provided written assurances to Israel, to Syria, to Jordan, Lebanon, and the Palestinians. In the spirit of openness and honesty, we will brief all parties on the assurances that we have provided to the other. We're prepared to extend guarantees, provide technology and support, if that is what peace requires. And we will call upon our friends and allies in Europe and in Asia to join with us in providing resources so that peace and prosperity go hand in hand.

Outsiders can assist, but, in the end, it is up to the peoples and governments of the Middle East to shape the future of the Middle East. It is their opportunity and it is their responsibility to do all that they can to take advantage of this gathering, this historic gathering, and what it symbolizes and what it promises.

No one should assume that the opportunity before us to make peace will remain if we fail to seize the moment....

May God bless and guide the work of this conference, and may this conference set us on the path of peace. Thank you.

GORBACHEV'S ADDRESS

... This [Arab-Israeli] conflict, the longest in the latter half of the 20th century, bears the heavy stamp of the so-called Cold War, and it was not until an end was put to that that ending this conflict became a tangible possibility, too....

... It was the will of history that without an improvement and then a radical change in Soviet-U.S. relations we would never have witnessed the profound qualitative changes in the world that now make it possible to speak in terms of an entirely new age, an age of peace in world history. Movement in that direction has begun. And it is only in this context that we can understand the fact that a tangible hope has emerged for an Arab-Israeli settlement.

Cooperation between the two powers and other members of the U.N. Security Council was indispensable in order to stop the aggression against Kuwait and to reaffirm the viability of a new criteria in international relations.

Directly after that, just as was agreed between President Bush and myself in September 1990 at our Helsinki meeting on the subject of the Gulf War, vigorous joint efforts began aimed at achieving a Middle East settlement.

All that we and the Americans have undertaken to that end signifies the right conclusions have been drawn from the Gulf War. Our joint participation in the process of settlement was prompted by a desire to offer our good offices, not any desire to impose solutions from outside that would run counter to the national interests of states in the region.

Thus, as a result of major bilateral and multilateral efforts, a signal was sent to the parties involved in the conflict. A signal of the need to negotiate, to work together towards finding a realistic balance of interests which alone may form the foundation for a durable peace.

Today we have a unique opportunity, and it would be unforgivable to miss this opportunity. Success is in everybody's interest, not only because the rights of the peoples and nations and of the individual are increasingly recognized today as the universal foundation for our world order.

But also for another reason of particular urgency and gravity, and that is the fact that the Middle East has become one of the most heavily armed regions in the world, where lethal weapons and nuclear technologies are building up, and where other weapons of mass destruction are also to be found.

There is justified cause for alarm. The international community is entitled to expect that this conference will come up with decisions that will put this concern to rest.

In my view, the conference can only succeed if no one seeks any victory for one side over the other. But all seek a shared victory over a cruel past. I'm speaking of peace rather than mainly a cessation of the state of war, and a durable peace implies the implementation of and respect for the rights of the Palestinian people.

We have restored diplomatic relations with Israel. Now that deep-rooted democratic changes are taking place in our country and in the world, and now that a real process towards settling the Middle East crisis is getting under way, the absence of relations with Israel was becoming senseless.

We hope, and we'll try to make sure that this will be a benefit to the peoples of our two countries and the entire Arab world. . . .

Our country, as a participant in the Middle East process, and a neighbor that has maintained longstanding and extensive ties with the nations of the region, has a special stake in the success of this conference. . . .

Ladies and gentlemen, it is for the delegations directly participating in the conference to sort out the details of this enormous task.

As co-chairman of the conference we will be in regular contact with our American counterparts, and we will do our utmost to find solutions for which your peoples and the entire world have long been yearning . . . I wish you every success.

SHAMIR'S ADDRESS

. . . The people of Israel look to this palace with great anticipation and expectation. We pray that this meeting will mark the beginning of a new chapter in the history of the Middle East; that it will signal the end of hostility, violence, terror and war; that it will bring dialogue, accommodation, coexistence and—above all—peace.

Distinguished co-chairmen, ladies and gentlemen;

To appreciate the meaning of peace for the people of Israel, one has to view today's Jewish sovereignty in the land of Israel against the background of our history.

Jews have been persecuted throughout the ages in almost every continent. Some countries barely tolerated us, others oppressed, tortured, slaughtered and exiled us.

This century saw the Nazi regime set out to exterminate us. The Sho'ah, the Holocaust, the catastrophic genocide of unprecedented proportions which destroyed a third of our people, became possible because no one defended us. Being homeless, we also rebelled against foreign imperialist rule. We did not conquer a foreign land. We repulsed the Arab onslaught, prevented Israel's annihilation, declared its independence and established a viable state and government institutions within a very short time.

After their attack on Israel failed, the Arab regimes continued their fight against Israel with boycott, blockade, terrorism and outright war. Soon after the establishment of Israel, they turned against the Jewish communities in Arab countries. A wave of oppression, expropriation and expulsion caused a mass exodus of some 800,000 Jews from lands they had inhabited from before the rise of the Islam. Most of these Jewish refugees, stripped of their considerable possessions, came to Israel. They were welcomed by the Jewish state. They were given shelter and support, and they were integrated into Israeli society together with half a million survivors of the European Holocaust.

The Arab regimes' rejection of Israel's existence in the Middle East, and the continuous war they have waged against it, are part of history. There have been attempts to rewrite this history, which depict the Arabs as victims and Israel as the aggressor. Like attempts to deny the Holocaust, they will fail. With the demise of totalitarian regimes in most of the world, this perversion of history will disappear.

In their war against Israel's existence, the Arab governments took advantage of the Cold War. They enlisted the military, economic and political support of the communist world against Israel, and they turned a local, regional conflict into an international powder keg. This caused the Middle East to be flooded with arms, which fueled wars and turned the area into a dangerous battleground and a testing arena for sophisticated weapons. At the UN, the Arab states mustered the support of other Muslim countries and the Soviet bloc. Together they had an automatic majority for countless resolutions that perverted history, paraded fiction as fact and made a travesty of the UN and its charter.

Arab hostility to Israel has also brought tragic human suffering to the Arab people. Tens of thousands have been killed and wounded. Hundreds of thousands of Arabs who lived in Mandatory Palestine were encouraged by their own leaders to flee from their homes. Their suffering is a blot on humanity. No decent person, least of all a Jew of this era, can be oblivious to this suffering.

Several hundreds of thousands of Palestinian Arabs live in slums known as refugee camps in Gaza, Judea and Samaria. Attempts by Israel to rehabilitate and house them have been defeated by Arab objections. Nor has their fate been any better in Arab states. Unlike the Jewish refugees who came to Israel from Arab countries, most Arab refugees were neither welcomed nor integrated by their hosts. Only the Kingdom of Jordan awarded them citizenship. Their plight has been used as a political weapon against Israel.

The Arabs who have chosen to remain in Israel—Christian and Moslem—will be discussed. There cannot be genuine peace in our region unless these regional issues are addressed and resolved.

We believe the goal of the bilateral negotiations is to sign peace treaties between Israel and its neighbors, and to reach an agreement on interim self-government arrangements with the Palestinian Arabs.

But nothing can be achieved without good will. I appeal to the Arab leaders, those who are here and those who have not yet joined the process. Show us and the world that you accept Israel's existence. Demonstrate your readiness to accept Israel as a permanent entity in the region. Let the people in our region hear you speak in the language of reconciliation, coexistence and peace with Israel.

In Israel there is an almost total consensus for the need for peace. We only differ on the best ways to achieve it. In most Arab countries the opposite seems to be true: the only differences are over the ways to push Israel into a defenseless position and, ultimately, to destruction. We would like to see in your countries an end to poisonous preachings against Israel. We would like to see an indication of the kind of hunger for peace which characterizes Israeli society.

We appeal to you to renounce the Jihad [holy war] against Israel. We appeal to you to denounce the PLO [Palestine Liberation Organization] covenant which calls for Israel's destruction. We appeal to you to condemn declarations that call for Israel's annihilation, like the one issued by the rejectionist conference in Teheran last week. We appeal to you to let Jews, who wish to leave your countries, go. And we address a call to the Palestinian Arabs: renounce violence and terrorism; use the universities in the administered territories—whose existence was made possible only by Israel—for learning and development, not agitation and violence; stop exposing your children to danger by sending them to throw bombs and stones at soldiers and civilians.

Just two days ago, we were reminded that Palestinian terrorism is still rampant, when a mother of seven children and a father of four were slaughtered in cold blood. We cannot remain indifferent and be expected to talk with people involved in such repulsive activities.

We appeal to you to shun dictators like Saddam Hussein who aim to destroy Israel; stop the brutal torture and murder of those who do not agree with you; allow us, and the world community, to build decent housing for the people who now live in refugee camps. Above all, we hope you finally realize that you could have been at this table long ago, soon after the Camp David Accords were first concluded, had you chosen dialogue instead of violence, coexistence instead of terrorism. . . .

. . . Today, the gulf separating the two sides is still too wide; the Arab hostility to Israel too deep; the lack of trust too immense, to permit a dramatic, quick solution. But, we must start on the long road to reconciliation with this first step in the peace process.

We are convinced that human nature prefers peace to war and belligerence. We, who have had to fight seven wars and sacrifice many thousands of lives, glorify neither death nor war. The Jewish faith exalts peace even to the extent that it considers it a synonym for the Creator himself. We yearn for peace. We pray for peace.

We believe the blessings of peace can turn the Middle East into a paradise; a center of cultural, scientific, medical and technological creativity. We can foresee a period of great economic progress that would put an end to misery, hunger and illiteracy. It could put the Middle East—the cradle of civilization—on the road to a new era.

Such a goal merits our devotion and dedication for as long as it is necessary until, in the words of the prophet Isaiah, we shall be able to turn "swords into ploughshares" and bring the blessings of peace to all the peoples of our region. . . .

Let us resolve to leave this hall with a united determination that from now on, any differences we may have will be solved only by negotiations, goodwill and mutual tolerance. Let us declare, here and now, an end to war, to belligerency and to hostility. Let us march forward together, to reconciliation and peace.

HAIDAR ABDUL SHAFI'S ADDRESS

. . . We meet in Madrid, a city with the rich texture of history, to weave together the fabric which joins our past with the future, to reaffirm a wholeness of vision, which once brought about a rebirth of civilization and a world order based on harmony in diversity.

Once again, Christian, Moslem and Jew face the challenge of heralding a new era enshrined in global values of democracy, human rights, freedom, justice and security. From Madrid we launch this quest for peace, a quest to place the sanctity of human life at the center of our world and to redirect our energies and resources from the pursuit of mutual destruction to the pursuit of joint prosperity, progress and happiness.

We, the people of Palestine, stand before you in the fullness of our pain, our pride, and our anticipation, for we have long harbored a yearning for peace and a dream of justice and freedom. For too long the Palestinian people have gone unheeded, silenced and denied—our identity negated by political expediency, our rightful struggle against injustice maligned, and our present existence subsumed by the past tragedy of another people.

Your excellencies, ladies and gentlemen, for the greater part of this century, we have been victimized by the myth of "a land without a people," and described with impunity as "the invisible Palestinians." Before such willful blindness, we refused to disappear or to accept a distorted identity. Our intifada [uprising] is a testimony to our perseverance and resilience, waged in a just struggle to regain our rights.

It is time for us to narrate our own story, to stand witness as advocates of a truth which has long lain buried in the consciousness and conscience of the world. We do not stand before you as supplicants, but rather as the torch bearers who know that in our world of today, ignorance can never be an excuse. We seek neither an admission of guilt after the fact, nor vengeance for past iniquities, but rather an act of will that would make a just peace a reality. We speak out, ladies and gentlemen, from the full conviction of the rightness of our cause, the verity of our history, and the depth of our commitment. Therein lies the strength of the Palestinian people today, for we have scaled the walls of fear and reticence and we wish to speak out with the courage and integrity that our narrative and our history deserve.

The co-sponsors have invited us here today to present our case and to reach out to "the other" with whom we have had to face a mutually exclusive reality on the land of Palestine. But even in the invitation to this peace conference, our narrative was distorted and our truth only partially acknowledged. The Palestinian people are one, fused by centuries of history in Palestine, bound together by a collective memory of shared sorrows and joys and sharing a unity of purpose and vision. Our songs and ballads, our folk tales and children's stories, the dialect of our jokes, the images of our poems, that hint of melancholy which colors even our happiest moments, are as important to us as the blood ties which link our families and clans.

Yet the invitation to discuss peace, the peace we all desire and need, comes to only a portion of our people. It ignores our national, historical, and organic unity. We come here wrenched from our sisters and brothers in exile to stand before you as the Palestinians under occupation, although we maintain that each of us represents the rights and interest of the whole. We have been denied the right to publicly acknowledge our loyalty to our leadership and system of government, but allegiance and loyalty cannot be censored or severed. Our acknowledged leadership is more than just the democratically chosen leadership of all the Palestinian people; it is the symbol of our national identity and unity—the guardian of our past, the protector of our present, and the hope of our future. Our people have chosen to entrust it with their history and the preservation of our precious legacy. This leadership has been clearly and unequivocally recognized by the community of nations, with only a few exceptions who had chosen, for so many years, shadow over substance.

Regardless of the nature and conditions of our oppression, whether the dispossession and dispersion of exile or the brutality and repression of the occupation, the Palestinian people cannot be torn asunder. They remain united, a nation wherever they are, or are forced to be.

And Jerusalem, ladies and gentlemen, that city which is not only the soul of Palestine but the cradle of three world religions, is tangible even in its claimed absence from our midst at this stage. Its apparent, though artificial, exclusion from this conference is a denial of its right to seek peace and redemption, for it too has suffered from war and occupation. Jerusalem, the city of peace, has been barred from a peace conference and deprived of its calling. Palestinian Jerusalem, the capital of our homeland and future state, defines Palestinian existence—past, present and future— but itself has been denied a voice and an identity. Jerusalem defies exclusive possessiveness or bondage. Israel's annexation of Arab Jerusalem remains both clearly illegal in the eyes of the world community and an affront to the peace that this city deserves.

We come to you from a tortured land and a proud, though captive, people, having been asked to negotiate with our occupiers, but leaving behind the children of the intifada, and a people under occupation and under curfew, who enjoined us not to surrender or forget. As we speak, thousands of our brothers and sisters are languishing in Israeli prisons and detention camps, most detained without evidence, charge or trial, many cruelly mistreated and tortured in interrogation, guilty only of seeking freedom or daring to defy the occupation. We speak in their name and we say: set them free.

As we speak, the tens of thousands who have been wounded or permanently disabled are in pain: let peace heal their wounds. As we speak, the eyes of thousands of Palestinian refugees, deportees, and displaced persons since 1967, are haunting us, for exile is a cruel fate: bring them home. They have the right to return. As we speak, the silence of demolished homes echoes through the halls and in our minds: we must rebuild our homes in our free state.

And what do we tell the loved ones of those killed by army bullets? How do we answer the questions and the fear in our children's eyes? For one out of three Palestinian children under occupation has been killed, injured or detained in the past four years. How can we explain to our children that

729

they are denied education, our schools so often closed by army fiat? Or why their life is in danger for raising a flag in a land where even children are killed or jailed? What requiem can be sung for trees uprooted by army bulldozers? And, most of all, who can explain to those whose lands are confiscated and clear waters stolen, the message of peace? Remove the barbed wire, restore the land, and its life-giving water.

The settlements must stop now. Peace cannot be waged while Palestinian land is confiscated in myriad ways and the status of the Occupied Territories is being decided each day by Israeli bulldozers and barbed wire. This is not simply a position; it is an irrefutable reality. Territory for peace is a travesty when territory for illegal settlement is official Israeli policy and practice. The settlements must stop now.

In the name of the Palestinian people, we wish to directly address the Israeli people with whom we have had a prolonged exchange of pain: let us share hope instead. We are willing to live side by side on the land and the promise of the future. Sharing, however, requires two partners willing to share as equals. Mutuality and reciprocity must replace domination and hostility for genuine reconciliation and coexistence under international legality. Your security and ours are mutually dependent, as entwined as the fears and nightmares of our children.

We have seen some of you at your best and at your worst, for the occupier can hide no secrets from the occupied, and we are witness to the toll that occupation has exacted from you and yours. We have seen you anguish over the transformation of your sons and daughters into instruments of a blind and violent occupation—and we are sure that at no time did you envisage such a role for the children whom you thought would forge your future. We have seen you look back in deepest sorrow at the tragedy of your past and look on in horror at the disfigurement of the victim turned oppressor. Not for this have you nurtured your hopes, dreams and your offspring.

This is why we have responded with solemn appreciation to those of you who came to offer consolation to our bereaved, to give support to those whose homes were being demolished, and to extend encouragement and counsel to those detained behind barbed wire and iron bars. And we have marched together, often choking together at the non-discriminatory tear gas or crying out in pain as the clubs descended on both Palestinian and Israeli alike. For pain knows no national boundaries, and no one can claim a monopoly on suffering. . . .

To the co-sponsors and participants in this occasion of awe and challenge, we pledge our commitment to the principle of justice, peace and reconciliation based on international legitimacy and uniform standards. We shall persist, in our quest for peace, to place before you the substance and determination of our people, often victimized but never defeated. We shall pursue our people's right to self-determination, to the exhilaration of freedom, and to the warmth of the sun as a nation among equals.

Bilateral negotiations on the withdrawal of Israeli forces, the dissolution of Israeli administration and the transfer of authority to the Palestinian people cannot proceed under coercion or threat in the current asymmetry of power. Israel must demonstrate its willingness to negotiate in good faith by immediately halting all settlement activity and land confiscation while implementing meaningful confidence-building measures. Without genuine progress, tangible constructive changes and just agreements during the bilateral talks, multilateral negotiations will be meaningless. Regional stability, security and development are the logical outcome of an equitable and just solution to the Palestinian question, which remains the key to the resolution of wider conflicts and concerns....

The process launched here must lead us to the light at the end of the tunnel, and this light is the promise of a new Palestine—free, democratic, and respectful of human rights and the integrity of nature.

Self-determination, ladies and gentlemen, can neither be granted nor withheld at the whim of the political self-interest of others, for it is enshrined in all international charters and humanitarian law. We claim this right; we firmly assert it here before you and in the eyes of the rest of the world, for it is a sacred and inviolable right which we shall relentlessly pursue and exercise with dedication and self-confidence and pride.

Let us end the Palestinian-Israeli fatal proximity in this unnatural condition of occupation, which has already claimed too many lives. No dream of expansion or glory can justify the taking of a single life. Set us free to re-engage as neighbors and as equals on our holy land.

To our people in exile and under occupation, who have sent us to this appointment laden with their trust, love and aspirations, we say that the load is heavy, and the task is great, but we shall be true. In the words of our great national poet, Mahmoud Darwish, "My homeland is not a suitcase, and I am no traveler." To the exiled and the occupied, we say: You shall return and you shall remain and we will prevail, for our cause is just. We will put on our embroidered robes and keffiyehs and, in the sight of the world, celebrate together on the day of liberation....

November

FIVE AMERICAN PRESIDENTS
AT REAGAN LIBRARY DEDICATION
November 4, 1991

Five U.S. presidents, present and past, made history merely by showing up November 4 at Simi Valley, California, to dedicate the Ronald Reagan Presidential Library. President George Bush noted that it was the first time so many U.S. chief executives and first ladies (six) had "gathered together in the same locale." George and Barbara Bush were joined by former presidents Reagan, Richard M. Nixon, Gerald Ford, and Jimmy Carter, their wives, and Lady Bird Johnson, widow of former president Lyndon B. Johnson.

All five presidents spoke at the ceremonial opening of the tenth presidential library, where many records of Reagan's White House years (1981-1989) and his mementos were assembled for the benefit of scholars and other visitors. "The doors of the library are open now and all are welcome," Reagan told an audience of friends and dignitaries. "The judgment of history is left to you, the people." Reagan, the fortieth president, quickly added that he had no fears of that judgment, "for we have done our best."

In his eighty years, Reagan observed, he had seen "war and peace, feast and famine, depression and prosperity, sickness and health ... the depths of suffering and the peaks of triumph." Referring to the fall of communism, he marveled that "within the course of only a few short years I have seen the world turned upside down and conventional wisdom utterly disproved."

President Bush, introducing his White House predecessor, declared that no leader since Winston Churchill in World War II used words so effectively as Reagan "to help freedom unchain our world." Bush quoted another former British prime minister, Reagan's friend Margaret Thatcher, as saying: "Ronald Reagan won the Cold War without firing a shot."

Nixon picked up this theme, crediting Reagan with restoring America's "military might that made it possible for George Bush to implement his brilliant strategy for victory in the Gulf war." Carter, the only Democrat among the five presidents, also commended Reagan as a president who "stood strong and resolute and made possible the beginning of the end of the Cold War."

But Carter also observed that it "takes several presidential administrations" to plan, design, test and produce weapons systems such as "those used recently in the Gulf." It was noted during the Persian Gulf War that some of the most effective American weaponry could be traced to research and development decisions made during Carter's presidency.

Carter joked that "one of the things that brings former presidents closest together is the extremely onerous and burdensome task of begging for enough money to build a presidential library from private sources ... and then turn it over to the federal government in perpetuity as a repository for the records of our great nation."

The Reagan library was preceded by libraries established in honor of former presidents Herbert Hoover, Franklin D. Roosevelt, Harry S. Truman, Dwight D. Eisenhower, John F. Kennedy, Johnson, Nixon, Ford, and Carter. The latest dedication was attended by several of Roosevelt's descendants, Kennedy's children, Caroline and John, Jr., and Johnson's daughter Luci.

Following are excerpts from speeches delivered at the dedication of the Ronald Reagan Presidential Library at Simi Valley, California, November 4, 1991, by President George Bush and by former presidents Reagan, Richard M. Nixon, Gerald Ford, and Jimmy Carter:

PRESIDENT BUSH'S
REMARKS

... This marks an historic occasion. For the first time, five Presidents and six First Ladies, past and present, have gathered together in the same locale. The four former Presidents—dedicated public servants—and these wonderful First Ladies—each has played a significant part in the American Story.

We begin with the 37th President, Richard Nixon, and the woman we know and love, as Pat. Mr. President, you were an innovator at home, a peacemaker and groundbreaker abroad. We'll never forget it. Here, too, are Betty Ford and America's 38th President, Gerald Ford. To this son of Michigan, we say: "We are very grateful for your quiet strength of character, your vigor and your just plain innate decency."

Next, we thank the 39th President, Jimmy Carter, and his wife Rosalyn.

America applauds your life-long commitment, sir, to peace, to human rights, to helping others. And it was most gracious of you to make such an extra effort to be here today.

And I feel very badly that you haven't met a Democratic president yet, but please don't do anything about that. And Lady Bird—Mrs. Johnson— we salute you for your dedication to our natural beauty, and also for your love of family that shines through every single day.

Today, we're here to honor "an American Life"—which is the title of his autobiography. We also honor an American Original. Ronald Reagan was born on February 6th—but his heart is the 4th of July.

And with his disarming sense of humor, President Reagan was something refreshingly different in Washington: a politician who was funny on purpose. And he also was, though, a visionary, a crusader, and a prophet in his time.

He was a political prophet—leading the tide toward conservatism. He was also a Main Street prophet. He understood that America is great because of what we are—not what we have. Politics can be cruel, can be mean and ugly and uncivil. And unfailingly, Ronald Reagan was strong and gentle. And he ennobled public service. He embodied the American character. He came from the heart of America geographically and culturally. Not even a bullet from the gun of a would-be assassin could stay his spirit.

I remember the terrible day in March of '81. He looked at the doctors in the emergency room and said, "I hope you're all Republicans." Well, Republicans or Democrats, his courage and humor made us all proud— proud to be Americans. And for eight years, I was very proud to be his Vice President. And I saw a man who was thoughtful, sentimental—sending money to strangers who touched him, writing letters on yellow legal paper and asking that they be retyped because he wanted to make it easier for the recipients to read.

As President, Ronald Reagan was unmoved by the vagaries of intellectual fashion. He treasured values that last, values that endure. And I speak of patriotism and civility and generosity and kindness—values etched in the American character. Once asked who he admired most in history, he simply responded, "The man from Galilee."

Mr. President, your faith is what is true and good, and that helped reaffirm our faith in the United States of America. Ronald Reagan believes in returning power to the people, and so he helped the private sector create more than 16 million jobs. He sought to enlarge opportunity, not government. So he lowered taxes and spending and cut inflation and helped create the longest peacetime boom in American history.

How ironic that the oldest President of the United States would prove as young as the American spirit. Here, as in Washington—here, as in Washington, he was aided by the true love of his life. As First Lady, Nancy championed the Foster Grandparents program, heightened breast cancer awareness. She refurbished the White House with the dignity that is her legacy. She sure left us a nice, cozy place to live, I might say. And to the scourge of drugs, she urged America's children to "Just Say No." And Nancy, for these things, and many more, all Americans salute you.

And finally, the President was a global prophet. Today, we've heard this, but the world is safer because he believed that we who are free to live our dreams have a duty to support those who dream of living free.

He predicted that communism would land in the dust bin of history— and history proved him right. And he knew that when it comes to national defense, finishing second means finishing last. So he practiced what he preached—supporting a strong military and pioneering the Strategic Defense Initiative. And his vision paid off for every American in the sea and sands of the Gulf. And America thanks him for that, too.

Mr. President, history will record the 1980s were not only among America's finest hours, they became perhaps democracy's finest era. Our friend—the Iron Lady—as usual, said it best. I speak of Margaret Thatcher—your fellow liege man of liberty.

Recently, she spoke of how great leaders are summed up in a sentence. Here's a quote: "Ronald Reagan won the Cold War without firing a shot. He had a little help—at least that's what he tells me." And looking here at men and women from presidencies of the last three decades, it occurs to me that help came largely from the American people, and you.

Here's part of what the historians will say of Ronald Reagan. He was the Great Communicator and also the Great Liberator. From Normandy to Moscow—from Berlin to the Oval Office—no leader since Churchill used words so effectively to help freedom unchain our world.

You were prophet and President—and I want to thank you for your many, many kindnesses to Barbara and to me. You love this country. You know America. And you have blessed America as few men ever have. Now, it is my distinct privilege and honor to introduce the 40th President of the United States, Ronald Reagan.

PRESIDENT REAGAN'S
REMARKS

Thank you very much, Mr. President, and to all the other distinguished speakers who hold that exalted title.

You know, I've been called, just recently, a great communicator. But I have to admit it's hard for me to communicate the emotions that crowd in at such a moment, and the humility that comes with tributes like those you've heard this morning. The pride I feel as I look over this audience and see so many old friends, for whom this library is a testimonial of love, loyalty, and idealism—to Lod Cook and the members of the Reagan Library Foundation, and to the thousands of donors the world over whose generosity is reflected in the building we dedicate this morning—there are no words to convey adequately the gratitude that both Nancy and I feel for all you have done.

And let me also thank President Bush and the former Presidents who have joined us today—the exclusive fraternity of Presidents has grown. And although we don't get together very often, when we do, well, as you can see, it generates quite a bit of interest.

At one time or another I've run against most of these gentlemen, and they've run against me. And yet, here we are. Which just goes to show that above personal ideologies and party politics, we stand united as Americans. . . .

The five Presidents on this platform span 22 years of challenge and triumph—from the first man on the moon to the last aggressor out of liberated Kuwait. . . .

Would you please join me, ladies and gentlemen, in expressing our gratitude to these great Americans, not just for their presence here today, but for their historic contributions to a world where, to a greater extent than ever before in our century, no one wields a sword and no one drags a chain. Together we gather for a single purpose: to give to the American people and the world a presidential library. . . .

Ever since Franklin Delano Roosevelt, presidents have built libraries in the midst of surroundings that have shaped their characters and molded their values. From West Branch, Iowa to the Simi Valley of California, these institutions reflect the genius of the American people for self-government.

Within their walls are housed millions of records for scholarly interpretation, along with thousands of objects that give both solid and symbolic substance to this nation's highest office and to the 40 men who have occupied it since Washington took his oath. Like the office they commemorate, presidential libraries are living institutions. Certainly it is my hope that the Reagan Library will become a dynamic intellectual forum where scholars interpret the past and policymakers debate the future.

It is said that after leaving the White House, Harry Truman once came into his living room to discover his wife, Bess, tossing their old love letters into the fireplace. "Think of history," said a horrified Mr. Truman. "I have," said Bess.

Well, in a few days, more than six million pages of documentation pertaining to my administration will be released to the public. In time, more than 50 million pages will be made available for researchers. But if the Reagan Library is anything like its counterparts, most of those who enter these doors will not be academics. No, they'll be ordinary people of all ages, backgrounds and political persuasions, eager to examine their past and explore a history not always learned in school. For them, this institution will be a time capsule of American growth and greatness, covering more than a single presidency, honoring more than a single president.

Here visitors will have a chance to tour and study at their leisure the accelerating changes in a fast-forward world. They will be able to trace the historic process by which mankind has stepped back from the narrow window ledge of mutually-assured destruction. They will observe an American President and a Soviet leader sitting in a boathouse on a shore of

Lake Geneva, striving to banish the nuclear nightmare from the dreams of all our children.

They will see tears of pride from the boys of Pointe du Hoc. They will hear the trusting engines of Challenger lifting off on a heartbreaking final mission. They will be introduced to a warm and selfless First Lady who reached out to a generation of young Americans threatened by the scourge of drugs, and who put a comforting arm around an older generation through the Foster Grandparents Program.

They'll catch the sinister crackle of a would-be assassin's weapon, one that forever changed the lives of Jim and Sarah Brady, while reconfirming my belief that whatever time remained to me was to be spent in service to the American people and in accord with the Lord's wishes.

No doubt many visitors will stand in the replica of my Oval Office. Perhaps they will sense a little of the loneliness that comes with decision-making on a global scale, or the stabbing pain inflicted by a terrorist bomb half a world away, or the dread sound of a telephone in the middle of the night with news of hostile actions.

They will also feel some of the immense pride that comes to any president in that office as he comes into daily contact with the American heroes whose faith in themselves, their mission and their mandate is a never-ending source of emotional renewal.

But then I was lucky. If I ever tired, all I had to do was look over my shoulder. Age has its privileges, and on this day of memory and reflection, I hope you will indulge me in recalling some very special people.

I remember a small woman with auburn hair and unquenchable optimism. Her name was Nellie Reagan. And she believed with all her heart that there was no such thing as accidents in this life; everything was part of God's plan. If something went wrong you didn't wring your hands, you rolled up your sleeves.

And I remember a story-telling salesman with the Irish gift of laughter and a certain American restlessness. In the spirit of his forebears who had settled on the endless sea of grass that was the Illinois prairies before the turn of the century, Jack Reagan took his family to many new beginnings.

Perhaps that was the root of my belief shared with Thomas Paine. But we Americans, of all people, were uniquely equipped to begin the world over. Jack had dreams. Nellie had drive. The Reagans of Dixon, Illinois, may have had little in material terms, but we were emotionally wealthy beyond imagination; for we were Americans—young people in a young land with the best days ahead. And we were part of a very special extended family.

I grew up in a town where everyone cared about one another, because everyone knew one another. Not as statistics in a government program, but as neighbors in need. Is that nostalgic? I don't think so. I think it is still what sets this nation apart from every other nation on the face of the Earth.

Our neighbors were never ashamed to kneel in prayer to their Maker. Nor were they ever embarrassed to feel a lump in their throat when Old

Glory passed by. No one in Dixon, Illinois, ever burned a flag. And no one in Dixon would have tolerated it.

Something else I learned and that every generation of young Americans must discover for themselves: I learned to admire the entrepreneurial spirit of this pioneering land where everyone has a chance to push out the boundaries of life. All this and more will greet visitors to this library and museum. If they're anything like me they will arrive with the conviction so reminiscent of what Nellie Reagan taught long ago in Dixon: that America itself is no accident of geography or political science, but part of God's plan—to preserve and extend the sacred fire of human liberty.

I, too, have been described as an undying optimist, always seeing the glass half full when some see it as half empty. And, yes, it's true, I always see the sunny side of life. And that's not just because I've been blessed by achieving so many of my dreams. My optimism comes not just from my strong faith in God, but from my strong and enduring faith in man.

In my 80 years—I prefer to call that the 41st anniversary of my 39th birthday—I've seen what men can do for each other and do to each other. I've seen war and peace, feast and famine, depression and prosperity, sickness and health. I've seen the depth of suffering and the peaks of triumph. And I know in my heart that man is good; that what is right will always eventually triumph; and that there is purpose and worth to each and every life.

A dynamic people, by rolling their sleeves up and getting government off their backs, can achieve economic renewal. They can slay the beast of inflation and break the record book when it comes to sustained economic growth. They can create millions of new jobs and show a watching world the success of free enterprise.

I remember a time when the growth of American government seemed inexorable, and the encroachment of that government on the lives and liberties of our citizens seemed unstoppable. I also remember a time when America was advised to keep a low profile in the world as if by hunkering down and muzzling her deepest beliefs she might avoid foreign criticism and placate her enemies. And I remember a time when walls divided nations and human rights were trampled in the name of corrupt ideologies; a time when the arms race was spiraling out of control and distrust stood between us.

Eighty years is a long time to live. And yet, within the course of only a few short years I have seen the world turned upside down and conventional wisdom utterly disproved.

Visitors to this mountaintop will see a great jagged chunk of that Berlin Wall, as you've been told already—hated symbol of, yes, an evil empire that spied on and lied to its citizens, denying them their freedom, their bread, even their faith. Well, today, that wall exists only in museums, souvenir collections, and memories of a people no longer oppressed.

It is also a reminder that a strong America is always desirable and necessary in our world.

Today a heroic people has cast off the chains of Marx and Lenin that gave rise to so much of this century's tensions. The Iron Curtain has rusted away. In churches and schools, in factories and on farms, the people of Eastern Europe have found their voice, and with it, a battering ram to knock down the walls of tyranny. Totalitarianism is melting like snow.

As the mythology of communism melts under the fierce heat of truth, our greatest enemy now may be complacency itself. Meanwhile, let us joyously invade our former opponents with Yankee ingenuity, entrepreneurs selling their wares, enthusiastic tourists all spreading the gospel of human freedom.

Prosperous democracies don't declare war on each other. They simply let their citizens build better lives for themselves. Western Europe soared like a Phoenix from the ashes of World War II. So can Eastern Europe from the ruins of totalitarianism. And the American people can help show the way. What a happy challenge for those looking for something to do after the Cold War.

Today is the latest chapter in a story that began a quarter century ago when the people of California entrusted me with the stewardship of their dreams. The latest, but far from the last, for 10 years after we summoned America to a new beginning, we are beginning still. Every day brings fresh challenges and opportunities to match. With each sunrise we are reminded that millions of our citizens have yet to share in the abundance of American prosperity. Many languish in neighborhoods bereft of hope. Still others hesitate to venture out on the streets for fear of criminal violence. Can't we pledge ourselves to a new beginning for them?

Around the world hope stirs in the Middle East, and our prayers are with the peacemakers as they strive to realize an historic opportunity to bring peace to that ancient cradle of faith. With the Cold War over, can't we achieve a new beginning wherever peace is threatened?

Proverbially, old men plant trees, even though they do not expect to see their fruition. So it is with presidents. The doors of this library are open now and all are welcome. The judgment of history is left to you, the people.

I have no fears of that, for we have done our best. And so I say, come and learn from it. My fondest hope is that Americans will travel the road extended forward from the arch of experience, never forgetting our heroic origins, never failing to seek Divine guidance as we march boldly, bravely into a future limited only by our capacity to dream.

May every day be a new beginning and every dawn bring us closer to that shining city upon a hill.

Thank you. God bless you all, and God bless America.

PRESIDENT NIXON'S REMARKS

... We have heard a great deal about the fact that this is an historic occasion because, for the first time, we have five Presidents and six First Ladies in attendance. But speaking as a politician, I think you should know that I'm much more impressed by the fact that there are four people here who served and were elected as Governors of their particular states. Over the past 45 years I have run for the House, have been elected to the House, I've been elected to the Senate, I've been elected as Vice President, I've been elected as President. I never made it for governor. But by losing in 1962, I made it possible for Ronald Reagan to be elected Governor in 1966.

This magnificent library is a deserved tribute to Ronald Reagan and to Nancy Reagan. But as far as Ronald Reagan's legacy is concerned, it does not need a building to make it live for all of us. Even without a building we always will remember that Ronald Reagan was the President who restored America's military might—the military might that made it possible for George Bush to implement his brilliant strategy for victory in the Gulf war.

But great as that victory was, Ronald Reagan will be remembered for something even more important. Throughout his career, he has been one who had profound beliefs, who had the courage to fight for those beliefs, and who had the eloquence to inspire his fellow Americans to support those beliefs. He believed in the simple things—he believed in freedom and democracy; he believed that America was on the right side of history, standing with the forces of good against the forces of evil in the world.

And some have dismissed him, therefore, as an ideologue, but Ronald Reagan has been justified by what has happened—history has justified his leadership and those strong beliefs. Permit me to use a personal example. Thirty-two years ago, when I was in Moscow, the Premier of the Soviet Union Nikita Khrushchev jabbed his finger into my chest and said, "Your grandchildren will live under communism." And I responded, "Your grandchildren will live in freedom." At that time, I was sure he was wrong. But I was not sure I was right. And now we know—thanks, in great part, to the strong, idealistic leadership of President Ronald Reagan, Khrushchev's grandchildren now live in freedom.

PRESIDENT FORD'S
REMARKS

... Well, here we are at the 10th and the newest presidential library, which is being dedicated, like the others, to the American people. Herein, they will find hanging the spurs that Ronald Reagan won—not just one pair, but several. He didn't stop with two successful acting and governor careers; he went on to be elected President of the United States by the third biggest landslide in history.

And what will history say of the Reagan presidency? This library contains the records that will document the details for unborn generations of scholars. But you know what they say about history. History is something that never happened written by those who weren't there. Let me give you my view as one who was there.

President Reagan, you will be remembered as a national leader who was able to articulate the highest hopes and deepest beliefs of the American people. You have a great gift for transforming the best instincts into the firmest articles of faith. . . .

President Reagan, for eight eventful years, you kept the faith. You stayed the course. President Reagan, very likely—I should say President Bush, very likely, you will be our last Commander-In-Chief who wore the uniform in World War II, as did all your predecessors beginning with President Eisenhower. A common policy of peace through strength can be seen running through these years, under both Democrats as well as Republicans.

The big question: Can the future learn from the past? Is there a lesson to be learned from the archives of the Cold War in Missouri, Truman; in Kansas, Eisenhower; in Massachusetts, Kennedy; in Texas, Johnson; in Michigan, Ford; in Georgia, Carter; and in California—two in California, where they always do things bigger and better?

My answer would be the records show the United State won the Cold War by staying strong and free. The freedom of our society enabled our adversaries to see our strength. They and their dependency came to see that our freedom was the source of our strength. They came to the conclusion that they could never bury us, that they would really rather become more like us. We welcome them. We should help the process along. But perpetuating peace may be even far more difficult than waging war. Though the Cold War may be over, global competition has only begun.

Europe without an Iron Curtain may dwarf the economic miracles of devastated Germany and Japan. Russia, in economic and political turmoil, remains an unguided giant. China is stirring restlessly. The so-called Third World is pocked with trouble spots. Much is the same; much has changed.

What course should the United States set in the years ahead? Our counsel, our advice is unchanged. Keep the faith. Be vigilant. Remain strong. Let freedom flourish. Let liberty live. Stay the course. Stay the course. Stay the course. . . .

PRESIDENT CARTER'S REMARKS

Yesterday morning, Rosalyn and I left Lusaka in Zambia, flew back and arrived here late last night so that we could be present at this historic event. On the way, on those long hours on the plane, I though about the significance of this assembly, unprecedented, of the leaders of our country.

What does it mean, as compared, for instance, with other nations? We participated in the election in Zambia and saw the vivid demonstration of the desire of people for true freedom and an honest election and real democracy after 27 years under a state of emergency, led by the same parties.

It was a wonderful occasion to witness that emerging into the democratic fold, side-by-side now with our great country. A few days before that we had been in Liberia, a country torn by war, named for freedom itself, founded by former slaves from the United States of America. Their capital is named after James Monroe, one of our early presidents.

We drove through Monrovia, a hollow shell of a city, reminiscent to me and Rosalyn of Beirut; we visited there just a few years ago. A country still at war, struggling to achieve a united nation, peace, and a chance again for freedom and democracy.

In the United States, we have those same kinds of differences—political differences. We have a heterogeneous population, wider dispersed in heritage, beliefs, language, than any other on Earth. But we have a solid, dependable, stable Constitution under which we all live. And what binds us together best of all is our common commitment to freedom. . . .

I read the morning paper. . . . And just glancing down the front page, you see the same kind of stories in the news that were there when I was President: civil rights, the debate over how to yield to our people the same kind of human rights in this country that we always expressed as a need in the foreign nations.

Abraham Lincoln was the one who opened up this panorama of opportunity for us. And it goes down to the present day. Environmental issues are with us. I was a President who was very proud of the fact that, under Richard M. Nixon, we saw the Congress and him work together to achieve the Environmental Protection Agency, pure air and water legislation, the Council of Environmental Quality.

We still struggle together, Democrats and Republicans alike, on basic issues that affect our country, the insurance of military strength. All of us who have been in that office know that to plan, design, test and produce a weapons system as those used recently in the Gulf, it takes several presidential administrations to bring those dreams into reality, that our fighting men and women have a chance to prevail.

Let me point out that we still have some unanswered questions: How to provide good health care for all our people; homes for those who don't have a place to dwell; better education for our children. These are the kinds of things that make a common tie among all us Presidents who have served.

I would say parenthetically that one of the things that brings former Presidents closest together is the extremely onerous and burdensome task of begging for enough money to build a presidential library from private sources, not from the government. And then turn it over to the federal government in perpetuity as a repository for the records of our great nation.

Under President Ronald Reagan, our nation stood strong and resolute and made possible the beginning of the end of the Cold War. This has led to a new opportunity for our country to exhibit its greatness which we accept for granted too often, more clearly to people around the world.

In the past, all during my lifetime as an adult, I've known both war in the Second World War period, and also since then the Cold War. That Cold War is now over. And instead of two superpowers constantly struggling one against another everywhere on Earth, almost, in intense competition, we have one superpower. It's a matter of pride, but it's also a matter of sober realization that the world is now looking to us to exhibit our greatness.

There are characteristics that do not change, that measure our nation's greatness: an adherence to truth, to justice, to freedom, and to human rights. All can see that this is a goal for us to strive to achieve.

The men behind me have helped make it possible for us to look to the future, when the greatness of our nation will be measured not by achievements at war, but by the true and unchallenged champion of peace on Earth.

MAGIC JOHNSON ON HIS
RETIREMENT FROM BASKETBALL
November 7, 1991

Basketball superstar Earvin "Magic" Johnson shocked his legions of admirers and the nation by announcing November 7 that he had tested positive for HIV (human immunodeficiency virus), and, on his physician's advice, was immediately retiring from the sport that had made him rich and famous. Johnson said he would become "a spokesman for the virus," which can lead to AIDS (acquired immune deficiency syndrome), and he encouraged the practice of "safe sex" to lessen the danger of acquiring the virus.

Johnson's announcement was the first time a prominent public figure acknowledged testing positive before being forced to do so, according to Peter Carpenter, a member of the California AIDS Commission. "In that respect it is a milestone," said Carpenter. Jerry Smith, a pass receiver during thirteen seasons with the Washington Redskins football team, was one of the first professional athletes whose death (in 1986) was caused by AIDS. From 1981 to 1991, the disease killed more than 125,000 Americans.

Noted for dazzling play in his twelve-year career with the Los Angeles Lakers, Johnson was instrumental in advancing the team to five National Basketball Association (NBA) championships and nine Western Conference finals. Three times he was voted the league's most valuable player. He entered the league after leading Michigan State University to the national collegiate championship in 1979. Many credited Johnson with popularizing professional basketball among vast numbers of Americans.

Johnson's announcement at a specially called news conference in

Inglewood, California, provoked a deluge of queries to AIDS hotlines and medical centers from people seeking information about the disease. The Rev. Carl Bean, head of the Los Angeles AIDS Project, said soon afterward, "He's made a big difference by proving that HIV is not discriminatory." Referring to misconceptions about the HIV virus, Johnson said in an exchange with reporters at his news conference: "I think we sometimes think only gay people can get it; it's not going to happen to me. And here I am saying that it can happen to anybody, even me Magic Johnson."

Bob Steiner, public relations director for California Sports Inc., the Lakers' parent company, said Johnson contracted the virus from having sexual relations with an infected woman. Johnson's pregnant wife, Earletha ("Cookie"), had not been infected. Medical research had established that the virus usually is transmitted through intimate sexual contact—either heterosexual or homosexual—the sharing of needles by intravenous drug users, contaminated blood transfusions, or HIV-infected blood from a mother to her fetus. The virus could not be spread through casual contact.

"We have all been a little too optimistic about [the lower chance of] heterosexual transmission," said Andrew Moss, an epidemiologist at the University of San Francisco. "We have been lulled by the apparently low rates of male-to-female transmission. It is time to have to think about it more."

Medical studies indicated that by late 1991 some 1 million to 1.5 million Americans were infected with HIV. Gay males were disproportionately affected. Of the 192,000 Americans diagnosed with AIDS, only about 6 percent had contracted the disease heterosexually. But the number of infected women and young children was reported to be growing rapidly.

When HIV enters the bloodstream it might remain dormant for ten or more years. When it attacks, it destroys essential blood cells, causing a person's immune system to fail. The person then becomes vulnerable to infections such as pneumonia and some types of cancer. AIDS symptoms include chronic fatigue, fever, swollen glands, rashes, night sweats, diarrhea, weight loss, and weakness. Although a few expensive drugs have slowed the progression of AIDS, most of its victims died within two years of diagnosis.

Experts agreed that, short of sexual abstinence, the use of a condom was the safest way to avoid infection during intercourse. But others argued that the advocacy of condoms condoned sexual promiscuity.

Following are remarks by Earvin "Magic" Johnson at a news conference November 7, 1991, about his retirement from professional basketball because he had contracted the virus that causes the deadly disease AIDS:

First of all, let me say good after—good *late* afternoon. Because of the HIV virus I have attained, I will have to announce my retirement from the Lakers today.

I just want to make clear, first of all, that I do not have the AIDS disease, because I know a lot of you want to know that, but the HIV virus. My wife is fine, she's negative, so no problem with her. I plan on going on living for a long time, bugging you guys like I always have. So you'll see me around. I plan on being with the Lakers and the league—hopefully [Commissioner] David [Stern] will have me for a while—and going on with my life. I guess now I get to enjoy some of the other sides of living—that [were missed] because of the season and the long practices and so on.

I just want to say that I'm going to miss playing. And I will now become a spokesman for the HIV virus because I want people, young people, to realize they can practice safe sex. And, you know, sometimes you're a little naive about it and you think it could never happen to you. You only thought it could happen to, you know, other people and so on and on. And it has happened.

But I'm going to deal with it and my life will go on. And I will be here enjoying the Laker games and all the other NBA games around the country. So life is going to go on for me, and I'm going to be a happy man.

Now, medical questions that you have, you have to direct them to Dr. [Michael] Mellman and he can answer all those questions for you. Anything concerning the Lakers and so on, we have [General Manager] Jerry West here, I'm sure—of course the league, we have our commissioner, who I want to thank. I want to thank everybody up here, as well as my teammates because they've been behind me all the way.

I want to thank Kareem [Abdul-Jabbar] for coming out here. Man, cool, cool. We stood side by side and won a lot of battles. Larry Drew, another good friend of mine who I played with. But the commissioner, David Stern, has been great in support of me and I will go on and hopefully work with the league and help in any way that I can.

I want to thank also Jerry West for all he's done [and] Dr. [Robert] Kerlan, Dr. Mellman, who will tell you who my other doctors are that will help me through this, as well as, like I said, my father in a sense, Dr. Jerry Buss [team owner] for, you know, just drafting me and me being here.

Now, of course, I will miss the battles and the wars and I will miss you guys. But life goes on.

RELEASE OF HOSTAGES IN LEBANON
November 18 and December 4, 1991

Nearly a decade after the first American was kidnapped by radical Arab factions in Lebanon, the last remaining hostage was released December 4. He was Terry Anderson, chief Middle East correspondent of the Associated Press, who had endured the longest captivity—2,454 days, since March 16, 1985.

The ordeal for Americans living in Lebanon began in the early 1980s. The country was torn by years of civil war between Moslem and Christian militias and had no effective central authority. A number of terrorist groups vied for recognition and popular allegiance. Often this could be achieved by kidnapping prominent Westerners in Beirut, the capital. David Dodge, acting president of Beirut University, was the first American to be taken. He was kidnapped July 19, 1982, and imprisoned about a year.

In all, seventeen Americans were abducted—five in 1984, four in 1985, three in 1986, four in 1987, and one in 1988. The last was William Higgins, a Marine Corp lieutenant colonel, who was kidnapped February 17, 1988, while serving on a United Nations truce-observer team. He was killed by his captors allegedly in retaliation for the abduction of a Shiite spiritual leader by Israeli commandos in Lebanon.

Anderson's release was immediately preceded by the freeing of two other long-held Americans, Joseph Cicippio and Alan Steen. Only three other Westerners who had been kidnapped in Lebanon were not accounted for. Two were German relief workers—Heinrich Strübig and Thomas Kemptner—missing since May 1989. Their captors had not publicly identified themselves. The third person was Alec Collette, a

British journalist kidnapped in March 1985 and believed to be dead.

The last known British captive, Terry Waite, was released November 18, along with Thomas Sutherland, an American. Sutherland was dean of agriculture at the American University in Beirut, where Cicippio was deputy controller; Steen was a journalism instructor at Beirut University.

Question of Waite-North Link

Waite's capture in January 1987 drew world attention. He was in Lebanon on behalf of American and Canadian churches attempting to negotiate the release of hostages. Waite already was widely known for his previously successful dealings with Arab militants. As a personal emissary of the Archbishop of Canterbury, he had negotiated the return of British missionaries from Iran in 1981 and of four Britons from Libya in 1984. He also was credited with winning the release of three American hostages in Lebanon in 1985-1986: Benjamin Weir, a Presbyterian clergyman; Lawrence M. Jenco, a Catholic priest; and David P. Jacobson, director of the American University Hospital in Beirut.

After Waite was freed, stories circulated in the American and British press about his dealings with Lt. Col. Oliver L. North, a Reagan White House staff member involved in a secret attempt to sell U.S. arms to Iran to win the release of American hostages. Waite's kidnapping was attributed to his captor's belief that he was an agent of the U.S. government. That he had met several times with North was revealed in the autumn of 1986 by an official investigation of the arms-for-hostages deal. Moreover, Waite had used an American military helicopter to travel from Beirut to Cyprus in 1986. Waite denied that he was a U.S. agent, and North concurred, in separate remarks after Waite's release. Both said they were drawn together on occasion by a common goal of attempting to free the hostages but that each operated independently of the other. However, Waite conceded that captors could have been misled by his contacts with North.

Accounts of Brutal Treatment

British and American hostages were turned over to Syrian authorities and released in Damascus. While expressing great delight in being free, they made remarks that were generally brief and restrained. When asked by a reporter in Damascus, "What kept you going?" Anderson answered: "Well, my companions. . . . My faith. Stubbornness, I guess." Sutherland credited Anderson with pulling him through.

Back on home soil, the ex-hostages were more willing to describe their prison experiences. While they generally appeared in better physical condition than many people expected, they told of enduring extreme hardship and brutality. Several said they were subject to death threats, even mock executions. Some were beaten severely. Steen suffered permanent neurological damage from being kicked in the head by his captors.

Cicippio, chained to a balcony during one winter, suffered frostbite. The individual accounts indicated that the treatment of hostages varied widely and generally improved with the passing years. But strict and usually isolated confinement, meager food, medical inattention, and verbal abuse were common.

Three Americans were killed outright: Higgins, Peter Kilburn, and William Buckley. Kilburn, an American University librarian, was seized in 1984 and shot to death in 1986, along with two British hostages, in retaliation for an American air raid on Libya. Buckley, the Central Intelligence Agency's station chief in Beirut, apparently died in October 1985 after eighteen months of captivity; his kidnappers said they killed him to avenge an Israeli air raid on Palestine Liberation Organization headquarters in Tunisia. His remains were found and identified in December 1991.

UN Secretary General's Key Role

How prisoners fared depended largely on which group of captors held them. Several groups operating under different names were believed to be allied with Hezbollah, a pro-Iranian Shiite Moslem movement. The break in the hostage situation that permitted the freedom of American captives came only after UN Secretary General Javier Perez de Cuellar persuaded Iran to use its influence to seek release of the hostages. When the Persian Gulf War ended with Iraq in defeat, de Cuellar met several times with Iranian diplomats to urge Iran to seize the opportunity to strengthen its position in that region and improve its relations with the West.

According to a New York Times account of those meetings, the secretary general deftly turned the discussion to the matter of hostages. The idea of releasing the hostages as a gesture of good will apparently took root in the Iranian government despite strong opposition. The first results of the secretary general's initiative came on August 8, when the Islamic Jihad released British journalist John McCarthy and gave him a letter for de Cuellar, which said that the organization was ready to release all Westerners as part of a global exchange of prisoners. On the day the letter was delivered, August 11, French relief worker Jerome Leyraud and American businessman Edward Tracy were released. Leyraud had been kidnapped only three days earlier, but Tracy had been a hostage since October 1986.

For weeks, Giandomenico Picco, a special emissary of the secretary general, shuttled from capital to capital carrying out hostage negotiations. On September 11 de Cuellar met in Teheran with Iranian president Hashemi Rafsanjani and reportedly obtained his direct backing. The same day Israel announced the release of fifty-one Arab prisoners and the bodies of nine slain Arab guerrillas, as demanded by pro-Iranian groups, upon confirmation that an Israeli serviceman missing in Lebanon was dead and that his body would be returned.

Among the Western hostages set free during the fall of 1991 was Jesse Turner, an American teacher at Beirut University. He emerged from *nearly five years of captivity on October 22. After Anderson's release, the United Nation officials said they would continue working to free the two German hostages and Arab detainees held by Israel and its surrogate militia in southern Lebanon and to resolve the fate of four Israelis missing in action in Lebanon since 1982-1983.*

Following are excerpts from remarks by Terry Waite and Thomas Sutherland at a news conference November 18, 1991, in Damascus upon their release from captivity and by Terry Anderson at a news conference December 4, 1991, in Damascus, upon his release:

WAITE'S STATEMENT

Your Excellence, ladies and gentlemen, I think first of all I would like to say to the Syrian Government our grateful thanks for their hospitality and care during the last few hours. Of course, there are so many people we need to thank—the British Government, the United Nations, churches, and more especially I think ordinary people around the world who have kept the name of the hostages and others alive, and that to us has been supremely important.

This afternoon, when we were sitting together in our cell, chained to the wall, as we have been chained to the wall for the last five years—and in some cases, as Tom and others, for seven years, 23 hours and 50 minutes today, one of our captors came in and told us that Tom and myself would be freed this evening. He also said to me: We apologize for having captured; we recognize that now this was the wrong thing to do, that holding hostages achieves no useful, constructive purpose. He went on to say that before the end of the month, Joseph Cicippio and Alann Steen would be released, we hope within the next five days.

He furthermore said that by the end of the month Terry Anderson would be set free. I asked him then about the German hostages, and I am sorry ... that at that point he could give me no further positive information, but he did say that he hoped very much that meant the two would be cleared up eventually, as soon as possible. . . .

SUTHERLAND'S REMARKS

. . . As some of you may know, I'm an old college prof from way back, and when I get up to speak, I generally get 50 minutes—which is about five times longer than I've had to go to the bathroom every day for the last seven years, but that's another story.

I would like to especially thank . . . the Government of Syria for all of the work that they have done in those past months and years on our behalf. And I can tell you that in the past hour or so—hour and a half perhaps—

we have been treated very, very nicely by some of the representatives of the Government of Syria. And we've had a very happy time joking with them and laughing out loud for the first time for a long time. . . .

I want to thank the Government of Iran as well . . . and Mr. Uri Lubrani has been quite instrumental in negotiating very well for our release.

Mr. Giandomenico Picco from the U.N. has also apparently played a reasonably key role in all of these negotiations and we are very, very grateful to him and to Secretary General de Cuellar. . . .

Like Terry Waite, I would say that his job is not done because we left Terry Anderson about three or four hours ago in Lebanon, and he is no longer chained to the wall, thank God, but he's still in a room that has very little fresh air and no daylight whatsoever.

All I can say, though, about the English, they take a hell of a long time to get things done. He [Terry Waite] came to get me out about five years ago and it's taken him five years to get me out, but finally he's taking me home.

Also to Iowa State University in Ames, Iowa. I was very, very moved when I heard on VOA a recording of "The Bells of Iowa State", which I particularly appreciated hearing when I was a student there on the campus. Walking to class every morning from quarter to 8 until 8, those bells played, so when I heard them ring out 72 bells on the occasion of my 72nd month, I was extremely happy.

So to Iowa State, I would say, keep the bells ringing, friends back there. . . .

*　　*　　*

Without Terry Anderson, I couldn't have made it six and a half years. Terry Anderson for me was a very big challenge for the first couple of years. He's very, very, very bright, and it was humiliating to me to have to cope with his tremendous brain. After a couple of years I came to grips with that, came to terms with it, and after that our sailing was free. . . .

And so I would just simply say to all of the friends of Terry Anderson, he is a man of whom all of you can be proud. He is in good health right now. He's in very good spirits. . . .

But he's a man who never should have been kidnapped. He was . . . doing his very best for the world and for Lebanon and reporting objectively about what was happening in Lebanon. And they never should have picked any of us up because I agree with Terry Waite that kidnapping is a great evil and that those who perpetrate it—I don't think they really thoroughly understand, many of these young men, what they were doing to us, putting those chains back on our legs every day. And Terry Anderson just said a couple of days ago, I simply couldn't do that to another human being; I simply couldn't do it.

. . . Things have been a lot better for us, and part of the reason why things have been better has been because two of the young men who were kind of the captains of the teams that alternated looking after us, one by the name of Mahmoud and one by the name of Jamil—I christened him Jamil. And those two men kept their other workers in line and they treated us with respect and they tried to give us the kind of things that we needed. . . .

WAITE'S FINAL REMARKS

I just want to say one final thing . . . that in the last years, we've lived through some of the suffering of the people of Lebanon. We've been under shellfire constantly, and to be under shellfire when you're chained to the wall.

But we've lived through that suffering. And we, all of us, all hostages would plead with those who are holding the people of south Lebanon—innocent people being held as hostages—to release them soon, to put an end to this problem, to put an end to terrorism, and to find peaceful, humane and civilized ways of resolving the very complex problems that face the people of the Middle East. We as hostages will give our utmost support to seeing this problem finished, not only for Western hostages, but for all in the Middle East who are held in that way.

ANDERSON'S REMARKS

I'm going to try to shake as many people's hands as I can after we get finished here. I mean you're all my friends, but I can't get to you all.

You can't imagine how glad I am to see you. I've thought about this moment for a long time. And now it's here, and I'm scared to death. I don't know what to say.

I have, of course, to thank the Syrian, Lebanese and Iranian governments for their cooperation and their work in helping to free so many hostages recently. I feel the deepest gratitude to Mr. [Giandomenico] Picco and the [U.N.] Secretary General [Javier Perez de Cuellar]. I don't know how to express it. I mean thanks just doesn't cover it.

Your support, all my colleagues, journalists, has been very important. I've heard so many things over the years—on the radio, in the few magazines and newspapers we've gotten—about your work for me. Again, I just can't say how grateful I am.

Also, for thousands and thousands of people, whom I don't know, never met, who don't know me, who I know have been working and praying for us all, all the hostages, your support, your prayers were important. They made a big difference, they made a difference for us in some very dark times.

My family, of course, my incredible sister, Peg, I will be thanking shortly myself and personally.

There are a couple of you I'd like to mention individually, obviously. Where's the BBC man? Here some place?

Press: Unidentified reporter: "He's not here."

Couldn't make it, huh? Well, after all the wonderful things that Tom [Sutherland] and Terry [Waite] said about the BBC, I suppose I should be a little critical and a little niggly here and there, but I haven't got the heart for it. I've spent a lot of time listening to the radio recently, most of the time to the BBC. Your news coverage always has been superb. My special thanks to the "Outlook" team ... for the many times and the much effort they spent to bring me messages from my family and my friends, and often their voices, and that was very, very important.

And I'd also like to thank my Lebanese colleagues, in the television and newspapers both, because each year they brought a message to me from my family on my birthday, on Christmas, and sometimes elsewhere. And they did this in midst of their own terrible troubles. And that shows a depth of concern and support that again, I just keep saying, I'm very grateful for.

I'm grateful to you all, to everyone.

Uh, we'll niggle a little bit. I was never a Marine captain, I was a Marine staff sergeant. And I'm very proud to have been that, by the way.

I spent the afternoon, interestingly enough, playing solitaire by candle-light and listening to the BBC reporting on my progress toward Damascus. Well, it was kind of fun in a weird kind of way, kind of like listening to your own obituary. You were very nice to me, thank you.

I'll try to answer a few questions, although you'll understand I have a date with a couple of beautiful ladies, and I'm already very late.

Press: Can you tell about your journey here and when you were actually freed?

Yesterday afternoon, my captors came in, brought some new clothes, new shoes—my first in seven years, and they hurt my feet, by the way—and they said that I would be going home today. They asked me to read a statement from them to the world about this kidnapping episode. And I did so on a videotape, which they said they took to the AP today.

Press: We got it!

OK, making very clear that it was their statement, not mine, but I felt it was worthwhile to listen to what they had to say. Spent the night awake mostly. Today, I spent the day pacing the room and playing solitaire and waiting. I think this last 24 hours has been longer than the whole 6½ years beforehand. I was taken from my cell about 6:20 or 6:30, and driven to a nearby place, turned over to Syrian officers, and brought, with a couple of brief stops, here and to face you. I almost walked in on you when I came in the door, except I heard a low growl go up and I figured I better go the other way.

Press: Tell us something more about what it's been like in captivity.

Oh Lord. Um, it would take a book. That's an idea, by the way.

Press: How do you feel about your title of longest-held hostage?

It's an honor I would gladly have given up a long time ago.

Press: What about the German hostages, you mentioned something about them. Did they mention anything about them?

I wish I had some news about them. I don't. I hope for their release. I hope for the release of all the Lebanese very, very soon and I know with fine men like Mr. Picco and Mr. de Cuellar working on it that there's a good chance it will happen. I don't have any news. My captors have always denied having any control or information or business to do with other hostages other than the ones that we knew about, the ones that were kept together with me. They always said [inaudible]

Press: What kept you going?

Well, my companions. I was lucky enough to have other people with me most of the time. My faith. Stubbornness, I guess. You just do what you have to do. You wake up every day, and you summon up the energy from somewhere, even when you think you haven't got it, and you get through the day. And you do it day after day after day.

Press: How did you occupy yourself . . . after you were the last one left?

Paced back and forth. I had a couple of plastic bottles that I filled up with water and used as dumbbells. Played a lot of solitaire—I had a deck of cards—and listened to the radio, mostly to the BBC.

Press: What were your last words to the kidnappers?

Goodbye!

BUSH ON JOB RIGHTS BILL
November 21, 1991

President George Bush on November 21 signed into law the Civil Rights Act of 1991, legislation that was two years in the making and once seemed doomed by his objection that it imposed hiring quotas for women and minorities. The president vetoed an earlier version of the bill in 1990, but he unexpectedly declared satisfaction with a compromise measure devised by Senate leaders in October 1991. It provided most of the job rights that congressional Democrats had sought.

The new legislation—like the vetoed bill—sought to counter the effects of Supreme Court rulings in recent years that had made it harder for workers to bring and win job discrimination lawsuits. (Court on Civil Rights, Historic Documents of 1989, p. 321) Additionally, for the first time limited money damages could be awarded to victims of workplace harassment and other intentional discrimination based on sex, religion, or disability.

White House negotiators insisted that the amounts be strictly limited and ultimately settled for liability ceilings of $50,000 to $300,000, depending on the size of the business. Those limits did not apply to members of racial minorities, who were already permitted to sue under a Reconstruction-era law.

Question of President's Position

Although the president's shift in position on the bill assured its prompt passage in the Senate (October 30) and House (November 7) by large bipartisan majorities, opposition remained on the Republican right. That opposition surfaced within the White House on the eve of the bill signing, reigniting a political debate on where the Bush administration stood on civil rights issues.

On November 20, White House Counsel C. Boyden Gray had circulated among administration officials the draft of a presidential statement directing all executive agencies to terminate federal affirmative action programs within their control, in effect, attempting to negate much of what the new law sought to accomplish.

News of the proposal was leaked to the press and created a furor. It angered civil rights activists and sponsors of the bill, including Sen. John C. Danforth, R-Mo., chief architect of the compromise agreement. The White House disowned the statement, saying that it was drafted without the president's knowledge or approval. That explanation appeared to mollify most critics, although some who were invited to the signing ceremony refused to attend. Rep. John Conyers, Jr., D-Mich., chairman of the Congressional Black Caucus, contended that the statement was a "trial balloon" floated on Bush's behalf and represented presidential "hypocrisy at its worst."

Retreat from "Quota Bill" Objections

At the ceremony in the White House Rose Garden, Bush did not mention Gray but pointedly asserted: "This administration is committed to action that is truly affirmative, positive action. Nothing in this bill overturns the government's affirmative action programs."

Job priorities based on race stem from a 1965 executive order signed by President Lyndon B. Johnson that required federal contractors to take "affirmative action" to add more black employees. In 1969 the Nixon administration developed "goals and timetables" to measure the progress of such hiring in the construction industry, where job discrimination was found to be widespread. A year later goals and timetables were applied to all federal contractors, and in 1974 affirmative action was extended to women. The Labor Department reported in 1991 that more than 93,000 companies employing 27 million workers held contracts worth $184 billion covered by the federal program.

Bush's past objection to "quotas bills" made him appear unsympathetic to affirmative action—and in step with the thinking of many white Americans, according to opinion polls. During the 1990 reelection campaign of Sen. Jesse Helms, R-N.C., the incumbent tapped into apparently strong feelings among white workers that affirmative action had cost them jobs. Many political analysts thought the president would play off the same sentiment in his own reelection campaign in 1992.

However, Bush's agreement to a compromise job rights bill indicated that he had shifted away from such a strategy. Some political analysts said the president wanted to separate himself from David Duke, a Republican former Ku Klux Klansman who ran a strong race for the Louisiana governorship, and to counter an unfavorable reaction among many women to hard-line Republican questioning of University of Oklahoma law professor Anita Hill's charges of sexual harassment against Supreme Court nominee Clarence Thomas at his Senate con-firmation hearings. (Confirmation of Supreme Court Justice Clarence Thomas, p. 549)

The legislative compromise, worked out immediately after the hearings and during the Louisiana election campaign, would allow women to sue for monetary damages over job-related sexual harassment.

Leaving Key Definition to Courts

In his Rose Garden statement, Bush retained one provision from Gray's proposal. The president said executive branch officials should consider "authoritative" an interpretation of the law's application that had been written by Gray and asserted in congressional debate by a dozen of the bill's Republican opponents. Upon the bill's passage, Democrats and Republicans submitted their separate views on the scope of the law in an attempt to influence future judiciary rulings on disputed meanings.

In a concession to the president, the bill's drafters deliberately left one key question for the courts to decide: What constituted a "business necessity" for not hiring women or minority groups? In 1971 the Supreme Court ruled in Griggs v. Duke Power Co. *that employers had to prove a "business necessity" to justify hiring practices that were seemingly fair but had an adverse impact on women or minorities. In 1989 the Court, having attained a conservative majority, held in* Wards Cove Packing Co. v. Atonio *that the burden of proof was on the workers to show that a company had no legitimate need to follow the hiring practices they challenged.*

Democratic sponsors of the bill succeeded in shifting the burden of proof back to employers but yielded to Bush's insistence that "business necessity" be defined by the courts—presumably by the Supreme Court, whose decisions generally were favorable to employers.

Other provisions of the new law, unrelated to past Supreme Court rulings, prohibited tests for hiring or promotion to be adjusted for race factors and provided for the president and Congress jointly to appoint a commission to determine why relatively few women and minorities rose to the top levels of corporate management.

Following are excerpts of remarks by President George Bush and a prepared statement he issued at the signing of the Civil Rights Act of 1991 at the White House on November 21, 1991:

REMARKS AT BILL SIGNING

... Today we celebrate a law that will fight the evil of discrimination while also building bridges of harmony between Americans of all races, sexes, creeds, and backgrounds. For the past few years, the issue of civil rights legislation has divided Americans. No more. From day one, I told the American people that I wanted a civil rights bill that advances the cause of equal opportunity. And I wanted a bill that advances the cause of racial harmony. And I wanted a bill that encourages people to work together. And today I am signing that bill, the Civil Rights Act of 1991.

Discrimination, whether on the basis of race, national origin, sex, religion, or disability, is worse than wrong. It's an evil that strikes at the very heart of the American ideal. This bill, building on current law, will help ensure that no American will discriminate against another.

For these reasons, this is a very good bill. Let me repeat: This is a very good bill. Last year, back in May of 1990 in the Rose Garden, right here with some of you present, I appealed for a bill I could sign. And I said that day that I cannot and will not sign a quota bill. Instead, I said that the American people deserved a civil rights bill that number one, insisted that employers focus on equal opportunity, not on developing strategies to avoid litigation. Number two, they deserved a bill that was based upon fundamental principles of fairness, that anyone who believes their rights have been violated is entitled to their day in court, and that the accused are innocent until proved guilty. And number three, they deserved a bill that provided adequate deterrent against harassment based upon race, sex, religion, or disability.

I also said that day back in 1990 that this administration is committed to action that is truly affirmative, positive action in every sense, to strike down all barriers to advancement of every kind for all people. And in that same spirit, I say again today, "I support affirmative action. Nothing in this bill overturns the Government's affirmative action programs."

And unlike last year's bill, a bill I was forced to veto, this bill will not encourage quotas or racial preferences because this bill will not create lawsuits on the basis of numbers alone. I oppose quotas because they incite tensions between the races, between the sexes, between people who get trapped in a numbers game.

This bill contains several important innovations. For example, it contains strong new remedies for the victims of discrimination and harassment, along with provisions capping damages that are an important model to be followed in tort reform. And it encourages mediation and arbitration between parties before the last resort of litigation. Our goal and our promise is harmony, a return to civility and brotherhood, as we build a better America for ourselves and our children. . . .

No one likes to oppose a bill containing the words "civil rights," especially me. And no one in Congress likes to vote against one, either. I owe a debt of gratitude to those who stood with us against counterproductive legislation last year and again earlier this year, as well as to those who led the way toward the important agreement we've reached today. I'm talking about Democrats, I'm talking about Republicans, and those outside the Congress who played a constructive role. And to all of you, I am very, very grateful, because I believe this is in the best interest of the United States.

But to the Congress I also say this: The 1991 civil rights bill is only the first step. If we seek—and I believe that every one of us does—to build a new era of harmony and shared purpose, we must make it possible for all Americans to scale the ladder of opportunity. If we seek to ease racial tensions in America, civil rights legislation is, by itself, not enough. The elimination of discrimination in the workplace is a vital element of the American dream, but it is simply not enough. . . .

The American dream rests on the vision of life, liberty, and the pursuit of happiness. In our workplaces, in our schools, or on our streets, this dream begins with equality and opportunity. Our agenda for the next American century, whether it be guaranteeing equal protection under the law, promoting excellence in education, or creating jobs, will ensure for generations to come that America remains the beacon of opportunity in the world. Now, with great pride—and thanks to so many people here in the Rose Garden today, especially the Members of Congress with us—with great pride I will sign this good, sound legislation into law. Thank you very much.

STATEMENT RELEASED AT SIGNING

Today I am pleased to sign into law S. 1745, the "Civil Rights Act of 1991." This historic legislation strengthens the barriers and sanctions against employment discrimination.

Employment discrimination law should seek to prevent improper conduct and foster the speedy resolution of conflicts. This Act promotes the goals of ridding the workplace of discrimination on the basis of race, color, sex, religion, national origin, and disability; ensuring that employers can hire on the basis of merit and ability without the fear of unwarranted litigation; and ensuring that aggrieved parties have effective remedies. This law will not lead to quotas, which are inconsistent with equal opportunity and merit-based hiring; nor does it create incentives for needless litigation.

Most of this Act's major provisions have been the subject of a bipartisan consensus. Along with most Members of the Congress, for example, I have favored expanding the right to challenge discriminatory seniority systems; expansion of the statutory prohibition against racial discrimination in connection with employment contracts; and the creation of meaningful monetary remedies for all forms of workplace harassment outlawed under Title VII of the Civil Rights Act of 1964. Similarly, my Administration has concurred in proposed changes to authorize expert witness fees in Title VII cases; to extend the statute of limitations and authorize the award of interest against the U.S. Government; and to cure technical defects with respect to providing notice of the statute of limitations under the Age Discrimination in Employment Act of 1967. I am happy to note that every one of these issues is addressed in the Act that becomes law today.

It is regrettable that enactment of these worthwhile measures has been substantially delayed by controversies over other proposals. S. 1745 resolves the most significant of these controversies, involving the law of "disparate impact," with provisions designed to avoid creating incentives for employers to adopt quotas or unfair preferences. It is extremely important that the statute be properly interpreted—by executive branch officials, by the courts, and by America's employers—so that no incentives to engage in such illegal conduct are created.

Until now, the law of disparate impact has been developed by the Supreme Court in a series of cases stretching from the *Griggs* decision in 1971 to the *Watson* and *Wards Cove* decisions in 1988 and 1989. Opinions by Justices Sandra Day O'Connor and Byron White have explained the safeguards against quotas and preferential treatment that have been included in the jurisprudence of disparate impact. S. 1745 codifies this theory of discrimination, while including a compromise provision that overturns *Wards Cove* by shifting to the employer the burden of persuasion on the "business necessity" defense. This change in the burden of proof means it is especially important to ensure that all the legislation's other safeguards against unfair application of disparate impact law are carefully observed. These highly technical matters are addressed in detail in the analyses of S. 1745 introduced by Senator [Robert] Dole on behalf of himself and several other Senators and of the Administration (137 Cong. Rec. S15472-S15478 (daily ed. Oct. 30, 1991); 137 Cong. Rec. S15953 (daily ed. Nov. 5, 1991)). These documents will be treated as authoritative interpretive guidance by all officials in the executive branch with respect to the law of disparate impact as well as the other matters covered in the documents.

Another important source of the controversy that delayed enactment of this legislation was a proposal to authorize jury trials and punitive damages in cases arising under Title VII. S. 1745 adopts a compromise under which "caps" have been placed on the amount that juries may award in such cases. The adoption of these limits on jury awards sets an important precedent, and I hope to see this model followed as part of an initiative to reform the Nation's tort system.

In addition to the protections provided by the "caps," section 118 of the Act encourages voluntary agreements between employers and employees to rely on alternative mechanisms such as mediation and arbitration. This provision is among the most valuable in the Act because of the important contribution that voluntary private arrangements can make in the effort to conserve the scarce resources of the Federal judiciary for those matters as to which no alternative forum would be possible or appropriate.

Finally, I note that certain provisions in Title III, involving particularly requirements that courts defer to the findings of fact of a congressional body, as well as some of the measures affecting individuals in the executive branch, raise serious constitutional questions.

Since the Civil Rights Act was enacted in 1964, our Nation has made great progress toward the elimination of employment discrimination. I hope and expect that this legislation will carry that progress further. Even if such discrimination were totally eliminated, however, we would not have done enough to advance the American dream of equal opportunity for all. Achieving that dream will require bold action to reform our educational system, reclaim our inner cities from violence and drugs, stimulate job creation and economic growth, and nurture the American genius for voluntary community service. My Administration is strongly committed to action in all these areas, and I look forward to continuing the effort we celebrate here today.

December

SUNUNU'S RESIGNATION AS BUSH'S CHIEF OF STAFF

December 3, 1991

In his first significant White House staff shakeup, President George Bush December 3 accepted the resignation of John H. Sununu, his embattled chief of staff. Sununu told the president in a letter released that day he would leave rather than "be a drag on your success" in the 1992 presidential election campaign. Bush, also in a letter, expressed gratitude for his chief aide's "distinguished service" and loyalty, which included intercepting "many of the 'arrows' aimed my way." Sununu had entered the White House with Bush in January 1989 after serving as governor of New Hampshire and figuring prominently in Bush's 1988 campaign.

Two days after the exchange of letters, Bush named Secretary of Transportation Samuel K. Skinner his new chief of staff, effective December 15. The president's decision to replace Sununu was seen as an attempt to alter the public's perception of White House confusion over domestic issues, especially in its dealing with a faltering economy. In December, Bush's job rating fell below the 50 percent mark for the first time in his presidency, according to a Washington Post-*ABC News Poll. The decline was attributed mostly to public discontent over a continuing recession.*

Sununu and budget director Richard G. Darman reputedly held firm control over White House formulations of domestic policy and advised Bush to give nothing but upbeat assessments of economic conditions. Two days after Sununu's departure as chief of staff, though, Bush, in an ABC News interview, conceded that the economy was "in trouble." (Greenspan on "Faltered" Business Recovery, p. 851) The White House and Sununu both promoted the resignation as voluntary. But it followed days of press reporting that the chief of staff was struggling to save his job and that the president's eldest son, George W. Bush, had told Sununu he was a "liability" to the president.

Sununu's "Pit Bull" Style

As a trusted and influential adviser of the president, Sununu championed political views of the Republican right and often carried out unpopular tasks to shield the president from criticism. With a combative political style and often arrogant manner, Sununu seemed to relish his role, comparing himself to a fierce pit bulldog. "I don't care if people hate me, as long as they hate me for the right reasons," Sununu once said. On other occasions, he said he worked for only one person—the president—and only his approval mattered.

Sununu's intense loyalty, or other attributes, previously had protected him from a host of detractors, including Republican colleagues and Democratic foes. In 1990 he weathered a round of public criticism over his use of military aircraft for ski trips and an out-of-town dental visit. But he was vulnerable to subsequent criticism over other White House missteps. In one instance, the president sent the stock market into a dive by remarking that the credit card interest rate should be lowered. Sununu, denying news reports that he had inserted the remarks, said Bush had ad-libbed them. Sununu thus failed to do what he was known for doing best: protecting his boss.

Contrasts

Although Sununu stepped down as chief of staff December 15, Bush said he would remain through March 1, 1992, as a counselor to the president with Cabinet rank. However, Sununu's commanding presence clearly ceased when Skinner moved into his vacated slot.

Both Sununu and Skinner were Republican leaders who were instrumental in Bush's 1988 presidential race. Sununu engineered Bush's crucial victory in the New Hampshire presidential primary, and Skinner ran Bush's successful general election campaign in Illinois. Their similarities, however, went no further. Skinner was known as a pragmatic politician with a calm management style and a willingness to compromise. He first gained prominence in the 1970s as a U.S. attorney in Illinois who convicted several Democratic officials, among them former governor Otto Kerner, of corrupt practices. But in later jobs, including that of transportation secretary, he worked effectively with Democrats. Before going to Washington, he directed the Chicago area transit system.

When announcing Skinner's appointment, Bush also named Secretary of Commerce Robert A. Mosbacher, who was his 1988 campaign finance director, general chairman of his 1992 reelection campaign. To assume the position, Mosbacher would have to resign his Cabinet seat.

Following are the texts of White House Chief of Staff John H. Sununu's resignation letter to President George Bush, and Bush's letter accepting the resignation, both dated December 3, 1991, and released that day by the White House:

Dear Mr. President,

A little over three years ago you asked me to be your Chief of Staff. I eagerly and appreciatively accepted.

Over these years it has been one of the most gratifying and satisfying experiences of my life to serve a President whom I admire, respect and will always consider a dear friend.

These have been amazing times for the world and the nation; they have been exciting and thrilling times for me. I am truly grateful for the opportunity to have been a part of it.

But most of all, from a purely personal perspective, I want to thank you for the fun we have had these last three years. In a way that will be very difficult for historians to capture, this White House was an unbelievably "fun place" to work. You, the Vice President, Scowcroft, Gates and I proved we could do very serious things well without taking the process or ourselves too seriously. I believe that chemistry, friendship, caring and irreverence was a singularly unique period for the Oval office, probably impossible ever to replicate. You were just great to let us do it that way.

I must also take this opportunity to tell you again how proud I am of the White House staff you allowed me to put together. They will eventually be recognized as the most talented, mutually supportive, cooperative team ever to serve a President. In fact, one of the challenges ahead of us will be to make very clear the significance of all you and they have accomplished in the domestic area as well as in foreign policy.

I have always said I wanted to serve as Chief of Staff as long as I could contribute to your success and help deal effectively with both the issues and the arrows. Until recently I was convinced that even with the distorted perceptions being created, I could be a strong contributor to your efforts and success.

But in politics, especially during the seasons of a political campaign, perceptions that can be effectively dealt with at other times, can be—and will be—converted into real political negatives. And I would never want to not be contributing positively, much less be a drag on your success. Therefore, as we enter the contentious climate of a political campaign, I believe it is in your best interest for me to resign as Chief of Staff to the President of the United States effective December 15, 1991.

As much as I will truly miss the opportunity to continue to work in the West Wing with you and my other friends there, I want you to know how strong and positive and upbeat I feel about doing this. I think you know that the responsibility and authority (contrary to the legends out there) never meant as much to me as the chance to assist you to be (and to be recognized) a great President. I intend to continue that effort as an ordinary citizen, with all the benefits that accrue to man and family in the private sector of our magnificent system.

I assure you that in pit bull mode or pussy cat mode (your choice, as always) I am ready to help.

I also want to thank Barbara and all the Bush clan for being such wonderful friends and strong supporters even during the toughest of days. Nancy and I and our family will always remember and cherish that kindness and friendship. I hope we will all have a chance to share a few laughs over the holidays.

Thanks again for the privilege of serving you and this wonderful country. It really has been great!!!

Sincerely and respectfully,

John H. Sununu

Dear John,

I now have your letter resigning as Chief of Staff effective December 15th. It is with reluctance, regret and a sense of personal loss that I accept your resignation as Chief of Staff.

I am very pleased, however, that you have agreed to remain as a Counsellor to the President, with Cabinet rank, through March 1, 1992.

During the period, December 15th to March 1, you will be an official member of my administration and I will continue to seek your counsel on the important issues facing our country.

John, I find it very difficult to write this letter both for professional reasons and for personal reasons.

On the professional side, thanks to your leadership we have made significant accomplishments for which you deserve great credit.

Working with others here in the White House, throughout the administration, and on Capitol Hill, you have played a major role in achieving some of our significant goals.

I will not attempt to list each legislative achievement for which you deserve an awful lot of personal credit. Having said that, your adherence to principle and your endless hours at the negotiating table were clearly instrumental in achieving good Clean Air Legislation; the ADA Bill and the Civil Rights Act of 91, both of which moved this country forward in a sensible way; groundbreaking Child Care legislation that strengthened the principle of family choice; and a budget agreement that for the first time in history put real enforceable caps on discretionary government spending. For all of this and much, much more, I am very grateful to you.

In your letter, you generously mention my family and our personal relationship. The longer I serve as President the more importance I place on true friendships—friendships tested by fire and time. Ours is such a friendship. Barbara feels this way. Our four sons feel this way and so of course does Dorothy.

You have never wavered in your loyalty to us and more importantly, your loyalty to the principles and goals of this administration. You have indeed helped with the issues and you have intercepted many of the "arrows" aimed my way.

Thank you from the bottom of my grateful heart for your distinguished service. I look forward to working with you in the future, first as Counsellor inside government and then as a trusted advisor outside government.

And, yes, from my vantage point and our families as well, the friendship we treasure is stronger than ever.

I hope you and Nancy, free of the enormous pressures of the office you have served so well, will enjoy life to its fullest. You deserve the best.

Most sincerely from this grateful President,

George Bush

FIFTIETH ANNIVERSARY
OF ATTACK ON PEARL HARBOR
December 7, 1991

In solemn ceremonies December 7 at Pearl Harbor, Hawaii, honoring the American dead from a Japanese surprise attack exactly fifty years earlier, President George Bush urged Americans not to harbor grievances against their enemies of World War II. Bush, a Navy flier shot down during Pacific combat in 1944, told a pierside gathering of war veterans and their families: "I have no rancor in my heart towards Germany or Japan, none at all. And I hope . . . you have none in yours. This is no time for recrimination. World War II is over. We won. We crushed totalitarianism, and when that was done we helped our enemies give birth to democracies."

The Japanese attack on Pearl Harbor precipitated U.S. entry into World War II, which cost 400,000 American lives. More than 2,400 of those deaths occurred in the brief attacks by carrier-based Japanese planes on U.S. warships in Pearl Harbor and shoreside facilities during the morning of December 7, 1941. Much of the U.S. Pacific fleet was destroyed or disabled in that raid. Bush spoke to the war veterans after a trip by barge to the USS Arizona Memorial, which bears the names of 1,177 crew members who died aboard the sunken battleship. Lying beneath the memorial structure, the ship's broken hull is the permanent gravesite for those whose remains could not be recovered.

The president and Mrs. Bush dropped flowers on the waters above the rusting vessel, and he spoke briefly at the memorial. As in his remarks at pierside and earlier ones at a daybreak ceremony at the National Cemetery of the Pacific, where 776 victims of the attack were buried, Bush balanced fulsome praise of Americans who fought in World War II with reminders that afterward "we made our enemies our friends." He said war "taught us isolation is a bankrupt notion" and—in support of that statement—cited the backing of many countries in the Persian Gulf War against Iraq.

At every place he spoke, the president praised Americans of Japanese descent who fought with U.S. forces in World War II, and he expressed regrets for the wartime removal of Japanese-American families—U.S. citizens and aliens alike—from their West Coast homes to internment camps in the interior. Bush called them "innocent victims who committed no offense."

Sensitivity to Japanese Reaction

The president appeared acutely aware of the effect his words would have in Japan as well as the United States, particularly on troubled U.S.-Japanese economic relations. He alluded to a trip he would make to Japan in early 1992 to try to open its markets to more American products. Japan's economic inroads in the United States were nowhere more evident than in Hawaii, where an influx of Japanese tourism and investment had enabled the state to prosper while much of the rest of the nation suffered from an economic recession.

Press reports from Tokyo portrayed the Japanese people as intensely interested in the Pearl Harbor anniversary and fearful that it might be the occasion for "Japan bashing" in the United States. Japanese television and newspapers reported the event fully and for months had featured articles and programs dealing with the war, Japan's close postwar involvement with the United States, and the cultural differences between the two countries.

According to polling in November sponsored jointly by the New York Times, CBS News, and Tokyo Broadcasting System, 77 percent of the Americans said they were generally friendly toward Japan, and 65 percent of the Japanese said they had the same feeling toward the United States. Whereas only 14 percent of the Americans who were polled said they held it against Japan for bombing Pearl Harbor, 65 percent of the Japanese thought that Americans did. And more Japanese (59 percent) than Americans (44 percent) thought that the Japanese government should formally apologize to the United States for the Pearl Harbor attack.

Question of Apology from Japan

The apology question caused problems for the Japanese government as the Pearl Harbor anniversary approached. The United States did not request an apology, but Japanese officials reportedly were sensitive to American contentions that Japan was reluctant to acknowledge its wartime role as an aggressor in Asia and the Pacific. A proposal to issue an apology arose within the Tokyo government but was sidetracked after an informal national debate developed over whether the United States should not, in turn, apologize for dropping two atomic bombs on Japan in 1945. To overcome that impasse, Prime Minister Kiichi Miyazawa expressed "deep remorse" at a Tokyo news conference December 6 for the attack. He went on to say that Japan owed its economic success "to the goodwill of the American people, to whom we are deeply grateful."

Following are excerpts from remarks by President George Bush in Hawaii, December 7, 1991, commemorating the fiftieth anniversary of the Japanese attack on Pearl Harbor, delivered to members of the Pearl Harbor Survivors Association at the National Cemetery of the Pacific on Oahu Island, at the USS Arizona Memorial in Pearl Harbor, and to World War II veterans and their families at Kilo Pier 8 in Honolulu:

REMARKS AT CEMETERY

... Americans did not wage war against nations or races. We fought for freedom and human dignity against the nightmare of totalitarianism. The world must never forget that the dictatorships we fought, the Hitler and Tojo regimes, committed war crimes and atrocities. Our servicemen struggled and sacrificed not only in defense of our free way of life, but also in the hope that the blessings of liberty some day might extend to all peoples.

Our cause was just and honorable, but not every American action was fully fair. This ground embraces many American veterans whose love of country was put to the test unfairly by our own authorities. These and other natural-born American citizens faced wartime internment, and they committed no crime. They were sent to internment camps simply because their ancestors were Japanese. Other Asian-Americans suffered discrimination, and even violence, because they were mistaken for Japanese. And they, too, were innocent victims, who committed no offense.

Here lie valiant servicemen of the 442d Regimental Combat Team and of the Military Intelligence Service, Americans of Japanese ancestry who fought to defeat the Axis in Europe and in the Pacific. Among these, the late Senator Spark Matsunaga, a combat hero and survivor who went on to help lead postwar Hawaii to American statehood.

I remember sharing danger and friendship in these skies and on this ocean. Some of my closest friends, like many people here, your closest friends, never came home. Perhaps because of this experience, I can better understand what you survivors of Pearl Harbor are sensing and feeling here today. As all the veterans here know, when a friend or comrade in arms falls in battle, war grabs a part of your soul.

My roommate aboard the carrier *San Jacinto*, CVL-30, was a guy named Jim Wykes. And as we were about to go into combat for the first time, a strike over Wake Island, Jim Wykes and his crew were sent out on a search mission from which they never returned.

Many more from our little torpedo squadron were to give their lives. And the names of many of these, and more than 18,000 other World War II servicemen lost in action in the Pacific, are engraved in the walls of this magnificent memorial.

During every passage of my life, I've often thought of those who never returned. Some left children behind, and today those children, like my own kids, are raising children of their own. And thank God, each surviving generation has honored the memory of our heroes of the Second World War. Each new generation has risen to meet the challenge of winning the peace.

After vanquishing the dictators of Japan and Germany and Italy, America's war generation helped those countries rebuild and grow strong in the exercise of democracy and free enterprise. They affirmed again that our quarrel had not been with races or nations.

The American victors welcomed the new leaders of Japan and Germany and Italy into alliances that won the cold war and helped prevent the third world war. America and our wartime allies joined hands with the liberated peoples of our former foes to create and nurture international organizations aimed at protecting human rights, collective security, and economic growth.

Winning the peace, then as now, demands preparedness. The cause of harmony among nations is not a call for pacifism. We avoided a third world war because we were prepared to defend the free world against aggressors. The Pearl Harbor generation saw its younger brothers go to Korea, its sons to Vietnam to resist communism. Pearl Harbor's grandchildren answered the call to the Persian Gulf to reverse Saddam's aggression against Kuwait.

How fitting it is that this great cemetery holds so many who died for the cause of Korean and Vietnamese freedom. How honored we are to stand on this ground, consecrated with the remains of Marine Lance Corporal Frank Allen of Hawaii, who gave his life just 10 months ago in the battle to free Kuwait.

Every soldier and sailor and airman buried here offered his life so that others might be free. Not one of them died in vain. Our men and women who served in Korea and Vietnam, whose sacrifices too often have been forgotten or even reviled, are nearing their day of greatest vindication. For I have confidence that the tragedy of totalitarianism has entered its final scene everywhere on this Earth.

This morning's sun will course the Pacific skies and illuminate the lands of Asia. And just as certainly, the movement of human freedom will supplant dictatorships that now hold sway in Pyongyang and Rangoon and Hanoi, and yes, in China, too. For a billion yearning men and women, the future means freedom and democracy.

This fair December dawn breaks on a world ready for renewal. A high tide of hope swells for those that are committed to peace and freedom. The nations pushed by tyrants into war against us half a century ago join us today as free and constructive partners in the effort for peace. The Soviet Communists' designs for world domination have collapsed before the free world's resolve.

We've reached this morning because generation after generation of Americans kept faith with our founders and our heroes. From the snows of Valley Forge, to the fiery seas of Midway and Pearl Harbor, to the sands of Iraq and Kuwait, Americans lived and died true to their ideals. They have prepared the way for a world of unprecedented freedom and cooperation. And thank God you Pearl Harbor survivors are here today to see this come to pass.

Today, as we remember the sacrifices of our countrymen, I salute all of you, the survivors of Pearl Harbor. And I ask all Americans to join me in a prayer: Lord, give our rising generations the wisdom to cherish their freedom and security as hard-won treasures. Lord, give them the same courage that pulsed in the blood of their fathers.

May God bless you all, and may God bless the United States of America. Thank you very much.

REMARKS AT USS *ARIZONA* MEMORIAL

... Today we honor those who gave their lives at this place, half a century ago. Their names were Bertie and Gomez and Dougherty and Granger. And they came from Idaho and Mississippi, the sweeping farmland of Ohio. And they were of all races and colors, native-born and foreign-born. And most of all, of course, they were Americans.

Think of how it was for these heroes of the Harbor, men who were also husbands, fathers, brothers, sons. Imagine the chaos of guns and smoke, flaming water, and ghastly carnage. Two thousand, four hundred and three Americans gave their lives. But in this haunting place, they live forever in our memory, reminding us gently, selflessly, like chimes in the distant night.

Every 15 seconds a drop of oil still rises from the *Arizona* and drifts to the surface. As it spreads across the water, we recall the ancient poet: "In our sleep, pain that cannot forget falls drop by drop upon the heart, and in our own despair against our will comes wisdom through the awful grace of God." With each drop, it is as though God Himself were crying. He cries, as we do, for the living and the dead: men like Commander Duncan Curry, firing a .45 at an attacking plane as tears streamed down his face.

We remember machinist's mate Robert Scott, who ran the air compressors powering the guns aboard *California*. And when the compartment flooded, the crew evacuated; Scott refused. "This is my station," he said. "I'm going to stay as long as the guns are going." And nearby, aboard *New Orleans*, the cruiser, Chaplain Forgy assured his troops it was all right to miss church that day. His words became legend: "You can praise the Lord and pass the ammunition."

Captain Ross, right here, then a warrant officer or was it a chief, was awarded the Congressional Medal of Honor for his heroism aboard *Nevada* that day. I salute him, the other Congressional Medal winners with us today, wherever they may be also.

For the defenders of Pearl, heroism came as naturally as breath. They reacted instinctively by rushing to their posts. They knew as well that our Nation would be sustained by the nobility of its cause.

So did Americans of Japanese ancestry who came by the hundreds to give wounded Americans blood, and the thousands of their kinsmen all across America who took up arms for their country. Every American believed in the cause.

The men I speak of would be embarrassed to be called heroes. Instead, they would tell you, probably with defiance: "Foes can sink American ships, but not the American spirit. They may kill us, but never the ideals that made us proud to serve."

Talk to those who survived to fight another day. They would repeat the Navy hymn that Barbara and I sing every Sunday in the lovely little chapel up at Camp David: "Eternal Father, strong to save, Whose arm hath bound the restless wave . . . O hear us when we cry to Thee, For those in peril on the sea."

Back in 1942, June of '42, I remember how Henry Stimson, the Secretary of War, defined the American soldier, and how that soldier should be, and I quote: "Brave without being brutal, self-confident without boasting, being part of an irresistible might without losing faith in individual liberty."

The heroes of the Harbor engraved that passage on every heart and soul. They fought for a world of peace, not war, where children's dreams speak more loudly than the brashest tyrant's guns. Because of them, this memorial lives to pass its lessons from one generation to the next, lessons as clear as this Pacific sky.

One of Pearl Harbor's lessons is that together we could "summon lightness against the dark"; that was Dwight Eisenhower. Another, that when it comes to national defense, finishing second means finishing last.

World War II also taught us that isolationism is a bankrupt notion. The world does not stop at our water's edge. And perhaps above all, that real peace, real peace, the peace that lasts, means the triumph of freedom, not merely the absence of war.

And as we look down at—Barbara and I just did—at *Arizona's* sunken hull, tomb to more than 1,000 Americans, the beguiling calm comforts us, reminds us of the might of ideals that inspire boys to die as men. Everyone who aches at their sacrifice knows America must be forever vigilant. And Americans must always remember the brave and the innocent who gave their lives to keep us free.

Each Memorial Day, not far from this spot, the heroes of Pearl Harbor are honored. Two leis are placed upon each grave by Hawaiian Boy Scouts and Girl Scouts. We must never forget that it is for them, the future, that we must apply the lessons of the past.

In Pearl Harbor's wake, we won the war and, thus, the peace. In the cold war that followed, Americans also shed their blood, but we used other means as well. For nearly half a century, patience, foresight, personal diplomacy helped America stand fast and firm for democracy.

But we've never stood alone. Beside us stood nations committed to democracy and free markets and free expression and freedom of worship, nations that include our former enemies, Germany, Italy, and Japan. This year these same nations stood with us against aggression in the Persian Gulf.

You know, the war in the Gulf was so different: different enemy, different circumstances, the outcome never in doubt. It was short; thank God our casualties mercifully few. But I ask you veterans of Pearl Harbor and all Americans who remember the unity of purpose that followed that momentous December day 50 years ago: Didn't we see that same strength of national spirit when we launched Desert Storm?

The answer is a resounding "yes." Once the war for Kuwait began, we pulled together. We were united, determined, and we were confident. And when it was over, we rejoiced in exactly the same way that we did in 1945— heads high, proud, and grateful. And what a feeling. Fifty years had passed, but, let me tell you, the American spirit is as young and fresh as ever. . . .

REMARKS TO VETERANS AT PIERSIDE

. . . I expect if we went around the room, all of us would remember. I remember exactly when I first heard the news about Pearl Harbor. I was 17 years old, walking across the green at school. And my thoughts in those days didn't turn to world events, but mainly to simpler things, more mundane things, like making the basketball team or entering college. And that walk across the campus marked an end of innocence for me.

When Americans heard the news, they froze in shock. But just as quickly we came together. Like all American kids back then, I was swept up in it. I decided that very day to go into the Navy to become a Navy pilot. And so on my 18th birthday, June 12th, 1942, I was sworn into the Navy as a seaman second class.

And I was shocked, I was shocked at my first sight of Pearl Harbor several months later, April of '44. We came into port on the CVL-30, on the carrier *San Jacinto*. Nearby, the *Utah* was still on her side; parts of the *Arizona* still stood silent in the water. Everywhere the skeletons of ships reached out as if to demand remembrance and warn us of our own mortality.

Over 2,000 men died in a matter of minutes on this site, a half a century ago. Many more died that same day as Japanese forces assaulted the Philippines and Guam and Wake Island, Midway, Malaya, Thailand, Singapore, Hong Kong. On that day of infamy, Pearl Harbor propelled each of us into a titanic contest for mankind's future. It galvanized the American spirit as never, ever before into a single-minded resolve that could produce only one thing: victory.

Churchill knew it as soon as he heard the news. He'd faced the Nazi conquest of Europe, the blitz of London, the terror of the U-boats. But when America was attacked, he declared there was "no more doubt about the end." He knew then that the American spirit would not fail the cause of freedom. The enemy mistook our diversity, our National diversity, for weakness. But Pearl Harbor became a rallying cry for men and women from all walks of life, all colors and creeds. And in the end, this unity of purpose made us invincible in war and now makes us secure in peace.

The next day, President Roosevelt proclaimed the singular American objective: "With confidence in our Armed Forces, with the unbounding determination of our people, we will gain the inevitable triumph, so help us, God." It was the steadfastness of the American people that would "win the war" and "win the peace that follows."

We triumphed in both, despite the fact that the American people did not want to be drawn into the conflict; "the unsought war," it's been called. Ironically, isolationists gathered together at what was known in those days as an "American First" rally in Pittsburgh at precisely the moment the first Americans met early, violent deaths right here at Pearl Harbor. The isolationists failed to see that the seeds of Pearl Harbor were sown back in 1919, when a victorious America decided that in the absence of a threatening enemy abroad, we should turn all of our energies inward. That notion of isolationism flew escort for the very bombers that attacked our men 50 years ago.

Again, in 1945, some called for America's return to isolationism, as if abandoning world leadership was the prerequisite dealing with pressing matters back home. And they were rudely awakened by the brutal reality of the Iron Curtain, the Soviet blockade of Berlin, and the Communist invasion of South Korea.

And now we stand triumphant, for the third time this century, this time in the wake of the cold war. As in 1919 and 1945, we face no enemy menacing our security. And yet we stand here today on the site of a tragedy spawned by isolationism. And we must learn, and this time avoid, the dangers of today's isolationism and its economic accomplice, protectionism. To do otherwise, to believe that turning our backs on the world would improve our lot here at home, is to ignore the tragic lessons of the 20th century.

The fact is, this country has enjoyed its most lasting growth and security when we rejected isolationism, both political and economic, in favor of engagement and leadership. We're a Pacific nation. And next month in Asia, I'll discuss with our Pacific friends and allies their responsibility to share with us the challenges and burdens of leadership in the post-cold war world.

The time has come for America's trading partners, in Europe, Asia, and around the world, to resolve that economic isolationism is wrong. To the leaders of Japan in particular, I say: This solemn occasion should reinforce our determination to join together in a future energized by free markets and free people. And so I'll continue to speak out against the voices of isolationism and protectionism, both at home and abroad.

Fifty years ago, we paid a heavy price for complacency and overconfidence. That too is a lesson we shall never forget. To those who have defended our country, from the shores of Guadalcanal to the hills of Korea, from the jungles of Vietnam to the sands of Kuwait, I say this: We will always remember; we will always be prepared, prepared to take on aggression, prepared to step forward in reconciliation, and prepared to secure the peace.

In remembering, it is important to come to grips with the past. No nation can fully understand itself or find its place in the world if it does not look with clear eyes at all the glories and disgraces, too, of the past. We in the United States acknowledge such an injustice in our own history: The internment of Americans of Japanese ancestry was a great injustice, and it will never be repeated.

Today, all Americans should acknowledge Japan's Prime Minister [Kiichi] Miyazawa's national statement of deep remorse concerning the attack on Pearl Harbor. It was a thoughtful, it was a difficult expression much appreciated by the people of the United States of America.

The values we hold dear as a Nation—equality of opportunity, freedom of religion and speech and assembly, free and vigorous elections—are not revered by many nations. Our greatest victory in World War II took place not on the field of battle, but in nations we once counted as foes. The ideals of democracy and liberty have triumphed in a world once threatened with conquest by tyranny and despotism.

Today as we celebrate the world's evolution toward freedom, we commemorate democracy's fallen heroes, the defenders of freedom as well as the victims of dictatorship who never saw the light of liberty. Earlier this year, when former adversaries joined us in the stand against aggression in the Persian Gulf, we affirmed the values cherished by the heroes of the Harbor.

The friends I lost, that all of us lost, upheld a great and noble cause. Because of their sacrifice, the world now lives in greater freedom and peace than ever before. It is right that all of us are here today. And it is right that we go on from here.

As you know, I just paid my respects to the *Arizona*, where it all began. And behind us stands the *Missouri*, where it came to an end. But the *Missouri* was also a beginning. Soon after that, Emperor Hirohito went to call on General MacArthur, who later noted that the Emperor "played a major role in the spiritual regeneration of Japan." Their meeting made history, and a hopeful future for a democratic Japan began to take shape.

I thought of that meeting with MacArthur when I attended the Emperor's funeral in 1989. I thought of it this morning, too, at the National Cemetery of the Pacific and then at the *Arizona* Memorial.

As you look back on life and retrace the steps that made you the person you are, you pick out the turning points, the defining moments. Over the years, Pearl Harbor still defines a part of who I am. To every veteran here, and indeed to all Americans, Pearl Harbor defines a part of who you are.

Recently a letter arrived from the son of a Pearl Harbor survivor, a Navy man named Bill Leu, who is with us here today. His son writes from his home, now in Tokyo, saying: "A half century ago, my father's thoughts were on surviving the attack and winning the war. He could not have envisioned a future where his son would study and work in Japan. But he recognizes that the world has changed, that America's challenges are different. My father's attitude represents that of the United States: Do your duty, and raise the next generation to do its."

I can understand Bill's feelings. I wondered how I'd feel being with you, the veterans of Pearl Harbor, the survivors, on this very special day. And I wondered if I would feel that intense hatred that all of us felt for the enemy 50 years ago. As I thought back to that day of infamy and the loss of friends, I wondered: What will my reaction be when I go back to Pearl Harbor? What will their reaction be, the other old veterans, especially those who survived that terrible day right here?

Well, let me tell you how I feel. I have no rancor in my heart towards Germany or Japan, none at all. And I hope, in spite of the loss, that you have none in yours. This is no time for recrimination.

World War II is over. It is history. We won. We crushed totalitarianism. And when that was done, we helped our enemies give birth to democracies. We reached out, both in Europe and in Asia. We made our enemies our friends, and we healed their wounds. And in the process, we lifted ourselves up.

The lessons of the war itself will live on, and well they should: Preparedness; strength; decency and honor; courage; sacrifice; the willingness to fight, even die, for one's country—America, the land of the free and the brave.

No, just speaking for one guy, I have no rancor in my heart. I can still see the faces of the fallen comrades, and I'll bet you can see the faces of your fallen comrades too, or family members. But don't you think they're saying, "Fifty years have passed; our country is the undisputed leader of the free world, and we are at peace."? Don't you think each one is saying, "I did not die in vain."?

May God bless each of you who sacrificed and served. And may God grant His loving protection to this, the greatest country on the face of the Earth, the United States of America.

Thank you all, and God bless you. Thank you very much.

END OF THE SOVIET UNION
AND GORBACHEV'S RULE
December 8, 12, 21, and 25, 1991

After months of crisis, the Soviet Union came to an end during the final weeks of 1991. The collapse became inevitable after Ukrainians voted for independence December 1; it might have come earlier except for the frantic efforts of Soviet president Mikhail S. Gorbachev to patch up the old system. (Plans for Restructuring the Soviet Union, p. 531) *Ultimately, he was powerless to prevent the Soviet republics from asserting self-rule and rearranging themselves into a loosely connected Commonwealth of Independent States under the guiding hand of Russia's president and Gorbachev's political nemesis, Boris N. Yeltsin.*

Bowing to reality, Gorbachev resigned December 25 as the leader of a country that had ceased to exist. In its dying, the Soviet Union continued to hold the world's attention as it had for nearly three-quarters of a century. The unfolding events created "one of the greatest dramas of the 20th century," President George Bush remarked shortly after Gorbachev resigned.

The Soviet Union's founding in 1922 originated in the 1917 Bolshevik Revolution overthrowing czarist Russia. The world's first Communist state was viewed from abroad with either fear or awe. Some saw a Red menace and others a developing utopia—at least until the onset of wholesale terrorism under Stalin. In World War II, Moscow and Washington were allied in the defeat of Nazi Germany, but cooperation soon turned to Cold War antagonism. The Soviet Union would be remembered by most Americans as the other nuclear-armed superpower whose containment became their obsession.

That tense rivalry evaporated only after Gorbachev became the Soviet leader in March 1985 and redirected the Kremlin's foreign policy toward peaceful cooperation with the United States. Washington's caution gradually turned to full acceptance of the proffered olive branch. Bush observed Gorbachev's departure by expressing gratitude on behalf of the American people for his "years of commitment to world peace" and "my personal respect for his intellect, vision, and courage."

Yeltsin's Post-Coup Dominance

At home Gorbachev's early popularity did not endure. By introducing half-measures of economic and democratic reforms, he set in motion a chain of events that swept him from office. The reforms were too much for the Communist old guard to swallow but did not go far enough to satisfy large numbers of reformers. The economy worsened and Yeltsin's populist challenge to the Kremlin grew stronger.

Yeltsin's dissent led to his expulsion from Gorbachev's inner circle in 1987 but laid the foundation for an astonishing comeback. In May 1990 Yeltsin won the first free election ever held for president of the Russian republic, a land of 147 million people stretching from eastern Europe to the Pacific. As leader of the dominant republic, he created a power base rivaling Gorbachev's. In July 1990 he left the Communist party and formed his own.

In August 1991 Yeltsin became a national hero with feats of personal courage—he rallied public opposition to a Kremlin coup and forced its hardline Communist instigators to give up and free Gorbachev, their hostage. (Failure of Soviet Coup Attempt, p. 515) Gorbachev was physically unharmed but politically weakened as a result of the coup attempt. Some of the coup makers were men he had appointed to high positions in a futile attempt to mollify the old guard. He could turn to neither the right nor the left for support. With the central government facing bankruptcy, Yeltsin placed many of its former functions under control of the Russian republic.

Ukraine's Vote Dooms USSR

When Ukrainians voted overwhelmingly December 1 to secede, the Soviet Union's days were numbered. Their republic, with more than 50 million people and larger than most European countries, was the industrial and agricultural heartland of the Soviet nation. The history of Ukrainians had been intertwined for more than a thousand years with the Russians, who also were predominantly Slavic. After the Ukraine referendum, Yeltsin promptly met with presidents Leonid M. Kravchuk of Ukraine and Stanislav Shushkevich of Byelorussia to devise an alliance supplanting the Soviet Union.

The three leaders met again December 8, this time in Moscow, and proclaimed a new Commonwealth of Independent States, a political structure for cooperation and some power sharing among the member republics—which otherwise asserted full sovereignty. "The USSR, as a subject of international law and geographic reality, is ceasing its existence," the three leaders declared.

In Washington, Secretary of State James A. Baker III approvingly agreed, saying: "The Soviet Union as we've known it no longer exists." Yeltsin telephoned Bush, but not Gorbachev, with the news of the commonwealth's founding. Bush praised Yeltsin's work. Gorbachev broke an initial vow of silence to complain bitterly that the republics could not properly secede "without the participation of all sovereign states and the will of their peoples." He had been left out of the negotiations and the Moscow ceremony.

Washington was concerned about who would gain control of the Soviet armed forces, especially the nuclear arsenal. The day after Ukraine's vote, Bush directed Baker to go to Kiev and discuss with the Ukranian leaders how they would handle the nuclear weapons on their soil. In a lengthy speech at Princeton University December 12, Baker outlined the steps Washington would take to help dismantle Soviet nuclear weapons, stabilize the economy, establish democratic institutions, and overcome shortages in food and medical supplies, but without significant increases in U.S. spending. The four republics with long-range missiles—Russia, Ukraine, Byelorussia (now called Belarus), and Kazakhstan—later agreed on joint weapons safeguards.

Kazakhstan was among eight republics that joined the commonwealth on December 21 at a ceremonial signing of documents in Alma-Ata, the Kazakh capital. All eleven republics were granted equal status, and each recognized the independence and borders of the others. The membership of Kazakhstan and central Asian neighbors Kyrgyzstan, Tajikistan, Turkmenistan, and Uzbekistan added a mostly Moslem population of about 50 million to the commonwealth, accounting for most of its non-Slavic people. The other new members were Moldova in eastern Europe and in Azerbaijan and Armenia in the extreme southeast along the Turkish and Iranian borders.

After Moscow recognized the independence of the Baltic states of Estonia, Latvia, and Lithuania in September, twelve Soviet republics remained. Of those twelve, only Georgia did not join the commonwealth. But like the others, Georgia declared its independence.

Following are an agreement signed by Russia, Ukraine, and Belarus in Moscow, December 8, 1991, to form a Commonwealth of Independent States; Secretary of State James A. Baker's speech at Princeton University on December 12, on U.S. aims with regard to the Soviet Union's collapse; a protocol to the commonwealth agreement recognizing eight new members, a separate declaration of common aims, and an agreement among four republics, all signed in Alma-Alta, December 21; Soviet president Mikhail S. Gorbachev's resignation speech December 25; and President George Bush's televised remarks on Gorbachev's resignation, and excerpts from Bush's address to the nation on the commonwealth, also December 25:

COMMONWEALTH PACT

We, the Republic of Byelorussia, the Russian Federation and Ukraine, as founding members of the Union of Soviet Socialist Republics, having signed the Union Treaty of 1922 and hereafter referred to as the agreeing parties, state that the Union of Soviet Socialist Republics, as a subject of international law and geopolitical reality, is ceasing its existence.

Based on historical commonalities of our peoples and on ties that were set up between them, considering bi-lateral agreements signed between the agreeing parties,

Striving to found democratic legal states and intending to develop our relations on the basis of mutual recognition and the respect of state sovereignty, the integral right to self-determination, the principles of equality and non-interference in internal affairs, the refusal to use force or pressure by economic or other means, the settlement of controversial problems through agreement, other common principles and norms of international law,

Taking into account that the further development and strengthening of relations of friendship, good-neighborliness and mutually beneficial co-operation between our states is consistent with the basic national interests of their people and serves in the interests of peace and security,

Confirming our commitment to the goals and principles of the United Nations Charter, the Helsinki Final Act and other documents from the Conference on Security and Cooperation in Europe,

Obliging to observe common international norms on human and national rights,

We agree on the following:

Article 1

The agreeing parties are founding a Commonwealth of Independent States.

Article 2

The agreeing parties guarantee their citizens, regardless of nationality or other differences, equal rights and freedoms. Each of the agreeing parties guarantees citizens of other parties and also people without citizenship who reside on its territory, regardless of nationality or other differences, civil, political, social, economic and cultural rights and freedoms in accordance with common international norms on human rights.

Article 3

The agreeing parties that wish to found unique ethno-cultural regions to contribute to the manifestation, preservation and development of ethnic, cultural, linguistic and religious distinctions of national minorities residing on their territories, will take them under their own protection.

Article 4

The agreeing parties will develop equal and mutually beneficial cooperation of their peoples and states in the spheres of politics, economics, culture, education, health care, environmental protection, science, trade, and humanitarian and other spheres, and will contribute to the wide exchange of information and will fully and strictly observe mutual obligations.

The parties consider it necessary to conclude agreements on cooperation in the above-mentioned spheres.

Article 5

The agreeing parties recognize and respect each other's territorial integrity, and the integrity of each other's borders in the framework of the commonwealth. They guarantee openness of borders, and the freedom for citizens to travel and exchange information within the framework of the commonwealth.

Article 6

Members of the commonwealth will cooperate to insure international peace and security and to carry out effective measures on limiting weapons and military expenditures. They are striving to liquidate all nuclear armaments, to have total and complete disarmament under strict international control.

The parties will respect each other's striving to achieve the status of a nuclear-free zone and neutral state.

Members of the commonwealth will preserve and support common military and strategic space under a common command, including common control over nuclear armaments, which will be regulated by special agreement.

They also mutually guarantee necessary conditions for the deployment, functioning, material and social maintenance of strategic armed forces. The parties are obliged to pursue consensual policy on questions of social protection and pensions for military personnel and their families.

Article 7

The parties recognize that the spheres of their mutual activities conducted on a mutual basis through common coordinating institutions of the commonwealth embrace:

- Coordination of foreign policy.
- Cooperation in forming and developing a common economic space, common European and Eurasian markets, in the sphere of customs policy.
- Cooperation to develop transport and communications systems.
- Cooperation on the sphere of environmental protection, participation in creating of the all-encompassing international system of ecological security.

- Questions of migration policy.
- The fight against organized crime.

Article 8

The parties are aware of the universal character of the Chernobyl disaster and are obliged to unite and coordinate their efforts to minimize and overcome its consequences.

They agreed to sign a special agreement on this matter, taking the consequences of the catastrophe into consideration.

Article 9

Disputes relating to the interpretation and usage of the norms of the current agreement are subject to be solved through negotiations between corresponding organs, and at the state and government level if necessary.

Article 10

Each party reserves the right to suspend the current agreement or its individual articles by notifying the agreement's participants a year in advance.

The current agreement can be supplemented or changed according to mutual consent of the agreeing parties.

Article 11

From the moment the current agreement is signed, the laws of third states, including the Union of Soviet Socialist Republics, are not valid on the territories of states which signed the current agreement.

Article 12

The parties guarantee the fulfillment of international obligations, treaties and agreements of the former Union of Soviet Socialist Republics, coming from these obligations.

Article 13

The current agreement does not concern obligations of the agreeing parties in relation to third states.

The current agreement is open to all state members of the former Union of Soviet Socialist Republics, and also to other states that share the goals and principles of the current agreement.

Article 14

The official location to station the coordinating organs of the Commonwealth is the city of Minsk.

The activities of the organs of the former Union of Soviet Socialist Republics on the territories of state members of the Commonwealth are stopped.

Finalized in three copies in the Byelorussian, Russian and Ukrainian languages in the city of Minsk, Dec. 8, 1991. All three copies bear equal weight.

BAKER'S PRINCETON SPEECH

Forty-one years ago this week, while I was in my junior year here at Princeton and reading the great authors, William Faulkner was already accepting the Nobel Prize for Literature. In his acceptance speech, he said the tragedy of the day—indeed, one might say the challenge of the generation—was "a general and universal physical fear" and that this fear was so great as to extinguish problems of the spirit. As he put it, "There is only one question: When will I be blown up?"

For my generation, Faulkner surely posed the right question. After 1945, one strategic, political, and moral imperative dominated American policy: to prevent war with the Soviet Union while upholding Western values and interests.

"Better Dead than Red," the saying went. But, in fact, there was no choice at all. While nuclear war would have destroyed us physically, Stalinism would have destroyed us spiritually. Everything else, unfortunately, had to be secondary.

To cope with this imperative, George Kennan—an illustrious son of this university who is with us today—articulated the logic and concept of containment. Soviet power, to Kennan, was a "fluid stream," one which moved unwaveringly toward the goal of filling "every nook and cranny available to it in the basin of world power."

Inherently antagonistic to what the West stood for, Stalinism had to be stopped. And the way to do this was through "patient but firm and vigilant containment." Containment and a cold war, rather than rollback and a hot war, might work, argued Kennan, because the Soviet system was profoundly at variance with human nature and, therefore, in the long-run illegitimate. The aim—or more realistically, the hope—was that containment would turn Soviet power on itself and hasten its decay. Eventually, the Stalinist threat would collapse of its own inner contradictions.

Four decades later, the simple fact of the matter is that containment worked. The state that Lenin founded and Stalin built held within itself the seeds of its demise. And when pressure from the outside was maintained—and its windows to the West were created—the Soviet state broke up from the inside out.

History has now answered Faulkner's question: We will not be blown up in a war with the Soviet Union. But that is not the end of the story.

Our policy was never solely about preventing a hot war or defeating Stalinism in the Cold War. What every President and every Congress have sought is a different world, free from the shadows of war, of political tyranny, of economic distress. These were and are our ideals. And these ideals, seasoned by a healthy sense of realism, must continue to drive our policy toward the peoples who were our Cold War enemies but now seek our friendship and support.

As a consequence of the Soviet collapse, we live in a new world. We must take advantage of this New Russian Revolution, set in motion with the defeat of the August coup, to cultivate relationships—relationships that can benefit not only America but the entire world. For unlike the Bolshevik Revolution, this revolution of 1991 contains the seeds of a brighter future, an enduring peace. It may even contain the potential for a flowering of democracy in places so long inhospitable to it.

No one, not even those making this revolution, can know the final outcome or *common entities* to be defined by these momentous events. These are being defined by the participants even as I speak. They, not we or any other outsider, will determine the outcome.

I am very conscious of the fact that events are moving quickly, altering history's course minute-by-minute. This is, after all, a revolution we are talking about. By its very nature, it will move into unforeseen territory. Undoubtedly, questions and problems will arise that no one can foresee today.

So, what I present to you today is not a fixed blueprint. Rather, it is the principles and approach which together define an agenda for action in a revolutionary, unpredictable situation—a situation in which the West can play an important supporting role.

We are not the leaders of this revolution, but neither are we mere bystanders. We are models for its leaders; we are partners in its progress; and we can be beneficiaries of its success for decades to come. Yet, the time for action is short.

Much as we will benefit if this revolution succeeds, we will pay if it fails—just as we paid with the collapse of the promising democratic revolution in Petrograd in February 1917. The pace of change is unrelenting; the transformation, radical. History is giving no one a breathing space.

So, today, I would like to tell you what's at stake—for my generation and for future generations—in the collapse of the Soviet empire. And then, I would like to suggest to you what needs to be done:

- What needs to be done so that the weapons of the Cold War do not become instruments of unintended and incalculable violence;
- What needs to be done to cultivate democratic values and tolerance in a region that is undergoing its own enlightenment; and
- What needs to be done to promote an economy where individual initiative creates its own reward and hope for a better future across the former Soviet Union.

Where We Have Been and Where We Are

Almost 3 years ago, President Bush foresaw the new opportunities in U.S.-Soviet relations when he said it was time to move beyond containment. His charge to me was clear: Engage with the Soviets and explore whether the promise of *perestroika* and new thinking could create a new reality for sustained U.S.-Soviet cooperation and the basis for a new era internationally. In the fall of 1989, I called this process the search for points of mutual advantage.

Looking back, I think it's fair to say that this search proved successful beyond anyone's expectations. Indeed, so successful that just a year later, in October 1990, I was able to say that the points of mutual advantage had become pathways of cooperation. In a very real sense, we and the Soviets had become partners, no longer competitors across the globe:

- Partners in facilitating the unification of Germany in peace and freedom;
- Partners in seeing Central and Eastern Europe peacefully liberated from communism's stranglehold;
- Partners in negotiating radical reductions in conventional and nuclear weapons;
- Partners in ending regional conflicts from Central America to Southern Africa to Cambodia;
- Partners in reversing Iraqi aggression and, subsequently, in promoting Arab-Israeli peace;
- Partners, in short, in ending the Cold War—the dangerous, but ultimately necessary, confrontation that defined and so badly distorted international life for my generation.

These achievements were possible primarily because of one man: Mikhail Gorbachev. The transformations we are dealing with now would not have begun were it not for him. His place in history is secure, for he helped end the Cold War peacefully. And, for that, the world is grateful and respectful. The same is true of his partner, Eduard Shevardnadze. Together new realities have been created by the new thinking in Soviet foreign and defense policy. But these polices were, themselves, the product of a parallel, but potentially far more important, change—the reforms they and other reformers began that transformed the Soviet Union itself.

Whatever the original intentions of *perestroika* and *glasnost*, by early August of this year, the all-powerful Stalinist state was well on its way to dissolution. A new civil society was breaking out across the Soviet Union. Democracy was replacing communism; power was moving from the center to the republics; and the old centrally planned economy was in the throes of collapse.

Then a small group of willful men—the embodiment of the Stalinist past and its institutions—sought to reverse this revolution by arresting President Gorbachev and summoning the tanks. But the Russian people and their courageous leader, Boris Yeltsin, surmounted those tanks with the will of the people.

By their heroic triumph, the Soviet internal revolution, in the space of 3 days, telescoped history years forward. As Alexander Yakovlev said to me on the day the coup failed, the coup plotters sought to kill the revolution, but they succeeded only in accelerating it. *Perestroika*, originally initiated for the purpose of humanizing and revitalizing Marxism-Leninism, ironically ended up producing its resounding defeat instead.

For the failed coup not only sounded the death knell of the Communist Party; those 3 days shook the Soviet world to its foundations. And in the 3 months that followed, the foundation itself has been uprooted. In its wake, the map and politics of Eurasia are being changed beyond recognition, and with them the assumptions that have guided American policy since World War II.

What's at Stake

The dramatic collapse of communism in Moscow and the unraveling of the centralized Soviet state confront the West with great opportunities as well as ominous dangers. Popularly elected leaders now run large and strategically important republics, including Russia, Ukraine, and Kazakhstan. They look to America and the West for guidance and help in launching genuine, far-reaching political and economic reform. If they can succeed, the centuries-old menace posed to the West, first by czarist autocracy and then by Soviet totalitarianism, will have been permanently altered.

The opportunities are historic.

- We have the chance to anchor Russia, Ukraine, and other republics firmly in the Euro-Atlantic community and democratic commonwealth of nations.
- We have the chance to bring democracy to lands that have little knowledge of it, an achievement that can transcend centuries of history.
- We have the chance to help harness the rich human and material resources of those vast lands to the cause of freedom instead of totalitarianism, thereby immeasurably enhancing the security, prosperity, and freedom of America and the world.

Yet, the dangers are equal in scale to the opportunities.

Economically, the old Soviet system has collapsed, multiplying every day the threats these reformers face—from social dislocation to political fragmentation to ethnic violence. Reconstructing economies that have been devastated by central planning is even more difficult than reconstructing from the devastation of war.

Politically, the dangers of protracted anarchy and chaos are obvious. Great empires rarely go quietly into extinction. No one can dismiss the possibility that darker political forces lurk in the wings, representing the remnants of Stalinism or the birth of nationalist extremism or even fascism, ready to exploit the frustrations of a proud but exhausted people in their hour of despair.

Strategically, both of these alternatives—anarchy or reaction— could become threats to the West's vital interests when they shake a land that is still home to nearly 30,000 nuclear weapons and the most powerful arsenal of conventional weaponry ever amassed in Europe.

What Has To Be Done

Taken together, these dangers serve as a call to action for America and the West. This historic watershed—the collapse of communist power in Bolshevism's birthplace—marks the challenge history has dealt us: to see the end of the Soviet empire turned into a beginning for democracy and economic freedom in Russia and Ukraine, in Kasakhstan and Belarus, in Armenia, Kyrgyzstan, and elsewhere across the former Soviet empire.

Here is what the West must do.

- As we organized an alliance against Stalinism during the Cold War, today, America can mobilize a coalition in support of freedom.
- Together with our NATO allies, Japan, South Korea, the other OECD [Organization for Economic Cooperation and Development] states, our Gulf coalition partners, and international institutions, we must pursue a diplomacy of collective engagement.
- Together with the new democrats in the former USSR, we can help create pathways of hope so that the new Russian revolution can fulfill the promise of the next generation.
- We, alone, cannot determine whether these new democrats will succeed. Their success lies in their hands, in the hard choices they make.

But history will count *our* efforts a success if we help the democrats hold open opportunities to determine a better future. This should be a major goal of the West: to help create a climate in which progress is possible— indeed, to help promote a process where even limited successes build hope and the authority of democrats over time.

To multiply the value of our efforts, the international coalition must divide its labors. The wreckage of communism is too large for any one nation to go it alone or to try and do everything. Working in concert, we must make use of the comparative advantages each of us holds.

For example, the United States could put to work the scientists at Los Alamos and Livermore who designed the weapons of the Cold War to help the Soviets destroy their weapons of mass destruction now. America— including state governments and private businesses in Alaska, Washington, Oregon and California—along with Japan and South Korea could help develop the resource-rich Soviet Far East. The Nordic countries could focus on the Baltics as well as St. Petersburg. And the IMF [International Monetary Fund] and World Bank could expand dramatically their engagement with reform-minded republics and any common entity to support comprehensive economic reform.

To crystallize this coalition, the President proposes that we begin by holding a *coordinating conference* to better divide our labor and responsibilities to help meet immediate and drastically increasing Soviet humanitarian needs. The United States will invite the advanced industrial democracies, the Central and East European states, the members of the Gulf war coalition, and the international financial institutions to join us in Washington in early January to discuss how best to meet ongoing humanitarian needs over the course of the next year.

This conference should work toward helping the Soviet peoples help themselves to get through the winter and to ensure that together we take the right steps this winter, spring, and summer to ensure a better situation *next* winter. Our work should focus on critical short—term needs: food, medicine, fuel, shelter. In the meantime, the United States will continue its ambitious food and medical assistance program that the President announced a year ago today.

But our collective engagement must extend beyond immediate humanitarian needs and should be organized around three tasks.

First and foremost, we must help the Soviets destroy and control the military remnants of the Cold War.

Second, we must help our former adversaries understand the ways of democracy to build political legitimacy out of the wreckage of totalitarianism.

Third, we must help free market forces stimulate economic stabilization and recovery in the lands of the former Soviet Union.

Obviously, one of the most vexing questions we face is: Who is the authority or authorities with whom we can deal? In a revolution where political authority has diffused and fractured, the possible interlocutors seem endless. In the face of such uncertainty, the West should stick to fundamentals and support those who put into practice our principles and values.

This means we will work with those republics and any common entity which commit to responsible security policies, democratic political practices, and free market economics. Fortunately, new leaders are emerging who are committed to these principles.

The three tasks I have outlined represent those areas where our principles matter most. They also represent the responsibilities members of the Euro-Atlantic community already have assumed. By accepting these responsibilities, new political entities in the former Soviet Union can join in the democratic commonwealth of nations, gain political acceptance, and justify our economic support.

Clearly, some—Russia, Ukraine, Kazakhstan, Armenia, and Kyrgyzstan—already are showing their intention to accept the responsibilities of the democratic community of nations. They understand that their success depends, above all, on their commitment to democracy and economic liberty.

Clearly, other governments—for example, Georgia—are showing already that communism can be replaced by governments that are authoritarian—and equally undeserving of our acceptance or support.

Let me turn now to discuss how these three tasks can serve as an agenda for action.

Responsible Security

The Cold War left tens of thousands of weapons littering the Soviet Union, and it created a massive military industrial complex. We must work with Russia, Ukraine, Kazakhstan, Belarus, the other republics, and any common entity to help them pursue responsible security policies. And that means first and foremost destroying and controlling the most dangerous vestiges of the Cold War: weapons of mass destruction.

One, we do not want to see new nuclear weapons states emerge as a result of the transformation of the Soviet Union. Of course, we want to see the START [Strategic Arms Reduction Treaty] Treaty ratified and implemented. But we also want to see Soviet nuclear weapons remain under safe, responsible, and reliable control with a single unified authority. The precise nature of that authority is for Russia, Ukraine, Kazakhstan, Belarus, and any common entity to determine. A single authority could, of course, be based on collective decision-making on the use of nuclear weapons. We are, however, opposed to the proliferation of any additional independent command authority or control over nuclear weapons.

For those republics who seek complete independence, we expect them to adhere to the Non-Proliferation Treaty as non-nuclear weapons states, to agree to full-scope IAEA [International Atomic Energy Agency] safeguards, and to implement effective export controls on nuclear materials and related technologies. As long as any such independent states retain nuclear weapons on their territory, those states should take part in unified command arrangements that exclude the possibility of independent control. In this connection, we strongly welcome Ukraine's determination to become nuclear-free by eliminating all nuclear weapons from its soil and its commitment, pending such elimination, to remain part of a single, unified command authority.

At the President's direction, we have begun exchanges between our experts on nuclear weapons safety, security, and dismantlement and their Soviet counterparts. This process has already begun, and we will accelerate it in the coming weeks. This is just one element of a larger effort to help enhance the safety and security of Soviet nuclear weapons and rapidly eliminate large numbers of them in a safe and environmentally sound manner.

I am pleased to announce that the Administration is prepared to draw upon the $400 million appropriated by Congress to assist in the destruction of Soviet weapons of mass destruction.

If during the Cold War, we spent trillions of dollars on missiles and bombers to *destroy* Soviet nuclear weapons in time of war, surely now we can spend just millions of dollars *to actually destroy and help control* those same nuclear weapons in time of peace. Nothing could be more in the national security interest of the United States.

That's neither charity nor aid; that's an investment in a secure future for every American. Surely, the American people will be willing to spend some of our defense budget at a cost of less than $2 per person in order to begin destroying nuclear weapons aimed at us.

Two, we want to see that proliferation of weapons of mass destruction and destabilizing conventional weaponry does not spread beyond the borders of the former USSR. While the nightmare of Orwell's *1984* is past, the terror of 1994 is that a Saddam Hussein or Muammar Qadhafi will use the black market to buy weapons from rogue military units or blueprints from unemployed engineers. We want to ensure that the creative talents of Soviet scientists and engineers are not diverted to dangerous military programs elsewhere in the world. And we expect republics and any common entity to establish strict export control policies and to put in place strict internal mechanisms capable of implementing those policies effectively.

The Administration will send a team of experts to brief republic leaders on what the international community expects in this area. We will work with the other members of the Nuclear Suppliers Group, the Australia Group, and the Missile Technology Control Regime to organize seminars and provide technical expertise to the republics and any common entity. We should promote programs in which Soviet scientists and engineers, possibly working with Western counterparts, can turn their talents to pressing global problems rather than the creation of new threats.

Three, "internal" arms races between former Soviet republics represent a potentially grave danger to European security. Already, we are seeing signs that some republican governments—notably Azerbaijan—are arming themselves for war against other republics. Those who pursue these misguided and anachronistic policies should know they will receive neither acceptance nor support from the West. In this regard, we are encouraged by efforts of Ukraine and Russia to establish a productive and non-threatening relationship.

We expect to see the CFE [Conventional Armed Forces in Europe] Treaty implemented by relevant authorities. And we will propose to broaden the CFE 1A negotiations so relevant republics will fall under its manpower provisions. Next week in Brussels, I will discuss with our NATO allies how we might reach out to those republics and any common entity which pursue responsible security policies, democratic political practices, and free market economics. By reaching out through NATO, we can reassure republics politically and dampen their desires to engage in destabilizing arms competitions with one another.

Four, we want to see the demilitarization of the Soviet economy and the transition to democratic civil-military relations, free markets, and a balance between social needs and reasonable and responsible security. Obviously, no one expects total disarmament, but the fact is that the Stalinist state *was* a military-industrial complex which robbed the people to benefit itself. That complex will continue to strangle democracy and any hope for economic recovery as long as it commands the bulk of Soviet resources.

Next Thursday, I will meet with NATO foreign ministers, and on the following day, together, we will meet with our eastern counterparts in the first North Atlantic Cooperation Council meeting. We have proposed that NATO create a defense conversion working group to facilitate the full range of political, economic, and social challenges associated with this undertaking. This will require that we draw upon all the resources at our disposal, including the participation of multilateral organizations.

Political Legitimacy

The most striking characteristic of the post-coup environment has been the dramatic shift of power from the center to the republics. This crisis of legitimacy of the Soviet empire has taken the form of an anti-communist revolution. But it is being driven by a parallel revolution of at least equal strength: an anti-imperialist revolution.

Together, the crisis of political legitimacy, the rebirth of nationalism, and economic collapse are driving Soviet dissolution. The result has been the severe undermining of central authority and the devolution of power to the republics, most of which have declared independence and created new authorities with new legitimacy. Now they must determine what that independence means in practice, for both their own peoples as well as for future inter-republic relations.

In the process, newly independent republics will find that they, too, cannot escape the problems of legitimacy and nationalism. We are reasonably hopeful that the republics will follow the democratic path and formulate a new legitimacy from the ground up. But while they may be better equipped to deal with these issues than a weakened center, the republics are clearly not immune to the forces of fragmentation. Even at the republic level, political authority divorced from the consent of the governed is being challenged. Likewise, ethnic minorities inside republics are demanding that their rights be accommodated.

Unless republic governments respond by complementing their independence with democracy and the equal treatment of persons belonging to minorities, they will soon find themselves suffering the very same cries of legitimacy, cohesion, and effectiveness that has caused the centrifugal devolution of power.

Without legitimacy, there will never be stability. Without stability, Western security will never be assured. As I noted when I laid out our five principles on September 4th, we will welcome into the community of democratic nations those new political entities who believe in democratic values and follow democratic practices; who safeguard human rights, including equal treatment of minorities; who respect borders and commit to changes only through peaceful and consensual means; and who will adhere to international obligations and to the norms and practices of the Helsinki Final Act and the Charter of Paris. But we will isolate those who cloak Stalinism or fascism in a facade of nationalist or liberal or democratic rhetoric.

Over a year ago, I called for a broad-based "democratic dialogue" with all levels of Soviet society. And, to that end, we have expanded our contacts and relations with republics and local authorities. Many of these new leaders want to follow us to build democracy and free markets. To help them, in addition, we propose:

- To discuss with our CSCE [Conference on Security and Cooperation in Europe] colleagues possible ways to integrate into CSCE those republics and any common entity which subscribe to and implement our five principles;

- To send our CSCE Ambassador to visit republics to discuss how CSCE norms can be put into practice; and
- To have USIA [U.S. Information Agency] expand its exchange programs to help states and localities in the United States promote expanded contacts. A large component of this might include a public policy training program for republic and local officials.

Economic Recovery

While we work with the Russians, Ukrainians, Kazakhs, and others to destroy weapons and cultivate democracy, the Russian winter—just as in 1812, 1917, and 1941—may again influence history's course. As the economy collapses with no bottom in sight, the onset of cold weather is exacerbating the situation and creating acute food, medicine, and energy shortages.

To meet these rapidly expanding needs, the United States has already this year shipped 18 million tons of food, the largest by far of any Western country. We've granted $4 billion in CCC [Commodity Credit Corporation] food and grain credits this year—$2.3 billion since the coup.

Through the President's Emergency Medical Initiative, we have shipped through Project Hope close to $20 million in medical supplies. We plan to double this amount over the next 18 months. These supplies—all donated by American firms and average citizens—have reached the Soviet peoples where they need them most: in the Urals and the Aral Sea region of Kazakhstan and Uzbekistan and the Chernobyl region of Ukraine; and in Armenia, Moscow, and soon Belarus. Over $8 million of these medical supplies have gone to the Baltic countries, and with their independence, the President has created a new and separate program for them.

To facilitate meeting humanitarian needs, we will deliver or expend the $165 million in Department of Agriculture grant funds to meet food shortages this winter, and we will draw upon the $100 million Congress has just authorized to transport humanitarian assistance.

We are also acting now to send food stocks left over from Desert Storm to regions in critical need—Armenia, the industrial cities of the Urals, Moscow, and St. Petersburg. The first shipments will be delivered by U.S. C-5 military aircraft to St. Petersburg and Moscow next week.

Beyond the humanitarian problems, we know that, at least over the near term, democracy and free markets are unlikely to succeed everywhere across the lands of the Soviet Union as we knew it. There are likely to be "islands" of democracy and free markets that have to stand as bulwarks against other "islands" of chaos or authoritarianism, even fascism. In this environment, the democrats in Russia, Ukraine, Kazakhstan, Armenia, and elsewhere must be able to offer pathways of hope to a better future.

We can help them define that path. For they will turn to us—America and Americans—as inspirations for the future, as sources of advice, and as partners in their work. And we can engage with our friends and allies by starting with human capital: people.

In this connection, the best way the West can help is to place Western experts on the ground and to bring Russians, Ukrainians, Kazakhs, and others here for training. The President has already approved an effort to put Americans on the ground to solve long-term food distribution problems; several U.S. firms have offered their executives and will cover their costs to assist this effort.

While much of this effort will have to be done through the private sector, assisted by organizations like the Citizens' Democracy Corps, the Administration is proposing several steps to augment our ongoing USIA efforts and expand the "human" factor.

- We will work with the Congress to support an expanded Peace Corps program in at least four republics. I would like to see at least 250 Peace Corps volunteers on the ground by next winter.
- We will expand Commerce's SABIT Business Training Program to accommodate 150 Soviet interns in the coming year.
- We will work with numerous voluntary organizations to look into ways they might expand their presence.

Clearly, the bulk of responsibility must lie with republic leaders who have already assumed primary control over economic policy and resources. They must make the hard choices necessary for economic recovery. And the choices they make must include free trade between republics. It would truly be a tragedy if Stalinist autarky that isolated the Soviet economy were replaced by republican autarky that will isolate and impoverish individual republics. Yet where comprehensive reforms are undertaken, we will work with other Western governments to form public-private partnerships that can help the democrats create opportunities for a better future.

For the Administration's part, we intend to be a catalyst for this partnership. We will work with the business community to help bring American business into Russia, Ukraine, Kazakhstan, Armenia, and other reforming republics. As part of this commitment, we plan to take the following immediate steps.

- As the President has announced, Deputy Secretary of State Lawrence Eagleburger will be the U.S. Government coordinator for our assistance efforts. With the President's full trust and authority, Deputy Secretary Eagleburger will be the champion of our assistance efforts.
- We intend to propose authorizing legislation to the Congress on its return to facilitate our efforts to provide assistance and technical cooperation. A major aim of this legislation will be to promote trade, business, and investment development by American companies in Russia, Ukraine, Kazakhstan, and other republics. In addition, the Administration will conduct a thorough review of barriers to American business operating there to make it easier for American businesses to join this effort.
- We will put together in consultation with Congress a $100-million

technical assistance program for the coming calendar year. Again, a major aim of this program will be to use government funds to catalyze private sector involvement. This money will, of course, not come from domestic accounts but from assistance to other foreign nations. Given the gravity of the situation, there is no other choice.

- The President will ask the heads of the Trade and Development Program, the Overseas Private Investment Corporation, and the Export-Import Bank to examine the possibility of focusing some of their efforts on facilitating the work of American business in the food distribution, energy, and housing sectors. These sectors are likely to be critical to the success of democracy and free markets, and while we help the Soviets, we would be supporting American business, too. The President will also ask them to see what they can do to facilitate the involvement of American business in defense conversion efforts.

- But these bilateral efforts must be complemented by the work of the international community. Through our G-7 initiative, we're forging a G-7 [Group of 7] debt deferral arrangement to permit continued flows of capital. To support the international community's involvement in support of democracy and free markets, we will support accelerated IMF and World Bank engagement to put together credible economic plans for those republics which follow the security and political responsibilities we have identified.

History's Precipice

Let me close by saying this: For the third time this century, we have ended a war—this time a cold one—between the Great Powers. After World War I, President Wilson—a president of this university and the inspiration for its School of International and Public Affairs—struggled in vain to call America to its historical mission. His cause was right, and his cause was just. And, above all, his cause was in the best interests of this country. But he was defeated; isolationism returned, and fascism and war followed. After World War II, our leaders—the Kennans of that generation—learned from the defeat of Wilson's vision. Surveying the wreckage made possible in part by America's isolationism of the 1920s and 1930s, they understood America had to stay engaged internationally. In a bipartisan way, they committed themselves to turn the war into an enduring peace.

Their work is plain to see, today, for its legacy is still with us: a democratic Europe and a democratic Japan, both prosperous and peace-loving. Now, their vision has been realized: We have skirted Faulkner's question and avoided nuclear war. And we have seen the demise of Stalinism.

Today, after the Cold War, we *again* stand at history's precipice. If, during the Cold War, we faced each other as two scorpions in a bottle, now the Western nations and the former Soviet republics stand as awkward climbers on a steep mountain. Held together by a common rope, a fall toward fascism or anarchy in the former Soviet Union will pull the West down, too. Yet, equally as important, a strong and steady pull by the West now can help them to gain their footing so that they, too, can climb above to enduring democracy and freedom. Surely we must strengthen the rope, not sever it.

From Odessa on the Black Sea to Vladivostok on the Pacific, the people are tired and hungry, disoriented and confused. These people must be able to see that democrats and reformers can deliver the goods, that there is some cause for hope, some sign that life will get better. For they are coming to grips with the fact that the ideas that have ruled their lives for 70 years—the ill-conceived ideas of Marx, Lenin, and Stalin—are not ideas at all but lies. Now these people who have lived under the lie must learn what it is like to live under freedom.

This will be hard work. It will be painful. And it may seem easy for them to slip from their commitment to freedom, to turn to the simplistic solutions of a new demagogue or dictator. And if they do, their problems will again manifestly become our concerns—as the turn of peoples toward fascism in the 1930s became a threat to our existence.

Ladies and gentlemen, what this means for America is that we face a simple choice: to follow our fears and turn inward, ignoring the opportunities presented by the collapse of the Soviet Empire, or to answer the summons of history and lead toward a better future for all.

When Faulkner spoke 41 years ago, he did not succumb to the paralyzing fear raised by the specter of nuclear armaggedon. Instead, he argued that the basest of all things is to be afraid, that we must conquer our fear, that man would not merely endure but prevail.

I believe that. I believe that having prevailed over the twin fears of nuclear war and Stalinism, we can prevail over the tyranny of the spirit that might threaten reform and democracy and bring darkness to our lives as well. We can prevail over the fearful isolationism that threatens to return us to the failures of the 1920s and 1930s. We can prevail over political paralysis to forge a bipartisan consensus about what has to be done, and then, united at home, we can join with our allies to form a new coalition: a coalition for a diplomacy of collective engagement; a coalition to create pathways of hope; a coalition to make of the end of the Cold War a new beginning for all the nations of the world. History *and* the American people expect no less of us.

PROTOCOL TO COMMONWEALTH PACT

The Azerbaijani Republic, the Republic of Armenia, the Republic of Byelorussia, the Republic of Kazakhstan, the Republic of Kirghizia, the Republic of Moldavia, the Russian Federation, the Republic of Tadzhikistan, Turkmenia, the Republic of Uzbekistan and Ukraine, on an equal basis, and as high contracting parties, are forming a Commonwealth of Independent States.

The agreement on the creation of the Commonwealth of Independent States comes into force for each of the high contracting parties from the moment of its ratification. Documents regulating cooperation in the framework of the commonwealth will be worked out on the basis of the agreement on the creation of the Commonwealth of Independent States, taking into consideration reservations made during its ratification.

This protocol is a constituent part of the agreement on the creation of the Commonwealth of Independent States.

Done in Alma-Ata, on Dec. 21, 1991, in one copy in the Azerbaijani, Armenian, Byelorussian, Kazakh, Kirghiz, Moldavian, Russian, Tadzhik, Turkmen, Uzbek and Ukrainian languages. All texts are equally valid. The authentic copy is kept in the archive of the government of the republic of Byelorussia, which will send the certified copy of this protocol to the high contracting parties.

ALMA-ATA DECLARATION

THE INDEPENDENT STATES—the Azerbaijani Republic, the Republic of Armenia, the Republic of Byelorussia, the Republic of Kazakhstan, the Republic of Kirghizia, the Republic of Moldavia, the Russian Federation, the Republic of Tadzhikistan, Turkmenia, the Republic of Uzbekistan and Ukraine,

SEEKING to build democratic law-governed states, the relations between which will develop on the basis of mutual recognition and respect for state sovereignty and sovereign equality, the inalienable right to self-determination, principles of equality and non-interference in internal affairs, the rejection of the use of force, the threat of force and economic and any other methods of pressure, a peaceful settlement of disputes, respect for human rights and freedoms, including the rights of national minorities, a conscientious fulfillment of commitments and other generally recognized principles and standards of international law;

RECOGNIZING AND RESPECTING each other's territorial integrity and the inviolability of the existing borders;

BELIEVING that the strengthening of the relations of friendship, good neighborliness and mutually advantageous cooperation, which has deep historic roots, meets the basic interests of nations and promotes the cause of peace and security;

BEING AWARE of their responsibility for the preservation of civil peace and inter-ethnic accord;

BEING LOYAL to the objectives and principles of the agreement on the creation of the Commonwealth of Independent States;

ARE MAKING the following statement:

Cooperation between members of the commonwealth will be carried out in accordance with the principle of equality through coordinating institutions formed on a parity basis and operating in the way established by the agreements between members of the commonwealth, which is neither a state nor a super-state structure.

In order to insure international strategic stability and security, allied command of the military-strategic forces and a single control over nuclear weapons will be preserved, the sides will respect each other's desire to attain the status of a non-nuclear or neutral state.

The Commonwealth of Independent States is open, with the agreement of all its participants, for other states to join—members of the former Soviet Union as well as other states sharing the goals and principles of the commonwealth.

The allegiance to cooperation in the formation and development of the common economic space, and all-European and Eurasian markets is being confirmed.

With the formation of the Commonwealth of Independent States, the Union of Soviet Socialist Republics ceases to exist.

Member states of the commonwealth guarantee, in accordance with their constitutional procedures, the fulfillment of international obligations stemming from the treaties and agreements of the former U.S.S.R.

Member states of the commonwealth pledge to observe strictly the principles of this declaration.

Proceeding from the provision, sealed in the agreement on the establishment of a Commonwealth of Independent States and in the Alma-Ata declaration, for keeping the common military-strategic space under a joint command and for keeping a single control over nuclear weapons, the high contracting parties agreed on the following:

The command of the armed forces shall be entrusted to Marshal Yevgeny I. Shaposhnikov, pending a solution to the question of reforming the armed forces.

Proposals concerning this question shall be submitted by Dec. 30, 1991, for the consideration of the heads of state.

A supreme body of the commonwealth—a "Council of the Heads of State"— as well as a "Council of the Heads of Government" shall be set up with a view to tackling matters connected with coordinating the activities of the states of the new commonwealth in the sphere of common interests.

The plenipotentiary representatives of the states of the new commonwealth shall be instructed to submit proposals concerning the abolition of the structures of the former Soviet Union, as well as the coordinating institutions of the commonwealth for the consideration of the Council of the Heads of State.

Member states of the commonwealth, referring to Article 12 of the agreement on the creation of the Commonwealth of Independent States,

PROCEEDING from the intention of each of the states to fulfill its duties stipulated by the U.N. Charter and to take part in the work of that organization as equal members;

TAKING into account that previously the Republic of Byelorussia, the U.S.S.R. and Ukraine were members of the United Nations organization;

EXPRESSING satisfaction that the Republic of Byelorussia and Ukraine continue to be U.N. members as sovereign independent states;

BEING full of resolve to promote the consolidation of world peace and security on the basis of the U.N. Charter in the interests of their nations and the whole of the world community;

HAVING DECIDED:

1. Member states of the commonwealth support Russia in taking over the U.S.S.R. membership in the U.N., including permanent membership in the Security Council and other international organizations.

2. The Republic of Byelorussia, the Russian Federation of Ukraine will help other member states of the commonwealth settle problems connected with their full membership in the U.N. and other intentional organizations.

Done in Alma-Ata on Dec. 21, 1991, in one copy in the Azerbaijani, Armenian, Byelorussian, Kazakh, Kirghiz, Moldavian, Russian, Tadzhik, Turkmen, Uzbek and Ukrainian languages. All texts have equal force. The original copy will be kept in the archive of the Government of the Republic of Byelorussia, which will send the high contracting parties a certified copy of this protocol.

For the Azerbaijani Republic
A. Mutalibov
For the Republic of Byelorussia
S. Shushkevich
For the Republic of Armenia
L. Ter-Petrosyan
For the Republic of Kazakhstan
N. Nazarbayev
For the Republic of Kirghizia
A. Akayev
For the Republic of Moldavia
M. Snegur
For the Russian Federation
B. Yeltsin
For the Republic of Tadzhikistan
R. Nabiyev
For Turkmenia
S. Niyazov
For the Republic of Uzbekistan
I. Karimov
For Ukraine
L. Kravchuk

NUCLEAR ARMS PACT

Byelorussia, Kazakhstan, the Russian Federation and Ukraine, called henceforth member states,

CONFIRMING their adherence to the non-proliferation of nuclear armaments;

STRIVING for the elimination of all nuclear armaments, and
WISHING to act to strengthen international stability, have agreed on the following:

[Article 1]

The nuclear armaments that are part of the unified strategic armed forces insure the collective security of all members of the Commonwealth of Independent States.

[Article 2]

The member states of this agreement confirm the obligation not to be the first to use nuclear weapons.

[Article 3]

The member states of this agreement are jointly drawing up a policy on nuclear matters.

[Article 4]

Until nuclear weapons have been completely eliminated on the territory of the Republic of Byelorussia and Ukraine, decisions on the need to use them are taken, by agreement with the heads of the member states of the agreement, by the R.S.F.S.R. [Russian Soviet Federated Socialist Republic] President, on the basis of procedures drawn up jointly by the member states.

[Article 5]

1. The republics of Byelorussia and Ukraine undertake to join the 1968 nuclear non-proliferation treaty as non-nuclear states and to conclude with the International Atomic Energy Agency the appropriate agreements-guarantees.

2. The member states of this agreement undertake not to transfer to anyone nuclear weapons or other triggering devices and technologies, or control over such nuclear triggering devices, either directly or indirectly, as well as not in any way to help, encourage and prompt any state not possessing nuclear weapons to produce nuclear weapons or other nuclear triggering devices, and also control over such weapons or triggering devices.

3. The provisions of paragraph 2 of this article do not stand in the way of transferring nuclear weapons from Byelorussia, Kazakhstan and Ukraine to R.S.F.S.R. territory with a view to destroying them.

[Article 6]

The member states of this agreement, in accordance with the international treaty, will assist in the eliminating of nuclear weapons. By July 1, 1992 Byelorussia, Kazakhstan and Ukraine will insure the withdrawal of tactical nuclear weapons to central factory premises for dismantling under joint supervision.

[Article 7]

The Governments of Byelorussia, Kazakhstan, the Russian Federation and Ukraine undertake to submit a treaty on strategic offensive arms for ratification to the Supreme Soviets of their states.

[Article 8]

This agreement requires ratification. It will come into force on the 30th day after the handing over of all ratification papers to the government of the R.S.F.S.R. for safekeeping.

Done in Alma-Ata in one certified copy in Byelorussian, Kazakh, Russian and Ukrainian languages, all texts being equally authentic.

GORBACHEV'S RESIGNATION

Dear compatriots, fellow citizens: As a result of the newly formed situation, creation of the Commonwealth of Independent States, I cease my activities in the post of U.S.S.R. president.

I am making this decision out of considerations based on principle. I have firmly stood for independence, self-rule of nations, for the sovereignty of the republics, but at the same time for preservation of the union state, the unity of the country.

Events went a different way. The policy prevailed of dismembering this country and disuniting the state, with which I cannot agree. And after the Alma-Ata meeting and the decisions made there, my position on this matter has not changed. Besides, I am convinced that decisions of such scale should have been made on the basis of a popular expression of will.

Yet I will continue to do everything in my power so that agreements signed there should lead to real accord in the society [and] facilitate the escape from the crisis and the reform process.

Addressing you for the last time in the capacity of president of the U.S.S.R., I consider it necessary to express my evaluation of the road we have traveled since 1985, especially as there are a lot of contradictory, superficial and subjective judgments on that matter.

Fate had it that when I found myself at the head of the state it was already clear that all was not well in the country. There is plenty of everything: land, oil and gas, other natural riches, and God gave us lots of intelligence and talent, yet we lived much worse than developed countries and keep falling behind them more and more.

The reason could already be seen. The society was suffocating in the vise of the command-bureaucratic system, doomed to serve ideology and bear the terrible burden of the arms race. It had reached the limit of its possibilities. All attempts at partial reform, and there had been many, had suffered defeat, one after another. The country was losing perspective. We could not go on living like that. Everything had to be changed radically.

That is why not once—not once—have I regretted that I did not take advantage of the post of [Communist Party] general secretary to rule as a czar for several years. I considered it irresponsible and amoral. I realized that to start reforms of such scale in a society such as ours was a most difficult and even a risky thing. But even today I am convinced of the historic correctness of the democratic reforms that were started in the spring of 1985.

The process of renovating the country and radical changes in the world community turned out to be far more complicated than could be expected. However, what has been done ought to be given its due. This society acquired freedom, liberated itself politically and spiritually, and this is the foremost achievement—which we have not yet understood completely, because we have not learned to use freedom.

However, work of historic significance has been accomplished. The totalitarian system that deprived the country of an opportunity to become successful and prosperous long ago has been eliminated. A breakthrough has been achieved on the way to democratic changes. Free elections, freedom of the press, religious freedoms, representative organs of power, a multi-party [system] became a reality. Human rights are recognized as the supreme principle.

The movement to a diverse economy has started, equality of all forms of property is becoming established, people who work on the land are coming to life again in the framework of land reform, farmers have appeared, millions of acres of land are being given over to people who live in the countryside and in towns.

Economic freedom of the producer has been legalized, and entrepreneurship, shareholding, privatization are gaining momentum. In turning the economy toward a market, it is important to remember that all this is done for the sake of the individual. At this difficult time, all should be done for his social protection, especially for senior citizens and children.

We live in a new world. The Cold War has ended; the arms race has stopped, as has the insane militarization that mutilated our economy, public psyche and morals. The threat of a world war has been removed. Once again I want to stress that on my part everything was done during the transition period to preserve reliable control of nuclear weapons.

We opened ourselves to the world, gave up interference into other people's affairs, the use of troops beyond the borders of the country, and trust, solidarity and respect came in response. We have become one of the main foundations for the transformation of modern civilization on peaceful democratic grounds.

The nations and peoples [of this country] gained real freedom of self-determination. The search for a democratic reformation of the multinational state brought us to the threshold of concluding a new union treaty. All these changes demanded immense strain. They were carried out with sharp struggle, with growing resistance from the old, the obsolete forces: for former party-state structures, the economic apparatus, as well as our habits, ideological superstitions, the psychology of sponging and leveling everyone out.

They stumbled on our intolerance, low level of political culture, fear of change. That is why we lost so much time. The old system collapsed before the new one had time to begin working, and the crisis in the society became even more acute. I am aware of the dissatisfaction with the present hard situation, of the sharp criticism of authorities at all levels including my personal activities. But once again I'd like to stress that radical changes in such a vast country, and a country with such a heritage, cannot pass painlessly without difficulties and shake-up.

The August coup brought the general crisis to its ultimate limit. The most damaging thing about this crisis is the breakup of the state. And today I am worried by our people's loss of the citizenship of a great country. The consequences may turn out to be very hard for everyone.

I think it is vitally important to preserve the democratic achievements of the last years. They have been paid for by the suffering of our whole history, our tragic experience. They must not be given up under any circumstances or any pretext, otherwise all our hopes for the better will be buried. I am saying all this straight and honestly. It is my moral duty.

Today, I'd like to express my gratitude to all citizens who supported the policy of renovating the country, got involved in the implementation of democratic reforms. I am grateful to statesmen, public and political figures, millions of people abroad, those who understood our concepts and supported them, turned to us, started sincere cooperation with us.

I am leaving my post with apprehension, but also with hope, with faith in you, your wisdom and force of spirit. We are the heirs of a great civilization, and its rebirth into a new, modern and dignified life now depends on one and all.

I wish to thank you with all my heart all those who have stood together with me all these years for a fair and good cause. Some mistakes could surely have been avoided; many things could have been done better. But I am convinced that sooner or later our common efforts will bear fruit, our nations will live in a prosperous and democratic society.

I wish all the best to all of you.

BUSH ON GORBACHEV'S RESIGNATION

Mikhail Gorbachev's resignation as President of the Soviet Union culminates a remarkable era in the history of his country and in its long and often difficult relationship with the United States. As he leaves office, I would like to express publicly and on behalf of the American people my gratitude to him for years of sustained commitment to world peace, and my personal respect for his intellect, vision, and courage.

President Gorbachev is responsible for one of the most important developments of this century, the revolutionary transformation of a totalitarian dictatorship and the liberation of his people from its smothering embrace. His personal commitment to democratic and economic reform through *perestroika* and *glasnost*, a commitment which demanded the highest degree of political and personal ingenuity and courage, permitted the peoples of Russia and other Republics to cast aside decades of dark oppression and put in place the foundations of freedom.

Working with President Reagan, myself, and other allied leaders, President Gorbachev acted boldly and decisively to end the bitter divisions of the cold war and contributed to the remaking of a Europe whole and free. His and Foreign Minister Eduard Shevardnadze's "New Thinking" in foreign affairs permitted the United States and the Soviet Union to move from confrontation to partnership in the search for peace across the globe. Together we negotiated historic reductions in chemical, nuclear, and conventional forces and reduced the risk of a nuclear conflict.

Working together, we helped the people of Eastern Europe win their liberty and the German people their goal of unity in peace and freedom. Our partnership led to unprecedented cooperation in repelling Iraqi aggression in Kuwait, in bringing peace to Nicaragua and Cambodia, and independence to Namibia. And our work continues as we seek a lasting and just peace between Israelis and Arabs in the Middle East and an end to the conflict in Afghanistan.

President Gorbachev's participation in these historic events is his legacy to his country and to the world. This record assures him an honored place in history and, most importantly for the future, establishes a solid basis from which the United States and the West can work in equally constructive ways with his successors.

BUSH ADDRESS TO NATION

During these last few months, you and I have witnessed one of the greatest dramas of the 20th century, the historic and revolutionary transformation of a totalitarian dictatorship, the Soviet Union, and the liberation of its peoples. As we celebrate Christmas, this day of peace and hope, I thought we should take a few minutes to reflect on what these events mean for us as Americans.

For over 40 years, the United States led the West in the struggle against communism and the threat it posed to our most precious values. This struggle shaped the lives of all Americans. It forced all nations to live under the specter of nuclear destruction.

That confrontation is now over. The nuclear threat, while far from gone, is receding. Eastern Europe is free. The Soviet Union itself is no more. This is a victory for democracy and freedom. It's a victory for the moral force of our values. Every American can take pride in this victory, from the millions of men and women who have served our country in uniform, to millions of Americans who supported their country and a strong defense under nine Presidents.

New, independent nations have emerged out of the wreckage of the Soviet empire. Last weekend, these former Republics formed a Commonwealth of Independent States. This act marks the end of the old Soviet Union, signified today by Mikhail Gorbachev's decision to resign as President.

I'd like to express, on behalf of the American people, my gratitude to Mikhail Gorbachev for years of sustained commitment to world peace, and for his intellect, vision, and courage. I spoke with Mikhail Gorbachev this morning. We reviewed the many accomplishments of the past few years and spoke of hope for the future.

Mikhail Gorbachev's revolutionary policies transformed the Soviet Union. His policies permitted the peoples of Russia and the other Republics to cast aside decades of oppression and establish the foundations of freedom. His legacy guarantees him an honored place in history and provides a solid basis for the United States to work in equally constructive ways with his successors.

The United States applauds and supports the historic choice for freedom by the new States of the Commonwealth. We congratulate them on the peaceful and democratic path they have chosen, and for their careful attention to nuclear control and safety during this transition. Despite a potential for instability and chaos, these events clearly serve our national interest.

We stand tonight before a new world of hope and possibilities for our children, a world we could not have contemplated a few years ago. The challenge for us now is to engage these new States in sustaining the peace and building a more prosperous future.

And so today, based on commitments and assurances given to us by some of these States, concerning nuclear safety, democracy, and free markets, I am announcing some important steps designed to begin this process.

First, the United States recognizes and welcomes the emergence of a free, independent, and democratic Russia, led by its courageous President, Boris Yeltsin. Our Embassy in Moscow will remain there as our Embassy to Russia. We will support Russia's assumption of the U.S.S.R.'s seat as a permanent Member of the United Nations Security Council. I look forward to working closely with President Yeltsin in support of his efforts to bring democratic and market reform to Russia.

Second, the United States also recognizes the independence of Ukraine, Armenia, Kazakhstan, Belarus, and Kyrgyzstan, all States that have made specific commitments to us. We will move quickly to establish diplomatic relations with these States and build new ties to them. We will sponsor membership in the United Nations for those not already members.

Third, the United States also recognizes today as independent States the remaining six former Soviet Republics: Moldova, Tukmenistan, Azerbaijan, Tadjikistan, Georgia, and Uzbekistan. We will establish diplomatic relations with them when we are satisfied that they have made commitments to responsible security policies and democratic principles, as have the other States we recognize today. . . .

This is a day of great hope for all Americans. Our enemies have become our partners, committed to building democratic and civil societies. They ask for our support, and we will give it to them. . . .

SUPREME COURT ON
NEW YORK COMPENSATION LAW
December 10, 1991

The Supreme Court December 10 declared unconstitutional New York's "Son of Sam" law, which sought to compensate the victims of a crime or their families with any profits the perpetrator might receive from publicizing his or her account of the crime. By an 8-to-0 vote, the Court ruled that the law violated the First Amendment's freedom of speech guarantee.

"Because the Federal Government and most of the States have enacted statutes with similar objectives, the issue is significant and likely to recur," Justice Sandra Day O'Connor said for the Court, explaining why it opted to review Simon & Schuster v. Crime Victims Board. *The statute's informal name was derived from a serial killer popularly known as Son of Sam, who terrorized New York in the summer of 1977. By the time David Berkowitz was identified as the killer and apprehended, the publication rights to his story were valuable.*

Berkowitz's opportunity to profit from his notoriety did not escape the attention of the New York legislature. It promptly passed a law to "ensure that monies received by the criminal under such circumstances shall first be made available to recompense the victims of the crime for their loss and suffering."

The law was later amended to require any publisher, broadcaster, or other media entity to withhold whatever income they would have paid an accused or convicted criminal, and to turn the money over to the state's Crime Victims Board. The money would be distributed to victims of the crime or their families who, within five years, successfully sued the defendant for damages.

Several people who committed highly publicized crimes in New York after the law's passage were denied payments for their stories. They included Jean Harris, convicted of murdering Dr. Herman Tarnower, the "Scarsdale Diet" author; Mark David Chapman, convicted of killing ex-Beatles star John Lennon; and R. Foster Winans, the former Wall Street Journal *columnist convicted of insider trading.*

Ironically, the law never touched Berkowitz. It applied only to criminals who had been convicted; Berkowitz was found incompetent to stand trial. However, the Crime Victims Board reported that Berkowitz voluntarily paid his share of royalties from the 1981 book Son of Sam *to the families of his victims.*

Wiseguy *Profits*

The case Simon & Schuster v. Crime Victims Board *arose over the publishing company's payments to Henry Hill, an organized crime figure, and his literary agent for its 1986 publication of the book,* Wiseguy: Life in a Mafia Family, *written by Nicholas Pileggi. Hill was arrested in 1980 and, in exchange for immunity from prosecution, testified against many of his former associates. From the safety of the federal witness protection program, Hill collaborated with Pileggi to produce* Wiseguy, *which colorfully depicted the day-to-day activities of those engaged in organized crime, mainly in Hill's first-person narrative.*

Wiseguy *sold more than 1 million copies and was made into the movie* Goodfellas. *Soon after the book was published, the board asked Simon & Schuster for copies of its contract with Hill and how much he had been paid; it also asked that future payments to him be suspended. The publisher complied, reporting that Hill's literary agent had received $96,250 in advances and royalties on Hill's behalf, and that it was holding $27,958 for payment to Hill.*

The board then determined that Simon & Schuster had violated the law by making payments to Hill, and ordered the company to turn over all money payable to him. Simon & Schuster refused. In August 1987 it asked a federal district court in New York to declare the law unconstitutional and to issue an injunction barring the law's enforcement. That court rejected the publisher's arguments, and the U.S. Court of Appeals for the Second Circuit (New York) affirmed its decision on a split vote.

Court's Decision

The Supreme Court was of a decidedly different opinion. The Court emphatically found that the law imposed a financial burden on speakers because of the content of their speech. "It singles out income derived from expressive activity, and is directed only at works with a specific content," Justice O'Connor wrote. She also wrote that a state had a compelling interest in compensating victims of crime but that the New York law was not tailored narrowly enough to achieve that goal without infringing on the Constitution.

Justice Anthony M. Kennedy wrote in a separate opinion that the

Court did not need to ask whether the state could show that the statute served a compelling state interest and was narrowly drawn to achieve that end. Kennedy feared that such an "unnecessary formulation ... [had] the capacity to weaken central protections of the First Amendment." He said that the Court should "recognize this opportunity to confirm our past holdings and to rule that the New York statute amounts to raw censorship based on content ... [and was] forbidden by the text of the First Amendment and well-settled principles protecting speech and the press. That ought to end the matter."

In another opinion, Justice Harry A. Blackmun also concurred in the Court's judgment but questioned its reasoning. He said most other states had laws similar to New York's and deserved more guidance from the Court "in this very sensitive area." Justice Clarence Thomas, the Court's newest member, did not participate in the case.

Following are the Supreme Court's majority and concurring opinions issued December 10, 1991, in the case Simon & Schuster Inc. v. Members of the New York State Crime Victims Board, *overturning the state's so-called Son of Sam law:*

No. 90-1059

Simon & Schuster, Inc., Petitioner *v.* Members of the New York State Crime Victims Board et al.	On writ of certiorari to the United States Court of Appeals for the Second Circuit

[December 10, 1991]

JUSTICE O'CONNOR delivered the opinion of the Court.

New York's "Son of Sam" law requires that an accused or convicted criminal's income from works describing his crime be deposited in an escrow account. These funds are then made available to the victims of the crime and the criminal's other creditors. We consider whether this statute is consistent with the First Amendment.

I

A

In the summer of 1977, New York was terrorized by a serial killer popularly known as the Son of Sam. The hunt for the Son of Sam received considerable publicity, and by the time David Berkowitz was identified as the killer and apprehended, the rights to his story were worth a substantial amount. Berkowitz's chance to profit from his notoriety while his victims and their families remained uncompensated did not escape the notice of

New York's Legislature. The State quickly enacted the statute at issue, N.Y. Exec. Law §632-a (McKinney 1982 and Supp. 1991)....

The Son of Sam law, as later amended, requires any entity contracting with an accused or convicted person for a depiction of the crime to submit a copy of the contract to respondent Crime Victims Board, and to turn over any income under that contract to the Board. This requirement applies to all such contracts in any medium of communication:

> "Every person, firm, corporation, partnership, association or other legal entity contracting with any person or the representative or assignee of any person, accused or convicted of a crime in this state, with respect to the reenactment of such crime, by way of a movie, book, magazine article, tape recording, phonograph record, radio or television presentation, live entertainment of any kind, or from the expression of such accused or convicted person's thoughts, feelings, opinions or emotions regarding such crime, shall submit a copy of such contract to the board and pay over to the board any moneys which would otherwise, by terms of such contract, be owing to the person so accused or convicted or his representatives." N.Y. Exec. Law §632-a(1) (McKinney 1982).

The Board is then required to deposit the payment in an escrow account "for the benefit of and payable to any victim . . . provided that such victim, within five years of the date of the establishment of such escrow account, brings a civil action in a court of competent jurisdiction and recovers a money judgment for damages against such [accused or convicted] person or his representatives." *Ibid.* After five years, if no actions are pending, "the board shall immediately pay over any moneys in the escrow account to such person or his legal representatives." §632-a(4). This 5-year period in which to bring a civil action against the convicted person begins to run when the escrow account is established, and supersedes any limitations period that expires earlier. §632-a(7).

Subsection (8) grants priority to two classes of claims against the escrow account. First, upon a court order, the Board must release assets "for the exclusive purpose of retaining legal representation." §632-a(8). In addition, the Board has the discretion, after giving notice to the victims of the crime, to "make payments from the escrow account to a representative of any person accused or convicted of a crime for the necessary expenses of the production of the moneys paid into the escrow account." *Ibid.* This provision permits payments to literary agents and other such representatives. Payments under subsection (8) may not exceed one-fifth of the amount collected in the account. *Ibid.*

Claims against the account are given the following priorities: (a) payments ordered by the Board under subsection (8); (b) subrogation claims of the State for payments made to victims of the crime; (c) civil judgments obtained by victims of the crime; and (d) claims of other creditors of the accused or convicted person, including state and local tax authorities. §632-a(11) (McKinney Supp. 1991).

Subsection (10) broadly defines "person convicted of a crime" to include "any person convicted of a crime in this state either by entry of a plea of guilty or by conviction after trial *and any person who has voluntarily and intelligently admitted the commission of a crime for which such person is not prosecuted.*" §632-a(10)(b) (emphasis added). Thus a person who has never been accused or convicted of a crime in the ordinary sense, but who admits in a book or other work to having committed a crime, is within the statute's coverage.

As recently construed by the New York Court of Appeals, however, the statute does not apply to victimless crimes. *Children of Bedford, Inc.* v. *Petromelis* (1991).

The Son of Sam law supplements pre-existing statutory schemes authorizing the Board to compensate crime victims for their losses, see N.Y. Civ. Prac. Law §§1310-1352 (McKinney Supp. 1991), providing for orders of restitution at sentencing, N.Y. Penal Law §60.27 (McKinney 1987); and affording prejudgment attachment procedures to ensure that wrongdoers do not dissipate their assets, N.Y. Civ. Prac. Law §§6201-6226 (McKinney 1980 and Supp. 1991). The escrow arrangement established by the Son of Sam law enhances these provisions only insofar as the accused or convicted person earns income within the scope of §632-a(1).

Since its enactment in 1977, the Son of Sam law has been invoked only a handful of times. As might be expected, the individuals whose profits the Board has sought to escrow have all become well known for having committed highly publicized crimes. These include Jean Harris, the convicted killer of "Scarsdale Diet" Doctor Herman Tarnower; Mark David Chapman, the man convicted of assassinating John Lennon; and R. Foster Winans, the former Wall Street Journal columnist convicted of insider trading. Ironically, the statute was never applied to the Son of Sam himself; David Berkowitz was found incompetent to stand trial, and the statute at that time applied only to criminals who had actually been convicted. N.Y. Times, Feb. 20, 1991, p. B8, col 4. According to the Board, Berkowitz voluntarily paid his share of the royalties from the book *Son of Sam*, published in 1981, to his victims or their estates. Brief for Respondents 8, n. 13.

This case began in 1986, when the Board first became aware of the contract between petitioner Simon & Schuster and admitted organized crime figure Henry Hill.

B

Looking back from the safety of the Federal Witness Protection Program, Henry Hill recalled: "At the age of twelve my ambition was to be a gangster. To be a wiseguy. To me being a wiseguy was better than being president of the United States." N. Pileggi, Wiseguy: Life in a Mafia Family 19 (1985) (hereinafter Wiseguy). Whatever one might think of Hill, at the very least it can be said that he realized his dreams. After a career spanning 25 years, Hill admitted engineering some of the most daring crimes of his day, including the 1978-1979 Boston College basketball point-shaving scandal, and the theft of $6 million from Lufthansa Airlines in 1978, the largest successful cash robbery in American history. Wiseguy 9. Most of Hill's crimes were more banausic: He committed extortion, he imported and distributed narcotics, and he organized numerous robberies.

Hill was arrested in 1980. In exchange for immunity from prosecution, he testified against many of his former colleagues. Since his arrest, he has lived under an assumed name in an unknown part of the country.

In August 1981, Hill entered into a contract with author Nicholas Pileggi for the production of a book about Hill's life. The following month, Hill and Pileggi signed a publishing agreement with Simon & Schuster. Under the agreement, Simon & Schuster agreed to make payments to both Hill and Pileggi. Over the next few years, according to Pileggi, he and Hill "talked at length virtually every single day, with not more than an occasional Sunday or holiday skipped. We spent more than three hundred hours together; my notes of conversations with Henry occupy more than six linear file feet." App. 27. Because producing the book required such a substantial investment of time and effort, Hill sought compensation. *Ibid.*

The result of Hill and Pileggi's collaboration was Wiseguy, which was published in January 1986. The book depicts, in colorful detail, the day-to-day existence of organized crime, primarily in Hill's first-person narrative. Throughout Wiseguy, Hill frankly admits to having participated in an astonishing variety of crimes. He discusses, among other things, his conviction of extortion and the prison sentence he served. In one portion of the book, Hill recounts how members of the Mafia received preferential treatment in prison:

> "The dorm was a separate three-story building outside the wall, which looked more like a Holiday Inn than a prision. There were four guys to a room, and we had comfortable beds and private baths. There were two dozen rooms on each floor, and each of them had mob guys living in them. It was like a wiseguy convention—the whole Gotti crew, Jimmy Doyle and his guys, 'Ernie Boy Abbamonte and 'Joe Crow' Delvecchio, Vinnie Aloi, Frank Cotroni.
>
> "It was wild. There was wine and booze, and it was kept in a bath-oil or after-shave jars. The hacks in the honor dorm were almost all on the take, and even though it was against the rules, we used to cook in our rooms. Looking back, I don't think Paulie went to the general mess five times in the two and a half years he was there. We had a stove and pots and pans and silverware stacked in the bathroom. We had glasses and an ice-water cooler where we kept the fresh meats and cheeses. When there was an inspection, we stored the stuff in the false ceiling, and once in a while, if it was confiscated, we'd just go to the kitchen and get new stuff.
>
> "We had the best food smuggled into our dorm from the kitchen. Steaks, veal cutlets, shrimp, red snapper. Whatever the hacks could buy, we ate. It cost me two, three hundred a week. Guys like Paulie spent five hundred to a thousand bucks a week. Scotch cost thirty dollars a pint. The hacks used to bring it inside the walls in their lunch pails. We never ran out of booze, because we had six hacks bringing it in six days a week. Depending on what you wanted and how much you were willing to spend, life could be almost bearable." Wiseguy 150-151.

Wiseguy was reviewed favorably: The Washington Post called it an "amply detailed and entirely fascinating book that amounts to a piece of revisionist history," while New York Daily News columnist Jimmy Breslin named it "the best book on crime in America every written." App. 5. The book was also a commercial success: Within 19 months of its publication, more than a million copies were in print. A few years later, the book was converted into a film called "Goodfellas", which won a host of awards as the best film of 1990.

From Henry Hill's perspective, however, the publicity generated by the book's success proved less desirable. The Crime Victims Board learned of Wiseguy in January 1986, soon after it was published.

C

On January 31, the Board notified Simon & Schuster: "It has come to our attention that you may have contracted with a person accused or convicted of a crime for the payment of monies to such person." The Board ordered Simon & Schuster to furnish copies of any contracts it had entered into with Hill, to provide the dollar amounts and dates of all payments to Hill in the future. Simon & Schuster complied with this order. By that time, Simon & Schuster had paid Hill's literary agent $96,250 in advances and royalties on Hill's behalf, and was holding $27,958 for eventual payment to Hill.

The Board reviewed the book and the contract, and on May 21, 1987, issued a Proposed Determination and Order. The Board determined that Wiseguy was covered by §632-a of the Executive Law, that Simon & Schuster had violated the law by failing to turn over its contract with Hill to the Board and by making payments to Hill, and that all money owed to Hill under the contract had to be turned over to the Board to be held in escrow for the victims of Hill's crimes. The Board ordered Hill to turn over the payments he had already received, and ordered Simon & Schuster to turn over all money payable to Hill at the time or in the future.

Simon & Schuster brought suit in August 1987, under 42 U.S.C. §1983, seeking a declaration that the Son of Sam law violates the First Amendment and an injunction barring the statute's enforcement. After the parties filed cross-motions for summary judgment, the District Court found the statute consistent with the First Amendment. A divided Court of Appeals affirmed.

Because the Federal Government and most of the States have enacted statutes with similar objectives, the issue is significant and likely to recur. We accordingly granted certiorari.

II

B

A statute is presumptively inconsistent with the First Amendment if it imposes a financial burden on speakers because of the content of their speech. As we emphasized in invalidating a content-based magazine tax, "official scrutiny of the content of publications as the basis for imposing a tax is entirely incompatible with the First Amendment's guarantee of freedom of the press." *Arkansas Writers' Project, Inc.* v. *Ragland* (1987).

This is a notion so engrained in our First Amendment jurisprudence that last Term we found it so "obvious" as to not require explanation. *Leathers*

v. *Medlock* (1991). It is but one manifestation of a far broader principle: "Regulations which permit the Government to discriminate on the basis of the content of the message cannot be tolerated under the First Amendment." *Regan* v. *Time, Inc.* (1984). In the context of financial regulation, it bears repeating, as we did in *Leathers*, that the Government's ability to impose content-based burdens on speech raises the specter that the Government may effectively drive certain ideas or viewpoints from the marketplace. The First Amendment presumptively places this sort of discrimination beyond the power of the Government. As we reiterated in *Leathers*, "The constitutional right of free expression is ... in the belief that no other approach would comport with the premise of individual dignity and choice upon which our political system rests."

The Son of Sam law is a such a content-based statute. It singles out income derived from expressive activity for a burden the State places on no other income, and it is directed only at works with a specified content. Whether the First Amendment "speaker" is considered to be Henry Hill, whose income the statute places in escrow because of the story he has told, or Simon & Schuster, which can publish books about crime with the assistance of only those criminals willing to forgo remuneration for at least five years, the statute plainly imposes a financial disincentive only on speech of a particular content.

The Board tries unsuccessfully to distinguish the Son of Sam law from the discriminatory tax at issue in *Arkansas Writers' Project*. While the Son of Sam law escrows all of the speaker's speech-derived income for at least five years, rather than taxing a percentage of it outright, this difference can hardly serve as the basis for disparate treatment under the First Amendment. Both forms of financial burden operate as disincentives to speak; indeed, in many cases it will be impossible to discern in advance which type of regulation will be more costly to the speaker.

The Board next argues that discriminatory financial treatment is suspect under the First Amendment only when the legislature intends to suppress certain ideas. This assertion is incorrect; our cases have consistently held that "[i]llicit legislative intent is not the *sine qua non* of a violation of the First Amendment." [citing] *Minneapolis Star & Tribune Co.* v. *Minnesota Comm'r of Revenue* (1983). Simon & Schuster need adduce "no evidence of an improper censorial motive." [citing] *Arkansas Writers' Project, supra.*

Finally, the Board claims that even if the First Amendment prohibits content-based financial regulation specifically of the *media*, the Son of Sam law is different, because it imposes a general burden on any "entity" contracting with a convicted person to transmit that person's speech. . . .

This argument falters on both semantic and constitutional grounds. Any "entity" that enters into such a contract becomes by definition a medium of communication, if it wasn't one already. In any event, the characterization of an entity as a member of the "media" is irrelevant for these purposes. The Government's power to impose content-based financial disincentives on speech surely does not vary with the identity of the speaker.

The Son of Sam law establishes a financial disincentive to create or publish works with a particular content. In order to justify such differential treatment, "the State must show that its regulation is necessary to serve a compelling state interest and is narrowly drawn to achieve that end." *Arkansas Writers' Project.*

B

The Board disclaims, as it must, any state interest in suppressing descriptions of crime out of solicitude for the sensibilities of readers. As we have often had occasion to repeat, "[T]he fact that society may find speech offensive is not a sufficient reason for suppressing it. Indeed, if it is the speaker's opinion that gives offense, that consequence is a reason for according it constitutional protection." (quoting *FCC* v. *Pacifica Foundation* (1978)). "If there is a bedrock principle underlying the First Amendment, it is that the Government may not prohibit the expression of an idea simply because society finds the idea itself offensive or disagreeable." (quoting *Texas* v. *Johnson* (1989)). The Board thus does not assert any interest in limiting whatever anguish Henry Hill's victims may suffer from reliving their victimization.

There can be little doubt, on the other hand, that the State has a compelling interest in ensuring that victims of crime are compensated by those who harm them. Every State has a body of tort law serving exactly this interest. The State's interest in preventing wrongdoers from dissipating their assets before victims can recover explains the existence of the State's statutory provisions for prejudgment remedies and orders of restitution. We have recognized the importance of this interest before, in the Sixth Amendment context. See *Caplin & Drysdale, Chartered* v. *United States* (1989).

The State likewise has an undisputed compelling interest in ensuring that criminals do not profit from their crimes. . . .

The parties debate whether book royalties can properly be termed the profits of crime, but that is a question we need not address here. For the purposes of this case, we can assume without deciding that the income escrowed by the Son of Sam law represents the fruits of crime. We need only conclude that the State has a compelling interest in depriving criminals of the profits of their crimes, and in using these funds to compensate victims.

The Board attempts to define the State's interest more narrowly, as "ensuring that criminals do not profit from storytelling about their crimes before their victims have a meaningful opportunity to be compensated for their injuries." Here the Board is on far shakier ground. The Board cannot explain why the State should have any greater interest in compensating victims from the proceeds of such "storytelling" than from any of the criminal's other assets. Nor can the Board offer any justification for a distinction between this expressive activity and any other activity in connection with its interest in transferring the fruits of crime from criminals to their victims. Thus even if the State can be said to have an interest in classifying a criminal's assets in this manner, that interest is hardly compelling.

We have rejected similar assertions of a compelling interest in the past. In *Arkansas Writers' Project* and *Minneapolis Star*, we observed that while the State certainly has an important interest in raising revenue through taxation, that interest hardly justified selective taxation of the press, as it was completely unrelated to a press/non-press distinction. Likewise, in *Carey* v. *Brown* (1980), we recognized the State's interest in preserving privacy by prohibiting residential picketing, but refused to permit the State to ban only nonlabor picketing. This was because "nothing in the content-based labor-nonlabor distinction has any bearing whatsoever on privacy." Much the same is true here. The distinction drawn by the Son of Sam law has nothing to do with the State's interest in transferring the proceeds of crime from criminals to their victims.

Like the government entities in the above cases, the Board has taken the *effect* of the statute and posited that effect as the State's interest. If accepted, this sort of circular defense can sidestep judicial review of almost any statute, because it makes all statutes look narrowly tailored. . . .

In short, the State has a compelling interest in compensating victims from the fruits of the crime, but little if any interest in limiting such compensation to the proceeds of the wrongdoer's speech about the crime. We must therefore determine whether the Son of Sam law is narrowly tailored to advance the former, not the latter, objective.

C

As a means of ensuring that victims are compensated from the proceeds of crime, the Son of Sam law is significantly over inclusive. As counsel for the Board conceded at oral argument, the statute applies to works on *any* subject, provided that they express the author's thoughts or recollections about his crime, however tangentially or incidentally. In addition, the statute's board definition of "person convicted of a crime" enables the Board to escrow the income of any author who admits in his work to having committed a crime, whether or not the author was ever actually accused or convicted.

These two provisions combine to encompass a potentially very large number of works. Had the Son of Sam law been in effect at the time and place of publication, it would have escrowed payment for such works as The Autobiography of Malcolm X, which describes crimes committed by the civil rights leader before he became a public figure; Civil Disobedience, in which there acknowledges his refusal to pay taxes and recalls his experience in jail; and even the Confessions of Saint Augustine, in which the author laments "my past foulness and the carnal corruptions of my soul," one instance of which involved the theft of pears from a neighboring vineyard. Association of American Publishers, Inc., has submitted a sobering bibliography listing hundreds of works by American prisoners and ex-prisoners, many of which contain descriptions of the crimes for which the authors were incarcerated, including works by such authors as Emma Goldman and Martin Luther King, Jr. A list of prominent figures whose autobiographies would be subject to the statute if written is not difficult to construct: The list could include Sir Walter Raleigh, who was convicted of treason after a dubiously conducted 1603 trial; Jesse Jackson, who was arrested in 1963 for trespass and resisting arrest after attempting to be served at a lunch counter in North Carolina; and Bertrand Russell, who was jailed for seven days at the age of 89 for participating in a sit-down protest against nuclear weapons. The argument that the statute like the Son of Sam law would prevent publication of *all* of these works is hyperbole—some would have been written without compensation—but the Son of Sam law clearly reaches a wide range of literature that does not enable a criminal to profit from his crime while a victim remains uncompensated.

Should a prominent figure write his autobiography at the end of his career, and include in an early chapter a brief recollection of having stolen (in New York) a nearly worthless item as a youthful prank, the Board would control his entire income from the book for five years, and would make that income available to all of the author's creditors, despite the fact that the statute of limitations for this minor incident had long since run. That the Son of Sam law can produce such an outcome indicates that the statute is, to say the least, not narrowly tailored to achieve the State's objective of compensating crime victims from the profits of crime.

III

The Federal Government and many of the States have enacted statutes designed to serve purposes similar to that served by the Son of Sam law. Some of these statutes may be quite different from New York's, and we have no occasion to determine the constitutionality of these other laws. We conclude simply that in the Son of Sam law, New York has singled out speech on a particular subject for a financial burden that it places on no other speech and no other income. The State's interest in compensating victims from the fruits of crime is a compelling one, but the Son of Sam law is not narrowly tailored to advance that objective. As a result, the statute is inconsistent with the First Amendment.

The judgment of the Court of Appeals is accordingly

Reversed.

JUSTICE THOMAS took no part in the consideration or decision of this case.

JUSTICE BLACKMUN, concurring in the judgment.

I am in general agreement with what the Court says in its opinion. I think, however, that the New York statute is underinclusive as well as over inclusive and that we should say so. Most other States have similar legislation and deserve from this Court all the guidance it can render in this very sensitive area.

JUSTICE KENNEDY, concurring in the judgment.

The New York statute we now consider imposes severe restrictions on authors and publishers, using as its sole criterion the content of what is written. The regulated content has the full protection of the First Amendment and this, I submit, is itself a full and sufficient reason for holding the statute unconstitutional. In my view it is both unnecessary and incorrect to ask whether the State can show that the statute "is necessary to serve a compelling state interest and is narrowly drawn to achieve that end." That test or formulation derives from our equal protection jurisprudence, and has no real or legitimate place when the Court considers the straightforward question whether the State may enact a burdensome restriction of speech based on content only, apart from any considerations of time, place, and manner or the use of public forums.

Here a law is directed to speech alone where the speech in question is not obscene, not defamatory, not words tantamount to an act otherwise criminal, not an impairment of some other constitutional right, not an incitement to lawless action, and not calculated or likely to bring about imminent harm the State has the substantive power to prevent. No further inquiry is necessary to reject the State's argument that the statute should be upheld.

Borrowing the compelling interest and narrow tailoring analysis is ill-advised when all that is at issue is a content-based restriction, for resort to the test might be read as a concession that States may censor speech whenever they believe there is a compelling justification for doing so. Our precedents and traditions allow no such inference.

This said, it must be acknowledged that the compelling interest inquiry has found its way into our First Amendment jurisprudence of late, even where the sole question is, or ought to be, whether the restriction is in fact content-based. Although the notion that protected speech may be restricted on the basis of content if the restriction survives what has sometimes been termed "the most exacting scrutiny," *Texas* v. *Johnson* (1989), may seem familiar, the Court appears to have adopted this formulation in First Amendment cases by accident rather than as the result of a considered judgment. . . .

The employment of the compelling interest test in the present context is in no way justified by my colleagues' citation of *Arkansas Writers' Project* v. *Ragland*. True, both *Ragland* and the case on which it relied, *Minneapolis Star & Tribune Co.* v. *Minnesota Comm'r of Revenue*, recite either the compelling interest test or a close variant, but neither is a case in which the State regulates speech for its content. . . .

The inapplicability of the compelling interest test to content-based restrictions on speech is demonstrated by our repeated statement that "above all else, the First Amendment means that government has no power to restrict expression because of its message, its ideas, its subject matter, or its content." *Police Dept. of Chicago* v. *Mosley* (1972).

There are a few legal categories in which content-based regulation has been permitted or at least contemplated. These include obscenity, or situations presenting some grave and imminent danger the government has the power to prevent. These are, however, historic and traditional categories long familiar to the bar, although with respect to the last category it is most difficult for the government to prevail. While it cannot be said with certainty that the foregoing types of expression are or will remain the only ones that are without First Amendment protection.... The use of these traditional legal categories is preferable to the sort of ad hoc balancing that the Court henceforth must perform in every case if the analysis here used becomes our standard test.

As a practical matter, perhaps we will interpret the compelling interest in cases involving content regulation so that the results become parallel to the historic categories I have discussed, although an enterprise such as today's tends not to remain *pro forma* but to take on a life of its own. When we leave open the possibility that various sorts of content regulations are appropriate, we discount the value of our precedents and invite experiments that in fact present clear violations of the First Amendment, as is true in the case before us.

To forgo the compelling interest test in cases involving direct content-based burdens on speech would not, of course, eliminate the need for difficult judgments respecting First Amendment issues. Among the questions we cannot avoid the necessity of deciding are: whether the restricted expression falls within one of the unprotected categories; whether some other constitutional right is impaired; whether, in the case of a regulation of activity which combines expressive with nonexpressive elements, the regulation aims at the activity or the expression; whether the regulation restricts speech itself or only the time, place, or manner of speech; and whether the regulation is in fact content-based or content-neutral. However difficult the lines may be to draw in some cases, here the answer to each of these questions is clear.

The case before us presents the opportunity to adhere to a surer test for content-based cases and to avoid using an unnecessary formulation, one with the capacity to weaken central protections of the First Amendment. I would recognize this opportunity to confirm our past holdings and to rule that the New York statute amounts to raw censorship based on content, censorship forbidden by the text of the First Amendment and well-settled principles protecting speech and the press. That ought to end the matter.

With these observations, I concur in the judgment of the Court holding the statute invalid.

REPORT ON DECLINING
STATE AID FOR THE POOR
December 11, 1991

Financially hard-pressed state governments cut programs for the poor more sharply during 1991 than at any time since the early 1980s, according to a report issued December 11 by two nonprofit study groups—the Center on Budget and Policy Priorities, in Washington, D.C., and the Center for the Study of the States, in Albany, New York. The report, entitled "The States and the Poor," focused on how state tax and spending decisions affected income support, medical care, and housing assistance for needy families and individuals. With few exceptions, the aid programs weakened by previous cutbacks were drained even further in 1991.

A nationwide economic recession delivered a double blow to state governments, retarding tax revenues and leaving more people jobless, sometimes homeless, and in need of assistance. A survey taken by the National Conference of State Legislatures in May 1991 revealed that two-thirds of the state governments faced deficits totaling $30 billion, forcing them to raise taxes or cut spending. Although most did some of each, popular resistance to higher taxation often resulted in deep slashes in welfare budgets.

According to the report, the value of benefits offered through the Aid to Families with Dependent Children program had fallen 42 percent since 1970 and was expected to decline further in 1991. General cash assistance programs were subject to the deepest cuts of all. Those programs primarily assist very poor single individuals and childless couples who are not elderly—typically persons who are temporarily disabled or awaiting a determination of whether they qualify for Social Security assistance.

Of thirty state-funded general assistance programs (in Michigan), one *was eliminated, fourteen suffered funding cuts, while thirteen others could not raise benefits to stay abreast of inflation. In Michigan, about 82,000 people lost their benefits. Emergency cash assistance programs—often a device of last resort to avert homelessness—were reduced in twelve states. Ten of twenty-nine state programs providing emergency housing of the homeless were pared back. Funding for those and other state affordable housing programs shrank by $246 million nationally, about one-fifth below the 1990 level of spending.*

The report's authors were the directors of the two study centers, Robert Greenstein in Washington and Steven D. Gold in Albany. Their coauthors were Isaac Shapiro, Mark Sheft, Julie Strawn, and Laura Summers, all in Washington. The writers applauded the efforts of some states to maintain support of assistance programs at or slightly above previous levels. But they deplored the decisions of other states to cut benefits for the poor more deeply than other services or to raise taxes to prevent such cuts.

> *Following are excerpts from the report entitled, "The States and the Poor," issued December 11, 1991, by the Center on Budget and Policy Priorities, in Washington, D.C., and the Center for the Study of the States, in Albany, New York:*

In 1991, states confronted their most serious fiscal crisis since the recessions of the early 1980s. The economic downturn both depressed revenue and increased the demand for services, aggravating state budget problems. Rising health care, prison, and education costs added to state budget problems. Rising health care, prison, and education costs added to state fiscal woes. According to a May 1991 survey by the National Conference of State Legislatures, prospective state deficits for fiscal year 1992 totaled more than $30 billion.

This study describes how poor people fared in the state tax and spending decisions made in 1991. These decisions primarily affected fiscal year 1992 state budgets, which typically began in July 1991. The report focuses on four important areas: income support, medical care, housing assistance, and tax policy.

In general, the policy choices states made in 1991 hit poor people hard. States cut programs for the poor more sharply than in any year since at least the early 1980s.

- Benefits in the Aid to Families with Dependent Children program were reduced more than in any year since at least 1981, with 40 states freezing or cutting benefits.
- States made cuts in general cash assistance programs that will affect nearly half a million people, about one-third of all GA [General Assistance] recipients nationwide. In some states, such as Michigan,

the cuts were especially deep and involved termination of benefits for large numbers of indigent people who are now eligible for no monthly cash aid from any level of government.

- Twelve states cut special needs payments and/or emergency cash assistance programs, which are designed in part to avert homelessness, while 10 of the 26 states that appropriate funds for low-income housing reduced these programs. Many of these reductions involved cuts of 20 percent to 100 percent.
- Most of the states that raised taxes in 1991 did so in a regressive manner, taking a larger share of income from the poor than from those at higher income levels.

These cuts come at a time when poverty is rising sharply. Between 1989 and 1990, the number of poor people in the United States rose two million; a still larger increase is expected in 1991. The cuts are especially biting because they coincide with a recession, precisely the time when the safety net is needed most. During recessions, jobs are scarce, and opportunities for upward mobility are diminished. Even many formerly middle-class people may have little choice but to rely on government assistance. A recession is not a time when the poorest and least skilled individuals can readily find employment. In such an economy, cutbacks in the safety net are certain to lead to increased hardship and even to homelessness.

Cash assistance programs for low-income people constitute only a small fraction of state expenditures—five percent nationwide. Nevertheless, in many states, low-income households were hit substantially harder than people at other income levels, losing more in benefits and also contributing a large share of their income in increased taxes.

Income Assistance

The most momentous state decisions affecting low-income people occurred in the area of cash assistance.

Aid to Families with Dependent Children

States determine benefit levels in the AFDC program, which assists families with children. At the start of 1991, AFDC was already providing far less support than in the past. Since 1970, the maximum benefit for a family of three with no other income had fallen 42 percent in the typical state, after adjusting for inflation. State actions in 1991 accelerated deterioration of AFDC benefits.

- In 40 states, the purchasing power of AFDC benefits declined in fiscal year 1992. (This figure includes the District of Columbia, which is counted as a state in this report.) Basic AFDC benefit levels have kept pace with or exceeded inflation in only 11 states this year.
- Nine states cut basic benefits below previous levels. Michigan cut benefits for families with no other income by 13 percent during winter months (and by six percent for the year as a whole). In California, benefits will fall 21 percent in purchasing power over a five-year

period. Tennessee, despite one of the lowest payment levels in the nation, cut benefits five percent and is considering an additional 15 percent reduction.

- An additional 31 states froze AFDC benefits. In these states, the benefits will lose further ground to inflation.

The net effect is the largest state-level reduction in AFDC in at least a decade. In the 10 years from 1981 to 1990, an average of 1.5 states cut benefits each year (compared to nine in 1991), and an average of 25 states either cut or froze benefits (compared to 40 this year). During this same period, an average of 26 states raised AFDC benefits each year, compared to 11 this year. Even during the recession of the early 1980s, the number of states cutting or freezing benefits was much lower than in 1991.

Special Needs and Emergency Assistance Programs

States may also make payments to cover "special needs" of AFDC recipients. These payments are often used to help prevent families from becoming homeless. Five of the 32 states with special needs payments reduced their programs in 1991, with the cuts being largely in California, Michigan, and Massachusetts. California cut a special needs program designed to prevent homelessness among AFDC families by 35 percent even though its cuts in AFDC benefits could place more families at risk of homelessness. Michigan, which cut AFDC benefits more deeply than any other state, terminated all special needs payment including those to pregnant women. Massachusetts ended special needs payments to help AFDC children buy winter coats and other clothing at the start of the school year.

Some states also run emergency assistance programs designed to provide short-term cash aid to households in crisis. States can restrict these programs to AFDC families only, or they can assist non-AFDC recipients as well. Emergency assistance payments are used for such purchases as preventing eviction by paying rent arrears, preventing utility shut-offs by paying utility bills past-due, or enabling homeless families to move to an apartment.

- Ten states cut emergency assistance programs in 1991. Michigan cut its program by one-third. Massachusetts eliminated $47 million in emergency aid to AFDC families and general assistance recipients. Ohio eliminated its program for GA recipients.
- Five states established new emergency assistance programs or expanded existing ones. With the exception of a $15 million expansion in New Jersey, however, these expansions were quite small.

General Cash Assistance

General assistance is the program of last resort for non-elderly poor people who do not qualify for AFDC or Supplemental Security Income. Typically, general assistance helps single individuals or childless couples who are not elderly, including individuals who are temporarily disabled or who are awaiting a determination of whether they are sufficiently disabled to qualify for SSI. These programs are funded entirely with state funds, local funds, or a combination of the two. No federal standards apply.

The 30 state-funded general assistance programs were hit harder in 1991 than any other set of low-income programs. Fourteen states cut their programs, often extremely deeply. In another 13 states, benefits were frozen and declined in purchasing power. Only three states with extremely small general assistance programs raised benefits.

- *Michigan* terminated its program, ending all monthly cash assistance to 82,000 people.
- *Ohio* slashed its program in half, reducing the maximum benefit for most single individuals to $100 a month—17 percent of the poverty line—and limiting benefits to six months in a 12-month period.
- *Massachusetts* is cutting at least 10,000 recipients from its roll.
- *Illinois* enacted reductions that could eliminate benefits for as many as 80,000 to 90,000 people for part of the year.
- *Minnesota* dropped 6,000 recipients from its program.

Altogether, the general assistance cuts affect nearly half a million people, over one-third of all general assistance recipients nationwide. Some of these recipients had their benefits reduced. Others lost all benefits, while some face the prospect of losing their benefits next year if they remain on the program for more than a specified number of months. Most of these people are unlikely to qualify for any other type of cash assistance from the government.

Supplemental Security Income

The SSI program provides cash assistance to poor individuals and couples who are elderly, blind, or disabled. The basic federal SSI grant leaves beneficiaries well below the poverty line. Consequently, 27 states provide supplemental SSI benefits. Unlike the federal grant, very few states index SSI supplemental benefits to inflation.

While failure to update these benefits for inflation has been widespread, benefit reductions have not been.

- This pattern changed in fiscal year 1991 as five states cut their SSI benefits. Four states cut these supplements in fiscal year 1992. Michigan slashed its benefits 54 percent this year, reducing assistance to elderly couples by $300 per year.
- Twenty states froze their SSI supplements in fiscal year 1992, which have declined in purchasing power as a result.
- Three states increased their supplements in fiscal year 1992, but in two states these increases simply restored part of large SSI cuts made the previous year.

Health Programs

The largest reductions in low-income health assistance resulted from the cuts made in general cash assistance programs. Twenty-seven states fund medical assistance programs for low-income residents who receive cash assistance from the state but do not qualify for Medicaid. These programs primarily aid general assistance recipients.

- In 10 states, the elimination of various categories of people from general cash assistance programs meant that some or all of these people lost eligibility for general medical assistance as well. For example, Michigan eliminated general medical assistance for all 82,000 poor people terminated from its general assistance program.
- In addition, eight states made specific cuts to their general medical assistance programs. For example, Illinois and Maryland eliminated all coverage for both inpatient and outpatient hospital services for GA recipients.

Changes in the Medicaid program were mixed. Some states reduced the program, while others expanded it. Some states cut one part of Medicaid but enlarged another. On the cutback side:

- Many individuals who were dropped from AFDC rolls as a result of the AFDC reductions lost Medicaid coverage as well.
- Five states—Florida, Kansas, Maine, Montana, and Oregon—eliminated or made cuts in the "Medically Needy" component of Medicaid, which assists certain low-income households who are not on AFDC or SSI and have large medical bills.
- Sixteen states eliminated or restricted coverage for some Medicaid services. Ten states scaled back prescription drug benefits. Five states reduced coverage for home health assistance. Some states also raised or instituted co-payments.

On the expansion side:

- Eleven states expanded Medicaid eligibility, with eight extending coverage to more near-poor pregnant women and infants.
- Some 20 states expanded services, with the most common action being expanded coverage for prenatal services for pregnant women.

This mixed Medicaid record may change sharply in the coming year. While Medicaid costs continue to grow rapidly, various "bootstrap" financing mechanisms that many states used to help fund their Medicaid programs in fiscal 1992 have been restricted, starting in fiscal year 1993, by a federal law enacted this November. With this funding stream restricted, states may enact deeper program cuts in the coming year.

Housing Programs

For fiscal year 1992, state funding for emergency housing assistance for the homeless fell $43 million, despite likely increases in the homeless population due to both the recession and some of the more severe state budget cuts.

- Ten of the 29 states with emergency housing programs for the homeless cut these programs, with five states cutting their programs more than 30 percent.
- Three of these five states—California, the District of Columbia, and Massachusetts—were states that also made significant cuts in AFDC, general assistance, or both. For example, California, which instituted sizable AFDC reductions, cut its homeless assistance program $22 million, or 35 percent. The District of Columbia cut its homeless housing assistance program $12 million, or 43 percent. Massachusetts sliced $47 million from its emergency assistance program, as noted above.
- Michigan and Ohio, two of the states making the deepest GA cuts, reduced their homeless programs 14 percent and 23 percent, respectively.

Ten states increased the amount spent on these programs. Most of the increase occurred in New Jersey and New York. The average increase in the other eight states amounted to a little over $1 million per state.

State programs to help low and moderate income households secure affordable housing were reduced substantially. Some 26 states appropriate funds for such programs, which include efforts to provide rental assistance to low-income households, facilitate homeownership, and promote new construction or rehabilitation of affordable housing.

- Overall, state affordable housing programs were but $246 million this year, or 22 percent.
- Ten of the 26 states reduced their affordable housing appropriations. Eight states cut their programs 20 percent or more.
- Ten states increased their budgets, but these increases tended to be quite small. The average increase in these 10 states was $3 million, while in the states that cut their appropriations, the average reduction was $27 million.

Tax Policy

While poor households in many states are being made poorer by program cuts, their taxes generally increased. Not only did state program cuts often hit the poor harder than other groups, but new taxes often hit the poor hardest as well.

This outcome reflects the traditional sources of revenue upon which states rely. The sales tax is the largest generator of state tax revenue. The sales tax is a tax on consumption, which is regressive because the percentage of income that households spend on consumption goods tends to decline as income rises. The one major tax that is progressive is the personal income tax; it typically takes a larger share of income from wealthy households than from poor or middle-income households. Income taxes, however, usually account for well under half of state tax revenues.

Among the 14 states that raised taxes the most for fiscal year 1992, only Connecticut and Rhode Island raised taxes in a clearly progressive manner. They relied primarily on income tax increases. By contrast, Nevada, New Hampshire, and Texas relied almost entirely on regressive taxes. Other states generally combined regressive and progressive taxes, but in most of them the net effect was regressive.

In addition to these 14 states, another 20 states raised taxes by smaller amounts. Their tax increases were overwhelmingly regressive.

Most states have recognized the impact of taxes on the poor by establishing programs that partially shield low-income households from taxation. Some states have followed the example of the federal government and eliminated income tax liability for working poor families, while others provide targeted relief through tax credits that reduce the burden of the local property tax, the sales tax, or the income tax.

This year, six states chose to provide new or expanded tax relief for poor families. On the other hand, three states reduced low-income tax relief programs. There is some overlap here, since two states reduced some relief programs while expanding others.

While the net effect of state tax changes made for fiscal year 1992 was regressive, the number of states incorporating progressive elements in their tax increases was larger than in most years in the recent past. In addition, targeted tax relief for poor households continued to grow in popularity among the states.

Different States, Different Choices

Eight states stand out for the depth and breadth of the cuts they instituted. Of these states, Michigan and Massachusetts made the most dramatic reductions. Both states instituted these cuts even though their unemployment rates stood at about nine percent, making it extremely difficult for poor people to make up the lost income through greater earnings.

- *Michigan* terminated both cash and medical assistance for approximately 82,000 general assistance recipients. It reduced basic AFDC benefits by 13 percent. eliminated all special needs payments for AFDC families—including a winter heating allowance and special needs payments for pregnant women—and cut by one-third the crisis assistance payments it provides to help AFDC families avoid utility shut-offs. The state also slashed SSI state supplements to the elderly poor more than 50 percent.
- *Massachusetts* cut its general assistance program by $56 million; at least 10,000 recipients will lose general cash and medical assistance. The state eliminated emergency assistance payments for GA clients, while sharply scaling back emergency aid for AFDC families. It also slashed its affordable housing program by $134 million.

Cuts in low-income programs were also deep in California, Maryland,

Ohio, Illinois, Maine, and the District of Columbia. Most of these eight states faced large budget deficits, but other states with deficits of a comparable size followed a less severe course.

The states that made the deepest cuts tended to be states with stronger-than-average safety nets. At the same time, however, these states tend to have above-average living costs. In addition, other states with stronger-than-average safety nets chose not to make cuts of this magnitude.

Some states were able to close large budget deficits while largely shielding the poor. For example, Pennsylvania faced a deficit equal to 19 percent of the state budget, but closed the deficit without cutting any of the programs examined here. In addition, nearly half of the tax increase Pennsylvania adopted came from the personal income tax; about one-fourth of the tax increase did come from clearly regressive measures, but these were accompanied by some low-income tax relief. Finally, Pennsylvania made some program expansions in the health area. Texas and Vermont are two other states that faced large deficits but chose deficit reduction measures that affected the poor less harshly than the policies of many other states.

The Overall Impact

The reductions states made in low-income programs predominantly affect those with little or no income besides their government support—that is, the poorest of the poor. By contrast, the large federal budget cuts in low-income programs enacted in 1981 primarily affected poor and near-poor families who worked or had other income besides their government assistance. It is likely the state cuts enacted this year in low-income programs will hit the very poor more sharply than any round of either federal or state cuts in recent memory, including the 1981 federal budget cuts.

Data are not available to conduct a detailed analysis across all states of how deficit reduction burdens were distributed among various income groups. It appears evident, however, that the poor shouldered a larger share of deficit reduction than other groups in some identifiable respects. The majority of states raised taxes that take a larger share of income from the poor than from those with higher incomes. Moreover, in states where general assistance and AFDC benefits were cut significantly, recipients of these programs are almost certain to have lost a larger share of their income than any other group.

Implications for the Future

It is entirely possible that poor households will be hit again in 1992—and hit substantially in a number of states. With the economy remaining weak, many states that believed they had balanced their fiscal year 1992 budget now find they face a deficit. Several states have already responded by instituting a second round of cuts, including cuts in programs for the poor. For example, Florida, Maryland, Arkansas, and Washington have recently instituted cuts in basic low-income programs. In addition, Tennessee's governor has proposed a 15 percent AFDC cut that would drop benefits to $157 a month, 17 percent of the poverty line, for a mother and two children with no other income. In California, the governor has proposed a 25 percent cut for families on AFDC at least six months as well as other AFDC and SSI reductions.

In addition, Maine's governor has proposed terminating general assistance; Maryland's governor has proposed terminating benefits for half the GA caseload and ending an emergency assistance program; and the New York Senate leadership has called for limiting GA benefits for nearly half of current recipients to 60 days out of the year. In the next few months, various states are expected either to call special legislative sessions to consider additional cuts or to institute such cuts by executive action.

The state fiscal picture for fiscal year 1993 is similarly bleak. State deficit forecasts for 1993 resemble those issued a year ago for 1992. Further deficit reduction measures will have to be adopted in many states.

Tax increases will be considerably tougher to pass in 1992, an election year, than in 1991. If taxes will play a smaller role in balancing budgets in 1992, program cuts will loom larger. In this environment, further cuts in programs serving the poor, a politically weak constituency, may appeal to policymakers.

States can, however, choose to approach deficit-reduction with an eye towards ensuring that those with the lowest incomes and those affected most severely by the recession do not bear excessive burdens. This is possible in part because many low-income programs constitute a small proportion of state budgets. For example, there are only four states where the total costs for all cash assistance programs for low-income people exceed six percent of the state budget.

In addition, tax increases should not automatically be ruled out. The vast majority of states did not increase taxes significantly in 1991; only a dozen boosted taxes by an amount equal to at least five percent of total state revenue. States electing to raise taxes can do so in ways that shield the poor. For example, states can choose to raise income taxes primarily or entirely on high income individuals, a course several states followed this year. If states rely more heavily on increases in regressive taxes, they can accompany these tax hikes with expanded tax relief provisions for low- and moderate-income households.

States can also follow a budget principle established at the federal level in recent years. After cutting programs for the poor substantially in the early 1980s, federal policymakers reached a general consensus these cuts had gone far enough (or too far, in some cases) and that further reductions would not be acceptable. From 1983 on, the federal government made few further reductions in major benefit programs for the poor. In fact, the Gramm-Rudman-Hollings law specifically exempts most major low-income benefit programs from the across-the-board cuts it triggers when deficit targets are breached.

Of course, federal policymakers could themselves play a much more constructive role in addressing state budget crises. Sharp federal cuts in grants to states and localities have contributed to state budget problems. The failure of the federal government to provide more anti-recession assistance has shifted more of that burden to states, as well.

Whether or not the federal government plays a more constructive role, however, the key policy decisions on how to balance state budgets remain in the states' hands. States establish their fiscal priorities. These priorities can reflect a commitment to protecting their poorest residents from large cuts or significant tax increases—or they can plunge those whose incomes already fail to meet society's standard for a minimum level of subsistence still deeper into poverty. . . .

Cuts Tended to Hit the Very Poor

Many of the state program cuts examined here squarely hit the poorest of the poor. The large federal budget cuts in low-income programs enacted in 1981 primarily affected poor and near-poor families with some income besides their government assistance; the working poor were the principal target of these reductions. By contrast, the cuts passed by states this year predominantly affect those with little or no income other than their government support. It is likely the state cuts enacted in low-income programs this year will hit the very poor more sharply than any round of either state or federal cuts in recent memory, including the 1981 federal budget reductions.

The new state budget cuts in low-income programs are especially biting because of the recession. With unemployment rates remaining high, low-income people whose benefits are terminated or reduced have limited opportunities to make up for this income loss by increasing their earnings. Michigan provides a particularly vivid example. More than 80,000 individuals, many of whom would have trouble finding employment in a booming economy, were dropped from general assistance rolls and told to find employment despite a state unemployment rate of about nine percent.

The large cuts made in state programs to prevent homelessness or to assist those already homeless warrant particular attention. Coming at a time when the economy is placing hundreds of thousands of people at increased risk of homelessness, these cutbacks diminish the nation's ability to respond to this problem.

Did Poor Households Bear a Disproportionate Share of the Deficit Reduction Burden?

Data are not available to conduct a detailed analysis across all states of how deficit reduction burdens were distributed among various income groups. It appears evident, however, that the poor shouldered a larger share of deficit reduction than other groups in some identifiable respects. The majority of states increased regressive taxes in 1991; these taxes take a larger share of income from the poor than from those in other income strata. Moreover, in states where general assistance and AFDC benefits were cut significantly, recipients of these programs are almost certain to have lost a larger share of their income than other groups. (The one exception to this rule would be state employees who lost their jobs.)

Some data on the distribution of deficit reduction burdens are available for one state, California. In the nation's largest state, AFDC families contributed a much larger share of their income to deficit reduction than any group of non-poor households.

- The incomes of most AFDC families in California will fall 6.7 percent in purchasing power in the 1991-1992 fiscal year, when both benefit cuts and tax increases are taken into account.
- By contrast, the wealthiest one percent of Californians are contributing an average of 1.6 percent of their income to deficit reduction.

Further Cutbacks Likely in 1992

Unfortunately, it is likely the harsh state policies of 1991 will continue in 1992. Despite budget-balancing measures adopted earlier this year, the two largest states—California and New York—project fiscal year 1992 deficits of $3 billion and $875 million, respectively. New York is currently contemplating cuts in Medicaid and general assistance that may total more than $1 billion. Numerous other states that believed they had balanced their fiscal year 1992 budgets now find they, too, face sizable deficits. Some states have already instituted further cuts, including new reductions in programs for the poor. Arkansas and Washington have scaled back some Medicaid services. Maryland implemented major cuts in AFDC and general assistance on December 1. Florida adopted large reductions in AFDC, emergency assistance, and Medicaid in a special legislative session that ended December 13.

Moreover, the recent cuts in these four states could be just the top of the iceberg. In recent weeks, a series of new proposal have surfaced that are stunning in their harshness. Tennessee's governor has proposed a further 15 percent AFDC cut that would reduce benefits for a mother and two children with no other cash income to $157 a month, one-sixth of the poverty line. In California, the governor has proposed a 10 percent AFDC benefit cut, followed by an additional 15 percent cut once a family has been on AFDC six months. The governor has also proposed terminating benefits for first-time pregnant women, reducing SSI state supplements over time, scaling back Medicaid coverage for low-income elderly and disabled people who are not on SSI but have high medical bills, and repealing the requirement that California counties run GA programs providing monthly cash assistance payments to indigent people not eligible for AFDC or SSI.

In addition, Maine's governor has proposed terminating general assistance entirely, while Maryland's governor has called for ending general assistance for half the caseload, terminating emergency assistance for GA recipients as well, and restructuring AFDC in ways that may cause sharp reductions in benefits for some families. The New York Senate has proposed limiting general assistance benefits for nearly half of its caseload to 60 days out of the year.

The state fiscal situation for fiscal year 1993 also is bleak. As governors and legislators prepare to work on their 1993 budgets, the deficit forecasts they are receiving sound ominously similar to those issued a year ago for fiscal 1992. In Massachusetts, a $1.6 billion shortfall is expected. In California, the combined deficit for the remainder of the current fiscal year and the new fiscal year starting July 1, 1992 is projected at $5 billion to $8 billion. When governors unveil their FY 1993 budgets in coming weeks, additional proposals for cuts in programs for the poor are likely to be offered in some states.

The two most important factors accounting for the dismal fiscal outlook are the economy and the Medicaid program. Weak economic growth results in stagnant revenue. The recession has cost states more than $10 billion annually in lost revenue and higher costs for social programs. Meanwhile, Medicaid is growing explosively, at more than a 20 percent annual rate. The "bootstrap" financing mechanisms in many states adopted to help finance Medicaid have now been restricted as a result of new federal legislation. This action diminishes the availability of a fiscal vehicle that states have increasingly relied upon to help balance their budgets without making still deeper reductions in programs.

These are not the only causes of budget woes. Prison spending, especially to fight the drug war, is increasing at a double digit rate in many states, and school enrollments are growing about one percent annually (and considerably more rapidly in some places). Courts are mandating higher spending for many programs, including mental health, corrections, and Medicaid. It is no wonder most states have deficit problems.

In 1992, tax increases will be considerably tougher to pass than in 1991. This is true for three reasons. First, it is an election year, and governors and legislators prefer to raise taxes after elections rather than shortly before them. Second, many families have lower real income than when the recession began, making them more resistant to tax increases. Finally, anti-incumbent fever has made elected officials more concerned than usual about voter anger; in this environment, state officials may be especially reluctant to support higher taxes.

If taxes play a smaller role in balancing budgets, program cutbacks will loom larger, as will one-shot measures that postpone difficult budget choices until after the election. (Such measures include the deferral of payments to suppliers and aid to local governments, acceleration of tax revenue, asset sales, loans from state accounts with "excess" funds, and reduction of pension fund contributions.)

In this environment, cutbacks in programs for the poor may appeal to many state policymakers. Not only do the poor lack the political clout of other groups, but it is possible some states will find it more acceptable politically to cut such programs now that other states have done so.

States Can Shield the Poor

States can, however, choose to shield the poor from further cuts. The events of the past year show that various states have followed different courses in determining whether to protect their poor residents. Some have approached deficit-reduction with an eye toward ensuring that those with the lowest incomes—and those hit hard by the recession—did not bear excessive burdens. Other states can also follow this approach.

On the program side, some states reduced large deficits without cutting deeply into low-income assistance. This is feasible because the low-income programs represent a small proportion of state budgets. AFDC expenditures make up five percent or more of state expenditures in only two states. Even when expenditures for other cash assistance programs such as general assistance and SSI supplements are added in, there are only four states where total costs for cash assistance programs for low-income people exceed six percent of the state budget.

States can use a combination of program cuts and revenue increases to balance their budgets. Contrary to popular impression, the vast majority of states did not increase taxes significantly for fiscal 1992. The state tax increases passed this year are estimated to total about $14 billion. While this has been described as the largest state tax increase in any year, that is misleading for two reasons:

- Approximately two-thirds of the total revenue increase occurred in California and Pennsylvania. In most other states, tax increases were relatively small. Only 12 states boosted taxes by an amount equal to as much as five percent of their total revenues. In short, most states had either modest tax increases or no tax increases at all.
- When measured as a proportion of total state tax revenues, the tax increases enacted nationwide were of about the same magnitude as the tax increases passed in state legislative sessions in 1983—and about half as large as those passed in 1971.

States that choose to raise taxes in the coming year can consider several different types of progressive tax packages. They can rely primarily on the progressive personal income tax to raise revenues, particularly through income tax increases aimed at those in the top brackets. Alternatively, if states rely more heavily on increases in regressive taxes, they can accompany such tax hikes with expanded tax relief provisions for low- or low- and moderate-income households, as five states did in 1991. Establishment or enlargement of state earned income credits, sales tax credits, and circuit breakers are options that warrant consideration.

Recent federal policies provide other examples of how deficits can be reduced while protecting those with the lowest incomes. In 1985, when Congress passed the Gramm-Rudman-Hollings Balanced Budget Act, it included a provision exempting most basic benefit programs for the poor from the across-the-board cuts triggered under the Act when deficit targets are missed. AFDC, SSI, food stamps, Medicaid, WIC, and child nutrition programs are exempt from the across-the-board cuts.

In addition, the federal budget reduction accord enacted in the fall of 1990 contained nearly $500 billion in deficit reduction measures over five years but managed to shield all major low-income benefit programs from cuts (and actually expanded Medicaid). Furthermore, the regressive gasoline, alcohol, and tobacco tax increases in the budget package were accompanied by a large increase in the federal earned income tax credit—so that the net effect on low-income households, as a group, was a slight reduction in tax burdens.

The 1990 federal budget agreement also illustrated one other point—how important it would be for state policymakers to have access to data showing the impact on households at different income levels of various tax increase or benefit reduction proposals. Such data played a critical role in the federal budget negotiations in 1990—and were responsible in significant part for major changes made during the budget negotiation process that led to more significant tax increases on the very wealthy (rather than on the middle-class and the poor) and to the inclusion of various provisions protecting these at low- and moderate-income levels. By contrast, few states had such data this year. State efforts to build the capacity to provide such data on a timely manner when deficit reduction measures are being considered, especially measures to raise revenues, would be very useful and could help lead to more balanced policies.

Implications for Federal Policy and Federalism

If federal policies are to be cited as any type of example, it should be noted that federal policies themselves have contributed in no small way to the state fiscal crisis. Over the past decade, the federal government has managed simultaneously to pursue policies greatly swelling the federal deficit and thereby weakening the national economy, while also cutting deeply into federal support for state and local governments. Federal grants to state and local governments, excluding grants for entitlements passed through to individuals in programs such as AFDC and Medicaid, fell 34 percent from fiscal year 1980 to fiscal year 1991, after adjustment for inflation. This has made it considerably more difficult for states to balance their budgets and meet the needs of their citizens.

In addition, with the federal budget deficit expected to surpass $350 billion in the current fiscal year, the federal government has largely foresworn the countercyclical measures typically used to "prime the pump" during recessions. The extension of unemployment benefits is the one exception to this pattern, and it came more than a year after the recession started—and only after the number of jobless workers exhausting regular unemployment benefits, without being able to receive any further unemployment assistance, reached its highest level in at least 40 years. Even with the additional unemployment benefits recently enacted, the unemployment insurance system remains significantly weaker than in previous recessions. And while the federal government may take some further actions to boost the economy in 1992, these are more likely to take the form of tax cuts (including tax cuts of dubious economic merit that would primarily benefit upper-income taxpayers and could increase the federal deficit over the long term) rather than countercyclical aid to hard-pressed state and local governments.

One lesson emerging from the painful budget crises in state capitals across the nation is that federal policies can have profound consequences on other levels of government. Of course, in a number of states, the fiscal crises reflect significant structural problems in state budgets themselves, as well as the effects of the recession and flawed federal policies.

Another lesson involving the federal government can be drawn. If poor households are to be shielded from deep cuts that can cause destitution and even homelessness, federal standards—accompanied by the requisite financial resources—are necessary. Such standards and the accompanying financing can be found in the food stamp program and the basic federal benefit structure in SSI. In addition, federal standards regarding AFDC coverage for two-parent families and Medicaid coverage for pregnant women, infants, and young children have led to increases in coverage for these groups in recent years and protected these groups from losing AFDC or Medicaid eligibility in state budget cuts this year. Furthermore, a federal law that threatens to terminate federal Medicaid matching funds if a state cuts AFDC benefits below the state's May 1988 benefit level may have helped prevent some states from instituting even deeper AFDC reductions than those already made.

In the current political atmosphere, however, the federal government seems unlikely to come forth with increased federal financing for these programs. As a result, a move toward stronger national standards is improbable. A case can be made for a realignment of federal and state roles in which the federal government assumes responsibility for a larger share of AFDC and Medicaid costs and establishes stronger national standards in these areas, while turning over to states (and reducing or ending federal financing for) a range of other, primarily non-low income programs. But such a case has been made before, and a realignment of this nature is not on the immediate political horizon.

In short, many of the most significant decisions regarding support for low-income people remain firmly in state hand. In 1992, many states will face decisions of profound importance to low-income families and individuals.

The roles played in this drama by the recession and by shortcomings in federal policy do not absolve states of responsibility for these decisions. States set their own budget priorities. These priorities can reflect a commitment to protecting their poorest residents from large cuts or significant tax increases—or they can plunge those whose incomes already fail to meet society's standard for a minimum level of subsistence still deeper into poverty.

EUROPEAN UNION TREATY
FOR A COMMON CURRENCY
December 11, 1991

Eleven of the twelve member nations of the European Community (EC) agreed December 11 to adopt a single currency and create a central bank by the end of the decade. Marks, francs, lire, pesetas, and the like—even pounds, if the holdout British later agreed—would give way to a European currency unit, or ecu for short. The intent was to create a truly common market. The countries previously committed themselves, beginning in 1993, to lifting all remaining restrictions on goods crossing their common borders. With a combined population of 328 million, the EC would form the world's largest trading bloc.

In closing a two-day summit at Maastricht in the Netherlands, several of the attending national leaders viewed the agreement as a historic milestone on the road to eventual economic and political union. President François Mitterrand of France called the treaty the most important agreement in Europe since the 1957 Treaty of Rome created a common market. "A great power is being born, one at least as strong commercially, industrially, and financially as the United States and Japan," he said.

German chancellor Helmut Kohl, a key figure in winning support for the treaty, said he was sure "a federally structured Europe" was in the making. "We have made enormous progress," he added. Germany's commitment to European unity pleased the countries that had feared that the unification of East and West Germany might revive German nationalism, as was witnessed in two world wars. France sought to speed up the timetable for political and economic integration to anchor Germany firmly within the European community. In accepting the new monetary agree-

ment, Germany would give up the mark, the strongest currency in Europe.

At Rome in 1957 the governments of France, West Germany, Italy, Belgium, the Netherlands, and Luxembourg laid the foundations for a common market, formally the European Economic Community, or EEC. Over the years Great Britain, Denmark, Ireland, Spain, Portugal, and Greece joined. In recent years the list of membership seekers grew longer; it included Norway, Sweden, Finland, Switzerland, Poland, Czechoslovakia, Hungary, and Turkey.

While the EEC was being enlarged, it and two similar European "communities"—one for coal and steel, and the other for atomic energy—were merged in 1967 to form the EC. With the merger came the development of a communitywide political structure. It included the creation of a European Parliament at Strasbourg, France; a European Commission, an executive arm, in Brussels; a policy-making Council of Ministers, whose presidency is rotated among the heads of member governments; and a European Court based in Luxembourg to arbitrate legal disputes between member countries.

EC's Political Centralization

The Maastrich agreement strengthened the EC's central authority, giving the community jurisdiction in areas such as industrial affairs, trade, environment, energy, tourism, and consumer protection but it left implementation to the national governments. In addition, the document created a political entity to be known as European Union for closer diplomatic cooperation in matters such as how to respond as a community to the Yugoslav civil war.

For the first time, the government leaders who met in Maastrich decided to work toward "the eventual framing of a common defense policy, which might in time lead to a common defense." That would be done by reviving an atrophied military pact known as the Western European Union, to which nine of the twelve members nominally belonged. The union could "elaborate and implement" community decisions on defense issues that were compatible with existing commitments to the North Atlantic Treaty Organization.

Britain Postpones Treaty Decision

Only Britain refused to sign the monetary pact, insisting on an "opt out" arrangement whereby the British Parliament would decide later whether to replace the pound with the ecu. Questions of yielding sovereignty to the EC long had troubled Britain, a member since 1973. At Maastrich, British prime minister John Major insisted that his country would stay out of an EC program for better working hours, minimum wages, and conditions of employment. And Major argued that the word "federal" in the draft treaty's preamble implied a loss of national sovereignty and persuaded his colleagues instead to endorse a goal of "ever closer union among the peoples of Europe."

However, Major appeared more cooperative than had Margaret

Thatcher, his predecessor, in earlier meetings. His position appeared to be based more on satisfying concerns within his Conservative party over the future fate of the pound sterling than on his personal views. British business generally was reported to favor full participation in Europe lest it be deprived of lucrative markets on the continent.

As agreed by the treaty signers, the EC would create a European Monetary Institute on January 1, 1994, as a precursor of a European Central Bank that would start operating no earlier than January 1, 1997. The bank would begin issuing the new common currency on or after January 1, 1999.

Following is a summary of major elements in a treaty to establish a single currency, issued by the European Community at Maastrich in the Netherlands December 11, 1991:

The EMU after Maastricht: Major elements of the Treaty

Economic and Monetary Union, which has been a political objective of the Community for more than 20 years, is now comprehensively laid down in the new Treaty which enters into force after ratification by the national Parliaments. The negotiations between governments lasted for about a year and took place in a very constructive climate with the active participation of all delegations including the UK (despite their reservations on EMU). The exercise has been a complex one, technically, intellectually and, of course, politically, but fortunately the groundwork was well prepared (Delors Report, etc.).

I. Monetary policy

1. ECB and ESCB

From the beginning of the negotiations, there has been agreement that in the final stage of EMU the Community will have a single monetary policy and a single currency—the ecu (leaving aside the UK reservations). This will require a new institution—the European Central Bank (ECB) which will form, together with the central banks of the Member States, the European System of Central Banks (ESCB). The ISCB will have as primary objective to maintain price stability. Without prejudice to this objective, it shall support the general economic policies in the Community. The ECB and the central banks of the Member States will be independent from instructions of governments of Member States and Community institutions.

2. National central banks

The central banks of the Member States are an integral part of the ESCB and act in accordance with the guidelines and instructions of the ECB. To the extent deemed possible and appropriate, the ECB shall have recourse to the central banks of the Member States to carry out the operations which are necessary to implement the monetary policy of the Community.

3. Decision-making bodies

The decision-making bodies of the ECB are the Governing Council and the Executive Board. The monetary policy of the Community will be formulated by the Governing Council, which is composed of the twelve Governors of the central banks of the Member States and of the members of the Executive Board. The Executive Board, consisting of the President of the ECB, the Vice-President and four other members, implements monetary policy and gives the necessary instructions to the national central banks. The term of office is 8 years for the members of the Executive Board and at least 5 years for the Governors.

4. Instruments of monetary policy

The ESCB will carry out open market and credit operations at its own discretion in order to pursue monetary policy. It may also impose *minimum* reserve requirements on credit institutions within limits to be specified by the Council (of Ministers). The ESCB's role in prudential supervision will be limited: it shall contribute to the smooth conduct of such policies and may offer advice on the scope and implementation of the relevant legislation. The ESCB Statutes include as enabling clause for more direct involvement in prudential supervision, but any such transfer of powers to the ECB requires a unanimity decision in the Council.

5. External monetary policy

Great care has been taken to find an adequate institutional balance with respect to the responsibility for exchange rate policy in Stage Three. A distinction has been made between, on the one side, formal agreements on an exchange rate system for the ecu vis-à-vis non-Community currencies, and on the other side—insofar as a formal exchange rate system does not exist—general orientations for the exchange rate policy. In both cases, the ultimate responsibility stays with the "political" authorities of the Community, in particular the Council. However, the ECB is protected against undue interference with its monetary policy in both cases by adequate references to the objective of price stability.

6. Inter-institutional cooperation and democratic accountability

The President of the Council and a member of the Commission may participate, without having the right to vote, in meetings of the Governing Council of the ECB. The President of the Council may submit a motion for deliberation to the Governing Council. Correspondingly, the President of the ECB will participate in Council meetings when matters of relevance for the ECB are discussed. The ECB will have to be consulted regarding any proposed legislation within its field of competence. It will be required to address an annual report to the other Community institutions, and the members of the Executive Board may be heard by the competant Committee of the European Parliament.

7. Financial provisions

The capital of the ECB is held by the national central banks in proportion to the individual countries' demographic and economic weight. The key is a weighted average of a country's share in population and GDP. The external foreign reserves of the national central banks are pooled at the ECB within certain limits. The sum of the seigniorage income of the ESCB as a whole is allocated to the national central banks according to the same key. The new Treaty does not affect the national practices with respect to the distribution of profits of the national central banks.

II. Economic policies

1. Coordination

In contrast to monetary policy, Member States will retain ultimate responsibility for non-monetary economic policies. They will, however, be required to conduct economic policies with a view to contribute to the achievement of the objectives of the Community, and to regard them as a matter of common concern. Economic policies will be coordinated at the Community level. For this purpose, the European Council will discuss a conclusion on the broad guidelines proposed by the Commission and the Council, before these guidelines are formally adopted by the Council as a recommendation to the Member States. The economic policies of the Member States will be monitored regularly against this background. In case economic policies are not consistent with the guidelines, the Council may address a specific recommendation to the Member State in question.

2. Budgetary policies

While each Member State remains responsible for its budgetary policy, the new Treaty reflects a long and thorough debate about safeguards against unsolid budgetary policies. Budgetary policies of Member States will be constrained by three rules:

- any extension of credit from the ECB or national central banks to public authorities will be prohibited; likewise, any privileged access of public authorities to the financial institutions will be banned;
- neither the Community nor any Member State will be liable for the commitments of any other Member State(s) (no bail-out);
- excessive government deficits shall be avoided.

It is up to the Council to decide after an overall assessment whether an excessive deficit exists. This decision is based on a recommendation from the Commission, whose task will be to monitor government finances with a view to identifying gross errors. The Commission shall in particular examine compliance with the budgetary discipline on the basis of two criteria:

- whether the government deficit exceeds 3 % of GDP and, if so, whether the ratio has not declined and has not come close to 3 % or, alternatively, whether the excess over 3 % is only exceptional and temporary;
- whether gross government debt exceeds 60 % of GDP and, if so, whether the debt ratio is not sufficiently diminishing and not approaching 60 % at a satisfactory pace.

In its report to the Council on a Member State which fails to pass this test, the Commission will also take into account all other relevant factors, including the size of the deficit relative to public investment and the medium-term economic situation and budgetary position of the Member State in question. When the Council has decided that an excessive deficit exists, it will address a recommendation to the Member State concerned, which may be made public after a while in case of non-respect. In a next step, the Council may prescribe measures for the reduction of the deficit. In case of non-compliance, it may impose or intensify one or more of the following sanctions:

- to require the Member State concerned to publish additional information before issuing bonds and securities;
- to invite the European Investment Bank to reconsider its lending policy towards the Member State concerned;
- to require the Member State concerned to make a non-interest-bearing deposit with the Community;
- to impose fines.

3. Financial assistance

The mutual balance of payments assistance according to Arts. 108 and 109 of the present Treaty will no longer be relevant for fully participating Member States, nor will it be available to them from the beginning of Stage Three. The new Treaty provides for a financial assistance facility for Member States which are threatened or hit by severe difficulties caused by exceptional occurrences beyond their control. The decision in the Council to grant such assistance requires unanimity except for natural disasters, where the Council acts by qualified majority.

III. Capital movements

The Treaty establishes the principle that all restrictions on the movement of capital between Member States and between Member States and third countries shall be prohibited. Restrictions vis-à-vis third countries are only possible in well-defined cases where unrestricted capital movements would invalidate measures taken in other policy areas (direct investment, establishment, provision of financial services, admission of securities to capital markets) or where capital movements would cause or threaten to cause serious difficulties for the operation of EMU.

IV. Transition

1. The European Monetary Institute

The second stage of EMU will begin on 1 January 1994. At this date, the European Monetary Institute (EMI) will be created. The EMI, which will have a President who is not a Governor of a national central bank, has as its basic tasks to strengthen the coordination of national monetary policies, to facilitate the use of the ecu and to oversee its development, and to prepare Stage Three. It may make recommendations to national central banks on the conduct of their monetary policies; it may make such recommendations public, acting unanimously. It shall also, at the latest before the end of 1996, specify the regulatory, organizational and logistical framework necessary for the ECB to perform its tasks from the first day of Stage Three. The EMI may hold and manage foreign exchange reserves as an agent for national central banks.

2. Other elements of Stage Two

The provisions on the coordination of economic policies including the setting of guidelines will be applicable as soon as the new Treaty is ratified. From the beginning of Stage Two, the following provisions will enter into force:

- the principle of free capital movements (Portugal and Greece may maintain existing restrictions for another 12 months);
- the ban on central bank overdrafts to public authorities and on privileged access to financial institutions;
- the no-bail-out rule;
- the monitoring of budget deficits and the possibility for the Council to decide that an excessive deficit exists and to address recommendations to the Member State in question. However, the unconditional ban over excessive deficits and the possibility to impose sanctions will only apply from the start of Stage Three.

During Stage Two, Member States will, as appropriate, have to start the process leading to the independence of their national central banks, so that their national legislation is compatible with the Statute of the ESCB when the ECB is established.

3. The passage to Stage Three

Having considered before the end of 1996 the state of convergence of the Member States and provided a majority of Member States pass a convergence test, the Council (meeting on this occasion in the composition of Heads of State or of Government) will decide on the basis of a qualified majority vote whether it is appropriate for the Community to move to the final stage of EMU and will, in the affirmative, set a date for the beginning of Stage Three. A country's convergence is examined in particular by reference to four criteria: rate of inflation close to the three best performers, sustainability of government financial position, successful participation in the narrow band of the EMS for at least two years, long-term interest rates close to the best-performers in terms of price stability.

Member States not participating form the start—provided that there are any—will be given a derogation which implies that the provisions on monetary policy and on sanctions with respect to excessive deficits do not apply to them. Specific rules will apply to the UK in case this Member State uses its right to abstain from EMU at the beginning of Stage Three. In case Denmark uses its right to have an exemption, the provisions on a derogation will apply. The UK and Denmark—in case they do not participate form the start—will not be included among the Member States when it is decided before the end of 1996 whether a majority passes the convergence test.

All central banks, including those not participating in the common monetary policy, will be members of the ESCB from the start of Stage Three. Likewise, all Governors will be members of the General Council of the ECB, which will be its third decision-making body and whose task will essentially be to contribute to the ESCB's tasks other than monetary policy in the strict sense.

If there is no decision at an earlier date, then 1 January 1999 will automatically become the starting date of the final stage. At this point in time, whichever Member States meet the convergence criteria (decided by qualified majority voting) will move forward to the final stage.

4. The ecu, single currency of the Community

The Treaty stipulates that the irrevocable fixing of exchange rates shall lead to the introduction of a single currency, the ecu. The present basket ecu has already become a major currency on the financial markets and has been stable vis-à-vis the strongest national currencies for a long time. Its stability will increase further in parallel with the achievement of greater convergence in the run-up to EMU. In order to add institutional strength, the new Treaty includes a provision that the present currency composition of the ecu basket will not be changed. This allows the present basket ecu to change into the final ecu of Stage Three without any disruption. At the start of Stage Three, the Council will adopt the definite conversion rates between their currencies and the rates at which the ecu will be substituted for these currencies.

The choice of the conversion rate of the ecu will by itself not modify the value of the ecu; in practical terms, this means that the prevailing market rate on the last day of the existence of the basket ecu will be the irrevocably fixed rate of the Stage Three ecu. The ecu will become a currency in its own right. National currencies may still circulate for some while after the start of Stage Three. However, the Treaty requires the Community to take the necessary measure for the introduction of the ecu as the single currency rapidly after that date. The ecu of Stage Three will be the currency of those Member States which participate fully in the single monetary policy.

GREENSPAN ON "FALTERED" BUSINESS RECOVERY

December 18, 1991

Congress received bleak news about the economy from Alan Greenspan, chairman of the Federal Reserve Board, in testimony December 18 before the House Ways and Means Committee. He said an upturn in business activity some had perceived earlier in the year "clearly has faltered." Although saying that the "economy is struggling," the Fed chairman cautioned that attempts to reignite it by cutting taxes would worsen the federal budget deficit and cause long-term harm. He counseled Congress to sit tight for the time being.

Greenspan's remarks came one day after President George Bush, in an ABC News interview, said he was aware that "the recession continues" and "people are hurting." In contrast to previous statements suggesting a recovery was under way or about to begin, Bush went on to say: "The economy is in trouble. It's sluggish; it has not responded the way all the experts felt it would." Greenspan tacitly acknowledged that he was among the analysts who underestimated the power of some adverse economic trends. He identified them as aftereffects of rampant speculation and debt in the 1980s. They led to a wave of business and household bankruptcies, bank closures, and job losses from plant shutdowns and production cutbacks. "The bottom line of this brief account," he said, "is that the national balance sheet has been severely stretched."

By late summer, he said, a recovery clearly was not under way. Most measurements of business activity continued to sag. Retail sales remained in a slump even through a normally brisk Christmas buying season. In December the jobless rolls climbed to 8.9 million, 7.1 percent of the workforce, the highest unemployment rate in nearly six years. Jobless benefit claims grew to the second-highest level in eight years.

The day Greenspan spoke, General Motors (GM) Corporation announced it would eliminate 74,000 jobs in American and Canadian plants during the next three years. GM's layoff announcement was preceded by sizable layoffs by other giant corporations such as International Business Machines, McDonnell Douglas, Tenneco, Westinghouse Electric, TRW, and Sears Roebuck.

Surveys indicated that consumer confidence was at an eight-year low in December—that many potential shoppers were crimped for spending money or else were fearful of losing their jobs and reluctant to buy anything but necessities.

Greenspan theorized that latent worries "about whether the current generation will live as well as previous ones" were brought to the surface when the expected recovery failed to materialize. "These events do not necessarily mean that a prolonged period of economic weakness is inevitable," he said, "but they do mean that policymakers must consider these unusual forces when shaping their responses to the current situation."

The Fed chairman did not suggest specific remedies for Congress to prescribe. But he urged that any change to the tax code "should give considerable emphasis to the encouragement of long-term economic growth through incentives for savings and investment." During most of 1991 the Federal Reserve Board sought to stimulate business by lowering the cost of borrowing money. Interest rates declined steadily, but the recession persisted. Then two days after Greenspan's testified, the Fed tried again, more boldly than before, in an apparent attempt to relieve some of the pressure building up in Congress and the White House for a tax cut.

On December 20 Federal Reserve banks sliced the rate on their lending to commercial banks—the so-called discount rate—by a full percentage point, an unusually large amount. This dropped the so-called discount rate to 3.5 percent, the lowest level in twenty-five years, barely above the rate of inflation. Several large banks followed suit, as expected, and reduced their rates to business and individual borrowers. But by early in 1992 whether the plan was having the desired effect on either the economy or politics was unclear.

> *Following is the statement of Alan Greenspan, chairman of the Federal Reserve Board, to the House Ways and Means Committee, December 18, 1991, on the state of the American economy:*

Mr. Chairman, members of the Committee, I appreciate the invitation to participate in these important hearings on tax policy. In your announcement, you made it clear that you intended to engage in a comprehensive review of the economic issues surrounding fiscal policy today, involving not only short-run, cyclical considerations, but also the implications of taxation for the longer-range growth of the economy. I applaud this broad scope; I believe that it is essential if we are to have the assurance that any action taken will truly serve the interests of the nation.

If I may, Mr. Chairman, I'd like to devote a few minutes to an assessment of the current economic situation. Obviously, we must know the nature of the problems we confront before we formulate a solution.

The upturn in business activity that began earlier this year clearly has faltered. It is apparent that the economy is struggling and that there have been some strong forces working against moderate cyclical revival. Now that we are well past the period of gyrations associated with the crisis in the Persian Gulf, we can better gauge the strength of the underlying disinflationary forces that were active well before the economy tilted into recession in the autumn of 1990.

During the 1980s, large stocks of physical assets were amassed in a number of sectors, largely financed by huge increases in indebtedness. In the business sector, the most obvious example is that of commercial real estate, with the accumulation of vast amounts of office and other commercial space—space that goes well beyond the plausible needs in most locales well into the future. Our financial intermediaries, not just depository institutions but other lenders as well, lavished credit upon developers, and they are paying the price today in the form of loan losses and impaired capital positions. The 1980s were also characterized by a wave of mergers and buyouts—purchases of corporate assets, often involving substitution of debt for equity and anticipating the sale of assets at higher prices. I needn't recount for you the subsequent disappointments, and the fall-out or holders of "below investment grade" bonds and related loans.

In the household sector, purchases of motor vehicles and other consumer durables ran for a number of years at remarkably high levels, and were often paid for with installment or other debt that carried extended maturities. In some parts of the country, the household spending boom reached to the purchase of homes, not simply for essential shelter, but as speculative investments—and often involving borrowing that constituted a heavy call on current and expected family incomes. The aftermath of all this is a considerable degree of financial stress in the household sector.

The bottom line of this brief account is that the national balance sheet has been severely stretched. While most analysts, of course, were aware of the increasingly disturbing trends of rising debt and elevated corporate leverage, it was not clear that these burdens had as yet reached a magnitude that would restrain the American economy for a moderate cyclical recovery in 1991.

Indeed, as inventory liquidation abated at mid-year, output moved up and closed the gap with the consumption of goods and services in much the same manner evident in the early stages of other recent business cycle recoveries. A range of leading indicators still were flashing positive signals on the economy's prospects.

By late summer, however, with half the recession losses recovered, it became clear that the cumulative upward momentum that characterized previous recoveries was absent. The growing propensity of households to pare debt and businesses to reduce leverage was a signal that the balance sheet restraints, feared by many for a long time, had indeed taken hold, working against the normal forces of economic growth.

These events do not necessarily mean that a prolonged period of economic weakness is inevitable, but they do mean that policymakers must consider these unusual forces when shaping their response in the current situation. It is essential that the direction of public policy be well targeted to the nature of the problem it is seeking to ameliorate.

For example, lower interest rates can reduce debt service burdens and their claim on current spendable incomes. Moreover, severely stretched private sector balance sheets must be reliquified if the economy is to return to normal growth. But only in the context of prudent, noninflationary expansion of money and credit are such improvements likely to be lasting.

In concept, private balance sheet liquification also could be facilitated by tax cuts for individuals or corporations if they are largely saved by the recipients. In effect, public debt would displace private debt on our nation's balance sheet. But if the markets were to perceive such policy initiatives as undermining long-term fiscal discipline, long-term interest rates would rise and debt service burdens again would mount. The heavy demand the government is already placing on the credit markets is a significant factor in the persistence of historically high real bond yields and mortgage rates, which is making the private balance sheet adjustment process all the more difficult.

The inference I draw from this is that the Congress should approach with great caution any proposal that would expand the structural budget deficit. At a minimum, care should be taken to ensure that any short-run stimulative action does not imply a widening of the deficit over the longer term.

Obviously, any policy that bolstered the asset side of the nation's private balance sheet or eased debt pressures without violating the goals of long-term federal budget balance or involving imprudent money creation could be of significant assistance in our current difficulties.

But there appears to be more that is required. It is certainly the case that stretched balance sheets are restraining expansion, and some relief is necessary to foster a resumption of sustained growth. But I have a suspicion that there is more to the story than that. Consumer confidence, which rebounded in a normal fashion as the cyclical recovery began in the spring, fell back as the recovery stalled, exacerbating the problems.

Consumers appear to be more apprehensive than one might expect, given the broad macroeconomic circumstances. For example, the level of employment and particularly the layoff rate are well below those experienced in periods of economic weakness; this would not seem to square with the deep concerns expressed in surveys about perceived labor market conditions.

It is true that homeowners sense some contraction, however small, in the market value of their most important asset, the equity in their homes. But it surely is no worse a concern today than it was in the spring. If anything, the data on home prices suggest it should be less so.

I suspect that what concerns consumers, and indeed everyone, is that the current pause may be underscoring a retardation in long-term growth and living standards. So long as the recovery proceeded, this latent concern did not surface, but as balance sheet constraints held the recovery in check, earlier worries about whether the current generation will live as well as previous ones resurfaced.

Such anticipations certainly need not be realized if we follow appropriate policies, and this suggests strongly that any current policy initiative should focus on some key fundamentals. Indeed, firm reliance on policies directed toward longer-term stability and incentives are likely to do as much, or more, for short-term economic expansion as a "quick fix."

What are the current restraints on growth and how can they be addressed? I, and others, have long argued before this Committee that the essential shortcoming of this economy is the lack of saving and investment. It's here that our major policy focus should rest. Investment is the key to enhanced productivity and higher living standards. While we have seen some improvement in productivity trends in the past decade, our performance leaves much to be desired—a fact reflected in our loss of international competitiveness in many industries and in the disappointing real incomes of too many American families.

Bolstering the supply of saving available to support productive private investment must be a priority for fiscal policy, and in that regard, reducing the call of the federal government on the nation's pool of saving is essential. Federal expenditure restraint is, in turn, crucial to this goal.

We also must recognize that private decisions about saving and investing can be powerfully affected by how various economic and financial transactions are taxed. Establishing the optimal structure of taxation is no simple matter, and there are inevitable conflicts among goals.

I would hope that any changes in taxation passed by the Congress in the coming months would give a heavy weight to promoting the capital formation process. In general, special attention should be given to the issue of the taxation of capital income. Our current system already does provide some incentives for saving in certain forms, such as retirement accounts or home equity, through favorable treatment of capital income. But in other areas the incentives are nonexistent or, worse, negative. As a more general matter, the structure of corporate taxation has long been recognized as distortive, and as an ingredient in the movement toward excessive leverage that we witnessed in the past decade.

As I have argued previously before this Committee, a reduction in the capital gains tax would be quite helpful. It is especially important considering our current difficulties with weak real estate property values. A capital gains tax cut would buoy property values, which would alleviate in part the collateral shortfalls that plague our financial institutions. This could induce greater financial intermediation and balance sheet liquification.

How far, and how fast, we can move toward a tax structure more conducive to capital formation is ultimately a political decision. My purpose this morning is not to advocate a particular agenda, but rather to suggest some principles that I think relevant to your deliberations. While I believe those principles—which relate basically to how fiscal policy can best contribute to the achievement of productivity, growth and higher living standards—are germane at all times, they may be of particular importance in today's economic circumstances. Traditional fiscal stimuli might provide a temporary boost to aggregate demand. But, if you accept the view that it is the concern of the American people for our long-term future that is at the root of our problem, then other instruments of policy might well be more effective.

Market forces are already addressing our stretched balance sheets. Record issuance of equity in our capital markets recently is contributing to deleveraging. And large bond issues are funding short-term debt and removing some of that strain. Finally, lower interest rates, as I indicated earlier, are lowering the debt service burden.

We have made a good deal of progress in the balance sheet adjustment process, and the payoff in the form of an easing of unusual restraint should begin to become evident in the reasonably near future. American industry is striving to enhance efficiency and competitiveness. The resulting increases in productivity, more than anything else, should dissipate the concerns of the American people about our economic future. Tax policy, in my judgment, should endeavor to reinforce these underlying trends.

In summary, then, an analysis of both the special factors affecting the economy at present and of the requirements for healthy growth of productivity and for international competitiveness over the longer run suggests that any changes made to the tax code should give considerable emphasis to the encouragement of long-term economic growth through incentives for saving and investment. Above all, we must not lose sight of the crucial need to eliminate the structural deficit in the federal budget over the coming years.

CUMULATIVE INDEX, 1987-1991

C